The Essential Sangharakshita

A HALF CENTURY OF WRITINGS

from the founder of the
Friends of the Western Buddhist Order

Urgyen Sangharakshita

Edited by Karen Stout (Vidyadevi)

WISDOM PUBLICATIONS • BOSTON

Wisdom Publications
199 Elm Street
Somerville MA 02144 USA
www.wisdompubs.org

Library of Congress Cataloging-in-Publication Data
Sangharakshita, Bhikshu, 1925–
 The essential Sangharakshita : a half-century of writings from the founder of the Friends
of the Western Buddhist Order / Urgyen Sangharakshita ; edited by Karen Stout
(Vidyadevi).
    p. cm.
 Includes bibliographical references and index.
 ISBN 0-86171-585-3 (pbk. : alk. paper)
1. Buddhism—Essence, genius, nature. 2. Buddhism—Doctrines. 3. Spiritual life—
Buddhism. 4. Buddhism art and symbolism. 5. Buddhism—Social aspects. I.
Vidyadevi, 1962– II. Title.
 BQ4055.S259 2009
 294.3'91—dc22   2008041528

13 12 11 10 09
5 4   3   2   1

Cover design by Phil Pascuzzo. Interior design by Gopa&Ted2, Inc. Set in Arno Pro,
11.6/15.2.

.

THE ESSENTIAL SANGHARAKSHITA

Urgyen Sangharakshita

Contents

PART TWO: BUDDHISM AND THE MIND

Editor's Preface

IN THE COURSE of his long career Sangharakshita has written a great deal, and more than fifty books are still in print: introductions to Buddhist history, thought, and practice, commentaries on texts from many parts of the Buddhist tradition, as well as several volumes of memoirs and poetry, book reviews and essays. He has made use of many genres, from polemic and academic exposition to story-telling, poetry and personal anecdotes. And he has written about many different Buddhist traditions, from the Theravada to the Tantra, from Abhidharma to Zen; as well as many Western traditions viewed from a Buddhist perspective. Some of the books began life in written form; others have their origins in talks and seminars which have been edited and published.

In assembling this collection of his writings, I wanted to include as many as possible of the aspects of Buddhist life and thought on which Sangharakshita has placed special emphasis. The first challenge was to decide what to include—or rather, what must be left out, despite the generous space allowed by Wisdom Publications. Once that was done, I found myself surrounded by a glittering but muddled heap of words. All my attempts to organize them seemed just to shift the heap into another heap; and the words, taken from their contexts, kept losing their luster. And then an idea came into my mind—or rather, an image. I decided to try organizing the collection according to a symbolic pattern to which Sangharakshita has returned many times in the course of his teaching: the mandala of the five Buddhas, from the Tibetan Buddhist tradition.

The mandala is based on the Enlightened qualities of Shakyamuni, the historical Buddha who lived two and a half thousand years ago. In the course of the hundreds of years of Buddhism's history in India and then Tibet, the Buddha's attributes came to be visualized in archetypal form, as mandalas of Buddhas, each Buddha embodying a particular quality of Enlightenment: compassion, wisdom, energy, purity, and so on. The mandala of the five Buddhas is one of the simplest of these. To borrow from a description by Sangharakshita, in the center is *the* Buddha—the primary Buddha, you could say. To his right and left are the Buddhas of the east and west, representing respectively wisdom and compassion, or the intellectual and emotional aspects of Buddhahood. This was a development of the Mahayana. Then, with the Tantra, appeared the Buddhas of the north and south, representing further aspects of Enlightenment—compassionate action and beauty. So now there were five: one at the center and one at each of the cardinal points.

It is this pattern that gives this book its shape. It is traditional to enter the mandala from the east, but here the starting point is the center. In the Tibetan tradition, there are many Buddhas to be visualized or depicted within the pattern of a mandala, but in the simple five-Buddha mandala, the Buddha at the center is often Vairocana, who is called the Illuminator; he is white in color and his hands are in the gesture of teaching. In this first section are gathered what might be called the essentials, the central concerns of Buddhism: who the Buddha was and what he taught; what makes a Buddhist and what might move anyone to become one; what are the unifying principles of Buddhism and how the different traditions express them.

In the east is the realm of Aksobhya the Imperturbable, the deep blue Buddha whose wisdom is described as mirror-like. This is the realm of the mind, and this section of the book covers Buddhism in its intellectual aspect: the importance of clear thinking, the nature of knowledge and the mind, key concepts such as conditionality and karma, and how Buddhism stands in relation to the other religions and philosophies of the world.

In the south is a very different world: the realm of Ratnasambhava the jewel-born one, the golden Buddha of beauty. Here are collected writings on the relationship of Buddhism with art, the Buddhist tradition as expressed in writing and scripture, the aesthetic aspect of Buddhist life, and the place of myth and symbol in the Buddhist tradition.

Continuing to move round the mandala, we come to the western realm of Amitabha, the red Buddha of infinite light. This is the realm of the heart, and one of the key themes here is the importance of the emotions to Buddhist life, and the role of faith and devotion in Buddhism. This section also explores the role of human relationships in spiritual life, especially friendship, and the nature of the relationship between teacher and disciple. Amitabha is especially associated with meditation, so this too is a theme here, as is our relationship to the natural world.

Then, in the northern realm of Amoghasiddhi, the deep green Buddha whose name means "unobstructed success," we move into another very different aspect of Buddhist life: the life of activity. Here we will consider what it is to lead an ethical life, and how the Buddhist relates to society as a whole, focusing especially on the spirit of altruism of the Bodhisattva. We will also encounter the heroic and active aspects of the Buddhist life, meet some of the most distinguished Buddhists of the last century, and look at what Buddhism has to say about the world's problems.

So that is the pattern into which the heaps of words have fallen, or been placed. I have been struck by how these different aspects of Buddhism really do seem like entirely different worlds: conceptual clarity and philosophy balanced with emotional warmth and devotional fervor, action in the world balanced with myths and dreams. Perhaps each of us will be drawn more to one of these "worlds" than the others; but the pattern also gives a sense of the mandala of Buddhism as a whole. As for Sangharakshita himself, it is difficult to guess in which of these realms he might feel most at home; to judge from these writings, he is happy in all of them. As he himself readily admits, he is a complex person, and his teachings happily reflect this complexity. This means, incidentally, that each section of the book contains a great variety of material: even on a particular theme, there are so many variations. Indeed, even in a book of these proportions it is hard to do justice to them.

While working on this project, I have thought a lot about Buddhism and about Sangharakshita's approach to it. I have thought also about my own relationship to this material, and have been glad to bring to mind again some favorite teachings, as well as persuading myself to consider some matters I would rather avoid. And I have also thought about you, the reader of this book, with frank curiosity. I wonder who you are, and what you want to know. I hope that, whatever it is, you will find it here, somewhere in this collection of the ideas, practical teachings, inspirations, and exhortations that this particular Buddhist teacher has thought or felt it important to express at this particular time in history. I hope that you will find inspiration, pleasure, and challenge in these words and the meanings they carry, as I have done, and will continue to do.

I am very grateful to Jnanasiddhi and Shantavira at Windhorse Publications—Jnanasiddhi for her encouragement and Shantavira for all his help with getting the text together. I must also add my appreciation for my fellow editor Jinananda, by whom many of the books quoted here were shaped and polished, and for all those who have given so much time and care to these literary endeavors over many years. Many thanks also to Josh Bartok, Gustavo Cutz, and Tony Lulek at Wisdom Publications for their encouragement, patience, and careful attention to detail; and to Wisdom for having the idea in the first place. I also very much appreciate all the other people who have so kindly given me their thoughts and advice; and above all I am immensely grateful to Sangharakshita, for his kindness and patience over the time this project has taken to bring to completion.

Karen Stout (Vidyadevi)

A Biographical Sketch of Sangharakshita

SANGHARAKSHITA (Dennis Lingwood) was born in London in 1925. His childhood was unusual in that a diagnosis of a heart problem (a misdiagnosis, it later turned out) confined him to bed for a period of years. He made good use of the time; he spent most of it reading, and—besides discovering a passion for literature—educated himself with the help of an encyclopedia. That was when he first came upon Buddhism, but it was later—when he was sixteen and living in wartime London—that he read the two texts which made him realize that he was a Buddhist, the *Diamond Sutra* and the *Sutra of Wei Lang*. He tracked down the Buddhist Society, which was continuing to meet and meditate despite the bombs falling on the city.

Then he was conscripted into the Army and, by a strange chance, was posted to India. Once the war was over, he and an Indian friend, determined to take their Buddhism seriously, gave away their possessions, destroyed their passports, and took to the roads as homeless wanderers in the time-honored tradition. They wandered the length of India for two years and met many sages and gurus (but few Buddhist ones) before they finally achieved their objective: Buddhist ordination.

Now ordained in the Theravada tradition and given his name (which means "one who is protected by the spiritual community"), Sangharakshita spent some time studying in Benares [Varanasi] with one of his first Buddhist teachers—Bhikkhu Kashyap—before settling in Kalimpong, a small town in the Himalayas, not far from the border with Tibet. Told by his teacher to "stay here and work for the good of Buddhism," he did just that, for the next fourteen years. He was there throughout the 1950s, when many Tibetan refugees came to Kalimpong, and was thus able to meet and learn from many lamas, from some of whom—Dhardo Rinpoche, Kachu Rinpoche, Jamyang Khyentse Rinpoche, Dilgo Khyentse Rinpoche, and others—he received formal initiations. He also learned from Yogi Chen, a master of Chan Buddhism who lived in Kalimpong. And he received many Western visitors and made many friends, including the German-born Lama Govinda, whose views on Buddhism—and especially on the role of art in Buddhism—Sangharakshita found to be very similar to his own.

While in Kalimpong he established a Buddhist magazine, *Stepping Stones*, which published the work of thinkers and scholars from all over the Buddhist world. His own contributions to the magazine, later published as *Crossing the Stream*, signaled many of the themes that would continue to concern him for many years: the unity of Buddhism, the benefits and pleasures of a simple life, the importance of thinking for oneself, the aesthetics of spiritual life, the value of friendship. He read everything he could about the Buddhism of all traditions, his motivation being—as he later explained—to try to understand why the Buddha said what he did, and what essential truths unified the Buddhist tradition in all its diversity. His thoughts and reflections found expression in many talks and writings, and especially in a substantial work, *A Survey of Buddhism*, published in 1957. At the same time he continued to write poetry in which he sought to express his love of nature, his devotion to the ideals of Buddhism, and his emotional and spiritual struggles and victories.

After some time and a lot of effort he eventually established a hermitage, to which one of his teachers gave the name "The place where the three ways flourish" (the three ways being the three major strands of Buddhist tradition). He relished living in the Himalayan foothills, with the view of snowy mountains in clear weather and—in the rainy season—the quiet months of reflection. But he had a new commitment which took him away from the mountains to the hot and dusty plains of India: a movement to change the situation of some of the most disadvantaged people in the subcontinent, about which he learned through his contact with Dr. B.R. Ambedkar. In 1956, while on a tour of northern India with other Buddhists from the border regions, he met Dr. Ambedkar, an eminent lawyer who had managed, despite his birth into what was known in the Hindu caste system as an "Untouchable" family, to overcome his circumstances and become the architect of independent India's new constitution. After searching for more than twenty years for a religion or philosophy according to which he and the rest of his community could live, and thus escape the degradation of the caste system, Ambedkar had declared that he was going to convert to Buddhism; and he did so, along with thousands of his followers. But he died just a few weeks after taking this step, and his followers were left without guidance, knowing that they were now "Buddhists," but uncertain what that meant and what they should do. Sangharakshita happened to be there, and he spoke to the grief-stricken crowds, explaining to them what being Buddhist involved and encouraging them to live according to the Dharma, as Ambedkar had wished. From then on, he spent each winter for several years touring the cities and plains of central India, giving talks and inspiring the new Buddhists to new efforts.

He might have gone on living in that way for many years; he never expected to leave India. But in 1964 he returned to England, in response to the growing interest in Buddhism there. On his return, however, it quickly became clear that although he had been invited there by members of the Buddhist "establishment," he was not going to fit into it very well. While in India he had reflected a great deal on the prevailing orthodoxies of Buddhism, according to which Buddhist practice consisted—for monks—of living according to monastic rules and—for lay people—of supporting monks to live in the way they did. Now that he was back in England, observing that people were apt to relate to him purely on the basis of his orange robes, he began to feel dissatisfied with the monastic lifestyle to which he had adhered so carefully in India. He let his hair grow, and wore his robes with a mixture of other eccentric garments, or sometimes jeans and a sweater instead. He didn't look out of place among the burgeoning hippy life of London, but he disappointed and even shocked those who expected him to look and behave like their idea of a respectable monk. Feeling that a new approach was needed, he decided that— although he didn't think that he necessarily had the qualities to succeed—he would attempt to begin a new Buddhist movement.

In 1967 he therefore founded the Friends of the Western Buddhist Order, and the following year the first members of the Order were ordained. This growing community of Buddhists emerged partly from a group of people who had been attending meditation classes led by Sangharakshita in the basement below a small shop in London's West End. They were very much part of the wave of experimentation with all manner of spiritual traditions that characterized the sixties, and interest in traditional meditation and other Buddhist practices was mixed with many strange fads and enthusiasms, but slowly a tradition which was definitely Buddhist and also distinctively Western began to emerge.

Seeking to help his students find ways of connecting with Buddhism, he gave talks on Buddhism and psychology, Buddhism and Western philosophy, even Buddhism as the path of the higher evolution. Some of the themes he addressed clearly reflected his personal interests. For example, while still in India he had published *The Religion of Art,* in which he asserted that the life of the artist and of aesthetic appreciation could be as much a living out of the spiritual life as the life of the monk or mystic. He also gave talks and seminars on classic Buddhist texts; the commentaries he has published on texts such as the *White Lotus Sutra,* the *Diamond Sutra,* and the *Satipatthana Sutta* have their origins in the transcripts of these seminars.

Although his teaching was shaped in part by his own interests and personality, it was above all designed to appeal to and inspire his audience, and help them to feel that Buddhism could give them a way to live and a sense that their life had meaning. Of all the meditation practices available in various forms of Buddhism, he especially encouraged people to practice two, the mindfulness of breathing and the development of loving-kindness (metta bhavana), believing that a combination of mindfulness and positivity was the best possible basis for living well and happily. Realizing that many Western people found it difficult to approach the ritual and devotion of Buddhist tradition, he sought both to explain its role in spiritual practice and to help people find ways to engage with it.

In particular, he emphasized that what mattered was not how you lived—whether you were celibate, married, or neither, whether you were "monastic" or "lay"—but the degree to which you were committed to living in accordance with the three ideals of Buddhism: the Buddha (the Enlightened teacher), the Dharma (his teaching), and the Sangha (the community of those who follow the Buddha's teaching). Over many years of practice, reflection, and contact with Buddhists of all schools, he had come to the conclusion that this—Going for Refuge, as it is traditionally called—rather than any particular style of life or practice, is what makes someone a Buddhist.

Inspired and challenged in equal measure, Sangharakshita's Western disciples set about trying to live according to the teachings to which he had introduced them. Those who were free to do so often chose to live in communities: mixed sex at first, and later, in an experiment which was unusual at that time in that culture, in single sex households; for some this emerged as a creative alternative to family life. Similarly, some people began to try out what came to be known as "right livelihood businesses": shops, vegetarian restaurants, and other ventures run by teams of Buddhists on a "give what you can, take what you need" basis. A distinctive feature of this new Buddhist movement was that women were given the same ordination as men, and encouraged to take their spiritual potential just as seriously. An important milestone was the founding of Taraloka, a retreat center run by and for women, and two more women's retreat centers have since been established.

In the course of the development of the FWBO, Buddhist centers have been established in cities in many countries, and retreats of many kinds are held. The movement has been developed in India, where it is called TBMSG (Trailokya Bauddha Mahasangha Sahayaka Gana), among the new Buddhists whom Sangharakshita befriended in the 1950s. In that context members of the Order have initiated and maintained educational and health projects as well as teaching meditation and Buddhism. Arts events and Buddhist festivals have also been important aspects of the movement's growth, as well as Buddhafield, which teaches meditation at music festivals as well as running its own retreats and gatherings. Perhaps the most important thing has been the development of a process by which men and women are prepared for ordination and ordained by other members of the Order. Sangharakshita himself, having handed on that responsibility, has continued to travel extensively, giving talks and meeting people, as well as spending long periods on retreat in Italy or Spain, or writing books—and answering letters—in his study wherever he happens to be living (currently he is in Birmingham).

During the forty years since his return to England, Sangharakshita has continued to be an unorthodox and controversial figure, and many aspects of his life and thought have received close scrutiny; he has attracted criticism from some and deep gratitude from others who say they owe their lives to the movement he founded.

PART ONE

The Essentials

1 ↩ Who Is the Buddha?

1. THE BUDDHA'S JOURNEY TO ENLIGHTENMENT

The ultimately unacceptable limitations of human life had impressed themselves upon Siddhartha's consciousness too forcibly for him to be able to ignore them, to put them aside and just "get on with his life."

T O CONTEMPLATE the biographical details of the Buddha's early life is to be concerned not just with the spiritual path followed by a man who lived two and a half thousand years ago. It is to contemplate a path which one can follow here and now, a path that one is committed to following if one is a Buddhist, if one has Buddhahood as one's ultimate goal. In other words, when as Buddhists we celebrate the Buddha's Enlightenment, we are not just rejoicing in a thing of the past. We are reminding ourselves that it is high time we started to think of our own Enlightenment, if indeed we have not already done so—and if we have, to think of it more persistently, more seriously, and more deeply.

I will sketch out an outline of the Buddha's early life, to give a general idea of the way to Enlightenment, and then take up for more detailed examination certain crucial episodes or feature of his biography that have a definite bearing on our own process of development toward Enlightenment. Like the story of the Buddha's life as a whole, these particularly notable elements are in substance historical, inasmuch as we know they did actually happen. However, the versions that have come down to us contain a certain amount of legendary material that helps to bring out the universal significance, the inner spiritual dimension, of the external events. The mythical aspect makes it clear, among other things, that these events are concerned not with one man's spiritual career, but with the career of every man and woman who aspires to grow and develop as an individual.

It is very often said that Siddhartha Gautama, who became the Buddha, was born in India, and a hundred years ago this would have been true. But owing to changing political boundaries we would have to say today that his birth took place in the southern part of what is now Nepal. He was born into a tribe called the Shakyans, who had inhabited that particular area in the foothills of the Himalayas for many centuries. Nor is it quite true—as it is, again, often said—that his father, Suddhodana Gautama, was the king of the tribe. He did certainly hold the title of rajah at the time of Siddhartha's birth, but today he would probably be called a president. Like other small tribes in northeastern India at that time, the Shakyans had a semi-republican form of government, with a leader elected from the clan assembly for a fixed period of twelve years. Toward the end of the Buddha's lifetime the little republics of India were swallowed up by the developing Magadhan empire, but at the time of his birth they were, for the most part, in a flourishing condition.

Siddhartha's mother, Mayadevi, was the daughter of the chief of a neighboring tribe, the Koliyas. It was then the custom, as it still is the custom in many parts of India, for the first child to be born in the house of the mother's parents. When she felt her time approaching, therefore, Mayadevi set off from Kapilavastu, the Shakyan capital, to make for her father's city, carried, as far as we know, in a palanquin. She was still only half-way there when, seized with the pangs of labor, she dismounted, and in a grove of sal trees at a little place called Lumbini gave birth to the future Buddha. She died shortly afterward—seven days later, according to tradition.

Siddhartha was reared by his maternal aunt, Mahaprajapati Gautami, whom his father had also married. There is really little more to be said about his childhood—it took place, after all, two thousand five hundred years ago. A single authentic incident stands out from it, one that took place when he was five, six, or perhaps seven years old, on the occasion of the annual ploughing ceremony. In primarily agricultural civilizations all over the world, the sowing of the first seed in the spring was a matter of magical and mythical significance, and the first ploughing was always undertaken by the king or chief. It was one of the duties of the old emperors of China, and until quite recently the emperor of Japan used to inaugurate the ploughing every year, so obviously this was one of the jobs that fell to Siddhartha's father to carry out. Later accounts tell us that it was done with a golden plough drawn by beautiful white oxen (storytellers love to embroider their material). But leaving aside the precise quality of the equipment used, what we can say with confidence is that Siddhartha's father performed this ceremony and that Siddhartha was brought along to watch.

The little boy was put on one side on a little bank in the shade of a jambu or rose-apple tree, and it was there that he had what we would describe nowadays as a spontaneous mystical experience. According to the Buddha himself, as he reminisced to his disciples a great many years later, what he experienced beneath the rose-apple tree was a sort of super-conscious state known as *dhyana*. So deep was his absorption that he never saw the ploughing at all, and he had still not emerged from the experience when they came to take him home. It is at this point that an interesting legendary anecdote finds its way into the episode. The legend has it that although it was noon when the ploughing started, and evening by the time the ceremony was all over, the shadow of the rose-apple tree had not moved during that time. On a literal level this would be what we call a miracle, but it is perhaps more meaningful if we take it symbolically. The obvious implication is that the sun stood still; and the implication on the symbolic level is that for the young Siddhartha time itself had stopped.

Later on, as we shall see, this experience—or rather the memory of this experience—was to have a crucial bearing on the direction of Siddhartha's spiritual career. But meanwhile, mystical experience or no mystical experience, he was a Kshatriya, a warrior, and he would have been brought up like one. That was his caste—the caste of the whole tribe. It was a Kshatriya tribe, and so he was literally born a warrior, as others were born Brahmins (priests), Vaishyas (traders and farmers), or Shudras (laborers)—just as they are today, although these four castes are now subdivided into some two thousand sub-castes.

The future Buddha spent his formative years not in the close study of philosophy or the observance of religious practices, but in the tiltyard, acquiring the arts of archery and spear-throwing, swordplay and the skillful handling of a war-chariot. With his patrician background he would have received the best martial training available. He would also have been initiated into the various traditions, customs, beliefs, and superstitions of the tribe, and he would have learned a little history and genealogy too. Of course, whatever he learned would have been by word of mouth from the elders of the tribe. It is not in fact clear whether the Buddha ever learned to read or write. We must imagine him as a man who was cultured, educated, and well-bred without ever having attended anything like a school (it is, in any case, questionable whether education has really anything to do with going to school). He led on the whole a quite comfortable, well-to-do life, had no particular responsibilities, and was doted on by his father.

Siddhartha's upbringing was not, however, quite as simple and straightforward as all that. Shortly after his birth, his father had taken him to a *rishi*, the sage Asita, to have his horoscope cast. This was common practice, as it still is in India today. There is hardly anybody, even among the Westernized so-called elite, who does not have this done for their children—especially for their sons. You want to know what is going to happen to your child, what sort of a career he or she will have, so you go to an astrologer. It is not known exactly how Siddhartha's horoscope was cast, but we know that he was placed in the arms of Asita, and that the *rishi* made his calculations. He predicted that the child would have a remarkable future: Siddhartha would either become a great Ksatriya, a great warrior and ruler, or else he would give it all up and become a great spiritual master.

Suddhodana was deeply disturbed at this prognostication, of course. He liked the idea of his son becoming an illustrious conqueror—he liked it very much—but he was appalled at the idea that the lad might take it into his head to retire from the world altogether and devote his talents to the spiritual quest. The older Siddhartha grew, the more Suddhodana turned the matter over in his mind. He thought, "I want him to grow up like me. I want him to be brave and strong and extend the territory of the tribe, and—if the *rishi* is right— to become a great ruler and maybe conquer all of India. He must not be allowed to waste his time over all this religious nonsense. Therefore he must be prevented from thinking too deeply about anything; he must not be introduced to the more unpalatable facts of life—at least not too early. His heart must be set firmly on worldly things."

So Suddhodana was determined that the young prince should want for nothing, that all he should learn about life should be how to enjoy it to the most refined pitch of sensual pleasure. The Buddha later related in one of his autobiographical discourses how his father had provided him with three beautiful mansions, one for each season, so that he should never feel discomfort from the heat or the cold or the rains. And he recounted also how these mansions were filled with alluring dancing girls and bewitching singing girls, and how his days and nights were spent in drinking, dancing, and singing, one pleasure succeeding another, with hardly a moment for sadness.

At sixteen he was married off to a cousin, Yasodhara. It was an arranged marriage, of course, just as in India today a marriage is nearly always negotiated by the families of the bride and bridegroom rather than by the young people themselves. He settled down happily enough and in this way for many years his life went on. All the same, he seems to have had an underlying sense of dissatisfaction with the life he was leading. He chafed at the bit. When the news was brought to him that his wife had given birth to a son his reaction was not the usual one of a proud father. Asked what the boy should be called, he said, "A fetter has been born to me. Call him Rahula"—for this is what the name Rahula means. It was as if he sensed what his father had been trying to do all his life. Somehow he knew that Suddhodana was trying to bind him down: bind him down with pleasure, bind him down with property, bind him down with power, with family, with wife and child. He knew what was happening. He neglected his martial exercises and lost interest in the amusements and distractions laid on for him indoors. Domestic life held no joy for him.

Increasingly he took himself off for long periods to give himself time to think, and at some point he evidently had some sort of spiritual crisis—though this is not of course how the early scriptures put it. This psychological and spiritual turning point is known among Buddhists everywhere in the form of a dramatic narrative called the Four Sights. Whether this is a legend, whether it is an external projection of an experience arising out of intense inner questioning, or whether it actually happened in something like the way the story has come down to us, it is impossible for us to say. What is certain is that the Four Sights crystallize in a very powerful form some of the fundamental teachings of Buddhism, as well as throwing light on the Buddha's own early spiritual development.

The story goes that one bright morning Siddhartha called his charioteer to harness the horses for an outing. "Let's see what is going on in the world, see what people are up to," he said. The charioteer shook his head. "I'm afraid we can't do that—it's more than my job's worth. You know the king has said you are not to go out among the people." But the young prince insisted: "Don't worry. I'll take full responsibility. If the king has anything to say about it, let him say it to me. But let's go." So the horses were whipped up and away they went. They drove out into the village and Siddhartha saw life going on much as he might have expected—until his attention was arrested by the sight of a very old man.

The traditional accounts give a graphic description of this old man's appearance—feeble, withered, and bent over, his bones sticking out, tottering along supported by a stick. He had a long white beard and the rheum was trickling from his eyes. If this seems to be laying it on a bit thick, it would not seem so in India. There, old people, even today—because of the climate and the hard life—can look very old indeed. At no more than fifty or sixty they can look about a hundred years old. We have to remember that according to the legend his father had deliberately secluded him from anything unpleasant about life, and this included old age. So when Siddhartha saw this very old man, he pointed at him and said, "Who—what—is that?"

The charioteer thought, "Well, he'll have to find out sooner or later," and he said, "It's an old man." "But why is he like that? Why is he so bent? Why do all his bones stick out? Why is that fluid trickling out from his eyes?" The charioteer was not used to fielding this sort of question, except perhaps from children. He said simply, "Well, he's just an old man." Obviously Siddhartha was not satisfied by this: "But how has he got like that?" "It just happens," the charioteer explained gently. "You don't have to do anything to get old—you just get old. It's natural, I'm afraid—everybody gets old." The young prince felt his flesh creep. "What, everybody?" he asked, and the charioteer said, "Well, yes, of course. Everybody." "What about me? Will I become like that?" The charioteer nodded: "The king, your father, the queen, your mother, your wife, myself, and you too—all of us—are subject to old age."

We are told that Siddhartha received this intelligence like an elephant struck by a thunderbolt, and he broke into a cold sweat with the shock. "What is the use of being young?" he lamented. "What is the use of this vitality and strength, if it all ends in such emaciation and frailty?" He was sick at heart. "That's enough for today, I think. Let's go home," he said, and as they rattled back to the palace he brooded over the knowledge he had been given.

This, then, is the legend of the first Sight. Siddhartha may or may not have literally clapped eyes on an old man for the first time in this way, but there is no mistaking the real significance of it. He might perhaps have seen many old men before, but somehow missed really seeing them. That day, perhaps, he saw an old man *as though* for the first time. This is what life is like, of course. We see a thing—we see it maybe every day of our lives, just as we see the sun rising and the sun setting—but we don't really see it because we are not aware and we don't think. We see but we don't see. We are blind. One might even work in an old people's home for years without taking in the fact of old age to any great depth. Then when we develop some awareness, some clarity, we find that things appear to us in such a fresh light that it is as if we never saw them before. So Siddhartha realized, truly realized for the first time in his life, that there was such a thing as old age, and that youth would be brief, even for him.

Shaken as he was by this realization, Siddhartha went out again a few days later—so the legend has it—and again he saw something he had never seen before. What he saw was a sick man, lying by the road-side with an attack of fever or something of that sort, tossing this way and that, with no one to care for him. Again Siddhartha asked the char-ioteer to explain to him what was going on: "Tell me what has hap-pened to this man. What is wrong with him? Why is he lying there beside the road? Why is he twitching? Why is he shaking and shiver-ing? Why are his eyes rolling so wildly? Why does his face look so ghastly?" Of course the charioteer had to tell him, "Well, he's ill." And Siddhartha, who had apparently enjoyed blooming health up to that time, wanted to know whether he too would be likely to suffer in this way: "Does this happen to other people? Will it happen to me?" So again the charioteer drove the point home: "All men, all women, are liable to sickness. It might come at any time. At any moment strength and health may go from us and then we must suffer sickness." So again Siddhartha had something to ponder over as he returned to the palace.

But after a few days off they went once more in the chariot, and this time he saw four men coming toward them carrying something between them on a sort of stretcher, the poles of which were balanced on their shoulders. Lying on the stretcher there was a man wrapped in a yellow sheet. His face was exposed, but there was something odd about it. He didn't move a muscle. The face was quite expressionless, stiff-looking, and the eyes were closed.

Of course, you can still see this sight any day of the week in India. An Indian funeral is rather different from what most of us are used to in the West. Here, when you die you are smuggled away in a box, and that's that. You are just quietly disposed of like so much garbage that no one wants to look at. You're put into the incinerator or into a hole in the ground which is swiftly covered over. But in India it isn't like that. In India you are laid out in the best room of the house and all your friends and relations come round to have a good look and say, "Well, he looks quite happy, quite peaceful. Yes, goodbye then, old fellow." They shed a tear and throw a few flowers on the corpse, and then it is hoisted on the shoulders of four strong men and borne through the streets with the face still uncovered. As the corpse is jolting along, crowds of people following behind in the heat, the people passing by look and say, "Oh yes, there's old so-and-so—didn't know he had died."

This sort of procession is what Siddhartha saw, and he said to the charioteer, "That's very strange. Why are they carrying that man like that? What are they doing? What's he done?" The charioteer replied in his usual laconic style, "Well, this is a dead body." We have to remember, of course, that death was one of those matters Siddhartha was supposed to have been kept in the dark about, so he was mystified by this explanation. "Dead? What do you mean dead?" And the charioteer again had to expatiate a little: "Well, you can see, he's stiff, lifeless, doesn't breathe, doesn't see, doesn't hear, doesn't feel. He's dead. They are taking him to the burning ground. They are going to burn the body. It's what happens at death." Siddhartha gasped with horror: "Does this too happen to everybody? Will everybody come to this, this death, as you call it? Will I too come to death?" The charioteer drew a long sigh. "Yes. Your father, your mother, your wife, your child—they must all die one day. I must die. You must die. Everybody who is born must die. There have been millions of men and women born since the world began and every single one of them has died. No doubt there will be millions more born in the future, but every single one of them will die. No one can ever escape the cold hand of death.

Death is king of all." So, sadder, more thoughtful, more anguished than ever, Siddhartha ordered the charioteer to turn round and head back to the palace.

Over these three outings with his charioteer he had come up against what nowadays might be called ineluctable existential situations: facts of existence from which you cannot escape. You don't want to grow old, but you can't help it. You don't want to fall sick, but it happens. You don't want to die, but die you will, like it or not. So you start asking yourself questions: "How do I come to be in this condition? I want to go on living forever, young and strong and healthy, but it isn't going to be that way. How is it that I have been given this urge to live when I am given not the remotest chance of escaping death? It's a riddle. But why am I presented with this riddle at all? Why this mystery? Is it God who is responsible? Is it fate? Or is this just the way it is? Is there an explanation? Or is there no explanation?"

Siddhartha was wrestling with the fundamental questions of life and death in this way when he took in the last of the Four Sights. Riding out again in his chariot he saw a man dressed not in the usual white garb, but in a yellow robe, and shaven-headed. This man was walking calmly along the village street with a begging-bowl, going from door to door. There was something in his mindful gait that Siddhartha found quietly compelling, and he asked the charioteer, "What manner of man is this that looks so at peace with himself and the world?" The charioteer replied, "This is one who has gone forth." "Gone forth?" said Siddhartha. "Gone forth from what?" "From the world," the charioteer explained. "He has gone forth from his home, from his family. He has simply left it all behind to devote himself to the search for Truth. He's trying to find an answer to the riddle of existence. To do this he has given up all worldly ties, all domestic responsibilities, all social and political obligations. In this way he has gone forth."

You may find such people in India even today, still wearing the saffron robe. They are called sadhus, which simply means "good people," and supporting them with alms is considered very meritorious. People give them food, invite them into their homes, and look after them.

Very much the same system is still in operation after two thousand five hundred years. And it was the sight of just such a figure that awoke in the young Siddhartha the inspiration to go forth himself. The ultimately unacceptable limitations of human life had impressed themselves upon his consciousness too forcibly for him to be able to ignore them, to put them aside and just "get on with his life." You can choose not to see them, but they are there all the time, and he knew this. But now he knew also that there was a way of penetrating through to the meaning of it all. After spending a long time thinking things over, he decided that there was nothing for it but to become a sadhu himself. He felt that these questions had to be answered and that he could not rest until an answer was found.

So one full-moon night when everything was quiet, Siddhartha bade a last farewell to his sleeping wife and child. He was not happy to leave them, but there could be no alternative. He had told no one about his decision except his faithful charioteer, who saddled the horse for him to ride out of the palace as a prince for the last time. We are told that the charioteer seized hold of the horse's tail and trotted behind, and that they traveled as far as a river marking the border of the Shakyan territory. There, Siddhartha cut off his beard and his long flowing black hair. Just then—it was the crack of dawn—a beggar came along, and Siddhartha offered to swap clothes with him. It did not take the beggar long to agree to this proposal, eccentric as it seemed, and he went on his way blinking with delight at the richly embroidered robes he now wore, the gold and silver buttons and buckles on them gleaming in the first rays of the sun. Siddhartha made his farewells to his faithful charioteer and his faithful horse, and watched them go. Then he plunged on into the jungle, alone.

He went in search of teachers who he hoped might have penetrated the ultimate mystery of existence. In those days in India, much as in India today, there were many who illumined the ways to the attainment of Truth. He went from one teacher to another; he practiced according to their instructions and mastered what they had to teach. But he was not satisfied. Good and profound as their teachings were, he knew that there was something beyond all they knew, something beyond all they had realized. He had no name for it. He did not know what it was. But he had to find it—he had to know. He had to carry on his search.

He was grateful for all that he had learned, but he moved on. He began a program of terrible austerities. This was a common practice in India, as it still is today, for it was thought that the thinner the veil of the flesh, as it were, the more transparent it was to the light of the spirit. For years Siddhartha mortified the flesh, and no one in India exceeded him in self-torture. The fame of his austerities was noised abroad, so it is said, like the sound of a great bell hung in the canopy of the sky, and he began to gather followers of his own. Eventually, however, something happened to make him wonder if he wasn't making a great deal of progress in the wrong direction. He fainted and collapsed into a river, from which, not having the strength to save himself, he was fortunate to be rescued. When he recovered he said to himself: "This is ridiculous. I'm getting no nearer to the Truth, for all this asceticism. I've been wasting my time. It's all been a big mistake."

So Siddhartha Gautama the great ascetic started taking regular meals again. His five disciples were not at all impressed. The fact was that they were not so much disciples as admirers, hangers-on. They relied on him to make the effort, and just hung on to his coattails in the hope that his achievements would somehow rub off on them. They thought that when he achieved his goal by virtue of his austerities they would be the first to benefit. So it was obviously a great disappointment to them when he made the decision to give his body the nourishment it needed. "He's backsliding," they said to one another, "He's gone back to the luxurious ways of the world. Clearly he's not the man we thought he was." And they trooped off in disgust. Once again, Siddhartha was on his own.

It was six years after he had left the palace when he came to the place that would mark the end of his quest. At a spot in the present-day state of Bihar called Uruvela, now known as Bodh Gaya, he found a copse of beautiful trees beside a river. It seemed an ideal location in which to sit and meditate. Then as he sat there in the shade, with a cool breeze blowing, he remembered something that suddenly seemed to show the way forward. He recollected his experience of thirty years before, sitting beneath another tree, while his father initiated the season's ploughing. He gently felt his way back to that integrated state of concentration—not trying to force it, but just letting it come, and letting go of whatever hindered its arising. As he did so a cowherd's wife from a neighboring village brought him some milk rice, which he took, and he was nourished and strengthened by it. A grass-cutter also came up to provide him with a heap of kusa grass to sit on, and he made himself comfortable on it. Tradition tells us that he then made the resolution, "I will not rise from this spot until I am Enlightened."

There is a beautiful and dramatic verse which is put into his mouth by some of the early compilers of the teachings: "Flesh may wither away, blood may dry up, but until I gain Enlightenment I shall not move from this seat." Then he settled down and gave himself to his meditative experience. He plunged deeper and deeper into it, through level after level of super-conscious states.

How long he sat there we do not know. It may have been days; it may have been weeks; it may even have been months. As he sat there he controlled and concentrated his mind, purified his mind, suppressed the mental hindrances, the defilements. And on Wesak night, the night of the full moon of May, just as the morning star was rising—just as he fixed his mind on that star glittering near the horizon—full illumination, full Enlightenment, arose.

It is obviously very difficult to describe this sort of state. We can say it is the plenitude of Wisdom. We can say it is the fullness of Compassion. We can say that it is seeing the Truth face to face. But these are only words, and they do not convey very much. So let us simply say that at that moment the "light" dawned, and Siddhartha Gautama became the Buddha.

In a sense this was the end of his quest. He had become the Buddha, the "one who knows." He had found the solution to the riddle of existence. He was Enlightened, he was Awake. But in a sense it was only the beginning of his mission. Deciding to make known to humanity the truth he had discovered, he left what we now call Bodh Gaya and walked to Sarnath, about one hundred miles away, gathered together the disciples who had left him when he gave up his austerities, and made known to them his great discovery.

Gradually a spiritual community grew up around the Buddha. He didn't stay permanently in any one place, but roamed all over northeastern India. He had a long life, gaining Enlightenment at the age of thirty-five and living to be eighty. So he had forty-five years of work, of active life, spreading his teaching. The pattern seems to have been that for nine months of the year he wandered from place to place teaching, and then for three months took shelter from the torrential monsoon rains. Whenever he came to a village he would, if it was time for his one meal of the day, get out his begging-bowl and stand silently at the doors of the huts, one after another. Having collected as much food as he needed, he would retire to the mango grove which, even now, is to be found on the outskirts of every Indian village, and sit down under a tree. When he had finished his meal the villagers would gather round and he would teach them. Sometimes brahmins would come, sometimes wealthy landowners, sometimes peasants, sometimes merchants, sometimes sweepers, sometimes prostitutes. The Buddha would teach them all. And sometimes in the big cities he would preach to kings and princes. In this way he gained a great following and became in his own day the greatest and best known of all the spiritual teachers in India. And when he died, when he gained what we call parinirvana, there were thousands, even tens of thousands, of his disciples to mourn his departure, both monks and lay people, men and women.

In outline, at least, such is the traditional biography of Siddhartha Gautama, the Indian prince who became the Buddha, the Enlightened One, the Awakened One, the founder of the great spiritual tradition which we call Buddhism. But does this really answer the question, "Who was the Buddha?" It certainly gives us all the facts, but does such a biography, however well documented, really tell us who the Buddha was? Do we know the Buddha—and the emphasis is on the "know"—from a description of the life of Siddhartha Gautama? What, in fact, do we mean by knowing the Buddha? Even from a worldly point of view, we may know a person's likes and dislikes, his or her opinions and beliefs, but do we really know that person? Sometimes even our closest friends do things which we find quite out of character, quite out of keeping with the ideas we had about them. This shows how little one really knows other people. We are not really able to plumb the deepest spring of their action, their fundamental motivation. Usually, the nearer people are to us, the less we really know them. There is an old saying: "It's a wise child that knows its own father." It is as though familiarity, or superficial closeness, gets in the way, so that what we know and relate to is not the other person but our own preconceptions, our own projected mental states, our own quite subjective reactions to that person. In other words, our "ego" gets in the way. In order really to know another person we have to go much deeper than the ordinary level of communication, which isn't real communication at all.

It is the same with regard to this question of knowing the Buddha. This question in its deeper sense has been asked since the very dawn of Buddhism. In fact it is a question which was put to the Buddha himself, apparently, soon after his Enlightenment: "Who are you?"

Journeying along the high road, the Buddha met a man called Dona.[1] Dona was a brahmin, and skilled in the science of bodily signs. Seeing on the Buddha's footprints the mark of a thousand-spoked wheel, he followed in his track along the road until he eventually caught up with the Buddha, who was sitting beneath a tree. As the Buddha was fresh from his Enlightenment, there was a radiance about his whole being. We are told it was as though a light shone from his face—he was happy, serene, joyful. Dona was very impressed by his appearance, and he seems to have felt that this wasn't an ordinary human being, perhaps not a human being at all. Drawing near, he came straight to the point, as the custom is in India where religious matters are concerned. He said, "Who are you?"

The ancient Indians believed that the universe is stratified into various levels of existence, that there are not just human beings and animals, as we believe, but gods and ghosts, *yaksas* and *gandharvas,* and all sorts of other mythological beings, inhabiting a multi-story universe, the human plane being just one story out of many. So Dona asked, "Are you a yaksa?" (a *yaksa* being a rather terrifying sublime spirit living in the forest). But the Buddha said "No." Just "No." So Dona tried again. "Are you a *gandharva?*" (a sort of celestial musician, a beautiful singing angel-like figure). Once again the Buddha said "No," and again Dona asked, "Well then, are you a *deva?*" (a god, a divine being, a sort of archangel). "No." Upon this Dona thought, "That's strange! He must be a human being after all." And he asked him that too, but yet again the Buddha said "No." By this time Dona was thoroughly perplexed, so he demanded, "If you are not any of these things, then who are you?" The Buddha replied, "Those mental conditionings on account of which I might have been described as a *yaksa* or a *gandharva,* as a *deva* or a human being, all those conditionings have been destroyed by me. Therefore I am a Buddha."

The word for mental conditionings is samskara, which means all kinds of conditioned mental attitudes. It is these conditioned mental attitudes, these volitions or karma-formations as they are sometimes called, which, according to Buddhism, and Indian belief in general, determine the nature of our rebirth. The Buddha was free from all these, and so there was nothing to cause him to be reborn as a yaksa, a gandharva, a god, or even as a human being, and even here and now he was not in reality any of these things. He had reached the state of unconditioned consciousness, though his body might appear to be that of a man. Therefore he was called the Buddha, Buddha being as it were an incarnation, a personification, of the unconditioned mind.

The human mind proceeds by degrees, from the known to the unknown, and this is what Dona tried to do. Seeing the glorious figure of the Buddha, he tried to apply to it the only labels he had at his disposal—the labels of *yaksa, gandharva,* etc.—but none of them would fit. This is very relevant to us because there are two of Dona's categories which represent mistakes which we still commit, here and now, when we try to understand who the Buddha was, or is. These are the categories of "God" and "man," the only two categories still available to us in the West. One school of thought says, "The Buddha was a very good man, even a holy man, but just a man and no more than that." This is the view taken by, for instance, some Christian writers about Buddhism. It is a rather insidious sort of approach. Though they may praise the Buddha for his wonderful love, wonderful compassion, and wonderful wisdom, they are careful to add that after all he was only a man, whereas Jesus Christ was the Son of God. The other school says, "No, the Buddha is a sort of God for the Buddhists. Originally he was a man, of course, but after his death his followers deified him because they wanted something to worship."

Both of these views are wrong. The Buddha was a man, yes, a human being, in the sense that he started off as every other human being starts off, but he wasn't an ordinary man, he was an Enlightened man. And such a being, or Buddha, is, according to Buddhist tradition, the highest being in the universe, higher even than the so-called gods. In Buddhist art the gods are represented in humble positions on either side of the Buddha, saluting him and listening to the teaching.

A certain amount of confusion has arisen in the West about the Buddha being a god, or God, because they see that he is worshipped—that Buddhists offer flowers to the altar, light candles, and bow down—and if you worship someone, we think, it means that for you that person is God. But that is quite wrong. Not only Buddhists, but people generally in the East, have got quite a different conception of worship. In India the same word puja is used for paying respect to the Buddha, to one's parents, to one's elder brothers and sisters, to one's teachers, spiritual or secular, and to any senior or respectable person. So what the Buddhists are doing when they offer flowers to the Buddha-image is respecting or honoring the Buddha as an Enlightened being, not worshipping him as God.

But let us get back to the question of knowing the Buddha. We have seen that "Buddha" means "unconditioned mind" or "Enlightened mind." Knowing the Buddha therefore means knowing the mind in its unconditioned state. So if at this stage we are asked, "Who is the Buddha?" we can only reply, "You yourself are the Buddha—potentially." We can really and truly come to know the Buddha only in the process of actualizing—in our spiritual life, our meditation, and so on—our own potential Buddhahood. It is only then that we can say from knowledge, from experience, who the Buddha is.

We cannot do this all at once. We have to establish, first of all, a living contact with Buddhism. We have to arrive at something which goes further than mere factual knowledge about Gautama the Buddha, about the details of his earthly career, even though it falls far short of knowing the unconditioned mind, of really knowing the Buddha. This something that comes in between the two is what we call Going for Refuge to the Buddha. This does not just mean reciting Buddham saranam gacchami ("To the Buddha for Refuge I go"), though it does not exclude such recitation. It means taking Buddhahood, taking the ideal of Enlightenment, as a living spiritual ideal, as our ultimate objective, and trying our utmost to realize it. In other words, it is only by taking Refuge in the Buddha in the traditional sense that we can really know who the Buddha is. This is one of the reasons why I have always attached such great importance to the Refuges, not only to Going for Refuge to the Buddha, but also to the Dharma (the Buddha's teaching) and to the Sangha (the community of his followers).

In conclusion, it is only by taking Refuge in the Buddha, with all that that implies, that we can really and truly answer, from the heart, from the mind, and from the whole of our spiritual life, the question, "Who is the Buddha?"

WHO IS THE BUDDHA? ~ 27

WHO IS THE BUDDHA? ~ 27

WHO IS THE BUDDHA? ~ 27

WHO IS THE BUDDHA? ~ 27

WHO IS THE BUDDHA? ~ 27

WHO IS THE BUDDHA? ~ 27

WHO IS THE BUDDHA? ~ 27

WHO IS THE BUDDHA? ~ 27

WHO IS THE BUDDHA? ~ 27

WHO IS THE BUDDHA? ~ 27

WHO IS THE BUDDHA? ~ 27

WHO IS THE BUDDHA? ~ 27

WHO IS THE BUDDHA? ~ 27

WHO IS THE BUDDHA? ~ 27

WHO IS THE BUDDHA? ~ 27

WHO IS THE BUDDHA? ~ 27

WHO IS THE BUDDHA? ~ 27

WHO IS THE BUDDHA? ~ 27

WHO IS THE BUDDHA? ~ 27

WHO IS THE BUDDHA? ~ 27

WHO IS THE BUDDHA? ~ 27

WHO IS THE BUDDHA? ~ 27

WHO IS THE BUDDHA? ~ 27

WHO IS THE BUDDHA? ~ 27

2. THE SYMBOLIC MEANING OF THE FOUR SIGHTS

Most of us are occupied, much of the time, with matters that are simply unworthy of the attention of a moderately aware human being.

LET US CONSIDER the Four Sights: Siddhartha's seeing for the first time—or as if for the first time—an old man, a sick man, a corpse, and a holy wanderer. Up to this point his father had apparently managed to protect him from the world by occupying him with his martial exercises by day and entertaining him with singing girls and dancing girls in one of his three mansions by night. In a sense Siddhartha had been secluded from real life, secluded even, you might say, from reality. For in Buddhist mythical literature the father sometimes represents ignorance, while the mother may represent craving (one being the more intellectual poison, and the other the more emotional source of suffering). So Siddhartha had been hemmed in, confined, by ignorance, the universal father of those beings who live without awareness. Lacking the wider perspective, he had lived in a little world of his own. He had not known what was going on outside. He had been hardly aware that there was a world outside at all—not so aware of it as to make any difference to the way he had occupied himself, anyway. The existential reality of his situation had not yet broken in upon his little world.

A different treatment of the same theme is to be found in the parable of the burning house from the *Saddharma Pundarika,* or *White Lotus Sutra.* In a huge crumbling mansion—so the parable goes—a lot of children are engrossed in their various childish games when a fire breaks out. While the fire blazes merrily and gradually takes hold of the ancient fabric of the building, the children pay no heed to the acrid smell in the air, or the smoke curling up from under the door, or the crackle and roar of the flames and the creak and crash of falling timbers at the heart of the conflagration. They are simply not aware of the danger. They just go on amusing themselves with their toys.

We are not concerned with the rest of the story here—suffice to say that the children are eventually saved. But the point of the opening of this parable hardly needs laboring. The burning house is this world, blazing with old age, disease, and death, while the children, of course, represent ourselves. The cosmos, conditioned existence itself, is on fire with existential suffering, yet we remain immersed in our trivial pursuits, our distractions and amusements. Most of us are occupied, much of the time, with matters that are simply unworthy of the attention of a moderately aware human being. Though we may catch glimpses of our real situation, of a real purpose to our existence, it is only too easy to slip back into the old ruts carved by social pressures and long habit.

Even when we are passionately absorbed in trivia, however, even as we waste our time over distractions, sooner or later something happens. One day, occupied though we may be with inconsequential personal things, something happens, something catastrophic, and our little world is shattered or so badly cracked, so badly dented, that we can never again be really comfortable living in it. It's as though we had, until then, never been born, like a chick in its egg; but suddenly our little world is broken open, and we find ourselves looking out through a crack into another, wider world. Reality has finally started to break in. We begin to see things as they really are. We feel as though we have grown up, and are no longer entranced by the toys and tales of childhood. Or it is as though we have woken from a dream. When we are immersed in our dreams, whatever happens seems as real, as vivid, as our waking experience. But when we wake up, the dream world rapidly fades. After a few minutes, or perhaps after a few hours, it is nothing, usually not even a memory. In the same way, when reality irrupts into our sleepy, cozy existence, we look back at our old life, all the old pursuits for which we have lost the appetite we once had, and we think, "How could I have lived in that way? Was that really me? Was I really so foolish, so deluded?"

As a result of this sort of experience our behavior changes, just as an adult behaves differently from a child. People may notice that we've changed, and may even wonder if there's something wrong with us.

"Is anything the matter?" they will ask, not unkindly—though privately they may think we're not quite in our right mind, because we're no longer taking interest in the sort of things that we used to, no longer doing the things that other people like to do.

The event which shatters one's private world is very often unpleasant—it may be a bereavement, or the loss of a job, or being dropped by a lover, or discovering the infidelity of a spouse. On the other hand the breakthrough can come about in a more agreeable fashion—you may get a sudden insight through art, perhaps, or music or poetry. Then again, it can occur through an experience that is neither pleasant nor unpleasant, nor even sudden: you just become discontented and dissatisfied. But whatever serves as the trip-wire, the experience which follows tends to be painful, disturbing, and all-consuming, because the old patterns are disrupted, the old molds are broken. This is the sort of experience that Siddhartha had, as illustrated by the Four Sights.

3. THE CHARACTERISTICS OF EXISTENCE

This is the essential religious question. How may the conditioned become the Unconditioned; how may the mortal become immortal? How may I conquer death?

IN THE *MAJJHIMA NIKAYA*, the medium-length discourses of the Pali Canon, there is one discourse that is of rather special interest on account of its autobiographical content. This is the *Ariyapariyesana Sutta,* in which the Buddha describes how he left home, how he became a wandering monk, how he strove for Enlightenment, and how he deliberated about whether or not to try to teach the Dharma.

What surprises some readers of this sutta is that there is no mention in it of the famous four sights, of how Siddhartha Gautama, the future

Buddha, sallied forth one fine morning in his chariot with his charioteer and saw a sick man, and then—on successive occasions—an old man, a corpse, and finally a wandering ascetic; and thus came alive to the existence of sickness, old age, and death, and the possibility of becoming a truth-seeking wanderer.

Instead, this account gives a comparatively naturalistic, even humanistic, description of how Siddhartha came to the decision to give up the household life. It is, so far as this account is concerned, a purely internal process, not connected with anything in particular that he saw or heard. Here he is represented—in his own words—as simply reflecting.

The Buddha relates how one day he was sitting at home in the palace, reflecting alone. We should imagine him perhaps under a tree in the compound; it is probably the early evening, when a cool, calm quiet descends over the Indian scene. He is there simply reflecting, "What am I? What am I doing with my life? I am mortal, subject to old age, sickness, and death. And yet, being such, what do I do? Being myself subject to birth, I pursue that which is also subject to birth. Being myself subject to old age I pursue that which likewise will grow old. Being myself subject to sickness, to decay, I pursue that which is subject to the same decay. And being myself subject to death, I pursue that which also must die."[2]

Then—as the Buddha goes on to relate to his interlocutor in this sutta, who is a Jain ascetic—there arose in his mind a different, almost a contrary train of reflection. It occurred to him: "Suppose now I were to do otherwise? Suppose now, being myself subject to birth, I were to go in search of that which is not subject to birth, which has no origin, which is timeless? Suppose, being myself subject to old age, I were to go in search of that which is immutable? Suppose, being myself subject to sickness, to decay, I were to go in search of that in whose perfection there is no diminution? Or suppose, finally, being myself subject to death, I were to go in search of the deathless, the everlasting, the eternal?"

As a result of these reflections, shortly afterward he left home.

There is no great drama in this sutta, no stealing out of the palace by moonlight on muffled hooves. It simply says that although his father and his foster-mother wept and wailed, he put on the yellow robe, shaved his head, cut off his beard, and went forth from home into the homeless life.

This is the story, in brief, of the Buddha's conversion—conversion in the literal sense of a "turning round," though in Siddhartha's case it was not an external turning round from one religion to another, but an internal one, from the conditioned to the Unconditioned. Siddhartha realized that he was a conditioned being, and that he was spending all his time and energy in pursuit of conditioned things—that is, in the *anariyapariyesana* or "ignoble quest." He realized, in other words, that he was binding himself to the endless round of existence, the wheel of life on which we all turn, passing from one life to the next indefinitely.

So he decided simply to turn round completely and go in search of the Unconditioned instead, to take up the *ariyapariyesana,* the "noble quest." In time, he would realize this quest as the spiral path leading from the endless round to the goal of Enlightenment or nirvana. But at this point he identified the course before him with this simple but strong, pre-Buddhistic expression, found in the oldest Upanishads: *esana,* urge, desire, will, search, aspiration, quest, pursuit. He could continue with the "ignoble quest," or he could undertake the "noble quest" instead.

The Buddha's conversion was not easy, we can be sure of that, because here and there, in other places in the scriptures, we get indications that a terrible struggle went on in his mind before he made his final decision. But stripped of all the legends and myths that have accumulated around it over the centuries, it was as simple—almost classically simple—as this. And it is in this most simple description of the first great insight of the Buddha-to-be that the essence of the spiritual life is to be found. Here we put our finger on the spring that works the whole mechanism.

This spring is the conditioned in pursuit of the Unconditioned, the mortal seeking the immortal: seeking, that is, not immortality of the self, but a self-transcending immortality. What Siddhartha was looking for was basically the answer to a question, one that we find asked (in the *Majjhima Nikaya*) by a young monk, Govinda, who spends a rainy season retreat—that is, a retreat of about three months—meditating on metta or universal loving-kindness, and as a result has a vision of the "eternal youth" Brahma Sanatkumara. The question Govinda asks Sanatkumara in this sutta is "How may the mortal obtain the immortal Brahma world?"[3]

This is the essential religious question. How may the conditioned become the Unconditioned; how may the mortal become immortal? How may I conquer death? Now it all sounds very fine put like that, but if one is going to take seriously the question of how to leave the conditioned and go in search of the Unconditioned, one will want a further question answered. What exactly does one mean by the conditioned? How do we identify the conditioned?

According to Buddhist tradition, that which is conditioned invariably bears three characteristics, or *laksanas,* by which it may be recognized as such. These three characteristics are sometimes called the "three signs of being," but more properly this should be the "three signs of becoming," as the nature of the conditioned is nothing as static as a "state of being."

The three *laksanas,* the three inseparable characteristics of all conditioned existence, are: *duhkha,* the unsatisfactory, or painful; *anitya,* the impermanent; and *anatman,* the emptiness of self, of essential being.[4] All conditioned things or beings whatsoever in this universe possess these three characteristics. They are all unsatisfactory, all impermanent, and all devoid of self. Of these three *laksanas* the first is in some ways the most difficult for most people to come to terms with, emotionally, so we shall look at it in rather more depth and detail than at the other two.

Suffering

The Sanskrit word here is *duhkha,* and the usual translation is "suffering," but a better one—if a bit cumbersome—is "unsatisfactoriness."

Best of all, perhaps, is to attend to its etymology: though the traditional account of the origin of the word *duhkha* is no longer universally accepted, it still leaves us with a true and precise image.

Duh- as a prefix means anything that is not good—bad, ill, wrong, or out of place; and *kha,* the main part of the word, is supposed to be connected with the Sanskrit *cakra,* meaning "wheel." So *duhkha* is said to have meant originally the ill-fitting wheel of a chariot, thus suggesting a bumpy, jarring ride, a journey on which one could never be comfortable, never at one's ease.

So much for a general picture of *duhkha.* As we look closer, though, we see that unease or suffering comes in many different forms—and the Buddha usually speaks of seven.[5] Firstly, he says, *birth* is suffering: human life starts with suffering. In the more poetical words of Oscar Wilde, "At the birth of a child or a star there is pain." In whatever way it is expressed, this is a great spiritual truth; it is significant that our life begins with suffering.

Birth is certainly physically painful for the mother, and consequently it is often emotionally painful for the father, while for the infant it is, we are told, a traumatic experience. It is very unpleasant to be suddenly thrust forth from a world of total harmony in the womb out into a cold, strange world, to which one is very likely to be welcomed with a slap on the bottom.

Secondly, the Buddha says, *old age* is suffering. One of the discomforts of old age is physical weakness: you cannot get about in the relaxed, agile way you used to. Then there is loss of memory: you can't remember names, or where you put things; you are not as agile and flexible intellectually as you were. Where this degeneration becomes senility it is a tragic thing to observe, most especially in once-eminent individuals. Perhaps most painful of all, when you are very old you are dependent upon others: you cannot do much for yourself, and you may even need constant looking after by a nurse or by your relations. Despite all modern comforts and amenities—and often as a result of modern advances in medicine—many of us will experience this suffering, especially if we survive to an extreme old age.

Thirdly, *sickness* is suffering. Whether it is a toothache or an incurable disease like cancer, no sickness is pleasant. It is not just the physical pain that is suffering: there is also the helplessness, the fear, and the frustration of it. Medical science may sometimes palliate the suffering of sickness, but there is no sign at all that we will ever banish it entirely. It seems that no sooner do we get rid of one disease than another comes along. As soon as one virus is defeated, a new, stronger strain of virus arises. And as soon as we feel physically quite healthy, we start to develop all sorts of mental ailments, more and more complex neuroses and mysterious syndromes, all of which involve suffering. Almost any sense of imperfection in our lives can develop into an illness of some sort: stress turns into heart attacks, fatigue turns into syndromes, habit turns into addictions. So it seems that sickness may change its appearance, but it doesn't go away.

Fourthly, *death* is suffering. We suffer when those dear to us die; we suffer as we watch the life ebbing from a physical body that we have long associated with the life of a loved one. We suffer in the knowledge that our loved ones will die, and we suffer in the knowledge of our own dissolution. Much of our suffering with regard to death, of course, is simply fear. Most of us will put up with a great deal of suffering before we will choose to die, such is our terror of the inevitable conclusion to our own existence:

> The weariest and most loath'd worldly life,
> That age, ache, penury, and imprisonment
> Can lay on nature, is a paradise
> To what we fear of death.[6]

People do not always feel ready to die. They are sorry to leave the scene of their labors and pleasures and achievements. Even if they do want to go, even if they are quite happy to pass on to a new life, or into they know not what, there is still the pain involved in the physical process of dissolution. And with this goes, sometimes, a great deal of mental suffering. Sometimes on their deathbeds, people are stricken with remorse: they remember terrible wrongs they have done, dreadful harm and pain they have visited on certain individuals; and they may have, in consequence, fears and apprehensions for the future. All this makes death a horrifying experience for many people, and one which, before it comes, they do their best not to think about.

Fifthly, *contact with what one dislikes* is suffering. We all know this. It may be that even in our own family there are people with whom we just don't get on. This is very tragic, especially when it is our own parents or children whom we dislike. Because the tie—even the attachment—of blood is there, well, we have to put up with a certain amount of contact, and this can be painful.

The work we do can also be a source of suffering, if we do it just because we need to earn a living and it is the only work we can get. Again, we may feel that we have to put up with what we dislike, and perhaps work with people we find uncongenial, for periods of time anyway, even though we would rather do something else.

There are, as well, all sorts of environmental conditions which are unpleasant: pollution, noise, weather. It is obviously not possible for everyone to go off and live in a Greek villa. So there seems to be no way of escape—certainly no way of escaping entirely. You just have to live with people, places, things, and conditions that you don't altogether like.

Sixthly, *separation from what one likes* is suffering. This can be a very harrowing form of suffering indeed. There are people we would like to be with, to meet more often—relations, friends—but circumstances intervene and it becomes simply impossible. This happens often in time of war, when families are broken up—men conscripted and taken to far-off battlefields, children sent away to places of safety, and people simply disappearing as refugees.

When I was in India during the war as a signals operator, many of my friends used to get letters from home regularly every week or so; and then a day might come when the letters would stop. They wouldn't know what had happened, but they would know that there were bombs falling in England, so after a while they would start suspecting the worst. Eventually, perhaps, they would get the news, either from another relation or officially, that their wife and children, or their parents, or their brothers and sisters, had been killed in an aerial bombardment. This is the most terrible suffering—permanent separation from those we love. Some people never get over such suffering, and brood over their loss for the rest of their lives.

Seventhly, *not to get what one wants* is suffering. There is little need to elaborate upon this. When you have set your heart on something (or someone) and you fail to achieve your goal, when the prize does not fall to you, then you feel disappointed and frustrated, even bitter. We have all known short-lived experiences of this kind, when we fail to get a job we particularly wanted, or fail to be selected for something, or find that someone else has got to something (or someone) before us.

Some people experience a lifetime of disappointment, frustration, and bitterness if they feel that life has short-changed them in some way—and of course the stronger the desire, the more the suffering. But even just in small ways, it happens almost every day, if not every hour—for example, when we find that all the cake has gone.

So these are the seven different aspects of *duhkha* identified by the Buddha. The Buddha once declared, "One thing only do I teach—suffering and the cessation of suffering"[7]—and emancipation from the bondage of suffering is indeed the keynote of his teaching. In the Pali scriptures he compares himself to a physician who attempts to relieve his patient of a tormenting disease—the disease of conditioned existence with which we are all afflicted.[8] Of course, we are not always willing patients, as the Buddha clearly found. But on the many occasions when he spoke about suffering, and tried to get people to see it in perspective, he would apparently sum up his discourse by saying that existence as a whole is painful, that the totality of conditioned sentient experience, comprising form, feeling, perceptions, volitions, and consciousness, is unsatisfactory.

Most people would say that this is going a bit far, that it is a pessimistic, if not morbid view of life. They would say that human existence can by no means be said to be unsatisfactory and painful all the way through. They will admit to birth being painful, they will agree that sickness, old age, and yes, death, are indeed painful. But at the same time they are reluctant to accept the conclusion which follows from all this, which is that conditioned existence itself is suffering. It is as though they admit all the individual digits in the sum, but they won't accept the total to which those digits add up. They say that yes, there is a certain amount of suffering in the world, but on the whole it's not such a bad place. Why be so negative? There's plenty to smile about. While there's life, there's hope.

And there is, of course. We have pleasant experiences as well as painful ones. But the Buddhist view is that even the pleasant experiences are at bottom painful. They are really only suffering concealed, glossed over, deferred—a whistling in the dark. And the extent to which we can see this, see the suffering behind the gilding of pleasure, "the skull beneath the skin," depends on our spiritual maturity.

Edward Conze has identified four different aspects of concealed suffering.[9] Firstly, something that is pleasant for oneself may involve suffering for other people, for other beings. We don't tend to consider this, of course. If we are all right, if we're having a good time, we don't worry too much or too often about others: "I'm all right, Jack" more or less sums up this attitude. The most common example of this is the frank enjoyment with which people eat the flesh of slaughtered animals. They go on merrily plying knife and fork without consciously thinking about the suffering of the animals.

But the unconscious mind is not so easily fooled. You can shut out an unpleasant fact from the conscious mind, but unconsciously you notice everything and you forget nothing. You may never be consciously aware of that unpleasant fact, but it will exert an influence on your mental state that is all the more powerful for being unseen. In this way we develop an "irrational" feeling of guilt, because in the depths of ourselves we know that our own pleasure has been bought at the expense of the suffering of other living beings. This guilt is the source of a great deal of uneasiness and anxiety.

Conze gives the example of wealthy people, who are nearly always afraid of becoming poor. This is, he says, because unconsciously they feel that they don't deserve to have their money. Unconsciously they feel that it *ought* to be taken away from them, and consciously they worry that perhaps it *will* be taken away from them. By contrast, it is noticeable that poor people who may not know where next week's food is coming from are rarely racked with anxiety over it. They are generally much more relaxed and cheerful than the rich.

Wealthy people may suffer from unconscious guilt feelings because they know, however much they may deny it consciously, that their wealth is "tainted," because its acquisition has brought suffering to other people, directly or indirectly. Consequently, they feel a constant need to justify themselves. They say, "I earn my money, I contribute to the well-being of the community, I offer a service that people want, I provide employment . . ." Or else they say, "Well, if I'm rich and other people are poor, it's because I work harder, I take risks—at least I don't ask to be spoon-fed . . ." If the feeling of guilt gets too much, then drastic measures are required to relieve it, and the most drastic measure of all is to give away some of that wealth—to the church, or to a hospital or some other deserving charity. Charity giving is a favorite option because it allows the giver to compensate for the suffering caused in acquiring the wealth by giving some of it to alleviate suffering. It is called "conscience money." If one has anything to do with religious organizations, one soon learns to recognize this sort of donation. Sometimes it is just put through the letter box in an envelope inscribed "from an anonymous donor." Then you know that someone's conscience is really biting.

Conze's second kind of concealed suffering is a pleasant experience which has a flavor of anxiety because you are afraid of losing it. Political power is like this: it is a very sweet thing to exercise power over other people, but you always have to watch your back, not knowing if you can trust even your best friend, or the very bodyguards at your door. All the time you are afraid of losing that power, especially if you have seized it by force, and others are waiting for their own chance to get their hands on it. Someone in such a position does not sleep easily. The traditional Buddhist illustration of this kind of experience is that of a hawk flying off with a piece of meat in its talons. What happens, of course, is that dozens of other hawks fly after it to try and seize that piece of meat for themselves, and the way they accomplish this is to tear and stab not at the meat itself but at the possessor of the meat, pecking at its body, its wings, its head, its eyes.[10] The highly competitive world of finance and business and entertainment is like this. Any pleasure that involves any element of power or status is contaminated by an element of anxiety, by the sense that others would like to be able to replace you at the top of your own particular dunghill.

The third concealed suffering indicated by Dr. Conze is something which is pleasant but which binds us to something else that brings about suffering. The example he gives is the human body. Through it we experience all sorts of pleasurable sensations that make us very attached to it; but we experience all sorts of unpleasant sensations through it as well. So our attachment to that which provides us with pleasant sensations binds us also to that which provides us with unpleasant sensations. We can't have the one without the other.

Lastly, Conze suggests that concealed suffering is to be found in the fact that pleasures derived from the experience of conditioned things cannot satisfy the deepest longings of the heart. In each one of us there is something that is Unconditioned, something that is not of this world, something transcendental, the Buddha-nature—call it what you like. Whatever you call it, you can recognize it by the fact that it cannot be satisfied by anything conditioned. It can be satisfied only by the Unconditioned. Whatever conditioned things you may enjoy there is always a lack, a void, which only the Unconditioned can fill. Ultimately, it is for this reason that—to come back to the Buddha's conclusion—all conditioned things are unsatisfactory, painful, either actually or potentially. It is in the light of the Unconditioned that suffering, *duhkha,* is clearly seen as characteristic of all forms of conditioned existence, and of sentient conditioned existence especially.

Impermanence

The second fundamental characteristic of conditioned existence, *anitya,* is quite easily translated. *Nitya* is "permanent," "eternal," so with the addition of the negative prefix you get "impermanent," "non-eternal." It is also quite easily understood—intellectually at least. It can hardly be denied that all conditioned things, all compounded things, are constantly changing. They are by definition made up of parts—that is, compounded. And that which is compounded, made up of parts, can also be uncompounded, can be reduced to its parts again—which is what happens, of course, all the time.

It should really be easier to understand this truth nowadays than it was in the Buddha's day. We now have the authority of science to assure us that there's no such thing as matter in the sense of actual lumps of hard solid matter scattered throughout space. We know that what we think of as matter is in reality only various forms of energy.

But the same great truth applies to the mind. There is nothing unchanging in our internal experience of ourselves, nothing permanent or immortal. There is only a constant succession of mental states, feelings, perceptions, volitions, acts of consciousness. In fact, the mind changes even more quickly than the physical body. We cannot usually see the physical body changing, but if we are observant we can see our mental states changing from moment to moment.

This is the reason for the Buddha's (at first sight) rather strange assertion that it is a bigger mistake to identify yourself (as a stable entity) with the mind than with the body.[11] But this is the Buddhist position. Belief in the reality of the "self" is a bigger spiritual mistake than belief in the reality of the body. This is because the body at least possesses a certain relative stability; but there is no stability to the mind at all. It is constantly, perceptibly changing.

Broadly speaking, the *laksana* of *anitya* points to the fact that the whole universe from top to bottom, in all its grandeur, in all its immensity, is just one vast congeries of processes of different types, taking place at different levels—and all interrelated. Nothing ever stands still, not even for an instant, not even for a fraction of a second.

We do not see this, though. When we look up we see the everlasting hills, and in the night sky we descry the same stars as were mapped by our ancestors at the dawn of history. Houses stand from generation to generation, and the old oak furniture within them seems to become more solid with the passing of the years. Even our own bodies seem much the same from one year to the next. It is only when the increments of change add up to something notable, when a great house is burnt down, when we realize that the star we are looking at is already extinct, or when we ourselves take to our deathbed, that we realize the truth of impermanence or non-eternity, that all conditioned things—from the tiniest particles to the most massive stars—begin, continue, and then cease.

Emptiness of Self

The third *laksana, anatman,* encapsulates the truth that all conditioned things are devoid of a permanent, unchanging self. So what does this mean exactly? When the Buddha denied the reality of the idea of the *atman,* what was he actually denying? What was the belief or doctrine of *atman* held by the Buddha's contemporaries, the Hindus of his day?

Actually, in the Upanishads alone there are many different conceptions of *atman* mentioned.[12] In some it is said that the *atman,* the self—or the soul, if you like—is the physical body. Elsewhere the view is propounded that the *atman* is just as big as the thumb, is material, and abides in the heart. But the most common view in the Buddha's day, the one with which he appears to have been most concerned, asserted that the *atman* was individual—in the sense that I am I and you are you—incorporeal or immaterial, conscious, unchanging, blissful, and sovereign—in the sense of exercising complete control over its own destiny.

The Buddha maintained that there was no such entity—and he did so by appealing to experience. He said that if you look within, at yourself, at your own mental life, you can account for everything you observe under just five headings: form, feeling, perception, volitions, and acts of consciousness. Nothing discovered in these categories can be observed to be permanent. There is nothing sovereign or ultimately blissful among them. Everything in them arises in dependence on conditions, and is unsatisfactory in one way or another. These five categories or aggregates are *anatman*. They don't constitute any such self as the Hindus of the Buddha's day asserted. Such a self exists neither in them nor outside of them nor associated with them in any other way.

The Three Liberations

Seeing conditioned existence, seeing life, in this way, as invariably subject to suffering, to impermanence, to emptiness of self, is called *vipasyana* (Sanskrit) or *vipassana* (Pali), which translates into English as "insight."

Insight is not just intellectual understanding. It can be developed only on the basis of a controlled, purified, elevated, concentrated, integrated mind—in other words, through meditative practice. Insight is a direct intuitive perception that takes place in the depths of meditation when the ordinary mental processes have fallen into abeyance. A preliminary intellectual understanding of these three characteristics is certainly helpful, but ultimately, insight is something that transcends the intellectual workings of the mind.

So in meditation, through insight, you see that without exception everything you experience through the five senses and through the mind—everything you can feel and touch and smell and taste and see and think about—is conditioned, is subject to suffering, is impermanent, is empty of self. When you see things in this way then you experience what is technically called revulsion or disgust, and you turn away from the conditioned. It is important to note that this is a spiritual experience, not just a psychological reaction; you turn away not because you are personally repelled by things as such, but because you see that the conditioned is not, on its own terms, worth having. When that turning away from the conditioned to the Unconditioned takes place decisively, it is said that you enter the "stream" leading to nirvana.

4. *Dukkha* as an Example of Conditionality

People often conclude that Buddhism is suffering-oriented, inward-looking, and self-centered, as though the idea was to become immersed in one's own suffering and how to alleviate it. But this is not what the Buddha is saying.

BUDDHIST TRADITION makes a distinction between those teachings that require interpretation and those that do not. The Buddha's statement in the *Dhammapada* that hatred never ceases by hatred is literally true, and the truth of it can be seen quite clearly in everyday life (except, of course, by those who are blinded by the desire for revenge). There are other teachings, however, that require us to go beyond the literal meaning, demanding a prior knowledge before we can understand them. The Buddha's teaching about *dukkha* is a good example of this kind of teaching. It is not often realized that when he speaks of suffering, its origin, and its cessation, he is using that as an *example* of how things arise and cease. It is not a definitive statement; in terms of another traditional distinction, it is method rather than doctrine.

It is worth giving careful thought to this. People often conclude that Buddhism is suffering-oriented, inward-looking, and self-centered, as though the idea was to become immersed in one's own suffering and how to alleviate it. But this is not what the Buddha is saying. What is usually translated as "suffering" is the Pali term *dukkha,* which points to the fact that conditioned existence, taken as a whole, is unsatisfactory and frustrating. But this does not mean that Buddhists view life as unremittingly painful and unpleasant, which it obviously is not. On the other hand, we can be sure that the Buddha did not choose this example of the workings of conditionality at random. It is salutary to reflect on the inherent unsatisfactoriness of things; this is an example of what is traditionally called "bending the bamboo the other way." We are not being asked to stop finding life agreeable, if that is our experience, but to acknowledge that however agreeable it may be, it is never wholly so. *Dukkha* is pain and sickness, but it is also lack of complete fulfillment; it is anxiety and loss, bitterness and cynicism, a sense of lengthening shadows. It is also the truth that even pleasant circumstances cannot last forever, inasmuch as they arise within conditioned existence.

5. THE BUDDHA'S VICTORY

According to the Buddha, the spiritual life is an active life, a strenuous life. We might even say that it is a *militant* life.

ALTHOUGH VERY FEW people in the West have so far had the opportunity to study or practice Buddhism to any great depth, most of us will have formed some sort of impression of it. We will have formed, too, some sort of impression of the Buddha. We meet people or we hear of people who have espoused Buddhism, we read articles about Buddhism in the newspapers, we hear people talking on the radio or the television about Buddhism—we may even, if we go to the cinema, see film stars impersonating the Buddha. Some of these impressions may be quite positive, even in some degree accurate, but inevitably there will be others which are very misleading. And, once established, misconceptions are notoriously difficult to eradicate. The most persistent misconceptions derive, in fact, from the earliest Western interpreters of Buddhism, who naturally saw it from the standpoint of their own religious tradition, a Victorian version of Christianity. They tended—naturally enough—to see the Buddha as a sort of oriental Jesus, and the popular Victorian conception of Jesus was a rather milk-and-water version of the real thing. If for the Victorians, as has been said, Christ was a ghostly figure in a white sheet gliding around Galilee and gently rebuking people for not believing in the Nicene Creed, a Victorian Buddha was likewise installed in the popular imagination as a ghostly figure in a yellow sheet gliding around India and gently rebuking people for not being kind to animals.

In this way, Buddhism began to be perceived as a rather passive, negative, or gutless teaching and tradition. This impression, unfortunately, can only be reinforced, perhaps unconsciously, by any acquaintance one may have with later Buddhist art, in which decadent phase the Buddha is depicted as a sweet, dreamy, effeminate figure. As for the mass-produced representations of the Buddha that are turned out in India today—usually on calendars—their attempts at the smile of Enlightenment leave the Buddha with the coquettish simper of a sentimental starlet. Such images cannot but influence the way we see the Buddha in our own minds.

In order to redress this imbalance we have to take a fresh look at what Buddhism is about; we have to rethink, perhaps, our whole attitude to the spiritual life. The aim of Buddhist teaching is the attainment of Enlightenment, or Buddhahood, a state of moral and spiritual perfection, and this ideal calls for the exercise, on the moral and spiritual plane, of heroic qualities. When we speak of the heroic ideal in Buddhism, we are not speaking of anything distinct from—much less still opposed to—the spiritual ideal. We are speaking of the spiritual ideal itself—an ideal that requires heroism in the highest degree.

Of course, "hero" is rather an unfashionable word these days, but it translates—more accurately than any less challenging term does—one of the titles by which Siddhartha Gautama was known after his Enlightenment. We know him as "the Buddha," or sometimes "the Compassionate One," but the Pali and Sanskrit texts also apply to the Buddha the epithets Mahavira, which means "Great Hero," and Jina, which means "Conqueror." In fact, the title Jina is almost as common in the earliest Buddhist texts as the one we are so familiar with, "the Buddha." He is the Conqueror because he has conquered the whole of conditioned existence within himself. He has conquered the world by conquering himself. According to the *Dhammapada,* "Though one may conquer in battle a thousand men a thousand times, yet he who conquers himself has the more glorious victory." Later, medieval Buddhism produced the idea of the Trailokya Vijaya, "the conquest of the three worlds"—conquest, that is, of the world of sensuous desire, the world of archetypal form, and the world of no form. So the Jina's victory is over these three inner worlds.

But victory usually implies victory over someone or something. Who or what, then, could this have been in the Buddha's case? The answer is simple: the Buddha conquered Mara, the "Evil One," and after conquering Mara, attained Enlightenment. In a sense, his conquest of Mara, his *Mara-vijaya* as it is called, *was* his attainment of Enlightenment.

It is possible that you have already encountered descriptions of the episode of the conquest of Mara. Perhaps you have seen it depicted in Buddhist art. If so, you will have seen the Buddha-to-be sitting on a heap of kusa grass beneath the spreading branches of the *ficus religiosus,* or sacred fig tree—which species was subsequently known, in honor of the Buddha, as the Bodhi tree, or "tree of Enlightenment." He is surrounded on all sides by thousands of fearsome figures, all horribly misshapen and deformed. Some of them are whirling enormous clubs, some are spitting fire; some are in the act of hurling great rocks, even whole mountains that they have torn up by the roots; some again are discharging arrows. These are the forces of Mara. Mara himself stands to one side directing his terrible army in its onslaught on the Buddha. But the Buddha takes no notice. He is completely surrounded by an aura of golden light. As soon as the various missiles touch this aura they turn into flowers and fall to the ground at the Buddha's feet as though in worship. The Buddha is undisturbed and carries on meditating. He does not take any notice even when Mara summons his three daughters and orders them to dance in the most seductive manner. So Mara retires defeated, his forces disappear, and his three daughters withdraw in confusion. The Buddha is left alone beneath the Bodhi tree on his heap of kusa grass, and carries on meditating. Sitting there in that way, he attains Enlightenment.

Such is the well-known episode. But like other-well known episodes in the Buddha's life, it is open to misunderstanding. We might of course realize that the episode is symbolic, but we may not understand that the episode of the *Mara-vijaya* was not the Buddha's only victory but rather the culmination of an entire series of victories. This is only to be expected, because spiritual life is like that. Just as one does not develop the fullness of wisdom or the fullness of compassion all at once, one does not develop the fullness of energy and heroism necessary to defeat Mara and his forces all at once. As with any spiritual quality, it is developed gradually. As the Buddha said in the *Dhammapada,* "As a pot becomes full by the constant falling of drops of water, so, little by little, does a man fill himself with good." Before the Buddha's great victory there were many other victories, without which the great victory could hardly have taken place. We shall now consider some of those lesser victories—lesser, of course, only in relation to the great victory over Mara. In themselves, these lesser victories are such as we might find hard even to imagine.

The Buddha's first victory, so far as we know at least, is generally described as the "Going Forth" from home into homelessness. We may not be accustomed to considering this as a victory, but that is what it was. Just suppose that you were the son or daughter of wealthy parents, with high social position and great prestige. Suppose you were young, healthy, and good looking. Suppose too that you were happily married, perhaps with a child. Would *you* have found it easy to give it all up? Would you have been able to "go forth" for the sake of you knew not what—for the sake of the "truth," for the sake of something "higher," something beyond anything you had yet experienced or imagined? This is exactly what Siddhartha, the Buddha-to-be, did.

There are several accounts of what happened on that occasion, some of them very colorful and romantic. They describe, for instance, how Siddhartha drew aside a curtain in the inner apartments of his palace and took his last long, lingering look at his peacefully sleeping wife and infant son. They describe how the gods of the various heavens silently opened the gates so that he could depart unseen and unheard. And they describe how those same gods supported the hooves of his horse on the palms of their hands so that there would be no noise. . . . But the oldest account is actually very simple. Reminiscing in his old age, the Buddha simply said to his disciples:

> Then I, monks, after a time, being young, my hair coal-black, possessed of radiant youth, in the prime of my life—although my unwilling parents wept and wailed—having cut off my hair and beard, having put on yellow robes, went forth from home into homelessness.[13]

Whether the description is elaborate or simple, what happened is sufficiently clear. The Buddha-to-be left home. He left his family, left the group. But in what sense was this a victory? What was it a victory over? It was a victory over the family, or rather, over the group, as represented especially by his parents. But it was also a victory in a deeper sense. It was a victory over his *attachment* to the group. It could not have been easy for Siddhartha to leave his family; his departure must have been preceded by a long internal struggle. But in the end he broke free from the group. This did not just mean leaving it physically: it meant overcoming group attitudes and group conditioning; it meant taking the initiative, doing something that he wanted to do; it meant thinking for himself, experiencing things for himself; it meant living his own life; it meant being an *individual*. Thus the "Going Forth" from home into homelessness was a victory over the "internalized" group.

Having gone forth, Siddhartha approached two famous spiritual teachers. These teachers, who seem to have been good and noble men, taught him everything they knew, taught him what they believed to be the highest truth. Siddhartha was a very good pupil, and learned what they had to teach. Whatever they taught him, he experienced for himself, very quickly becoming their equal. Realizing this, they offered to share with him the leadership of the communities they had founded. But he refused and, leaving them, returned to his solitary wanderings.

This too was a victory, a victory over spiritual complacency and spiritual ambition. Siddhartha had experienced for himself everything that his teachers had to teach, but he knew that there was still something "beyond," something higher which he had not yet realized—

and which he wanted to realize. He knew that he was not yet fully Enlightened, despite what his teachers were telling him. In other words, he did not settle down with a limited spiritual experience— even though by ordinary standards it was quite an exalted experience. It was not the highest, and Siddhartha *knew* that it was not the highest. In this way he overcame spiritual complacency. Moreover, his teachers had offered to share with him the leadership of their communities. What an opportunity was this for a young man! But Siddhartha refused. He was not concerned with leadership. He was concerned with truth, he was concerned with Enlightenment. In this way he overcame spiritual ambition.

It is interesting to note that Siddhartha overcame spiritual complacency and spiritual ambition at the same time. The two are closely connected. If you are spiritually ambitious, in the sense of seeking a position of spiritual leadership, you are likely to become spiritually complacent. Similarly, if you are spiritually complacent, you will tend to seek a position of spiritual leadership by way of compensation for your lack of real spiritual effort.

Continuing his quest alone, Siddhartha decided to live in the depths of the forest, far from any human habitation. He lived somewhere where it was very difficult to live, even for those committed to the spiritual life. Furthermore, he stayed in what we would call haunted places, places inhabited, at least according to popular belief, by ghosts and spirits—places in which feelings of fear and terror were likely to arise. And those feelings of panic, fear, and terror *did* arise in his mind. So what did Siddhartha do on these occasions? If the fear and terror arose while he was walking to and fro, he continued walking to and fro until he had overcome them. He did not run away, did not try to escape from those feelings. Similarly, if they arose while he was sitting still, or while he was lying down, then that is where he faced and overcame them. In this way he was victorious over fear.

Even today, of course, many people have this experience of fear and terror, panic and dread—or of anxiety at least—especially when they are alone. But however and wherever we have this sort of experience, it is important to face it. It is important not to run away, whether literally or metaphorically. If we face it we will eventually overcome it, as Siddhartha did.

Even though Siddhartha had overcome fear, he had still not attained Enlightenment. He now embarked upon a course of extreme "self-mortification." The Buddhist scriptures give us full details of the various torments that he inflicted upon himself. Suffice it to say that he subsequently asserted that no one else had ever gone to such extremes of self-mortification. Indeed, he very nearly died. But there were compensations. He became famous. In those days it was popularly believed that you could attain Enlightenment by means of self-mortification—the more extreme the better. He therefore attracted, in particular, five close disciples, who intended to remain with him until, as a result of his self-mortification, he attained Enlightenment.

But Siddhartha did not attain Enlightenment in this way. Apparently, he remained as far from it as ever. He therefore gave up self-mortification, even though he had been practicing it for years, and—to the shock of his disciples—started taking solid food again. The five disciples immediately left him, deeply disappointed that he was not the man they had thought he was. He had weakened, they thought, and had returned to a life of luxury. Once again Siddhartha was left alone.

On the face of it this may look like a defeat, but it was actually a great victory. Siddhartha had overcome the very human tendency to refuse to admit that one has made a mistake, that one has been on the wrong path, and that one must now retrace one's steps and start all over again. After all, when one has invested a great deal of energy, not to speak of time, money, and all sorts of other things, in making that mistake, one does not like to admit, even to oneself, that all that effort has in a sense been wasted. But Siddhartha did not mind doing this. He did not mind losing his disciples; he did not mind being on his own again. It would have been easy, in comparison, to continue with his self-mortification, easy to become more and more famous, easy to attract great numbers of disciples. But instead he admitted that he had made a mistake, and continued his quest.

Eventually, it took him to the foot of the Bodhi tree. There he sat down, as we have seen, and was attacked by Mara and his forces. But who, or what, is Mara? I have already described this episode as it is depicted in Buddhist art, but I must now pay some attention to its significance—even though the symbolic terms in which the episode is described do communicate their own message. If we do not understand what Mara represents, we will not be able to understand the true significance of the Buddha's victory over Mara.

The word *Mara* means "killing," "destroying," it means bringing death and pestilence. Mara is therefore the principle of destruction. Sometimes this principle is personified, and thus it happens that the Buddhist texts mention no less than *four* Maras. These are (in Pali) MaccuMara, KhandhaMara, KilesaMara, and DevaputtaMara. We will look at each of them in turn.

First of all comes MaccuMara. Here, Mara simply means "death" or "destruction." Death, of course, is usually very unwelcome. Sometimes people are surprised when it comes, even though they should have known it would come some time. Because death is so unwelcome, people tend to regard it as an evil. But in itself death is neither good nor evil: it is just a fact of existence and has to be recognized. That is what MaccuMara represents.

Secondly, rather more metaphysically, there is KhandhaMara. This Mara represents a sort of extension of MaccuMara. Here we remember that death is not just an abstraction, not just a word. Death is a concrete reality. Death means that there are things and beings which die, which are destroyed. And these things and beings between them constitute a world. In other words, there is a world which is under the sway of death. This is the world of what are called the *khandhas,* in Pali (Sanskrit *skandhas*). These *khandhas,* or "aggregates," as the word is often translated, are five in number: *rupa,* or material form, *vedana,* or feeling, *samjna,* or perception, *sankhara,* or volition, and *vijnana,* or consciousness. These five *khandhas* are well known; if you know anything at all about Buddhism you will be familiar with them. Between them they represent the whole of conditioned, mundane existence, or, in more traditional terms, the whole of samsara. That is what KhandhaMara represents.

Thirdly, there is KilesaMara. *Kilesa* comes from a root meaning "to adhere" or "to stick to," and is cognate with the word for "slime"; it means "stain," "soil," or "impurity," or, in an ethical sense, "depravity," "lust," or "passion." Broadly speaking, *kilesa* corresponds to what are otherwise called *akusalacittani*, unskillful mental states. The five principal *kilesas*, or "defilements," as they are generally called in English, are: craving, aversion, ignorance, conceit, and distraction. The first three of these—craving, aversion, and ignorance—correspond to the three *akusalamulas* or "roots of unskillfulness" which are represented by the cock, the snake, and the pig that we see at the center of the Tibetan Wheel of Life. It is these three that keep the wheel turning. In other words, it is because our minds are dominated by the *kilesas* that we are reborn within samsara, reborn in the world of conditioned existence, the world that is under the sway of death. This is what KilesaMara represents.

And then there is DevaputtaMara. Deva means "god," with a small G, and *putta* means "son." So Devaputta means "son of god," which is to say, a god—just as "son of man" means a man. DevaputtaMara is Mara as an actually existing being or person. He is the being who appears in the episode of the Buddha's *Mara-vijaya*. Sometimes DevaputtaMara is regarded as being simply a personification of the *kilesas* or defilements, but he cannot really be reduced in this way. Naturally he is dominated by the defilements, just as are most beings within samsara; but at the same time he has his own being and position in the universe, his own place in Buddhist mythology.

Buddhism sees the universe as consisting of various planes and worlds, which are the objective counterparts—or correlatives—of mental states, both positive and negative. Just as there is a "world" of human beings, according to Buddhist cosmology, so also is there a "world" of animals, a "world" of gods, a "world" of demons, and so on.

Mara belongs to one of these worlds, in fact to one of the lower heaven worlds. Low though it is, however, Mara rules over this world; indeed, he rules over all the worlds belonging to what is called the *kamaloka,* or "realm of sensuous desire," which includes our own human world. In a wider sense, of course, Mara rules over the entire universe, the whole of conditioned existence, because it is subject to *death,* which Mara primarily represents. But he rules particularly over the *kamaloka,* the realm of sensuous desire.

In order to understand why this should be we must first realize that above the realm of sensuous desire there is the *rupaloka* or "realm of archetypal form." This realm corresponds to the various mental states of higher meditative consciousness. From these states, from the *rupaloka,* it is possible to gain Enlightenment—which it is not possible to do from the *kamaloka.* Mara is therefore particularly anxious to stop people reaching the *rupaloka,* that is, stop them escaping from the *kamaloka.* This is why Mara, with the help of his forces and his daughters, tried to interrupt the Buddha's meditation beneath the Bodhi tree. Perhaps he sometimes tries to interrupt *your* meditation. Perhaps that little distraction which arises in your mind, perhaps even that little tickling sensation that distracts you, is none other than Mara.

Perhaps now I have said enough about Mara to place us in a better position to understand what it was that the Buddha conquered. We can now return to the *Mara-vijaya* itself. As we have seen, there are four Maras: MaccuMara, KhandhaMara, KilesaMara, and Devaputta-Mara. The Buddha overcame all four of them; his victory was therefore a fourfold victory. Let us look at each of them in turn.

How did the Buddha overcome MaccuMara? How did he overcome death? He overcame death by overcoming birth, for where there is birth there will inevitably be death. He overcame birth by overcoming the unskillful mental states that lead to birth—that is to say to rebirth. In other words, the Buddha overcame death by attaining what in Pali is called the *amatapada,* the "deathless state," the state which is free from death, free from birth—that is, *nibbana* (Sanskrit *nirvana*). He overcame death by attaining Enlightenment, a state which is above and beyond conditioned existence. It is not that after attaining Enlightenment the Buddha could not be reborn in the human world if he wanted to be. But he would not be reborn there out of compulsion, as a result of previous *kamma* (Sanskrit *karma*) that he had committed. He would be reborn—if he was reborn at all—out of compassion, in order to continue to help ordinary, unenlightened human beings.

How did the Buddha overcome KhandhaMara? How did he overcome conditioned existence? He overcame conditioned existence by overcoming the *kilesas,* the defilements, which lead one into conditioned existence. He did this at the time that he attained Enlightenment. In a sense, the two things were synonymous. According to tradition, however, the Buddha did not finally overcome the *khandhas* until his *parinibbana* forty-five years later. At the time of his *parinibbana* he severed all connection with the physical body, and all connection with the *khandhas.* For this reason the *parinibbana* is also known as *khandhanibbana,* or *anupadisesanibbana,* that is to say, "Nibbana without remainder in the form of a physical body."

But *how* did the Buddha overcome the *kilesas?* So much depends upon this. As we have seen, there are five principal *kilesas:* craving, aversion, ignorance, conceit, and distraction. The Buddha overcame craving by means of tranquillity, aversion by means of friendliness and compassion, ignorance by means of wisdom, conceit by means of selflessness, and distraction by means of awareness or mindfulness. Naturally, it was not easy even for the Buddha to do this. Qualities like tranquillity, friendliness and compassion do not just appear—not even when one is seated beneath the Bodhi tree. They have to be developed. But they *can* be developed. It is one of the central teachings of Buddhism that our mental states are in our own power and can be changed. Furthermore, Buddhism not only exhorts us to change them, but also tells us just how to do it; it gives us specific meditation methods.

Tranquillity is developed by means of the three contemplations:

the contemplation of the repulsiveness of the physical body, the contemplation of death, and the contemplation of impermanence. The first of these, the contemplation of the repulsiveness of the physical body, is the most extreme, and generally takes the form of contemplating the ten stages in the progressive decomposition of a corpse. Perhaps I should add that it is usually taught only to those who are psychologically and spiritually mature. The other two are less extreme and are therefore taught more widely. But whichever method we practice, whether the contemplation of death or the contemplation of impermanence, or even the contemplation of the repulsiveness of the physical body, we can succeed in developing tranquillity. And by developing tranquillity we overcome craving.

We develop friendliness and compassion by means of *metta bhavana,* or the "cultivation of universal loving-kindness." This practice consists in the systematic development of goodwill toward oneself, toward a near and dear friend, toward a "neutral" person, toward an "enemy," and, finally, toward all living beings. The *metta bhavana* is one of the best known and most popular of all Buddhist meditation methods. By practicing it we can develop friendliness and compassion, and by developing friendliness and compassion we overcome aversion.

We can develop wisdom by means of the contemplation of the twelve *nidanas,* or "links." For a detailed discussion of these, I must refer readers to my other writings (in particular *A Survey of Buddhism* and *The Three Jewels*). Broadly speaking, we develop wisdom by reflecting on the conditionality of mundane existence, on the fact that whatever mundane phenomenon arises or comes into existence does so in dependence on certain definite causes and conditions. Reflection on the conditionality of mundane existence is also roughly tantamount to reflecting on *sunyata* or "voidness." In these different ways we develop wisdom, and by developing wisdom we overcome ignorance.

We develop selflessness by reflection on the six elements: earth, water, fire, air, space, and consciousness. In this practice we reflect that there exists in our own physical body the element *earth* in the form of flesh, bone, and so on. We then further reflect that the earth element in our physical body does not really belong to us. We may point to our bodies and say "this is me," "this is mine"; but it does *not* belong to us. The earth element within our physical bodies has been borrowed, literally borrowed, from the earth element in the universe, and one day we shall have to give it back. If we see a corpse—even the corpse of a little bird—in the process of decomposition, we can see this happening, especially if the corpse is lying on the earth. We can see the flesh and bone that once belonged to the body returning to the soil, returning to the earth, returning to the earth element in the universe from which it came. Similarly, one day, we too shall have to give our body back to the earth element. We should therefore not be attached to it. We should not identify with it by saying "this body belongs to me." We then continue to reflect in this way with regard to all of the six elements. As we do so, we develop selflessness, and by developing selflessness we overcome conceit.

Finally, we develop mindfulness, or awareness, by means of *anapanasati,* or the "recollection of breathing." Here we simply "watch" our breath, without interfering with it in any way, allowing our minds to be increasingly focused, increasingly concentrated on the breath. By practicing *anapanasati* we develop mindfulness, and by developing mindfulness we overcome distraction, overcome the wandering mind.

Thus the five principal *kilesas* are overcome by these methods of meditation. This is how the Buddha overcame them. He overcame craving by means of tranquillity, aversion by means of friendliness and compassion, ignorance by means of wisdom, conceit by means of selflessness, and distraction by means of mindfulness, or awareness. In this way the Buddha overcame KilesaMara.

There is one Mara left. How did the Buddha overcome Devaputta-Mara, or "Mara the son of a god"? To understand this we must return to the episode of the *Mara-vijaya,* or victory over Mara, as depicted in Buddhist art. In the traditional representations of this incident we see the Buddha seated beneath the Bodhi tree, his eyes closed, or half closed, and we see Mara with his forces and his daughters. The Buddha is not paying Mara any attention at all. We could therefore say that the Buddha overcame DevaputtaMara simply by ignoring him.

In ordinary life, of course, to ignore someone usually means that we have a rather negative attitude toward him or her. But the Buddha could not possibly have had a negative attitude toward anyone—not even toward Mara. So we must try to put things a little more positively. It is not so much that the Buddha ignored Mara: rather, he overcame Mara simply *by being himself.* He overcame him by being the Bodhisatta, by being the Buddha. According to the medieval Indian commentator Mallinatha, the word *jayati,* or "to conquer," means to surpass everything else by means of one's own excellence. It means to be the "highest." Thus the Buddha's victory over Mara was not the result of a fight on Mara's terms; he defeated Mara simply by being himself, by virtue of the sheer excellence of his moral and spiritual qualities.

Thus the Buddha's victory over Mara was complete. Because it was complete he attained Enlightenment. One would have thought, therefore, that there was nothing left for him to do, nothing left for him to overcome. In a sense this is true, but after the *Mara-vijaya* there is in fact another episode that represents yet another victory, perhaps the ultimate victory. This is the episode of Brahma's request. Let us now witness it in our mind's eye:

The Buddha has attained Enlightenment; he is enjoying the freedom and bliss of Enlightenment. He is also reflecting that the truth he has discovered is very deep indeed, and therefore very difficult to understand. As he reflects in this way he is inclined not to try to communicate this truth—the Dhamma—to other human beings: it will be just too difficult. After all, he reflects, beings are deeply immersed in worldly pleasures, and thus they will not be able to understand the Dhamma he has discovered. Just then, Brahma Sahampati, the "Lord of a Thousand Worlds," another figure from Buddhist mythology, appears. He pleads with the Buddha, pointing out that there are at least a few beings who *will* understand. He implores that for their sake the Buddha should communicate the truth he has discovered. In the end the Buddha agrees, saying: "Opened for those who hear are the doors of the Deathless, Brahma, let them give forth their faith."[14]

Here the Buddha has overcome the temptation to keep his Enlightenment to himself, or even to think that he *could* keep it to himself. He has overcome spiritual individualism. The Buddha has overcome the Buddha—and has therefore become truly the Buddha. This is the last and greatest of all his victories. He has overcome the group, including the internalized group. He has overcome spiritual complacency and spiritual ambition. He has overcome fear. He has overcome the tendency to refuse to admit that one has made a mistake. He has overcome all four Maras. Now, finally, he has overcome spiritual individualism. He has been victorious all along the line. He is not only the Buddha, not only the Enlightened One, but he is also the *Jina,* the "Victorious One."

In the West we are accustomed to using the title "Buddha." But we should not forget that the Buddha is also commonly known as the Jina. Similarly, followers of the Buddha are usually called "Buddhists," but perhaps they could just as easily be called "Jinists": followers of the Jina, the Victorious One. The Buddha did in fact once tell his disciples that they were *ksatriyas,* or "warriors," fighting for *sila,* fighting for *samadhi,* fighting for *panna*—that is, they were fighting to live an ethical life, fighting for higher states of consciousness, and fighting for transcendental wisdom. According to the Buddha, the spiritual life is an active life, a strenuous life. We might even say that it is a *militant* life. We have to take the offensive against Mara. We should not wait for him to come and tap us on the shoulder. Attack is the best method of defense; prevention is better than cure.

For this reason, Western Buddhists should beware of taking too soft a view of the spiritual life. Perhaps we do not meditate hard enough, study hard enough, work hard enough, even play hard enough. Perhaps we have not committed ourselves to the Three Jewels with sufficient depth and intensity. Perhaps we do not really want to spread the Dhamma. Perhaps we are just playing at being Buddhists. If that is the case then we will not get very far: we will not be truly successful or genuinely happy. We will not be real Buddhists, and we certainly won't be real Jinists, real spiritual warriors.

Nowadays there is so much to be overcome, both in ourselves and in the world. There is so much to be transformed by the "Golden Light." As the life of the Buddha reminds us, we have to overcome the group; we have to overcome spiritual complacency and spiritual ambition; we have to overcome fear; we have to overcome that very human tendency to refuse to admit that we have made a mistake; we have to overcome Mara; and we have to overcome spiritual individualism. In short, we have to overcome everything that the Buddha overcame so that we can attain Enlightenment just as he did, and benefit the world just as he benefited it.

This is certainly not easy, and no real Buddhist has ever said that it was. But a human being should be ashamed not to attempt that which is difficult. A human being should be ashamed not to attempt that which is the most difficult of all. A human being should be ashamed not to be fighting against the odds. Sometimes we may feel that we are being overwhelmed. We may feel that we are having to hack our way through a dense jungle: the jungle of *samsara,* the jungle of conditioned existence. The Buddha must have felt like that too at times. After his Enlightenment he gave some of his disciples the following parable:

> Just as if, brethren, a man traveling in a forest, along a mountain height, should come upon an ancient road, an ancient track, traversed by men of former days, and should proceed along it: and as he went should come upon an old-time city, a royal city of olden days, dwelt in by men of bygone ages, laid out with parks and groves and water tanks, and stoutly walled about—a delightful spot.
>
> Then suppose, brethren, that this man should tell of his find to the king or royal minister, thus: "Pardon me,

sire, but I would have you know that while traveling in a forest, along a mountain height, I came upon an ancient road, an ancient track, traversed by men of former days, and proceeded along it. And as I went I came upon an old-time city, a royal city of olden days, dwelt in by men of bygone ages, laid out with parks and groves and water tanks, and stoutly walled about, a delightful spot. Sire, restore that city."

Then suppose, brethren, that king or royal minister were to restore that city, so that thereafter it became prosperous, fortunate, and populous, crowded with inhabitants, and were to reach growth and increase.

Even so, brethren, have I seen an ancient Path, an ancient track traversed by the Perfectly Enlightened ones of former times. And what is that Path? It is this Ariyan Eightfold Path.[15]

This parable tells us a number of things. It tells us that the Buddha was a pioneer. It tells us that the state of Enlightenment is like a wonderful city inhabited by innumerable people. It tells us that there is a way to that city, a way to that state. Above all, however, the parable reminds us that the Buddha's teaching is something that can be lost. The Three Jewels can be lost. Values can be lost. Fortunately, we are living at a time and in a place where the Dhamma is still known, and can still be practiced. We can still tread the ancient road to the city. But the jungle has started to encroach. Fewer people now live in the city; parts of the city are in a derelict condition, and entire sections of the road are overgrown.

Even though we are not being called upon to be pioneers in the way that the Buddha was, there is still a lot for us to do. We have to hack away at the jungle; we have to be spiritual warriors; we have to be not just Buddhists, but Jinists: we have at least to make an effort to overcome what the Buddha overcame.

6. Archetypal Symbolism in the Biography of the Buddha

In the course of our spiritual life, especially as we practice meditation, these archetypes tend to emerge in various ways into consciousness.

IF WE LOOK below the rational, conceptual surface of the human mind, we find vast unplumbed depths which make up what we call the unconscious. The psyche in its wholeness consists of both the conscious and the unconscious. The unconscious, non-rational part of us is by far the larger part of our total nature, and its importance is far greater than we generally care to recognize. Consciousness is just like a light froth playing and sparkling on the surface, while the unconscious is like the vast ocean depths, dark and unfathomed, lying far beneath. In order to appeal to the whole person, it isn't enough to appeal just to the conscious, rational intelligence that floats upon the surface. We have to appeal to something more, and this means that we have to speak the language of images, of concrete form. If we want to reach this non-rational part of the human psyche, we have to use the language of poetry, of myth, of legend.

This other, no less important, language is one which many modern people have forgotten, or which they know only in a few distorted and broken forms. But Buddhism does very definitely speak this language and speaks it no less powerfully than it speaks the language of concepts, and it is through the latter that we are going to approach our subject, changing over from the conceptual approach to the non-conceptual, from the conscious mind to the unconscious. Here, we shall be beginning to descend into this language, encountering there some of what I have called the "Archetypal Symbolism in the Biography of the Buddha." To allow for this encounter, we have to be receptive, to open ourselves to these archetypal symbols, to listen to them and allow them to speak in their own way to us, especially to our unconscious depths, so that we do not just realize them mentally, but experience them and assimilate them, even allowing them eventually to transform our whole life.

The Language of Buddhism

Some people are under the impression that Buddhism speaks only the language of concepts, of reason; that it is a strictly rational system, even a sort of rationalism. When they hear the word Buddhism, they expect something very dry and abstract—it is as though they almost heard the skeleton rattle! Such a misunderstanding is in a way quite natural in the West. After all, ninety percent, if not ninety-nine percent, of our knowledge is derived from books, magazines, lectures, TV programs and so on, so that, although we may not always be aware of this, our approach is in terms of intellectual understanding. It addresses our rational intelligence, our capacity to formulate concepts. In this way we get a very one-sided impression of Buddhism. But if we go to the East we see a very different picture. In fact, we may even say that in the Eastern Buddhist countries they tend to the other extreme. They tend to be moved and influenced by the divinities and images all about them without easily being able to give a mental formulation of what they actually believe. When I first went to live in Kalimpong, up in the Himalayas, I was surprised to find that many of my Tibetan, Sikkimese, and Bhutanese friends who were ardent practicing Buddhists had never heard of the Buddha!—or, if they had heard of him, they thought he was a very unreal, distant historical figure. Archetypal forms such as Padmasambhava, or the "Five *Jinas*," or Maitreya, were real to them, but not the historical facts and figures.

So far as Buddhism in the West is concerned, much more attention has been given to the conceptual, analytical, intellectual approach. We now have to give much more time and much more serious attention to the other type of approach, to begin to try to combine both these approaches, unite both the conceptual and the non-conceptual. In other words, we need a balanced spiritual life in which both the conscious and unconscious mind play their part.

But let us define our key terms. What do we mean by archetypal symbolism? What is an archetype? Broadly speaking, an archetype is the original pattern or model of a work, or the model from which a thing is made or formed. In Jung's psychology—and it was Jung who familiarized this term in the modern psychological context—the term is used in a much more specialized sense. I must say, I find it rather difficult to elucidate the precise sense in which Jung uses this word. His use of it is very fluid and shifting. The meaning is not always conceptually clear and he tends to rely on examples, which he cites profusely. In doing this, he no doubt proceeds deliberately. Perhaps it is better to follow him in this and make the meaning of this term clear by citing examples.

And what do we mean by symbolism? A symbol is generally defined as a visible sign of something invisible. But philosophically and religiously speaking it is more than that: it is something existing on a lower plane which is in correspondence with something existing on a higher plane. Just to cite a common example, in the various theistic traditions, the sun is a symbol for God, because the sun performs in the physical universe the same function that God, according to these systems, performs in the spiritual universe: the sun sheds light, sheds heat, just as God sheds the light of knowledge, the warmth of love, into the spiritual universe. One can say that the sun is the god of the material world, and in the same way God is the sun of the spiritual world. It is the same principle manifesting on different levels in different ways. This is, of course, the old Hermetic idea: "As above, so below."[16]

Two Kinds of Truth

Various Western scholars in modern times have tried to write full, detailed biographies of the Buddha. There is quite a lot of traditional material available. Quite a number of biographies were written in ancient India, for instance the *Mahavastu* (which means the Great Relation). This is essentially a biography of the Buddha, though it does contain a great deal of other matter, especially *Jatakas* and *Avadanas*.[17] It is a bulky work—three volumes in the English translation, altogether about 1,500 pages—which contains some very ancient and interesting material. Then there are the *Lalita-vistara* and the *Abhiniskramana Sutra*, both Mahayana sutras. The *Lalita-vistara* is a highly poetic work and has great devotional appeal and literary value. In fact, Sir Edwin Arnold's famous poem, *The Light of Asia*, is primarily based on it. These works are in Sanskrit, but we also have in Pali the *Nidana*, Buddhaghosa's introduction to his own commentary on the *Jataka* stories. Then again, we have Asvaghosa's *Buddhacarita* (which means the Acts of the Buddha), a beautiful epic poem in classical Sanskrit.

Western scholars have explored this abundant material thoroughly, but having gone through the various episodes and incidents, they divide them into two great "heaps": on one side, they put whatever they consider to be a historic fact—that the Buddha was born into a certain family, that he spoke a certain language, that he left home at a certain age, etc. On the other side, they put what they consider to be myth and legend. This is all right so far as it goes, but most of them go a step further and start indulging in value judgments, saying that only the historical facts—or what they consider to be the historical facts—are valuable and relevant. As for the myths and legends, all the poetry of the account, they usually see this as mere fiction and therefore to be discarded as worthless.

This is a very great mistake indeed. There are two kinds of truth: there is what we call scientific truth, the truth of concepts, of reasoning; and in addition to this—some would even say above this—there is what we may call poetic truth, or truth of the imagination, or the intuition. Both are at least equally important. The latter kind of truth is manifested, or revealed, in what we call myths and legends, as well as in works of art, in symbolic ritual, and also quite importantly in dreams. The archetypal symbolism of the biography of the Buddha belongs to this second category—it is not meant to be historic truth, factual information, but poetic, even spiritual, truth. We may say that this biography—or partial biography—of the Buddha in terms of archetypal symbolism is not concerned with the external events of his career, but is meant to suggest to us something about his inner spiritual experience and, therefore, to shed light on the spiritual life for all of us.

This archetypal symbolism is often found in Buddhist biographies, for example, in the life of Nagarjuna,[18] of Padmasambhava,[19] of Milarepa.[20] In all these so-called biographies, there are many incidents which are not based, and are not supposed to be based, on historical facts, but which have an archetypal symbolic significance pointing to inner experience and inner realization. Sometimes it is difficult to distinguish between the two categories, to make up one's mind whether something belongs to the historical or to the symbolic order. Very often we find that the Buddhist tradition itself does not clearly distinguish between the two. It usually seems to take the myths and legends just as literally as the historical facts, as though in early times people almost didn't possess the capacity, or perhaps even the willingness, to distinguish in this way. Everything was true, everything was fact, of its own kind, in its own order. There is no harm in our trying to make up our minds what constitutes the factual, historical content of the Buddha's biography, and what represents its archetypal and symbolic content, but we should be careful not to undervalue the mythical and the legendary elements.

Buddhist Symbolism

The Buddha, according to the traditional account, gained Enlightenment at the foot of a pipal tree. It is significant that, from a historical, factual point of view, we don't really know whether he sat under a tree or not: the oldest accounts don't mention this. We may assume quite naturally that he did because, after all, he gained his Enlightenment in the month of May, which is the hottest time of year in India; so it is more than likely that he was sitting under a tree, just for the sake of shade and shelter from the heat. But we don't know. Gradually, it seems, as the legendary and mythical element grew in the biographies, the Buddha came to be more and more associated at the time of his Enlightenment with sitting at the foot of a tree. A tree's roots go deep down into the earth, but at the same time its branches tower high into the sky. So the tree links heaven and earth, is a symbol of the union, or harmony, of opposites.

The World Tree is found in most mythologies. For instance, we have the Norse Yggdrasil, which is the World Ash—roots deep down, branches right up in the heavens, all the worlds as it were suspended on the branches. And one often gets this identification of the Christian cross with a World or Cosmic Tree. I have seen a representation of the crucifixion where branches were growing out of the sides of the cross, and the roots went deep down into the soil. The cross also, like the World Tree, links heaven and earth cosmically in the same way that Christ unites the human and the divine natures "psychologically."

Closely associated with the idea of a tree is the image of the central point. In all the traditional legendary accounts of the Buddha's gaining Enlightenment, he is represented as sitting on what is called the *vajrasana,* which literally means the Diamond Seat, or Diamond Throne as it is sometimes translated. The diamond, the *vajra,* the *dorje,* in Buddhist tradition always represents the transcendental element, the metaphysical base.[21] According to tradition, the *vajrasana* is the center of the universe. One can compare this with the corresponding Christian tradition that the cross stood on the same spot as the Tree of Knowledge of Good and Evil, from which Adam and Eve had eaten the apple, and that this spot represents the exact center of the world. This centrality in the cosmos of the *vajrasana* suggests that Enlightenment consists in adopting a position of centrality.

I could go on in this way almost indefinitely—the traditional biographies are full of material of this sort. But now I want to look at a whole sequence of symbols which are connected with the most important event in the Buddha's whole career, his attainment of Enlightenment. These symbols are represented by certain incidents usually regarded as historical, or partly historical, though their actual significance is much deeper.

The first of these incidents is traditionally known as the Victory over Mara,[22] the Evil One, the Satan of Buddhism. According to some of the later legendary accounts, the Buddha—or the Bodhisattva (Pali *Bodhisatta*), the Buddha-to-be—was seated in meditation at the foot of the tree when he was attacked by terrible demon hosts, by all sorts of foul, unsightly, misshapen figures, led by Mara. These hosts and their attack are vividly depicted in Buddhist art as well as in poetry. They were partly human, partly animal, hideously deformed, with snarling, leering, angry, and wrathful expressions, some of them lifting great clubs, others brandishing swords, all very menacing and frightful indeed. But all the stones, arrows, and flames, on reaching the edge of the Buddha's aura of light, turned into flowers and fell at his feet.

The significance of this is obvious and doesn't need to be explained, only to be felt. The Buddha wasn't touched, wasn't moved, by this terrible attack. His eyes remained closed, he remained in meditation, with that same smile on his lips. So Mara sent against the Buddha his three beautiful daughters, whose names are Lust, Passion, and Delight. They danced in front of the Buddha, exhibiting all of their wiles, but the Buddha didn't even open his eyes. They retired discomfited.

All this represents the forces of the unconscious in their crude, unsublimated form. The demons, the terrible misshapen figures, represent anger, aversion, dislike, and so on. As for the daughters of Mara, they represent, of course, the various aspects of craving and desire. Mara himself represents primordial ignorance or unawareness, on account of which we take birth again and again. Incidentally, the literal meaning of the name Mara is simply "death."

The second incident is known as the Calling of the Earth Goddess to Witness.[23] After he had been defeated, after his armies had returned discomfited, Mara tried another trick. He said to the Buddha-to-be, "You are sitting on the central point of the universe, on the throne of the Buddhas of old. What right have you, just an ordinary person, to sit on that Diamond Throne where the previous Buddhas sat?" So the Buddha said, "In my past lives I have practiced all the paramitas, all the Perfections, that is to say, Perfection of Giving, Perfection of

Morality, Perfection of Patience, Perfection of Energy, Perfection of Meditation, Perfection of Wisdom.[24] I have practiced all these, and I have reached a point in my spiritual evolution where I am ready now, where I am about to gain Enlightenment. Therefore I am worthy to sit on this Diamond Throne like the previous Buddhas when they gained Enlightenment."

Mara wasn't satisfied. He said, "All right, you say that you practiced all these Perfections in your previous lives, but who saw you? Who is your witness?" Mara takes on the guise of a lawyer; he wants a witness, he wants evidence. So the future Buddha, who was seated on the Diamond Throne in the position of meditation, with his hands resting in his lap, just tapped on the earth—this is the famous bhumisparsa mudra,[25] the earth-touching or earth-witnessing mudra, or position—and up rose the Earth Goddess, bearing a vase in her hand. She bore witness, saying, "I have been here all the time. Men may come and men may go, but the earth always remains. I have seen all his previous lives. I have seen hundreds of thousands of lives in which he practiced the Perfections. So I bear witness that on account of his practice of these Perfections he is worthy to sit in the seat of the Buddhas of old."

This scene is also often depicted in Buddhist art—sometimes the Earth Goddess is shown as dark green in color, sometimes a beautiful golden-brown, always half-emerged from the earth, very much like the figure of Mother Erda in Wagner's *Ring*. (Erda of course means the earth, and Erda and the Earth Goddess are the same as Hertha, as in Swinburne's famous poem of that name.) The significance of the Earth Goddess is a whole subject in itself and there is a whole literature on it. Basically, she represents the same forces as those represented by Mara's daughters. But whereas Mara's daughters represent them in their crude, negative, unsublimated aspects, the Earth Goddess, as she bears witness, represents them in their tamed, subdued, even in their sublimated aspect, ready to help, not hinder.

The third incident is known as Brahma's Request.[26] After his Enlightenment, the Buddha was inclined to keep silent. He reflected, "This Truth, this Reality, which I have discovered, is so abstract, so difficult to see, so sublime, that ordinary people, their eyes covered with the dust of ignorance and passion, are not going to see it, to appreciate it. It is better to remain silent, to remain under the Bodhi tree, better to remain with eyes closed, not to go out into the world and preach." But then another great apparition arose. A great light shone forth, and in the midst of the light an ancient figure, the figure of Brahma Sahampati, Brahma the Great God, Lord of a Thousand Worlds, appeared before the Buddha with folded hands. He said, "Please preach, preach the Truth. There are just a few with only a little dust on their eyes. They will appreciate it, they will follow it." The Buddha opened his divine eye and looked forth over the universe. He saw all beings, just like lotuses in a pond, in various stages of development. And he said, "For the sake of those with just a little dust over their eyes, those who are like lotuses beginning to blossom, I will preach the Dharma."

We shouldn't of course take this incident literally in the historical sense. The Buddha was Enlightened; he didn't need to be asked to preach. Brahma's Request represents the manifestation within the Buddha's own mind of the forces of Compassion which eventually compelled him to make known the Truth he had discovered.

The fourth and last episode is the Mucalinda episode.[27] For seven weeks after his Enlightenment, the Buddha sat at the foot of the Bodhi tree and other trees in its vicinity, and in the middle of the seventh week there arose a great storm. The Buddha was Enlightened in the month of May, so seven weeks takes us to the middle of July, the beginning of the rainy season. In India, when the rainy season begins, in a matter of instants the whole sky becomes black and rain descends not in bucketfuls but in absolute reservoirfuls. The Buddha was out in the open, under a tree, with just a thin robe—he couldn't do much about it. But another figure arose out of the undergrowth, out of the shadows: a great snake, King Mucalinda, the Serpent-King. He came and wrapped his coils around the Buddha and stood with his hood over his head like an umbrella, and in this way protected him against the downpour. This episode is often depicted in Buddhist art, sometimes almost comically: you see a coil, like a coil of rope, with the Buddha's head just poking out, and the hood like an umbrella over him. Then the rain disappeared, the storm-clouds cleared up, and the Serpent-King assumed a different form, that of a beautiful youth about sixteen years of age, who bowed before the Buddha.

Some scholars try to take this episode literally, try to force some factual meaning from it, saying, "Oh yes, it is well known that in the East snakes are sometimes quite friendly with holy men, and come and sit near them, and this is what must have happened." But we cannot accept this pseudo-historical type of explanation. We are on a different plane, a different level of meaning altogether. All over the world, water—or the sea, or the ocean—represents the unconscious. And in Indian mythology—Hindu, Buddhist, and Jain—the nagas, that is to say, the serpents, or the dragons, live in the depths of the ocean. So the *nagas* represent the forces in the depths of the unconscious in their most positive and beneficent aspect—and Mucalinda is the king of the *nagas*.

The falling of the rain, the torrential downpour after seven weeks, represents a baptism. All over the world, pouring water on someone or something represents the investiture of that person or that object with all the powers of the unconscious mind. For example, in Christianity there is a baptism with water and with fire, an investiture with the forces of the unconscious mind and with the forces of the spirit.

The rain, we saw, falls at the end of the seventh week, and Mucalinda wraps his coils seven times around the seated figure of the Buddha. This repetition of the figure seven is no coincidence. Mucalinda also stands for what the Tantras call the Chandali, the Fiery Power, or the Fiery One, which the Hindus call the Kundalini, or the Coiled-up One, or the Serpent Power. This represents all the powerful psychic energies surging up inside a person, especially at the time of meditation, through the median nerve. The seven coils, or the winding seven times round the Buddha, represent the seven psychic centers[28] through which the Kundalini passes in the course of its ascent. Mucalinda's assuming the form of a beautiful youth represents the new personality which is born as a result of this upward progression of the Chandali, or Kundalini. Mucalinda in the new form bows to the Buddha: this represents the perfect submission of all the powers of the unconscious to the Enlightened mind.

It is obvious from all this that these four incidents all have a deep psychological and spiritual significance. They are not just pseudo-history, and they are not just a fairy tale (though even fairy tales have a significance). They are invested with a powerful symbolic and archetypal meaning.

The Four Principal Archetypes

Going a little further, we may say that the four main figures with which we have been concerned form a very definite set: Mara the Evil One, Vasundhara the Earth Goddess, Brahma, and Mucalinda, in that order. Now I am going to draw what some people may feel is a bold analogy, but I think it has great significance and suggestiveness. It seems to me that these four figures are to some extent analogous to the four principal archetypes according to Jung and that their appearance in this order represents an integration of these contents into the conscious mind—in other words, it represents, on a higher level, what Jung calls the individuation process. Mara corresponds to what Jung calls the Shadow, that darker side of ourselves of which we are ashamed, which we usually try to keep hidden. The Earth Goddess represents the Anima. (In Jung's analytic psychology, the Anima is the inner feminine part of the male personality, while the Animus is the inner masculine part of the female personality. The Buddha, being a man, had an Anima—in the case of a woman it would be an Animus.) Brahma represents the archetype of the Wise Old Man. He is seen in Buddhist art with white hair and a beard, a sort of God-the-Father figure. And Mucalinda is the archetype of the Young Hero.

There is also a correspondence with the principal figures of Christian mythology, Mara corresponding to Satan, the Earth Goddess to the Virgin Mary, Brahma to God, and Mucalinda to Christ. I don't think this is too far-fetched. If we study these matters carefully, go into them deeply, we should see the analogy. In Tantric Buddhism, there is a similar set: the Guardian (or Protector, as he is sometimes called), the *dakini,* the guru, and the *yidam.*

Though I have drawn these analogies, there is a great difference of principle between the Buddhist and the Christian approaches to, or attitudes toward, the archetypes of their respective traditions. In Buddhism, it is always clearly, even categorically, stated that all these appearances, all these archetypal forms, are ultimately phenomena of one's own True Mind, or projections from one's own unconscious, and that they are all to be integrated. But in Christianity the corresponding archetypes are regarded as objectively existing beings. One cannot really resolve an archetype in the sense of incorporating it as representing unconscious contents into one's conscious mind, one's conscious attitudes, or one's new self, unless one realizes that, in the last analysis, it isn't something objectively existing, but something which one has projected from some depths, from some hidden source within oneself.

On account of this limitation, in the Christian tradition—with the exception perhaps of a few heretical mystics—there is no full resolution of the archetypal figure, whereas in Buddhism, on account of a more deeply metaphysical and spiritual background, such a resolution is possible. In Buddhism all the archetypes can be dissolved, can be drawn back into one's own conscious attitude and integrated there so as to enrich, perfect, and beautify it. In other words, the individuation process can be carried to its absolute conclusion, Enlightenment.

We have only touched on a few of the archetypal symbols occurring in the biography of the Buddha. I would have liked to mention many more, for instance the Buddha's begging-bowl. There are many legends about it, some of them very interesting indeed. In fact, we may say without any exaggeration that it occupies in Buddhist legend and history a position analogous to that of the Holy Grail in Christianity, and carries much the same significance.

The archetypes are not just of historic or literary interest, not something foreign to us. Each and every one is present within us all;

WHO IS THE BUDDHA? ~ 73

or we can say that we are all present in them. We share them, we have them all in common, or they share us, have all of us in common. And in the course of our spiritual life, especially as we practice meditation, these archetypes tend to emerge in various ways into consciousness. Sometimes they show themselves, at least by way of a glimpse, in dreams, in meditation, or in waking fantasies. We all have to encounter the Shadow, for instance. This is the dark, unpleasant side of ourselves which appears in dreams, for example, as a dark snarling hound snapping at our heels which we want to get rid of, but cannot; or as a dark man, perhaps. We have to face the Shadow, come to terms with it, even assimilate this darker side of ourselves, just as the Buddha faced and overcame Mara and his hosts. And here, just as in the case of Mara, repression is no solution. The Shadow, or the content represented by the Shadow, must be saturated with awareness and resolved. The Buddha himself didn't start emitting flames to counteract the flames of Mara's hosts; but when the flames touched his aura, they were transformed into flowers, transmuted. This is also the sort of thing we have to do with our own Shadow—just see it, recognize it, accept it, and then transform and transmute it into what Tantric tradition calls a Guardian, or Protector.

We too have to call up the Earth Goddess, which means in psychoanalytical language that we have to face, and free ourselves from, the Anima—in the case of a man—that is to say, we have to bring and integrate into our conscious attitude our unconscious femininity, just as a woman has to bring up and integrate her unconscious masculinity. If this is done, there will no longer be any question of projecting these unconscious, unrealized contents onto members of the opposite sex, and the "problem," as it sometimes called, of sex will have been resolved. This is a very important aspect of the spiritual life.

Next, we all have to learn from the Wise Old Man. Sometimes we may quite literally have to sit at the feet of a teacher, or at least have some ideal image to which we owe allegiance. Then, perhaps after many years, we have to incorporate into ourselves the qualities which that figure represents—wisdom, knowledge, and so on.

And then, finally, each one has to give birth within himself or herself to the Young Hero; in other words, create the nucleus of a new self, a new being, or in traditional Buddhist language, give birth within ourselves to the Buddha.

If we face our own Shadow, call up our own Anima or Animus, learn from our Wise Old Man, and give birth within ourselves to our own Young Hero, we shall live out, we shall recapitulate within ourselves in our own lives, at all levels, in all aspects, the archetypal symbols which appear in the Buddha's biography.

7. Inspiration from the Buddha's Life

After all those years, in which he had heard so much, the overall impression the Buddha had made upon Ananda is summed up in those few words: "He who is so kind." Half of Buddhism is in that remark.

When the Buddha died, to many of his followers it was as though Enlightenment itself had disappeared from the universe. Some people exclaimed, "The Eye of the World has disappeared!"[29] And although this wasn't really true—a cloud had moved across the face of the sun, but the sun was still shining—it *felt* true, and they were devastated. According to tradition, even the animals were affected.

But even though the disciples felt that the light of the world had gone out, still, slowly, they recovered from their grief, as we all have to recover on these occasions, and started to take stock of the situation. Unbelievable as it seemed at first, the Buddha was gone and they had to settle down to life in a Buddha-less world—which, especially for those who had lived in his presence for many years, was a terrible change. But eventually they started trying to understand what they were left with. And some—perhaps the intellectuals among them—said, "Well, we've got the teachings the Buddha gave us: the doctrines, the rules of behavior, and so on. That's enough, surely." (One can imagine that these were the kind of people who went on to spend their lives happily analyzing and classifying the teachings, and later began the tradition that became what is known as the Abhidharma.)[30] But there were many among the disciples of the Buddha who, while they had nothing against the teachings or the rules, felt there was something missing from their lives now that the Buddha had gone. We can imagine that even when they were supposed to be thinking of the teachings and committing those long lists of terms to memory, they couldn't help thinking of the Buddha, and recalling incidents in his life that exemplified his personal qualities.

For instance, some of them no doubt remembered the occasion when the Buddha was going round from one hermitage to the next and found in one hut an elderly monk lying on the floor in a terrible condition; he had dysentery. It was obvious that he had been lying there for days without receiving any help at all. The Buddha asked the old man why the other monks weren't looking after him, and he said, "Well, I'm useless to them now. Why should they bother to look after me?" So the Buddha sent his companion, Ananda, to fetch warm water, and together they lifted the old monk onto a bed, washed him, and made him comfortable. Then the Buddha called all the monks together and said, "Monks, you have neither father nor mother, brother nor sister. You've given up the world. You must be brother and sister, mother and father, to one another. He who wishes to serve me, let him serve the sick."[31]

Incidents like this, incidents which show the Buddha's practical compassion, must surely have remained in the minds and hearts of many of his disciples. Some of them, especially the lay disciples, might also have remembered the story of Kisagotami. In India in those days, as now, infant mortality was very high, and the story goes that a young woman called Kisagotami lost her only child when he was only a few years old. Unable to believe he was dead, crazed with grief, she took his body in her arms from house to house, asking for medicine to make him well again. Eventually someone had the good sense and kindness to suggest that she should go to the Buddha for help, so she went to him and asked him to bring her baby back to life.

He didn't refuse. He didn't give her a sermon—he knew that would be useless, grief-stricken as she was. In fact, he didn't respond to her request directly at all. He just said, "Bring me just a few grains of mustard seed—but bring them from a house where no one has died." So off she went, going from one house to another. Everywhere she went the people were more than willing to give her some mustard seed. But when she asked, "Has anyone died in this house?" they said, "Do not remind us of our grief. The dead are many, but the living are few." At every house she learned the same lesson: death comes to all. Eventually she laid her child's body to rest in the jungle, came back to the Buddha, and sat quietly at his feet. She didn't say anything for a long time. Then at last she said, "Give me a refuge," and she became a nun.[32]

Such incidents added to the general stock of stories and anecdotes which must have been fresh in the hearts and minds of his disciples. Many of them must have felt that these stories communicated something of tremendous importance, something the formal teachings did not convey: the effect the Buddha had on those with whom he came in contact, the direct impact of an Enlightened being, which is above and beyond all words.

No one could have been a better judge of this than the Buddha's cousin Ananda, who for more than twenty years was the Buddha's personal attendant, and went with him everywhere. If the Buddha was invited to lunch, Ananda went too. If the Buddha went to give a sermon, Ananda went along. If the Buddha received visitors, or answered questions, Ananda was present. He was always there, like the Buddha's shadow. And the Buddha, we gather, meant everything to him. When the Buddha was about to die, Ananda, understandably, felt it more deeply than anybody. According to the *Mahaparinibbana Sutta*, as the Buddha lay in the sal grove, Ananda left him and went to a nearby lodging-house. There he stood at the door of the hut and leaned against the doorpost. As he stood there, he tried to realize that the Buddha was going to die in a matter of days or even hours. Weeping bitterly, he said to himself, "The Master is about to pass away from me: he who is so kind."[33]

These words are of the greatest significance. In the course of the twenty years Ananda had spent with the Buddha he must have heard the Buddha deliver hundreds of discourses, including many abstruse, philosophical, deeply mystical teachings. He had heard him answer thousands of questions. He must have admired his brilliance, his affability, the ease with which he handled difficult questions. No doubt he had witnessed all sorts of supernormal happenings. But it was not the Buddha's wisdom or his understanding of philosophy, his skill in debate or his ability to work miracles, his courage or his tireless energy, that stood out. For Ananda the Buddha's outstanding quality was his kindness. After all those years, in which he had heard so much, the overall impression the Buddha had made upon Ananda is summed up in those few words: "He who is so kind."

Half of Buddhism is in that remark. The Buddha's wisdom is revealed in his doctrinal teachings, but his love, his compassion, which so deeply impressed Ananda, is revealed in his personal example. This is what those disciples who could not identify Buddhism exclusively with the verbal teaching of the Buddha were getting at. They were saying that Buddhism was not just wisdom, as represented by the teaching, but also love and compassion, as exemplified by the Buddha's life; and in any formulation of Buddhism, both should be taken into consideration. Yes, we should try to attain Enlightenment, to awaken, to see the Truth; this is the wisdom aspect. But we should try to attain wisdom for the sake of all sentient beings; this is the compassion aspect. These two together form the Bodhisattva ideal.

2 ← Going for Refuge

1. "Coming Home" to Buddhism

The system of spiritual teaching and training that we call Buddhism is, in reality, neither Eastern nor Western, any more than we ourselves, in the depths of our being, are either Eastern or Western.

O N THE OCCASION of their first contact with Buddhism, whether that contact takes the form of reading a Buddhist book, seeing an image of the Buddha, or paying a visit to a Buddhist spiritual community, many people experience a paradoxical feeling of absolute newness and, at the same time, complete familiarity. They feel not just that they have gained something infinitely precious but that they have *re*gained it. They feel that, after many wanderings, they have not only arrived at last at the gates of a glorious palace but also that, incredible as it seems, they have "come home." Some of them seek to account for this feeling of complete familiarity by saying that to them Buddhism represents what they have, in fact, always believed, though without fully realizing it. Others seek to account for it by saying, with varying degrees of conviction, that they must have been Buddhist in a previous existence. However they may account for the feeling, or even if they choose not to account for it at all, such Western Buddhists are naturally astonished when somebody tells them, as somebody occasionally does, even today, that he or she is unable to understand how it is possible for one born and brought up in the West, as a member of Western society and in the midst of Western culture, to accept an Eastern religion like Buddhism or, in other words, to accept a religion that is foreign and exotic. But such a thing is possible, as is daily becoming more evident, and the reason why it is possible is that the system of spiritual teaching and training that we call Buddhism is, in reality, neither Eastern nor Western, any more than we ourselves, in the depths of our being, are either Eastern or Western. When we accept the so-called Eastern religion of Buddhism we accept it, even as we encounter it, on a level where the terms Eastern and Western no longer have any meaning.

If a few words of personal confession may be permitted, this was very much my own experience many years ago when, at the age of sixteen, I had my first real contact with Buddhism. That contact took place when I read two short but exceptionally profound Buddhist scriptures of great historical and spiritual significance. These were the *Diamond Sutra,* a work belonging to the "Perfection of Wisdom" corpus, and the *Sutra of Wei Lang,* a collection of discourses by the first Chinese patriarch of the Ch'an or Zen school, who is better known as Hui Neng. Reading these two works, I realized that although in one sense the truth they taught, or the reality they disclosed, was new to me, in another sense it was not new at all but strangely familiar. I certainly did not feel that I was accepting an Eastern religion, or a religion that was foreign and exotic. Rather I felt that contact with Buddhism was, at the same time, contact with the depths of my own being: that in knowing Buddhism I was knowing myself, and that in knowing myself I was knowing Buddhism.

2. What Going for Refuge Is

We too are capable of gaining Enlightenment. This is what committing one-self to the Buddha means.

A Buddhist is one who "goes for Refuge" to the Buddha, the Dharma, and the Sangha, one who totally *commits* himself or herself, with body, speech, and mind, to the Buddha, the Dharma, and the Sangha. There are many stories in the ancient Buddhist scriptures which illustrate what this means. When we read those scriptures, especially the Pali scriptures, we encounter the Buddha as he wanders from place to place, begging for food as he goes. In the course of his wanderings he might meet somebody under a tree, or in a village, and the two of them get into a conversation. Maybe it's a brahmin priest, or a farmer, or a well-to-do merchant, or a young man about town. Maybe it's a wandering ascetic, or a housewife, or a prince . . . but in one way or another they get talking.

Sooner or later this person asks the Buddha a question, perhaps about the meaning of life, or about his teaching, or about what happens after death. The Buddha might reply at considerable length, giving a detailed discourse, or he might answer with just a few words. If he is very inspired he might reply in verse, "breathing out" what is called an *Udana*. He might even give one of his famous "lion roars," a full and frank, almost defiant, declaration of his great spiritual experience and the path that he teaches; or he might reply with complete silence—a wordless communication that says so much more than words. But whatever the Buddha says or does not say, if the listener is receptive, the result is the same. He or she feels deeply affected, deeply moved, deeply stirred. They are so stirred, so thrilled, in fact, that their hair may stand on end, or they may shed tears, or be seized by a violent fit of trembling. They feel as if they are seeing a great light; they have a tremendous sense of emancipation; they feel as if a great burden has been lifted from their back, or as though they have been suddenly let out of prison. At such a moment, the listener feels spiritually reborn. And at that extraordinary turning point they respond to the Buddha and to the Dharma with a cry that breaks spontaneously from their lips. According to those ancient Pali texts, they say; "*Buddham saranam gacchami, Dhammam saranam gacchami, Sangham saranam gacchami*," which means, "To the Buddha for Refuge I go, to the Dharma for Refuge I go, to the Sangha for Refuge I go."[34] This is their response: they go for Refuge, commit themselves, because the Buddha has shown them a vision of inner truth, of existence, of life itself in all its depth and complexity. This vision is so great that all one can do is give oneself to it completely, live for it, and if necessary die for it.

But what does one actually mean when one says, "To the Buddha for Refuge I go; to the Dharma for Refuge I go; to the Sangha for Refuge I go"? The English word "refuge" is not very satisfactory. It is a literal translation of the Pali and Sanskrit word *sarana,* but does not give its real meaning. There is certainly no question of running away from anything when one goes for Refuge, no question of taking shelter with anyone. Going for Refuge really means commitment: committing oneself to the Buddha, committing oneself to the Dharma, committing oneself to the Sangha. So what does this mean?

Committing oneself to the Buddha does not mean handing oneself over to the Buddha or blindly obeying the Buddha. It means taking the Buddha as one's ideal, taking *Buddhahood* as an ideal. The historical Buddha, Gautama, was a human being. By his own human efforts he developed higher and ever higher states of being, states that eventually culminated in what we call Enlightenment, the highest conceivable state of moral and spiritual perfection, a state of supreme wisdom, infinite compassion, and absolute purity. We too are human beings; we too, therefore, according to Buddhism, are capable of developing higher and higher states of being and consciousness. We too are capable of gaining Enlightenment. This is what committing oneself to the Buddha means. It means recognizing the Buddha as the living embodiment of the highest conceivable state of human perfection. It means recognizing Buddhahood as a practical ideal for all human beings, and actually devoting all one's energies toward the realization of that ideal.

What is meant by "committing oneself to the Dharma"? The Dharma is the teaching of the Buddha, and it is concerned mainly with two things: with the goal of Enlightenment, or Buddhahood, and with the path leading to that state. Committing oneself to the Dharma therefore means actually following the path in order to realize the goal. The path consists of several steps and stages which are variously enumerated according to the particular point of view adopted. One popular enumeration of the stages of the path is that of the three stages of morality, meditation, and wisdom. Another enumeration is that of the Noble Eightfold Path. This is not really a path of eight stages, as is generally thought, but a path of two stages: a stage of vision and a stage of transformation. The stage of vision is a vision of the goal—not just a theoretical idea but an actual spiritual experience—and the stage of transformation is the gradual transformation of all aspects of one's being, from the highest to the lowest, in accordance with that vision. There is also the path of the six perfections—of generosity, morality, patience, vigor, meditation, and wisdom. So committing oneself to the Dharma means following the path in any of these various ways. It means committing oneself to the process of one's development as an individual by whatever means one can.

The Sangha is the spiritual community—that is, the community of the spiritually committed. The Dharma, as we have seen, is a path which consists of various steps and stages, and naturally different individuals are on different steps and at different stages. Some are more advanced than we are, some are less advanced, and some are equally advanced, and to these people we naturally adopt different attitudes. We reverence those who are more advanced, we are receptive to their spiritual influence, and assist them in their spiritual work. We help those who are less advanced than we are, giving advice and moral support as and when we can. And we enjoy spiritual friendship with those who are at the same stage as ourselves. Indeed, we can enjoy spiritual fellowship with all members of the Sangha in different ways and to differing degrees. This is what is meant by committing ourselves to the Sangha.

Certainly each individual must develop for him- or herself, by his or her own efforts, but we will develop more easily and more enjoyably if we do so in spiritual fellowship with others. We could even say that spiritual fellowship is necessary to individual development. In the spiritual community all help each, and each helps all. In the end, all narrow, pseudo-religious individualism is transcended; there is only a spiritual community of individuals who are, as it were, transparent to each other, individuals through whom the light of Enlightenment shines.

So this is how one can know that someone is a Buddhist. A Buddhist is one who goes for Refuge in response to the Buddha and his teaching. A Buddhist is one who gives him- or herself to the Buddha and the Dharma and the Sangha. This was the criterion in the Buddha's day two thousand five hundred years ago, and it remains the criterion today.

In many traditionally Buddhist countries this profound change of heart is institutionalized in the form of a ceremony called "taking the Refuges." In this form it inevitably tends to get trivialized. Any public meeting, even a political meeting, it is sad to say, will start with everyone "taking" the Refuges and precepts—that is, reciting them—just to show that they are all good Buddhists. Another way that Going for Refuge gets cheapened is when it is taken as something you do once and for all, like baptism in Christianity, so that it is assumed that when you have "taken the Refuges" from a monk, you are safely a Buddhist.

As a committed Buddhist one goes for Refuge—or tries to—all the time. As one's appreciation of the Three Jewels grows, one's Going for Refuge becomes correspondingly more profound. And this can sometimes have surprising results. It may mean that what brings you to Buddhism in the first place becomes, as you progress in your practice, not more but less important, as your deepening understanding comes to displace the comparatively superficial appreciation of Buddhism that was sufficient to get you going in the first place.

For instance, one may have heard it said that whereas Christianity is a religion of faith, Buddhism is a religion of reason, and one may be drawn to Buddhism on that basis. (One may have heard, for example, that faith in Buddhism is not "blind," but traditionally based on three things: intuition, reason, and experience.) But as one goes more deeply into it, one finds that it isn't quite like that. One finds that while reason is given a definite and honored place in Buddhism, it is by no means enthroned as its governing principle. But one remains a Buddhist because one has gone deep enough not only to be able to put reason in its proper place, but also to find other aspects of Buddhist practice profoundly meaningful.

Thus Going for Refuge is an experience—a spiritual experience—that is deepening and growing more multidimensional all the time. One accepts the ideal of Enlightened humanity, exemplified by the historical Buddha, as being more and more relevant to oneself personally; one takes that ideal as one's personal goal in life more and more to heart; and one tries to practice the Dharma in such a way as to realize that ideal more and more effectively.

3. GOING FOR REFUGE AND THE CONCEPT OF ESCAPE

The fact that the word *sarana*, refuge, is so firmly embedded in Buddhist tradition makes it extremely important to bring out its positive implications, otherwise we get a one-sidedly negative picture of the spiritual life, like talking about escape from the bud without mentioning the flower.

ONE OF THE COMMONEST criticisms of the spiritual life is that it is escapism, and that those who try to practice some such thing as Buddhism are escapists. What people mean by this probably comes quite close to the dictionary definition of escapism: "the tendency to seek distraction and relief from reality." As we shall see, nothing could be less like a description of Buddhism.

But escape—"to get away, as by flight or other conscious efforts; to break away, get free, or get clear, from or out of detention, danger, discomfort, or the like, as to escape from prison"—*is* quite a good description of the spiritual life, at least as looked at from a certain point of view. It may not be the whole truth about spiritual life, but it is a substantial part of it. When one sets out to live a spiritual life, one is—or one should be—making a conscious effort to break away, to get free, to get clear of all sorts of entanglements, involvements, and complicated murkiness. Or, to put it another way, one is trying to make the transition from lower to higher states of being and consciousness, trying to develop, trying to evolve. This is what the spiritual life is substantially about.

So why might we try to do this? What makes us want to escape, to develop, to rise from a lower to a higher state of being and consciousness? We are impelled, even compelled, to do it because we experience our present state as restrictive, cramped, limiting, confined, unsatisfactory, even dangerous. In our present state and circumstances, we feel only too often as though we are imprisoned, even caged, on a treadmill. Naturally we have the urge to get out, to *break* out if necessary, to get free and clear.

The Pali Canon contains a passage attributed to the Buddha in which he tries to explain to some of his disciples what it feels like to be Enlightened. Obviously they are very curious to know how it feels when you've got there. What does it feel like to be liberated? What does it feel like to be a Buddha? In his attempt to put across the inner content of the experience, rather than offer a conceptual explanation, the Buddha chose to use three similes.[35] He said, suppose that on a hot and dusty day you've been carrying an enormous burden for many miles; and suppose that after you've been staggering along with it for mile after mile, hour after hour, you are at last able to lift that load off your shoulders and put it down, free from that tremendous, oppressive weight. Becoming Enlightened, he said, is like that. You feel as though you have set down all your burdens. There's no weight for you to carry, nothing oppressing you. You are light and buoyant; you can float free.

Then again, he said, suppose you've been engaged in some trade, and suppose as the result of your business enterprise—or lack of enterprise—you've got heavily into debt. You owe a lot of money to a lot of people and you have no idea how you are going to pay them back. Your creditors are knocking on your door, following you about, wanting their money. Before you is the prospect of going to prison. Then one day, by some miracle, you suddenly acquire a large sum of money and can discharge all your debts. At last you can look everybody in the face again, free from that terrible anxiety. Becoming Enlightened, the Buddha said, is a bit like that.

Then a third image: becoming Enlightened, the Buddha said, is like being released from prison. Imagine how it might feel to have been shut up in prison for years on end. Then, one day, the door is flung open. Suddenly you are free to walk out into the sunlight and go wherever you please. Being Enlightened is just like that—you've escaped from the prison of the world itself.

Through these three similes, the Buddha tried to express something of how it feels to become Enlightened. You feel light, buoyant, carefree. You may even strike unenlightened people as being rather irresponsible, as not taking life seriously enough. You feel completely unconcerned about the past, because there is nothing left over that you have to deal with, and you are not concerned about the future either. Above all, you feel free, absolutely free, because you have at last escaped in the fullest possible sense.

It is therefore quite appropriate to describe the spiritual life as being, at least from one point of view, about escape. As for escapism, that is something else entirely. If an escapee is one who breaks out of prison, an escapist is one who tries to forget that he is in prison at all, who pretends to himself that the prison is not a prison, and that he is really free. Broadly speaking, this kind of escapism takes two forms: the non-religious and the religious. Of these two, non-religious escapism is probably the more common these days. It consists in trying to forget that one is in prison by becoming absorbed in whatever activities can be carried on within the prison walls. Religious escapism, on the other hand, consists in trying to forget that one is in prison by becoming absorbed in books on how to escape from prison.

Closely related to the idea of escape in Buddhism generally, and much more familiar, is the idea of "refuge," which the dictionary defines as "that which, or one who, shelters, protects from danger, distress, calamity, etc., a place inaccessible to the enemy." In Buddhism, refuge—a means of escape and a place to escape to—is provided by the Three Jewels, or Three Refuges: the Buddha, the Enlightened teacher; the Dharma, the teaching; and the Sangha, the more highly developed members of the spiritual community. Between them the Three Refuges represent not only the means of escape from lower to higher levels of consciousness; they also represent what we escape to, those higher levels themselves. The act of Going for Refuge to the Buddha, the Dharma, and the Sangha is the central act of the whole Buddhist life; it is Going for Refuge that makes one a Buddhist. For the Buddhist tradition, therefore, Going for Refuge is identical with the following of the spiritual path itself.

All of this finds expression in the very earliest Buddhist texts, most famously in the *Dhammapada,* in which the Buddha is recorded as making a clear distinction between what could be called false refuges and true refuges, the main point being that no mundane thing can give refuge in an absolute sense. He says:

> Many people, out of fear, flee for refuge to sacred hills, woods, groves, trees, and shrines. In reality this is not a safe refuge. In reality this is not the best refuge. Fleeing to such a refuge one is not released from all suffering. He who goes for refuge to the Enlightened One, to the Truth, and to the Spiritual Community—and who sees with perfect wisdom the Four Ariyan Truths—namely, suffering, the origin of suffering, the passing beyond suffering and the Ariyan Eightfold Way leading to the pacification of suffering—for him this is a safe refuge, for him this is the best refuge. Having gone to such a refuge, one is released from all suffering.[36]

Just to clear up possible misunderstanding, it should be observed that the idea of Going for Refuge as a way of escaping from all that is unsatisfactory does not do full justice to the ideals and practice of the spiritual life. The spiritual life also involves committing oneself to all that is truly satisfactory, and the point of escaping is to leave yourself free to make that commitment. There is nothing wrong in escaping if there is something to escape from, but to escape is not the be-all and end-all of the spiritual life any more than it is of worldly life. The fact that the word *sarana,* refuge, is so firmly embedded in Buddhist tradition makes it extremely important to bring out its positive implications, otherwise we get a one-sidedly negative picture of the spiritual life, like talking about escape from the bud without mentioning the flower.

3 ← The Path to Enlightenment

1. "What Is Your Dharma?": The Buddha's Answer to Mahapajapati Gotami

The Dharma is whatever helps us to rise from wherever we are now, and from whatever we are now.

THERE ARE MANY different versions of Buddhism, and many interpretations. Indeed, the word "Buddhism" itself represents an interpretation. Buddhism was not originally called Buddhism at all. It was never called Buddhism in India, and it was certainly never called Buddhism by the Buddha. It was called the *Dharma* in Sanskrit, or *Dhamma* in Pali. And the word *Dharma,* or *Dhamma,* means Reality or Truth; it means law, doctrine, or teaching. Or, one may say, it represents Reality or Truth as communicated in the form of a teaching from the Enlightened to the unenlightened mind. The originator of this Dharma, this vision of reality as a teaching, is, of course, Gautama the Buddha. He communicates to his followers a reality, a truth which he has personally experienced—the experience of which constitutes Enlightenment. The Buddha is therefore the best spokesman, the best interpreter, of Buddhism. So what does the Buddha himself say that the Dharma is? In this connection we can refer to an episode in the Pali scriptures, for the Buddha himself was once asked this very question, namely: "What is your Dharma? What is your teaching?"

The person who asked this was Mahapajapati Gotami, the Buddha's aunt and foster-mother. She had brought him up since childhood, since the death of his mother when he was just a few days old. In later years Mahapajapati Gotami had not only become a follower of his teaching, but had "gone forth," as we say, after hearing those teachings from his own lips. She had been so impressed by them that she had wanted to give up all her other interests, connections, and ties so as to be able to devote her entire life to practicing the Dharma. She had therefore gone forth, leaving her home, leaving her family, leaving her husband, leaving the city of Kapilavastu, and wandering from place to place, meditating and seeking to practice the Dharma.

At the time of our episode, Mahapajapati Gotami had passed a period of time without any direct contact with the Buddha, and so there was a certain amount of confusion in her mind. She wanted to practice the Dharma, but she was not quite sure what the Dharma was. This is not such an uncommon thing. Sometimes, at least, many of us may find ourselves in the position of wanting to practice the truth without being quite sure, or even at all sure, what the truth actually is.

Although Mahapajapati Gotami was in contact with some of the Buddha's disciples and was able to ask them what it was that the Buddha taught, the interpretations they gave her were often very different; they each had their own point of view. In the end she decided to go and ask the Buddha himself what it was that he did fundamentally teach. She therefore made the journey to the place where the Buddha was staying and asked, point blank as it were, "What is your Dharma? How can we know what you actually teach? What is the criterion?" Here is a translation of what, according to the tradition, the Buddha said to Mahapajapati Gotami on that occasion:

> Gotami, those things of which you know, "These things
> lead to passion, not to dispassion; to attachment, not to

detachment; to amassing, not to dispersal; to ambition, not to modesty; to discontent, not to content; to association (association with the group, that is), not to seclusion (from the group); to idleness, not to energy; to luxury, not to frugality," of them, you can quite certainly decide: "This is not the Dharma, this is not the Vinaya, this is not the Master's teaching."

But those things of which you know, "These things lead to dispassion, not to passion; to detachment, not to attachment; to dispersal, not to amassing; to modesty, not to ambition; to content, not to discontent; to seclusion (from the group), not to association (with the group); to energy, not to idleness; to frugality, not to luxury," of them you can quite certainly decide, "This is the Dharma, this is the Vinaya, this is the Master's teaching."

So here in the Buddha's own words is the criterion; this is the principle. The Dharma is whatever contributes to the spiritual development of the individual. It is whatever the individual finds, in his or her own experience, does actually contribute to his or her spiritual development.

In this passage, as in others, individuals are clearly seen to be living, growing, and developing. And in this connection we may also remember the Buddha's "vision" of humanity immediately after his Enlightenment. At that time, the Buddha was undecided as to whether or not he should teach the truth he had discovered. It was, he knew, very deep, very difficult, and abstruse. But he eventually decided that he would go out and teach, he would communicate the truth he had discovered to other beings. And at that moment, we are told, he opened his eyes and looked out over the world to see those living beings as a bed of lotus flowers. It was as if he could see a vast bed of lotuses spreading in all directions, as far as the eye could see. This was humanity. This was the human race. Some of these "flowers"—some of these people—were clearly sunk in the mud. Others had risen just a little way out of it and were struggling free. Others still had broken out of the mud altogether and were rising above the surface of the water so that their petals could open out to receive the light of the sun.

This is how the Buddha saw humanity at that moment. He saw all beings as individuals, and he could see that they were all at different stages of development, all growing but needing the sunlight of the Dharma in order to grow and develop further.

In another passage, in the great Mahayana sutra called the *Saddharma Pundarika* or "White Lotus" Sutra, there is another very beautiful comparison. Here, individuals are compared not just to lotuses emerging from the mud and slime, but to many different kinds of plants. They are compared to grass, trees, flowers, and shrubs, while the Buddha's teaching is compared to a great rain-cloud. During the winter and summer in India it is very hot and dry for many months. Everything becomes very withered and parched. But then, suddenly, at the beginning of the rainy season, a great black cloud arises in the midst of the sky. There is thunder, lightning, and then the rain falls, very heavily and very steadily, day in and day out, sometimes for weeks on end. And as it rains, everything grows. Everything that was so parched and dry becomes green again and starts springing up. All the leaves, all the grass, trees, flowers, and shrubs, start to grow again. And everything grows in its own way. The tree grows as a tree, the shrub grows as a shrub, the grass grows as grass, the flower grows as a flower; each grows in its own way. This is important to the Buddha's analogy, for the Dharma is just like that rain-cloud: it gives us just the nourishment we each need. It leads us from where it finds us, its starting point—so far as we are concerned—being where we are now, because everyone needs the Dharma in his or her own way. The Dharma is whatever helps us to rise from wherever we are now, and from whatever we are now. The Dharma is therefore defined as whatever contributes to the development of the individual. That is the criterion.

This may sound rather broad and general, but it is not really so. The Dharma—the Buddha's teaching—is embodied in a number of actual spiritual practices. This is made clear in another episode from the Pali scriptures. In this episode we are reminded that there were a number of spiritual teachers in India during the Buddha's time. One of the best known of these was Nigantha Nataputta, as he is called in the Pali texts, who is usually identified with Mahavira, the founder of Jainism. Nigantha Nataputta died shortly before the Buddha, and after his death his monk followers split into two factions. These factions disagreed so vehemently about what their master had taught that they almost came to blows. Ananda, who seems to have been something of a gossip, told the Buddha about this, adding that he hoped there would be no such disputes after the Buddha himself had gone.

The Buddha replied that such a thing would be impossible. He was confident that there were not even two monks among his followers who would describe his teachings discordantly. He then reminded Ananda what those teachings were. There were the four foundations of mindfulness: mindfulness of the body, of the feelings, of thoughts, and of Reality. There were the four "right efforts": the effort to prevent the arising of unskillful mental states that have not arisen; the effort to abandon unskillful mental states that have arisen; the effort to develop skillful mental states that have not arisen; and the effort to maintain in existence those skillful mental states that have already arisen. He reminded Ananda about the four bases of success, the five spiritual faculties, the five powers, the seven factors of Enlightenment, the Noble Eightfold Path. . . . All these things constituted the Dharma that he had taught and he was confident that there would be no dispute about them after his death even between two of his disciples.

The immediately noticeable thing about this list of teachings is that they are all practical. They are all *practices.* There is nothing theoretical here; the Buddha says nothing about nirvana, nothing about *sunyata,* nothing about the mind. He does not even mention dependent origination. It is as if he is saying that the teachings he has given his disciples are all practical teachings and cannot therefore really be described differently by different people. After all, practical teachings involve actual practice and so the experience would be the same for all who practiced. It is much the same in ordinary life; we may disagree about theory, but we do not very often disagree about practice. We may disagree, for example, about the nature of electricity, but we are unlikely to disagree about how to mend a fuse. Similarly, the Buddha's disciples might disagree about theoretical teachings, but they could hardly disagree about practical teachings, provided of course that they had actually practiced them. So the Dharma is embodied primarily in spiritual practices, in things you do.

There is another interesting point which arises in connection with this episode. Despite the Buddha's answer, Ananda was not satisfied. He now said, "Well, even though they may all agree about the teaching, there might still be disputes about livelihood, or there might be disputes about the code of rules (Pali *patimokkha,* the hundred-and-fifty rules observed by the monks, still observed in many cases)." The Buddha's reply to this is very important. A dispute over livelihood, or a dispute over the code of rules, he said, would be a trifling matter. Only disputes over the path, or disputes over the way of practice, would be disastrous.

2. THE ARISING OF VISION

The aim of this great Buddhist teaching of the Path of Vision and the Path of Transformation is to enable us to bring the whole of our life up to the level of its highest moments.

ACCORDING TO the Indian Buddhist tradition the Noble Eightfold Path naturally falls into two great divisions: the Path of Vision (*darsana-marga*) and the Path of Transformation (*bhavana-marga*). Thus the Noble Eightfold Path is made up of two lesser "Paths," in the sense of two successive stages, the Path of Vision, which corresponds only to the first *anga,* or so-called step, Perfect Vision, and the Path of Transformation, which corresponds to the seven remaining "steps":

Perfect Emotion, Perfect Speech, Perfect Action, Perfect Livelihood, Perfect Effort, Perfect Awareness, and Perfect Meditation. The significance of this division is that Perfect Vision represents the phase of initial spiritual insight and experience, whereas the rest of the Eightfold Path represents the transformation of one's whole being, in all its heights and depths, in all its aspects, in accordance with that initial insight and experience. The Path of Transformation represents a complete and thoroughgoing transformation of one's emotional life, speech, communication with others, livelihood, and so on. One may transform one's livelihood, which is the fifth "step," before one's speech, which is only the third; but eventually, in one way or another, the whole being is to be transformed, in its heights and in its depths, conscious and unconscious.

This initial spiritual experience—this Perfect Vision or Path of Vision—may arise in different ways for different people. There is no uniform pattern. Indeed the great variety that exists among people shows itself in the spiritual life generally, as well as in the way people enter upon the spiritual path. For some people the Path of Vision arises as the result of personal tragedy, bereavement, or loss. Their whole existence is disturbed and upset as though by a great earthquake in which everything they had cherished or held dear is laid low. In this wreck, this ruin of their lives, they start questioning, start looking deeper, start wondering about the meaning and purpose of existence.

For others Perfect Vision may arise by way of a spontaneous mystical experience. (I don't like this word "mystical," which for many people is redolent of mystery and mystery-mongering, but we don't have a better one.) A number of such mystical experiences are described in Bucke's *Cosmic Consciousness,* a book published in 1901 which is still worth reading. It is surprising how many people have had an experience of this kind, some rare moment of ecstasy, or insight, or tremendous love, which apparently without any preparation possessed them, swept them away, lifted them up into a new dimension, and completely altered their outlook on life. Also under the heading of mystical experience we can include our experience of nature, as when we are overwhelmed by the sight of some wonderful sunset, or when in the midst of the countryside we experience a great, all-pervading peace, stillness, and tranquillity.

Sometimes the Path of Vision can arise as a result of looking at a beautiful painting, or listening to music. On such occasions we can be carried away into a new dimension of existence. Sometimes it can arise as a result of deep and prolonged thought. Some people endeavor to reach out and grasp the truth by means of the intellect. They try to plumb the depths of being with reason and logic. This is the way of the thinker, the philosopher, the sage. Some people actually *think* their way through to Reality, to the Path of Vision.

For others it may arise in quite a different way, as the result of the practice of meditation. When the mind has been systematically stilled, and when, although thoughts have been banished, clear consciousness still persists, under these conditions also, Perfect Vision may arise.

Sometimes it may arise for those who are engaged in altruistic activities, such as nursing the sick or looking after the old. For those who are sacrificing themselves and their personal interests, and who are completely selfless on the plane of work and action, even in the midst of their activity Perfect Vision may arise.

Finally it may arise, for some people at least, out of their whole experience of life—especially as they grow older, and (it is to be hoped) more mature. When all the different threads seem to come together, and the pattern of their lives seems to make some kind of sense, to reflect some glimmer of meaning, then out of the depths of their simple human maturity Perfect Vision may arise. I am not suggesting that wisdom comes automatically with age. Far from it! If that were the case, we would not need to take the trouble to acquire wisdom when young. But certainly for those who have led a truly human life, as they mellow and perhaps sweeten a little, and as their experience clarifies, the Path of Vision may sometimes arise.

Thus the Path of Vision arises for different people in all these different ways. For some it has even arisen in a dream. But however it does arise we should be very careful not to lose it, not to forget it. This happens very easily, for as the poet says, "the world is too much with us." We may have an experience so wonderful that we might think we will never forget it. But after a short time, after a few days or weeks, it is no longer there; indeed, it is as though it had never been. So we should cherish it, cultivate it, dwell upon it—try to deepen it, clarify it, develop it—all the time. We should eventually try to allow it to permeate and transform our whole being, our whole life.

To sum up we may say that the aim of this great Buddhist teaching of the Path of Vision and the Path of Transformation is to enable us to bring the whole of our life up to the level of its highest moments. This is what it means to evolve spiritually. This is what it means to follow the Noble Eightfold Path. It means to achieve Perfect Vision by one means or another, and then transform our whole being in accordance with that vision.

3. The Connection Between Philosophy and Practice

Buddhism is not a system of abstract thought, and it does not attempt to satisfy mere intellectual curiosity by giving a rationally coherent account of the universe.

About a century ago, Schopenhauer, who was more deeply influenced by and imbued with the spirit of ancient Indian philosophy than any other Western thinker, ventured a striking prediction. He said that the renaissance which would be brought about by the discovery, in the nineteenth century, of the treasures of oriental literature would be incomparably more glorious than that which had been ushered in during the fifteenth and sixteenth centuries by the rediscovery of the classics of Greece and Rome. This bold prediction of the nineteenth century is now being fulfilled, or at least beginning to be fulfilled. What was merely political and commercial contact between the nations of the East and the West has begun to deepen into cultural exchanges and inter-religious fellowship. Throughout every Western land, men and women are now to be found—few in number, indeed, but increasingly influential—who are convinced that now as ever light comes from the East: *Ex Oriente lux.*

Of the rays into which that light, shooting through the spectrum of human understanding, is broken up, none confronts occidental eyes with a steadier radiance, or shines forth with a more blindingly brilliant effulgence, than the hitherto unknown splendor to which the West, startled into awareness of a whole new world of values, has given the name "Buddhism." Yet often is that splendor dimmed by the opacity of the medium through which it is transmitted. Even today, when the Pali Text Society of London and other bodies, as well as distinguished scholars working independently in the field of Buddhist studies, have between them published a small library of Pali, Sanskrit, Chinese, and Tibetan Buddhist texts and their translations, the writers of articles and compilers of popular handbooks on Buddhism, ignoring this mass of authentic material, are frequently found repeating the same old misunderstandings about nirvana and other points of Buddhist doctrine.

Such misunderstandings, when they are not due to ineradicable religious prejudice, such as still animates many Christian writers on non-Christian religions, may be traced to a misconception of the very nature of Buddhism. This misconception has its roots deep down in the history of Western thought. Briefly stated, it consists in regarding Buddhism as a system of philosophy in the modern academic sense.

To the ancient Greeks and Romans, philosophy was not merely an opinion, but a passion; it meant not only loftier thinking, but nobler living. A philosopher was expected to leave his hair and beard untrimmed, to wear but one long simple garment, to sleep on the bare ground, and to eat sparingly. With the irruption of Christianity into the Greco-Roman world, the old classic ideals of moderation, balance, and harmony were destroyed. Wisdom was replaced by faith, while for the harmless and helpful philosophic life was substituted one of aggressive good works (which included the conversion of the heathen, by force, if necessary, and the burning of heretics). Between faith and works some kind of harmony was indeed sought to be maintained, but, covering as these did only a small part of the scale of human potentialities, this harmony was not rich or full enough to be long sustained, and, before many centuries had passed, the shrill note of faith first dominated and then drowned all others.

The modern scientific attitude of mind developed in part as a protest against the unverifiable dogmas of medieval Christianity, and every advance in scientific knowledge was made in the teeth of determined ecclesiastical opposition; for the schoolman, no less than the scientist, was aware that the victory of science spelled the defeat of faith. With the abandonment of Christian doctrine came the tacit repudiation of the Christian way of life, and though individual thinkers continued to conform to Christian ethical standards and even, in some cases, professed to accept the Christian revelation, Western thought came more and more under the influence of science and developed with increasing freedom from religious preconceptions. The introduction of psychological and epistemological interests strengthened still further the theoretical and speculative tendencies in modern thought, and, by the time Schopenhauer arose to challenge the academic and professorial conception of philosophy, despite artificial attempts at reconciliation the divorce between religion and philosophy had been made absolute.

A division between concrete living and abstract thinking continues to characterize modern Western culture. Philosophy is taught at universities as a purely theoretical subject; it does not demand from its votaries the adoption of a distinctive mode of life, nor does it have as a whole any bearing upon practical affairs. For the philosophic life, as it was understood by the Greeks and Romans in even their most degenerate days—the passionate pursuit of beauty, truth, and goodness, and the endeavor to reflect them in one's own life—has been substituted by the detached and barren study of the history of philosophical opinions.

When the star of Buddhism first rose above these icy academic horizons, its dependence on reason rather than faith, its freedom from credulity and superstition, not unnaturally caused it to be regarded as an ethico-philosophical system rather than as a religion in the Christian sense of the term. Owing to the congenitally abstract proclivities of Western thought, the close connection between the practical and the theoretical aspects of Buddhism was gradually ignored, and topics such as the nature of nirvana came to be discussed as though they had a simply theoretical import that could be determined by the exercise of speculative reason. The fact that Buddhism is, above all, a way of life was forgotten.

Most of the problems, and many of the misunderstandings, which have arisen in connection with Buddhism may be traced to this wrong habit of considering the significance of its profoundest teaching in complete dissociation from their pragmatic consequences in the actual Buddhist way of living. It therefore becomes necessary to stress the fact that Buddhism is not a system of abstract thought, and that it does not attempt to satisfy mere intellectual curiosity by giving a rationally coherent account of the universe. Buddhism is a way of life that leads to a spiritual experience; in fact, to a number of experiences. These experiences link up into a series that culminates in the supreme experience of nirvana.

4. THE ESSENCE OF THE DHARMA

The Buddha compares the state of mind of one gaining Enlightenment to that of someone who has come safe out of a dangerous jungle, or been freed from debt, or released from prison.

MANY STUDENTS of Buddhism are at first staggered by the vastness of the field before them and bewildered by the abundance of material. This is natural. Like Christianity and Islam, Buddhism is not only a teaching but a culture, a civilization, a movement in history, a social order, in fact a whole world in itself. It comprises systems of philosophy, methods of meditation, rituals, manners, and customs, clothes, languages, sacred literature, pagodas, temples, monasteries, calligraphy, poems, paintings, plays, stories, games, flower-arrangements, pottery, and a thousand other things. All this is Buddhist, and often immediately recognizable as such. Whether it is a stone Buddha seated cross-legged in the jungles of Anuradhupura, a Tibetan sacred dance, a cup of tea between friends in Japan, or the way in which a bhikshu answers a question in London, everything is invisibly signed with the same mysterious seal. Sometimes it floats with the clouds between heaven and earth, shines in the rainbow, or gurgles over pebbles in the company of a mountain stream. "Looked at, it cannot be seen; listened to, it cannot be heard."[37] Sooner or later, however, the student tries to identify it. He wonders what it could be that gives unity to all these diverse expressions, so that however remote in space and time, and however different their respective mediums, one perfectly harmonizes with another, creating not the dissonance that might have been expected but "a concord of sweet sounds." Eventually a question shapes itself in his mind, and at last he enquires, "What is the essence of the Dharma?"

The best answer to this question would be the "thunder-like silence" with which Vimalakirti, in the Mahayana sutra that bears his name, answered the bodhisattva Manjusri's question about the nature of Reality. Can we describe even the color of a rose? But this apparently negative procedure the student would not find very helpful. Concessions must be made. Buddhism is essentially an experience. "An experience of what?" Before answering this second question, let us try to explain why, of all the words in the dictionary, "experience" is the first term on which one falls back when compelled to abandon the "thunder-like silence." Unlike thought, experience is direct, unmediated; it is knowledge by acquaintance. Hence it is characterized by a feeling of absolute certainty. When we see the sun shining in a clear sky we do not doubt that it is bright; when a thorn runs beneath our fingernail we do not speculate whether it is painful. In saying that Buddhism is essentially an experience, we do not suggest that the object of that experience in any way resembles the objects of sense-experience, nor even that there is an object at all. We simply draw attention to its unique unconceptualized immediacy. The relation between sense-experience and the kind with which we are now concerned is merely analogical. For this reason it is necessary to go a step further and complete our definition by saying that the essence of the Dharma, of Buddhism, consists in a *spiritual* or *transcendental* experience. This is what in traditional terminology is called Enlightenment-experience.

Apart from conveying an impression that the subject has now been lost sight of in the clouds, the mere addition of these adjectives is inconclusive. They themselves need definition. But inasmuch as this will involve the use of terms even more abstract, more remote from concrete experience, such definition will set up a process of conceptualization as a result of which the reflection of Enlightenment-experience in our minds will be in danger of complete distortion, like the moon's reflection in a pond the surface of which the wind has chopped into waves. Concepts had therefore better be treated as symbols, the value of which lies not in their literal meaning so much as in their suggestiveness. They should be handled in the spirit not of logic but of poetry; not pushed hither and thither with grim calculation like pieces on a chessboard, but tossed lightly, playfully in the air like a juggler's multicolored balls. Approaching the subject in this spirit we may define Enlightenment-experience as "seeing things as they are" (*yathabhutajnanadarsana*). This is the traditional definition. Here also, it will be observed, the use of the word "seeing" (*darsana*)— which primarily denotes a form of sense-perception—emphasizes not only the directness and immediacy of the experience but also its noetic character. Enlightenment-experience is not just a blind sensing of things, but, as the English word suggests, the shining forth of a light, an illumination, in the brightness of which things become visible in their reality. Such expressions should not mislead us into thinking that there is any real difference between the subject and the object of the experience, between the light and the things illuminated (which disposes of the second question raised above—that is, "What is Buddhism an experience of?"). Were it not for the fact that all words indicative of existence have for Buddhism a disagreeable substantialist flavor, it might even be preferable not to speak of Enlightenment as an experience at all but to call it a state of being. Fortunately other ways of surmounting the difficulty are available. The *Avatamsaka Sutra*, for instance, depicts the world of Enlightenment-experience as consisting not of objects illuminated from without but entirely of innumerable beams of light, all intersecting and intersected, none of which offers any resistance to the passage of any other. Light being always in motion, this striking similitude has the additional advantage of precluding the notion that Enlightenment is a definite state in which one as it were settles comfortably down for good, instead showing that it is a movement from perfection to greater perfection in a process in which there is no final term, the direction of movement alone remaining constant.

If spiritual or transcendental experience is a state of seeing things as they are, its opposite, mundane experience, wherein all unenlightened beings are involved, must be one of seeing them as they are not. The cause of this blindness is twofold. Being creatures of desires, human beings are concerned with things only to the extent that they can be made to serve our own ends. We are interested not in truth but in utility. For us things and people exist not in their own right but only as actual or possible means of our own gratification. This is the "veil of passions" (*klesavarana*). Usually we do not like to acknowledge, even to ourselves, that our attitude toward life is often no better than that of a pig rooting for acorns. Motives are therefore rationalized. Instead of admitting that we hate somebody, we say he is wicked and ought to be punished. Rather than admit we enjoy eating flesh, we maintain that sheep and cows were created for our benefit. Not wishing to die, we invent the dogma of the immortality of the individual soul. Craving help and protection, we start believing in a personal God. According to the Buddha, all the philosophies, and a great deal of religious teaching, are rationalizations of desires. This is the "veil of (false) assumptions" (*jneyavarana*). On the attainment of Enlightenment both veils are rent asunder. For this reason the experience is accompanied by an exhilarating sense of release. The Buddha compares the state of mind of one gaining Enlightenment to that of someone who has come safe out of a dangerous jungle, or been freed from debt, or released from prison. It is as though an intolerable burden had at last been lifted from one's back. So intense is this feeling of release from pain, suffering, conflicting emotions, and mental sterility and stagnation that many of the older canonical texts speak of the Enlightenment-experience exclusively in terms of freedom or emancipation (*vimukti*). One of them represents the Buddha himself as saying that even as the great ocean had one taste, the taste of salt, so his teaching had one flavor, the flavor of emancipation.[38] Besides a psychological aspect, *vimukti* has an intellectual and an existential aspect. In the first place it is a freedom from all theories and speculations about Reality; and in the second, from any form of conditioned existence whatever, including "re-becoming" as a result of karma. The freedom into which one breaks through at the time of Enlightenment is not limited and partial, but absolute and unconditioned.

This introduces an aspect of Enlightenment-experience which is not always properly understood. Freedom, to be really unconditioned, must transcend the distinction between conditioned and unconditioned, *samsara* and *nirvana*, bondage and liberation, all of which are really mental constructions and, as such, part of the "veil of assumptions." In the ultimate sense there can therefore be no question of escaping from the conditioned to the Unconditioned as though they were distinct entities. To speak paradoxically, in order to be truly free one has to escape not only from bondage but from liberation, not only from samsara into nirvana but from nirvana back into samsara. It is this "escape" or descent that constitutes the *mahakaruna* or "Great Compassion" of the Buddha, which is in reality his realization of the non-duality of the conditioned and the

Unconditioned as that realization appears from the viewpoint of the conditioned. The Enlightenment-experience is therefore not only one of illumination and freedom but also of infinite and inexhaustible love, a love which has for object all sentient beings, and which manifests as uninterrupted activity in pursuit of their temporal and spiritual welfare.

5. The Path as a Symbol

One is not following the Buddhist path if one feels that one is being driven along it like a sheep, rather wishing one could stray off and have a nibble on some succulent wayside shrub or flower.

ACCORDING TO BUDDHISM our predicament arises out of our ignorance. Ignorance (Sanskrit *avidya*) is traditionally likened to drunkenness, while the volitions (*samskaras*) that arise from ignorance are compared to actions committed while in a state of drunkenness. This perception of the human condition may seem extreme, but it is no more than sober fact. Sometimes we don't realize the extent of the damage we do simply because we don't know what we are doing. We initiate things, we say things, we get involved with people, and in doing so we inevitably set up problems. Although we sometimes become aware that our lives are more or less made up of the problems we create in this way, very often we don't even see them as problems—and this is a problem in itself.

Of course, there is no question of trying to stay on the safe side by putting off doing anything at all until we are Enlightened; to live, we must act, and we are therefore bound to make mistakes. But if we can understand what we are doing, we can break the reactive patterns that cause us to create the same problems over and over again. And the way to break those reactive patterns that bring us so much suffering is to set up different patterns of thought, feeling, and behavior.

When you see your predicament clearly, when you know where you are starting from, you are in a position to perceive the choices before you, which gives you a certain degree of freedom. It isn't absolute freedom—you can't choose your starting point—but you are free to choose what you make of your situation. Where you are is less important than whether or not you *know* where you are. There is a freedom which arises out of knowing oneself and knowing the possibility of evolving beyond one's present condition.

That freedom is, however, double-edged. The mind is not a thing; it is not, as Guenther puts it in the introduction to his translation of *Mind in Buddhist Psychology*, "a static entity or a mere state or function of consciousness."[39] It consists solely in its activities. "It" is therefore always changing, always moving. But it can move either creatively or reactively. At every moment the mind is confronted with the choice of repeating old patterns and going round in circles or rearranging the pattern and setting up more positive conditions for spiritual growth. At every moment there is the possibility of moving forward and also the possibility of just moving round and thus not really moving at all. We are free to develop our awareness of the spiritual path, to look for solutions; and we are also free to sink back into unconsciousness and stop asking questions. Furthermore, mental states cannot be compartmentalized. Painful and harmful states of mind cannot be shut away somewhere while we develop mindfulness, joy, and kindness. At any one time we are either encouraging positive mental states or reinforcing negative ones.

If one makes the effort to develop in a positive direction, one's life assumes a more serious meaning as one takes responsibility for it. One realizes for oneself the necessity, almost, of a certain way of living. This is what it means to follow the Buddhist path. Buddhism is presented as a path or way, but this is only a manner of speaking. The path is a symbol, representing the fact that we can change, we can develop. If we know what we are now and what we can become, we can take steps to effect that transition. We have the capacity, and the freedom, to perceive and to realize our best interests.

According to the Pali idiom, we *develop* the path.[40] It is not something out there, an objective thing. We *are* the path. If we think of it as something out there, like a road or track, we may get stuck with an unhelpful notion of the spiritual discipline required in order to follow it. One is not following the Buddhist path if one feels that one is being driven along it like a sheep, rather wishing one could stray off and have a nibble on some succulent wayside shrub or flower.

There is certainly an objective criterion of development which one has to understand and act upon, but the path itself is not out there; it is in here. There is no question of forcing yourself to follow a particular track or go in a particular direction. The path simply represents the individual solution to your own particular predicament. If you know and understand yourself as you are now, that puts you in a position to develop in your own way. The path is you in the process of organizing your mental states in such a way that growth and development will take place in a positive direction.

6. Spiritual Growth: Developmental or Immanent?

There is no point in saying that one believes in the Buddha, even if the Buddha can be demonstrated to have lived, if one makes no effort to close the gap between oneself and the Buddha.

IT IS ONLY too easy to think of the Bodhisattva's path in a very literal way, as though it leads to Buddhahood just as the garden path leads to the door of a house. We think that following the path will mean going along step by step until one day we reach the wonderful gateway of nirvana, all glistening and golden. There it is, and we go in. It is very natural for us to think in this way—but it isn't really like that. When you come to the end of the Bodhisattva path, you don't find a gate or doorway, or any sort of celestial mansion waiting for you. You don't find anything at all. There's nothing there. The path just ends—and there you are at the end of it.

In fact, you find yourself—to use another metaphor, which is also not to be taken literally—at the edge of a precipice. The path has gone on nicely, step by step, stage by stage, mile after mile. You have counted all those milestones, and you were expecting to arrive in comfort at the entrance to a great house. But no—you find that the path ends right at the edge of a precipice. So there you are, standing on the edge, and the drop goes down not just a few feet, but what seems like miles. Somehow you know that it's bottomless, infinite. What are you going to do?

The Zen people put it another way. They say that the spiritual life is like climbing a high and greasy flagpole.[41] When, after a great deal of effort, you get to the top, you find that there's nowhere to go. You obviously can't go any further up—and you can't come down, because at the bottom there's a Zen master with a big stick. Nor is there a little platform at the top of the flagpole on which you can settle down like Saint Simeon Stylites.[42] There's nothing there but empty space. And, of course, you're too high up to jump. You can't go up, you can't go down, you can't stay there, and you can't jump off. What are you to do? Well, it is quite impossible to say.

This predicament arises out of the fact that "path" and "goal" are discontinuous. Contrary to our usual metaphorical mode of description, Enlightenment is not reached by following a path. But this doesn't mean that the path should not be followed. Paradoxically enough, you follow the path knowing that it doesn't lead anywhere.

Not even the "right" path will take us to Enlightenment. The path, one may say, is in the dimension of time, while the goal is in the dimension of eternity. We will never reach eternity by going on and on in time. That is, one does not arrive at eternity by an indefinite prolongation of time, any more than one can arrive at a two-dimensional figure by the prolongation of a one-dimensional line. The two—eternity and time, the goal and the path—are by definition discontinuous, discrete. The Bodhisattva represents the dimension of time because the Bodhisattva path is followed in time. It's something that happens—it has a past, a present, and a future—and it doesn't go beyond time. But the Buddha represents the dimension of eternity. The Buddha represents the goal, and the goal is attained out of time. One reaches the end of the path within time, but one shouldn't think that one attains the goal in time: one attains the goal out of time or, to put it another way, the goal is eternally attained.

There are two ways of looking at spiritual development. It can be seen in terms of advancing from stage to stage, but it can also be seen in terms of deepening one's experience of what is already there. We need both. If one thinks one-sidedly of the spiritual life as a progression from stage to stage, one is liable to become too goal-oriented. But if one thinks only in terms of deepening one's present experience, unfolding from a deep center within oneself, one may become rather inert. It is perhaps best to think of operating in both modes at the same time, or alternating between them at different periods of one's life.

We have said that one follows the path knowing that it doesn't lead anywhere. One also follows it with no guarantee that it is the *right* path. However, it is possible to resolve this contradiction and uncertainty by balancing the model of the path with the model of unfolding. Sometimes people are overconcerned that they have got exactly the right teacher, the right mantra, the right book—that they are doing the right thing that will get them to the right Enlightenment. In a sense, it isn't possible to know. If someone came along and said, "You are on the wrong path. You are definitely going to hell," what could you say? You couldn't prove the person was wrong. You don't "know" in that logical, demonstrable fashion. But is that sort of knowledge applicable or appropriate to Enlightenment, and the path to Enlightenment?

If it is possible to know that one is on the path to Enlightenment, it can only be because there is something within one already, however embryonic, that corresponds to what is fully developed in the Buddha. Without that consonance, one could never follow the path or gain Enlightenment. An unenlightened human being and an

Enlightened human being are both human beings; so one has something in common with the Buddha, and the Buddha has something in common with oneself. What one is trying to do is increase what there is in common so that there will be less and less difference between the Buddha and oneself. When there is no difference at all, one will oneself be Enlightened.

All we can do is say, "Here I am, and there is the Buddha—or at least we have what purport to be records of a being of that sort. When I examine those records I can see that I have certain things in common with the Buddha, and although he had those qualities to a much greater degree than I do, the teachings suggest that I can develop them. So, provisionally accepting that there might be something in these teachings, I will see if I can. For instance, this text says that the Buddha was extremely kind. I can be kind myself on occasion, but I can see that I could be a lot kinder. Is it possible for me to develop more kindness?" So we try, and we find that, yes, it is possible. Then we conclude, "Well, if I can develop a bit more kindness, I can surely develop a lot more." And so we go on.

It all comes down to one's own practice. There is no point in saying that one believes in the Buddha, even if the Buddha can be demonstrated to have lived, if one makes no effort to close the gap between oneself and the Buddha. It is a continuous refinement through which one becomes progressively happier and more integrated. And there will be something in oneself which insists that when one becomes more emotionally positive and more mindful, one is on the right path. When you feel healthy, no one can say, "Ah no, you're very ill." You *know* that you're in a state of health, at least if it lasts for a little while. In the same way, if you are full of friendliness and compassion and mindfulness, no one can convince you that you are on the wrong path. The naturally self-transcending nature of the conscious being means that when you are all the time transcending yourself, you know that you are on the right path, because such a path corresponds to your innermost nature.

Sometimes you may feel as though you are unfolding like a flower; at other times spiritual life may feel more like climbing a mountain. The two modes correspond to the nature of the *bodhicitta* (the bodhicitta being the "will to Enlightenment"). The absolute *bodhicitta* is Enlightenment itself, while the relative *bodhicitta* is the *bodhicitta* everlastingly in the process of attaining Enlightenment. The two together are the ultimate realization. Thus in our spiritual life we are trying all the time to achieve that which we already have. We have to do both: realize that we already have it, but at the same time go all out to achieve it. One without the other leaves us out of balance.

We can get a sense of the possibility of combining the two from our dream life. Say, for example, you wake up with a memory of having been dreaming about traveling in India. At the same time, you are aware that this dream was really about painting a picture of a flower. Somehow you have to accept that the same dream was about both things. To your waking consciousness they seem like two alternatives, but the dream experience was both, in a mysterious way that the waking consciousness cannot apprehend. The spiritual life is rather like that. You have to have a sense of racing forward all the time, moving from stage to stage, climbing that mountain. At the same time, you have to be absolutely still, just realizing more and more deeply where you are now.

7. WHAT IS NIRVANA?

The question we should be asking is not "What is nirvana?" but "Why am I interested in nirvana? Why am I reading this book rather than another, or rather than, say, watching television?"

THE FIRST QUESTION Buddhists get asked when they meet non-Buddhists is, as likely as not, "What is nirvana?" Certainly when I was a Buddhist monk traveling about India, I used to find on trains that no sooner had I taken my seat than someone would come up to me (for in India people are by no means bashful when it comes to getting into conversation) and say, "You seem to be a Buddhist monk. Please tell me—what is nirvana?"

Indeed, it is a very appropriate question to ask. The question is, after all, addressing the whole point of being a Buddhist. You may see Buddhists engaged in all sorts of different activities, but they all have the same overall purpose in view. You may see shaven-headed Japanese monks in their long black robes sitting in disciplined rows, meditating hour after hour in the silence and tranquillity of a Zen monastery. You may see ordinary Tibetans going in the early morning up the steps of the temples, carrying their flowers and their candles and their bundles of incense sticks, kneeling down and making their offerings, chanting verses of praise to the Buddha, the Dharma, and the Sangha, and then going about their daily business. You may see Sri Lankan monks poring over palm-leaf manuscripts, the pages brown with age. You may see lay-folk in the Theravadin countries of Southeast Asia giving alms to the monks when they come round with their black begging-bowls. You may see Western Buddhists working together in Right Livelihood businesses.

When you see unfolded this whole vast panorama of Buddhist activities, the question that arises is: Why? What is the reason for it all? What is the moving spirit, the great impulse, behind all this activity? What are all these people trying to do? What are they trying to achieve through their meditation, their worshipping, their study, their alms-giving, their work, and so on?

If you asked this of any of these people, you would probably receive the traditional answer: "We're doing this for the sake of the attainment of nirvana, liberation, Enlightenment." But what then is this nirvana? How is it to be understood, explained? How is it to be fitted in to one's own particular range of mental furniture? One naturally gropes after analogies. If one has a Christian background one will try to envisage nirvana as a sort of eternal life in heaven after death. If one takes it outside the usual religious framework altogether, one may even think of it as a state of complete annihilation or extinction.

But in fact there is no excuse for these kinds of badly mistaken views. It is not difficult to give a clear account of nirvana, because the ancient canonical texts are pretty clear as to what it is and what it isn't. If one does have the job of presenting the topic of nirvana, one will probably need to begin by discussing the etymology of the word *nirvana*—whether it means a "blowing out" or a "cooling down." One will no doubt go on to explain that, according to the Pali texts at least, nirvana consists in the extinction of all craving, all hatred, and all ignorance of the true nature of things.[43]

At some point it is customary to say that nirvana is a state of incomparable bliss, to which the bliss of this world cannot be compared.[44] And if one wants to get a bit technical, one may want to describe the two kinds of nirvana: the *klesa nirvana,* consisting in the extinction of all passions and defilements; and the *skandha nirvana,* consisting in the extinction of all the various processes of psychophysical existence, an event that takes place upon the death—as we call it—of someone who has already gained *klesa nirvana* during their lifetime.[45]

One may then go on to the different interpretations of nirvana in the various different schools of Buddhism—the Theravada, the Madhyamaka, the Yogacara, the Tantra, Zen, and so on. Finally, it is always necessary to emphasize that nirvana is neither eternal life in the Christian sense, nor annihilation or extinction in the materialist sense—that here, as elsewhere, one has to follow the middle path between two extreme views.

So this is how nirvana is traditionally delineated. Above all, perhaps, nirvana is conventionally defined as the *goal* of Buddhism. And it is in respect of this particular way of positioning the concept that my approach here will appear to some people—mistakenly, in my view—to be perhaps rather unorthodox.

The Psychology of Goal-setting

There are all kinds of groups of people in the world—religious groups, political groups, cultural groups, charitable groups, and so on—and each of these groups has its goal, be it power, or wealth, or some other satisfaction, and whether it is for their own good or the good of others. And it would seem that Buddhists likewise have their own particular goal that they call nirvana. So let us look at what is meant by this idea of a goal to be attained or realized, and then establish to what extent it is applicable to nirvana.

It should be clear at once where this procedure is going to lead us. The fact is that whenever terms get to be used rather loosely, without any lucid consideration of what they mean, you get the beginnings of serious misunderstandings. This is particularly the case when we transfer terms and expressions derived from mundane experience, like "goal," to spiritual or transcendental experience, like "nirvana." If they don't quite fit then we need to be aware of this, and if they don't fit at all, then we need to think through the whole question afresh.

With this in mind, let us examine the idea of a "goal" a bit more closely. A goal is an objective, something you strive for. You could, if you like, draw a distinction between striving to *be* and striving to *have*. But actually, the two come to the same thing: "having" is a sort of vicarious "being." A goal is in the end something that you want to *be*. Suppose, for instance, your goal is wealth: you can say that your goal is to possess wealth, or that your goal is to be wealthy, but obviously the possessing, the having, is reducible to the being, the existing.

There is one really crucial (if obvious) precondition for setting a goal: it must represent something you aren't. You don't want to have or to be what you already have or are. You can only want to be what you aren't—which suggests, obviously, that you're dissatisfied with what you are. If you're not dissatisfied with what you are, you will never strive to be what you aren't.

Suppose, for example, that your goal happens to be money and material possessions. Well, you will have made these things your goal because you're dissatisfied with being poor. Or if, say, you make knowledge your goal, if you want to add to your understanding, investigate fundamental principles, and so on, then you want to do this because you're dissatisfied with your present state of being ignorant.

We don't always see it in quite these stark terms, but this is the basic pattern or procedure involved in setting ourselves goals; and it is quite an appropriate way of proceeding on its own level. But we get into a tangle when we extend it into the spiritual life—and by this I don't mean some elevated sphere of experience far removed from everyday concerns. By the spiritual life I mean something very close to home.

Any complex of problems we may have can be boiled down to the most basic problem of all, which is unhappiness in one form or another. A case of bad temper, for example, is a problem because it makes us miserable, and one could equally well say the opposite, that being miserable makes us bad-tempered. Even though we don't usually think of the problem we have as unhappiness as such, that is what, in the end, it is.

So we try to get away from unhappiness and attain happiness. The way we go about this is to try to ricochet, as it were, from the experience of feeling miserable or discontented into an opposite state or experience of feeling happy; and this usually involves grasping at some object or experience that we believe will give us the happiness we seek.

When we feel unhappy, we set up this goal of happiness, which we strive to achieve. And as we all know, we fail. All our lives through, in one way or another, we are in search of happiness. No one is in search of misery. And there is no one who could possibly say they're so happy that they couldn't imagine being happier. Most people, if they're honest with themselves, have to admit that their life consists of a fluctuating state of unease and dissatisfaction, punctuated by moments of happiness and joy which make them temporarily forget their discomfort and discontent.

So this possibility of being happy becomes everybody's goal—a goal which can never be realized because happiness is by its nature fleeting. We all continue to set up this phantom goal, however, because the alternative is too challenging for us. The alternative is simply to be aware.

The setting up of goals—which means trying to get away from one's present experience—is really a substitute for awareness, for self-knowledge. Even if we do develop a measure of self-knowledge, we don't tend to maintain it because to do so would be just too threatening. We always end up setting up goals rather than continuing to be aware.

To take a simple example, suppose I have something of a problem with my temper: I get irritated, even angry, rather easily—even a small thing can spark me off—and this bad temper of mine makes life difficult, and perhaps miserable for myself and others. And suppose that I wake up one day and decide that enough is enough, that it's time it came to a stop. What do I do? I set up a goal for myself—the goal of being good-tempered. I think "Well, here I am now—I'm undeniably bad-tempered: my goal, however, is to be sweet-tempered and amiable, always returning the soft answer, always ready to turn the other cheek."

What actually happens, though? One almost invariably fails. The intention—even the degree of self-knowledge—is admirable. But after a while one's resolve falters. In the face of the same old provocations, one is back again in the same old rut—and probably blaming the same old people and the same old external circumstances for it. So why is this? Anybody who has ever begun to recognize that their problems are, at least to a degree, of their own making will also recognize that this is what happens. But why does it happen?

The reason is that we are continuing to tackle the symptoms rather than the disease. If we try to get away from our unhappiness simply by trying to be good-humored, we are still unaware of the fundamental cause of our being bad-tempered. And if this isn't resolved, if we don't know why we are bad-tempered, if we don't know what is prompting the angry answer or the violent reaction, then we can't possibly hope to become good-tempered.

Whatever our problem, we automatically—almost instinctively— set up a goal of being happy in order to get away from our unhappiness. Even if a little awareness, a little insight, does arise, it is not sustained. We revert automatically to setting up a goal of one kind or another rather than continuing to be aware, and trying to understand very deeply why that problem arises. Setting up goals is an automatic reflex to short-circuit the development of awareness and self-knowledge—in short, to get away from ourselves.

How do we change this? To start with, we need a change of attitude. Rather than trying to escape from ourselves, we need to begin to acknowledge the reality of what we are. We need to understand—and not just intellectually—why we are what we are. If you are suffering, don't just reach out for a chocolate. You need to recognize the fact that you suffer and look at it more and more deeply. Or—as the case may be—if you're happy, you need to recognize that fully, take it in more and more deeply. Instead of running from it into guilt, or into some sort of excitable intoxication, you need to understand why, what the true nature of that happiness is, where it really comes from. And again, this isn't just intellectual; it's something that has to go very deep down indeed.

For some people this sort of understanding, this sort of penetration or insight, will come in the course of meditation. Meditation isn't just fixing the mind on an object, or revolving a certain idea in the mind. Meditation really involves—among other things—getting down to the bedrock of the mind, illuminating the mind from the bottom upward, as it were. It is about exposing to oneself one's motives, the deep-seated causes of one's mental states, one's experiences, one's joy, and one's suffering, and so on. In this way real growth in awareness will come about.

But where is all this leading? What has all this to do with nirvana? It may seem that we have strayed rather from our subject, but in fact we have been doing some necessary preparing of the ground. With some things, if one tackles them too directly, one can easily miss the mark. What we can now do is open up some kind of perspective on the way nirvana is traditionally described—or rather on the effect on us of these traditional descriptions.

Suppose, for example, I have been going through rather a difficult, upsetting period, and am feeling rather miserable. Then one day I pick up a book in which it is stated that nirvana is the supreme happiness, the supreme bliss. What will be my reaction? The likelihood is that I will think, "Good—that's just what I want—bliss, happiness." I will make nirvana my goal. And what this means is that effectively I will be making lack of awareness my goal. I will be latching on to nirvana—labelled as the supreme bliss—because it happens to fit in with my subjective needs and feelings at this particular time. Such a reaction has of course nothing to do with being a Buddhist, but it is the way that a lot of us approach Buddhism, and indeed use Buddhism, in a quite unaware, almost automatic way. Unconsciously we try to use nirvana to settle problems which can only really be resolved through awareness.

We do not succeed in banishing unhappiness by pretending to ourselves that we are happy, by shoving our misery out of sight. The first step is to acknowledge the reality of our condition: if there is an underlying unhappiness to our lives, we must face up to the fact. It is certainly good to be cheerful and positive, but not at the expense of fooling ourselves. One has only to look at the faces of the people you see in any city to see the "marks of weakness, marks of woe"[46] that William Blake saw in London two hundred years ago, and yet few people will admit that they are miserable even to themselves.

No progress can be made until we come to terms with our actual experience, until we get to know our unhappiness in all its comings and goings, until we learn to live with it and study it. What is it, at bottom, that makes us unhappy? What is its source? We will get nowhere by looking for a way out of our misery, by aiming for the goal of happiness, or even nirvana. It is a mistake, at least, to postulate the goal of nirvana too quickly or too unconsciously. All we can do is try to see more and more clearly and distinctly what it is in ourselves that is making us unhappy. This is the only way that nirvana will be attained.

In this sense nirvana cannot be seen as an escape from unhappiness at all. It is by trying too hard to escape from unhappiness that we fail to do so. The real key is awareness, self-knowledge. One way—a paradoxical way—of putting it would be to say that the goal of Buddhism consists in being completely and totally aware at all levels of your need to reach a goal. We can also say, going a little further, that nirvana consists in the full and complete awareness of why you want to reach nirvana at all. If you understand completely why you want to reach nirvana, then you've reached nirvana. We can go further even than this. We can even say that the unaware person is in need of nirvana, but is unable to get a true idea of it. An aware person, on the other hand, is quite clear about this goal, but doesn't need it. That's really the position.

So there we have the basic drawback to conventional accounts of nirvana as being this or that. We simply accept or reject this or that aspect of nirvana in accordance with our own largely unconscious needs. If the underlying—and therefore unconscious—drive of our existence is toward pleasure, then we will find ourselves responding to the idea of nirvana as the supreme bliss. If on the other hand we are emotionally driven by a fundamental need to know, to understand, to see what is really going on, then almost automatically we will make our goal a state of complete illumination. And again, if we feel oppressed or constrained by life, if our childhood was one of control and confinement, or if we have a sense that our options in life are restricted by our particular circumstances—by poverty, by being tied down to a job or a family, or looking after elderly relatives—then we will be drawn to the idea of nirvana as freedom, as emancipation.

In this way there takes place a half-conscious setting up of goals based on our own psychological or social conditioning, instead of a growing understanding of why we feel dissatisfied, why we feel somehow "in the dark," or why we feel tied down. Nirvana becomes simply a projection of our own mundane needs.

Hence when we consider the subject of nirvana, the goal of Buddhism, the question we should be asking is not "What is nirvana?" but "Why am I interested in nirvana? Why am I reading this book rather than another, or rather than, say, watching television?" Is it curiosity, is it duty, is it vanity, is it just to see how Sangharakshita is going to tackle this thorny topic? Or is it something deeper?

Even these questions will not settle the matter. If it is curiosity, well, why are we curious about nirvana? If it is duty, toward what or whom do we really feel dutiful? If it is vanity, why do we want to preen ourselves in this particular way? What is underneath our interest? If there is something deeper in our motivation, what is it?

This line of questioning might appear unconventional or unorthodox, and in pursuing it we may not learn much about Buddhism or nirvana in the purely objective, historical sense. But we will learn a great deal about what the ideas of Buddhism really represent. If we follow this particular line, constantly trying to penetrate to the depths of our own mind, we may even get a little nearer to the goal of nirvana itself.

4 ↞ Buddhism—One or Many?

1. VARIETY AND UNITY IN THE BUDDHIST TRADITION

Divergences in both institutional religion and personal religion being so numerous, and in many cases so radical, are we justified in speaking of Buddhism at all?

AS EVEN THE MOST superficially interested visitor cannot fail to observe, the Dharma assumed in every land in which it took root a distinct, unique, and unmistakable national form and local coloration. The history of the *stupa,* as it evolves from the burial mound of the Indian original into the bell-shaped beauty of its Sinhalese type, the *chortens* of Tibet, the almost Gothic perpendicularity of the graceful gilded Thai *chedis,* the streamer-swathed *chaityas* of Nepal, each of their four sides alive with a pair of hypnotically staring eyes, the city-like formations of Java and Cambodia, and the many-storied pagodas of China and Japan, may be taken as an architectural illustration of the richness and diversity of the Dharma on the institutional side. Of India one does not speak: though later systems incorporated a number of its teachings, here Buddhism as an institutional religion no longer exists. Let us go southward to Sri Lanka, for centuries the stronghold of Theravada, and where even now are to be found the most intelligent and cultured exponents of this ancient school. The sky is an abyss of cloudless blue, and our eyes are almost blinded by the sunlight reflected from the dazzling white walls of squat, bungalow-like viharas, each with red-tiled roofs and deep verandas, and of the larger and grander temple buildings nearby: the dagobas are so white that they seem flat rather than round, shapes cut out of enormous sheets of white paper and pinned on to the landscape. Coconut palms are everywhere—in groves, in clumps and clusters, and singly. Their trunks are bent at angles of various degrees of acuteness toward the earth, and when silhouetted against the sky seem to be interlaced; their plumes sweep the ground; the green nuts are high up, hanging in clusters, and seem quite small until we see a tiny turbaned figure scramble up and start hurling them to the ground. It is still early morning. Slowly and quietly there comes along the road—so slowly and so quietly that at first there seems to be only a patch of color in almost imperceptible motion—a figure draped in brilliant yellow with bowed and shaven head. He clasps in his two hands a large black bowl. His countenance is impassive. His eyes seem to be shut, for they are fixed upon the ground in front of him. With dignity and deliberation he moves from door to door, and is received with respectful salutations. Halting for a moment, he lifts the lid of the bowl to receive the alms of the faithful, who, from their reverential demeanor, evidently feel that they are indebted to him rather than he to them. More and more yellow figures as it were materialize on the scene, appearing in the alternate bars of brilliant sunshine and purple shadow lying along the dusty road like the silent unfolding of yellow flowers. They are not seen for long, though, and as the sun mounts and the shadows shorten no human figures are visible save a few coolies whose blue-black bodies, glistening with sweat, stagger along under enormous loads. The rickshaw puller sleeps between the shafts of his vehicle in a scrap of shade. Earth and sky begin to vibrate with heat. Presently a haze flickers in front of the eyes, blurring the landscape, which now jumps and dances as though seen through a tongue of flame . . . perspiration . . . exhaustion . . . prostration. . . . The click of the fan above the bed . . . then unconsciousness.

When we awake the land is steeped in deep, cool shadows. A light breeze brings unimaginable refreshment. The palm trees rustle above our heads, and looking up through the fronds we see that the unclouded sky is ablaze with stars. The tom-toms begin to throb from the temple nearby; the clarinets wail; the air, which had vibrated all day with the intensity of heat, now vibrates with the fury of sound. Already white figures are flitting through the shadows of the trees. Each one bears a tray on which is a heap of five-petalled temple flowers—ah! the incredible sweetness of their fragrance as it floats through the dusk—a few sticks of incense, and a tiny lamp. Let us follow them to the temple. We shall bow down together at the feet of the Exalted One. Squeezing in, we find that the shrine is densely packed with white-clad worshippers, and the air oppressive with the fumes of thousands of brightly burning lamps of coconut oil. Progress is slow; the men and women are either silent or muttering prayers; there is no impatience, no pushing. Inch by inch, we move forward with the crowd; at last the pressure relaxes; we find ourselves standing with waist pressed against the edge of the great altar. Flowers are everywhere; the smell of the incense is overpoweringly sweet; thousands of candles splutter and burn. Lifting our eyes we see behind the altar, clad in robes of the same brilliant yellow, a dozen or so serene figures who smile benignly at the worshippers. Above and beyond them towers the brightly painted image of the Buddha, upon its face the smile of eternal peace. But our contemplation cannot last long. A gentle pressure from behind reminds us that it is time to give place to others, and before many minutes have passed we find ourselves outside in the cold night air. We stand beneath the palm trees watching the streams of worshippers passing through the temple gates. A line of elephants, gorgeously caparisoned and surrounded by troops of excitedly shouting boys, comes swaying through the darkness, their triumphal progress illuminated by flaring torches. Parties of strongly built male dancers, with black oil-bright bodies that reflect the ruddy glare of the torches and fantastic headdresses, pirouette on either side, their bare feet stamping upon the hard ground in time with the rhythm of the tom-toms. The tumult is deafening. But only for a few moments. As swiftly as it had come the procession disappears from sight. In an hour's time the last worshippers have left the temple and gone home. Silence reigns. But hour after hour, and even long after we have gone to bed, we can still hear the faint insistent beat of the tom-tom ... *tom-tom ... tom-tom. ...*

Geographically speaking, the distance between Sri Lanka, the Theravadin stronghold, and Tibet, the inmost citadel of Mahayana tradition, is only two thousand miles. But on the spiritual plane, at least so far as the institutional aspect of religion is concerned, the gulf dividing them is seemingly immeasurable. Crossing the snow-clad peaks of the Himalayas, the largest and the loftiest mountain barrier in existence, we find ourselves on the Roof of the World. An icy wind blows furiously, cutting through quilted garments and furs; lightly but steadily comes the snow, driven almost horizontally by the wind. Soon our eyes are sore with looking at the blinding whiteness of the earth and the pitilessly brilliant blueness of the sky. Every now and then the tempest shrieks suddenly past, giving mighty buffets as though it were a legion of devils seeking to send us rolling from our horses down the five-thousand-foot precipice yawning beneath our feet. We cling on tightly, gripping the horse's mane with numbed fists. At last we feel the animal between our knees slithering down the stony slopes of the mountainside . . . our three-week-long journey to the Land of Religion is nearing its end. Painfully we open our gummed lids with the help of our fingers. Around us the unbroken circle of the horizon makes a sharp edge against the sky. We realize that we had never known before the meaning of space. Here and there are patches of light green color; but no trees, hardly a shrub. Only a vast expanse of waving grass as smooth and flat as a billiard table, with what look like specks of stone but are really Tibetan homesteads, and the black dots of grazing yaks and nomad tents scattered over it at enormous intervals: they are so small that at first sight the landscape seems deserted.

As we ride forward, and as the days pass, what at first had seemed a slight corrugation of the horizon becomes a long low range of mountains blue-black in the far distance. Gradually, as we approach, they thrust themselves higher and higher into the sky, and eventually the central peak towers above our heads seemingly halfway up to heaven. Saddle-sore, we dismount at the foot of a flight of stairs hewn as though for the feet of a giant out of the rock. Slowly we ascend. Each turn of the path reveals a fresh flight and each flight contains thousands of steps. We dare not look down. At last, on the next ridge, only a few hundred feet above our heads, we see red and white striped walls and gilded roofs. Where the mountain ends and the monastery begins is difficult to say, though, for they are built of the same material and on the same colossal scale. The black mouth of an enormous door yawns before us. Stalwart figures are mounting guard on either side, their bulk prodigiously increased by swaths of maroon-colored woolen cloth, their already exceptional stature heightened by yellow headgear shaped like the helmet of Achilles, and yet more terrible; in their hands are enormous staves studded with brass. As we approach their eyes narrow suspiciously in their grimy faces; but they say nothing, and we are allowed to pass. The iron door slams shut behind us; there is a rattling of chains. After a full half-minute has passed the sound is echoed as though from the very heart of the earth. Slowly we grope our way forward through the pitch darkness, tripping and stumbling over the uneven ground. We are aware of flittings to and fro on either side of us; suddenly a hand seizes hold of our arm, and we are pulled roughly along. A misty light shines forth; a door has opened. With the sudden lifting of a curtain the mist becomes a blaze and a deep roaring and groaning noise of trumpets, inexpressibly moving, that had been hitherto muffled by the thickness of the stone walls, blares mournfully in our ears.

We find ourselves in an enormous chamber. On the floor sit rows and rows of maroon-colored figures: there must be thousands of them. From the ceiling hang huge cylinder-shaped Banners of Victory, every flounce of a different color. Before each monk is a bowl of steaming tea; some are sipping, some adding their voices to the deep-throated rumbling chorus that the assembly sends rolling wave-like from one end of the long chamber to the other. Armed with a whip, a figure resembling those we saw at the main entrance strides up and down the central aisle. A few vertical shafts of misty sunshine, penetrating from some aperture above, illumine the faces of the celebrants, some of whom are obviously very old, others astonishingly youthful; but all, despite bent backs and rounded shoulders, are sturdily built and all are shaven-headed. In the far distance, ranked on a long narrow table running almost the entire width of the room, hundreds of golden butter-lamps are steadily burning. Behind them is the altar, whereon have been arranged various artistically molded offerings. To the left, high above the heads of the worshippers, is a magnificently carved, painted, and gilded throne. In front of this, a white silken scarf in our hands, we now find ourselves. Cross-legged upon its brocade cushions sits an old man, magnificently clad in garments of dark red silk. The smile with which he looks down at us as we make our obeisance is not of this earth; it is the smile of Enlightenment. Far more brightly than any ray of earthly sunshine it penetrates our heart. Within his small, twinkling eyes all knowledge seems to dwell, and we are aware that not even our most secret thoughts are hidden from him; yet we do not feel afraid.

When, a few minutes later, we stand in front of the main altar, it is the same smile which, as though from the moon itself, calmly and tenderly shines from the central face of the eleven-headed white image behind the glass doors of the tabernacle. A thousand arms, each ending in a hand which either bears an emblem or makes with tapering fingers a graceful symbolical gesture, radiate from its shoulders like spokes from the hub of a wheel. We are face to face with Universal Compassion.

Five minutes later we are face to face with Death. After being hurried through dimly lit corridors, the noise behind us receding further and further into the distance, we are ushered into a small black hole. A single lamp is burning. Fearfully, as though in unwilling obedience to a command, a monk lifts the heavy curtain of iron rings that hangs before the inmost shrine. Involuntarily we recoil from the sight. The figure that stares down upon us with bulging eyeballs is full of menace. His huge, powerful body, deep blue in color, is festooned with garlands of skulls. His four arms are raised threateningly, and his hands grasp various weapons. One brawny knee is uplifted as he tramples upon the enemies of the Dharma. His face is that of a horned beast, and his red tongue lolls out from between his rows of gleaming fangs as though thirsty for blood. Round his waist is a tiger-skin. Clinging to his bosom, her slender arms clasped tightly round his bull-neck, her legs wrapped round his thighs, and her mouth strained passionately to his, is the small white figure of his consort. They are locked in sexual embrace. Round them roars a halo of flames. Terrible but strangely fascinating, vibrant with power incalculable, are the Father and the Mother, the transcendental pair whose union symbolizes the inseparability of wisdom and compassion, of Doctrine and Method—or, returning to the much more limited point of view wherefrom we started, the metaphysical unity of the institutional and personal aspects of religion—as they tower in all their preternatural vigor before us until, with a ringing clash, the curtain falls, and we are left with the smoky lamp throwing against the ceiling the fantastic shadows of the huge stuffed animal carcasses suspended there.

Two strikingly dissimilar pictures indeed! Could a greater contrast be imagined, the reader may wonder, than that between the Buddhism of Sri Lanka and the Buddhism of Tibet? For, though I freely own up to a deliberate heightening of color, a calculated distribution of lights and shades, the diptych I have painted is nevertheless a faithful illustration of the differences prevailing at the institutional level between the various distinct and mutually independent branches of Buddhist tradition. No wonder, then, that those who have been born or brought up within an environment dominated, from the religious point of view, by any one form of institutional Buddhism, to the exclusion of the rest, should find it difficult to avoid falling into the pitfall of thinking that the form with which they have been familiar since childhood is the one true form, while less familiar forms are false. For although there does exist a Basic Buddhism which is the common foundation of all schools, the doctrines by which one line of tradition is distinguished from another are almost always placed, by those belonging to that line, at the very center of their picture of Buddhism, and receive the highlight, while the remainder, their shapes hardly discernible in the gloom, are distributed toward the circumference, some in fact being cut in half owing to the necessity of having a frame. It is hardly astonishing, therefore, that even a conscientiously impartial student of the Buddhist schools should discover, more often than not, mutual opposition and contradiction rather than agreement and harmony. Differences regarding doctrine, no less than a variety of institutions, do exist: the fact cannot be ignored; and of those who become aware of them without having transcended the intellectual standpoint what can we expect but a violent reaction toward an even more bigoted belief in the exclusive truth and authenticity of the traditions of their own school?

Modern Theravadins, insisting that progress upon the path depends solely upon one's own efforts, wax eloquent over the fact that we are each our own savior, that we ourselves are the architects of our fortunes, the captains of our souls and the masters of our fates, and that heavens and hells are the creations of our own good and evil deeds. The Buddha is simply a guide pointing out to us the path, which, whether we like it or not, we must perforce tread with our own two feet. He is like a schoolmaster (a comparison for which several exponents of this school exhibit a special fondness) who can explain to us a difficult algebraical problem on the blackboard but who cannot, unfortunately, give us the intelligence with which to do our own sums. One of their favorite texts is *Dhammapada* verse 165, which says:

Evil is done by self alone, by self alone is one stained; by self alone is evil left undone, by self alone is one purified. Purity and impurity depend on one's own self. No man can purify another.

This individualistic doctrine the Jodo Shin School repudiates as dire heresy. Emancipation, it believes, depends not on our own efforts but entirely upon the grace of Amitabha Buddha; attempting to save ourselves is as ridiculous as trying to hoist ourselves up into the air by tugging at our own bootlaces. Good deeds, far from being of any help, only intensify the feeling of individual selfhood, thus obstructing the operation of the saving grace or "other-power" of Amitabha. Hence the paradoxical saying, no less popular with Jodo Shin followers than the *Dhammapada* verse is with Theravadins, "Even the good man will be saved. How much more so the evil man!" Instead of striving to win Enlightenment in this world and in this life by means of our own unaided efforts, we should, with a heart full of love and faith, simply invoke the name of Amitabha and pray to be reborn in Sukhavati, the Land of Bliss he has established in the West.

No less extreme is the difference which exists between certain Tantric schools, on the one hand, and the non-Tantric schools, on the other, regarding the importance of morality. Though both parties agree in recognizing the instrumental function and relative value of ethical observances, the recognition is accorded from positions so wide apart as in effect to amount to a radical divergence of views. To the non-Tantric schools, the fact that morality is a means to Enlightenment adds to, rather than detracts from, its importance; for in the absence of the proper means, the desired goal becomes impossible to attain. Morality is not only the means, but the indispensable means to Enlightenment; hence it is an absolute value. Some of these schools therefore strive for a rigid observance not only of the major precepts of morality but even of the minor monastic obligations which, though many of them are in reality without ethical significance, are all comprehended in the traditional Buddhist conception of morality.

Against this view, which can so easily harden into a petrified ethical formalism, the followers of various Tantric schools contend that the fact that morality is only a means to an end, instead of proving its absoluteness, demonstrates its relativity. The sole absolute value is compassion; even wisdom is only a means for the realization of that supreme end. However indispensable at the time of sickness, medicines may be emptied down the drain when we are restored to health; the Perfected Ones, having by means of ethical observances attained full Enlightenment, thereafter have personally no further use for them, and henceforth may act according to circumstances either in an "ethical" or in an "unethical" manner. Their sole concern is with the welfare of all sentient beings, for the sake of which they are prepared to sacrifice every other consideration. If by their merely apparent violation of the ethical precepts they can assist in his progress along the path a single pilgrim soul they do not shrink from committing what, in the case of an unenlightened person, would be a deadly sin, even though they thereby forfeit their own reputation for sanctity (one of the subtlest fetters, this) and incur the disapprobation of society. The biography of more than one Tantric teacher is replete with episodes in which he deprives animals and even human beings of life, appropriates to his own use the property of others, freely indulges in sexual intercourse, tells lies, and partakes of strong drink to the point of inebriation. They appear far indeed from the sobriety and restraint, the almost pathetic eagerness to "keep up appearances" in the eyes of the world, even though not always in the mirror of one's own conscience, which characterizes ordinary practitioners! Where even the major ethical precepts are treated with so little ceremony, the minor monastic obligations, indeed the very idea not only of monasticism but of any formally religious life at all, can expect nothing but a rude dismissal. All pretenses to respectability are abandoned; dignity, decorum, and even ordinary decency are flung to the winds. In place of the noble bearing and refined manners of the true monk we see the reckless demeanor and abandoned behavior of the outcasts of society. Among non-Tantric schools, the appearance of saintliness is easily achieved even by those who are in reality furthest from saintliness; in some Tantric schools, however, the opposite is the case: the saintliest appear as the least saintly. It is not difficult to see that the doctrine of ethical relativism is fraught with grave dangers; the frailty of human

BUDDHISM—ONE OR MANY? ~ 133

nature is only too willing to believe that since the Perfected Ones may, upon occasion, act "unethically," one who acts unethically is a Perfected One, and that the easiest and the quickest way of gaining Enlightenment is by breaking, one after another, all the moral laws. In the Tantric schools, too, may be found those who follow the letter rather than the spirit of tradition. Whatever our own attitude toward ethical relativism may be, the fact is that, in the extreme form we have described, the doctrine is far from being upheld by all Tantric schools, the majority of which are as exacting in their ethical demands as any of the schools belonging to the non-Tantric group.

Differences of this kind are by no means rare in Buddhism; the two somewhat extreme cases we have described, far from being exceptional, are only illustrative of a hundred divergences of opinion on doctrinal issues—some of them of fundamental importance. Ere long the student of the Dharma discovers, rather to his amazement, that whereas the dharmas are for one school realities, for another they are merely words; on the one hand he is exhorted to work out his own salvation with diligence, on the other to dedicate his life to the emancipation of all sentient beings; for *this* school the Buddha is merely a man who attained Enlightenment, while for *that* he is the wholly transcendental and eternally Enlightened Reality itself in human form; one party tells us that meditation and wisdom are inseparable, and that with the attainment of the former the latter is attained automatically, but this view the opposite party denies, saying that meditation is not necessarily associated with wisdom; here we see vegetarianism upheld, there meat-eating permitted; one school defines Reality as absolute consciousness, another as complete emptiness; in some teachings nirvana and samsara are identical, in others an irreducible duality; on one side we see a celibate monastic order, on the other an association of married priests. And so on. The catalogue is without end.

Divergences in both institutional religion and personal religion being so numerous, and in many cases so radical, are we justified in speaking of Buddhism at all? Or are we not rather concerned with a number of practically independent religious movements, all more or less nominally Buddhist? Is Buddhism one or many? Obviously, there is no external uniformity. There is not always even unity of Doctrine. What, then, constitutes the fundamental ground of unity in Buddhism?

The unity of Buddhism consists in the fact that, through differences and divergences of doctrine innumerable, all schools of Buddhism aim at Enlightenment, at reproducing the spiritual experience of the Buddha. The Dharma is therefore to be defined, not so much in terms of this or that particular teaching, but rather as the sum total of the means whereby that experience may be attained. Hence it can even be considered as being in principle and function, though not always in institutional form and specific intellectual content, identical for all schools of Buddhism.

2. The Forms of Eastern Buddhism

There is no harm in dressing up as an Indian, or pretending to be Japanese, or imagining that you are a Tibetan. It is quite harmless—except to the extent that it represents an alienation from your own culture. But it has nothing to do with being a Buddhist.

HISTORICALLY SPEAKING at least, Buddhism is an Eastern religion. It originated in India, and for 2,500 years it has been virtually confined to the East. It is only quite recently, in the course of the last hundred years in fact, that it has become known in the West at all. So what is the relation between Western Buddhists and Eastern Buddhism?

In attempting to answer this question, the first thing that has to be said is that there is no such thing as Eastern Buddhism. In fact, there are a number of Eastern Buddhisms, in the plural. Broadly speaking there are four of these extant in the Eastern Buddhist world: South-East Asian Buddhism, Chinese Buddhism, Japanese Buddhism, and Tibetan Buddhism.

South-East Asian Buddhism is found in Sri Lanka, Burma, Thailand, and Cambodia—as well as, here and there, in Singapore and Malaysia. This form of Buddhism belongs to the Theravada school, whose scriptures are contained in the Pali Tipitaka—in some forty-five volumes in the Royal Thai edition.

Chinese Buddhism is found mainly in China, Taiwan, Korea, Vietnam, and, again, in parts of Singapore and Malaysia. (I am ignoring recent political developments which have certainly altered the situation to some extent.) Chinese Buddhism belongs to what we may call "general," or non-sectarian, Mahayana, and its scriptures are contained in the Tsa-tsan, or "Three Treasuries," corresponding to the Tipitaka, in fifty-five volumes. These volumes are very much bigger than the volumes of the Pali Tipitaka. In this particular collection there are no less than 1,662 independent works, a few of which are almost as long as the Christian Bible.

Japanese Buddhism is found, of course, in Japan, but also in Hawaii, and among Japanese immigrants in mainland USA. It comprises various schools of what may be described as "sectarian" Mahayana, the best known of which are Zen and Shin. There are also various modern schools which have been developed even in the last century. The scriptures of Japanese Buddhism are the Chinese Tsa-tsan plus various Japanese works according to sect—which may in practice sometimes displace the Tsa-tsan.

Tibetan Buddhism is found in Tibet, Mongolia, Sikkim, Bhutan, Ladakh, parts of China, and even parts of the former USSR. It consists of four main traditions, all of which follow all three of the *yanas*—that is, Hinayana, Mahayana, and Vajrayana. The differences between these four traditions occur mainly in respect of Vajrayana—that is to say Tantric—lineages. Their scriptures are all contained in the Kangyur, which means the "Buddha-word," in 100 or 108 (according to the edition) xylographed volumes, plus special collections like the *Rinchen-Terma* of the Nyingmapas and the *Milarepa Kabum* of the Kagyupas.

These are the four extant Eastern schools of Buddhism. There are many intermediate forms, and sub-forms, and sub-sub-forms, but for the sake of simplicity I have ignored them. For practical purposes Western Buddhists find themselves confronted by four Eastern Buddhisms rather than by just one monolithic Eastern Buddhism with complementary unitary features.

Perhaps I could just add here that we do not find ourselves confronted by an Eastern mind, or by an Eastern psychology either. Some writers speak of the Western mind and the Eastern mind as though they were two completely different minds, and it is suggested that it is very difficult for the Eastern mind to understand the Western mind, and vice versa. Buddhism of course is supposed to be a product of the Eastern mind, which is why, we are sometimes told, it is difficult for Westerners to understand Buddhism. Speaking from experience, however, I have found no evidence for any such belief. Wherever I went during my twenty years in the East, whether I was associating with Indians, Tibetans, Mongolians, Thais, or Sinhalese—or even Europeans—I found that I could understand them, and they could understand me. Buddhism is admittedly difficult to understand, but not because it is a product of the "Eastern mind." It is difficult to understand because it is a product of the *Enlightened* mind, a mind which transcends the conditionings of both the East and the West.

Another popular myth which I might as well mention in this connection is that there is a division between a "spiritual" East and a "materialistic" West. This really is another myth. The West is no more materialistic than the East. One might say that the West has simply been more "successful" in its pursuit of materialism—and even this is changing.

However, to return to the theme of Western Buddhists and the four Eastern Buddhisms, the four Eastern Buddhisms are differentiated from each other in two main ways. They are differentiated, first of all, according to the doctrinal school of Buddhism to which they belong. Secondly, they are differentiated according to the regional or national culture with which they are associated.

From a practical point of view, at least, the regional, cultural asso-ciation is probably the more important since, as a consequence, the Buddhism that most people come across in the West, whether in con-tent or in practice, is not really Buddhism. We could even say that many Western Buddhists never really encounter Buddhism at all. What they encounter is a particular school or sub-school of Buddhism associated with a particular national or regional culture. They may encounter the Theravada, for instance, which is associated with South-East Asian—specifically Sinhalese—culture. Or they may encounter Zen, which is associated with Japanese culture, and so on.

But the situation is even more complicated than that. Buddhism arose in India, a country with a very rich and ancient culture. From its very beginning, from the moment it emerged from the Buddha's mouth, so to speak, Buddhism was associated with Indian culture, indeed with Indian cultures, because in the course of the 1,500 years during which Buddhism was alive in India, Indian culture went through several different phases of development, each with very strongly marked characteristics.

When Buddhism went from India to China, what actually "went" was Buddhism plus Indian culture. Then, in China, Buddhism assumed cer-tain Chinese cultural characteristics before going on to Japan. In Japan, of course, Buddhism assumed certain Japanese characteristics. So today, Japanese Buddhism consists of Buddhism plus Indian culture plus Chi-nese culture plus Japanese culture. *That* is the Buddhism which is com-ing to the United States of America, to Britain, to Australia, and so on. Sometimes, of course, Buddhism succeeds in penetrating all the layers of culture which are superimposed upon it, but sometimes it does not.

Confronted by these different Eastern Buddhisms, the first thing that the Western Buddhist has to do is learn to distinguish what is really Buddhism from what is actually South-East Asian, or Chinese, or Japanese, or Tibetan, or even Indian culture. It is not that there is anything wrong with any of those cultures; they are often very beauti-ful indeed. But they are not the same thing as Buddhism, not the same thing as the Dharma.

However, some Western Buddhists are unable to make this distinction between Buddhism and Eastern culture. They think that they are attracted by Buddhism when in reality they are attracted to an exotic oriental culture. Sometimes they think that they are trying to be Buddhists when in reality they are just trying to copy Indians, Japanese, or Tibetans—or at least to look like them. This is quite harmless, of course. There is no harm in dressing up as an Indian, or pretending to be Japanese, or imagining that you are a Tibetan. It is quite harmless—except to the extent that it represents an alienation from your own culture. But it has nothing to do with being a Buddhist.

In some parts of the West we now have a very strange situation indeed. All four of the main Eastern Buddhisms have now been introduced. They have their Western followers, all of whom are supposedly Buddhists; but because they follow different Eastern cultures, they are unable to live together or to practice Buddhism together.

I remember an example of this sort of thing from the very early days of the FWBO. Not far from London lived a group of English Zen Buddhists. They decided that they would like to join one of our FWBO communities, and, after some discussion, we agreed—even though I had my own misgivings. Almost as soon as they had moved in, a difficulty arose: they refused to join in the puja—that is, the evening devotions. The reason for this was that our puja was recited in Pali and English, and their guru (who was, incidentally, an English woman who had spent some time in Japan) had told them that they should do their puja only in Japanese. So while some members of the community performed their puja in English and Pali these English Zen Buddhists waited outside the shrine-room; they would not even sit in the room and listen.

Another example comes to mind in connection with this same guru. Japanese culture is what sociologists call a "shame culture." In Japanese culture shame is used as a technique of social control. (Our Western Christian culture is probably a "guilt culture.") In traditional Japanese society, when a young person misbehaves, an older person will proceed to imitate him—but greatly exaggerating the misdemeanor. If the young person has been noisy, the older person will be four or five times as noisy. If he or she has slammed a door the older person must go and slam it three or four times very, very loudly. The young person then feels ashamed; realizing that he or she has been corrected, he or she desists from that particular misbehavior out of shame. At some stage this technique of control through shame was transferred to the Japanese Zen temple. If the disciple misbehaved, the master would imitate him. If the disciple slouched during meditation, the master would immediately slouch right over; the disciple would notice, feel ashamed, pull himself up straight, and in that way he would learn. The technique was known as "mirroring."

Now, an English/Japanese Zen guru happened to pass through London some years ago. It seems that she did not very much like what some of the English Buddhists, who had not been to Japan, were doing. So she started mirroring them. Her head monk, an American who was accompanying her, started mirroring them as well. For example, thinking that English Buddhists ate far too much while on retreat, he started mirroring them, and took a second helping of everything, just to show them how greedy they were. However, the English Buddhists, not being Japanese, did not understand what was going on. They thought the poor fellow must be hungry, and gave him a third helping of everything. The guru, I heard, was quite annoyed. She said that English Buddhists were stupid because they could not appreciate her mirroring technique. But really it was she who could not understand that mirroring was part of Japanese culture; it had nothing to do with Buddhism, and it was not appropriate in the West.

3. THE IDEAL APPROACH TO BUDDHISM

To identify Buddhism with one particular version, on whatever grounds, is ridiculous.

IN THE *Udana*[47] the Buddha relates the Parable of the Blind Men and the Elephant. A number of men, blind from birth, are asked to feel the body of an elephant and then describe the beast. Those who felt the head declared it to be like a pot, those who grasped the ear said it was like a winnowing-basket, those who handled the tusk opined it was a ploughshare, and so on. Eventually, each one vehemently maintaining his own opinion, they began to quarrel and fight. The parable illustrates not only the one-sidedness of the sectarian teachers of the Buddha's own time, in connection with whom it was originally told, but also the wide divergences that can be noticed between the different approaches to Buddhism adopted by modern writers.

Until very recently three approaches were most common. They may be termed respectively the sectarian, the fundamentalist, and the encyclopedic. The basic error of the sectarian approach is that it mistakes the part for the whole. Quite early in the history of Buddhism, perhaps within a century of the parinirvana, there arose within the Buddhist community circumstances which eventually led to the formation of different schools. Though differing on various doctrinal and disciplinary points, these schools shared a common tradition which united them to a far greater extent than their points of difference divided them. As time went on, however, and they started occupying different geographical centers, not only in India but throughout Asia, their differences gradually grew more pronounced. The result is that instead of consisting of one version of the Dharma only, Buddhism now comprises a number of different versions laid as it were side by side and overlapping in varying degrees. To identify Buddhism with one particular version, on whatever grounds, is ridiculous. As Dr. Edward Conze says,

> The doctrine of the Buddha, conceived in its full breadth, width, majesty and grandeur, comprises all those teachings which are linked to the original teaching by historical continuity, and which work out methods leading to the extinction of individuality by eliminating the belief in it.[48]

Unfortunately, some corners of the Buddhist world have not yet awoken to the truth of these words. Books, pamphlets, and articles continue to be produced which naively present a single branch as the whole tree. This is not to say that the branch is not a noble branch, nor that individual accounts of the different Buddhist schools are not needed. I refer to something quite different: the practice of presenting, as complete accounts of Buddhism, what are in fact expositions of the tenets of one school based on a highly selective reading of a single branch of the canonical literature, usually the Pali Tipitaka. Some writers go to the extreme of explicitly repudiating as "not the pure Dharma" all Buddhist traditions but their own. Despite occasional absurdities of this kind, however, the sectarian type of approach to Buddhism is fortunately on the wane. Throughout the Buddhist world the conviction is steadily gaining ground that so far as the Dharma is concerned, the truth, to apply the Hegelian dictum, is the whole.

The fundamentalist approach is concerned with what the Buddha "really" said. It has two forms. The first to some extent coincides with the sectarian approach which, in one of its forms, maintains even in the face of abundant internal evidence to the contrary that the Pali Tipitaka consists entirely of the *ipsissima verba* of the Buddha. The second, the intellectually respectable form, is a product of modern scholarship, largely non-Buddhist. By means of textual criticism, comparison with archaeological and epigraphical evidence, etc., it endeavors to separate the passages belonging to earlier from those belonging to later strata of the canonical literature. Broadly speaking, this attempt has met with some success. The fundamentalist desires, however, a greater degree of certainty than the nature of the subject allows. Even if it is possible to isolate the most ancient texts, the problem of the relation of these to the oral tradition which preceded them and of this to the Buddha's own utterances remains insoluble. It is doubtful whether any known Buddhist text contains a line which preserves the Dharma in the same language or dialect in which it was originally expounded by the Buddha. The more strictly scientific methods are applied, the greater likelihood there seems to be that the fundamentalist will eventually be left with nothing but the Buddha's "noble silence." Some, indeed, horrified by the void confronting them, have sought to fill it with their own arbitrary constructions of what they imagine the Buddha "really" taught. Both forms of fundamentalism commit the mistake of assuming that the Teaching is bound up with a certain form of words, and that unless these are known it cannot be properly understood.

The encyclopedic approach emphasizes breadth rather than depth of knowledge. It tends to confuse knowledge *about* Buddhism with knowledge *of* Buddhism. It is concerned more with facts than with principles, tries to see from without instead of feeling from within. For a century it has profoundly influenced, if not dominated, the world of non-traditional Buddhist scholarship. Since it is not an isolated phenomenon, but has its roots deep in the soil of the modern scientific outlook, whose general tendencies it exemplifies within its own special field, this approach is likely to remain important for some time to come. Provided its limitations are understood, and any mischief to which they might give rise guarded against, this is not necessarily a bad thing for Buddhism. Such scholarship has accomplished much useful work. Moreover, during the last decade it has been leavened and enlivened, in the case of one or two well-known writers, by elements of sympathy and understanding which were originally lacking. Nevertheless, this does not alter the basic fact that, owing to the vast extent of Buddhist literature, which includes thousands of works regarded as canonical, besides innumerable non-canonical works, its aim of achieving complete factual knowledge about Buddhism and from this inferring its nature is impossible of attainment.

The ideal approach to Buddhism incorporates elements from the sectarian, the fundamentalist, and the encyclopedic approaches, shorn of their imperfections. It has for basis an insight into the Dharma derived from the actual practice of a system of spiritual discipline which, owing to the specialized nature of such techniques, is necessarily that of a particular school—Japanese Zen, say, or Tibetan Mahamudra, or the Thai "Samma Araham" method. Despite this fact, it will be vividly aware and warmly appreciative of the multiple richness of the Buddhist tradition, and however firmly it may grasp a particular thread will never lose sight of its connection with the whole fabric. While accurately distinguishing earlier formulations of the Teaching from later ones, and even preferring the former for introductory purposes, it will not commit the mistake of treating the age of a formulation as the sole criterion of its spiritual authenticity, nor consider the Dharma to be limited to its verbal expressions. Depth will not, however, exclude breadth. Besides keeping abreast of developments in the field of non-traditional Buddhist studies, the ideal approach to Buddhism will not only take all Buddhism for its province but will enforce its conclusions by drawing upon as wide a range of scriptural reference as possible. Above all, it will be concerned to exhibit the living spirit of Buddhism.

4. WHAT DO ALL THE SCHOOLS OF BUDDHISM HAVE IN COMMON?

A clue through the labyrinth, a switch that, when turned on, will light up the whole edifice—in short, a principle of unity that will enable us to see the schools as all "parts of one tremendous whole" which is Buddhism—does exist.

LIKE ALMOST ALL PRODUCTIONS of the Indian mind Buddhism is characterized by richness, profusion, amplitude, and diversity. In the course of fifteen centuries of uninterrupted development on Indian soil its inherent spiritual vitality has found expression in a multitude of forms. Organizationally, it consists of an immense number of schools, all of which are branches of, or divisions within, the one Sangha, and all of which, besides sharing in the common heritage, have their own distinctive doctrines and practices, their own lineages of teachers, and their own literatures. Pluralistic realism, absolutism, and idealism all flourished in turn, each being regarded by men of the highest philosophical genius as the correct interpretation of Buddhist thought. Now wisdom is recommended as the principal means to deliverance, now meditation, and now faith and devotion. One great spiritual movement proclaims emancipation of self alone as the goal of the religious life, another Supreme Enlightenment for the sake of all sentient beings. And so on and so on. These differences, amounting sometimes to logical contradictions, give to Buddhism an appearance not only of multifariousness but of confusion. Like a traveler lost in some enormous, architecturally complex Indian temple, the student tends to be so overwhelmed by the lavish abundance of the ornamentation as to be incapable of appreciating the simplicity and grandeur of the design. Since there is an almost complete absence of historical records, Chinese pilgrims and Tibetan historians being sometimes the sole available sources of information for crucial periods, the student moreover finds himself alone in the temple at night—its immensities dimly lit by lamps that allow him, as he gropes his way around, no more than a glimpse of a column here and an archway there.

A clue through the labyrinth, a switch that, when turned on, will light up the whole edifice—in short, a principle of unity that will enable us to see the schools as all "parts of one tremendous whole" which is Buddhism—does however exist. The unity of Buddhism consists in the fact that, through differences and divergences of doctrine innumerable, all schools of Buddhism aim at Enlightenment, at reproducing the spiritual experience of the Buddha. This unity is not rational but transcendental. That is to say, the doctrinal and other differences between the schools are not resolved by being reduced on their own level one to another or all to a conceptual denominator, but transcended by referring them to a factor which, being supra-logical, can be the common object of contradictory assertions. According to the Prajnaparamita sutras, indeed, recourse to paradoxes or propositions involving a logical oppugnancy, as when the Bodhisattva is urged to deliver sentient beings who do not exist,[49] is inevitable if justice is to be done to the non-conceptual nature of Reality and of the spiritual experience which has Reality for its "objective" counterpart. The specific differences between the schools are due to the fact that they approach the transcendental factor, Enlightenment or nirvana, from opposite directions.

This can be made clearer by a reference to the Five Spiritual Faculties, the *pancendriya,* a set of "cardinal virtues" figuring prominently in the early literature. The five are faith (*sraddha*), vigor (*virya*), mindfulness (*smrti*), concentration (*samadhi*), and wisdom (*prajna*). All these the disciple develops equally, counterbalancing, by means of mindfulness, faith and wisdom, and vigor and concentration, in such a way as to attain a state of perfect psychological and spiritual equilibrium (*indriya-samatta*). Sona Kolivisa is rebuked for developing vigor at the expense of concentration. In a famous simile, the Buddha tells him that, just as a lute is unfit for playing when the strings are either too taut or too slack, so does too much output of vigor conduce to restlessness and too feeble a vigor to slothfulness. He should, therefore, determine on evenness of vigor.[50] Full development of the Five Spiritual Faculties makes one an Arahant.[51] After the Buddha's *parinirvana,* or "final passing away," however, different schools tended to specialize, as it were, in one particular faculty and to approach Enlightenment from that "direction." Thus, for example, the Abhidharmikas and the Madhyamikas developed wisdom, the Yogacarins concentration, the popular devotional movements faith, and the esoteric Tantric traditions vigor.

The Five Spiritual Faculties can also be cultivated one after another.[52] It is also possible, therefore, to regard them as representing so many successive stages of spiritual development. Explaining how those unworthy beings who are hard to tame are brought to subjugation, the Lord says in the *Hevajra Tantra:* "First there should be the public confession (*posadha*), then they should be taught the ten rules of virtuous conduct, then the Vaibhasya teachings and then the Sautrantika, after that the Yogacara and the Madhyamaka. Then when they know all mantra-method, they should start upon Hevajra."[53] Usually, however, when arranged according to the order of their spiritual progression the schools are subsumed under the three *yanas,* that is to say the Hinayana, the Mahayana, and the Vajrayana, representing the three phases of the Buddha's personal teaching and the three stages of its historical development. By cultivating each yana in turn, taking the earlier as the basis for the understanding and practice of the later, the disciple attains Supreme Enlightenment. The triyana system is, therefore, not just a philosophical synthesis, but the most practical possible expression of the unity of Buddhism.

Inasmuch as all were regarded as aiming, in one way or another, at the same goal, it is not surprising that between the different schools of Buddhism there was a relationship of mutual respect and tolerance. This is not to say that doctrinal differences were not keenly felt and vigorously debated, or that sectarian feeling did not sometimes run high; but such differences were always settled peacefully, by means of discussion, no attempt ever being made to enforce conformity. Persecution, or "arguing by torture," was unknown. Neither was anyone ever consigned to hell by his opponent for holding unorthodox views. The Pudgalavadins, who believed in the real existence of the Person, were constantly refuted by other schools; but no one ever questioned their ability to gain Enlightenment. Such, indeed, was the harmony that prevailed, that monks of different schools sometimes occupied the same monastery, observing a common rule and sharing in the same corporate monastic life, but devoting themselves, in addition, each to his own special studies and meditations.

PART TWO

Buddhism and the Mind

1 ꧅ Thinking Clearly

1. "The Impossibility of Retracting an Opinion I Believe to Be True"

SATYAPRIYA, the friend with whom I traveled and was ordained in India, was so morbidly sensitive, and so quick to take offense, that he seemed to imagine differences where none existed. It was as though he had to create a difference in order to give himself an excuse for losing his temper. Something of this sort happened two or three days after we had stopped observing silence. We were bathing in the icy waters of the pool, eight or ten feet across and very deep, that lay beneath an overhanging fragment of rock, a few yards along the cliff face from the temple. Something I said, which he interpreted as expressing a difference of opinion, upset him, and despite all my efforts to calm him down he succeeded in gradually working himself up to a pitch of murderous fury such as I had never before witnessed. He had had enough of me, he hissed, his eyes bloodshot with rage. He had allowed me to torment him with my unreasonable behavior too long already. Now he was going to kill me. He would drown me in the pool. No one would ever know. He would tell them that I had died accidentally. Looking at him, I knew that he meant it. For the first time in my life I was actually face to face with death. Strange to say, though I was frightened, and though at one stage Satyapriya was actually clutching me by the arm and preparing to hold me down under the dark water until I drowned, I had no intention whatever of with-drawing the offending remark. On the contrary, I became aware of the existence within me of a rock-bottom of obstinacy that made it utterly impossible for me to retract or disown any opinion which I genuinely believed to be true even to save my life. How the episode ended I no longer recollect.

2. The Voice Within

Buddhism has been described as "the proudest assertion ever made of human freedom" because it stands up boldly, even defiantly, against the ponderous brute mass of externality that threatens to grind out of existence the moral and spiritual life of humanity.

Human beings are today less free to think and feel simply, naturally, and spontaneously than at any other period in history. The pitiless pressure of education and environment tends to grind down even the feeblest manifestation of independent and original thought or feeling. Our ideas and emotions are manufactured for us by those to whose advantage it is that we should think or feel as they hypocritically tell us it is good for us to think and feel. Lurid billboards scream at us that this or that particular beverage will give us vitality and strength. News-paper advertisements assure us with expressions of the fondest solici-tude that yet another undreamed of article is indispensable to our well-being. Political columnists tell us with an air of infallible author-ity which nation is right and which wrong, while popular orators inform us which ideological group we ought to love and which to hate. The propaganda machines of governments and political parties pour out an incessant stream of ready-made opinions on every possible subject, from the latest international crisis to the most recent scien-tific discovery. Critics of literature and art, with their "Book of the Month" and "Picture of the Year," save us the trouble of having to judge for ourselves which books and paintings deserve our attention and which do not. The synthetic emotion of the latest popular song renders deep and genuine feeling superfluous. Cinemas and radios, newspapers and school text-books, billboards and public speeches, together with a thousand other devices for the mass-production and wide dissemination of prefabricated thoughts and emotions, opinions and ideas, are doing our thinking and feeling for us. We no longer create, but passively receive the cartoned products of mechanical efficiency. And that which does not create does not live. Stunned and deafened by the clamorous pressure of the external, we are no longer masters of ourselves, and therefore no longer masters of our environment. Our heads are full of ideas which we do not truly think, our hearts of emotions we do not sincerely feel. A thousand voices from the world without beat upon our ears as relentlessly as the surf upon the sea-beach. The Voice Within is silent.

Not only in the sphere of politics and commerce, literature and art, education and journalism, but in the sacred sphere of religion also, the same intolerable weight of the external is felt. Here, in fact, it has been felt longer than anywhere else. The tyranny of cinema and radio, of popular slogan and newspaper advertisement, is a thing of yesterday and today; but the tyranny of religion dates back three or four millennia at least, to the time when divinely-inspired scriptures, infallible prophets, and mediatorial priesthoods made their first attempts to smother nascent spiritual life. As advertisements tell us what to buy, and stump-orators how to vote, so do the Vedas, Bibles, and Korans tell us what to believe, and the prophets and priests who manipulate them, how to invest our money in celestial stocks and shares so as to obtain the largest possible dividends. When the poor investor eventually realizes who really profits from the whole transaction, he may be pardoned if he doubts equally the good faith of his political, commercial, and ecclesiastical advisers! Religious life, instead of being a voyage of spiritual self-discovery, thus becomes an uncritical acceptance of creeds and dogmas which serve the selfish interests of some particular class or community. Independent thought and unbiased investigation are discouraged and, if possible, suppressed by force, while blind faith (the blinder the better!) is heaped with superlatives and extolled as the one infallible means of obtaining salvation. Divinely-revealed sacred books, infallible prophets, mediatorial priesthoods, and irrefragable dogmas have thundered so loud and long in the ear of humanity that it has been almost deafened by the sound. Once again, the Voice Within is silent or, if not silent, at least unheard.

Buddhism has been described as "the proudest assertion ever made of human freedom" because it stands up boldly, even defiantly, against the ponderous brute mass of externality that threatens to grind out of existence the moral and spiritual life of humanity. It not only teaches us that our first duty is to understand things as they really are, but gives us the courage necessary to make the attempt. It exhorts us never to allow ourselves to be overwhelmed by the flood of thoughts and emotions which come pouring in upon us from all sides, but to weigh and test each one of them in the light of our own knowledge and experience. We should be equally critical of the claims of an advertisement, an election poster, and a religious teaching. That which we find wrong and harmful we should at once reject, while that which we find true and good we should accept and endeavor to put into practice. We should in all circumstances think clearly and feel sincerely. Then we will act rightly, too. For Buddhism does not take up such an independent attitude toward the external world simply for the sake of display, but in order to make room for the full development of the latent spiritual-creative powers of men and women. Pressure from without is wrong and bad only because it crushes the life which is struggling to flower forth from within.

This does not mean that we should allow free play to whatever instincts and impulses happen to spring up within us, but that the purpose of external discipline should be understood before its restraints are accepted. The Buddha said that his disciples should try his words as gold is tried by fire. They were neither to accept them nor reject them without examination. Their confidence in him should be like that of a patient in his doctor, or of a student in his teacher. The books in which his words have been recorded are not, therefore, regarded by his followers as a revelation in which they must blindly believe, but as a guide to practice with which they may experiment. For this reason Buddhism does not lend itself very easily to the manipulations of priestcraft, and wherever it has remained pure it has contributed to the liberation of the creative forces of the human spirit.

When the eyes and ears are blinded and deafened by the very multiplicity of the sights and sounds which come surging in upon them, the mind grows bewildered and independent thought on the situation grows impossible. The Buddha therefore taught us that if we want to see things as they really are, if we desire to act nobly and powerfully in the affairs of life, we must first learn to retire within ourselves and hear, or rather feel, the whisper vibrating through the silence there. We must be our own island of refuge, our own light; we should not look to any external refuge. We should be deaf to all the voices that thunder at us from without so that we can listen to the Voice Within. Then only will we be the masters of ourselves, and masters of our environment. Then only will we be able to see and tread the path that will lead us, one day, even to the heart's Enlightenment.

3. Getting a Clear Idea of Buddhism

The reason we so often fail to put in the commitment required to realize our ideals is that we have not addressed our underlying doubt and indecision about them.

DOUBT AND INDECISION lie at the root of our difficulties with the spiritual life, and that is where we have to bring clear thinking to bear. If one doesn't really believe that it is possible to develop as an individual, one won't be able to put into that development the energy that will enable one to develop. If one is unsure about the value or effectiveness of meditation, so that one does it with an attitude of just seeing how it will turn out, hoping something will come of practicing it, one probably won't get very far. One can't start off with no doubts whatsoever, but there must be at least some sort of willing suspension of disbelief; one must have a degree of conviction sufficient to fuel one's practice with the requisite energy and decisiveness and thus produce a result tangible enough to confirm the rightness of the original decision. In this way there is a possibility of something tentative and provisional being proven on the anvil of experience.

For example, perhaps one believes that psychological development is possible but one is not sure about the whole idea of spiritual development—or vice versa. Either way, one has to be clear about what these notions actually amount to before one decides to commit oneself to them. The reason we so often fail to put in the commitment required to realize our ideals is that we have not addressed our underlying doubt and indecision about them.

Does one, for instance, really believe in the non-reality of the self? What *is* the self? In what sense is it unreal? And has one thought out one's position as regards oriental Buddhism and Buddhism in the West? As regards the three *yanas*—the Hinayana, the Mahayana, the Vajrayana? As regards the Arahant ideal and the Bodhisattva ideal? Is one trying to be an Arahant, or a Bodhisattva? Or has one vaguely kept the two ideas (which are supposed to be ideals) in different compartments of one's mind, unsure how they might hang together—except that one day one somehow feels that it's time to get down to being an Arahant, while the next it's the Bodhisattva spirit that seems to be the thing.

One probably feels that it is hardly worth thinking about, but inasmuch as one cares about these ideals at all, one hopes that in the long run they will turn out to be more or less the same thing. Perhaps one likes to be pragmatic: perhaps one thinks that abstract theorizing and metaphysics are all right if you like that sort of thing, but they butter no parsnips. One has perhaps picked up the idea that the truth of things is not to be approached through the rational mind at all, but that it will suddenly vouchsafe itself while one is muddling along, and then everything will become clear.

But it is not going to be like this. One penetrates beyond the rational by way of exhausting the resources of the rational mind. The thing is not going to be achieved except through the tension of the rational mind stretching itself to its limit. Even more immediately practical matters require more clear thinking than we generally like to afford them. Why exactly should one be a vegetarian, for instance— what are the principles involved? Or why does one meditate—what actually is the point? You can't just say, "If you're a Buddhist, these are the things you do." Well, you can, but you won't thereby make much of an impression on a skeptical non-Buddhist.

It may be true that not everything one does as a Buddhist is fully susceptible to rational analysis. The Dharma does point toward something beyond the grasp of the rational mind. But there are rational considerations that certainly do arise, and which may be communicated in response to enquiries about why you do what you do. There can be a false humility in admitting that you have no clear idea about what you are doing.

4. Learning to Think

From the point of view of learning to think clearly, argument is better than agreement.

To reflect on the Dharma is to reflect on the expression of fundamental truth in terms only barely accessible to human thought; without intellectual clarity we will be unable to grasp the essence of the teaching in all its subtlety and depth. If we are to practice Buddhism effectively, in short, we will need to learn to reflect.

It is not easy, however, to concentrate the mind and direct one's thoughts undistractedly for sustained periods. When you are engaged in a discussion or absorbed in a book, you might be able to hold your mind to a train of thought, but if you leave it to its own devices you are likely to find your attention wandering and your concentration starting to flag. You might set yourself to reflect for an hour on, for instance, the three *lakkhanas,* but it takes a lot of practice to manage more than a few minutes. (Anyone who doubts this should try it and see what happens.)

Thinking should be under one's control, and when it isn't objectively necessary one just shouldn't engage in it. The Buddha used to exhort his disciples to maintain a noble silence (*ariya-mona*) rather than indulge in unprofitable talk, and one could say that the same should go for thought-processes. The alternative to clear and mindful thinking should not be idle mental chatter; one should be able to maintain inner silence. Again, it is obviously a lot easier to say this than to do it—but it is possible.

One way to improve one's ability to think in a directed way is to plan time for thinking. One can learn to take up and put down one's thinking according to one's own needs, not just circumstances. Why not plan thinking time just as you schedule other activities? This is in effect a practice of *sampajanna,* mindfulness of purpose. We all have plenty to think about but our trains of thought seldom reach a conclusion. We are forever dropping one thing and picking up another, then when we sit down to meditate, unfinished business resurfaces and hinders our concentration. Such muddled mental activity is an obstacle to action of any kind and means that we often end up making decisions on the spur of the moment rather than thinking them through. If it is necessary to make a decision it is best to sit down, apply oneself to the matter in hand, and come to a well-considered conclusion. But if we sit down to reflect at all, we often turn the matter over in our mind in such a half-hearted way that quite soon our thoughts have wandered away to irrelevant topics. Unable to come to any clear conclusion, we just make the decision on the basis of how we happen to be feeling at the time, or in response to some quite incidental external pressure. We cannot afford to do this if our decisions are going to count for anything.

We should think about things when we have time to do them justice.

Just as mealtimes, meeting friends, and making time for exercise and meditation involve making definite arrangements, mental activity can also be planned. You could apportion, say, an afternoon each week for thinking about things that really matter, things that are of much more consequence than day-to-day practicalities, although they might not be so pressing. If you keep yourself free of thinking about your deeper problems until the appointed time, you might also find everyday difficulties easier to deal with. If you try this out, though, make sure you are going to be free from interruption for however long you need—half an hour or an hour, or even weeks or months together. A chain of sustained and directed thinking can be very subtle, and to have it snapped by untimely and trivial interruptions is painful. The idea of planning in a period of thinking at two o'clock on Tuesday afternoon might come as a shock, but anyone with a busy life already has to do this to some extent. There are always urgent matters to attend to, but these should not be allowed to push the really important questions to the margins of our consciousness.

Whether planned or not, the best way to improve one's directed thinking is simply to think more. Just as physical exercise is the way to become fit, so thinking is the way to improve the capacity for thought. It is a good idea to take any opportunity you get to consider views and opinions with a logical, questioning attitude. Reasoned discussion with a friend or in a small group—the smaller the better—gives different angles on an issue and brings an enjoyable stimulus to thinking. Because our views tend to be emotionally based, if you are thinking about something on your own, there is always the temptation to come to a premature conclusion and resist thinking along lines that run counter to that conclusion. Collaborative thinking forces you to be more objective, to look for a truth that does not necessarily suit you. There is something about the physical presence of another person that generates interest and a keenness to get at the truth, and if you are talking with someone whose intellect is quite active, you might find that you have to get used to organizing and articulating your thoughts more carefully, to avoid non-sequiturs and short-cuts in your argument.

Your friends might convince you, or you them. You might even end up convincing yourself, if you were not sure at the outset of the discussion what you really thought. Writing also helps to develop clear thinking—your argument has to be more rigorous than when you are speaking to people you know, and you have to be more careful to make logical connections between the ideas you present.

From the point of view of learning to think clearly, argument is better than agreement. If you only ever have discussions with people whose views you share and read books you agree with, you will never be obliged to address any faulty reasoning that might underpin your view of things. A valid conclusion does not guarantee the logic of any and every argument used in its support. A statement based on a poor line of argument—or no argument at all—might go unchallenged because everyone agrees with the conclusion anyway, regardless of how it is reached. It can therefore be a good idea to seek out a bit of opposition: there is nothing like meeting criticism for improving one's ability to frame a logical argument and make it watertight. Even though sound arguments are unlikely to win over someone with a deep emotional investment in the views they hold, trying to win that person over can make you aware of the strength or weakness of your logic. On the other hand, if your arguments do hold water, the confidence this gives you will help you to be more open to new ideas, because you will know that you have the ability to sift through them without getting muddled or feeling threatened.

5. More and More of Less and Less

"The books and letters which you do not practice—give them up!"

ON AN INTELLECTUAL LEVEL, Buddhism, historically, is characterized by clarity, honesty, and rigor of thought. The problem from our point of view is that most of us aren't accustomed to analyzing situations and propositions, to rigorously drawing conclusions from evidence properly adduced. We tend to go on hunches, bits and pieces of information, and little scraps of knowledge, from which we draw all sorts of weird and wonderful conclusions.

As Buddhists, therefore, we need to challenge one another to think more clearly. We don't have to be nit-picking or unnecessarily controversial, but we do need to make sure that we know what we are talking about. For example, what do the words we use really mean? If they are translations from, say, the Pali or Sanskrit, do we know how accurate they are? Indeed, are we really clear about the meaning of the terms we use in our own language? Dictionaries are full of interesting surprises.

We don't all have to be intellectuals, but whenever we use language we can try to use it clearly and precisely; otherwise it will give us vague and inaccurate ideas. One does not avoid the undoubted dangers of intellectualism by being sloppy; and sloppy thinking may even hinder one's spiritual development. It is true that transcendental insight itself is independent of conceptual thought, but it doesn't just appear out of nowhere. It arises on the basis of the conceptual expression of the Dharma. It is on the basis of thinking about the concept of impermanence, say, that you develop *insight* into the truth of impermanence. Intellectual understanding comes first; it's a sort of springboard.

Intellectual clarity is not attained by becoming better educated, reading more books, or becoming an intellectual. Indeed, becoming engrossed in theory is as unhelpful as woolly thinking. Wanting to know more and more about the theory and philosophy of Buddhism in a vain attempt to consume as much Buddhism as we can as fast as we can will just give us intellectual indigestion.

Many modern expositions of Buddhism deal so much in concepts, talk so much about Buddhist thought, Buddhist philosophy, and so on, that one can get the impression of something one-sidedly, even overwhelmingly, intellectual. It can seem as if to understand it you have to undergo a rigorous course in logic, metaphysics, and epistemology. But in ancient India, when spiritual teaching was entirely a matter of oral transmission, people were given exactly what they needed at the time. You couldn't read a book describing the stages of the path to Enlightenment. Perhaps you would be completely ignorant of the very idea of Enlightenment. You would go along to a teacher and he would say, after a bit of conversation or just looking you up and down, "Go away and do this practice." You would go away and do it, perhaps for several years, and when you had mastered it thoroughly he would give you some further teaching to practice. You certainly wouldn't be given a theoretical preview.

These days we are constantly being given theoretical previews. We know the path, we know all about the different stages, we know all about prajna, we know all about the different degrees and levels of sunyata. Because we are so familiar with this material theoretically, it is hard for us to distinguish between theoretical knowledge and the kind of knowledge that comes only from experience. And to recognize the difference, we may have to unknow what we know and unlearn what we have learned.

What are we to do, given the amount of Buddhist theory by which we are surrounded? The key, probably, is more and more of less and less: in other words, to focus on a very few texts or teachings or approaches to the Dharma, and deepen our experience of them through reflection and practice and questioning. Indeed, that reflection and questioning itself should be real. Our reflections and questions should be our own—not just a game of rearranging concepts. A real question springs out of one's own experience, even one's own conflict. "The books and letters which you do not practice—give them up!" is the robust statement of the great Buddhist teacher Padmasambhava.[54]

Western culture being what it is, we are probably going to want to make at least a rapid survey of the whole field. But having made it we should get back to where we actually are, and practice and study accordingly. The Buddha used the language of clear conceptual analysis, but the purpose of that analysis was never merely theoretical.

Sometimes the Buddha made this point by using a completely different language to communicate the Dharma—as when, according to the Zen tradition, on one occasion, in the midst of a gathering of monks, he spoke no words, but simply held up a golden flower. Of all the disciples gathered there just one, Mahakasyapa, understood what was being communicated, and responded with a smile. And that, they say, is how Zen began. That great spiritual movement, which spread throughout the Far East and produced hundreds of Enlightened masters, sprang not from a system of philosophy, not from a lengthy discourse, but from that one simple action: the holding up of a golden flower, in whose petals all the wisdom of the Buddhas was to be discerned.[55] That is what Mahakasyapa understood, and that is why he smiled. He probably thought to himself that the Buddha had never done anything more wonderful in his whole life than to hold up that golden flower, which even now is continuing to transmit its beauty.

The language of symbolism is a language that we too have to learn to speak. We may be ready, even glib, with the language of ideas and concepts—we may discuss Buddhist philosophy endlessly—but this must be complemented by the language of images. This dimension of communication may be comparatively unfamiliar to us, but by immersing ourselves in legends, myths, and symbols, we can learn to understand and even speak that language.

2 ← Mind Reactive and Creative

1. SONNET

Reading some books, you'd think the Buddha-Way,
As though macadamized, ran smooth and white,
Straight as an arrow, billboards left and right,
And that the yellow buses, thrice a day,
Whirled past the milestones, whose smug faces say,
"Nirvana 15 miles . . . By 10 tonight
You'll all be there, good people, and alight
Outside the Peace Hotel, where you're to stay."
But those who read their own hearts, inly wise,
Know that the Way's a hacked path, roughly made
Through densest jungle, deep in the Unknown . . .
And that, though burn a thousand baleful eyes
Like death-lamps round, serene and unafraid,
Man through the hideous dark must plunge alone.

2. THE PATH OF REGULAR STEPS AND THE PATH OF IRREGULAR STEPS

Western Buddhists tend to pick and choose from the material available and to select not according to their real spiritual needs but according to quite subjective and superficial whims and fancies.

THE DISTINCTION between the Path of Regular Steps and the Path of Irregular Steps is a very ancient one. It goes back to sixth century China, and to the great Chinese teacher Chih-i, well known as the virtual founder of one of the greatest and most important of all the schools of Chinese Buddhism, the T'ien-T'ai School—a school which, though one of the greatest Buddhism has known, has so far been rather neglected by Western Buddhists. In the course of his lifetime Chih-i preached the Dharma widely, founded monasteries, and by reason of his profound spiritual attainments was able to attract an extraordinarily large number of disciples. These disciples he addressed from time to time, commenting upon the scriptures, speaking about the spiritual life, and especially, it seems, speaking about meditation. In the course of his discourses on meditation, many of which have come down to us, Chih-i spoke of Meditation by Regular Steps, of Meditation by Irregular Steps, and also of Meditation Without Any Steps at All.[56]

On the present occasion we are concerned only with regular steps and irregular steps, and we are concerned with them because Chih-i's distinction between meditation by regular steps and meditation by irregular steps is applicable not only to the practice of meditation but to the practice and experience of the whole spiritual path, in all its stages and all its aspects.

What, then, is the Path of Regular Steps? What is the Path of Irregular Steps? In attempting to answer these questions I propose to be a little irregular myself and deal with the second Path first.

MIND REACTIVE AND CREATIVE ~ 165

The Path of Irregular Steps

In order to understand what the Path of Irregular Steps is, we must first look at Buddhism as it exists in the Western world today, whether in Britain, in continental Europe, or in the Americas. When we look, the first thing that we see is books—hundreds of books—about Buddhism. This is the most conspicuous feature of Buddhism in the West.

If we are young and enthusiastic, and have lots of time, we start trying to read these books—all of them if possible, or at least as many as we can of the better-known ones. Usually we read quite a lot—some of us may even get around to reading the Buddhist scriptures themselves. In this way, by virtue of our miscellaneous reading, we start getting an impression of Buddhism and even start forming ideas about it. These ideas are usually very confused. They are so confused that in many cases we do not even begin to realize how confused they are until years afterward. In some cases we may never realize it. But meanwhile, we think we understand Buddhism because we have read about it.

The position is, however, that we do not understand Buddhism *at all*. When I say "at all" I mean this quite literally. It is not that we have a little understanding of Buddhism, that we have grasped just a portion of it. The position is that we do not understand Buddhism *at all*. But we think we do. From this a very important consequence follows.

When we understand a thing—whether we really understand it or just think we do—we become as it were superior to that thing. Understanding means appropriating; it means taking the subject of knowledge unto oneself. It means taking it *into* oneself and making it one's own, making it part of oneself. For this reason, because understanding means appropriating—we speak in terms of "mastering" a subject. Thus we speak of mastering accountancy, or mastering mathematics. We even speak—or at least think—of mastering Buddhism. So because we have, as we think, understood Buddhism—because we have appropriated it, and made it part of ourselves—we start feeling superior to Buddhism, because we have "mastered" it. Because we feel superior to Buddhism we do not look up to it; we do not feel toward Buddhism any real devotion or reverence. We are in fact devoid of any such feelings. We have simply "mastered" the subject.

This kind of attitude is not new, and is by no means confined to modern Western Buddhists. It has been widespread in the Western world for quite a long time. We find the great poet and thinker Coleridge complaining about this kind of attitude—complaining, of course, within a Christian context—one hundred and fifty years ago. On 15 May 1833 he delivered himself of these sentiments:

> There is now no reverence for anything. And the reason is that men possess conceptions only, and all their knowledge is conceptional only. Now, as to conceive is a work of the mere understanding, and as all that can be conceived may be comprehended, it is impossible that a man should reverence that to which he must always feel something in himself superior. If it were possible to conceive God in a strict sense, that is, as we conceive of a horse or a tree, even God himself could not excite any reverence. . . .

And reverence, Coleridge goes on to say,

> . . . is only due from man and is only excitable in man toward ideal truths which are always mysteries to the understanding, for the same reason that the motion of my finger behind my back is a mystery to you now, your eyes not being made for seeing through my body.[57]

This is what Coleridge said on the subject of lack of reverence. At about the same time we find in Germany an even greater poet and thinker saying much the same thing, though rather more briefly. Goethe says: "The finest achievement for men of thought is to have fathomed the fathomable, and quietly to revere the unfathomable."[58]

MIND REACTIVE AND CREATIVE ~ 167

It is this quiet revering of the unfathomable, of that which, in Buddhist terminology, is *atakkavacara,* or beyond the reach of thought—beyond the reach of understanding and conception—that until recently has been so lacking among Western Buddhists. We have been much too quick to "understand," much too ready to speak, even about the unfathomable. In fact, we have been much too ready to speak *especially* about the unfathomable.

This is not altogether our fault. To a great extent it is the result of the situation in which we find ourselves. There are so many books on Buddhism, so many translations of ancient Buddhist texts, and we have to admit that some of this material is extremely advanced. Some of it—the sutras—is addressed to disciples of a high degree of spiritual development. The opening scene of some of the great Mahayana sutras may be familiar. The Buddha is seated in the midst of a great concourse of disciples, perhaps in some heaven or archetypal realm. All around him are Arahants and great Bodhisattvas, even irreversible Bodhisattvas, that is, Bodhisattvas who cannot regress from the ideal of Supreme Buddhahood and who have, as it were, nirvana in the palm of their hand, and the sublime teachings that the Buddha proceeds to give are addressed to these great beings—beings who exist on a very high level of spirituality, beyond all that we can conceive or imagine.

Many of these Mahayana sutras have now been translated and thus, in a sense, made available to us. So we read this or that sutra, and we think we have mastered its contents, and thinking we have mastered it we tend to adopt a cool, superior, even patronizing attitude toward Buddhism. So much is this the case that some of us may even think it unnecessary to call ourselves Buddhists at all—after all, we have "gone beyond" all that—and may even look down somewhat on those simple-minded folk in the West who do choose to call themselves Buddhists, who pay their respects to images, who offer flowers and light candles, and who try to observe the precepts. We may think our attitude more advanced, but the truth is that it is purely theoretical, purely mental, and devoid of any deep and genuine feeling of reverence and devotion.

Because of this lack of all "quiet revering of the unfathomable," until recently Western Buddhism has tended to be a rather shallow and superficial thing. Western Buddhists tend to pick and choose from the material available and to select not according to their real spiritual needs but according to quite subjective and superficial whims and fancies. Thus you find people saying, "I like this bit, but I do not like that bit. I am happy with the idea of karma, but I do not like the idea of rebirth." Or you find people being drawn by the doctrine of *anatman* (Pali *anatta*). For some reason or other, the idea that they do not have a soul or a self seems rather to attract some people—though at the same time they find the thought of nirvana rather depressing. Thus people tend to pick and choose, and to select—and of course their likes and dislikes change. For a while one may be into Zen, because one rather likes the idea that one is already a Buddha, already "there," and that there is nothing to do. It seems to make life a lot easier: one does not have to practice anything, apparently! One does not have to give up anything. So you rather like Zen—for a while. But eventually you get rather bored with being a Buddha, so you start getting into the Tantra, and Tantra, of course, immediately conjures up visions of sex, and you start getting into the yoga of sex (theoretically, of course!). In this way the average Western Buddhist has been browsing and dabbling for all these years.

Even so, despite all these difficulties—and they are difficulties which every one of us has experienced—some Western Buddhists do get around to practicing Buddhism. On the basis of my personal experience, seeing so many people coming and going, I would say that perhaps, at a liberal estimate, one in twenty Western Buddhists gets around to trying to practice Buddhism. Eventually it dawns on them that Buddhism is not just a collection of interesting ideas—not just a philosophy, not just something to think about. It dawns on them that Buddhism is something to be applied, even something to be experienced. So they start trying to practice it; start trying to put it into operation. But, unfortunately, so strong is the force of conditioning and habit that even when they start trying to practice Buddhism the same old pattern, derived from their previous theoretical approach, persists. Their attitude is still shallow and superficial. They still tend to pick and choose.

In the first half of this century there was very little Buddhism in the West in any form, books or otherwise. Now the situation is different. We could even say that there is too much Buddhism around. There are so many books, so many practices, so many teachers, so many schools represented! There is such a bewildering confusion and profusion of forms of Buddhism. In our excitement and greed we snatch first at this and then at that, sampling a bit here and a bit there, like a greedy child in a sweet shop. We are in the transcendental sweet shop of Buddhism, with all these beautiful spiritual goodies around us, and so we grab this and grab that: Zen, Tantra, Theravada, ethics, meditation of one sort and another. But nonetheless, we do make some progress. The Path of Irregular Steps is a path, and it does give us some experience of Buddhism.

But only up to a point. As we practice in this way—as we follow the Path of Irregular Steps—we find, sooner or later, that we are slowing down, as though we have come up against an invisible obstacle. We are still going through the motions of following the Path of Irregular Steps, but nothing is happening: it has all come to a standstill. If we want to overcome this invisible obstacle—if we want to make progress and continue to make progress—there must be a radical change, and that change consists in making the transition from the Path of Irregular Steps to the Path of Regular Steps.

The Path of Regular Steps

Now why is this? What is the Path of Regular Steps? How does it differ from the Path of Irregular Steps, and why does further progress depend on our making a transition from the one to the other? These questions cannot be answered without our first understanding the nature of the path in general, that is to say, the path from that which Buddhists call samsara, or the round of mundane existence, to nirvana; the path from conditioned to Unconditioned being; the path from unenlightened humanity to the Enlightened humanity of the Buddha.

This great path is traditionally divided into three successive stages: the stage of *sila* or morality, the stage of *samadhi* or meditation, and the stage of *prajna* (Pali *panna*) or wisdom. Though there are other ways of dividing, and even subdividing, the path, this threefold division remains the most important and the most fundamental.

Sila or morality is simply skillful action: action which benefits oneself, and helps one to grow and develop; and action which benefits others, too, and helps *them* to grow and develop. Not that *sila* is a matter of external action divorced from mental attitude; it is both the mental attitude and the mode of behavior in which that attitude naturally expresses itself. Thus *sila* is skillful action in the sense that it is action arising from, or based upon, skillful mental states, especially states of love, generosity, peace, and contentment. *Sila* is everything one does out of, or because of, these skillful mental states. That, essentially, is what morality or ethics is in Buddhism: actions expressive of skillful mental states.

Samadhi or meditation is a word with many different meanings, on a number of different levels. First of all it consists in the gathering of all one's scattered energies and bringing them together into a single focus. Most of the time our energies are divided, and go in different directions; they are not unified, not integrated. So first of all we have to integrate them. This does not mean forcibly concentrating on a particular point; it means bringing together all our energies, both conscious and unconscious, and harmonizing them in a natural and spontaneous manner. Thus concentration, in the sense of the complete unification of one's psycho-spiritual energies, is the first grade or level of *samadhi*.

Next, *samadhi* consists in the experience of progressively higher states of consciousness—states extending into what are called the *dhyanas* or superconscious states. In these superconscious states we transcend the body and, eventually, transcend the mind in the sense of discursive mental activity. We also experience bliss, peace, joy, and ecstasy—but we do *not* experience Insight, since we are still within samsara, still within the realm of the mundane. Finally, *samadhi* includes the development of such supernormal—though not "supernatural"—powers of the mind as telepathy, clairvoyance, clairaudience, and the recollection of one's previous existences—powers which sometimes arise quite naturally and spontaneously in the course of meditation.

Prajna or wisdom means direct insight into the Truth or into Reality. This direct insight into, or personal contact with, Reality is at first only momentary, like a sudden flash of lightning that, on a dark night, lights up the landscape just for an instant. As the flashes of insight become more frequent, however, and more continuous, they eventually become a steady beam of light that is capable of penetrating (as it were) into the depths of Reality. When fully developed this wisdom or insight is what we call *bodhi* or Enlightenment—though at that level it is not to be spoken of in exclusively cognitive terms but also in terms of love and compassion, or rather, in terms of the transcendental counterpart of the emotions which we usually designate by those names.

The division of the path into these three stages is not arbitrary. The stages are not mere chalk marks, as it were, but are inherent in the Path itself, and represent natural stages in the spiritual and transcendental growth of the individual, like stages in the growth of a plant. First there is the seed; from the seed comes forth a little shoot; the shoot grows into a stem; then leaves are produced; and finally buds and flowers appear. Of course, we must not push an analogy of this sort too far. The whole process of the flower's growth is unconscious. The flower does not have to decide whether to grow or not; nature "decides" for it—whereas in the case of a human being, spiritual development is conscious and deliberate, and by its very nature must be so. Each of us is dependent for our further growth on our own individual, personal effort—though this is not a matter of one-sided, egoistic willing but of the growth and development, in awareness, of the whole being. Spiritual development can also be compared with the construction of a house or any multi-story building. First we lay the foundation, then the first story, then the second, and finally we put on the roof. We cannot reverse the sequence, which is determined by the nature of the structure itself.

In Buddhism, as it has come down to us, there are many different teachings, and these teachings correspond to different stages of spiritual and transcendental development. When we practice the Dharma we should therefore practice those teachings which correspond to the stage of development which we have actually reached—reached not mentally or theoretically but with our whole being. This is the traditional method, or at least the predominant traditional method.

First we practice morality: we observe the precepts; we become thoroughly ethical individuals, both inwardly and outwardly—and this may take several years. Then, when our ethical individuality has been established relatively firmly, we take up the practice of concentration: we learn to tame the unruly wandering mind, and to concentrate at will on any object for any length of time. This may take several more years. Then, slowly, we start raising the level of consciousness: we experience the first *dhyana,* the second *dhyana,* and so on, gradually training ourselves not just to touch them but even to dwell in them. Finally, perhaps after many years of endeavor, one raises one's purified and concentrated—one's elevated and sublime—mind, together with the integrated energies of one's whole being, to the contemplation of Reality itself. This is the Path of Regular Steps.

On the Path of Regular Steps progress is systematic. One consolidates an earlier stage of the path before proceeding to the next, or a later, stage. But in the Path of Irregular Steps one does not do this. Following the Path of Irregular Steps involves starting with a more or less mental or theoretical idea of Buddhism, or of the Path (and a confused and incomplete idea at that) and then beginning to practice— usually, in the West, without a teacher. One does not start practicing those teachings which correspond to the stage of development one has reached, because one does not know that anyway: one starts practicing what appeals to one, or perhaps what appeals to one's vanity.

One might, for instance, start practicing the Perfection of Wisdom. Now even for an absolute beginner to practice the Perfection of Wisdom is not absolutely impossible. After all, the seed of Buddhahood is there, however deeply hidden. Deep down there is an affinity with the Perfection of Wisdom, so that it is not absolutely impossible even for the beginner to start practicing the Perfection of Wisdom on the basis of a purely theoretical understanding of the subject. Such a person may even succeed, to a very slight extent. By sheer force of the egoistic will one may succeed in holding oneself, just for an instant, at a level of concentration where one gets a glimpse even of the Perfection of Wisdom: even of the Void (*sunyata*). But one will not be able to keep it up. One will slip, one will sink, one will fall, and there will even be a reaction—a reaction from the being and consciousness as a whole, which is simply not at that level and not ready to practice the Perfection of Wisdom. Then, one has to go back and practice meditation, thereby developing higher states of consciousness and in this way creating a firm basis for the practice of the Perfection of Wisdom. Having done that, one can go forward again.

Going Back to Go Forward

Following the Path of Irregular Steps thus usually involves forcing the process of spiritual development. It is like trying to make a plant grow by forcibly opening the tiny buds with one's fingers, or like trying to put on the upper story of a house before the foundation is complete. Sooner or later we discover that it cannot be done. It is no use trying to open the buds; you have to water the roots. It is no use trying to put on the upper story; you have to strengthen the foundation. As Buddhists, the flower that we want to see blooming is the thousand-petalled lotus itself (the lotus which blooms only with the development of Insight), so plenty of water is needed. The tower we want to build is the tower that reaches up into the very heavens, so a firm foundation is needed. To state the matter axiomatically, we may say that a higher stage of the Path cannot be developed in its fullness, or even to a moderate extent, before a lower stage of the Path has been developed in its fullness. This is the basic principle. If we want to experience the higher stage, or higher level, with any intensity or any permanence, we must first perfect the lower stage, on the basis of which, alone, the higher stage is to be established. This is why, sooner or later, we have to make the transition from the Path of Irregular Steps to the Path of Regular Steps. We have to go back in order to go forward.

But how far back do we have to go? One could say "Back to morality": that is quite a popular slogan nowadays! Or one could say "Back to the individual path." But in fact we have to go back even further than that. We have to go back to something even more basic and fundamental than morality, even more basic and fundamental than the individual path—we have to go back to the Three Jewels. We have to go down on our knees, as it were, and go for Refuge saying, "*Buddham saranam gacchami, Dhammam saranam gacchami, Sangham saranam gacchami.* To the Buddha for Refuge I go, to the Dharma for Refuge I go, to the Sangha for Refuge I go." This is where Buddhism really begins. This is the root, the foundation, the absolute bedrock of our spiritual life. This is how we really start practicing the path—by Going for Refuge.

3. What Do We Really Know?

We have to learn the value of silence, not only physical silence but the silence of thoughts, the silence of the mind.

WE SAY WE KNOW this or know that. But what do we really mean? We mean, surely, that we have read it somewhere, or heard about it, or seen it on television. We have very little *direct* knowledge. It is all based on hearsay, on second-hand, third-hand, and tenth-hand information, on conjecture and gossip. We consider, for instance, that we know what is going on in the world at large, what is happening in distant places. But whence is our "knowledge" derived? From words and letters, the radio and the newspapers, snatches of conversation overheard on the train, chance remarks at parties. How great is our dependence! The thought is quite horrifying. But if there were no radios, no newspapers, we would "know" very little of what went on in the world. We would have fewer thoughts, fewer ideas. Being less cluttered up mentally, we would be better able to concentrate on things near at hand. We would be able to live more intensely. Perhaps we would be closer to Reality.

This was, of course, the condition of our ancestors in bygone days, even as it is still the condition of many people in the "undeveloped" countries. Compared with us, our ancestors knew very little of what was going on in the wide world that lay outside the gates of their own village or township. Vague rumors reached them from the distant capital, and usually that was all. Sometimes, of course, they saw armies marching past, and sometimes armies devastated with fire and sword, but despite beating drums and flying colors, ordinary folk did not understand what the war was about or who was fighting whom. Occasionally men were conscripted. Otherwise, apart from natural calamities, the stream of life flowed on placid and undisturbed from year to year and from generation to generation. I am not trying to idealize the past. I am only trying to point out how much our knowledge depends upon words and letters and how little on direct personal experience, and that this dependence is, moreover, both proportionally and absolutely, greater now than ever before in history.

This is true in all fields. Take any subject that we think we "know." Take botany, or the history of art, or any other branch of human knowledge, from astronomy to zoology. By far the greater part of our knowledge of these subjects, if not the whole of it, is secondhand. Hardly any of it is original, the result of our own independent thought and discovery. Inheriting as it were a great stockpile of knowledge from the past, we go through life, for the most part, without adding to it so much as a single grain of our own. Originality would seem to be the prerogative of genius.

In everyday life, all this, though perhaps regrettable, does not matter very much. We manage to get along somehow. From the Zen point of view, however, it is important to realize what is actually happening. It might be interesting to perform an experiment. As you sit here, fold your hands and close your eyes, just as you do for meditation. Forget all you have ever learned from books, newspapers, magazines, radio, television, and advertisements. Forget even talks, lectures, and discussions. How much knowledge would you then have left? The answer must be: very little indeed. If we were to perform the experiment regularly the experience would be quite salutary. We should then realize how little we really know. And to know that we do not know is the beginning of wisdom.

From our general dependence on words and letters let us now turn to our dependence on them where spiritual things are concerned. We have, let us assume, a certain amount of religious knowledge. We know about Buddhism. We know about the Four Noble Truths and the Noble Eightfold Path; about karma and rebirth, nirvana and dependent origination; about *sunyata,* bodhisattvas, and the Pure Land. What a lot we know! We even know about Zen. Now where has all this knowledge come from? From books and lectures. Ultimately, of course, it comes from the scriptures, which consist of words and letters. On words and letters, therefore, is our knowledge of Buddhism dependent. It is all secondhand, not based on direct, personal experience and perception.

Let us perform another experiment. Let us put aside all knowledge of Buddhism that depends on words and letters, all that we have not experienced and verified for ourselves. Probably we shall have to discard quite a lot. Do we really know what nirvana is? What about *sunyata?* Put them aside too if necessary. At the end of the experiment how much real knowledge is left? Perhaps none at all.

We should not think we have lost anything, however. In fact there is a great gain. Zen is concerned with the experience of the living spirit of Buddhism, and with the transmission of that spirit. For Zen nothing else matters. Nothing must be allowed to stand in the way. This is what makes Zen so ruthless. Zen has no hesitation about burning holy Buddha-images or tearing up sacred books if these get in the way. But what is it that gets in the way more than anything else? What is it that most of all prevents us from having a real knowledge of Buddhism, based on our own experience? Surely the greatest obstacle is to think that we know. Until this obstacle has been removed, no progress is possible. Here, more than anywhere else, is the beginning of wisdom. It is also the beginning of Enlightenment, the beginning of progress: to know that we do not know.

Such knowledge involves distinguishing between what we know at secondhand, from the scriptures, and what we know from experience. This is what Zen means when it urges us not to confuse the two kinds of knowledge. If we do confuse them, no spiritual progress is possible. Unfortunately we are guilty of this confusion all the time. It is, in fact, part of our general psychological conditioning. Having failed to distinguish thoughts from things, we then fail to distinguish words from thoughts. We think that if we can label a thing we have understood it. Take, for example, nirvana. This is essentially a spiritual principle, or transcendental Reality, and can be thought of in various ways. For instance, it can be thought of in terms of the complete cessation of craving. Since we understand what is meant by the words "cessation of craving" we think that we know what nirvana is. When, therefore, in some non-Buddhist work, we come across the idea of freedom from craving, we at once triumphantly exclaim, "Ah yes, nirvana!" At once we slap on the label. We think we "know" that the state of freedom from craving mentioned in the non-Buddhist work and the Buddhist nirvana are one and the same. But all that we have in fact done is to equate thoughts and words. We are not dealing directly with things, with realities, at all. At best we are dealing with thoughts about things, or often with just words.

Conceptualizing and verbalizing activity of this sort is only too common in the West. People talk far too much. They always want to affix ready-made labels to their experiences. It is as though they were unable to enjoy the beauty of a flower until they had given it its correct botanical classification and a Latin name. We have to learn the value of silence, not only physical silence but the silence of thoughts, the silence of the mind. In this connection I remember an anecdote told me, many years ago, by an Indian friend of mine, an elder brother in the Order. Some years previously this friend had paid a visit to Germany, where he gave some lectures on Buddhism. One morning a German Buddhist lady came to see him. As he was in the midst of writing a letter, and wanted to catch the post, he asked her to wait in an adjoining room. He had only been writing for a few minutes, however, when the door suddenly burst open, and the German lady violently exclaimed, "I shall go mad if I stay here much longer. *There's no one to talk to!*" As he came to the end of the story my friend threw up his hands in mock despair, as if to say, "What hope is there of spreading Buddhism among such people?" And, of course, such people are to be found in all countries, Western and Eastern.

There are some things that can be experienced and also thought about and described in words. Others, though capable of being experienced, transcend thought and speech. At best they can only be indicated, or suggested, or hinted at. Such are the realities, or aspects of Reality, of which we speak in such terms as "Enlightenment," "nirvana," "Buddhahood." All these terms are used only provisionally. They give us a certain amount of practical guidance, some idea of the quarter in which to look, the direction toward which we have to orient our spiritual strivings, but their validity is only relative. They do not really define the goal. In using them we say, therefore, in the absolute sense, nothing at all. Hence in the *Lankavatara Sutra* the Buddha declares that from the night of his Supreme Enlightenment to the night of his final passing away he has not uttered a single word. Between the two events lay forty-five years of untiring earthly ministry. During that period he had taught thousands, perhaps hundreds of thousands, of people. Hardly a day had gone by without discourses, dialogues, answers to questions. Yet in reality nothing had been said because nothing can be said about Reality. All his words had been pointers to what is beyond words. As Asvaghosa says, "We use words to get free from words until we reach the pure wordless Essence."

4. MIND REACTIVE, MIND CREATIVE

The creative mind loves where there is no reason to love, is happy where there is no reason for happiness, creates where there is no possibility of creativity, and in this way "builds a heaven in hell's despair."

TAKING A BIRD'S-EYE VIEW of human culture, we see that there exist in the world numerous spiritual traditions. Some of these are of great antiquity, coming down from the remote past with all the authority and prestige of that which has been long established; others are of more recent origin. While some have crystallized, in the course of centuries, into religious cults with enormous followings, others have remained more of the nature of philosophies, making few concessions to popular tastes and needs. Each of these traditions has its own system, that is to say, its own special concatenation—its own network— of ideas and ideals, beliefs and practices, as well as its own particular starting-point in thought or experience out of which the whole system evolves. This starting-point is the "golden string" which, when wound into the ball of the total system, will lead one in at the "heaven's gate, built in Jerusalem's wall" of the tradition concerned.

Like other traditions, Buddhism possesses its own special system and its own distinctive starting point. The system of Buddhism is what is known as the "Dharma," a Sanskrit word meaning, in this context, the "Doctrine" or the "Teaching," and connoting the sum total of the insights and experiences conducive to the attainment of Enlightenment or Buddhahood. Its starting-point is the mind.

That this, and no other, is the starting-point, is illustrated by two quotations from what are sometimes regarded as the two most highly antithetical, not to say mutually exclusive, developments within the whole field of Buddhism: Theravada and Zen. According to the first two verses of the *Dhammapada,* an ancient collection of metrical aphorisms included in the Pali Canon of the Theravadins,

> Experiences are preceded by mind, led by mind, and produced by mind. If one speaks or acts with an impure mind, suffering follows even as the cart-wheel follows the hoof of the ox. Experiences are preceded by mind, led by mind, and produced by mind. If one speaks or acts with a pure mind, happiness follows like a shadow that never departs.

The Zen quotation is if anything more emphatic. In a verse which made its appearance in China during the T'ang dynasty, Zen itself, which claims to convey from generation to generation of disciples the very heart of the Buddha's spiritual experience, is briefly characterized as:

> A special transmission outside the Scriptures.
> No dependence on words and letters.
> Direct pointing to the mind.
> Seeing into one's own nature and realizing Buddhahood.

From these quotations, representative of many others which could be made, it is clear that the starting-point of Buddhism is not outside us. In the language of Western thought, it is not objective but subjective. The starting-point is the mind.

But what do we mean by mind? In the *Dhammapada* verses the original Pali word is *mano;* in the Chinese Zen stanza it is *hsin,* corresponding to the Sanskrit and Pali *citta.* As both these terms can be quite adequately rendered by the English "mind" there is no need to explore etymologies and we can plunge at once into the heart of our subject.

To begin with, mind is twofold. On the one hand there is Absolute Mind; on the other, relative mind. By Absolute Mind is meant that infinite cosmic or transcendental Awareness within whose pure timeless flow the subject-object polarity as we ordinarily experience it is forever dissolved. For mind in this exalted sense Buddhism employs, according to context, a number of expressions, each with its own distinctive shade of meaning. Prominent among these expressions are the One Mind, the Unconditioned, Buddha-nature, the Void. In the more neutral language of philosophy, Absolute Mind is Reality. It is the realization of Absolute Mind through the dissolution of the subject-object polarity—the waking up to Reality out of the dream of mundane existence—which constitutes Enlightenment, the attainment of Enlightenment being, of course, the ultimate aim of Buddhism.

By relative mind is meant the individual mind or consciousness, functioning within the framework of the subject-object polarity, and it is with this mind that we are now concerned. Like mind in general, relative mind or consciousness is of two kinds: reactive and creative. While these are not traditional Buddhist expressions, neither of them rendering any one technical term in any of the canonical languages, they seem to express very well the import of the Buddha's teaching. In any case, the distinction which they represent is of fundamental importance not only in the system of Buddhism but in the spiritual life generally and even in the entire scheme of human evolution. The transition from "reactive" to "creative" marks, indeed, the beginning of spiritual life. It is conversion in the true sense of the term. What, then, do we mean by speaking of "reactive mind" and "creative mind"?

In the first place, we should not imagine that there are literally two relative minds, one reactive, the other creative. Rather should we understand that there are two ways in which relative mind or the individual consciousness is capable of functioning. It is capable of functioning reactively and it is capable of functioning creatively. When it functions in a reactive manner, it is known as the reactive mind; when it functions in a creative manner, it is known as the creative mind. But there is only one relative mind.

By the reactive mind is meant our ordinary, everyday mind, the mind that most people use most of the time, or, rather, it is the mind that uses them. In extreme cases, indeed, the reactive mind functions all the time, the creative mind remaining in complete abeyance. People of this type are born, live, and die animals; though possessing the human form they are in fact not human beings at all. Rather than attempt an abstract definition of the reactive mind let us try to grasp its nature by examining some of its characteristics.

In the first place, the reactive mind is a *re*-active mind. It does not really act, but only *re*-acts. Instead of acting spontaneously, out of its own inner fullness and abundance, it requires an external stimulus to set it in motion. This stimulus usually comes through the five senses. We are walking along the street; an advertisement catches our eye, its bright colors and bold lettering making an instant appeal. Perhaps it is an advertisement for a certain brand of cigarette, or for a certain make of car, or for summer holidays on the sun-drenched beaches of some distant pleasure resort. Whatever the goods or services depicted, our attention is attracted, arrested. We go and do what the advertisement is designed to make us do, or make a mental note to do it, or are left with an unconscious disposition to do it as and when circumstances permit. We have not acted, but have been activated. We have *re*-acted.

The reactive mind is, therefore, the conditioned mind. It is conditioned by its object (e.g. the advertisement) in the sense of being not merely dependent upon it but actually determined by it. The reactive mind is not free.

Since it is conditioned the reactive mind is, moreover, purely mechanical. As such it can be appropriately described as the "penny-in-the-slot" mind. Insert the coin, and out comes the packet. In much the same way, let the reactive mind be confronted with a certain situation or experience and it will react automatically, in an entirely mechanical, hence predictable, fashion. Not only our behavior but much of our "thinking" conforms to this pattern. Whether in the field of politics, or literature, or religion, or whether in the affairs of everyday life, the opinions we so firmly hold and so confidently profess are very rarely the outcome of conscious reflection, of our individual effort to arrive at the truth. Our ideas are hardly ever our own. Only too often they have been fed into us from external sources, from books, newspapers, and conversations, and we have accepted them, or rather received them, in a passive and unreflecting manner. When the appropriate stimulus occurs we automatically reproduce whatever has been fed into our system, and it is this purely mechanical reaction that passes for expression of opinion. Truly original thought on any subject is, indeed, extremely rare, though "original" does not necessarily mean "different," but rather whatever one creates out of one's own inner resources regardless of whether or not this coincides with something previously created by somebody else. Some people, of course, *try* to be different. This can, however, be a subtle form of conditionedness, for in trying to be different such people are still being determined by an object, by whatever or whoever it is they are trying to be different from. They are still re-acting, instead of really acting.

Besides being conditioned and mechanical, the reactive mind is repetitive. Being "programmed" as it were by needs of which it is largely unconscious, it reacts to the same stimuli in much the same way, and like a machine therefore goes on performing the same operation over and over again. It is owing to this characteristic of the reactive mind that human life as a whole becomes so much a matter of fixed and settled habit, in a world of routine. As we grow older, especially, we develop a passive resistance to change, preferring to deepen the old ruts rather than strike out in a new direction. Even our religious life, if we are not careful, can become incorporated into the routine, can become part of the pattern, part of the machinery of existence. The Sunday service or the mid-week meditation become fixed as reference points in our lives, buoys charting a way through the dangerous waters of freedom, along with the weekly visit to the cinema and the supermarket, the annual holiday at the seaside, and the seasonal spree.

Above all, however, the reactive mind is the unaware mind. Whatever it does, it does without any real knowledge of what it is doing. Metaphorically speaking, the reactive mind is asleep. Those in whom it predominates can, therefore, be described as asleep rather than awake. In a state of sleep they live out their lives; in a state of sleep they eat, drink, talk, work, play, vote, make love; in a state of sleep, even, they read books on Buddhism and try to meditate. Like somnambulists who walk with eyes wide open, they only appear to be awake. Some people, indeed, are so fast asleep that for all their apparent activity they can more adequately be described as dead. Their movements are those of a zombie, or a robot with all its controls switched on, rather than those of a truly aware human being. It is with this realization—when we become aware of our own unawareness, when we wake up to the fact that we are asleep—that spiritual life begins. One might, indeed, go so far as to say that it marks the beginning of truly human existence, though this would imply, indeed, a far higher conception of human existence than the word usually conveys—a conception nearer what is usually termed spiritual. This brings us to the second kind of relative mind, to what I have termed the creative mind.

The characteristics of the creative mind are the opposite of those of the reactive mind. The creative mind does not *re*-act. It is not dependent on, or determined by, the stimuli with which it comes into contact. On the contrary, it is active on its own account, functioning spontaneously, out of the depths of its own intrinsic nature. Even when initially prompted by something external to itself it quickly transcends its original point of departure and starts functioning independently. The creative mind can therefore be said to *respond* rather than to react. Indeed, it is capable of transcending conditions altogether. Hence it can also be said that whereas the reactive mind is essentially pessimistic, being confined to what is given in immediate experience, the creative mind is profoundly and radically optimistic. Its optimism is not, however, the superficial optimism of the streets, no mere unthinking reaction to, or rationalization of, pleasurable stimuli. By virtue of the very nature of the creative mind such a reaction would be impossible. On the contrary, the optimism of the creative mind persists despite unpleasant stimuli, despite conditions unfavorable for optimism, or even when there are no conditions for it at all. The creative mind loves where there is no reason to love, is happy where there is no reason for happiness, creates where there is no possibility of creativity, and in this way "builds a heaven in hell's despair."

Not being dependent on any object, the creative mind is essentially non-conditioned. It is independent by nature, and functions, therefore, in a perfectly spontaneous manner. When functioning on the highest possible level, at its highest pitch of intensity, the creative mind is identical with the Unconditioned; that is to say, it coincides with Absolute Mind. Being non-conditioned the creative mind is free; indeed, it is Freedom itself. It is also original in the true sense of the term, being characterized by ceaseless productivity. This productivity is not necessarily artistic, literary, or musical, even though the painting, the poem, and the symphony are admittedly among its most typical, even among its most striking, manifestations. Moreover, just as the creative mind does not necessarily find expression in "works of art," so what are conventionally regarded as "works of art" are not necessarily expressions of the creative mind. Imitative and lacking true originality, some of them are more likely to be the mechanical products of the reactive mind.

Outside the sphere of the fine arts the creative mind finds expression in productive personal relations, as when through our own emotional positivity others become more emotionally positive, or as when through the intensity of their mutual awareness two or more people reach out toward, and together experience, a dimension of being greater and more inclusive than their separate individualities. In these and similar cases the creative mind is productive in the sense of contributing to the increase, in the world, of the sum total of positive emotion, of higher states of being and consciousness.

Finally, as just indicated, the creative mind is above all the aware mind. Being aware, or rather, being Awareness itself, the creative mind is also intensely and radiantly alive. The creative person, as one in whom the creative mind manifests may be termed, is not only more aware than the reactive person but also has far greater vitality. This vitality is not just animal high spirits or emotional exuberance, much less still mere intellectual energy or the compulsive urgency of egoistic volition. Were such expressions permissible, one might say it is the Spirit of Life itself rising like a fountain from the infinite depths of existence, and vivifying, through the creative person, all with whom it comes into contact.

5. THE PERFECTION OF WISDOM—THE FLAVOR OF IRRELEVANCE

It's refreshing to have something which in a way you understand, but which in another way you don't understand at all.

AS SERIOUSLY PRACTICING BUDDHISTS we do need to be able to relate traditional teachings to our own personal experience. We need to work out how the Dharma bears upon our own lives, how it applies to the world we live in, and how to interpret ancient texts so as to be of practical and immediate concern to the situation in which we find ourselves. But on another level we should not be overconcerned with what is relevant to "me," interesting to "me," applicable to "my" situation in the West. It is all very well to expect Buddhism to be meaningful to where we are, here and now—but where is here and when is now? Is our conditioned existence all we are? In the end there needs also to be some element of the Dharma which is not relevant to our spiritual development at all. When it comes to transcending conditioned existence, the last thing we need is something useful. In fact it takes something quite irrelevant to transcend conditions—and then the pointless becomes the most relevant thing of all.

So in the *Diamond Sutra* we are still concerned with the Dharma, but we are not concerned with any of the things that we usually think of as constituting the Dharma—the things that we settle down and feel comfortable with. We are taking a rest from looking at ethics or meditation or impermanence; instead we are getting a breath of nonsense, a touch of Lewis Carroll or Edward Lear (without suggesting by this analogy that *Alice in Wonderland* is some kind of Zen text, of course).

The Perfection of Wisdom is like salt. An exclusive diet of it wouldn't do you much good, but you need a pinch of it in your spiritual diet all the time. It gives it a little flavor—the flavor of irrelevance. Otherwise, if it all becomes too relevant, well, you take it all too seriously—you think too much in terms of yourself as you are now. It's refreshing to have something which in a way you understand, but which in another way you don't understand at all.

What we have in the *Diamond Sutra* is a comprehensible but irrelevant meaning, with a further significance or purport that is relevant but is *not* comprehensible. It is not difficult to get at the meaning of the sentences, but to get at what I am calling the purport, the direction in which the words are pointing above and beyond the verbal meaning, is much more difficult. It may also sometimes be difficult to explain the connection between the meaning and the purport. What we may be sure of is that we can only get at the purport by constantly bearing the meaning in mind. One way to do this is to recite the words constantly, as one does in some visualization practices, repeating certain short verses over and over again. If we repeat the comprehensible but irrelevant words often enough, as monks have been doing for hundreds of years in the monasteries of Japan and the lamaseries of Tibet, something of the purport will begin to dawn on us.

6. The Shattering Nature of Reality

The experience of reality in what the Tantras call its "nakedness" can be a shattering experience.

THE PERFECTION OF WISDOM is one of the most important themes of the Mahayana, and it is dealt with principally in the group of scriptures known as Prajnaparamita sutras. There are more than thirty-five of these, some of enormous length and some very short indeed. One of the best known and most important of them is the *Vajracchedika Prajnaparamita* sutra, the discourse on the transcendental wisdom that pierces like the thunderbolt or cuts like the diamond. What transcendental wisdom pierces or cuts is our illusions, our wrong ideas, our false notions, our projections. We can even go so far as to say that it is destructive. It destroys our intellectual assumptions, usually adopted so unthinkingly. It destroys the psychological conditionings in which we are enmeshed. It destroys the emotional hang-ups to which we are so attached. It destroys, in short, ourselves as we are at present.

It is not always understood that wisdom, the *experience* of reality, is destructive. It is tempting to think of it as a pleasant extra, something comfortably added on to what we already are. But it isn't like that at all. The experience of reality in what the Tantras call its "nakedness" can be a shattering experience. One can even go so far as to say that any shattering experience has an element of reality in it. If an experience shatters, it is real—and if it doesn't shatter us, its authenticity may be questioned. This is not to say that this experience of breaking through or shattering needs to be traumatic—it can be very joyful.

Whether one can expect to have this kind of experience oneself all depends on the way one goes about one's spiritual practice. If you meditate for half an hour or an hour a day over a period of years, you will get results, but they will be slow in coming. However, if you meditate for ten or twenty hours a day, and keep that up, you can expect something much more dramatic to happen. Breaking through depends not so much on the kind of meditation you do as on the intensity with which you do it. And, of course, most people tend to take things quite easily. There is certainly room for a great deal more intensity in the spiritual practice of most western Buddhists. This should include concentrated attention upon the views that direct that intense practice, and a robust faith with which to meet the strong reactions and inner resistance that such intensity tends to provoke.

7. "ABOVE ME BROODS . . ."

Above me broods
A world of mysteries and magnitudes.
I see, I hear,
More than what strikes the eye or meets the ear.
Within me sleep
Potencies deep, unfathomably deep,
Which, when awake,
The bonds of life, death, time, and space will break.
Infinity
Above me like the blue sky do I see.
Below, in me,
Lies the reflection of infinity.

3 ← Views and Truths

1. WRONG VIEWS, RIGHT VIEWS, AND PERFECT VISION

…the total vision of the total human being…

TRADITIONALLY Buddhism distinguishes two kinds of view: wrong view and Right view. We may understand in general terms the difference between the two kinds of "philosophical" view or vision by making a simple analogy with ordinary physical vision. With good vision we see clearly and for a great distance. Good vision is unblinkered: we can see all around us. Good vision is also undistorted; nothing clouds or colors or refracts it. Conversely, poor vision may be weak in that we do not see very far or distinctly; it may be blinkered, restricted to a narrow field so that we see only what is straight in front of us; or it may be distorted, as when we look through a thick fog or through colored glass or bottle-glass.

Wrong view is very much like poor vision. First of all, it is weak. Our mental vision is weak when it lacks the concentrated energy to be derived from meditation. It is this energy that transforms a purely conceptual understanding of the truth into direct experience. If this energy is not there, then we do not see deeply into the true nature of things. We do not see things clearly or distinctly; we do not see them as they truly are.

Secondly, wrong view is blinkered. It is limited to a narrow range of experience, to what can be experienced through the five physical senses and the rational mind. It is to have just this narrow viewpoint from which to draw conclusions, to be unaware of other possibilities of perception or experience. On a very basic level this kind of wrong view is exemplified by the poverty of outlook of people who are interested only in their job, their family, the National Lottery, and television programs. Having no interest in world affairs, the arts and sciences, or personal development, they see life simply in terms of their own limited existence.

Thirdly, wrong view is distorted. Vision can be distorted by our mood—whether we are feeling happy or gloomy. It can be distorted by our likes and dislikes. If we dislike someone they seem to us to have all sorts of faults, whereas if we like someone we may see in them all sorts of perfections that they do not really possess. Our vision may be distorted, too, by prejudices regarding race, class, religion, or nationality. Thus wrong view is weak, limited to a narrow range of experience, and distorted by personal feelings and prejudices.

Right view, obviously, is the opposite of this. Right view is powerful. Based on the concentrated energy of meditation, it gives rise not just to conceptual understanding but also to direct experience of the truth. For this reason, it does not remain on the surface, but penetrates deep into the heart of things, and sees everything clearly and distinctly. Secondly, Right view is unlimited. It ranges over the whole field of human experience; it is not confined to what can be experienced through the physical senses or the rational mind. If it generalizes at all, those generalizations are made from the entire range of human experience in all fields, at all levels. Lastly, Right view is not distorted by emotion or prejudice; it sees things as they are.

The distinction between wrong view and Right view is of supreme importance in Buddhism. A view does not, after all, exist in the abstract, somehow apart from people. It belongs to someone. So if we can identify two kinds of view, we may also identify two kinds of people. People whose view of existence is limited, restricted, and distorted are known in Buddhism as *prthagjanas*—the "many-folk"—and as the name implies, they constitute the majority of people. Most people have not worked to develop themselves at all and consequently are just as nature made them, so to speak. On the other hand, there are those whose view is unlimited in extent, unrestricted in scope, and without any distortion whatsoever. These are known as *aryas,* the "spiritually noble." Such individuals, having worked to attain some degree of personal development, have remodelled themselves, at least to some extent. Of course, the crucial point about these categories is that it is possible to move from the one to the other—by developing awareness, by cultivating positive emotions, by raising the level of consciousness, and, above all, by discarding wrong views and developing right ones.

So these two—wrong view and Right view—are what we have to work with, practically speaking. However, there is a third kind of view—Perfect View, or rather Perfect Vision. Perfect Vision is Right view developed to the fullest possible extent. It is the total vision of the total human being at the highest conceivable level of his or her development. It is the unconditioned vision of the unconditioned reality. It is the vision that does not just look beyond space and time but is totally unconditioned by it, that totally transcends the ordinary framework of perception. Perfect Vision is the vision of the Enlightened One, the Buddha, the one who sees with wisdom and compassion.

For the most part, our own view is wrong view. Moreover, we tend to rationalize our wrong views, presenting them in systematic conceptual form. These rationalizations are the worldly philosophies, the various -isms and -ologies. Only occasionally do we have a flash of Right view—and such sparks of Right view derive ultimately from Perfect Vision. They become available to us through the Perfect Vision of the Buddha. If we can attend to what the Buddha has communicated of his vision of existence, we can momentarily rise to that level, at least in imagination, and see exactly where we stand. We will have a true philosophy that will enable us to understand the general principles that underlie the whole process of personal development, and that will give meaning and purpose to our lives.

2. No "Ready-made" Buddhist Answers

On the whole, people want to know what to think, which means something black and white. They want certainty. What they are certain about is less important to them than the certainty itself.

Most people put their faith and trust in someone who makes a strong impression, someone who is very emphatic and certain and self-confident. If you try to be careful about what you are saying, introducing qualifications where appropriate and suggesting that yours is only a certain way of looking at things, that there are other ways, and that one will have to make up one's own mind, you will make a comparatively feeble impression. On the whole, people want to know what to think, which means something black and white. They want certainty. What they are certain about is less important to them than the certainty itself. They will believe any farrago of nonsense as long as they have permission to believe in it absolutely. It is not clarity but certainty they are looking for. Certainty is security; and being exposed to the difficulties and confusions of having to think seriously is to be thrown into insecurity.

Many people seem to want to rush to take up views where, one may say, angels fear to tread. I have noticed this in, for example, Hindus with a smattering of religious knowledge. I remember on one occasion when I took the public jeep from Kalimpong to Siliguri, I was sitting in the front next to the driver when there was a hold-up of some sort, and the Bihari policeman who was controlling things, seeing there was a sadhu in yellow robes—myself—waiting there, and having nothing better to do for the moment, strolled up and started asking the usual questions: "Are you a holy man?" and so on. Then he began to tell me all about how the universe had evolved from Brahman, and how it was all unreal, and how the soul was the same as God. He held forth in this way for about fifteen minutes and then strolled off again. There was a Tibetan Buddhist sitting behind me who had observed all this with mounting horror: "That man was talking about the Dharma," he said at last, as if he couldn't believe his ears. That someone with a few undigested religious notions rattling around in his head should shoot his mouth off about them, in public, to a total stranger, had left him almost speechless.

As a Buddhist one finds that one has to resist a tendency in people to look for absolutist views. They might ask about a certain gifted but wayward Buddhist teacher, "Is so-and-so a Bodhisattva or is he a total fake?" Of course, the fact is that such a person is a complex human being and worthy of more than a snap judgment either way—or even somewhere precisely in between. Or someone might say, "What is the Buddhist view on such and such: hanging, abortion, astrology, extra-marital sex?" What they want is a definite, simple answer to take away with them.

But there is no "Buddhist view" as such; there is no hierarchy of authority from which to draw one's views. One can have one's own view as a Buddhist, but it will not have the stamp of authority that Christians have from God or the Bible or the Pope. And people generally want the kind of security one gets from a source of authoritative judgments. As a Buddhist, the best one can do sometimes is to say, "Here are the Four Noble Truths. Do what you can with these."

By looking for ready-made "Buddhist" answers—the party line—people also want to be able to categorize one as a Buddhist. Just as people say "He's an Aries," or or "She's an accountant," and think they've got that person dealt with, classified, docketed, likewise, if they can categorize Buddhism, then they can put one in the Buddhist category. Again, one needs to resist this tendency. It's a way of dismissing you, disposing of you, not being concerned with you as an individual. What to think of you has been settled by the fact that you are a Buddhist. This is not to say that one should be afraid of saying that one is a Buddhist—or an accountant, for that matter—but that one should not imagine (or hope) that being a Buddhist puts one as an individual in a category.

3. THE *ANATTA* DOCTRINE

The idea that the doctrine of no-self declares life to be worthless, meaningless, and in fact non-existent, is simply not Buddhist.

TRADITIONALLY, the extreme views that are held to be representative are eternalism and nihilism: the view that the self is eternally existent, and the view that the self is totally non-existent.[59] In ancient India these two views concerned whether or not the self survived death in some form. The eternalist view was that the self persisted unchanged from life to life; this is akin to the Christian view of the soul, that it survives death intact and goes on to heaven, hell, or limbo. The nihilistic view was that the whole psycho-physical organism was totally annihilated at the moment of death—which is of course the common, modern, secular view.

Such is, we may say, the psychological aspect of these two extreme views. They may also be put in a more metaphysical context. This version offers the view that mundane existence, in terms of the five *skandhas,* is ultimately real in some way, and at the other extreme the view that it is completely unreal and illusory at every level.

Thirdly, in ethical terms, nihilism and eternalism may be interpreted as the two extremes of self-indulgence and self-torture. It is possible to see self-indulgence—in the philosophy of "eat, drink, and be merry, for tomorrow we die"—as a form of nihilism. And it is possible to see self-torture—for the purpose of releasing the eternal soul from its prison—as a form of eternalism. However, this is just from the viewpoint of the traditional idea of the two extremes as representing attitudes to the possibility of life after death. It is probably more true to the psychological reality to say that self-indulgence expresses a belief in the absolute reality of mundane existence, while self-torture expresses self-hatred, and thus a desire for self-destruction and, by extension, for the destruction of mundane existence.

The Buddhist doctrine of *anatman,* no-self, is unfortunately sometimes interpreted in such terms as to appeal to this tendency toward self-destruction. If this teaching is interpreted as a total negation of the self, it will be very attractive to people who want to express their own self-hatred. Quite a few people seem to have this sort of attitude, a fascination with the *anatman* doctrine as an essentially life-denying principle. But the idea that the doctrine of no-self declares life to be worthless, meaningless, and in fact non-existent, is simply not Buddhist.

The *anatman* doctrine can also be used as a way of avoiding personal responsibility, or of sitting on one's natural energies. Anything one decides to do, particularly in an energetic or wholehearted way, becomes an expression of ego and thus doctrinally suspect. Again, this is a wrong view. The goal of Buddhahood is to go beyond the individual self, not to regress from the achievement of individual selfhood.

The ego is no more than the tendency to absolutize one's present state of being. It is not a thing, but a faulty interpretation. One is seeing something that just isn't there. The individual is there in a process of continuous change and therefore of ever-present potential development; delusion may also be there, in the form of a belief in a fixed, unchanging self or essence or soul. But that fixed, unchanging self or essence or soul or ego is not there; it never was, and it never will be. And because it isn't there, one can't do anything with it—get rid of it, go beyond it, or whatever. The best thing to do as far as the ego is concerned is just to forget about it.

We are not just an absence of self; we are an absence of *fixed* self, a flow of ever-changing components, physical and mental. The Buddha himself was evidently a powerfully distinct individual, with a very clear idea of who or what he was. To have a self-view means to identify oneself with a sort of cross-section of the flow of *skandhas* and imagine that one can arrest the flow at that point. It is just a state of arrested development, like being a child who says, "When I grow up I'm going to fill my house with toys and eat sweets all day," unable to imagine the transformation involved in growing up.

4. BREAKING THE FETTERS

We could even say that each one of us is simply a habit—probably a bad habit.

ACCORDING TO Theravada teaching, Stream-entry is achieved by breaking the first three of the ten fetters that are said to bind us to the Wheel of Life. These three fetters are usually described as: firstly, the fetter of belief in an essential, unchanging self; secondly, the fetter of doubt and indecision with regard to the Dharma; and thirdly, the fetter of attachment to religious observances as ends in themselves. Here, however, we are going to approach them in very general, even basic—or down-to-earth—terms, as: firstly, the fetter of *habit;* secondly, the fetter of *superficiality;* and thirdly, the fetter of *vagueness.*

The Fetter of Habit

A habit is something we are said to *have.* We have "the tendency or disposition to act in a particular way." However, as this dictionary definition makes clear, a habit consists of action, and action is an essential part of us, not just something added on, something we have. In fact, according to the Dhamma-Vinaya we are our actions. And this is the way we usually think of, and refer to, a person: someone is the sum total of his or her actions of body, speech, and mind, and doesn't exist apart from these.

The fact that we have a "tendency or disposition to *act* in a particular way" means, therefore, that we have a tendency or disposition to *be* in a particular way. We are not just the sum total of our actions; we are the sum total of our habits. We are our habits. We could even say that each one of us is simply a habit—probably a bad habit. The person we think of as George or Mary, and recognize as acting in a particular way, is simply a habit that a certain stream of consciousness has got into.

But since it has got into it, it can get out of it. It is like a knot tied in a piece of string: it can be untied. Breaking the fetter of habit means, essentially, getting out of the habit of being a particular kind of person.

It is only a habit you have got into. You don't *have* to be the way you are. There is no necessity about it. Breaking the fetter of habit means, therefore, getting rid of the old self, the past self. It means becoming a true individual; that is, becoming continually aware and emotionally positive, continually responsible, sensitive, and creative—continually creative of one's one self.

This is the meaning of the Buddhist doctrine of anatta or "no-self." It is not so much that we never have a self as that we always have a new self. And if each new self is a better one than the last, then we can say that spiritual progress is taking place.

It is not easy to get out of the habit of being the kind of person that we are. One of the reasons for this is other people. Not only have we ourselves got into the habit of being in a particular way, but other people have got into the habit of experiencing us as being in the habit of being in a particular way.

The people who experience us as what we were rather than as what we are—or what we are in process of becoming—represent a collective way of thinking, feeling, and acting. They represent the group as opposed to the individual. The group is the enemy of the individual— of the true individual—inasmuch as it will not allow the true individual to emerge from its ranks. It insists on dealing with you not as you are but as you were, and to this extent it tries to deal with someone who no longer exists. This tends to happen, for example, when one visits one's family after some time.

Becoming free of the group does not, of course, necessarily mean actually breaking off relations with the group. What it means is breaking away from the influence—the habit-forming influence—of the group.

The Fetter of Superficiality

To be superficial means to act from the surface of ourselves and, in consequence, to act without thoroughness or care; it is about acting in outward appearance rather than genuinely or actually. Now why should we do this? Why should we act superficially?

The reason is that we are divided. More often than not, the conscious rational surface is divided from the unconscious emotional depths. We act out of intellectual conviction but do not succeed in carrying the emotions with us. Sometimes, of course, we do act out of the fullness of our emotions but then, only too often, the rational mind holds back, and even, perhaps, does not approve. In neither case do we act totally, wholeheartedly. We do not act with the whole of ourselves and, therefore, in a sense, do not really act at all.

This state of affairs is very general. Superficiality is one of the curses of the modern age. Matthew Arnold, more than a hundred years ago, spoke of our "sick hurry," our "divided aims"—and that just about describes the situation. We are neurotically busy, without any real focus, any singleness of purpose. We don't truly, authentically, do anything. We don't do anything with the whole force of our being. When we love we don't really love, and when we hate we don't really hate. We don't even really think. We half do all these things.

It is the same, only too often, when we take up the spiritual life and try to follow the Dharma. When we meditate, it is only with part of ourselves. When we communicate, or when we work, again it is only with part of ourselves. Consequently we don't get very far: we don't really grow; we don't really develop. We don't carry the whole of our being along with us, so to speak. A small part of us is prospecting ahead, but the greater part is lagging far behind.

Breaking the fetter of superficiality therefore means acting with the whole of oneself: acting with thoroughness and care; acting genuinely and actually. It means, in a word, commitment. It means committing oneself to the spiritual life, committing oneself to being a true individual.

The Fetter of Vagueness

"Vague" means "indistinct, not clearly expressed or identified, of uncertain or ill-defined meaning or character." So why should anyone be vague? The fact is, we are vague when we are undecided, vague when we don't *want* to decide, and, above all, vague when we don't want to commit ourselves. Our vagueness is, therefore, a dishonest vagueness.

After all, spiritual life is very difficult. Growth and development is often a painful process (even though it is always enjoyable). Therefore we tend to shrink back. We keep our options open. We keep a number of different interests, or a number of different aims, on which we can fall back, and allow ourselves to oscillate between them, even to drift between them. At all costs we remain vague: woolly, foggy, shapeless, indistinct, unclear.

Breaking the fetter of vagueness means being willing to think clearly. It means giving time to thinking things out, having the determination to think things through. It means being prepared to look at what the alternatives really are, and to sort out one's priorities. It means being ready to make up one's mind. It means making a decision to choose the best and then to act wholeheartedly upon that choice. It means not postponing the moment of decision.

Creativity, Commitment, and Clarity

The three fetters—of habit, of superficiality, and of vagueness—are broken by means of Insight, that is, by means of knowledge and vision of things as they really are. In less traditional terms, they are broken by our becoming creative (in the sense of creative of our own new self), by becoming committed, and by becoming clear. When Insight arises, one enters the Stream, the Stream that leads directly to Enlightenment: one becomes a Stream-entrant and, being a Stream-entrant, one becomes a true individual. And as a true individual, one can experience *vimutti* (this being the Pali term for "freedom", "release", describing the state of mind of the Stream-entrant), one can enjoy the taste of freedom.

Two key points emerge from all this. The first is that only the true individual is really free; the second, that one becomes a true individual only by developing Insight: that is, by breaking the three fetters and thereby becoming creative, committed, and clear. This is freedom.

5. LIFE IS KING

Hour after hour, day
After day we try
To grasp the Ungraspable, pinpoint
The Unpredictable. Flowers
Wither when touched, ice
Suddenly cracks beneath our feet. Vainly
We try to track birdflight through the sky trace
Dumb fish through deep water, try
To anticipate the earned smile the soft
Reward, even
Try to grasp our own lives. But Life
Slips through our fingers
Like snow. Life
Cannot belong to us. We
Belong to Life. Life
Is King.

6. THE BUDDHIST ATTITUDE TO DEATH

After all, death is just as natural as life.

EVERYTHING IS IMPERMANENT. From the solar system to one's own breath, from instant to instant everything is changing, flowing, transient. When one remembers this, one can view things as being like clouds passing through the sky. One can't hang on to anything very determinedly when one knows that sooner or later one will have to give it up.

Every day the newspapers are full of reports of fatal accidents, and this gives, as well as the occasion for compassion, an opportunity for reflection. Human life is liable to unexpected termination; one may not live to a ripe old age. As Pascal said, just a grain of dust is sufficient to destroy us if it gets into the wrong place.[60] Life is very precarious. Such reflections can be sobering and fruitful; but they will be counterproductive if what they produce is a kind of neurotic timidity. One has to be sensitive to one's own nature in this regard.

A skull or a few bones, preferably human ones, can also be useful objects of reflection. It might sound strange or even amusing—we are sometimes inclined to laugh at death to cover up our fear of it—but this is standard practice among Tibetan Buddhists. (Of course, we have a precedent for it in the Western tradition, in Hamlet's contemplation of Yorick's skull in Shakespeare's play.) In fact, Tibetans tend to surround themselves with all kinds of things made of human bone: bone rosaries, thigh-bone trumpets, skull-cups. They take a common-sense view of death; they don't think there's anything morbid or macabre about it.

In the West, though, the very word death is supposed to send a shiver down one's spine. Not that the Christian tradition avoids the straightforward facts of death. Many ancient tombstones bear representations of skeletons and skulls, in some burial places bones are kept for visitors to see, and monks practice the constant recollection of death. Corpses are laid out for friends and relations of the dead person to come and have a look—and of course there is the tradition of the wake. Indeed, if we sweep death under the carpet in our modern culture, perhaps it is partly because the Christian tradition is less important to us than it used to be. The problem in our culture is not really denial but the tendency to identify the total self with the body, even when the soul has departed. According to some kinds of popular Christianity, the teaching of the resurrection of the body means the literal resuscitation of the corpse. It follows that when a man is buried the worms are eating *him*—not just his body, but him. This identification of the decomposing corpse with the deceased person gives death a peculiar sort of horror mixed with fascination.

But this is not the Buddhist way of looking at death—nor, come to that, the Hindu or Muslim way of looking at it. After all, death is just as natural as life. Tagore, the great modern Bengali poet, says, "I know

I shall love death, because I have loved life."[61] Life and death are opposite sides of the same thing. If you love life, you will love death; and if you can't love death, you haven't really loved life. It sounds paradoxical, but it is deeply true.

7. Reflections on Impermanence

Impermanence is what makes the path possible, for without it there could be no transformation or creativity.

REFLECTING ON IMPERMANENCE is so important because through it we begin to break down the tendency to over-identify with the body, and thus the delusion of a fixed self is weakened. This is the heart of the matter. An experience of bereavement, for all its pain, is a precious opportunity to grow. If everything changes, indeed must do so, then you can change too. You can develop and grow; you need not be confined to what you are at present, or have been in the past. Impermanence is what makes the path possible, for without it there could be no transformation or creativity. You would be stuck with your old self forever, with no hope of release. Think how terrible that would be! You might be able to put up with it for quite a while, but eventually life would become truly unbearable. Yet, paradoxically, here we are, clinging to this fixed view of self for all we are worth.

Impermanence is what enables us to turn our whole lives toward the ideal of Enlightenment. To speak of death is not necessarily to lapse into pessimism—it is just being realistic. Old age, grief, lamentation, and death are after all just facts. But life can still be positive, even though it sometimes involves having to face things we find unpleasant. If we are to grow, we will need to face those things, acknowledge them, and go beyond them. The overall process is positive, and the Buddhist vision expresses that positivity without seeing everything through a rosy mist or refusing to face unpleasant facts.

The recollection of death should therefore be as familiar to the Buddhist as it is strange to people who haven't given any thought to the fact that they will one day die. If you have never reflected on impermanence in any serious way, you will be in a difficult position when the time of your own death draws near. You won't suddenly be able to intensify your mindfulness if you haven't already developed sufficient momentum in your practice of it. This is when you will need to call your spiritual friends around you, to give you help and moral support. But although they will be able to help you to some extent, the best and wisest thing is to keep up your spiritual practice as an integral part of your life when you are free from sickness and danger. Do not leave it too late. One does not wish to be morbid, but we are reminded sometimes that we never know when we are going to be run over by the proverbial bus. The best policy is to concentrate your energies and pour them wholeheartedly not just into your practice of meditation or study, but into the whole of your spiritual life.

8. How to Reflect

Simply taking note of certain objective facts about existence is crucial to the process of growing up, of maturing in a truly human way.

THE SO-CALLED CORPSE MEDITATIONS are traditionally recommended for people of the greed type, the passionate type of person, because if you have always concentrated on the bright, agreeable, pleasant side of human life, you must remind yourself that there is another side. You may be very much attached to someone physically, for example, but if you are going to be truly aware of what you are attached to, you must ask yourself what is going to happen to it in ten, fifteen, thirty, a hundred years' time. The point of cultivating a deeper awareness of the more challenging aspects of human experience is not to take the sparkle out of life, but to help detach yourself from an over-preoccupation with the kind of beauty that is bound up with craving, and thus make yourself free to experience a more refined beauty.

But if you are of the hate type, it might not be good for you to practice these meditations because you already see life as essentially disagreeable, or even disgusting. You will need rather to remind yourself that life, and especially the aspect of life that concerns other people, has a bright side, an agreeable aspect. In such a case, the metta bhavana, the development of loving-kindness, will be a more suitable meditation practice.

Even if you are of the greed type, going out in search of corpses to meditate on is not necessarily the best approach. If you are so greedy by temperament that you are completely obsessed with material things and with other people on the purely physical level, then a visit to the cemetery, or a burning ground if you could find one, might be salutary (though with such a temperament you would be unlikely to go out of choice). But if you aren't of that extreme type, you can reflect upon death or even just upon impermanence. It will not have the kind of dramatic effect that trying to force oneself into an awareness of death may have. However, simply taking note of certain objective facts about existence is crucial to the process of growing up, of maturing in a truly human way. If you apply what you understand and experience to yourself, you will gradually deepen that awareness of impermanence to allow real insight to emerge.

Merely taking in one's natural surroundings can help with this exercise. It is easier in the countryside than in the city, but even in the city you can see impermanence as an immediate reality. When I lived in the East End of London there was a tree outside my window which I used to enjoy looking at, noticing its annual flourishing and withering: in the spring covered in blossom, in the summer in full leaf, and in the winter with no leaves at all. Even where there is no turning of the seasons to observe, one can still catch striking glimpses of the same reality. When I visited New Zealand, for example, although the native bush was virtually all evergreen, in the midst of the green I noticed skeletons of trees, bleached white by the sun. That was quite odd, a real memento mori, a skeleton at the feast. It was as if you were to go down to a beach full of healthy, bronzed people sunbathing and see at intervals human skeletons, bleached white, reclining among the sunbathers.

The Romans allegedly had skeletons at their feasts, dressed up with garlands of roses, to remind them that the feasting was going to end one day, for everybody. To us this would no doubt seem an unnecessarily morbid addition to our guest list. We don't even keep flowers in our rooms once the petals have begun to fall. But if you live in the countryside, you cannot pick and choose from its seasons, and that does give you a sense of the evanescence of things, if you are observant. You can also nourish this sense with the arts: reflections on transitoriness are of course the constant theme of both English nature poetry and Chinese and Japanese Zen Buddhist poetry.

In all these different ways one may deepen one's awareness of one's own existence, becoming more alert to the shortness of one's life, and learning to see things more constantly from this truer perspective. Nor is such a perspective at all negative—rather the opposite. As you start recognizing the impermanence of things, you realize that change is not just about decay and deterioration—things can also change for the better. Indeed, you can *make* them change for the better, so that change becomes not just change but transformation. This is symbolized by the Hindu figure of the dancing Shiva: although Shiva is apparently a violent, destructive figure, the symbolism is essentially positive because it represents the potential for transformation. Likewise, in Buddhist tradition, the Bodhisattva Avalokitesvara who appears in all the six realms of existence of the Wheel of Life reminds us that the possibility of transformation exists in every one of those realms.

Facing up to impermanence before old age forces us to do so helps us to make the most of life. Whereas many people start to take full advantage of life only when they get older and a bit wiser, if you are fortunate enough still to have youth on your side, you can reflect, while you are still young, "Here I am, alive, and with luck I will live for a few more years. In that time, I can really do something with my life, make it worthwhile, so that at the end of it I can look back and think, 'Well, I have had a wonderful opportunity, and thank heaven I have been able to take advantage of it.'"

The corpse meditation is therefore only the most hair-raising way of contemplating impermanence. There are many other practices concerned with the same basic theme and purpose that are better suited to most people's spiritual needs. It is said that one should do the corpse meditation in the full manner only if one has strong nerves—and indeed one should approach any version of the practice with caution and seriousness and a firm foundation of mindfulness and metta—especially metta toward oneself.

9. KARMA AND REBIRTH

From the Buddhist point of view the universe is an ethical universe.

OLD AGE, sickness, and death were the spurs to Siddhartha Gautama's quest, and what he realized when he became the Buddha somehow put an end to these things. It was not just that he came to terms with death; it was not even that he looked forward to death. He realized something—not intellectually but by way of direct perception—that transformed him into a new species of being to whom birth and death simply did not apply. At first, the Buddha doubted the possibility of communicating this alchemical insight—what he called "the truth of *pratitya-samutpada*"—to anyone else. But communicate it he did, deep and subtle as it was. And though his seminal formulation of *pratitya-samutpada* engendered, over the years, a vast and rich array of teachings, it remains the basis, the very foundation, of all of them. In philosophical terms, at least, it is the realization of this truth of universal conditionality which constitutes the essence of the Buddha's Enlightenment. Hence we describe it as the fundamental principle of Buddhism.

It originally took the form in his mind of a laconic, even bleak statement: "This is conditioned by that. All that happens is by way of a cause." However, the most renowned version of this principle derives, perhaps significantly, from an occasion when it was being communicated—and with dramatic success. In this particular instance it was in fact communicated not by the Buddha himself, but by one of his disciples, and it was imparted to a seeker after the truth who was to become the Buddha's chief disciple.

It was a few months after the Buddha's Enlightenment. A young brahmin from Bihar called Sariputra had gone forth from home, just as the Buddha had, along with his childhood friend Maudgalyayana. He was now on his own because the two of them had agreed that they would go off in different directions, and that whichever of them found an Enlightened teacher first would tell the other, thus doubling their chances, so to speak.

In the course of his travels, Sariputra happened to meet one of the Buddha's first five disciples, called Asvajit, who had by this time become Enlightened himself and gone forth to teach the Dharma. Very much impressed by the appearance of this wandering monk, who radiated tranquillity and happiness, Sariputra approached him, greeted him, and asked "Who is your teacher?" This might seem to us a rather direct way of addressing a total stranger. In Britain we generally open a conversation with a remark like "Nice weather we're having" or "Looks like it's beginning to clear up a bit now." But in India they tend to come straight to the point. So Sariputra asked the question that people in India still ask each other when they meet in this way, and Asvajit answered, "My teacher is Shakyamuni, the Sage, the Wise One of the Sakya tribe, the Buddha." Sariputra then put to Asvajit the second standard question—standard, but in this case, anyway, also momentous: "What does he teach?" Asvajit said, "Frankly, I'm a beginner. I really don't know much about the Dharma. But I can tell you in brief what it's about." And what he then said has since become famous throughout the Buddhist world in the form of a short Pali verse of just two lines. He said, or pronounced—or perhaps even declaimed:

> Of all those things that proceed from a cause, the Tatha-gata[62] has explained the cause, and also its cessation. This is the teaching of the great *sramana*.[63]

It seems that this stanza made a shattering, and at the same time liberating, impression on the mind of Sariputra. He had an instantaneous glimpse of the truth that it embodied. Transcendental insight arose in him, and he became a Stream-entrant on the spot. Obviously, the ground had been so well prepared that this most compressed exposition of the Dharma was enough to tell him his quest was at an end. He could go to his friend, Maudgalyayana, and tell him with confidence that he had found the Buddha.

You will find this verse of Asvajit's recorded, honored, and worshipped all over the Eastern Buddhist world. In Tibet, China, Japan, Thailand, Sri Lanka, it is found carved on stone monuments and clay tablets, printed on strips of paper to be stuffed inside images, and inscribed on plates of silver or gold. It is, we may say, the credo of Buddhism. If it seems rather dry and abstract, academic, uninspiring even, it certainly did not seem so to Sariputra. And when you really think about the principle of *pratitya-samutpada*—in whatever form it is put—when you meditate on it, when you really follow through its implications, you begin to understand the extraordinary impact it has had on the world. Whatever comes into existence on whatever level does so in dependence on conditions, and in the absence of those conditions it ceases to exist. This is all it says. But if anything is Buddhism, this is Buddhism.

What it is saying is that, from the viewpoint of the Enlightened mind, the outstanding feature of all phenomena, whether physical or psychical, is that they are conditioned. The unceasing flux of things, both material events and states of mind, is a process of interdependent stages, each of which comes about through the presence of conditions and, in its turn, conditions the stages succeeding it. Rainfall, sunshine, and the nourishing earth are the conditions from which arises the oak tree, whose fallen leaves rot and form the rich humus from which the bluebell grows. A jealous attachment will have consequences that may lead to murder. Nothing phenomenal is spontaneously produced without preceding conditions, or itself fails to have consequences. And it is the process of becoming aware of this law of conditionality that gradually liberates us from all conditions, leading to the freely functioning, spontaneous creativity of Enlightenment.

If we are reasonably clear about what it was that constituted the Buddha's realization, we can move on to look at how it actually dealt with the questions that Siddhartha originally set out to answer. What about old age, sickness, and death? Where do the immutable facts of our physical decay fit into the whole process of conditionality? Does this "unceasing flux of things" continue beyond death—or is death the end? These questions, of course, are not abstract or theoretical for us. The mystery of death which so troubled primitive humanity is still a mystery. Even these days, when we apparently know so much, you only need to give a talk called "The Tibetan Book of the Dead" or "What happens after death" or "Where you go when you die" to draw record crowds. And there is always a healthy market for books about death and dying. We may think things have changed immeasurably since primitive times, but they haven't changed much when it comes to our understanding of death. Indeed, if anything, the "problem" of death has become more pressing.

We are not, however, talking here about one single problem of death common to everyone. The way we feel about death, and the way we come to terms—or not—with death, is not exactly the same as the way other people feel about it. And people's feelings and ideas about death have changed over time, over the centuries, as well. Putting the problem of death into some kind of historical perspective, we may say that it all really began when mankind first started growing crops, in the age of the great river valley civilizations. This was perhaps ten or fifteen thousand years ago. At that time the world began to take on an aspect that was less hostile and mysterious, but people were still in the dark about the greatest of all mysteries—death. The mystery, in fact, grew deeper and darker, and it seemed to weigh on people's minds more oppressively than ever before. And there was a reason for this. People no longer wandered about in roving bands; they lived in villages and towns, even in great cities. Civilization as we know it, so to speak, had begun. Life had become more secure and comfortable, and people enjoyed it more. And having begun to enjoy it, they wanted to go on enjoying it. They didn't want to leave their wives or husbands, their children, their houses and their neatly cultivated fields, their singing and their dancing, their games of chance and their religious rites—but one day they would have to, and they knew it. The thought of death threw a shadow over the sunlight of their lives. What was life for, if it had to end so soon? You had just a few short years of youth, pleasure, and prosperity, and after that, just a blank, a void, with nothing apparently surviving—perhaps some ghostly wraith twittering in the darkness, but nothing more.

What could you do about it? It seemed that you could do nothing at all. Most people just tried to forget about it and enjoy life as much as possible while they could. "Eat, drink, and be merry, for tomorrow we die," expressed the substance of their philosophy. A few who were made of sterner stuff immersed themselves in action. They performed heroic deeds—went about slaying monsters, fighting battles, conquering kingdoms. They tried to make a name for themselves so that even though they might perish—probably sooner rather than later— their names would live on after them, so they hoped, forever. But even these heroes, in their more reflective moments, saw that this was all a bit pointless.

Human life, it seemed, was not just a mystery, but a tragedy. This mood is reflected in the traditions and tales of ancient cultures, which were eventually written down to become the earliest examples of our literature. We find it in the Babylonian epic of Gilgamesh, from around 3000 BCE, and in Homer's account of the fall of Troy, the

Iliad, composed over 2,000 years later. It is there in the Anglo-Saxon epic poem *Beowulf,* dating from the eighth century, and it is perhaps even more powerfully and bitterly expressed in the Bible, in the Book of Ecclesiastes, the "Book of the Preacher." The vanity of human ambition in the face of death, the great leveller, is a favorite theme in ancient literature, and has inspired the same sort of thing in more recent times:

> The boast of heraldry, the pomp of pow'r,
> And all that beauty, all that wealth e'er gave,
> Awaits alike th'inevitable hour:
> The paths of glory lead but to the grave.[64]

But this was not the whole story. It was only half the story—the western half. Further east, people had started to take a different attitude, and had, in fact, arrived at some sort of solution to the mystery of death, which of course also meant some sort of solution to the mystery of life. What they perceived was that death was not the end. Human beings did not just vanish. After a time, they came back in a new body, in accordance with the nature of the deeds they had performed in their previous life. This perception made its first appearance in India at about the time of Homer (ca. 800 BCE), and from India thereafter spread widely. The first clear reference to it is found in the *Brihadaranyaka Upanishad,* in which the idea is represented as a highly esoteric teaching, to be communicated only to the chosen few. But as the idea spread, it became known, in a more organized, systematized form, as the teaching of karma and rebirth.

When people in the West go flocking along to a lecture on karma and rebirth, or the *Tibetan Book of the Dead,* what they really want to know is: "What is going to happen to me when I die? Is death the end, the absolute full stop, or not?" The fact is, if we could be assured that death was not the end, there would be no problem at all. If people knew with absolute certainty that they weren't going to just disappear when they died, they would be a lot less inclined to go and hear a lecture on karma and rebirth, or to snap up the latest commentary on the *Tibetan Book of the Dead*. For us, death is the problem. But in the East, especially the Hindu and Buddhist East, it is rather different. People are not so bothered about death there. For them, death is natural and inevitable—and so is rebirth. You die and you are reborn, you die again and you are reborn again—that's just the way it is. It's not a matter for speculation at all. In the East it is not death that is the problem. The problem is how to escape from the whole process of birth and death. How can you reach a state in which you will no longer be subject to birth and death? The problem is dying and being born time and time again, through endless ages. So the question is carried a stage further: what for the West is a solution of the problem is for the East a problem in itself, requiring a further solution. And this is where the Buddha's discovery of the universal principle of conditionality comes in.

When, in the course of the Enlightenment experience, the Buddha surveyed the whole vast range of conditioned existence, he saw that everything, from the lowest to the highest, was subject to the universal law of conditionality. And he also saw that this universal law operates in two distinct modes: a cyclical mode and a spiral mode. In the cyclical mode, there is action and reaction between opposites. We experience pleasure and pain, vice and virtue, birth and death—and usually what happens is that we swing back and forth between them. Life is followed by death, which is in turn followed by new life. Pain is followed by pleasure which is again followed by pain. At all levels of life—physical, biological, psychological, sociological, historical—this same cyclical process can be found to be operating. Empires rise only to fall; growth must be succeeded by decay; health, wealth, fame, and status have old age, sickness, death, loss, and oblivion as their inevitable outcome.

In the spiral mode of conditionality, on the other hand, there is the possibility of real and permanent growth. Each factor in this process, rather than reversing the effect of the previous one, increases its effect. For example, instead of an oscillation between pleasure and pain, you go from pleasure to happiness, then from happiness to joy, from joy to rapture, from rapture to bliss, and so on indefinitely. And this spiral mode can be applied to life and death just as much as to anything else. The Buddha saw that as well as being subject to the endless round of birth and death, it was possible for human beings to enter the spiral path of spiritual development, which was "the way to the door of the Deathless," the way beyond the opposites of life and death.

When applied to the process of life and death, the principle of conditionality gave rise to one of the most famous and important—and most frequently misunderstood—of Buddhist teachings: karma and rebirth. And this is the first thing to understand about karma, that this is all it is. It is just an application of the principle of conditionality. Nothing mysterious, nothing odd, nothing strange, nothing occult. Karma, in the most general terms, represents the law of conditionality at work on a certain plane of existence. This has to be emphasized, because one major source of confusion seems to be the idea that karma *is* the Buddhist teaching of cause and effect, and that it is universal—which is not the case. The universal principle is conditionality, and karma is only one of the ways in which conditionality operates. This point may be clarified by referring to a Buddhist teaching which dates from considerably later than the Buddha's own lifetime: the teaching of the five *niyamas,* which comes from the analytical and systematizing philosophical tradition of the Abhidharma. These five *niyamas* are a very useful formulation because, as is the way with the Abhidharma, they draw together strands which are otherwise rather loose and disconnected as we find them in the original suttas.

The word *niyama* is a term common to Pali and Sanskrit meaning a natural law, a cosmic order. According to this teaching there are five of them, showing the law of cause and effect at work on five different levels. The first three are straightforward enough, as they can be related to Western sciences. Firstly, there is *utu-niyama. Utu* means non-living matter. Nowadays people are beginning to doubt whether there is any such thing as non-living matter, but let's call it that for the time being. In other words, this is the physical, inorganic order of exis-tence. *Utu-niyama* is therefore the law of cause and effect as operative on the level of inorganic matter. It very roughly embraces the laws of physics and chemistry and associated disciplines.

The second *niyama* is *bija-niyama*. *Bija* means "seed," so *bija-niyama* deals with the world of living matter, the physical organic order whose laws constitute the science of biology.

Then there is *citta-niyama*. *Citta* is "mind," so *citta-niyama* is con-ditionality as operative in the world of mind. The existence of this third *niyama*, therefore, implies that mental activity and development are not haphazard, but governed by laws, and it is important that we understand what this means. We are used to the idea of laws operat-ing on the level of physics, chemistry, and biology, but we are not so used to the idea that similar laws might govern mental events. In the West we are more inclined to the view that mental events just happen, without any particular causation. To some extent and in some quar-ters, the influence of Freud has begun to shift this assumption, but the idea that mental phenomena arise in dependence on conditions is not one that has yet penetrated deeply into popular thinking. It is there in Buddhism, however, in this teaching of *citta-niyama*, the law of cause and effect as operative in the world of mind—and we may say that it is a concept which corresponds to the modern science of psychology.

Fourthly: *kamma-niyama*. *Kamma* (Pali) is of course more popu-larly known in its Sanskrit form, *karma*, and it means "action," but in the sense of deliberately willed action. So it is traditionally, and para-doxically, said sometimes that karma is equivalent to *cetana* (voli-tional consciousness), that is, that action equals volition: "for as soon as volition arises, one does the action, whether by body, speech, or mind." *Kamma-niyama* therefore pertains to the world of ethical responsibility; it is the principle of conditionality operative on the moral plane.

It is perhaps difficult for those of us with a background of Western thought on morality to understand how this works. In ordinary social life, if you commit a crime, you are arrested and brought before the judge or magistrate, tried and convicted, sentenced, and sent to jail or fined. Committing the crime and being punished are quite separate events, and there is someone or something—society, the police, the judge, the law—who punishes you. Our tendency is to apply this legal model when it comes to morality as a whole. We think of sin and the punishment of sin, virtue and the reward of virtue. And traditionally we have tended to think in terms of a judge too: somebody who sees what you do, and punishes or rewards you accordingly—the judge being, of course, God. People imagine God as holding a sort of tremendous quarter sessions, with everybody hauled up in front of him, and the angels and demons standing around like police witnesses. It is still official Christian doctrine that when you die you face your judge, and this is a terrible thought for the orthodox Christian— that you are going to be put in the dock before the Transcendental Beak and then bundled off wherever he sends you. The dramatic possibilities inherent in the doctrine have made for some terrific literature, music, drama, and art—Michelangelo's tremendous painting of the Last Judgment in the Sistine Chapel is just one notable example. But it also makes for rather poor philosophy, and a mode of thinking from which we are still suffering a ghastly hangover.

The Buddhist point of view is totally different, and it may seem distinctly odd to us, with our approach to ethics—almost whether we like it or not—underpinned by Christian theology. In Buddhism there is a law but no lawgiver, and no one who administers the law. I have heard Christian missionaries arguing with Buddhists and insisting that if you believe in a law, there must be a lawgiver—but this is quite specious. After all, there is a law of gravity, but there isn't a god of gravity pushing and pulling things. The law of gravity is just a generalized description of what happens when objects fall. In the same way we don't have a god of heredity, or a god of sexual selection. These things just happen; they work themselves.

It is much the same on the moral plane, according to Buddhism. The law administers itself, so to speak. Good karma naturally results in happiness, and bad karma naturally results in misery. There is no need for anybody else to come along, look at what you've done, and then fit the punishment or the reward to the deed. It happens of its own accord. "Good" and "bad" are built into the structure of the universe. This might sound dreadfully anthropomorphic—and I am putting it rather crudely here—but what it really means is that from the Buddhist point of view the universe is an ethical universe. Putting it more precisely, the universe functions according to conditionality, and this operates at the karmic level in a way which we could describe as ethical, in that it conserves ethical values. This is *kamma-niyama.*

The fifth and last *niyama* is *dhamma-niyama. Dhamma (dharma* in Sanskrit), which is a word with a number of different possible applications, here means simply spiritual or transcendental as opposed to mundane. So the principle of conditionality operates on this level too. Exactly how it does so, however, has not always been made very clear. It must be said that some of the more popular traditional examples of the functioning of this *niyama* are rather childish and superficial. For example, many legends report that when the Buddha gained Enlightenment, and also when he died—and indeed on other momentous occasions—the earth shook and trembled in six different ways; and this, according to some commentators, was due to the operation of *dhamma-niyama.*

In fact we do not have to look very far in order to locate a more sensible and helpful interpretation. The obvious key, it seems to me at least, is in the distinction between the two types or modes of conditionality. The first four *niyamas,* including *kamma-niyama,* are all types of conditionality in the cyclical sense, in the sense of action and reaction between pairs of opposites. But *dhamma-niyama* corresponds to the spiral type of conditionality, and as such constitutes the sum total of the spiritual laws which govern progress through the stages of the Buddhist path.

Thus karma is not the law of conditionality in general, but only that law as operating on a certain level—the ethical level, the plane of moral responsibility. This means we cannot assume that what befalls us necessarily does so as a result of our past actions, because karma is only one of the five levels of conditionality. What happens to us may be a result of physical, biological, psychological, ethical, or spiritual factors. In all likelihood, it will involve a complex combination of factors, bringing several of the *niyamas* into play.

10. IS IT NECESSARY FOR A BUDDHIST TO BELIEVE IN REBIRTH?

The very survival of human life on this planet seems to many of us more pressing than any consideration of future rebirths.

THERE IS NO NEED to assent to the idea of karma and rebirth in order to be a practicing Buddhist. Any account of Buddhism as traditionally handed down tends to bring it in at some point, but there are plenty of texts and teachings which present the path simply as the path, making no reference to karma and rebirth at all. If the Buddhist tradition holds good, then as our understanding deepens, the truth of karma and rebirth will presumably become clearer. After all, Buddhists have disagreed over many things, but no teacher of any school or sect has ever suggested that belief in karma and rebirth might be a wrong view—except in the sense that time itself, mundane existence itself, is not ultimately real. The idea of rebirth, one could say, follows logically upon the fundamental tenet of Buddhism that actions have consequences. However, one doesn't have to be completely logical in order to follow the Buddhist path, and it is possible to draw motivation for one's practice by considering the operation of karma in this life without necessarily taking rebirth into account.

Of course, however logical belief in it may be, rebirth is not the only possible answer to the universal question "What happens when we die?" For many people the Buddhist conception of rebirth seems more or less self-evident. But there are, obviously, other views on the matter. In fact there are three, or possibly four, views to choose from. The first view is that one will exist after death—in heaven or elsewhere, though not again on earth—but that one did not exist before this life. This is the Christian view, or, at least, that is the view which has been held almost universally throughout Christian history. One or two of the early Greek Christian scholars, like Origen, did believe in some sort of pre-existence before physical birth. Their idea was that the soul, which one inherited from one's parents, ultimately came from Adam. This belief—which amounted to a belief in a sort of group soul of which one's individual soul is a part—was known as Traductionism (because one's soul is "traduced" or conveyed from Adam).

Christian opinion is more divided on what happens after death. Some believe that the soul created by God is immortal, and that it eventually goes to heaven or hell—or, in the case of unchristened babies, to Limbo—for all eternity. Others take the view that the soul is created mortal and dies with the death of the body until it is revived, either shortly after death or—according to, for example, Seventh Day Adventists and Jehovah's Witnesses—at the time of the Last Judgment. Then one goes either to heaven or to hell—though the Seventh Day Adventists replace eternal torment with a much kinder final solution for the condemned, which is that God simply annihilates them.

The second possible view is the strictly materialist one: the belief that there is just this life with no kind of existence whatsoever before or after. The third possible view is purely theoretical; it would be the view that there is just this life and a succession of previous lives, but no next life—but no one, to the best of my knowledge, actually holds this view. Finally, the fourth possible view is that there is a past life or lives, a present life, and a future life or lives.

Most people find that one of these views seems more satisfactory than the others. No one view is altogether free from difficulties; but personally I have come to the conclusion that the idea of rebirth fits best. And the most telling confirmation of its likelihood would seem to lie not in some objective intellectual demonstration but in a feeling—a quite definite and powerful feeling—that develops through one's life.

This is something one can't appreciate when one is young, unless one is rather exceptional. But as one gets older, one starts seeing that one's whole life has had a certain clear direction or tendency which cannot be accounted for fully by any accumulation of circumstances within this present life, but which definitely seems to originate from what one can only assume is a previous life. Furthermore, one gets a strong feeling that this trend isn't just going to stop, but will continue after one's death. If one is relatively observant and reflective I think one cannot but entertain quite seriously the idea that one has come into this life with a propensity, even an agenda, already in place and that one will project it—project oneself—beyond the conclusion of one's life.

One can get a sense of this from telling one's life story to a friend or friends. This is a useful and powerful practice which often brings to the surface half-forgotten aspects of one's life and allows one to discover patterns in one's experience. And one theme that frequently emerges as one tells one's life story is a sense that in the business of growing up something important has been lost along the way. Quite a number of people have this feeling, that when they were young, before they got caught up in worldly responsibilities, they really did have a sense of what life was all about, before it all got overlaid by the dense complex of adult experience. It's as though we lose contact with our true feelings, our true self, even—not just in a psychological way that requires some psychotherapeutic solution, but in a definitely spiritual way.

In our early years many of us have experiences or feelings that seem to belong not to this world but elsewhere—or that even seem to indicate that we belong elsewhere. A few years later, when one starts to think and feel as an individual without yet being weighed down with responsibilities, one wants to find one's way back to one's origins, back to a truer, more innocent experience, and take that as one's starting point.

All this is not to suggest that there is some kind of primeval innocence about a child, or that children are in some way in touch with the

222 ~ THE ESSENTIAL SANGHARAKSHITA

Absolute. Unfortunately, one can get a sentimental and mistaken impression of this sort from some of the English poets: Vaughan, for example—"Happy those early days when I / Shined in my Angel-infancy"; or Wordsworth—"trailing clouds of glory do we come / From God who is our home." Wordsworth himself is a very clear, though unusual, example of someone who achieved a true vision in early adolescence which he managed to sustain well into his thirties. William Blake is another—indeed, he never really lost contact with his childhood. Though he was a very mature person he never grew up at all in the sense of becoming corrupted with (in Traherne's phrase) "the dirty devices of the world."

There will always be people who say that it is a necessary part of one's development to taste something of the dirty devices of this world, but this is a wrong view. Ideally, one should try to remain an adolescent in this positive sense for as long as possible. One should seek to deepen one's vision, to mature it—but not to lose it. To return to the idea of rebirth, it's as though when we are young we are in touch with something from a previous life. One may not be aware of it as a small child, but as one comes up to adolescence one becomes old enough to have a sense of it—though not, perhaps, old enough to appreciate how precious it is, or how easily it is lost.

Such experiences lead many people to see the idea of rebirth as quite reasonable, even obvious. However, if we find it difficult to take it to heart, we do not thereby lose our motivation for the spiritual life—at least, not necessarily. In fact, in some Buddhist countries the doctrine of karma and rebirth sometimes provides an excuse for postponing any real spiritual effort. It is even said that it isn't possible to gain Enlightenment any longer—the Buddha lived so long ago and there aren't any Enlightened teachers around any more—so our best bet is to accumulate merit, hope for good rebirths, and wait a few thousand years for the next Buddha to reappear, in the hope that we will get a chance to become his disciples. That will be the time to make an effort to gain Enlightenment. So some people believe—but it is a disastrously wrong view. It is better to disbelieve in karma and rebirth and follow the path anyway than to believe in karma and rebirth and make that one's excuse for not following the path here and now.

The traditional assumption that it is concern for one's future rebirth that motivates one to take up Buddhism is simply not the way most people think in the West today. People tend to become interested in Buddhism, or start practicing meditation, because it seems to offer a solution to psychological problems, or an intellectually respectable alternative to a purely materialist philosophy. Many practicing Buddhists may be said to take a frankly agnostic or even skeptical attitude to the idea of rebirth. The very survival of human life on this planet seems to many of us more pressing than any consideration of future rebirths.

Nowadays we can see things happening much more quickly than people could in more traditional and stable societies. It seems as though the whole process of life has speeded up, so that we can see the results of karma in this life itself. We are continually made aware through the media that we are teetering on the edge of global catastrophe, and this deepens our sense of responsibility. Never mind future lives; if we don't act now something terrible will happen in *this* life. (Of course, one can also think in terms of the consequences of our actions for future generations.) On a more personal level, too, one may conclude that only through some kind of spiritual development will one be able to transcend one's immediate painful conditions in this life. In these ways it is possible to accept the principle of karma within the much narrower context and more limited timescale of a single lifespan. Some people derive sufficient inspiration from thinking in terms of transforming their lives and the world around them, without needing to consider a long view of futurity at all.

Alternatively, one can take a completely opposite, more positive, perspective to the traditional one. Within the framework of karma and rebirth one is usually thinking in terms of escaping from something. Some Tibetan lamas teaching in the West make a point of describing in vivid detail all the different hells and heavens that await us—what will happen to you if you do this, what will happen to you if you do that—and this uncompromising, even dogmatic laying down of traditional doctrine evidently has a strong effect. But many western Buddhists see this approach as unnecessarily fundamentalist. For them the spiritual life has its own intrinsic appeal which overrides the fear of any unpleasant contingencies attendant upon the worldly life, whether here and now or in the future. This innate love for the spiritual life should be encouraged. There are people who do not need to be told that they will suffer if they follow the worldly life, because they see spiritual development as good in itself.

Of course, the doctrine of karma and rebirth need not be intimidating. Some people are positively invigorated by the prospect of practicing the spiritual life for life after life after life, gathering momentum over eons of time and visiting all sorts of Buddha-worlds as described in the Mahayana sutras. That others will find the mind-boggling duration of three *asamkheyyas*[65] of lifetimes simply depressing testifies to the necessity of developing an appropriate motivation of one's own.

But whatever we think about rebirth, we can still take karma seriously. Karma, it should be noted, is only one of the five levels on which conditionality operates (see previous section). This is an aspect of the teaching that is not always made explicit in the Mahayana, although it is standard Theravadin teaching.[66] (Indeed, not all Mahayana Buddhists would even agree that conditionality is multi-faceted in this way; in some Mahayana traditions karma has become very dominant indeed.) But taking the Theravadin line on this, we can say that everything that happens does so as the result of a network of conditions, involving causal links which can be of a physical, biological, psychological, karmic, or transcendental nature. While karma—the level on which our skillful actions bring happiness for us and our unskillful actions bring suffering—is a causal factor in our lives, it does not follow that everything that happens to us is a result of our karma. Nonetheless, an understanding of the karmic level of conditionality is crucial to us because it is something on which we can rely. If we act skillfully, joy is sure to follow; if we act unskillfully, we are letting ourselves in for suffering we could have avoided.

This insight can be traced back to the very earliest Buddhist teachings, to the first two verses of the *Dhammapada,* which state:

> Unskillful mental states are preceded by mind, led by mind, and made up of mind. If one speaks or acts with an impure mind suffering follows him even as the cart-wheel follows the hoof of the ox.

> Skillful mental states are preceded by mind, led by mind, and made up of mind. If one speaks or acts with a pure mind happiness follows him like his shadow.[67]

As these verses make clear, there is a connection between our mind and the nature of our future life or lives. According to the doctrine of karma and rebirth, our actions have a direct effect on our own being by modifying the patterns of habit, the conscious and unconscious volitional drives, which constitute the most essential part of us. This "essential nature" is not unchangeable; on the contrary, it can change in any direction at any time. It carries on through death and into another rebirth, in accordance with the karma that has accumulated during the previous life.

4 ⤝ Buddhism among -isms and -ologies

1. Religion as Revelation or Discovery

Religion-as-Discovery would envisage the dharmic or normative life not as the engraftment of some exotic blossom on the barren stock of humanity but as the flowering forth of its native perfection from the seed within.

T HE PROBLEM of whether Religion is essentially a revelation of truth *to* humanity or a discovery of truth *by* humanity is the intellectual formulation of a spiritual difficulty which each one of us experiences in the course of his or her quest for Reality. The most obvious and natural grouping of the various religious sects of the world is, therefore, into those for whom Religion consists in revelation, and those for whom it consists of discovery, of the Truth. This division is not simply theoretical, since each of these definitions of Religion has exercised a profoundly modifying influence upon the entire body of the beliefs and practices of the religions which were, whether consciously or unconsciously, dominated by it. Nor is this division wholly new. Far-Eastern Buddhists have long been familiar with the classification of religions into those depending on "self-power," in Japanese *jiriki,* and those depending on "other-power," or *tariki.* And in India religious aspirants are sometimes spoken of as displaying the characteristics of the young monkey, which clings fast to the hair of its mother's belly, and of the kitten, which is simply carried about helpless in her mouth.

Religion-as-Revelation holds that the existence of Religion in the world, and therefore the possibility of the attainment of Salvation or Emancipation by man, is ultimately dependent on the Object, the Other, and that the initiative in the matter belongs wholly to It or Him. It conceives the spiritual life not as the progressive actualization of a perfection potentially present in human beings but as the acceptance of something which we would never have been able to acquire by means of our own unaided efforts. Consequently, it tends to stress the weakness and sinfulness of human nature and to emphasize the necessity of extra-terrestrial intervention in the affairs of humanity. It is therefore only natural that Reality should be conceived as personal, and that the founders of the various religions and sects should be regarded as prophets or messengers sent from, or as full or partial incarnations of, Him. The written record of the message, teaching, or life of each such founder is invariably regarded as the word of God Himself, and to doubt, question, or criticize it is considered not only to preclude all possibility of salvation but even to run the risk of eternal damnation. Religion-as-Revelation therefore places the strongest possible emphasis on faith in God, faith in His prophet, messenger, or incarnation, faith in His infallible Word, faith in His Church, faith in His priest. Unfortunately, the beliefs of the various founders, scriptures, and churches which are included in this group of religions often disagree not only among themselves but also with those which are included in the other group. Hideous fanaticism and ferocious persecution thus ensue. Since each such religion regards its own particular revelation as the supreme and incontrovertible source of Truth the possibility of an appeal to reason and experience is automatically precluded. Obviously God would not wittingly contradict Himself. One revelation must therefore be true, and the remainder false, that is to say, not revelations at all but simply human fictions and inventions. Moreover, Religion-as-Revelation's house is divided not only against itself but against many other houses as well—against Science, for instance, which has succeeded in demonstrating the fallibility of many an infallible scripture.

Religion-as-Discovery, on the other hand, holds that Religion is essentially a manifestation of the human spirit, that as human beings we are able to discover the Way to Truth ourselves by means of our own unaided human efforts, that the attainment of liberating knowledge depends upon the subject or self, and that the initiative in the matter rests ultimately within one's own volition. It would envisage the dharmic or normative life not as the engraftment of some exotic blossom onto the barren stock of humanity but as the flowering forth of its native perfection from the seed within. Consequently, it is inclined rather to inspire us by appealing to our innate strength and goodness than to discourage us by dwelling upon our mistakes and failures. Instead of imagining an arbitrary divine intervention to be the most important event in history it asserts the supremacy of natural law and maintains that the aspiration toward emancipation must, like every other process, proceed in accordance with an eternal and universal order (*sanatana dharma*). It is therefore hardly surprising that Religion-as-Discovery conceives Reality as a supra-personal principle of knowledge or state of consciousness or that it regards the religious founder simply as one who, after realizing that principle or state, teaches humanity the way thereto. The records of his life and teachings are only a map describing the Way, a raft to cross the stream, or a finger pointing to the moon. They demand not blind faith but clear-sighted understanding, and they appeal not to some infallible authority but to reason and experience. Religion-as-Discovery is therefore not only tolerant of all other religious beliefs and practices, howsoever divergent from its own, but is able to join hands with earnest seekers after truth in every sphere of human activity. It sees Science not as an enemy but as a friend and fellow worker.

2. The Buddha's Attitude toward the Teachings of his Time

He knew that a positive method of teaching was more appealing, more likely to find entrance into the hearts and minds of his auditors, than a purely negative and destructive one, however correct and logical the latter might be.

> "Now Kalamas, do not ye go by hearsay, nor by what is handed down by others, nor by what people say, nor by what is stated on the authority of your traditional teachings. Do not go by reasoning, nor by inferring, nor by argument as to method, nor from reflection on and approval of an opinion, nor out of respect, thinking a recluse must be deferred to. But, Kalamas, when you know, of yourselves: 'These teachings are not good; they are blameworthy; they are regarded with contempt by the wise: these teachings, when followed out and put in practice, conduce to loss and suffering'—then reject them."[68]

THE REAL IMPORT of this oft-quoted but much misunderstood passage should be carefully noted. It was not intended as a vindication of "free thought"; neither does it give *carte blanche* to rationalistic skepticism. Rationalism is in fact explicitly rejected. The Kalamas were no more disposed to question the possibility of a transcendental attainment than the Buddha himself was; but they were confused by the impossibility of reconciling the claims made on behalf of one method of reaching the goal with the claims made on behalf of other methods. All the rival teachers could not be speaking the truth. If one was right, the others must be wrong. The Buddha's reply is not an invitation to question the existence of a transcendental state, nor an encouragement to doubt whether the realization of such a state is within the reach of human effort. It simply affirms that we are to decide between the rival claims of religious teachings, firstly on the basis of their results as revealed in our own experience and secondly (a statement which is almost always ignored) in accordance with the testimony of the Wise. Who the Wise are, and how we may recognize them, is told elsewhere. One of their characteristics is that, unlike the recluses and brahmins who had disturbed the minds of the Kalamas, they do not indulge in acrimonious disputes.

The Buddha's reply to Maha-Pajapati, the Gotamid, who had asked him to show her a teaching, hearing which from the lips of the Exalted One she might dwell "alone, solitary, zealous, ardent, and resolved," formulates in much more positive terms, and in a more definitely Buddhist context, the general principle that was the burden of his discourse to the Kalamas:

> Of whatsoever teachings, Gotamid, thou canst assure thyself thus: "These doctrines conduce to passions, not to dispassion; to bondage, not to detachment; to increase of (worldly) gains, not to decrease of them; to covetousness, not to frugality: to discontent, and not content; to company, not solitude; to sluggishness, not energy; to delight in evil, not delight in good": of such teachings thou mayest with certainty affirm, Gotamid, "This is not the Norm. This is not the Discipline. This is not the Master's Message."
>
> But of whatsoever teachings thou canst assure thyself (that they are the opposite of these things that I have told you)—of such teachings thou mayest with certainty affirm: "This is the Norm. This is the Discipline. This is the Master's Message."[69]

These well-known passages from the Pali Canon make perfectly clear the nature of the principle by which the Buddha's attitude toward contemporary teachings was governed. He was prepared neither to accept nor to reject them absolutely. With complete intellectual detachment and freedom from preconception, he surveyed them all from the standpoint of Enlightenment—just as one who has

ascended a mountain height can look back and see clearly that, of the
numerous paths winding up from the valley below, some come to an
end at the edge of a precipice or a foaming torrent, while others lead
safely to the summit—and followed the Middle Path of accepting as
part of his own teaching whatever was conducive to the attainment of
the beyondless heights of Liberation, and rejecting as false and wrong
whatever hindered, or retarded, or even merely did not help, in the
process of spiritual ascent.

Thanks to the unexampled intellectual fertility of the Indian mind
in that age, and to the unrestrained exuberance of its religious imagination, which ran riot through a thousand brilliantly colored forms
and fancies, as well as to the fanatical enthusiasm with which a thousand zealots experimented with the most fantastic methods of salvation, there was no lack of material for the Buddha to work upon. What
he himself described as the "jungle of views," which flourished so
richly and so rankly in those days, seems to have produced the sublime and the ridiculous, the more than divine and the hardly less than
bestial, in the way of religious ideals, with the same perfect indiffer-
ence with which the great subtropical forests of the Himalayan region
produce at the same time the marvelous blossoms of the rare and
lovely orchid, and the monstrous growth of the common poisonous
datura. This luxuriant crop of ideas the Buddha had partly to uproot,
partly to prune, and partly to train to grow in the right direction. One
has only to read the *Brahmajala Sutta,* the opening discourse of the
Digha Nikaya (collection of "long discourses") with which the Sutta
Pitaka, the first of the three great divisions of the Pali canonical scriptures, begins—where no fewer than sixty-two contemporary "false
views" are classified—to realize the immensity of the work of religio-
philosophical criticism accomplished by the All-knowing One. It
may, in fact, be said that it was he who laid down the main lines for the
development of Indian spirituality, not only in its Buddhist but in its
non-Buddhist forms, for thousands of years to come.

Though the Buddha rejected in the most categorical manner a great
many of the beliefs and practices current in his time, references to which

will be found scattered all over the pages of the scriptures, it should not be concluded that his attitude toward contemporary trends of thought was entirely negative, much less unsympathetic or hostile—words which have no meaning in relation to a fully Enlightened and wholly compassionate One. He was as ready to accept as to reject; in fact, more ready. For he knew that a positive method of teaching was more appealing, more likely to find entrance into the hearts and minds of his auditors, than a purely negative and destructive one, however correct and logical the latter might be. Consequently we find the Buddha constantly putting—if we may be permitted a metaphor which he probably would not have used, even if he had known it—the new wine of his teaching into old bottles. He does not condemn the practice of ceremonial ablution, for instance, so much as insist that real purification comes by bathing, not in the Ganges as people thought, but in the cleansing waters of the Dharma. He does not ask the brahmin to give up tending the Sacred Fire, with which so many ancient traditions and so much religious emotion were bound up, but to remember that the true fire burns within, and that it feeds not on any material object but solely on the fuel of meditation. These examples of the Buddha's capacity to utilize Indian traditional practices for the purposes of his own teaching could be paralleled by a hundred others from the same canonical sources. Though self-torture had been definitely rejected as a means to Enlightenment, he permitted thirteen ascetic practices, called *dhutangas,* out of hundreds of similar ones, to the members of his Order, not because he considered them necessary, but because there was a popular demand for them and because they were in any case not positively harmful.

This spirit of adaptation and assimilation was one of the causes which enabled Buddhism to spread so rapidly and easily, and with the minimum of opposition, among races and peoples whose traditions and cultural background were in many ways quite different from those of India. The Dharma, while remaining in essence changeless, was capable of assuming a thousand forms, because, as we have already seen, it is in principle simply the means to Enlightenment. With this criterion constantly in view, Buddhism, both in India and

abroad, was able not only firmly to reject beliefs, customs, and observances that hindered the living of the holy life, but also freely to accept
those by which it was helped, regardless of their origin. The illustration by means of which we sought to elucidate the relation of Buddhism to contemporary teachings may here be of further service to us.
In the soil of the pot there are found not only particles of earth which
contain various nutritious elements, but also potsherds and fragments
of stone containing none. Among the doctrines current in northeastern India during the life of the Buddha, there were some which could
provide materials for the growth and development of the seed of the
Dharma, and others which could not provide such materials. The former were of course utilized, and not so much incorporated into the
Buddha's teaching as recognized as being in truth already a part of it.
The latter were simply picked out and thrown away.

What we need most of all to remember is the fact that whatever the
part played by the contents of the pot may be, the seed out of which
grew up the mighty spreading banyan tree of the Dharma came not
from inside but from outside it. Only if we grasp this idea will it be
possible for us to comprehend the traditional conception of the Buddha and his teaching.

3. The Transcendental Critique of Religion

We need to grow, we need to become free, and we need something to help
us do so. If we agree to call that thing "religion," how are we to make sure
that religion does not become a means of enslaving or stultifying, even of
crushing, the individual?

ONCE OUR BASIC NEEDS for food, clothing, shelter, and leisure have
been met, what do we need more than anything else in life? What is our
essential need as human beings? Surely it is freedom. The real meaning
of human life is to develop our distinctively human characteristics:

awareness, emotional positivity, responsibility for ourselves and others, and creativity. But we cannot develop, we cannot grow, unless we have space—both literally and metaphorically—to grow into. We need freedom: freedom from all that restricts us, both outside us and within us, freedom from our own conditioning, even freedom from our old self.

And what helps us to be free—apart from our own efforts—is, or at least is considered to be, religion. In Buddhism the spiritual life is frequently described in terms of freedom, but Buddhism is not alone in this. The followers of other religions, at least the universal religions, would probably also say that their religion stands for the freedom of the individual. The Christian might quote from the New Testament the words: "You shall know the truth, and the truth shall make you free."

But if we consider what it is that stops us from becoming free—apart from our own sloth and torpor, laziness, neglect, forgetfulness, and so on—we encounter a tremendous paradox. Strangely enough, religion, rather than helping us to become spiritually free, only too often helps to keep us enslaved, and even adds further shackles to our chains. To many people, the very idea that religion has anything to do with freedom sounds like an absurd contradiction in terms. Some people, and I must confess that I am among them, feel uncomfortable using—in a sense being obliged to use—the word "religion" at all.

We find it so difficult to associate religion with freedom not because of what religion is in principle, but rather because of its historical record. It is fairly obvious that we cannot develop as individuals unless we are free at least to think for ourselves. But organized religion often fails to allow the individual that freedom.

Not only has organized religion often refused to allow individuals to think for themselves, it has made them think in ways actually detrimental, actually inimical, to their own personal development. It has made them think of themselves as miserable sinners, as weak and powerless, made them think that being independent and taking the initiative is wrong, if not positively sinful.

So what went wrong? How is it that religion has become not a liberator but a jailer? The short answer is that religion has become an end in itself. The forms which religion takes—doctrines, rituals, institutions, rules—have become ends in themselves. It has been forgotten that religion is a means to an end—that end being the individual's development from ignorance to Enlightenment, from mundane consciousness to transcendental consciousness.

What are we to do in this situation? We need to grow, we need to become free, and we need something to help us do so. If we agree to call that thing "religion," how are we to make sure that religion does not become a means of enslaving or stultifying, even of crushing, the individual? We need something that will constantly remind us of the limitations of religion, something that will constantly remind us that religion is only a means to an end. In other words, we need a transcendental critique of religion.

This critique has always been part of Buddhism. The Buddha said "I teach the Dharma under the figure of a raft." In other words, just as a raft is useful for getting you across the water, but you wouldn't carry it with you once you had reached dry land, so the Buddha's teaching is useful for carrying us across the waters of samsara, but we will have no need for it when we have reached the other shore of Enlightenment. This sort of emphasis is particularly strong in the Mahayana, and strongest of all, perhaps, in Zen. You get Japanese and Chinese pictures of the Sixth Patriarch tearing up the *Diamond Sutra.* There is the story of the traveling monk who needed fuel because he was cold, and chopped up the wooden Buddha images in the temple at which he was staying. And there is the master who famously said to his disciple, "If you meet the Buddha on the road, kill him!"

These are all rather extreme, rather bizarre ways of underlining the same message: that Buddhism is only a means to an end. It is because Buddhism has always been aware of the difference between means and ends that down the centuries it has remained spiritually alive. For the same reason, it has not on the whole been dogmatic or intolerant. It has never persecuted the followers of other religions, and the followers of one form of Buddhism have rarely persecuted the followers of another.

Some people think that one should not criticize religion at all. But such criticism is essential in revealing obstacles to one's development as an individual. It is only by means of a critique that we can ensure that the means to the development of the individual remains a means and does not harden into an end in itself.

We should therefore apply this critique, even this criticism, to everything that presents itself to us as religion. We should apply it to Christianity, apply it to Buddhism, apply it to the Hinayana, apply it to the Mahayana, apply it to the Vajrayana.

We need, of course, to make sure that we apply our critique appropriately; sometimes it is more appropriate to express appreciation. A guiding principle might be to apply the critique first and foremost to oneself. If we all applied this transcendental critique to our own spiritual practice, there would hardly be any need for a transcendental critique of religion in general, or of our own religion in particular. We must be careful not to knock away the very ladder by which we are climbing—not, at least, until we are ready to do without it. We need to apply the critique to whatever practices we undertake—whether it is meditation or devotional practice, reading books or attending lectures, living in a community or working in a Right Livelihood business. We need to stay alive to the crucial question: is it helping me to develop? We should never allow any of these things to become ends in themselves; they are all means to an end.

4. THE INDIVIDUAL AND THE GROUP

For the person who is essentially a member of the group, an individual—who does *not* belong to the group, whose being is not totally submerged in the group—is rather difficult to conceive.

THE WORLD TODAY has certain special problems, problems that did not exist in the past quite in the way that they exist now. These problems are not entirely new, but they happen to be more acute now, and confront us in a more urgent form—which means that their solution has become more urgent. You may immediately think of economic problems or ecological problems, according to your particular interest, but the biggest problem of all, at least in human or spiritual terms, is the problem of the *individual:* the survival of the individual.

It is very difficult for the individual to survive nowadays. It is very difficult for the individual to grow and develop. And that which threatens the survival of the individual is clearly, in one word, the *group.* That the individual—as such—needs to be protected might be a new idea to some people. We are familiar with the idea that children should be protected; we are even familiar with the idea that animals should be protected. But nowadays, the individual too needs to be protected. The individual is threatened by the group, is threatened, even, with extinction. By now you will have realized that I am using the terms "group" and "individual" in a rather special way. To explain what I mean I will have to go back a little in history, even pre-history, and attempt a few definitions.

The group, of course, came before the individual, before the "true individual." Anthropologists tell us that human beings have always lived in groups; the group was necessary to survival. This was true not only of humans but of all our pre-hominid ancestors as well: they all lived in groups of various sizes, containing anything from a dozen to two or three dozen members of various ages, and of course of both sexes. In this way they formed a sort of extended family group. This pattern was followed by human beings, but with the difference that in our case, the group gradually became bigger. Extended families merged to form tribes, tribes merged to form nations, nations founded states, and states even merged to form empires. This process extended over a period of many thousands of years, gradually accelerating toward the end when we reach the period of recordable, datable history, which begins around 8000 BCE.

Whether the group was large or small, in principle it remained unchanged. We can therefore define the group as a collectivity organized for its own survival, in which the interests of the individual are subordinated to those of the collectivity. The group, or collectivity, is also a power-structure in which the ultimate sanction is force. The group did not just make survival possible for its members; in the case of humans, it made it possible for them to enjoy higher and higher levels of material prosperity and culture. It made possible the emergence of folk art and ethnic religion; it made possible the emergence of civilization. But there was a price to be paid by the proto-individual, and that price was conformity with the group. The individual was regarded as being essentially *a member of the group.* The individual had no existence separate from the group, or apart from the group.

Let me give you an illustration of this from my own experience. Living in India for twenty years, I made many Hindu friends. Some of them, being very orthodox and rather old fashioned, used to be rather puzzled by the fact that I did not have a caste. Sometimes they would ask me, "What is your caste?" because, in their view, I *had* to belong to a caste. When I told them that I did not have a caste, first of all because I was born in England, where we don't have caste, and secondly because I was a Buddhist, and in Buddhism we do not recognize the system of hereditary caste, they would say, "But you *must* have a caste! Every human being must have a caste." They could not conceive of someone who did not belong to one of the two thousand or so castes of Hinduism. They could not conceive of someone who did not belong to a group of some kind. There is something a little parallel to this in the West in that we cannot conceive of someone who is not of a particular nationality. But caste is even harder, even stricter, than that.

For the person who is essentially a member of the group, an individual—who does *not* belong to the group, whose being is not totally submerged in the group—is rather difficult to conceive. Because such a person is essentially a member of the group, he does not think for himself, he thinks and even feels just as the group does, and acts as other members of the group act. It does not even occur to him that he can do anything else. It does not occur to an orthodox Hindu that you need not have a caste. Whether we are talking about pre-historic times or nowadays, a group member, as such, is perfectly content with this state of affairs, because the group member is not an individual—not in the sense of being a true individual. He or she may have a separate body, but there is no really independent mind, no independent consciousness. The group member shares in the group consciousness, so to speak. We can call this sort of individual a "statistical individual." He can be counted, he can be enumerated, but he doesn't exist as an individual in the true sense. He is simply a group member.

However, at some stage in human history, something remarkable happened. A new type of consciousness started to develop, a type of consciousness that we usually call "reflexive consciousness," or self-consciousness, or self-awareness. Reflexive consciousness can be contrasted with "simple consciousness." With simple consciousness, you are aware of sights, you are aware of sounds, you are aware of trees, houses, people, books, flowers, and so on, but you are not aware of being aware. But when one has reflexive consciousness, consciousness as it were doubles back upon itself, and one is *aware of being aware.*

When one is aware of being aware, one is conscious of oneself as an individual, conscious of oneself as separate from the group. One is conscious of one's ability to think and feel and act differently from the group, even against the group. An individual of this type is a true individual. Such a person is not only self-aware but is emotionally positive, full of good will toward all living beings. He or she is also spontaneous and creative because he or she is not determined in his thinking, feeling, or acting by previously existing mental, emotional, and psychological patterns—whether his or her own or those of other people. The true individual is also responsible, aware of his or her own needs, aware of others' needs, and prepared and willing to act accordingly.

True individuals started appearing on the stage of history in relatively large numbers in the course of what we call—to use Karl Jaspers' term—the Axial Age. This Axial Age, a crucial turning point in human history, was a three-hundred-year period extending very

roughly from around 800 BCE to around 500 BCE. The true individuals who started to emerge during this period appeared in Palestine,
Greece, Persia, India, and China, in fact in most of the great centers of
civilization. Some of them were great thinkers; others were prophets
and mystics; others again were poets, sculptors, and founders of religions. In Palestine we have such figures as the prophets Isaiah, Jere-
miah, and Amos, as well as the unknown author of "The Book of Job."
In Greece we have Pythagoras and the great philosopher Plato; we
have the Attic dramatists, the great poet Pindar, the sculptor Phidias,
and so on. In Persia we have the prophet Zoroaster. In India we have
the Upanishadic sages like Yagnavalkya; we have Mahavira, the
founder of Jainism, and we have the Buddha. In China we have Con-
fucius and Lao Tse, the two most important individuals to arise in the
whole history of Chinese culture. Of course, some of these individuals went far beyond the stage of mere self-consciousness. At least
some of them developed what may be called "Transcendental consciousness," and even "Absolute consciousness."

In this way, the Axial Age was a period of efflorescence of the true
individual. Indeed, from this time onward we can see two factors at
work in human cultural, religious, and spiritual history. On the one
hand there is the individual, and on the other hand there is the group.

Between the true individual and the group there was always a certain creative tension, the group pulling one way—in the direction of
conformity—and the individual pulling the other—in the direction
of nonconformity, of freedom, of originality, of spontaneity. In this
dialectical relationship, the group provided the individual with his
raw material. We find this, for example, in Greek drama. Here, certain
myths and legends, themselves a product of the collective unconscious, provided the dramatists with stories which they adapted in
such a way as to give expression to their own highly individual vision
of existence. In this way the individual influenced the group, reacted
upon the group, raising the statistical individuals who still belonged to
the group, at least momentarily, to a higher level, bringing them closer
to true individuality.

This relationship was in force for about two thousand years. On the whole it was a lively and a healthy one. Sometimes it broke down, as when the medieval Catholic Church started persecuting those "heretics" who dared to think differently from the Church. (By this time, of course, the Church was no longer a spiritual community, as it had once been, but simply a religious group, a sort of ecclesiastical power structure.) But on the whole, the relationship between the true individual and the group continued to be fairly healthy for about two thousand years. Generally speaking, the group at least tolerated the individual—provided he or she did not impinge too uncomfortably upon the group. During the last two hundred years, however, a change has taken place to such an extent that a serious imbalance now prevails between the individual and the group. There are various reasons for this, but I will only summarize some of the more important ones.

To begin with, the population of practically every country in the world has greatly increased in recent years. Because we have so many more people in the world, almost everywhere, it has become much more difficult to get away from one's fellows, much more difficult to get away from the group. This is especially the case in small, densely populated countries like Holland and the United Kingdom, and in some parts of the bigger countries.

Secondly, there is the increase in the power of the corporate state. Today's corporate state, we may say, is the group *par excellence,* and it controls so many aspects of our lives. In most countries, this control is increasing rather than decreasing. These corporate states now divide the whole world between them. There is no portion of the Earth's land surface which is not controlled by one or another corporate state, and they have even started staking out claims to the sea. There used to be some nice empty spaces, terra incognita, between them, where you could go if you wanted to get away from the state. But those spaces no longer exist; there are no spaces anywhere in the world where no state exercises any authority. Every individual has to belong to a state, whether they like it or not. From time to time we hear about a few miserable people who have been declared stateless. Their condition is considered a terrible calamity because, these days, you just have to belong to a state. You have to have a passport, for without one you cannot travel from one state to another. This is a fairly recent development; passports came into general use only after the First World War. Before that it was not so necessary to have one, but now they are really indispensable.

Thirdly, there is the growth of modern technology. This is in many ways a helpful development, but it has its disadvantages. It means that, among other things, the corporate state can now keep track of its citizens far more efficiently. A computer system can be set up to tell its operators a person's date of birth, when he or she last paid taxes, how many parking offenses they have ever committed, where they spent their holiday last year, whether they have ever had measles, and so on. With this information at its fingertips, the state finds it much easier to exercise control over the individual.

Fourthly, there is our higher standard of living. This too is a blessing up to a point, but it does make us dependent on the group. We are dependent on the group for such good things of life as motor cars and television sets, not to speak of petroleum and electricity, since it is very doubtful whether we could produce these things by ourselves. Generally, we are so helpless, so dependent, that we cannot even grow our own food, or make our own clothes. The general principle would therefore seem to run thus: the higher our standard of living, the bigger and more complex the state to which we have to belong—and, therefore, the more control it exercises over our lives and the less freedom we have. There is something a little paradoxical about this. If we have a car, for instance, we have greater freedom in the form of more personal mobility. But that freedom is taken away from us in certain other respects by the fact that, in order to possess and to drive a car, we have to be part of a society which is geared to the production of cars—which may not necessarily be the best kind of society. For these reasons we can now see that there is an imbalance between the individual and the group.

Now I have said that the state is the group *par excellence.* But within the state there are many other smaller groups. The state is in fact a sort of interlocking system of groups, some of which are very powerful indeed when set against the individual. There is the political party, the trades union, the chamber of commerce, the church, the bank, the school. Some of these impinge on us in certain respects more strongly and more directly than does the state itself. The result is that we are left with a virtually powerless individual in a virtually all-powerful state. The group has practically overwhelmed the individual, who feels, very often, that he is quite unable to influence the group, even in those matters which most closely concern his own life.

This is the state of affairs in the world today, especially in the Western democracies, in the old Communist states, and in various military dictatorships. It is a state of affairs which is becoming more and more widespread. And the result is that the true individual is dissatisfied. The "statistical individual," very often, is not dissatisfied; very often he or she is happy with what the group provides, whether it is bread and circuses, as in the case of ancient Rome, or motor cars and television sets as is the case today. Such people's only complaint is that they would like to have more of these things more frequently! But the true individual is frustrated. In extreme cases, his frustration may sometimes find expression in violence. We know that violence is on the increase in our cities—and I am certainly not saying that frustration of the kind I have mentioned is the sole cause of this violence, but it is certainly one factor. What, then, are we to do?

To begin with, and above all, we have to restore the balance between the individual and the group. This means that we need a philosophy, a way of looking at things, which can provide the perspective within which we will be able to see the possibility of restoring the balance. We need a philosophy that recognizes the value of the individual, a philosophy that shows the individual how to grow, how to be a true individual. This is where what nowadays we call Buddhism (but which calls itself, in its own habitat, the Dharma) comes in.

Buddhism places the individual in the very forefront of its teaching.

The Buddha's teaching is concerned solely with the individual, both alone and in free association with other individuals. It shows the individual how to grow, shows him or her, by means of actual methods, how to develop awareness, how to develop emotional positivity, how to live spontaneously and creatively, how to accept responsibility for oneself and for others, how, in other words, to be more and more of a true individual.

Gautama the Buddha, the original teacher, was and is an example of a true individual. He was an individual of the highest kind: an *Enlightened* individual. He was an individual who had developed not only reflexive consciousness, but also "Transcendental" consciousness and "Absolute" consciousness. If we take even a cursory glance at the Buddha's life, we can see how the Buddha's individuality demonstrated itself right from the start. Quite early in his life he cut himself off from the group; that was the first significant step he took. He left his parents, left his wife and child, left his city, left his tribe, and gave up his social position to wander alone from place to place. Occasionally he joined various religious groups and cults, but in the end he cut himself off from them too. They too were hindrances, they too were groups. He was left entirely alone—in a way that perhaps no one had ever been alone before. Being alone, he was able to be himself; being himself, he was able to be an individual; being an individual—looking at things as an individual, seeing things as an individual—he was able to see the Truth for himself, able to experience it for himself. Being able to see the Truth, he was able to become what we call a Buddha, an Enlightened individual. And having become an Enlightened individual, he was able to help others to become such. From that moment, we may say, the power of the group, the power of Mara—the power of the gravitational pull of conditioned existence—was diminished.

In the Buddha's day the power of the group was perhaps not as great as it is today, but the Buddha's teaching and example were needed all the same. The Dharma is needed, we may say, whenever and wherever the survival of the individual is threatened, wherever there is an imbalance between the individual and the group, especially when that imbalance is as extreme as it is in the world today. There is no political or economic solution to such a problem. There is only a *spiritual* solution, a solution which takes the individual into account. If put into operation, that solution will of course have political and economic implications and consequences, but it has to be a solution that respects and emphasizes the value of the individual.

This is a radical view of things. After all, how many people respect the individual? You can meet so many people who do not respect you as an individual, who don't even *see* you as an individual. Sometimes when you go into a shop or into a government office and try to deal with the people there, they do not see you as an individual at all, but just as a sort of public zombie who has drifted in. But the solution we need is a solution that *sees* the individual, respects the individual, allows the individual, even, to make his or her own mistakes; that does not hold the individual's hand all the time. This attitude is very well illustrated by an incident in the Buddha's life.

A brahmin once came to see the Buddha and asked whether he taught all his disciples the way to nirvana equally. When the Buddha affirmed that he did, the brahmin asked, "But do they all, equally, attain Enlightenment?"

When the Buddha replied that some did, while others did not, the brahmin was rather puzzled and asked, "Well, why is this? If they all get the same teaching, why don't they all realize nirvana?"

The Buddha gave him the following example: "Over there," he said, "is the city of Rajagriha. Now, you know the city of Rajagriha; you know the way to the city of Rajagriha. So suppose two men come to you and both say, 'Please tell me the way to Rajagriha.' And suppose you give quite detailed instructions: 'Go along this road, pass that bush, turn that corner, go through that grove of mango trees, and then you'll get to the city.' Suppose you give both of them these directions, and suppose one follows your directions and arrives, but the other does not follow your directions and does not arrive, because he makes a mistake. Would it be your fault? Would you be to blame for that?"

"No," said the brahmin. "If, after I had given the proper directions, one of them found the way but the other did not, it wouldn't be any fault of mine. I wouldn't be to blame. I am only the shower of the way. I only give directions."

"It is the same in my case," said the Buddha, "I am only a shower of the way."

The Buddha is only the shower of the way, but it is up to the individual to follow that way, to decide whether he or she is going to follow that way or not. We may say that this attitude shows tremendous respect for the individual. It shows great confidence in the potential of the individual. It shows an appreciation of the fact that the individual cannot be forced. He must want to change; he must want to develop. All that one can do is show him how, show him an example, encourage him, and, if one can, inspire him. You can't force him, you can't bribe or threaten him; you can only show him the way. That is to say, if you are an individual, and are trying to deal with him as an individual, then you can only show him the way and leave it to him to follow or not to follow.

This attitude is the basis of Buddhism's well-known spirit of tolerance. Buddhism is deeply conscious of human differences, deeply conscious of the fact that we are not all the same. We each have our own temperaments, characters, and ways of looking at things. We therefore have to be allowed to develop, each one of us, in our own manner. This is why, in the whole of its two thousand five hundred-year history, Buddhism has never persecuted anybody for their beliefs. There is no such thing as heresy in Buddhism. There are such things as "wrong views," views which hold us back and prevent us from developing, but these wrong views are to be corrected—if they are to be corrected at all—by discussion and not by force. Force has absolutely no place in Buddhism, no place in the spiritual life.

Buddhism recognizes the value of the individual. Buddhism shows the individual how to grow, how to become more and more of an individual; it allows him or her to develop in his or her own way. It also gives us the inspiring example of the Buddha and the support of the

Sangha, or spiritual community, of other *individuals* with whom we are in direct personal contact.

5. THE IDEAL STUDENT OF BUDDHISM

One of the most original contributions of the Buddha to human knowledge is the discovery that theories are rooted in desires.

NOWADAYS BUDDHISM has more often to pray for protection from its friends than from its enemies. The number of those who like Buddhism for the wrong reason, or who, more correctly, are attracted by what they wrongly imagine is Buddhism, is increasing, and by reason of their very sincerity they constitute a growing threat to the purity and integrity of the doctrine that they profess to support. Such people will generally be found to have developed strong religious convictions prior to their study of Buddhism. These convictions they do not wish to have unsettled, and although genuinely attracted by certain aspects of the Dharma they do not hesitate to challenge, misinterpret, or simply explain away whatever other aspects of the teaching are in conflict with their preconceived ideas. One of the most original contributions of the Buddha to human knowledge is the discovery that theories are rooted in desires, and the very tenacity with which, in the face of the clearest textual evidence to the contrary, such students persist in clinging to their erroneous interpretations of the Dharma, is an unmistakable indication of the extent of their emotional commitment. Theories of a personal God and an immortal soul are so deeply rooted in the soil of the human heart that belief in them has often been regarded as synonymous with religion itself. Such belief is not synonymous with the Dharma. The Buddha in fact taught that belief in a personal God and an immortal soul were rationalizations of desires, of our craving for love and protection, our attachment to our own personalities, and our thirst for life. Enlightenment can be attained by the renunciation not only of selfish desires but of the religious theories or "views" (*drsti*) that are based on those desires. Belief in a personal God and immortal soul are not helps but hindrances to one who would follow the Buddhadharma, and the student who is strongly attached to such beliefs and who feels at the same time attracted by certain aspects of Buddhism, or who shrinks from the suggestion that so distinguished a tradition should deny his or her most cherished convictions, will be compelled by his or her emotional needs to blunder into misunderstandings and misinterpretations of the Dharma. "The Buddha *must* have believed in God," cry some such people, "he *could not* have denied the existence of the *atman*," protest others; but unfortunately for them the Buddha did do both "shocking" things. The wisdom of the Tathagata is not to be measured by the yardstick of human intelligence, nor limited by the cravings of the human heart.

The ideal student of Buddhism would be one who, whether scientifically trained or not, was prepared to admit the possibility of a spiritual experience which would transcend the physical senses and the rational mind, and who would be willing to give unprejudiced consideration to the Buddha's claim that he had achieved this experience himself and that by following his teaching others might achieve it for themselves too. Such a person would not commit the mistake of thinking that the intellect, though capable of performing useful preliminary work, was able to penetrate the inner meaning of Buddhism, or that Truth would reveal itself to any faculty save to intuition awakened by spiritual practice. He or she would be free from beliefs which, though they pass for religious doctrines in the world, are in fact born of fear, craving, and other egocentric emotions. Resolved fearlessly to pursue, frankly to examine, and faithfully to accept and follow whatever the truth about Buddhism might turn out to be, such an ideal student could be said to be fairly well equipped for the study of Buddhism, and to approach the Dharma with at least an approximation to Right Motive in the specifically Buddhist sense.

6. FORMULATIONS OF THE BUDDHIST PATH

Traveling on a path implies a journey, and it is of a journey that both the scriptures and history often speak.

SPEAKING IN THE CLEAREST and most general terms, Buddhism is a Path or Way. It is a Path leading from the impermanent to the permanent, from sorrow to happiness, from the darkness of ignorance to the light of perfect wisdom. This is the Path for which the Buddha himself, in the days before his Enlightenment, is represented as searching. For the sake of this Path he went forth from home into homelessness. For the sake of this Path he sat at the foot of the Bodhi tree. This is the Path he discovered at the time of his Supreme Enlightenment, this is the Path which, after initial hesitation, he made known to mankind. In his own words, as recorded in the *Dhammapada,*

> Walking this Path you shall make an end of suffering.
> This is the Path made known by me when I had learnt to
>   remove all darts.

This Path it was that, for the forty-five years of his teaching life, in one formulation or another made up the principal content of the Buddha's message. The formulations were indeed very numerous. Perhaps the most basic was that of the Path as consisting of the three great stages of right conduct (*sila*), meditation (*samadhi*), and wisdom (*prajna*).

> Great becomes the fruit, great the advantages of medita-
> tion, when it is set round with (that is, supported by)
> upright conduct. Great becomes the fruit, great the advan-
> tage of wisdom, when it is set round with meditation.[70]

Such was the gist of the "comprehensive religious talk" which the Buddha delivered in eleven out of the fourteen places he visited in the course of the last six months of his life. No less important, and even better known, is the formulation of the Path as Eightfold, that is to say, as consisting in the gradual extension of Perfect Vision—the vision of the transcendental—successively to one's emotional attitude, one's communication with other people, one's actions, one's means of livelihood, one's energy, one's recollection, and one's overall state of being and consciousness. Much rarer is a formulation which in fact occurs only once in the Pali Canon. This is the formulation of the Path in terms of the Seven Stages of Purification—ethical, emotional, intellectual, and so on. Together with right conduct, meditation, and wisdom, this formulation provides the double framework of Buddhaghosa's great exegetical work the *Visuddhimagga* or "Path of Purity," the standard work of Theravada Buddhism, i.e. of the Pali Buddhism of Sri Lanka, Burma, Thailand, Cambodia, and Laos.

In the Mahayana scriptures many other formulations are found. Some of these are extremely comprehensive in scope, so that with them the Path begins to take on a more universal character. Among these more comprehensive formulations the most important, both historically and spiritually, is that of the Path of the Ten Perfections, the Ten Perfections being Generosity, Right Conduct, Patience and Forbearance, Vigor, Meditation, Wisdom, Skillful Means (Compassion), Salvific Vow, Strength or Power, and Knowledge or Transcendental Awareness. This Path of the Ten Perfections is, of course, the Path of the Bodhisattva, "he whose nature or essence is Bodhi," the great spiritual hero who instead of aiming at the inferior goal of individual Enlightenment, that is, Enlightenment for oneself alone, out of compassion seeks to attain the universal Enlightenment of a Buddha, so as to be able to deliver all sentient beings from suffering. For the accomplishment of this sublime purpose he practices the Ten Perfections not for one lifetime only but for an unthinkable number of lifetimes, being reborn in many different worlds, and on many different planes of existence. In this way he traverses the ten great "levels" (*bhumis*) of spiritual progress—another formulation—from that called "the Joyful" right up to "the Cloud of Dharma," at which stage he

252 ~ THE ESSENTIAL SANGHARAKSHITA

becomes a Buddha. Thus he fulfills the Bodhisattva Ideal, as it is called—an ideal which the Mahayana regards the historical Buddha as himself exemplifying. Yet another formulation of the Path found in the Mahayana scriptures is that of the eleven "abodes" (*viharas*), which are also stages of spiritual progress traversed by the Bodhisattva, and which coincide to some extent with the ten "levels." Perhaps the most comprehensive of all formulations of the Path is that of the Nyingma school of Tibetan Buddhism, according to which the total Path consists of nine ways (*yanas*) which between them cover all the three major *yanas*—the Hinayana, the Mahayana, the Vajrayana—conceived not only as stages in the historical development of Indian Buddhism but as stages in the spiritual evolution of the individual Buddhist.

The number and importance of these abstract formulations of the Path should not blind us to the fact that the Path also finds vivid concrete embodiment in actual human lives, whether as depicted in the scriptures or as recorded by profane history. The Path in truth is the pilgrim, and the pilgrim the Path, so that—to quote from Madame Blavatsky's *The Voice of the Silence*—"Thou canst not travel on the Path before thou hast become the Path itself." Traveling on a path implies a journey, and it is of a journey that both the scriptures and history often speak. Thus in the *Gandavyuha* or "Flower-Array" Sutra the youth Sudhana, in order to achieve what the text calls "the highest knowledge of Enlightenment," goes on a journey that takes him to various parts of India in the course of which he visits more than fifty spiritual teachers. Similarly, in the *Prajnaparamita* or "Perfection of Wisdom" Sutra (the version in 8,000 lines), the Bodhisattva Sadaprarudita or "Ever-Weeping," advised by a divine voice, goes east in search of the perfection of wisdom, encountering many adventures on the way until, in the city of Gandhavati, he meets with the Bodhisattva Dharmodgata and hears his demonstration of the Dharma. On a more mythic level, in the *Saddharma Pundarika* or "White Lotus of the True Dharma" Sutra the journey is a *return* journey not unlike that of the king's son in the Gnostic "Hymn of the Pearl." In more strictly geographical terms there are Yuan Chwang's and Monkey's famous pilgrimages from China to the West—that is, to India—related in the Chinese classical novel *Journey to the West*. There is also Basho's "Journey to the Far North."

Though a picture of Buddhism has now been drawn, and though the rough outline of the Path has been filled in with details of abstract formulations and concrete embodiments in actual human lives, this is by no means enough. If we are really to understand what Buddhism is we must understand what the Path is *in principle,* that is, we must understand what it is that makes the Path the Path. In order to understand this we shall have to go back, so to speak, to the fundamental principles of what, in the absence of any more suitable term, we are obliged to call Buddhist philosophy. This will bring us close to the very essence of Buddhism.

Philosophy takes for its object all time and all existence. It is the science which, as metaphysics, investigates the most general facts and principles of reality (this is the dictionary definition). The fundamental principles of Buddhist philosophy, from which all its other principles derive, are therefore principles that embody its understanding of the nature of existence in the most general sense—though in the case of Buddhism this understanding is the product not of systematic reflection on sense experience but of direct spiritual vision. According to Buddhism the nature of existence is best described in terms of change, or becoming. This does not mean that existence changes, in the sense of being subject to change but distinct from it, but that existence itself *is* change, *is* becoming. One of the fundamental principles of Buddhism, therefore, is that which finds embodiment in the well known equation "Existence (or Reality) = Change (or Becoming)." This change or becoming is not fortuitous, but takes place in a certain fixed manner, in accordance with a certain definite law. (Not that the law really exists apart from the changing physical and mental phenomena it is said to govern. The law simply describes the way in which physical and mental phenomena behave in accordance with their inherent nature.) The general formula for this law, a formula

254 ~ THE ESSENTIAL SANGHARAKSHITA

which according to the Pali scriptures goes back to the Buddha himself, is that "This being, that becomes; from the arising of this, that arises. This not being, that does not become; from the ceasing of this, that ceases." The law is thus a law of conditionality or, in more specifically Buddhist language, it is a law of dependent origination or conditioned co-production, as the term *pratitya-samutpada* is variously translated. Just as existence is change, so change is conditionality. The Vision that Buddhism sees—the Vision that the Buddha saw on the night of his Enlightenment—is a vision of existence in terms of an infinitely complex, constantly shifting network of physical and mental phenomena, all arising in dependence on certain conditions and ceasing when those conditions cease.

Universal though it is in scope, however, the law of conditionality is not uniform in operation—not all of one same kind, so to speak. Within the infinitely complex, constantly shifting network of physical and mental happenings—within the totality of existence—it is possible to distinguish two distinct trends or types of conditionality. In the one case there arises, in dependence on the immediately preceding factor in a "dependently originating" series, a factor which is the opposite of the preceding one, as when good arises in dependence on evil (or vice versa), happiness in dependence on suffering, death in dependence on birth. In the other case there arises, in dependence on the preceding factor, a factor which far from being the opposite of the preceding one, and thus negating it, is what may be termed its positive counterpart, so that it actually augments it, as when joy arises in dependence on happiness, rapture in dependence on joy, bliss in dependence on rapture. One trend or type of conditionality consists in a rotary movement between pairs of factors which are opposites, and the order of conditionality is therefore said to be cyclical in character. The other consists in a cumulative movement between factors which are counterparts or complements, and the order of conditionality is therefore said to be progressive. The first trend or type or order of conditionality the Buddha saw as a wheel endlessly turning round—a wheel of birth and death. The second type he saw as a spiral constantly ascending—a spiral of spiritual development. We are now in a position to understand what the Path is in principle, and therefore what Buddhism really is. The Path is in principle identical with the progressive order of conditionality. The Path is essentially an ascending series of mental factors or mental states.

7. Buddhism and Evolution

Our project as Buddhists must be to replace a mechanistic universe with one that has meaning, one that carries throughout its fabric intimations of spiritual values.

Buddhism is a vast subject. Although in this context I want to consider it in relation to a concept which is familiar to the modern Western mind, this is not like finding a big box into which we can fit a smaller box. It is a matter rather of laying out the Buddhist system of thought in terms that should be sufficiently familiar to all of us—as a way of looking at the world—not to require much explanation. And the idea that functions most comprehensively in this way is the principle of evolution, derived from the biological sciences. No great *tour de force* is needed to bring Buddhism and modern evolutionary ideas together.

We now know that the theory of evolution was anticipated by a number of thinkers, by Kant, Hegel, and others—even, according to some, by Aristotle. But Darwin was the first to trace the operation of evolution in detail within the field of biology. To attempt to refute the principle of evolution in that field today would be like saying the earth is flat. It is the given basis for all the biological sciences. If anything, the idea has invaded all sorts of other disciplines, from politics to astronomy, so that one could fairly say that just as the Elizabethan age was dominated by the concepts of order and hierarchy, so the modern world is dominated by the concept of evolution.

In taking up an idea that is generally understood in scientific or at least academic applications and applying it in a spiritual context, we have, of course, to draw some precise boundaries. Scientific knowledge depends on the evidence of the senses—but, just because Buddhism has never tried to resist the evidence of the senses, that does not make it a "scientific religion." It is certainly true that Buddhism's appeal in the West owes much to the spirit of empirical, open-minded inquiry which the Buddha laid down as axiomatic to the spiritual quest—and this lack of dogmatism does align Buddhism in some important respects with the Greek scientific spirit rather than with the dominant religious traditions of the modern West. Equally axiomatic to the Buddhist notion of the spiritual quest, however, is the recognition of a transcendental Reality—which is not, of course, a provable scientific hypothesis. As a practicing Buddhist one starts from the evidence of one's own experience, which will tend to support more and more the idea of a spiritual order of evolution, and it is on the basis of this evidence that biological evolution carries conviction—not the other way round. Therefore, if we look at ourselves as in any way constituting some kind of key to the universe, then on the basis of our own experience of progression we may fairly conclude that progression is in some way inherent in the universe.

In this respect, at least, Buddhism inclines more toward a traditional, pre-scientific viewpoint. If we look at a traditional civilization, we find that everything, every activity, every piece of knowledge, is linked with ideas of a metaphysical order. Ordinary things, ordinary events, accepted ideas, are not just of practical use. They have a symbolic value, they point beyond themselves, they have meaning. Amid our own fragmented, "specialist," economically defined culture we may find it difficult to appreciate this attitude, but it is the basis for the Tantra, and it was the world view of our own society until comparatively recently. According to this view everything is interconnected and nothing can ever really be ordinary—in the sense of being without a deeper meaning—at all. Rather than look for scientific proof of spiritual realities, we may say, paraphrasing G.K. Chesterton, that it is because we no longer believe in the gods that we no longer believe in ourselves. Our project as Buddhists must be to replace a mechanistic universe with one that has meaning, one that carries throughout its fabric intimations of spiritual values.

Buddhism therefore looks at the rational knowledge derived from the senses in the light of a knowledge that is derived not from the senses and reason alone, but from a fusion of reason with emotion in a higher faculty of archetypal knowledge which we may call "vision," "insight," or "imagination." It is not a question of justifying Buddhism in scientific terms, but rather of understanding sense-derived knowledge by means of knowledge that is not sense-based. In other words, the knowledge that is derived from the senses fits into a much larger pattern of knowledge that is not derived from the senses. From a Buddhist point of view, there is a hierarchy of levels of being and consciousness, a hierarchy of degrees of spiritual attainment, which seems to be reflected in, or as it were anticipated by, the whole process of biological evolution. It seems to make sense, therefore, to regard both biological evolution and the hierarchies of spiritual development as being—from the Buddhist point of view—in their separate spheres, exemplifications of a single law or principle.

It is clear that according to the principle of evolution life is not just existence. It is a process—a process of becoming—and humankind is not something apart from the rest of nature, as the theistic religions usually teach. Humankind itself also comes under the operation of this great process of becoming. It too is evolving and developing, not just toward new forms of existence and organization, but toward new and higher levels of being.

Of the two general scientific theories of evolution, that it is a mechanistic, random process, and the opposite view, that it could not have taken place without some kind of purpose or direction, the Buddhist approach would go with the second view. It is very broadly "vitalist" in that it recognizes a will to Enlightenment somehow present in all forms of life and manifesting in any gesture of consideration or act of intelligent good will. With the beginning of the evolutionary process you get the impression of a sort of fumbling, with a lot of false starts—it seems a bit hit-or-miss. But then as you follow it further, whatever it is that stands behind the evolutionary process seems to become surer of itself, as it were, and to define itself more clearly as time goes by. And with the emergence of the aware individual human being undertaking the spiritual path it becomes fully conscious of itself, thereby speeding up the whole process.

The Buddhist has to tread very lightly in this area to avoid misunderstanding. Evolution is just a metaphor or model for Buddhism, a temporal model. If we speak in terms of developing from one stage to another, that is to look at reality in temporal terms. But if we speak of what is there all the time, the absolute reality which is always here and now, that is to speak in spatial terms. So this is the function of the "Will to Enlightenment" or *bodhicitta,* in this context—to transcend these spatio-temporal models. It is not a sort of cosmic life principle—not the life-force of the universe, or any kind of causative first principle—but a liberation principle, a will to transcend the universe or samsara.

In fact, transcendence, self-transcendence, is what the whole of evolution, from the amoeba upward, is about. Furthermore, this evolutionary principle of self-transcendence is expressed in its highest and most fully self-conscious form in the figure of the Bodhisattva, the one who, according to Mahayana Buddhism, dedicates himself or herself to the cause of helping all sentient existence to Enlightenment. The Will to Enlightenment of a Bodhisattva is a fully committed volition to perpetual self-transcendence. And from the Bodhisattva to the Buddha there is only, as it were, a step.

It is from this perspective, seeing spiritual development in terms of perpetual self-transcendence, that we can best appreciate the often half-understood Buddhist concept of *anatman,* or "no-self." This is sometimes interpreted as meaning that we don't really exist, that there's a sort of hole where one imagines one's self to be. In fact, the point of this teaching is that we have no *unchanging* self. Indeed, putting it more dynamically and experientially, we can say that for radical change, radical development, to take place—for a fully conscious self-transcendence to be possible—there *can* be no unchanging self.

We may look at Buddhism from a purely academic perspective as just an activity or philosophical position of a number of individuals calling themselves Buddhists. On the other hand, we can take the vast and awe-inspiring perspective of the Buddha's teaching itself. From this latter perspective, we are all frail, impermanent beings, born into the world and passing out of it with apparently little to show for our trouble—but at the same time we embody the universal possibility of Enlightenment. Just as the scientific concept of evolution involves a progression toward new biological organisms through periods of time that are practically unimaginable, so, according to Buddhism, our own lives take their place in a context of literally unimaginable temporal duration, in which, however, they are of literally cosmic importance. For among all the life-forms in the universe, from the amoeba to the highest realms of the gods, it is only the kind of sentient life to which human beings conform that can be, in the words of Lama Govinda, "the vehicle for the rediscovery of the transcendental and inconceivable nature of mind or consciousness"—that can become, in short, a Buddha.

PART THREE

Art, Beauty, and Myth in the Buddhist Tradition

1 ← The Place of Beauty in the Spiritual Life

1. SANGHARAKSHITA I AND SANGHARAKSHITA II

"SANGHARAKSHITA I" wanted to enjoy the beauty of nature, to read and write poetry, to listen to music, to look at paintings and sculpture, to experience emotion, to lie in bed and dream, to see places, to meet people. "Sangharakshita II" wanted to realize the truth, to read and write philosophy, to observe the precepts, to get up early and meditate, to mortify the flesh, to fast and pray. Sometimes Sangharakshita I was victorious, sometimes Sangharakshita II, while occasionally there was an uneasy duumvirate. What they ought to have done, of course, was to marry and give birth to Sangharakshita III, who would have united beauty and truth, poetry and philosophy, spontaneity and discipline; but this seemed to be a dream impossible of fulfillment. For the last two and a half years Sangharakshita II had ruled practically unchallenged. Aided and abetted by Buddharakshita (the friend with whom I wandered in India and sought Buddhist ordination), who strongly disapproved of poetry, he had in fact sought to finish off Sangharakshita I altogether, and but for the timely intervention of Swami Ramdas, who firmly declared that writing poetry was *not* incompatible with the spiritual life, Sangharakshita I might well have died a premature death in Muvattupuzha.

However, despite the bludgeoning that he had received he had not died, and after leading a furtive existence in Nepal he was now coming into his own again at Buddha Kuti. Kashyapji's dealings were of course mainly with Sangharakshita II (the Venerable Jagdish Kashyap was the learned Buddhist monk with whom I studied Pali, Abhidhamma and logic at Benares [Varanasi]), but he had no objection to Sangharakshita I being around, and even spoke to him occasionally. Soon Sangharakshita I was feeling strong enough to demand equal rights. If Sangharakshita II devoted the afternoon to *The Path of Purity,* Sangharakshita I spent the evening immersed in the poetry of Matthew Arnold, which for some reason or other exerted a powerful influence during this period. When the former wrote an article on Buddhist philosophy, or edited the second edition of Kashyapji's *Buddhism for Everybody,* the latter composed poems. Sometimes, while one self was busy copying out extracts from the books he had been reading, the other would look idly out of the window and watch the falling of the rain. One day there was a violent clash between them. Angered by the encroachments of Sangharakshita I, who was reading more poetry than ever, and who had written a long poem which, though it had a Buddhist theme, was still a poem, Sangharakshita II suddenly burned the two notebooks in which his rival had written all the poems he had composed from the time of their departure from England right down to about the middle of their sojourn in Singapore. After this catastrophe, which shocked them both, they learned to respect each other's spheres of influence. Occasionally they even collaborated, as in the completion of the blank-verse rendition of the five *paritrana sutras* that had been started in Nepal. There were even rare moments when it seemed that, despite their quarrels, they might get married one day.

2. BEAUTY AS A CHARACTERISTIC OF LIFE

Life is fleeting, life is transient, but life is also beautiful.

As stars, a fault of vision, as a lamp,
A mock show, dewdrops, or a bubble,

A dream, a lightning flash, or cloud,
So should one view what is conditioned.

THESE COMPARISONS are taken from a well-known Buddhist text, the *Diamond Sutra,* and they are meant to illustrate the impermanence of all conditioned things. The lightning flash doesn't last very long, the dewdrop doesn't last very long, the cloud drifts by, the dream comes and goes. All these things are evanescent, impermanent. Life is like that.

But there is something else to notice about these comparisons: they are all beautiful. They may be illustrating impermanence, but they also illustrate the beauty of the world. The cloud is beautiful as it floats through the sky. The dewdrop is beautiful as it glistens in the early morning sunlight. The lightning flash is beautiful in its brief, awesome power. The bubble on the stream, reflecting myriad hues—like a rainbow sometimes—is also beautiful. So to my mind there is a twofold message in that particular verse: life is fleeting, life is transient, but life is also beautiful.

In the early Buddhist scriptures—those, that is, which can be said to reflect the historical circumstances under which the Buddha taught—there is evidence of a very great sensitivity to the natural world. The Buddha himself, like his immediate disciples, lived close to nature. He was born in an orchard—his mother holding on to the branch of a tree. He gained Enlightenment at Bodh Gaya sitting underneath a tree. He died in the sal tree grove of the Mallas, stretched out between two sal trees. And of course he spent much of his time wandering from place to place, from village to village, in the open air.

So Buddhism had its origins in the open air, and this open-air background to the scriptures inevitably affected the way the Dharma was taught by the Buddha and experienced by his disciples. For instance, there is a set of verses in the *Theragatha* ("Verses of the Elders"), attributed to one of the Buddha's senior disciples. In it he describes a cloud—a heavy, black, or rather, dark blue, cloud—and how a white bird flies across the dark cloud. The beauty of this sight seems to send him into a sort of ecstasy.

Scholars have a tendency, perhaps, to overlook this aspect of Buddhism in their intent to present Buddhism as a *teaching*, sometimes, even, as quite a dry, methodical, analytical teaching. But if you look at the life of the Buddha, and those of his close companions, you see the natural world very much *there* in their lives, in their practice of the Dharma. And there is therefore a close connection, I would say, between early Buddhism and the natural environment.

The most common symbol in Buddhism is the lotus flower. It goes right back to the time immediately after the Buddha's Enlightenment, when he was wondering whether or not he would ever be able to communicate his experience to others. He looked out over the world and saw human beings as lotus flowers growing in a pond. Some were deep down in the mud, some had just raised their petals above the water, and some were standing completely free of the water, opening their petals to the sunlight. This was the Buddha's vision of humanity. And through it he knew that human beings could grow and expand and open up to receive the sunlight of the Dharma—and that like blossoms, some individuals were more developed and mature—and therefore more receptive to the Dharma—than others.

So it does seem that the Buddha himself was not just conscious of the natural environment but felt deep sympathy with it. The Buddhist scriptures are full of references to nature spirits—spirits of the trees, spirits of the ponds, spirits of the streams, even spirits of flowers. There's a story in one of the scriptures of a monk who goes and smells a lotus flower growing in the water, and the spirit of the flower comes out and says "Why are you stealing my scent?"—which obviously gives the monk something to think about. In future he won't thoughtlessly take from nature without asking permission in some way. He won't even think to smell a lotus flower without the flower's permission. After all, it isn't *his* scent—it's the flower's scent.

This does, perhaps, convey to us some kind of environmentalist message about the way we exploit nature. The idea that we shouldn't so much as smell a flower without seeking the flower's permission might seem a bit sentimental, but there is a philosophy underlying it which has some quite far-reaching implications for us today—that there can be a sort of imaginative identification between man and nature.

3. Learning to See

We have to learn to look at things themselves, for their own sake, untainted by any trace of subjectivity, personal preference, or desire.

MOST OF THE TIME, we are only vaguely conscious of the things around us, and have no more than a peripheral awareness of them. We are not really aware of our environment, of nature, of the cosmos, and the reason for this is that we seldom or never really stop and look at them. How many minutes of the day—not to speak of hours—do we spend just looking at something? Probably we do not even spend seconds in this way. And the reason we usually give is that we have no time. This is perhaps one of the greatest indictments of modern civilization that could possibly be made—that we have no time to stop and look at anything. We may pass a tree on the way to work, but we have no time to look at it, or even to look at less romantic things such as walls, houses, and fences. This makes one wonder what this life, and this modern civilization of ours, is worth if there is no time to look at things. To quote from "Leisure," by the English poet W.H. Davies:

> What is this life if, full of care,
> We have no time to stand and stare?

Of course the poet has used the word "stare" for the sake of the rhyme, and what he really means is not staring in the literal sense but just looking and seeing. The fact that we have no time for this is something of which we need to remind ourselves. Yet even if we do have time to stop and look and try to be aware we hardly ever see things in themselves. What we usually see is our own projected subjectivity. We look at something, but we see it through the veil, the curtain, the mist, the fog of our own mental conditioning.

Some years ago in Kalimpong I went for a walk with a Nepalese friend, and we happened to stop at the foot of a magnificent pine tree. As I looked up at the smooth trunk and the mass of deep green foliage I could not help exclaiming, "Well, isn't that a beautiful tree!" My Nepalese friend, who was standing beside me, said, "Oh yes, it is a beautiful tree. There's enough firewood there for the whole winter." He did not see the tree at all. All he saw was a certain quantity of firewood. Most of us look at the world of material things in just this way, and it is an attitude from which we have to free ourselves. We have to learn to look at things themselves, for their own sake, untainted by any trace of subjectivity, personal preference, or desire.

This attitude or approach is much emphasized in Far Eastern Buddhist art, that is, in the art of China and Japan. In this connection there is the story of a certain apprentice painter who once asked his master, a celebrated artist, how to paint bamboos. The master did not say that you take your brush and make certain strokes on the silk or the paper. He did not say anything about brushes or pigments, or even about painting. He only said, "If you want to learn to paint bamboos, first learn to *see* bamboos." This is a sobering thought—that one might rush to paint something without having even looked at it—but this is what many artists do, or at least what many amateurs in art do. So the disciple, we are told, just looked. He went about *looking at bamboos*. He looked at the stems, and he looked at the leaves. He looked at them in the mist, and in the rain, and in the moonlight. He looked at them in spring, in autumn, and in winter. He looked at large bamboos, and he looked at small bamboos. He looked at them when they were green, and when they were yellow, when they were fresh and springy, and when they were dry and decayed. In this way he spent several years, just looking at bamboos. He became genuinely aware of the bamboos. He really *saw* them. And seeing them, being aware of them in this way, he became one with the bamboos. His life passed into the life of the bamboos. The life of the bamboos passed into his life. Only then did he paint bamboos; and of course you may be sure that it was real bamboos that he painted. In fact we might say that it became a question of a bamboo painting bamboos.

According to Buddhism, at least according to Far Eastern Buddhism—the traditions of China and Japan and, above all perhaps, the traditions of Ch'an and Zen—this should be our attitude toward all material things. This should be our attitude toward the whole of nature: not only toward bamboos, but toward the sun, the moon, the stars, and the earth; toward trees and flowers and human beings. We should learn to look, learn to see, learn to be aware, and in this way become supremely receptive. Because of our receptivity we shall become one with, or at least fused with, all things; and out of this oneness, this realization of affinity and deep unity, if we are of artistic temperament we shall create, and truly create.

4. Bamboos

Among all branched things, I for beauty choose
The yellowness and slimness of bamboos,
Whose bunched leaves twinkle on a gusty day
And back and forth the clattering branches sway.
And when from frozen skies the pure snows fall
In large white flakes that softly mantle all
The loaded branches stoop without a sound
Till their green leaf-tips almost touch the ground.
Then, when they seem a kind of crystal tree
Sparkling with diamond buds and silvery
Shoots, by the snowflakes' overburdening

And their own patience freed, the lithe boughs spring
Up, and in powdery showers the white snow flies
Flung by the wind across the freezing skies,
While, as the bamboos dance in wind and rain,
Like stars the bunched leaves twinkle forth again.
Hence, among branched things I for beauty choose
The yellowness and slimness of bamboos,
Which taught me, more than what in books is writ,
That life is conquered when we yield to it.

5. THE GREATER MANDALA OF AESTHETIC APPRECIATION

We usually think of "aesthetic appreciation" as a little separate part of life within a much larger area that is utilitarian and "practical," but really it needs to be the other way around.

THE ENLIGHTENMENT of the Buddha was not a cold, detached knowledge. He saw with warmth; he saw with feeling; what is more, he saw everything as being pure, or *subha,* which also means beautiful. The Buddha saw everything as pure beauty because he saw everything with compassion—just as, conversely, when you hate someone, they appear ugly. When, out of metta, you see things as beautiful, you naturally experience joy and delight. And out of that joy and delight flow spontaneity, freedom, creativity, and energy. This flow from metta to joy to freedom and energy is the constant experience of the Bodhisattva. The Bodhisattva's wisdom in the fullest sense therefore includes metta. In a sense, we could even say that metta *is* wisdom, is *prajna.*

We may further dispel any impression a superficial look at the *Prajnaparamita* (the Perfection of Wisdom literature) may give that the Bodhisattva is a sort of glorified logic-chopper by looking at another word used to describe the Bodhisattva's experience: *vidya*. *Vidya* is the opposite of *avidya*, "ignorance," and is usually translated as "knowledge." However, Guenther renders it as "aesthetic appreciation" (like *prajna* but without the element of analysis), which comes much closer to its true meaning. *Vidya* is a sort of relishing of things, a harmony with the world; and its opposite, *avidya*, conveys a sense of alienation and conflict—certainly not an absence of *knowledge* in the usual sense of the word.

When one is said to *know* something, this carries the suggestion that the knowledge is utilitarian. One knows what the thing is good for; one knows what one can do with it. If what we see is the utilitarian value of something, we are relating to it from a need, which becomes desire, which turns to craving for the object conceived as fulfilling that desire. The tree is seen not as existing in its own right, for its own sake, but as something to fulfill our need. If, however, we have no desires to be fulfilled, there is no subject and no object. That is the state of the Bodhisattva—empty of any desire to use things for any particular purpose. All that is left is aesthetic appreciation. If you are a Bodhisattva you enjoy the world much as you enjoy a work of art or an artistic performance—with the difference that you do not experience a division between yourself and something "out there." Normally—though less so in the cinema—people in an audience retain a sense of themselves as subjects separate from what they are experiencing as an aesthetic object, and to that degree remain alienated from it. But the Bodhisattva's experience of the world is more like

> Music heard so deeply
> That it is not heard at all,
> But you are the music
> While the music lasts[71]

and like the experience of the woman in the stalls who forgets it is "only" a play and shouts to Othello that Desdemona is innocent.

The "purpose" of a Bodhisattva, if one may speak in that way at all, is in no degree passive, however. It is not unlike the function of the artist—except that a painter can rarely just enjoy the world without starting to think of how to make a picture out of it. What the Bodhisattva creates is something different. The Bodhisattva, quite unpurposefully, rearranges the whole universe and turns it into a gigantic mandala.

What does this mean? Well, what is a mandala? Putting aside the more conventional descriptions, let us take this short definition by a Tibetan teacher, Rongzompa Chokyi Zangpo: "To make a mandala is to take any prominent aspect of reality and surround it with beauty." Why you should select one particular aspect of reality over another will be a matter not of attraction as a form of craving, but of spiritual affinity. It will be a facet of reality that you value and appreciate enough to want to surround it with a harmonious pattern of beautiful images. You take, say, a particular Buddha figure—one that you find particularly appealing, sublime, or precious—as the aspect of reality you want to focus on, and you decorate it with, for instance, other Buddha figures at the points of the compass. Then you might place the four elements in between, and use all the other things in nature as materials with which to fill the spaces so as to make a harmonious and pleasing configuration.

The Bodhisattva creates a mandala through a response to the world that is aesthetic and appreciative rather than utilitarian. To sustain life you have to engage in a certain amount of practical activity—you have to think about things and understand how the world works—but if you are a Bodhisattva all this takes place within an overall context of aesthetic appreciation. We usually think of "aesthetic appreciation" as a little separate part of life within a much larger area that is utilitarian and "practical," but really it needs to be the other way around. Our overall attitude, our overall response to life, should be purely aesthetic. We should not seek to use things, but just enjoy them, appreciate them, feel for them. We don't have to think of our mandala of aesthetic appreciation as something the size of one of those Tibetan *thangkas* sitting in a corner of the great big real world of important practical business. Instead, we can think of ourselves as living *within* a "greater mandala" of aesthetic appreciation, of which all our practical mundane affairs, and the fulfillment of all our (non-neurotic) needs and wants, occupy just a tiny corner. The real values are aesthetic, not utilitarian.

There is a story of a Taoist sage who was sitting by a river with a fishing rod when someone came along and asked him how he could reconcile trying to catch fish with being a Taoist sage. He replied "It's all right, I'm not using any bait." He was just enjoying the fishing; he didn't need to try and catch anything. We don't *really* have anything to do—well, do we? Most of the time we could just be sitting back, as it were, and enjoying the universe. That's our major occupation. That's our real work—not to work. We need to get food to eat, clothing, a roof over our head, healthcare, a few books, transport of some kind . . . but the rest of our time and energy we can just devote to the contemplation of the universe, simply enjoying it all. This is how a Bodhisattva lives, anyway.

I am not talking about some lotus-eating, daydreaming, navel-gazing ideal here. The Bodhisattva is the greatest worker of all, constantly responding to the objective needs of a situation, but at the same time he or she operates within the greater mandala of aesthetic appreciation. It is not even as though the sphere within which the Bodhisattva operates is a sphere of "practical activity" that exists apart from the greater mandala. Bodhisattvas do not absent themselves from the mandala of aesthetic appreciation when they carry on their practical activities. The greater mandala interpenetrates that limited sphere, so that those practical activities are an expression of the values of the greater mandala within a certain context and for the sake of certain people.

6. LEARNING TO STAND STILL

We have to listen to the exhortation of the Buddha—to the voice of our own immanent Buddhahood—and learn simply to "stand still" at all levels of our being, both physical and mental.

WHAT IS THE EFFECT of the acceleration of the speed at which we can now travel—indeed of the pace at which we now live—on the general human consciousness? Physical speed and the sense of duration being intimately related, the more quickly we are able to do anything, the less time there appears to be in which to do it. Conversely, the less time there appears to be in which to do a thing, the more quickly we desire to do it, whether the action concerned be that of traveling or anything else. Such is the vicious circle in which a rapidly increasing section of the human race now finds itself involved. In the experience of time, there would seem to operate a principle analogous to the law of diminishing returns in economics, in accordance with which the more time-saving devices are placed at one's disposal, the more pressed for time one becomes. Under such conditions the activities of humanity are increasingly characterized by a feverish haste which eventually results in physical exhaustion, nervous strain, and mental breakdown.

Angulimala the bandit, pursuing the Buddha along the jungle path with drawn sword, found himself in a similar predicament. However fast he ran, he was unable to catch up with the Enlightened One, though the latter was walking at a slow, dignified pace. Eventually, exhausted by his efforts and terrified at the inexplicable phenomenon, he called to the Master to stand still. Back came the reply, "I am already standing still (i.e. have attained nirvana); it is you who are running (i.e. round and round in samsara, impelled by the force of ignorant desire)."

The more desperately we strive to catch up with the future the more it eludes our grasp. Like Angulimala, we have to listen to the exhortation of the Buddha—to the voice of our own immanent Buddhahood—and learn simply to "stand still" at all levels of our being, both physical and mental. This can be done, initially, only by becoming aware that we are running. Awareness of speed, of duration, of the three tenses, eventually enables us to realize that past and future are concepts only. With this realization comes about a subsidence, a calming down and dying away, of all those emotions—desires and fears, anxieties and regrets—which are based on these concepts. We begin to live in the present in the true spiritual sense, and, thus living in the present unobsessed by the passage of time, find that we have time enough in which to do all things. Having reached such a state, we shall be able to board a Boeing 747, if circumstances so require, or even go for a weekend on the moon, with the same unruffled composure, the same freedom from all sense of haste, with which we walk at night in our garden among the fragrance of tranquil flowers.

7. Pauses and Empty Spaces

Truly did a Chinese sage say that it is only because of empty space that the wheel is able to revolve, and houses to be made use of.

WHEN THE COMPOSER Mozart was asked what was the most important part of his music, he did not reply that melody, or harmony, or counterpoint, or even orchestration was the most important, but simply "the pauses."

As in the music of Mozart, so in the paintings of the Far Eastern (Chinese and Japanese) masters of the art of landscape. It is the empty spaces which are the most important parts of the picture. The vast empty spaces of sky, or snow, or water are not only themselves charged with mysterious significance as a cloud with lightning, but they somehow infuse that significance into the single blossomless branch, or tiny floating boat, or solitary human figure, which stands almost lost at the edge, or in the center, of the huge blank expanse of paper, or faintly tinted silk.

And just as the pauses are the most important part of music, and the empty spaces the most important part of a picture, so are silence and emptiness the most important part of life. A life which consists of a frantic stream of external activities, without one moment of inward recollection, is like music which is an uninterrupted succession of sounds, or a picture which is crammed with figures: all three are not only meaningless, but positively painful.

As music is born of silence, and derives its significance therefrom; and as a painting is born of empty space, and derives its significance therefrom; so are our lives born of silence, of stillness, of quietude of spirit, and derive their significance, their distinctive flavor and individual quality, therefrom. The deeper and more frequent are those moments of interior silence and stillness wherein, transcending all sights and sounds, tastes and touches, we experience Reality as it is, the more rich in significance, the more truly meaningful, will our lives be.

It has been said that there is a silence of words, a silence of desires, and a silence of thoughts. Only when the egoistic will itself is "silent," that is, no longer operative, will be heard the True Sound. Only when our hearts are utterly empty of all self-will shall we behold the True Form. And since this Silence and Emptiness are not states of mere negation, but dynamic and full of life, our thoughts and words and deeds, even the most insignificant, will be charged with a mysterious potency, like two or three notes of a flute sounding in the midst of a great pause in a symphony, or a few delicate twigs sketched in the corner of an empty scroll.

Truly did a Chinese sage say that it is only because of empty space that the wheel is able to revolve, and houses to be made use of.

It is the pauses which make beautiful the music of our lives. It is the empty spaces which give richness and significance to them. And it is stillness which makes them truly useful.

8. The Simple Life

The truly simple life glows with significance, for its simplicity is not the dead simplicity of a skeleton but the living simplicity of a flower or a great work of art.

MEN AND WOMEN bewildered by the ever-increasing complexity of modern civilization cry out for the simple life as a drowning man gasps for air. Visions of cool trees and quiet cottages arise before eyes almost blinded by the glare of neon lights; and ears well nigh deaf with the thunder of traffic and shriek of machinery seem to catch, during brief interludes of silence, the sound of white surf as it sweeps hissing up the beach or the song of a bird as it floats sweet and clear through the moonlight from the darkness of distant trees.

But the simple life is by no means one of ease and idleness, as the town-dweller, with his sentimental "idealization" of life in the country, is apt to suppose. Nor is it necessarily associated with lonely hermitages wreathed in mountain mist or gleaming coral beaches fringed with languorous palms, although the relative freedom from external distractions and irritations which such places enjoy may make them more helpful to the leading of a simple life than others less fortunate. For the simple life is also a strenuous one, being the product of a process of simplification, a reduction of life to its barest essentials; and the successful accomplishment of this process is, amid the monstrous jungle-growth of the complexities of modern living, a task calling for unremitting endeavor and inflexible resolve. Nor does it involve merely the simplification of the external mode of one's existence, but something far more fundamental upon which hinges not only this but every other mode of existence as well.

But before we can reduce life to its essentials we must determine what those essentials are, otherwise the expression remains a mere gaudy flower of rhetoric barren of all fruition in experience. And before we can determine what are the essentials of life and what its adventitious trappings, we must ask ourselves the question: Essential to what? For life as we ordinarily live it is obviously not an end in itself, but only a means to an end, and until we know what that end is it is impossible for us to judge what in our lives is essential, and what inessential, to the attainment of it.

Buddhism posits *bodhi,* or the realization of Transcendent Wisdom, as the ultimate goal not only of every human being but of every other form of sentient existence as well. Life is for the sake of Enlightenment. The essentials of life are those things which are helpful to the attainment of Enlightenment, and it is back to these naked boughs that the luxuriant foliage and innumerable buds of our life-tree must be ruthlessly stripped and pruned if ever it is to bear its loveliest blossoms and most ambrosial fruit. The truly simple life is that which is dedicated solely to the attainment of Supreme Wisdom, and wherein each thought, word, and deed is integrated to the achievement of that end. Killing, stealing, wrong means of livelihood, and all other forms of unskillful bodily action must be given up until those actions alone remain the performance of which abounds in spiritual significance. Thus bodily action is simplified into Mudra. The use of false, frivolous, abusive, and obscene speech must be gradually restricted until no word is uttered without some background of spiritual recollection behind it. Thus speech is simplified into Mantra. Greedy, malicious, and deluded thoughts must be eliminated until the concentrated mind admits only thoughts that are pure, compassionate, and illumined. Thus thought is simplified into Samadhi. As the Bodhisattva disciplines himself in this way his body, speech, and mind gradually become as it were transparent, and through each thought, word, and deed streams into the world the effulgence of Great Compassion, just as the beams of the rising sun leap through the windows of a room and dispel the darkness within. The truly simple life glows with significance, for its simplicity is not the dead simplicity of a skeleton but the living simplicity of a flower or a great work of art. The unessential has melted like mist from life and the Himalayan contours of the essential are seen towering with sublime simplicity above the petty hills and valleys of the futilities of mundane existence.

Far Eastern aesthetics make extensive use of a term which may be interpretively translated as "aesthetic impoverishment." This kind of art finds its highest expression in ink drawings which reveal a whole world of significance with three strokes of the brush, and tiny verses which seem almost to exhaust the possibilities of poetic expression within the compass of thirty-seven syllables, although the principle on which it is based is not peculiar to the realm of art but penetrates every phase of the life and culture of the Far Eastern peoples. In fact, it is an aesthetic application of the principle on which the simple life, in the sense of the Bodhisattva career, is founded—the principle that the more rigorous the simplicity of the outward form the more clearly is the significance of the inner spirit revealed.

It is the presence of this parallelism which makes it possible to speak of the spiritual life as a work of art, as the greatest of all works of art, and which perhaps explains the aesthetic pleasure with which we contemplate the Bodhisattva ideal, an ideal which seems not only good and true but also incomparably beautiful. For the simple life is in fact all three, and where goodness, truth, and beauty abound happiness is of a surety not far to seek.

2 ⬿ Buddhism and Art

1. THE TRANSFORMATIVE POWER OF ART

Buddhism and art are both indispensable to a balanced spiritual life.

FROM THE DUAL viewpoint of subject matter and quality of inspiration, four categories of art can be distinguished. The first is neither religious in form nor spiritualizing in effect. Tabloid newspapers, pulp magazines, and the majority of popular films may be mentioned in this category. The second category of art is that which is formally, but not essentially, religious. Such are the lithographed pictures of gods and saints and religious teachers which one finds in the possession of devout people all over the world. Though religious in theme, they are executed in mechanical fashion, without feeling, and do not produce an expansion of consciousness so much as condition a devotional reflex. Thirdly, we have a type of art that is essentially, though not formally, religious. Chinese landscape painting springs at once to mind as the almost classic example of this category of art. Though devoid of any formally religious content, such paintings are in the deepest sense spiritual. The extraordinary sense of liberation and infinite expansion of consciousness that they produce in the spectator is sufficient proof of the tremendous height of inspiration whence, like a cataract that "smokes upon the mountainside," they descend through brushes and black ink onto rolls of silk.

The fourth and last of our categories includes works of art that are both formally and essentially religious. Enough has been said of the three previous categories to make clear, without need of further explanation, the nature of this one, the crown and flower of them all. The ancient Buddhist art of India and Sri Lanka, China and Japan, Tibet and Cambodia, may without reproach of partiality be allowed the honor of representing this supreme class. Though it is difficult, even impossible, to single out any one type of Buddhist art as being more typical of the whole group than are others, it will no doubt be conceded that the image of the Buddha seated in meditation is the most popular and widely known of all. Here the meaning of Buddhism and the value of art coalesce upon the lips of the Buddha into a smile that expresses what is, perhaps, the greatest expansion of consciousness that it is possible for the plastic arts to meditate.

From how high a quality of inspiration the work of art issued, we hardly dare to guess. How tremendous an effect it can have upon the whole character may be understood from a story I heard from a French lady, a scholar in Sanskrit and poet in her own language, and a Buddhist nun in India. She told me that she had received so deep an impression—a spiritual shock of such high voltage—from an image of this kind which she had seen in the Musée Guimet in Paris, that she resolved to consecrate her whole life to the study and practice of Buddhism, so as to experience for herself, to however small an extent, that liberation of consciousness, that wisdom and compassion, which shone through those stone features as though they had been transparent to a light within.

An archaic torso of Apollo that the poet Rilke saw in a museum seems to have produced a similar transformation in his consciousness; but the transformation was not so much reflected in his life as registered in his art. Not that he was unaware of the spiritual significance of deep aesthetic experience. He was, perhaps, more conscious of the inner relations between the experience of the saint and the experience of the artist than any other modern poet, and this consciousness makes him, in an age when external contact between religion and art has been broken off, an artist whose work is of very special significance and value. If the first twelve and a half lines of his sonnet, "An Archaic Torso of Apollo," show how deep, how heartfelt, was his experience of beauty, the concluding one and a half lines, which mark an abrupt, almost a violent, transition from the descriptive to the reflective mood, reveal how clearly he understood the ethical and spiritual demands of that experience, and how little afraid he was to meet and grapple with them. His meaning is unmistakable, as feeling abruptly deepens into insight and he cries out

> Here is no place
> That does not see you. You must change your life.

This change of life, this transformation of character and attitude, constitutes not only the message of the Buddha image and of the archaic torso of Apollo, but, as I have tried to show, the essence and meaning of Buddhism and the real value of art as well.

Buddhism and art both effect an expansion in consciousness, and the practical results that they achieve are of the same kind, however greatly such results may vary in degree, and however dissimilar may be the methods employed to bring them about. Buddhism effects an expansion of consciousness by acting directly on the understanding and the will, while art produces a change of life indirectly, by appealing to our sense of beauty. Since we possess an emotional as well as an intellectual and a volitional nature, and are capable of responding to beauty no less than to truth and goodness, it is necessary for us to develop and expand simultaneously the emotional, intellectual, and volitional aspects of our personalities. Buddhism and art, therefore, are both indispensable to a balanced spiritual life. Not that I intend to suggest an absolutely exclusive distribution of functions between them, allotting to Buddhism the sole responsibility for developing the mind and to art the sole responsibility for developing the emotions. Every thought possesses emotional coloring, however obscure. Buddhism, though acting primarily on the intellect, certainly makes a powerful secondary appeal to the emotions, especially to the devotional feelings, which are developed as fully in members of the Buddhist community as in people belonging to religions that appeal more to the heart than to the head, to faith rather than to reason. Art, though it operates on the imagination directly, does not fail to influence the understanding. In poetry especially, it is impossible to dissociate the emotional impact of a work of art from the framework of objective reference to which it is attached and which constitutes its "meaning" for the intellect.

Whether the life of any particular person will be dominated more by interests pertaining to Buddhism, or more by interests pertaining to art, is a question that will be determined by the relative strength in him or her of reason and of emotion. We are concerned only to insist first of all that the meaning of Buddhism coincides with the value of art; and secondly, that the development of understanding and insight through the one, and of imagination and sensitiveness to beauty through the other, is, for modern men and women, in whom the emotional life and the intellectual life are of almost equal vividness and vigor, not only a need, but almost a necessity.

2. Art as an Integral Part of Spiritual Life

"Art and meditation are creative states of the human mind."

WHEN ONE HAS looked forward to meeting two people as much as I had been looking forward to meeting Lama Govinda and Li Gotami—and as they, apparently, had been looking forward to meeting me—there is always the possibility of mutual disappointment. In this instance, this was far from being the case. Within half an hour of their arrival at "The Hermitage" a definite rapport had been established between us and we were talking as freely as if we had known each other for years. As might have been expected, I felt a greater rapport with Lama Govinda than I did with Li Gotami. Nevertheless, I appreciated Li Gotami for her liveliness and intelligence, as well as for her delightful outspokenness, which at times bordered on the outrageous. Though her religious affiliations were by no means exclusively Buddhist, she knew enough about Buddhism to be able to take a serious interest in the subject and there was, therefore, no question of her being excluded from the lengthy discussions in which Lama Govinda and I soon became involved.

What these discussions were about it would be difficult to say. It was as though in the course of the five days that my two guests spent with me in Kalimpong, as well as the seven days that I spent with them in Ghoom immediately afterward, Lama Govinda and I ranged over practically the whole field of Buddhist thought and practice. On whatever topic we happened to touch, we found ourselves in agreement to an extent that would have been surprising had we not been familiar with each other's writings and had we not already exchanged ideas in a number of letters. Indeed, as the cloudless autumn days went by, my feeling that we were kindred spirits received more abundant confirmation than I had dared to hope, and I was left in no doubt whatever that despite the fact that he was a married lama and I was a celibate monk I had more in common with Lama Govinda than with any other Buddhist I had ever met.

One of the most important topics on which we touched, and in fact touched more than once, was that of the relation between Buddhism and the spiritual life, on the one hand, and literature and the fine arts, on the other. Besides being a Buddhist by conviction, Lama Govinda was himself an artist and poet of no small repute. He had held exhibitions of his paintings in a number of major Indian cities, and had brought out two small volumes of poetry in his native German. For my part, I had written poetry since the age of eleven or twelve, and was even now thinking of putting together some of my more recent poems for publication in book form. A few of these poems had already appeared in the pages of the *Illustrated Weekly of India,* which had financed Lama Govinda's expedition to Tsaparang in Western Tibet and afterward serialized Li Gotami's account of their experiences, and from the nature of these poems he was well aware that I was no more indifferent to the claims of Beauty than I was to those of Truth or Goodness.

The fact that Lama Govinda and I cultivated literature and the fine arts did not, however, mean that he painted pictures or that I wrote poems *in addition to* doing such specifically Buddhist things as observing the precepts, meditating, studying the Dharma, and giving lectures. For him as for me the painting of pictures and the writing of poems was an integral part of the spiritual life itself. The relation between Buddhism and the spiritual life, on the one hand, and literature and the fine arts, on the other, was not, therefore, one that was merely external, as between different material objects. On the contrary, there was a deep inner connection between them. For this reason there could be no question of the cultivation of literature and the fine arts being inconsistent with the practice of Buddhism and the living of the spiritual life, as I had for a time supposed (or had been led to suppose), much less still of the one being actually inimical to the other. Thanks largely to his intimate acquaintance with Tibetan Buddhist art in all its forms, Lama Govinda's understanding of this important truth was at that time much clearer and more explicit than my own. In particular he had a deep appreciation of the relation between art and meditation. "Art and meditation are creative states of the human mind," he had written in a little book on the subject that he afterward gave me, "Both are nourished by the same source, but it may seem that they are moving in different directions: art toward the realm of sense-impressions, meditation toward the overcoming of forms and sense-impressions. But the difference pertains only to accidentals, not to the essentials. First of all, meditation does not mean pure abstraction or negation of form—except in its ultimate illimitable stages—it means the perfect concentration of mind and the elimination of all unessential features of the subject in question until we are fully conscious of it by experiencing reality in a particular aspect or from a particular angle of vision. Art proceeds in a similar way: while using the forms of the external world, it never tries to imitate nature but to reveal a higher reality by omitting all accidentals, thus raising the visible form to the value of a symbol, expressing a direct experience of life. The same experience may be gained by a process of meditation. But instead of creating a formal (objectively existing) expression, it leaves a subjective impression, thus acting as a forming agent on the character or the consciousness of the meditator."

3. Buddhism and Western Culture

Just because something is labelled "Buddhist" does not mean that you can call it an expression or even a part of Buddhist culture.

CAN BUDDHISM be separated from Eastern culture? Well, not only can it be separated; it *must* be separated, or at least distinguished. Buddhism is not Eastern culture, however beautiful Eastern culture may be. Buddhism is not culture at all. The Dharma is not culture. Culture is only the medium. Unfortunately, many Eastern Buddhists, including those who come to the West hoping to teach, do not understand this. Sometimes they think they are preaching the Dharma when they are only propagating their own national culture, and this causes great confusion in the minds of at least some Western Buddhists.

Second question: Is an acquaintance with Eastern culture necessary to the understanding of Buddhism? Yes and no. Historically Buddhism has found expression in terms of Eastern culture, and if we want to approach the Dharma we therefore need to have some acquaintance with Eastern culture, at least to begin with. In the *Sutra of Golden Light*, for example, the Dharma is expressed very much in terms of Indian culture, so that unless one has some understanding of Indian culture, the message of the sutra remains more or less inaccessible. An acquaintance with Eastern culture can be dispensed with only if one is in personal contact with a spiritual teacher who does not have to rely on Eastern culture as a medium of communication.

There is, I think, very little purely "Buddhist" culture. In my view there are very few cultural forms or artifacts which can be said purely to express the spirit of Buddhism. Just because something is labelled "Buddhist" does not mean that you can call it an expression or even a part of Buddhist culture. At the same time you need, generally speaking, a cultural context of some kind for the practice of Buddhism. So, although a Western Buddhist practicing in the West does not have to adopt Eastern culture in principle, until Western Buddhist cultural equivalents have emerged we shall have to use or adapt some elements of Eastern Buddhist culture, for instance in such matters as robes, style of chanting, and iconography. In the East it is probably best for the Western Buddhist to conform completely to the local Buddhist culture—while being careful not to mistake that culture for the Dharma. However, it is becoming less and less necessary for the Western Buddhist to go East at all. Now we have everything we need at home.

Third question—and this is quite a complex one: how can Western culture place itself at the service of Buddhism? Western Buddhists can at least make a start by establishing points of contact with great artists, and other great Western creative figures who, at least at times and to a limited extent, have made some approach to the Dharma: people like Goethe, Schopenhauer, Nietzsche, Blake, Wordsworth, and even D.H. Lawrence. I certainly hope that one day a Western Buddhist culture will be developed, and there are signs that beginnings are being made. But you can only really hope to create a Western Buddhist culture if you are deeply imbued with the spirit of Buddhism. In a sense, Buddhism comes first and Buddhist culture follows. However, it can work the other way round as well. Involvement with culture in the best sense helps to refine the emotions, and the refinement of the emotions is important, even essential, for one's spiritual development as an individual. The practice of Buddhism and the development of Buddhist culture must go together.

4. The Dharma in Western Poetry

WE STUDIED each poem word by word and line by line, appreciating the appropriateness of an adjective and exploring the implications of a metaphor or simile, yet trying at the same time not to lose sight of the poem as a whole. Nor was that all. Whether it was a poem by Wordsworth, or Keats, or Shelley, or any other poet, as winter gave way to spring and bamboo orchids were succeeded, in the garden of "The Hermitage," by camellias and gardenias, Sachin and I (Sachin was a Nepali student to whom I gave tuition in Kalimpong) went through each poem not once but many times and I dictated to him not paraphrases—one cannot really paraphrase a poem—but extensive critical notes. The greater the number of times we went through a poem the more deeply we were able to penetrate into its meaning— a meaning that seemed, in the case of some poems, to coincide with the meaning of Buddhism itself. Once again I realized what I had first realized three years earlier, namely, that in explaining a poem—a poem such as Shelley's "The Cloud" or one of Keats's Odes—I was in fact teaching Buddhism, especially when I was explaining it to, or studying it with, a dear friend. It was therefore not surprising that at the time when Sachin and I were going through the poetry he was studying for his exam together I should have been impressed by Rilke's idea that poetry is not *about* existence but *is,* itself, a new kind of existence, or that I should have thought of writing an article on what I called "the metaphorical nature of reality," as well as an article on the Buddhist element in the plays of Sophocles. (Next to Yeats, Rilke was my favorite poet at this time, and Sophocles I was re-reading with great enjoyment after a lapse of some years.) Neither of the two projected articles was ever actually written, but the kind of ideas I had intended to express in them were henceforth to be a permanent part of my thinking.

5. STRETCHING THE MIND THROUGH ART

Time and again the literalness and abstractness of philosophic and religious terminology introduce confusions which vitiate the spiritual strivings of humanity.

IN HIS BOOK *The Meaning of Art*, Herbert Read says that "art *stretches the mind*." . . . How difficult it would be to find a more appropriate verb! It connotes a continuity, and, at the same time, a progressive development, of experience through higher and higher levels of sub-tilization not suggested by cruder and more abstract terms such as "transcend," or even by concrete ones like "overstep" and "pass beyond," all of which imply that the mind is somehow lifted up bodily over the "limits of the rational," like a small boy over a fence, and dumped down safely on the other side. The rational is not external to the mind, but the mind itself at one stage of its development, and to transcend the rational does not mean to transfer the mind unchanged from the rational to the super-rational plane (such transferrals are possible only for physical bodies), but to continue changing it until a complete transformation takes place and it enters the super-rational stage of its development by becoming itself super-rational.

Time and again the literalness and abstractness of philosophic and religious terminology introduce confusions which vitiate the spiritual strivings of humanity. Most of these confusions, like that from which Herbert Read saves himself by speaking of stretching the mind, arise from the misconception that the mind, or soul, or whatever else it may be called, is not a flux, a process—a *santana*, as the expressive Pali word has it—in a state of continuous change and development, but an inert, unchanging *thing* subject only to external changes of time and place, and therefore differing from a stone in no observable particu-lar. From this fatal misconception, which is in fact the rationalization of ordinary human egoism, the Religion of Art, no less than other forms of spiritual culture, promises to deliver us. If within the sphere of art itself the delusion that the mind is an immutable non-material "substance" arises, the possibility of transforming the mind through art is precluded, and works of art are regarded not as engines of delight but solely as instruments of selfish pleasure, with the consequence that the pseudo-aesthetic life depicted by Tennyson in "The Palace of Art," together with the ruin which inevitably overtakes such a life, of necessity ensues in place of the train of lofty consequences set in motion by the Religion of Art.

We should do well, therefore, to think of the function of art as being quite literally to stretch the mind (the implied comparison with a piece of elastic is far less objectionable than a covert comparison with a stone) further than the limits of its own rationality into the "distance beyond" of Beauty, as this will enable us to see more clearly in what consists the value of the Religion of Art to its average devotee. Works of art are valuable to him because they stretch his mind. Usually, his mind is stiff and unyieldingly rigid; changes take place in it, but there is no development. The egoistic pattern of his life remains the same, though the elements composing it may vary from time to time. To a "tough" mind like this, conventional religion nowadays often appeals in vain. Tug and pull as she may, it stubbornly refuses to be stretched or, even if she does succeed in stretching it for just a fraction of an inch, the minute her grip is relaxed it flies back to its former position more obstinately than ever. Then along comes the artist. Gently, very gently, he takes hold of the reluctant mind; slowly, oh so slowly, he starts drawing it out of itself, caressing and coaxing it all the time. Then, little by little, with infinite patience and inexorable firmness, he stretches and stretches it until it passes, no longer coarse and thick but delicate as the thread of a spider's web, over the limits of selfhood into that realm of selflessness which is the homeland of true art no less than of true religion.

At first the mind shrinks from the artist's touch; but it soon discovers that to be stretched is, after all, not such an unpleasant experience as it had supposed. Eventually, the experience becomes a positive delight, dearer, perhaps, and more rewarding, than any hitherto known. The spiritual life claims another devotee. So irresistible are the charms of Art. As Irwin Edman has written, "Values translated into immediately loved images have a powerful suasion on the imagination." A single smile of Beauty can bring about greater transformations of character than all the frowns of Righteousness.

3 ↤ The Creative Life

1. After Rilke

The poet is the world's interpreter,
At least to his own self. He recreates
In his own heart the things he contemplates,
And brings them forth transformed from what they were
Into a beauty-truth that cannot err,
That cannot fade or die. Though dull ingrates
May mock, no vile disparagement abates
The benefits the poet's words confer.
A tree is not a tree, unless within
The poet's all-transmuting mind it grows
Refined, reborn—by his own power redeemed
Into a truer life. The poet's kin
Are Memnon, Orpheus, Merlin. History shows
The best but live what once the poet dreamed.

2. ENTERING A SPIRITUAL DIMENSION THROUGH WRITING

THE REQUEST to write on the theme of my "entrance/access to a spiritual dimension/realm" did not evoke an immediate response. As a Buddhist, my principal "entrance" to the dimension or realm in question has been through Buddhism or, perhaps I should say, through being a Buddhist, in the sense of being one who goes for Refuge to the Three Jewels: the Buddha, or perfectly Enlightened teacher; the Dharma, or principal means to Enlightenment; and the Sangha, or spiritual community of all Buddhists, past, present, and future. Basically, my "entrance" has been the act of Going for Refuge, as that deepens from provisional to effective Going for Refuge, and from effective to Real.

Nonetheless, the theme on which I had been invited to write must have remained at the back of my mind, and eventually it produced a kind of eureka experience. The thought struck me that besides Buddhism and Going for Refuge I had another entrance to a spiritual dimension—an entrance which had in fact been under my nose all the time and on which it might be possible for me to offer a few reflections. This other entrance was the experience of writing—the experience of transferring ideas and emotions to the written and, eventually, the printed page.

After all, writing had long been an important part of my life. Over the years I must have spent thousands of hours at my desk, and the written and printed word had been, with the spoken word, the principal means by which I had communicated the Dharma—the Buddha's teaching—to hundreds of thousands of people in both the East and the West. Let me therefore try to explain how it is that, for me, writing is an entrance/access to a spiritual dimension/realm.

But before that, I would like to explain what I understand by "spiritual," as well as by "dimensions/realms." Though the word spiritual is widely used, its meaning is not very clear. According to the dictionary, it means, primarily, "relating to the spirit or soul and not to physical nature or matter; intangible." This leaves us none the wiser, as we are not informed what the spirit or soul (apparently the two terms are synonymous) is in itself. In my own usage, standardized over many years, the word spiritual has two meanings, one narrower than the other. In its narrower sense, "spiritual" corresponds to the Buddhist term *kusala,* literally, skillful (sometimes translated as "wholesome"), which means characterized by the mental states of freedom from craving, freedom from aversion, and freedom from delusion or, more positively, by contentment, (non-erotic) love, and wisdom. Thus a spiritual life is a life devoted to the cultivation of such states, a spiritual practice one that conduces to their development, and a spiritual teaching one that is concerned with them either theoretically or practically or both.

In its broader sense "spiritual" corresponds, in my personal usage, not only to the term *kusala* but also to the still more important term *lokuttara,* literally, "the beyond-world" or, as we may say, the transcendental or Nirvanic. When the word spiritual is taken in this broader sense, the spiritual life is one that is devoted not only to the cultivation of skillful mental states but also to the attainment of the transcendental or Nirvanic state. For Buddhism it is axiomatic that there is no attainment of the transcendental or Nirvanic state except on the basis of a mind dominated by the skillful mental states of freedom from craving, freedom from aversion, and freedom from delusion.

In what way, then, does writing, for me, constitute an entrance into a spiritual dimension/realm? Nowadays a distinction is often made, at least implicitly, between "creative writing," as it is called, and writing that is not creative. I doubt very much if the distinction is a hard and fast one. Creative writing does not form a distinct genre, as a piece of writing in any genre may be either creative or non-creative. Nonetheless certain genres undeniably give greater scope to pure creativity than do others. Such, for example, are the poem, the novel and short story, and the drama. Others, like the scientific treatise and the business letter, give it minimal scope. As for genres such as history and biography (including autobiography and memoirs), these come somewhere in the middle, for though all are concerned with facts, the author has a good deal of freedom in the arrangement and presentation of those facts. Here I shall draw principally on my experience of writing my most recent volume of memoirs, an experience which lasted, on and off, for three years.

In the first place, writing involves concentration. By concentration I do not mean the forcible fixation of one's attention on a single object but rather the gradual mobilization of one's energies around a single point, which for me as a writer is the point where pen meets paper and inner experience is transformed into outer expression. My usual practice is to write in the morning (as I am doing now), starting immediately after breakfast. Especially when I have been writing daily for several weeks, I find that I become concentrated as soon as I sit down at my desk and take up my pen—having not yet succumbed to the blandishments of modern technology in the form of the word processor.

Here there is a definite parallel with my experience as a meditator, for especially when I have been meditating regularly I find, more often than not, that I become concentrated as soon as I sit down on my cushion, cross my legs, and close my eyes. The parallel illustrates the fact that writing, like meditation, is able to form an entrance to a spiritual dimension by virtue of the element of concentration it involves, though it should be emphasized that for writing, as for meditation, the concentration in question is "skillful" concentration, that is, concentration that is associated with the mental states of freedom from craving, freedom from aversion, and freedom from delusion. The writing of a pornographic novel, for instance, would not be an entrance to a spiritual dimension inasmuch as the concentration involved would be associated with unskillful mental states.

My life has consisted of a series of incidents and experiences, and writing my memoirs means writing about those incidents and experiences. But first they have to be recalled. This I do not find too difficult, at least in certain respects. For instance I have a good visual memory, and can recall the way certain people and places looked, even though

I saw them forty and more years ago. What I cannot recall so easily is conversations. I can recall the substance of what was said, whether by myself or others, but very rarely can I recall the actual words that were spoken, much less still a whole series of verbal exchanges. My memoirs therefore contain no conversations, which from a purely literary point of view is a serious defect. On the few occasions when I do place my own or another person's remarks within inverted commas the reader may be sure that the words quoted were spoken exactly as given, and that I must have remembered them because they made a deep impression on me at the time.

Autobiographies and memoirs often contain conversations. A few of them consist of little else. In some cases the author may have had a good memory for conversation, or have made notes or kept a diary; in others, I suspect, he or she simply invented the conversations and dialogue, thus doing with real-life characters what the novelist does with imaginary ones. In writing my own memoirs I was determined to include nothing that was not factual even if that meant leaving some unsightly gaps in my narrative. I was determined not to usurp the function of the novelist. With regard to each incident and experience I asked myself "What actually happened?" and only when this was clear did I describe it. In other words I was concerned that my memoirs should be strictly truthful, and truthfulness is an entrance to a spiritual dimension. Certainly there can be no entry to such a dimension without it.

But truth is subjective as well as objective. One can be truthful not only with regard to outer events but also with regard to inner feelings. In writing my memoirs I therefore had to ask myself not only what happened, but also what I felt on a particular occasion, or in a certain situation. Sometimes this was obvious. Sometimes, however, it was not, and I had to recall the occasion or situation in detail, dwell upon it, and coax forth into present consciousness the feeling I then experienced. Only when I had done this did I seek to describe the feeling.

Occasionally it so happened that I was able to coax forth feelings of which I had not been fully cognizant at the time or to which I had been unwilling to admit. For example, I saw that there were occasions when my real feeling had not been just one of mild annoyance, as I then thought, but actually one of anger. I was also able to see more deeply into the motives which had led me to adopt a particular course of action or behave in a certain way. I saw how I had missed opportunities and failed to take full advantage of favorable circumstances. All this meant that in writing my memoirs I got to know myself better, at least as I had been in the past; and that self-knowledge is a means of entrance to a spiritual dimension there can be little doubt.

As I described incidents and experiences, seeking to ascertain feelings and exploring motives, and as I got to know my past self better, I began to see my life more as a whole, or at least to see more as a whole the part of it covered by my third volume of memoirs. Seeing it as a whole I was able to see it more objectively and, in a way, even to distance myself from it. Distancing myself from it I could see how one thing had led to another and how in dependence on events which were, in themselves, seemingly insignificant, there had arisen others which were of considerable importance.

In a word I saw my life as conditioned, and to the extent that one truly sees the conditioned as conditioned one is free from the conditioned, in the sense of being free from attachment to it, and has access to the unconditioned. The unconditioned being synonymous with the spiritual in the broader sense of the term, seeing one's life as a whole and as wholly conditioned is an entrance to a spiritual dimension. Not that one can see one's life as a whole only if one writes an autobiography or memoirs, or that writing these will necessarily enable one to see one's life as a whole and as conditioned, but writing them certainly enables one to focus on one's life in a sustained and systematic way that otherwise is hardly possible outside meditation.

Concentration, truthfulness both objective and subjective, and self-knowledge are all entrances to a spiritual dimension/realm, and as writing, including the (semi-creative) writing of memoirs, can involve all three, writing itself can be an entrance to that dimension. I for one have certainly found it to be so.

3. A Creative Relationship with the World

Creativity is not limited to the exercise of the fine arts; everyone is creative.

ONE OFTEN HEARS people saying—sometimes apologetically, sometimes defiantly, sometimes wistfully, sometimes ironically— "I'm not very creative." What they usually mean by this is that they cannot paint pictures, write poetry, compose music, or throw pots. Artistic creativity seems to be in vogue these days; everyone is supposed to be creative. But what do we mean by being creative? Is it just a matter of being able to paint pictures?

Creativity involves a distinction between subject and object. On the one hand there is you, the artist; on the other, the material out of which you create your work of art, as well as the idea in accordance with which you create it, an idea that may be more or less conscious. And the material out of which the artist creates may be of several kinds. There's the obvious physical stuff out of which a work is made—clay, paint, sound, language, or whatever. Then there's the involvement of the artist's own person: the voice, the physical body, the mental and emotional states. And other people also become artistic material, either as merely passive material for the artist's creativity (like a sculptor's model), or actively co-operating with it, themselves creative in relation to the artist's creativity (like an orchestra or a cast of actors). In the latter case, there is no absolute distinction between the artist and the material—the people—from which they create.

Generally we experience ourselves as subjects in relation to the "object" of the whole external world in the broadest sense. But we are not passive in relation to the external world. We do not merely register impressions. The world impinges on us, and we also impinge on the world, on our own environment, or a part of it. We impinge on our own selves, on ourselves considered as objects to ourselves (that is, considered reflexively), and we also impinge on other people. Not only do we impinge on the world; we affect it in various ways. We alter it, we arrange it, we *re*-arrange it—at least to some extent, however slight. And not only that. There is a pattern to the way in which we impinge on the world. We don't impinge on it at random, but in accordance with a certain idea, a certain pattern, image, gestalt, or myth, within ourselves—even, we could say, a pattern which *is* ourselves.

It is rare for us consciously to realize this, but what it means is that our relationship with the world is essentially creative. We are creating all the time. Creativity is not limited to the exercise of the fine arts; everyone is creative. It is only a question of the quality of our creativity—greater or lesser success, greater or lesser clarity, greater or lesser positivity. We are creative when we speak, when we decorate a room, when we write a letter. This is the basic principle of what we may call "applied Zen"—Zen applied to the art of living itself.

4. Should Buddhists Have a Sense of Humor?

It is important to cultivate a sense of proportion with regard to oneself and one's own achievements and affairs.

IT HAS BEEN SAID that to worldly people, "spiritual" people appear frivolous because they don't care about the things that matter to worldly people. If you are spiritually minded and you lose something, or you are not given something you were expecting, you tend to take it quite lightly, whereas a more worldly minded person would take it very seriously indeed. In the same way, the spiritually minded person regards as a joke things that worldly people don't find at all funny, because he or she has a greater sense of proportion. It has been said that one of the elements of humor is a sense of proportion, a sense of relative fitness. For instance, one might see a politician delivering a speech so pompously and with such self-importance that one can't help laughing, because one can see that he is not as important as he thinks he is, or as he is trying to appear.

According to the Pali Canon, the Buddha did say on one occasion that to laugh in such a way as to show the teeth is to be mad,[72] but perhaps one shouldn't take this too literally. Perhaps he was thinking of uncontrollable laughter—just abandoning oneself to it, throwing oneself around and laughing in a raucous, crude, unmindful way. The Buddha himself is almost always represented with a gentle smile; and even the Abhidharma—and you can't get much more austere than that—lists "the smile of the Arahant" among its classifications.[73] So the Abhidharma itself has a place for something like lila, something spontaneous, just for its own sake—for the smile of the Arahant is said to be without karmic significance. Perhaps the Buddha's smile arises from his perception of the incongruity between the conditioned and the Unconditioned; or perhaps he smiles a little at the mess unenlightened human beings get themselves into, though at the same time he responds to them with deep compassion.

Does a sense of humor have a part to play in the life of a Buddhist? Here one has to be very careful. Humor is often negative, and sometimes cruel, even sadistic or cynical. Cynicism can represent a fear of positive emotion, including one's own positive emotion, and a fear of being taken in; and sometimes it can be a more or less refined expression of basic negativity and anger. People are often unaware of this; it can be interesting to examine more closely the things that one finds oneself laughing at. There is also a certain style of humor that goes with one's nationality; one needs to be aware that what one thinks is funny may be simply unintelligible to people from another culture.

But humor can be a good thing. Freud speaks of wit in terms of energy release;[74] sometimes if you really let yourself go, notwithstanding the Buddha's dim view of extravagant laughter, innocent merriment can have an energizing and freeing effect. At its most innocent, humor has to do with not taking oneself too seriously. It is easy to fall into an attitude of regarding some trivial aspect of one's own life or work as being of world-shattering importance. It is important to cultivate a sense of proportion with regard to oneself and one's own achievements and affairs. You need be no less serious or hard-working, but you won't be taking yourself seriously in that self-absorbed, egoistic way.

This idea of spiritual life as a playful bubbling up of transcendental energy is a prominent feature in Indian thought and religious life. Some people take religion very seriously, even to the extent of feeling that it is somehow blasphemous to laugh in church—but the Bodhisattva's life isn't like that. It's a game, a play, a sport. That is, it is an end in itself, uncalculating, natural, and enjoyable.

5. THE PLAYFUL ARTS

You haven't come into existence after all these millions of years of evolution just to sit down in front of a typewriter, or to keep accounts.

THE DIFFERENCE between work and play is that play is not necessary. It is not harnessed to any goal; it serves no purpose. In Sanskrit the fine arts are called *lalitakala,* the "playful arts," because they're of no earthly use. You can live without the arts: no one ever dropped dead from lack of art. It is quite superfluous—which is why it's so necessary. Likewise, the Bodhisattva's life—the life that is depicted in the *Prajnaparamita*—is useful, curiously enough, precisely because it is useless. All that meditation and study and Right Livelihood culminates in the experience of being happy just being yourself, with nothing in particular to do. You might just be dancing around the room, aimlessly, unselfconsciously—not trying to be playful or spontaneous, but just being yourself. Some busybody will then turn up, of course, and say "Come on, what are you wasting your time like that for? There's work to get on with." But that's putting the cart before the horse (or rather, harnessing the horse to the cart).

Someone came to me once and said that he did not feel that he could be very useful because he had no particular talent. I told him, "Think of yourself as an unspecialized human being." People think that if they can't make themselves useful in some way—they can't type, they can't keep accounts, they can't cook, they can't write or give a talk or paint or play a musical instrument—there's something wrong with them. But consider: this apparently useless human being is the product of millions upon millions of years of evolution. You are the goal; you are what it has all been for. You don't have to justify your existence by being useful. You yourself are the justification for your existence. You haven't come into existence after all these millions of years of evolution just to sit down in front of a typewriter, or to keep accounts. *You* are the justification of that whole process. You are an end in yourself. All that you can really be said to be here for is to develop into some higher form of human life—to become a Bodhisattva, to become a Buddha. So don't be ashamed of sitting around and doing nothing. Glory in it. Do things spontaneously, out of a state of inner satisfaction and achievement. It is a virtue to be ornamental as well as useful.

If you take this seriously, you have to be watchful for people trying to work on your feelings of guilt. How can you be spontaneous if you're riddled with guilt? So don't let people get at you with any kind of emotional blackmail. If someone starts saying to you, "Look how hard I'm working for the Dharma! Don't you feel bad just sitting there doing nothing, letting me do it all?" you should just say, "No, I feel fine. I'm really enjoying watching you do it all." It is important not to give in to this sort of emotional arm-twisting; it is highly unskillful, appealing to negative emotions in order to get things done instead of arousing an enthusiasm to work for the joy of it. Don't take your Buddhist activities too earnestly. I am not advocating irresponsible frivolity or a frittering away of energy in unmindful hilarity. But even while you are doing your best to succeed at whatever you are doing, remember that you are essentially at play—and you don't lose sleep over a game; it isn't worth it. Being serious doesn't mean being solemn, just as practicing puja in front of a shrine does not call for long faces and a "dim religious light."

There is something further to take into account when we look at the spirit in which we approach Dharmic activities: the question of psychological types or temperaments. For example, there are people who are "organized," and there are others who are "non-organized." Organized types tend to do the organizing, and non-organized types are the people the organized types organize, often whether the non-organized like it or not. But just because you don't function in that organized way, it doesn't necessarily mean that you are lazy or less committed, or even that you are doing less than those who *are* organized. It is possible to function positively and creatively and energetically in a way that is anathema to the organized type.

Unfortunately, any kind of collective Buddhist activity nearly always caters for those who like being organized—and those with the opposite sort of temperament tend to get roped in willy-nilly. But why not cater for the non-organized person occasionally? Why not a have a non-organized retreat, with no program at all? Call it a "Dharma holiday"—all the retreat facilities would be there, but it would be up to you how you went about benefiting from them. Some people might want to get together, elect a leader, and organize a program, but others would go their own way and still have a very productive retreat. Some might even decide—in the most mindful, objective, responsible, and positive way—that the best thing to do with this Dharma holiday would be to get up late and sit in the garden doing nothing. For some people this could be quite a challenge; even on a retreat it is possible to fill up the day with useful activities in such a way as to lose sight of the greater mandala.

The Bodhisattva has resolved this opposition or antithesis between aesthetic contemplation on the one hand and practical activity on the other, and feels no conflict. But so long as we have to switch over from the one to the other, and so long as the presence or experience of the one implies the absence or non-experience of the other, there will always be some difficulty in the transition. All we can do is somehow try to carry the aesthetic experience into the practical activity—which is exactly what the Bodhisattva does, as represented in the Perfection of Wisdom—a very difficult process. We can make a start by adopting a more lighthearted attitude toward practical things. By all means be

useful, but only within the much larger context of complete useless-
ness. Taoism is quite good on this whole theme. Taoists say that the
man of Tao is like a great tree, which is so big that it is good for nothing—the branches are too thick for making axe-handles, and so on.
One should try to be too big to be useful. However important the
work a Bodhisattva does, he or she sees, in the Perfection of Wisdom,
that it takes place in a tiny circle within the greater mandala of quite
pointless appreciation.

4 ↩ A "Buddhist Bible"?—Buddhist Scriptures and Where They Come From

1. THE SEA OF BUDDHIST LITERATURE

The essence of the Dharma is not a limited quantity which becomes diluted, as it were, with each successive addition to Buddhist literature.

IT IS TRUE that Buddhist literature is a sea, and that none but the most laborious scholars will ever be able to wade through the oceanic extent of all the Buddhist books in Sanskrit, Pali, Tibetan, Chinese, and Japanese. But it is not necessary for the ordinary Buddhist even to attempt such a feat. Far from there being any need for a person who wants to know the essence of Buddhism to study whole libraries of volumes, all that such an enquirer has to do is to understand and thoroughly assimilate a single one out of the numerous chapters or even verses, into which that essence has been concentrated.

For the essence of the Dharma is not a limited quantity which becomes diluted, as it were, with each successive addition to Buddhist literature (as a small amount of milk might be diluted by liberal additions of water), so that one who wishes to know it has to master an ever increasing number of books. Such a way of thinking is an example of the fantastic literalness into which a purely rational and "practical" intelligence may sometimes be betrayed. If any comparison were needed, the essence of Buddhism might be more fittingly, though still imperfectly, represented by the flame of a lamp, which is able to kindle the flames of other lamps without the least diminution of its own brilliance.

A contributory source of the erroneous notion that a Buddhist ought to make himself acquainted with the whole enormous bulk of Buddhist sacred literature is to be found, perhaps, in the Protestant Christian belief that, since the Bible is the Word of God, the believer should acquaint himself with every single word of it, as ignorance of a single letter, even, might prejudice his chance of salvation.

It is hardly necessary to point out how utterly foreign such conceptions are to Buddhism, or to emphasize how serious is the mistake of trying to import them into it. The fundamental principles of the Dharma are few in number, and these can be explained in a very few pages well enough for most practical purposes. The multiplicity of Buddhist scriptures is due to the desire of generations of writers to elaborate these principles to the furthest possible extent, to pursue their implications into the remotest fields of thought and, above all else, to their eagerness to adapt them to the understanding and temperament of inconceivably numerous classes of sentient beings—an eagerness which has its origin in Compassion, in the aspiration that every birth-and-death-doomed creature should one day open the Door of the Immortal.

2. THE ORIGIN OF THE BUDDHIST SCRIPTURES

The words "Thus have I heard," with which almost every Buddhist scripture begins, represent Ananda's personal testimony that what follows is a reliable account of what the Enlightened One actually said.

THE BUDDHA HIMSELF, the historical Shakyamuni, never wrote anything. It is not even certain that he *could* read and write. In his day, writing was not a very respectable occupation. Businessmen used it for keeping their accounts, but the idea of committing anything as sacred as spiritual teachings to writing was simply unthinkable. The Buddha taught, therefore, not by writing spiritual bestsellers, but by talking to people, passing on his teachings through conversation, discussions, and discourses. For their part, his disciples made a point of remembering what he said. Sometimes, indeed, his words were so memorable that no one within earshot could possibly forget them. But even if some disciples did forget, there were others who remembered, and in due course passed on the teachings they had heard to their own disciples. In this way the Buddha's teaching was orally transmitted in India for many, many generations, spanning hundreds of years.

Not only did the early disciples remember hundreds and thousands of teachings, they also managed to arrange, edit, and even index them orally, without even beginning to put pen to paper—or rather stylus to palm leaf: surely a tremendous feat. The key figure in this whole extraordinary process was Ananda, who was the Buddha's cousin and his constant companion for the last twenty years of his life. Wherever the Buddha went, Ananda went. If the Buddha went for alms, Ananda would be just a few paces behind him. If the Buddha accepted an invitation, Ananda was naturally included. And if the Buddha gave a discourse, Ananda was present in the audience. For twenty years the Buddha was very rarely to be seen without Ananda in tow, committing everything his master said to a prodigiously retentive memory.

I must confess to having harbored doubts about Ananda's superhuman memory, until I actually met someone with comparable powers of recollection, a man who could remember everything he had ever heard me say word for word—together with where I had said it, when, and even why I had said it. This was enough to satisfy me that such an individual as Ananda is unusual, but no chimera.

It was shortly after the Buddha's death—his *parinirvana*—that Ananda's gift really came into its own. This was when the Buddha's followers gathered together in a great cave near Rajagriha in modern Bihar for the purpose of what has since become known as the First

Council. But this name for it comes nowhere near evoking the true nature of the occasion. The Sanskrit word used to describe this gathering is *sangiti,* which literally means "a chanting together" or even "a singing together." The monks—and there are supposed to have been five hundred of them—chanted or sang together whatever they could remember of the Buddha's teaching. The *sangiti* was dominated, however, by Ananda's contribution to what might be called the collective memory of the spiritual community.

So the words "Thus have I heard," with which almost every Buddhist scripture begins, represent Ananda's personal testimony that what follows is a reliable account of what the Enlightened One actually said. They mean that Ananda had been there, or that if he had not been present the Buddha had repeated it all to him afterward. They are believed to guarantee the authenticity of that text. "Thus have I heard at one time" is used like a general imprimatur, so to speak, for the content of any scripture.

3. How to Read Buddhist Texts

Sutras can be approached as sources of inspiration and enjoyment, not as texts that you have to slog your way through because you happen to be a Buddhist.

THE BUDDHIST SCRIPTURES—as we call them in English—do not, like the Bible, constitute some infallible revelation from God. They are a record of the life and teaching of a supremely and perfectly Enlightened human being, a human being who was the living embodiment of absolute Wisdom and infinite Compassion. Nonetheless, some people probably do read a sutra as though it *were* Holy Writ, and feel that they have no choice but to accept whatever the Buddha says in it, whether they like it or not; and such a projection of authority may create in them some resistance to the sutra's message.

But if a particular text is not actually labelled a sutra, we can avoid the mistake of regarding it as "spiritually authoritative." We can read it, in fact, more or less as we would read any other work of the imagination—a novel, a poem, or a short story. If we can read Buddhist texts as literature rather than dogma, as poetry rather than scientific fact or philosophical truth, we may perhaps be more open to their spiritual message. We may even allow ourselves to be captivated—at least a little—by their atmosphere and their magic. (Conversely—this is just a thought—we might try reading works of imagination as though they were sutras, and in this way open ourselves to their real spiritual content.)

What I am getting at is that sutras can be approached as sources of inspiration and enjoyment, not as texts that you have to slog your way through because you happen to be a Buddhist. You may have to put in some additional study and reflection—it may take some time and many readings to understand a sutra deeply and really appreciate it—but some phrases or images may affect you quite powerfully straight away. It is true that we may well feel more at home with Western literature. Most of it is easier to read because it has been written by unenlightened people like ourselves—with all sorts of little glimmers of insight here and there—and it deals generally with ordinary human predicaments with which we can easily identify. But human frailty is not the only possible subject for literature; it is certainly not always the most inspiring and uplifting one. We can also read literature which takes us away from our ordinary human life and its frailties. And this is what the Mahayana sutras are all about—to take us away from the ordinary, to give us a taste of the magical.

Obviously it is difficult to rise to that level of experience, so it is going to be difficult to read sutras, just as it is difficult to read some of the great works of Western literature. Any work of literature has an effect commensurate with the effort one makes to understand it. It is really a matter of getting into the habit of stretching oneself a bit. If you have a strong enough desire to understand, you will make the effort.

4. BUDDHIST STORIES

Whether told by monk or minstrel, or enacted in dramatic form, the story of Vessantara is as well known to the Tibetan nomad as to the Burmese farmer, and moves both equally to tears.

HUMAN BEINGS have always loved stories, and the people of India have been, perhaps, even more addicted to this form of entertainment than those of other lands. Dialogues and anthologies could hardly be expected to vie with them in popularity. Quite early in the history of the religion, therefore, the followers of the Buddha lighted, either by design or by accident, on the happy idea of appropriating the entire wealth of ancient Indian folklore, including fables, proverbs, fairy tales, anecdotes, ballads, riddles, humorous stories, jokes, novels, romances, moral narratives, and pious legends, and incorporating them *en bloc* in their own rapidly growing oral-cum-literary tradition as the simplest and most effective means of propagating the truths of the Dharma among the common people. In this way the Jatakas and Avadanas came into existence.

The stories themselves are of numerous types. Among the animal fables of the first *nipatas,* which contain the shorter Jatakas, there are several that parallel those of Aesop—the stories of the ass in a lion's skin and the jackal who, to get some fruit, praised the crow for her fine voice are examples. Who borrowed from whom we do not know. The fairy tales, of which there are many genres, include tales of grateful animals and ungrateful human beings, of strange adventures with ghostly women and lovely cannibal demonesses, of superhuman beings of various types, both quaint and monstrous, as well as tales of mystery and magic. Humorous sketches, satires, and tales in which the Bodhisattva, as hero, exhibits his ready wit, good judgment, cleverness, and skill by answering riddles, resolving dilemmas, and accomplishing all kinds of seemingly impossible tasks are also plentiful. Of great interest from a sociological, and even from a literary, point of view, are the picaresque tales in which robbers, vagabonds, gamesters, and courtesans play the principal roles, as well as the sometimes coarse, but evidently highly popular, stories dealing with all manner of sexual improprieties.

Besides material of this sort, the connection of which with Buddhism is at times obscure, the Jataka book contains, as might be expected, a good number of patently didactic moral tales. Much the greater part of the work, however, especially in its later sections, is taken up by various types of legend. These are often of great beauty. Some of them occur in that ancient Indian epic-cum-encyclopedia the *Mahabharata.* They inculcate the old grave moral virtues, such as service to one's parents, truthfulness, and chastity, and teach the impermanence of all worldly things and the happiness of renunciation. These latter themes often feature in the purely Buddhist stories among the Jatakas, especially those illustrating the practice of the *paramitas.* As Winternitz observes, they are characterized by "exceeding kindness and gentleness, and self-sacrifice transcending by far the bounds of what is natural."[75] The King of the Sivis sacrifices his eyes; Prince Kanha, renouncing all he possesses, goes to the Himalayas as a hermit; Khantivadin, the "Preacher of Patience," remains free from anger even when barbarously mutilated by an enraged potentate; Prince Vessantara gladly gives away not only the palladium of his father's kingdom but his wife and two young children. The superiority of the golden rule is also inculcated. In spirit if not in form, some of the tales of grateful or heroically virtuous animals belong to the same category. The monkey-chief, in order to save his retinue, makes himself into a bridge; the Banyan deer, moved by the plight of the pregnant doe, offers his own life to the king as a ransom for hers.

Popular as the whole of the Jataka book undoubtedly is, it is the legends of sublime self-abnegation and absolute altruism that have most deeply and decisively influenced the religious outlook of the Buddhist peoples of South-East Asia. So much might be said, indeed, of China, Japan, and Tibet; for there exist Sanskrit collections of Jatakas which, in translation, are no less familiar to the followers of the Mahayana. Whether told by monk or minstrel, or enacted in dramatic form, the story of Vessantara is as well known to the Tibetan nomad as to the Burmese farmer, and moves both equally to tears. Most of the finest Bodhisattva stories are, in fact, the common heritage of the entire Buddhist world, and one of its greatest unifying influences.

5. The Bible Designed to Be Read as Literature

The possibility of fundamentalism exists wherever a canonical literature exists.

In 1940 I was in Torquay, a seaside town in south-west England to which I was sent as a teenager to avoid the bombing in London. One day, in the window of a bookshop in the main street, I saw a new publication on sale: *The Bible Designed to be Read as Literature.* It was a large, thick volume, and since it lay there open I could see that it was printed like an ordinary book, the text not being divided into the usual numbered verses. At that time the idea that the Bible could be read as literature was comparatively new, at least to the wider reading public. It was certainly new to me. From school and church I had imbibed the idea that the Bible was essentially a repository of texts. Texts lay side by side in the Bible like bullets in a bandolier, and these bullets could be fired off at anyone with whom one happened to be having an argument, whether about religion or about anything else. To quote a text —or texts—from the Bible settled the matter. This kind of attitude still prevails, of course, among fundamentalist Christians of all denominations. But reading the Bible as literature meant, so far as I remember, reading it in much the same way as one would read the works of Shakespeare, and the layout of the volume that I saw in the window of the Torquay bookshop was intended to facilitate this process. It was intended to encourage one to think of the Bible as a book rather than as a collection of bullets, and to approach it accordingly. Thus *The Bible Designed to be Read as Literature* was the Bible designed to be read for enjoyment. It was the Bible designed to be read as a whole—or rather as a series of wholes—rather than chopped up into bits in the form of numbered "verses." It was the Bible designed to be read, in the case of some of its books, as poetry rather than as prose. It was the Bible designed to be read for its own sake rather than for the sake of some ulterior purpose. To the fundamentalist, reading the Bible in this way was irreverent, even blasphemous. How could one possibly read the Bible as one read the works of Shakespeare? The Bible was the Word of God. How could one possibly compare profane literature, however great, with literature that had been inspired, even dictated, by the Holy Spirit?

In Buddhism there is no such thing as full-blown fundamentalism in the Christian sense. Buddhists have never chopped up the Buddhist canonical literature into bits and used the bits as bullets. Nevertheless, it has to be admitted that in some Buddhist circles there exists a sort of quasi-fundamentalism that could, if it were to develop, be as antithetical to our approaching Buddhist canonical literature as literature as Christian fundamentalism is to the appreciation of *The Bible Designed to be Read as Literature*. This quasi-fundamentalism takes the form of appealing to the authority of the canonical literature in support of a particular belief or practice but only in a general way, that is, without actually citing any individual text or texts. An appeal of this sort is usually couched in such language as "the Buddha says," or "according to the Tipitaka," or "it is stated in all the Sutras and Tantras." This quasi-fundamentalism is strengthened by the fact that in many parts of the Buddhist world the beautifully written and richly bound volumes of the canonical literature are often ceremonially worshipped rather than read—even in the case of those very bhikkhus and lamas who appeal to their authority in this manner. This is not to say that there is anything wrong in making the volumes of the Buddhist canonical literature an object of ceremonial worship. Such is far from being the case. But ceremonial worship of the volumes of the Buddhist canonical literature is no substitute for the actual reading of that literature. Unless we read the canonical literature we cannot understand and practice the Buddha's teaching and—what is of particular relevance to the present discussion—unless we read the canonical literature there can be no question of our approaching it as literature.

Even the quasi-fundamentalism that exists in some Buddhist circles is not easy to eradicate, however. Indeed, it may be said that despite the fact that in Buddhism there is no full-blown fundamentalism in the Christian sense, the possibility of fundamentalism exists wherever a canonical literature exists, irrespective of whether that literature is regarded as the Word of God or as the written record of the utterance of a supremely Enlightened human teacher. Such being the case, it should be possible for us to apply the same general principles that were responsible for the appearance of the thick volume of *The Bible Designed to be Read as Literature* in the window of that Torquay bookshop to the Buddhist canonical literature, in such a way as to enable us to understand what it actually means, in practical terms, to approach Buddhist canonical literature as literature.

Thus, to approach Buddhist canonical literature as literature means, in the first place, reading the canonical literature for enjoyment. This does not mean reading it for the sake of amusement, or simply to while away the time. Reading the canonical literature for enjoyment means reading it because in so doing we find ourselves immersed in an emotionally positive state of being such as—outside meditation—we hardly ever experience. Reading the canonical literature for enjoyment means reading it without any sense of compulsion. We do not *have* to read it. Whether as represented by the *Dhammapada* or the *White Lotus Sutra,* the *Middle Length Sayings* or the *Perfection of Wisdom "in Eight Thousand Lines,"* the Buddhist canonical literature is not a sort of prescribed text on which we are going to be examined at the end of the year and rewarded or punished in accordance with how well—or how badly—we have done. Reading the canonical literature for enjoyment means reading it because we want to read it. It means reading it because we have an affinity with it, and are drawn to it naturally and spontaneously. Having said this, however, I must add that I always find it a little strange when someone who professes to be a committed Buddhist does not read at least some parts of the canonical literature for enjoyment, especially if he or she enjoys reading other kinds of literature.

To approach the Buddhist canonical literature as literature also means reading it as a whole. This does not mean reading the whole of that literature (it is in any case fifty times more extensive than the Bible) but rather reading this or that item of canonical literature as a whole. Reading the *Sutta-Nipata,* or the *Vimalakirti-nirdesa,* for example, in this manner, means not reading it piecemeal, not concentrating on the parts at the expense of the whole, but reading it in such a way as to allow oneself to experience its total impact. Only if we read it in this kind of way will we be able to grasp the fundamental significance of the work or, if you like, its gestalt. This is particularly the case, perhaps, where the work in question possesses a definite artistic unity and where it has been cast in poetic form. In the latter case, to approach the Buddhist canonical literature as literature means, of course, reading it as poetry. It was one of the special features of *The Bible Designed to be Read as Literature* that it printed the poetical books of the Old Testament as poetry, which gave them a rather Whitmanesque appearance, instead of chopping them up into numbered bits as though they were prose. (Not that even prose should really be treated in this way.) In the case of Buddhist canonical literature there is no danger of works, or parts of works, that are in poetic form being chopped up into numbered bits—at least, not when they are printed in the original. The danger is that when they are translated into a modern language they will be translated not into poetry but into prose and read accordingly.

Finally, and perhaps most importantly, to approach the Buddhist canonical literature as literature means to read it for its own sake rather than for the sake of some ulterior purpose. The ulterior purposes for the sake of which it is possible to read the canonical literature are very numerous. I shall mention only a few of them, leaving you to think of the rest for yourself. Buddhist canonical literature can be read simply for the sake of the languages in which it has come down to us, that is, it can be read with a view to furthering our knowledge of linguistics. Similarly, it can be read for the sake of the light it sheds (particularly in the case of the agamas/Nikayas and the Vinaya-Pitaka) on the political, social, economic, and religious condition of India at the time of the Buddha and his immediate disciples. Buddhist canonical literature can also be read for the sake of its contribution to comparative religion and mythology and to the intellectual history of mankind. It can even be read for the purpose of refuting Buddhism, as when a Christian missionary reads it before going off to work in a Buddhist country. With the possible exception of the last, there is nothing wrong with reading the Buddhist canonical literature for the sake of any of these purposes. But the fact remains that they are all ulterior purposes—ulterior, that is, to the purpose that the Buddhist canonical literature exists to serve and for the sake of which, therefore, it should really be read.

The purpose that the Buddhist canonical literature exists to serve is the happiness and welfare—the highest happiness and highest welfare—of all sentient beings, and we read that literature for its own sake when we read it with this in mind. The Buddhist canonical literature is, after all, the *Buddhavacana,* the word or utterance of the Enlightened One. It is a communication from the heart and mind of an Enlightened human being to the hearts and minds of those who are as yet unenlightened. It is a communication from the Buddha to us. Reading the canonical literature for its own sake therefore means reading it in order to listen to what the Buddha has to say to us— which means listening seriously. Indeed, we cannot really listen in any other kind of way. I have more than once said of the poets—especially the great poets—that far from merely indulging in flowery language they in fact mean exactly what they say, and that they are trying to communicate to us something which they think worth communicating. How much more so is this the case with the Buddha, and how much more seriously, therefore, ought we to listen to the words of the *Buddhavacana!* How much more seriously ought we to read the Buddhist canonical literature!

This, then, is what it means, in practical terms, to approach the Buddhist canonical literature as literature. It means reading the Buddhist canonical literature for enjoyment, reading it as a whole, reading it—wherever appropriate—as poetry rather than as prose, and reading it for its own sake rather than for the sake of some ulterior purpose. But when I speak of approaching Buddhist canonical literature as literature I do not mean to imply that it is all equally literature, or all literature in the same sense of the term. A distinction made by De Quincey will be useful here. According to De Quincey, there are two kinds of literature. He says, "There is first the literature of knowledge, and secondly, the literature of power. The function of the former is to teach; the function of the second is to move; the first is a rudder, the second an oar or a sail. The first speaks to the mere discursive understanding; the second speaks ultimately, it may happen, to the higher understanding of reason." In another place De Quincey goes so far as to suggest that the literature of knowledge is not really literature at all. "All that is literature seeks to communicate power: all that is not literature seeks to communicate knowledge." In the last analysis the difference between the two kinds of literature, or two kinds of communication, would seem to be one of degree rather than one of kind. Literature is not all equally literature, nor all literature in the same sense of the term, in that some works of literature communicate more power—and therefore move us more—than others. In the case of the Bible, the Book of Job moves us more than the Book of Leviticus, even though the Book of Leviticus contains a great deal more information about the ancient Jewish sacrificial system. Thus the Book of Job belongs to the literature of power. It is literature proper. It is "great literature."

Applying this to the Buddhist canonical literature, we may say that the narrative power of the *Mahaparinibbana Sutta*, which describes the Buddha's last days, moves us more than does a (to some) abstruse philosophical work like the Abhidhamma *Dhatu-katha* (I am taking extreme examples to make the distinction clear), the imaginative sweep of a Mahayana sutra like the *Vimalakirti-nirdesa* more than the subtle logic of a Perfection of Wisdom text like the *Suvikrantivikrami-paripriccha* (also of the Mahayana tradition), and the stirring "Confession" chapter of the *Sutra of Golden Light* (the *Suvarna-prabhasha Sutra*) more than the hard-to-fathom "Sunyata" chapter of the same work. Thus the *Mahaparinibbana Sutta,* the *Vimalakirti-nirdesa,* and the "Confession" chapter of the *Suvarna-prabhasha Sutra* all belong to the literature of power, while the *Dhatu-katha,* the *Suvikrantivikrami-paripriccha,* and the "Sunyata" chapter of the *Suvarna-prabhasha Sutra* all belong to the literature of knowledge. Since it is the literature of power that constitutes literature in the real sense, or great literature, reading the Buddhist canonical literature as literature therefore means reading such works as the *Mahaparinibbana Sutta* rather than such works as the *Dhatu-katha.* Indeed, we might even go so far as to say that just as literature is not all equally literature so canonical literature is not all equally canonical literature, and that it is the more truly canonical the more deeply it moves us. This is not to say that, from the Buddhist point of view, there is a real distinction between teaching, which according to De Quincey is the function of the literature of knowledge, and moving, which according to De Quincey is the function of the literature of power. From the point of view of Buddhism, the Buddha teaches by moving, because his "teaching" is addressed not to what De Quincey calls "the mere discursive understanding" or what we might call the alienated intellect, but rather to what De Quincey calls "the higher understanding of reason" or what we might call the heart, in the sense of the deepest part of our being, or the spiritual intuition, or the whole person. Reading the Buddhist canonical literature as literature therefore means reading it as the literature of power and allowing ourselves to be moved by that power to the fullest possible extent.

One last point. I have said that when works, or parts of works, of Buddhist canonical literature that are in poetry are translated into a modern language there is the danger that they will be translated into prose and read accordingly. The danger consists in the fact that poetry is the literature of power *par excellence,* which is the reason why poetry is capable of moving us to a far greater extent than prose, so that when poetry is translated into prose it loses much of its original power and, therefore, much of its capacity to move. In reading works of Buddhist canonical literature in translation we should be careful to read them, wherever possible, in translations which do justice to their poetic quality. Otherwise we shall be unable to read them as literature in the fullest sense and thus will not be moved by them to the extent that we might have been.

If we are able, however, to read poetry as poetry, if we are able to understand the real nature of literature, if we are able to see to what extent we are justified in approaching Buddhist canonical literature as literature, and able to see what it actually means, in practical terms, to approach it in this way, if we allow ourselves to feel the power of works like the *Mahaparinibbana Sutta* and the *Vimalakirti-nirdesa,* then we shall obtain at least a glimpse of the glory of the literary world, and gain a better understanding of the real nature of Buddhist canonical literature.

6. PALI SCRIPTURES AND MAHAYANA SUTRAS

If we really allow ourselves to become absorbed in a Mahayana sutra, we become part of it. We join the great assembly and experience ourselves right in the midst of it, taking part in the events of the sutra as they unfold.

IF YOU READ the Pali scriptures and then the Mahayana scriptures—say two or three volumes of each, enough to give you a taste of them—you will notice that you get something from the Mahayana scriptures that you do not quite get from the Pali texts. This is not by any means to dismiss the unique historical and spiritual importance of the Pali scriptures. They give us a vivid and deeply moving picture of the life and teaching career of the human historical Buddha. They contain all the basic spiritual principles and practices from which all

322 ~ THE ESSENTIAL SANGHARAKSHITA

the subsequent forms of Buddhism developed. They are rich in content and full of inspiration. We cannot possibly dispense with the Pali scriptures; as Buddhists, we are enormously indebted to them. Humanity, in fact, is indebted to them. They cannot be praised enough and we cannot be sufficiently grateful for them.

They do not, however, contain everything that everybody needs. There is an element missing, and it is this element that we find in the Mahayana scriptures. Reading the Mahayana scriptures, we are emancipated from the contingent and the determinate, from time, space, and causality, from historical reality. We experience archetypal reality, myth, the realm of undefined meanings. In technical terms, we encounter the *sambhogakaya.* That is, we encounter the Buddhas and Bodhisattvas of the Mahayana in their archetypal forms. Through this experience we contact something within us of which we were not previously aware. Something is sparked off that even the Pali scriptures were unable to spark off. And this happens because the realm of archetypal reality, of myth, of undefined meanings, corresponds to something within us.

According to the *Tibetan Book of the Dead,* we experience this realm directly when we die. In the intermediate state between death and rebirth we experience all sorts of visions, including visions of Buddhas and Bodhisattvas in both their peaceful and their wrathful forms. And the Buddhist tradition tells us not to be afraid, but to recognize all these visions, all these Buddhas and Bodhisattvas, as our own thought forms, as phenomena of our own true mind. If we can do this, we attain liberation on the spot.

As a writer, one inevitably notices a difference in feeling between the experience of composing passages of conceptual prose and the experience of writing something more creative, more inspired or poetic. It is this kind of shift we feel when we make the transition from the prose of the Pali scriptures to the poetry of the Mahayana scriptures, the transition from history to myth on a grand scale.

Unfortunately, some people cannot make this transition. Take the well-known case of Charles Darwin. As a young man Darwin loved poetry and literature, especially Shakespeare, but for the greater part of his life he immersed himself in scientific research. When as an old man he tried to get back to Shakespeare, he found to his dismay that poetry held no meaning for him any more; he had lost his capacity to enjoy it. In the course of his years, even decades, of scientific research, a whole side of him had withered and died. Much the same happened to John Stuart Mill, at least for part of his life. Even as a small boy his favorite subjects were logic and political economy; and as he grew older he found that he became more and more cut off from poetry. It is not just that he was cut off from poetry in the literary sense; he was—to put it rather poetically—cut off from the poetry of life.

Today we are all exposed to this sort of danger. We all suffer from this sort of deprivation, at least to some extent. We have been suffering from it, in fact, since the Industrial Revolution, at the beginning of which William Blake warned against the loss of what he called "the divine vision." He criticized Bacon, Newton, and Locke so vigorously because he felt that they tended to limit humanity to the realm of historical reality, the realm of time, space, and causality. In his own literary and visual creative work Blake, of course, was not limited in this way. In his Prophetic Books especially he explores the deeper levels of human experience. Blake's profound concern with archetypal forces and forms must explain why he continues to hold such a fascination for people today.

Our desire to contact the realm of the archetypal also explains the popularity of tales of myth and fantasy, whether traditional, like the stories of King Arthur, or modern, like *The Lord of the Rings* and some forms of science fiction. Such works explore facets of humanity's quest for meaning, and in reading them we are trying, perhaps unconsciously, to break out of the prison of merely historical reality, seeking to experience a deeper meaning to our existence.

Meaning is not a thing that you can grasp by looking in a dictionary. Meaning must be meaning *for you,* something that you personally experience. Our quest for meaning is therefore our quest for ourselves, our quest for the totality, the wholeness, of our own being. On one level we belong to the realm of historical reality; but on another, we belong to the realm of spiritual reality. The Mahayana scriptures reveal this world to us. So does myth; so does poetry. And they reveal it to us not as something external to ourselves, but as our own world, as a world in which we ourselves actually live, usually without knowing it.

It was a maxim of the Neo-Platonists that the eye could not behold the sun unless it had within its nature something sun-like, something akin to the sun.[76] Similarly, we can experience the archetypal realm only because we ourselves are, on another level, archetypal beings. If we really allow ourselves to become absorbed in a Mahayana sutra, we become part of it. We join the great assembly and experience ourselves right in the midst of it, taking part in the events of the sutra as they unfold.

But although we can make the transition to the realm of archetypal reality, this does not mean that we leave the realm of historical reality behind. We cannot—we must not—opt for myth and discard history. We need both, because we exist in both realms. We exist in them both all the time, whether or not we are aware of it. And of course a lot of the time we are not aware of it. Our relation to the archetypal realm is analogous to our relation to the dream state. When we are asleep and dreaming, we exist, one might say, in the dream realm, and we have all sorts of experiences. When we wake up, we are no longer in the dream state, but the emotions we experienced while we were dreaming continue. It's like an underground river that we descend into from time to time through a hole in the ground: just as the river is flowing all the time, so there is continuity between dreams. You can even have a dream, wake up, and then fall asleep again and continue with the same dream, as though it has been going on all the time.

In a sense we are living in that dream realm all the time. And we can extend that to the realm of archetypal experience. Just as a very strong dream continues to have its effect when we have woken up, so the archetypal realm continues to affect us, whether or not we are conscious of it.

5 ⟿ Dreams, Myths, and Symbols

1. THE NATURE OF TANTRIC BUDDHISM

Tantric Buddhism is concerned not with theories or speculations, not with formal religiosity or external piety, but with the direct experience, in the depths of one's being, of what one truly and essentially is.

I WELL REMEMBER my early impressions of the Tantra. As I tried to penetrate a little into it, to see what it was about and how it connected with other forms of Buddhism and with modern thought (psychology, comparative symbolism, and so on), I felt more and more that it was a jungle—a jungle in which one could very easily get lost. There seemed to be so many different traditions within it. There were so many meditation methods and forms of ritual observance, so many kinds of offerings, even so many kinds of ceremonial robe— and, indeed, ceremonial hat.

I used to tell my Tibetan friends that I found the Tantra far too vast and complicated to study as a whole, and that I was therefore going to confine myself to the study of one little corner of it. My chosen field of study, I said, would be the hats, some of which were very weird and wonderful indeed. I would make a collection of at least a hundred kinds of Tantric hat, and then write a book about them. Of course, I never did. But even when I began to study the Tantra in earnest, there were so many images in the temples, so many scroll paintings, so many figures of Buddhas and Bodhisattvas and gurus, and dakas and dakinis and dharmapalas, that for a long time I continued to feel that the Tantra was truly a vast jungle.

This is likely to be the experience of any Westerner beginning to investigate the Tantra. The impression one gets of richness and variety, growth, fertility, and abundance is quite bewildering to begin with. But a feeling of being lost among the creative symbols of Tantric Buddhism is no cause for alarm. Indeed, to become *intellectually* lost in the context of the Tantra is quite a positive thing. One may find oneself moved or stirred by the symbols without being able to say exactly how or why. With more experience, one comes to discover that the Tantra is not really the jungle it appears to be. It is more like a garden or, rather, a complex of gardens. Despite the richness of the Tantra, despite its incredible profusion, its superabundance of material and its exuberance, there is a pattern running through it, or a number of interlocking patterns. These patterns are not intellectual but spiritual. They are not imposed on the Tantra from the outside, but unfold from within it, expressing its innermost nature and essential purpose.

What is that purpose? Tantric Buddhism is concerned not with theories or speculations, not with formal religiosity or external piety, but with the direct experience, in the depths of one's being, of what one truly and essentially is. It seeks to reveal to us our essential nature—not just psychologically but existentially, metaphysically, even transcendentally. So far as the Tantra is concerned, this experience cannot be mediated by concepts. In fact, concepts give no idea of it at all, do not lead to it or point to it in any way. It is beyond words, beyond thought, beyond the conscious mind and personality. But this direct experience can be evoked, conjured up, or at least glimpsed, with the help of symbols. The whole Tantric path to Enlightenment is strewn with symbolic images, mantras, and rituals. You stumble over them at every step; indeed, the Tantric path largely consists of them. And they are all intended to reflect, or lead to, or give a glimpse of, this direct experience.

2. THE VALUE OF THE DREAM STATE

Marvelous to relate, we are alive.

THESE DAYS most of us imagine we have so many things to do that we can't afford to spend much of our precious time sitting about reflecting on life. But if we do happen to find time to turn things over in our minds a little more seriously than usual, we may well have to acknowledge certain things about ourselves, things that we may not find altogether pleasant to accept, things that aren't entirely to our credit. And one of the things that on reflection we may be forced to acknowledge is that as human beings we take quite a lot for granted. There are certain things which we know we possess, we know we experience, but of the value and significance of which we are totally unaware—so unaware, indeed, that we might as well not possess them at all.

Suppose that when you were a baby, you had been given a pebble to play with. And suppose you kept that pebble and played with it every day, every hour, so that it became as familiar to you as your own hand. You would gradually become so used to the pebble that you would probably not take any particular care of it or attach any particular value to it. You might never realize, in fact, that the "pebble" was not a pebble at all, but a priceless precious stone.

One of the things we tend to treat as a pebble, instead of the precious stone it really is, is life itself. We fail to understand the significance of the bare fact that we are alive. But it *is* significant. After all, we might just as easily be dead, or never have existed at all. But we do exist. There was, we could say, some unique, unrepeatable combination of circumstances, and here we are. It may have been a billion to one chance, but it has come off. Marvelous to relate, we are alive. We are sitting here. How wonderful!

This is surely what the old Zen monk was celebrating when he cried out "How wonderful! How miraculous! I draw water and I carry fuel." He had realized that until then he had taken his ordinary, everyday life for granted, utterly failing to realize its value and significance.

Another thing that we take for granted is our "ordinary" human consciousness, the normal waking state. We take it for granted that we can see and hear. We take it for granted that we can think. We take it for granted that we can be aware. More often than not, we simply fail to realize the unaccountable singularity of it all.

And in the same way, we take sleep for granted—such a wonderful, such a refreshing thing as sleep—unless of course we are unfortunate enough to have to resort to sleeping tablets. We even, most of us, take our dreams for granted. You get bad dreams—this is what our grand-mothers used to tell us—if you eat too much cheese at night, and that's all there is to it. Or else—this is another popular theory—dreams are just a jumbled reminiscence of the events of the previous day.

But if you think about it, the dream state is a rather strange thing. In the dream state, the physical sense organs are not functioning, but nonetheless we see, we hear, we even smell and taste. In the dream state we're oblivious to the physical body, but we do seem to have a sort of body. We are free to move about, free to go places—in fact, we have more freedom than we do when we are awake. We can go any-where, by any method. Sometimes we can even fly.

And in dreams we experience a different kind of time, a different kind of space—even a different kind of world. Usually the dream world is a recognizable extension of the world of everyday waking consciousness, but not always. Sometimes it's a completely different world, a world of which we have had no previous experience in any form. It's almost as though we have passed through the dream state into quite another state of consciousness, quite another mode of being—even into a higher state of consciousness, a higher mode of being. To suppose that higher states of consciousness are accessible only from the waking state is pure assumption. It's just another of those things that we take for granted. The fact is that we certainly can have access to these higher states from or through the dream state.

In Buddhism, especially in the Mahayana and the Vajrayana, the value of the dream state is recognized as being twofold. In the first place, it shows us that it is possible to experience a state of consciousness other than the waking state. This is quite an obvious point, but no less profound for that. And secondly, certain dreams show us that we can experience states of consciousness which are not only different from the waking state but higher than it. For this reason, dreams play an important role, sometimes even a crucial role, in the transformation of the individual.

3. What Is Myth?

How as Western Buddhists will we engage in the creation of myth?

THE WORD MYTH, in the sense I intend it, does not mean something false or imaginary. A myth, one might think, is a story about gods and goddesses, and in a way this is so—but we have to ask what those gods and goddesses are, or what they represent. They are beings or powers or forces that exist on some other level, some other plane of being. So when our life is inspired by a mythic dimension, we are working out on the historical plane something that is of archetypal significance. And the *bodhicitta,* one could say, is the myth that inspires the Buddhist spiritual community.

Whatever the rational, conceptual, historically-oriented consciousness may comprehend, there is an imaginative or archetypal dimension to life that will always elude that rational consciousness. An analogy can be drawn here with our dream life. We may have a rich and vivid dream life—more vivid, sometimes, than our waking life. If we are to give a complete account of ourselves, we must describe not only our waking life but also our dream life; but this, significantly, most of us find very difficult to do. We often don't remember our dreams; and when we are dreaming we rarely remember our waking life. They go along more or less separately, occupying their different planes. Likewise, if one does a lot of meditation, not much may be happening on the material plane—one may be on retreat and therefore not "doing" very much at all—but a lot will be happening on that other plane of existence which is meditative consciousness.

If one's inner experience finds a collective expression in some kind of spiritual movement, one could think of that movement as having a dream life, or a mythic life, of its own. Perhaps it does have an existence on another level. Indeed, if it did not, if it were merely an organization on the material plane, it would wither away very quickly. It needs to have very deep roots—roots in the sky.

A myth comes into being when people have very strong feelings about something, feelings which are not adequately supported by the existing state of affairs. The Mahayana Buddhists, it seems, felt a need to create a myth able to reflect not only their positive emotions but also the higher truths of Buddhism. Unable to nourish themselves on the dry bread—as they saw it—of the Abhidharma, they *had* to believe in the sort of Buddhism those myths represented. So one isn't to think that the Mahayanists decided on rational grounds that it was about time there was a bit of myth in Buddhism. Their myths emerged out of spiritual necessity. The creation of these myths was, as with all myths, a collective rather than an individual process. And the myths were not created out of thin air; there were elements in the teachings going right back to the time of the Buddha that the myth-makers could build on. The Pali Canon is very rich in mythical and legendary material, although the modern Theravada tends to ignore that aspect of its literature.

Indeed, in the Pali Canon one may even see myths in the process of emerging. There is an episode in the *Mahaparinibbana Sutta* of the *Digha Nikaya* in which Ananda asks the Buddha if he is really going to gain parinirvana in the little wattle-and-daub township of Kusinara. Couldn't he choose a more distinguished place? But the Buddha says, "Don't say that, Ananda. Formerly this was the capital of a very great kingdom."[77] Then another sutta of the *Digha Nikaya*, the *Mahasudassana Sutta,* gives what is clearly an amplified version of this same episode, including a lot of imagery along almost Mahayanistic lines.[78] The *Sukhavati-vyuha* sutras of the Mahayana may be said to carry on from where this Pali sutta leaves off; certain references (to rows of jewel trees, for example) are very similar indeed.[79]

The question for us now is how we may renew this mythical dimension. How as Western Buddhists will we engage in the creation of myth? On the one hand we have the whole Buddhist tradition, together with the mythology of Western culture, to inspire us. On the other, we have so much theoretical knowledge getting in the way of that inspiration. The creation of myths will depend on our own very deep feelings and profound aspirations, feelings that go beyond our present personal situation, and even the existing world situation. If we have these feelings and aspirations, eventually there will be a need for them to be projected in an objective form, as myth. In the meantime it is important to recognize myths like the bodhicitta for what they are, and to appreciate what their mythical status means.

4. The Emergence of Myth in Buddhism

The Buddha is clearly a historical figure who is concerned with teaching individuals how they may develop as human beings. It is only later on, especially in the Mahayana and then in the Vajrayana, that myth appears.

To contemporary Buddhists it might seem that myth, by which I mean not "untruth" but something that is deeply true, an expression (through image or story) of truths beyond the direct grasp of our intellect, is an integral part of Buddhism—but in fact it was quite a late development. By contrast, in the historical development of Christianity the myth came first—the myth of the savior, the son of God who is slain by his enemies, then comes back to life and returns to his father in heaven, taking his worshippers with him. The strength—and the weakness—of Christianity is that it is based on a myth of this kind. As time went on, the myth was gradually turned into history; ethical and spiritual teachings were incorporated into it, but the myth came first.

Then, the myth being firmly established as history, came the teaching. This is reflected in the Creed which is still recited today: the striking thing about it is that it is nothing but myth. The teaching, a certain amount of which evidently did take place, according to the Gospels, is just passed over, apparently regarded as being of no significance. A Christian is not someone who believes in the Sermon on the Mount— after all, such teachings are found in other religions too—but some-one who believes in the virgin birth, the crucifixion, the resurrection, and the ascension—in other words, someone who believes in myths.

In Buddhism it is the other way round: first teaching, then myth. The Buddha is clearly a historical figure who is concerned with teach-ing individuals how they may develop as human beings. It is only later on, especially in the Mahayana and then in the Vajrayana, that myth appears. This is illustrated by the development of the mandala of the five Buddhas. First of all you simply have the Buddha Shakyamuni, in the different phases of his career: in meditation under the Bodhi tree, then calling the earth to witness, then teaching, then reassuring his dis-ciples, then offering the gift of the Dharma to his disciples and to the world. From this naturalistic basis developed specific Buddha icons, each Buddha making a gesture or mudra to illustrate each situation. If the Buddha were depicted with his hands folded in his lap, that would represent him meditating under the Bodhi tree, and if the tips of his fin-gers were touching the earth, that would represent calling the earth to witness, while if he were displaying a mudra as though turning a wheel, that would represent the turning of the wheel of the Dharma.

In this way there emerged a set of five episodes with five mudras, and these gradually became almost like five different Buddhas. The whole idea of Buddhahood was gradually raised to a more ideal or archetypal level, giving a richer and more multifaceted—even multi-dimensional—expression to the content of the original, historically embodied Buddha ideal. Thus was formed the mandala of the five Buddhas. In the center was *the* Buddha—the primary Buddha, you could say. (Over the course of time, as different traditions developed, this central position could be occupied by whichever Buddha was central to a particular tradition, or even to a particular practitioner.) To the right and left of the central Buddha were the Buddhas of the east and west, representing respectively wisdom and compassion, or the intellectual and emotional aspects of Buddhahood. This was a development of the Mahayana. Then, with the Tantra, appeared the Buddhas of the north and south, representing further aspects of Enlightenment—compassionate action and beauty. So now there were five: one at the center and one at each of the cardinal points.

The five Buddhas are sometimes referred to as the *Dhyani-Buddhas*, but this is not a truly Buddhist term, and never occurs in Buddhist texts. It was coined by someone writing about Nepalese Buddhism in the nineteenth century (the word was derived from the Sanskrit *dhyana*, which refers to states of meditative concentration), and then taken up and popularized by the Theosophists. The five Buddhas are more correctly spoken of as the five Jinas—that is, the five Conquerors—or the five Tathagatas. Each Jina or Buddha can be regarded as having an active aspect, personified in the form of his attendant Bodhisattva, or even two attendant Bodhisattvas, representing his compassion and his wisdom, or his wisdom and his activity, or his activity and his compassion. These were sometimes split up into further aspects, each of which was separately represented. In the Vajrayana a major development was the introduction of female counterparts to all these aspects.

All these developments represent a gradual filling out of the original Buddha ideal. It is as though you had an uncut diamond: its surface would not catch and reflect the light, and consequently its true beauty would easily be missed. But worked upon by a master jeweler, its facets would sparkle with reflected light and iridescent color, and its beauty would be revealed. That is how the mandala of the five Buddhas gradually took shape.

The five Buddhas represent an attempt to communicate something of the multifaceted nature of Enlightenment. If you define Buddhahood as "the wisdom of reality," this description may be true, but it is hardly very beautiful or inspiring. What kind of wisdom is it, what kind of reality? To illuminate this, the wisdom of the Buddha is described as having four principal aspects—the mirror-like wisdom, the wisdom of equality, the discriminating wisdom, and the all-performing wisdom—and this gives a fuller and richer idea of what Buddhahood is like, bringing out its nature more explicitly so that it can be seen more clearly.

Many of the Buddhas and Bodhisattvas within the mandala became the objects of cults; they were visualized and meditated upon, and their mantras were recited, until in Vajrayana Buddhism, and Tibetan Buddhism especially, they became the foundation of a vast range of spiritual practices and experiences, as if refracting rainbow light from the thousands of facets of the mandala.

As for dividing each Buddha into masculine and feminine, into a Buddha and his consort, this helped to bring out the passionate engagement that is part and parcel of transcendental wisdom. If the wisdoms of the Buddhas seem a bit cold, the Buddhas themselves, with their consorts, counteract that feeling. The attendant Bodhisattvas who also appear in the mandala have their own effect too, each bringing out a specific aspect of the activity of the Buddhas. The dharmapalas, the guardians of the Dharma, bring out further aspects still. And then, in a rich and complex mandala, there may be wrathful as well as peaceful Buddhas to bring out more and more aspects of Enlightenment.

5. TAKING MYTHS LITERALLY

The whole point about the realm of myth is that it is a realm not of clearly defined meanings, but of undefined, even indefinable meanings.

IF YOU TAKE A MYTH in the modern, sophisticated sense, it has its effect on you, but if you are able to believe that the myth is literally true, it has a much greater effect. For instance, if you are a Christian and you believe that the resurrection of Christ has a deep symbolical significance, even though he didn't literally rise from the dead, the resurrection is a very meaningful symbol for you. But if as a traditional Christian you believe that Christ literally rose from the dead because he was the son of God and he had that power inherent in him, your belief will have much deeper foundations, or at least you will be more strongly motivated. The nature of our approach to "myth" is one of the basic questions that have to be faced nowadays, not only by Christians but by Buddhists as well.

For Buddhists, however, it is not such a key issue, because in Buddhism, especially early Buddhism, the taking of myth as literal truth doesn't occupy such an important place. If you read, for example, that the Buddha walked up and down in the air emitting water and fire at the same time, you can believe that quite literally and no doubt find it inspiring. But taking that myth literally doesn't occupy the kind of central place in Buddhism that belief in the resurrection of Christ occupies in Christianity. There is no doubt, however, that if you are able to take myth as being literally true, you are likely to practice your religion more zealously and energetically. Of course, such literal belief can go to the undesirable extreme of fanatical fundamentalism. But in avoiding that, perhaps we need to take care not to fall into too sophisticated or rational an approach to myth. The whole point about the realm of myth is that it is a realm not of clearly defined meanings, but of undefined, even indefinable meanings. It is the same realm to which belong such things as symbols, archetypal images, the imagination itself, and poetry.

6. THE TIBETAN WHEEL OF LIFE

In fact the Wheel of Life is not a picture at all. It is a mirror, in which we see—what else?—ourselves.

THE TIBETAN WHEEL OF LIFE did not originate in Tibet; it is described in early Buddhist scriptures and in Mahayana sutras, and those traditions were preserved in the Tantric context, while at the same time the symbol was imbued with a distinctively Tantric spirit. In fact, the wheel is only partly symbolic. While some parts of its complex structure are true symbols (that is, they stand for certain things without actually depicting them), others are only illustrative, representing in pictorial form teachings which can be expressed in other terms. Here we shall be dwelling more on the symbolic than on the illustrative elements of the wheel.

Starting with a simple description, what do we see when we look at the wheel? Basically, we see a lot of little pictures. The wheel consists of four concentric circles—that is, four circles of different sizes, one inside the other. Within the innermost circle, at the hub of the wheel, are to be seen three animals: a cock, a snake, and a pig. They appear head-to-tail in a sort of triangular relationship, each animal biting the tail of the one in front.

The circle surrounding the hub is divided into two halves, one light, the other dark. In the light segment are human beings moving upward as though on a sort of celestial escalator. They have peaceful, joyful expressions, and they are decently clad. In the dark segment there are what seem to be human beings too—but are they really human? They are plunging headlong as though into a pit, naked and chained together, with expressions of fear and horror on their faces.

Moving outward, the next circle is divided into six equal segments. In the first segment, right at the top of the circle, we see the world of the gods. Heaven opens before our eyes: a world of pleasures and delights where the gods live in beautiful palaces among trees and gardens, a world where every wish is instantly gratified. As soon as the desire for something floats—however vaguely—into your mind, that thing instantly appears in front of you, or in your hands, or your mouth, or on your body. This is how the gods live.

In the second segment, moving clockwise, is the world of the asuras, the demigods, the Titans. These are fierce, war-like beings— usually depicted as well-muscled, not to say heavily built—and they are engaged in perpetual warfare with the gods, fighting especially for the possession of the *kalpataru,* the magic tree that grants all wishes and fulfills all desires.

The third segment depicts the world of the *pretas,* the hungry ghosts. These beings are naked and horribly deformed: they have enormously swollen bellies, very thin necks, and mouths no bigger than the eye of a needle. Suffering all the time from ravenous hunger, they grasp at food and drink, trying desperately to cram it into their needle-eye mouths, but as they do so, the food and drink turns into excrement and liquid fire.

In the fourth segment, right at the bottom of the wheel, is the world of tormented beings: hell. At the center of this world is a fearsome figure sitting enthroned. This is Yamaraja, the King of Death, dark blue in color, clad in a tiger skin and surrounded by flames. In his hand he holds a mirror—the mirror of karma—and as beings are dragged before him, beings who have just died, he looks into the mirror and sees everything they have done, everything they have said, everything they have thought. If they have done more evil than good in the course of their preceding life, he orders that they should be taken away and punished. It should be said that this world is more of a purgatory than a hell, because it isn't a permanent state—but even so, in it we see guilty people suffering torments so terrible that it is painful to think about them, let alone describe them. The air is full of the sound of wailing and roaring and lamentation.

In the fifth segment is the world of animals, both wild and domesticated. They are shown in pairs, male and female, and they seem to be living a peaceful, idyllic existence—almost like the lion and the lamb in the biblical story. It isn't a very Darwinian picture, at least as depicted in Tibetan Buddhist art. There's no nature red in tooth and claw—the animals all seem very placid. Perhaps it is intended to show the animal's life from the animal's point of view, because, after all, animals don't worry about what's going to happen tomorrow.

The sixth and last segment is the world of human beings, and there men and women buy and sell, read, talk, work in the fields, meditate under the trees, and are finally carried as corpses to the cremation ground.

There is one important feature in each realm that hasn't yet been mentioned. In each of the six worlds there appears a Buddha figure of a particular color, offering to the beings in that world something they need. In the world of the gods there appears a pure white Buddha holding a stringed musical instrument—usually in the paintings it's an Indian vina, which is rather like a medieval lute. This Buddha plays to the gods a sweet, penetrating melody: the melody of impermanence. Nothing lasts, the tune is saying; everything changes. In the world of the asuras, there appears a Buddha of a beautiful emerald green color, holding in his right hand a flaming sword. It is on fire because it is the sword of transcendental wisdom, and he brandishes it at the asuras as they're fighting. In the world of the pretas, the hungry ghosts, there appears a ruby red Buddha who showers upon the pretas food and drink that they are able actually to consume. In the world of tormented beings there appears a Buddha the color of smoke, bluish-grey, and he regales the beings in hell with *amrta,* the food or drink of the gods known in the western tradition as nectar or ambrosia. In the world of the animals there appears a dark blue Buddha who is showing something to the animals: a book. And in the human world there appears a golden yellow Buddha, bearing the twin insignia of the spiritual life in ancient India: the begging-bowl and the staff with three rings. These six Buddhas represent the introduction into the symbolism of the Wheel of Life of a Mahayanistic element, the element of great compassion, which, conjoined with wisdom, sees and responds appropriately to the needs of all beings.

The outermost circle of the wheel is divided into twelve segments, in each of which is a tiny picture. Clockwise from the top, these are: (1) a blind man with a stick, (2) a potter with a wheel and pots, (3) a monkey climbing a flowering tree, (4) a boat with four passengers, one of whom is steering, (5) an empty house with five windows and a door, (6) a man and woman embracing, (7) a man with an arrow stuck in his eye, (8) a woman offering a drink to a seated man, (9) a man gathering fruit from a tree, (10) a pregnant woman, (11) a woman in childbirth, and (12) a man carrying a corpse to the cemetery.

The whole wheel is gripped by a monstrous, demoniacal figure: his face peers over the top of the wheel, his clawed hands and feet grip the sides, and his scaly reptilian tail coils below. He is impermanence personified, and he wears a crown made of five human skulls, a Tantric touch that hints at radical transformation. (We shall be looking at this key aspect of the Tantra when we come to consider the symbolism of the cremation ground and the celestial maidens.)

Above the wheel and to the right is the figure of Shakyamuni Buddha, floating on clouds and stretching out his arm to point out the path to Enlightenment. On the left is the full moon, in which can be discerned the figure of a hare.

This is the Tibetan Wheel of Life as it is—or used to be—depicted on the walls of temples and monasteries, and on painted scrolls, all over Tibet and the adjacent Himalayan region. But what does it all mean? As to that, much of it—the symbols, at least—cannot, as I said, be explained at all. The main thing for us to do is just look at the wheel: not only at it, but into it—because in fact the Wheel of Life is not a picture at all. It is a mirror, in which we see—what else?—ourselves. Perhaps we could say that the Wheel of Life is made up not of four concentric circles, but of four mirrors. Or we could say that we look into the mirror four times, each time seeing more and more of ourselves, experiencing more of ourselves, realizing more of ourselves. The Wheel of Life is a sort of magic mirror or crystal ball into which we can gaze.

So let us look now into that mirror—not just four times but as many times as may be necessary—and let us have the courage to see ourselves in it. Some courage, indeed, will be needed. The very first time we look into the mirror, we see the three animals: the cock, the snake, and the pig. Usually it is said that they represent greed, hatred, and ignorance and that these three poisons are present in our own hearts. But this explanation is letting us off far too lightly; it is a kind of defensive rationalization. It is much more of a shock to look into the mirror and see not the human face we expected, but the face of an animal—a bird, a reptile, a pig. That's us, and uncomfortable as it may be, indeed should be, we should take a long look. This reflection is giving us a direct experience of our own animal nature. We see that we are not quite so human, so civilized, as we had thought. We're just an animal, a beast. And this realization is the beginning of spiritual life. We see ourselves as we are on the most basic level, we accept ourselves, and we go on from there.

Going on from there means taking another look in the mirror: once we have recovered from the shock of seeing that animal face, we take a second look. This time we see two paths, one going up, the other going down, one light, the other dark. So we are faced with two alternatives: up or down. It's as simple as that. We can either evolve or regress; the choice is before us. And this choice is before us every minute of the day, in every situation in which we find ourselves. Shall we go up or shall we go down? Shall we follow the light path or the dark path? It's up to us to decide.

If we do decide, after thinking it over, to follow the light path, the next question is, how? What must we do to grow spiritually? What is the next step? This clearly depends on where we are now. And to find that out, we need to look into the mirror a third time. This time we see one of the six worlds: the world of the gods, the world of the asuras, the world of the hungry ghosts, the world of tormented beings, the world of animals, or the world of human beings. In other words, we see where we are at any given moment or over any given period of time. Sometimes when we look into the mirror we see a happy, peaceful, cheerful face: the face of a god. Sometimes we see the angry, aggressive face of an asura. Sometimes we see a famished, hollow-eyed face, with a pinched mouth and a dissatisfied expression: the face of a hungry ghost. Sometimes we see the miserable, tormented face of someone in hell. Sometimes we see a face with a long snout and whiskers or big sharp teeth: the face of an animal. And sometimes we see just an ordinary human face. But whatever we see, we see ourselves.

The six segments into which this circle of the Wheel of Life is divided can be considered literally as realms of existence into which living beings are reborn as a result of their karma and in which they live until that karma has been exhausted. But this is only half the truth that the symbol represents. The segments can also be seen as representing states of mind that we can experience here and now, in the course of our everyday human existence. Sometimes our experience of these states of mind is so strong that for the time being we seem actually to be living in heaven or in hell or among the hungry ghosts. In other words, we experience them almost as states of being rather than just states of mind.

Viewed in this light, the world of the gods represents a happy state of mind, a state of relaxation, content, and repose. It's a state in which everything seems to flow smoothly, and there are no obstacles or problems. It is a state of aesthetic experience and artistic enjoyment as well as of meditation in the sense of deep concentration or *samatha,* though not in the sense of insight into reality or *vipasyana* (Pali *vipassana*).

The world of the asuras, by contrast, represents an aggressive, competitive state of mind. Here there is a lot of energy—perhaps too much—and it all turns outward. There is restlessness, suspicion, jealousy. Just as the asuras fight for possession of the wish-fulfilling tree, the asura-like state of mind is one that strives for an ever higher standard of living, more and more money, and so on. It is a state of assertive egotism, a state in which one wants to be better or more distinguished than other people, and even to control and exercise power over them.

The world of the hungry ghosts is the state of neurotic desire. Desire is neurotic when it seeks from its object more than that object can give, or even something quite different from what it can give. An obvious example is the neurotic desire for food. Sometimes people gobble down huge quantities of food, especially sweet things, but they don't really want food at all. It's a substitute for something else—for affection, very often, psychologists tell us. Neurotic desire in this sense is very often present in personal relationships, especially those of the more intimate kind—to such an extent in some cases that the two people involved are like hungry ghosts trying to devour each other.

The world of the tormented beings is the state of acute mental suffering, nervous frustration, mental breakdown, even insanity. This state is brought about in various ways: by the long-continued frustration of natural human impulses, by sudden bereavement, by unconscious mental conflicts, and by many other conditions and causes.

The world of the animals represents the state of purely sensual indulgence, the state in which one is interested only in food, sex, and material comforts, all the pleasures of life. When these needs are satisfied, one is quite gentle and tame, but when they are frustrated, one becomes snappy and even rather dangerous.

Finally, the world of human beings is the state of distinctively human consciousness, the state which is neither ecstatic nor agonized, neither fiercely competitive nor mindlessly sensual nor yet neurotically desirous. It's a state in which we are aware of our own self and aware of other people, a state in which we satisfy our objective human needs but at the same time see that they have their limitations, a state in which we devote ourselves to spiritual development. We call it the human realm, but in reality the truly human state is one that most "human beings" only intermittently—or perhaps never—experience.

Our third look into the mirror has shown us where we are, whether we are—for the moment—a god or an asura, a hungry ghost or a tormented being, an animal or a human being. When we have seen where we are, we know the next step we have to take—and that draws us to the six Buddhas appearing in the midst of the six worlds. According to the Tibetan Buddhist teaching, these Buddhas are all manifestations of Avalokitesvara, the Bodhisattva who embodies the compassion aspect of the Enlightenment experience. Each of these six Buddhas holds, as we have observed, a particular object, something needed by the beings of the world in which he appears. As we shall see, the nature of the object the Buddha holds gives us a clue as to how to move on from that world, or that state of mind.

In the world of the gods the white Buddha holds a lute upon which he plays the melody of impermanence. This suggests that when we are in a state of aesthetic enjoyment, the next step is to remind ourselves that it won't last and also that aesthetic pleasure, however great, is not to be mistaken for the supreme bliss of Enlightenment. Although things may be going well now, we still have a long way to go. The Buddhist tradition stresses that prolonged happiness can be spiritually dangerous, if not disastrous. If we are happy and contented all the time, if things go easily and we have our own way, we meet no problems or obstacles, we tend to become self-satisfied, complacent, and even careless. We tend to forget that we are mortal, that life is short and time is precious. This applies even to the enjoyment of meditation, as well as to the appreciation of the fine arts. We need to make the transition from the heights of mundane experience to the experience of the transcendental.

Notice that the white Buddha doesn't stand up among the gods and deliver a lecture on impermanence; he conveys his message by playing a melody on a lute. Nor is this just a symbolic notion, if we are to believe a story told about Asvaghosa, to whom tradition ascribes the seminal text called *The Awakening of Faith in the Mahayana*. As well as being a great philosopher and spiritual teacher, Asvaghosa was also a great musician, and he traveled throughout the India of his day playing his lute. The Chinese traveler Hsuan-Tsang, who followed in his footsteps a few centuries later (in the seventh century CE), reports in his account of his sojourn in India that the effect of Asvaghosa's music was still remembered all those years later. Apparently, when people heard it, they immediately got a sense of the impermanence of things. Somehow the melody conveyed the message that everything conditioned is unsatisfactory, all worldly things are unreal and insubstantial, nirvana is the only reality. Just listening to Asvaghosa's music gave people that direct understanding. The music played by the white Buddha in the realm of the gods has the same effect. It wakes up those who are in this complacent and self-satisfied state, making them aware of higher truths and realities, not through philosophy, religion, or intellectual discussion, but through music.

In the world of the asuras a green Buddha appears, brandishing a flaming sword, the sword of wisdom, transcendental wisdom—not just intellectual knowledge, but penetration into reality as a spiritual experience. This suggests that when we are in a state of competitiveness and aggressiveness, the next step is to develop intellectual insight into truth and reality. The battle, in other words, is relocated to the intellectual front. But why is wisdom symbolized by a sword? In an essay on "Hate, Love, and Perfect Wisdom," the great Buddhist scholar Dr. Edward Conze asserts that there is an affinity between hatred and wisdom.[80] If you experience a lot of anger and hatred, he says, you should be able to develop wisdom fairly easily.

This sounds odd at first, but a little thought shows the sense of it. The characteristic of hatred is to seek to destroy the hated object. If you hate something or someone, you want to finish them off, to smash them to smithereens, to make just one big nothing where they used to be. We may not always admit it to ourselves, but this is what we would like to do. And the characteristic of transcendental wisdom is also to destroy: to destroy conditioned existence itself, to reduce to dust everything that isn't reality, isn't truth, isn't Buddhahood. This is why transcendental wisdom is symbolized by the vajra, the thunderbolt, which is said to smash and destroy all obstacles.

Thus there is this affinity between hatred and wisdom, although the one is highly unethical and the other entirely ethical. It is noticeable that a hot temper and a highly developed intellect often go together, even when that intellect is applied to Buddhism, which should be the epitome of equanimity. Scholars specializing in Buddhist studies can be bad-tempered and quarrelsome to a remarkable degree, especially among themselves—an example being Dr. Conze himself, who was celebrated not only for his tremendous scholarship and intellectual penetration, but also for his peppery temper. It is as though the destructive force that expresses itself in hatred can be diverted into intellectual channels and used to fuel the discovery and realization of truth.

Dr. Conze points out that the Perfection of Wisdom tradition is associated with the Buddha Aksobhya, called the Imperturbable, one of the set of five archetypal Buddhas. Aksobhya is said to be the patron Buddha of people of predominantly choleric temperament. In this way the Tantric tradition seems to recognize an affinity between hatred and wisdom. It seems that an asura-like person has a natural ability not only to fight with the gods, but also to conquer truth itself, at least intellectually, more effectively than other people who may be easier to get on with.

Having said this, one must be careful not to make a necessary connection out of a mere correspondence between two quite separate spheres, between an aspect of psychological conditioning and an aspect of reality. This suggestion of an affinity between hatred and wisdom originates with Buddhaghosa, the great commentator on the Pali Canon who lived in the sixth century CE. But what he actually said—as near as we can make it out—was that just as hatred seizes upon the negative aspects of things, in the same way wisdom seizes upon the faults of conditioned existence. He draws an analogy between hatred and wisdom, but no more than that. In other words, people with critical, intellectually aggressive minds may have a greater potential to follow the path of wisdom, but unless they actually do so they are no closer to true wisdom than anyone else. By the same token, someone who is warmly affectionate is not, without taking steps to realize their potential, any closer to developing true compassion than less demonstrative people.

In the world of the hungry ghosts there appears a red Buddha who showers the suffering denizens of that state of existence with food and drink that they can actually consume. Now what does this mean for us in practical terms? It means that when we are in a state of neurotic desire, the next step is to get back to an accurately objective perception of the situation, which also means getting back to the present moment. We must see what the desired object can give us and what it cannot. We also need to discover what we really desire, and where that desire is coming from. Once we have done so, we can either give our desire its proper satisfaction, if that is possible, or—if it is inappropriate or unskillful—do our best to let go of it.

The *amrta* or nectar with which the smoke-colored Buddha regales the beings in hell can be interpreted in at least two—rather contradictory—ways. Most obviously it signifies that when we are in a state of intense mental suffering, the next step is simply to gain a respite from it, some ease and relaxation. That is often the best we can do in the circumstances. But at another level of meaning, this nectar is both more challenging and more profound. Amrta is usually translated as "nectar" or "ambrosia," but in many Buddhist texts it is a synonym for Enlightenment itself: the *amrtapada,* the state of nectar, the deathless, eternal state. So the smoke-colored Buddha gives the beings in hell not just nectar but nirvana. The suggestion—which in a way seems quite outrageous—is that when we are in a state of intense suffering, the next step is to gain Enlightenment. But it does make sense. There's nothing else for us to do. All worldly hope has foundered. All we can do is head straight for Enlightenment. It's as though there were another strange affinity between a supremely negative state and a supremely positive one—this time between intense mental suffering and an aptitude for the highest spiritual attainment.

In the world of animals, the blue Buddha shows the animals a book. Surely this suggests that when we are in a state of barbarism and savagery, our next step is to become civilized, to acquaint ourselves with the arts and sciences, with the cultural life of mankind, because these things have a refining influence. It is difficult, if not impossible, to go from a barbaric state straight into a life of spiritual development. This is one of the reasons why Buddhism has always been a bearer of culture. As well as spiritual teachings, Buddhists took Indian higher culture all over Asia, because that refined, humanistic culture provided a foundation for the spiritual life. Hence, the Bodhisattva, the ideal Buddhist, is presented in Mahayana texts as a master of arts, sciences, and even handicrafts—quintessentially in the figure of Manjughosa, the great Bodhisattva of wisdom, who is said to preside over the arts and sciences.

Finally, the yellow Buddha who appears in the world of human beings carries the begging-bowl and three-ringed staff that are the insignia of the religious mendicant and therefore of the spiritual life in general. The point of this is clear: when we find ourselves in a truly human state, the next step is to devote ourselves wholeheartedly to the task of spiritual development. Once we have reached the truly human state, this should be our main interest in life.

The general message from the presence of the different Buddhas is that within each of these realms or states of existence there is the potential for development. There is always a next step. One of the fundamental teachings of Buddhism, especially Mahayana Buddhism, is that all sentient beings are capable of Buddhahood. Indeed, above and beyond the world of time and phenomenal particularity, all beings *are* Buddha, *are* Enlightened. And within time all beings are capable— eventually—of gaining Enlightenment.

But beings are not all equally capable of becoming Enlightened from their present state, whatever it is. In the Chinese Mahayana tradition it is said that some people are endowed with more "Buddha seeds" than others. According to this tradition, there are three kinds of seed, three kinds of potentialities, in sentient beings. There are good seeds (red seeds, as they are sometimes called), bad seeds (black seeds) and Buddha seeds (yellow or golden seeds). Buddha seeds represent potentialities for spiritual growth. The distinction between good seeds and Buddha seeds is a reminder that being good does not necessarily make you a Buddha, although if you are a Buddha you can't help being good, presumably. All three kinds of seed are present in all beings, in all six realms, in varying—and sometimes rather surprising—proportions.

In the world of the gods, there are no bad seeds. The gods have no potentiality for evil—and you do get people like that, people who wouldn't hurt a fly. Almost all the seeds in the god realm are good seeds because the gods really are very good—happy, holy, contented, peaceful, and kind. But what is perhaps surprising is the fact that they possess very few Buddha seeds; the potentiality of the gods for Enlightenment is very limited.

The seeds in the world of the asuras are two thirds bad, one third good, with only a single Buddha seed. In the world of hungry ghosts there are no good seeds at all and a predominance of bad seeds, but quite a lot of Buddha seeds. It's almost exactly the same in the world of tormented beings, except that there are even more Buddha seeds. In the world of the animals there are very few good seeds—so they don't have a very happy time of it after all, it would seem—a predominance of bad seeds and a few Buddha seeds, about twice as many as the good seeds there. And in the world of human beings the three kinds of seed are present in roughly equal proportions.

Some of the conclusions that follow from all this are quite obvious. The asuras—warlike, competitive people—have the least potential for Buddhahood. By analogy, if you are in a highly competitive environment—big business, for example, or politics—you will have only the very smallest potential for Enlightenment, it would seem. This is not to say that all competition must be removed from the spiritual life. Competitiveness can be negative and destructive, but it can also be healthy and positive. It is possible to use the competitive spirit as a means of getting oneself to make more spiritual effort without having any antagonistic feeling toward the person with whom one is competing. For example, you might feel competitive with a friend about the relative consistency of your meditation practice. But if he or she manages to get up early to meditate more often than you do, you don't in the end mind being beaten, because you have got the best out of yourself in the process, and that is what matters.

The competitiveness of the asuras, though, is completely antithetical to the spiritual life. It is not just using competitiveness in a playful way to get yourself to make more effort; it is aimed at victory, conquest, doing the other person down. This does sometimes occur even among those trying to live a spiritual life. It manifests most frequently in a reluctance to cooperate, but it can be expressed just through talking and joking. If we come to realize that we tend to be uncooperative, we need to make the effort to be more willing to go along with what other people want, and not to have very strong views about very small things. Bitter disputes so often arise over trivialities—because, of course, the issue isn't really whether to do this or that, but whether I have my way or you have your way. It is a good practice to be very slow to take a stand on anything other than a real matter of principle. Very often the situation isn't worth arguing about, but the asura element in one's nature whispers, "Why should I do what he wants? Why should I always be following him?" It is a mistake to listen to that little voice. In most situations, the more wholehearted and warm the cooperation, the better it is for everyone.

It is sobering to observe that the gods have a smaller potential for Enlightenment than either the hungry ghosts or the tormented beings. It is very difficult, unfortunately, to gain Enlightenment from a state of unadulterated happiness and pleasure. It is much easier, though still extremely difficult, to make spiritual progress from a state of intense suffering. Suffering acts as a catalyst, it makes us more aware. People undergoing serious illness, going through physical changes and pain, or suffering intense distress, sometimes have spiritual experiences of a depth and intensity that do not occur so readily under more pleasant circumstances. We are more sensitive at such times, and thus more susceptible to spiritual influences. Self-inflicted suffering is, of course, another matter, and the Buddha was clear that self-mortification takes one as far from the middle way, the path to Enlightenment, as self-indulgence, which is the other extreme.

So has life in the god realm nothing to recommend it from a spiritual point of view? Is it just a waste of time? Not necessarily. It is analogous to sleep, which we know is not mere time-wasting, but necessary to our good health and indeed our very existence. If you have led a healthy, positive life, a period in the god realm represents a rest from mundane existence, an opportunity to assimilate and digest experience. Then, as a residue of the skillful deeds that have caused you to be reborn among the gods, you may have a happy and positive human rebirth—like someone waking refreshed from a good sleep—and can make another positive spiritual effort. But while you are actually in the realm of the gods, as in dreams, it is difficult (though not impossible) to make any effort at all.

Contentment is, of course, perilously close to complacency, and this is the fatal flaw of life in the god realm. In *The Jewel Ornament of Liberation,* the Tibetan teacher Gampopa says:

> How is it that we have not already obtained Buddhahood? The fault lies in people like ourselves having come under the power of four obstacles by which the attainment of Buddhahood is prevented. They are: attachment to sensuous experiences during this life, to sensual pleasures in this world, to self-complacency, and to ignorance about the means of realizing Buddhahood.[81]

Hindered by the first of these obstacles, you take it for granted that your particular world will continue. Hindered by the second—taking pleasure as the highest value—you seize the pleasure of the moment and forget your long-term interests. And in the grip of the third—self-complacency—you are satisfied with yourself as you are, and what could be a greater obstacle than that? You say, "Well, I'm all right, I'm quite happy, I'm doing well, I meditate every day"—and you lose your sense of urgency with regard to spiritual development.

It is crucial to understand this obstacle *as* an obstacle. Once you feel established on the spiritual path, once you are meditating, going on retreat and associating with people who share your values, you naturally and rightly feel very pleased about the state of affairs. But that is the time to say to yourself, "I must beware of complacency. I must keep on growing." You have to keep asking yourself if the situation you are in is helping you to keep growing spiritually.

At the same time you can't overcome complacency simply by making life difficult for yourself. It is also possible to be complacent about being someone who has to struggle and make a lot of effort in life. You are not necessarily growing just because you are struggling, especially if you feel quietly pleased with yourself because you are always the one who is making the effort. So while in general greed types are more prone to complacency than hate types, hate types are also susceptible to it in their own way.

If the teaching of the seeds is anything to go by, our best bet, if we want to make spiritual progress, would seem to be to seek rebirth in the human realm, where "joy and pain are woven fine," as Blake says. But this is not easy either. In the *Dhammapada,* the Buddha says, "Difficult is the attainment of the human state."[82] One can look at this statement in two ways, one traditional and the other more contemporary. The traditional view is that it is literally difficult to attain a human birth, and this view is illustrated by means of a simile. The chances of being born human are likened to the chances that a blind turtle who only emerges from the depths of the ocean once every hundred years will happen to put his head through a wooden yoke floating on the surface.[83]

This is probably not to be taken literally. No doubt the statistical probability that any living being will be born human is remote, given how many billions of insects, fish, and all sorts of other creatures there are—one could perhaps look at human birth as being rare in that way. But it is unlikely that those who have been human beings in previous existences will not be reborn human. In approaching this idea that it is difficult to attain the human state, it is more fruitful to ask what it really means to be a human being. This brings us to the more contemporary interpretation of the statement. What is the human state? Are you necessarily a human being because you bear a remote resemblance to the higher apes? What *is* a human being?

To speak of being *born* as a human being is clearly to refer to being human in the ordinary biological sense. But to speak of *attaining* the human state is to suggest that it is not enough to be human merely in the biological sense. You have to develop certain qualities to qualify as a human being. The process of becoming human consists in the full development of such qualities as self-awareness, emotional positivity, responsibility, fidelity, and cooperativeness. So it isn't easy to be human; the human state is, as the Buddha says, "difficult of attainment."

We have to ask ourselves the purpose of this teaching of the seeds. It is not saying that there are literally so many red, black, and yellow seeds in an animal, so many in a human being and so on. It is not meant to be scientific. It is simply a reminder that as human beings we have great potential for spiritual development, and that we should therefore make the effort to develop whatever potential we have. Whether the six realms of existence are taken literally, or whether they are regarded as being contained within human life, the whole teaching is meant to be encouraging, meant to remind us that there is always some potential for Enlightenment. If you are a *human* human being, the potential is greater. But even if you are in a hellish or preta-like state of mind, even if you are neurotic or aggressive, your potential for spiritual development is not altogether obscured—you can still make progress. Inasmuch as you are a human being, Buddha seeds are there.

Having taken our third long look into the mirror, we have seen where we are, the mental state we are in, and the next step to be taken. Now we must look into the mirror again. This time we see the images depicted around the rim of the Wheel of Life: the old blind man with his stick, the potter with his wheel and pots, the monkey climbing the flowering tree, and so on. These are the twelve *nidanas* or links that show how it all happens, how we pass from one state of existence to another, one state of mind to another. This is the process of what I have termed the reactive mind. And seeing it, really seeing it, we are free of it. We have seen through the reactive mind and we pass beyond it. And after a while, we look into the mirror again.

This time we see the monster in whose grip the wheel is tightly clutched. We come face to face with death, with the fact of universal, cosmic impermanence. We see that conditioned existence—that is to say, existence that comes into being in dependence on causes and conditions—is not only impermanent but also ultimately unreal. But we see at the same time, in the depths of the unreality of conditioned existence, gleaming like a pearl at the bottom of the sea, the real, the ultimately, absolutely real. It is not even really separate from the unreal, but constitutes another dimension of it.

When we look into the mirror once more, we see the Buddha—this time not up in the corner of the picture, but right in the center of things. We see, in short, Enlightenment itself. In Zen terms, we see our own original face. We experience directly what we truly and essentially are, in the depths of our being. And then we see the Bodhisattva. This is what the hare in the full moon represents: the Bodhisattva—that is, the Buddha in one of his previous lives. According to the traditional Jataka stories, the Buddha-to-be was reborn as a hare, and sacrificed his body in the fire to provide a meal for a hungry guest. As so often in legends of this sort, the guest turned out to be a king in disguise—in this case Indra, the king of the gods. He restored the hare to life and drew his picture on the full moon as an everlasting testimony to his spirit of generosity and self-sacrifice.[84] This is why, according to Indian legend, you see the hare in the moon (not the man in the moon, as our legend is in the West), even today. Every time you look up at the hare in the moon, you are reminded of the Bodhisattva's generosity and self-sacrifice.

The Bodhisattva does not represent just one individual. Seeing the Bodhisattva means seeing the spirit of Enlightenment at work in the cosmos, and seeing ourselves as participating in that work. Having seen the Buddha, our own original face, outside time, we see that same Buddha principle at work within time, through time, in the activities of the Bodhisattva.

Looking in the mirror for the last time, we don't see anything at all. In fact, the mirror disappears. There's nothing to see and nobody to see it. And yet at the same time, mysteriously, everything is seen. Everything is heard. Everything is understood. Everything is realized. The symbolism of the Tibetan Wheel of Life has been transcended—and fulfilled.

7. The Parable of the Burning House

Today the burning house is burning more merrily than ever; we only have to open our newspapers or turn on the television any day of the week to know that.

ONCE UPON A TIME there was a great elder, a very rich old man who lived in a huge mansion with his hundreds of servants and his many children. The story does not speak of wives or mothers, but we know that the elder had as many as thirty children, and they were all quite young. The house in which they lived had once been magnificent, but now it was old and tumbledown. The pillars were decaying, the windows were broken, the floorboards were rotting and the walls were crumbling. And in the nooks and crannies of this tumbledown house there lurked all sorts of ghosts and evil spirits.

One day the house suddenly caught fire. Because it was so old and the timbers were so dry, the whole building was burning merrily in no time. As it happened, the elder was safe outside the house when the fire started, but his children were playing inside. Too young to realize that they were in danger of being burned to death, they just carried on playing and made no effort to escape.

The elder was very afraid for his children, of course, and wondered how on earth to save them. At first he thought of carrying them out of the house one by one, for he was strong and able, but he soon realized that it would be impossible to get them all out in time. Instead, he decided to try calling out to the children. He shouted "The house is on fire! You're in terrible danger! Come out quickly!" But the children had no idea what their father could mean by danger. They just carried on playing their games, glancing at the elder occasionally as they ran to and fro, but taking no serious notice of him at all.

The elder saw that there was no time to lose, for the house would crash to the ground at any minute. In desperation he hit upon another plan. He would try to trick the children into coming out of the house. Knowing the different nature of each child, he knew that they liked different kinds of toys, some liking one kind and some preferring another. So he called out to them "Come and look at the toys I have brought for you! There are all kinds of carts, some drawn by deer, some drawn by goats and some drawn by bullocks, and they are all standing just outside the gate. Come quickly and look!" And although the children had been deaf to all his warnings, this time they heard him. They all came rushing and tumbling helter-skelter out of the burning house, pushing and shoving each other in their eagerness to get the new toys.

When the elder was sure that all the children were safely out of the house, he sat down with a great sigh of relief; and at once, of course, the children came clamoring round him demanding the toys he had promised them. The elder was extremely fond of his children, and wanted to give them whatever their hearts desired. And, fortunately, he was extremely wealthy—in fact his wealth was infinite—so he could afford to give them the best of everything. Instead of the carts of different kinds which he had promised them, therefore, he gave to each of them a magnificent bullock-drawn cart, bigger and better than they could have imagined in their wildest dreams. Although he had promised them one thing and gave them something else, this was not deceitfulness on his part, because it was motivated by his desire for the welfare and the safety of his children.

So this is the parable of the burning house.[85] In a way there is no need to say any more, because a parable speaks directly in its own symbolic language. It means just what it says it means, and we simply have to let it all sink in. It can be useful, however, to dwell on the events of the story and see what significance they have for us.

The elder, of course, is the Buddha, the Enlightened One, and the mansion in which he lives is the world—not just this earth, but the whole universe, the whole of conditioned existence, all worlds. The mansion—the universe—is inhabited by many beings—not just human beings, according to Buddhism, but beings of all kinds, some less developed than human beings and some even more developed. And just as the mansion is old and decayed, this universe is subject to all kinds of imperfections. For a start, it is impermanent, changing all the time. We cannot stay in it for long; it is more like a hotel than a home. The mansion has ghosts in the corners too, which suggests that this world of ours is haunted. Haunted by what? By the past. We like to think that we live in the present, but more often than not the ghosts of the past are all around us. We may think that we are experiencing objectively existing beings and situations, but often they are really the projections of our unconscious minds, the ghosts of the past that we carry along with us all the time.

In the parable the mansion catches fire at a certain time, but in reality the mansion of the world is constantly blazing and burning. The use of fire as a symbol is very common in Buddhism, and in Indian religion generally. The Buddha used it in a teaching known as the Fire Sermon which he gave not long after his Enlightenment, on an occasion when he was speaking to a company of his disciples who had previously been "matted-hair" ascetics and whose main religious practice had been fire-worship. No doubt the Buddha was alluding to their previous practice when he led a thousand of them to the top of a hill and said to them, "The whole world is ablaze. The whole world is burning. Burning with what? It is burning with the fire of craving and neurotic desire. It is burning with the fire of anger, hatred, and aggression. It is burning with the fire of ignorance, delusion, bewilderment, and lack of awareness."[86] This was surely not just an idea of the Buddha's, not just a concept he happened to think up. He surely saw the world, as though in a vision, just like this. Perhaps before he spoke he had been looking down from the hilltop into the jungles below, and had seen a forest fire burning in the distance. Then he may have seen, in his spiritual vision, that not only was the forest burning, but the houses were burning, people were burning, the mountains were burning, the earth was burning, the sun, moon, and stars were burning— everything conditioned was burning with the threefold fires of craving, hatred, and delusion.

Fire, incidentally, far from being just a negative symbol in Buddhism, has many positive associations. It is associated with change—

in fact fire, the process of combustion, *is* change, and not just change but transformation. In Indian spiritual life fire is therefore a symbol not just of destruction but also of renewal and spiritual rebirth. In Vedic times, long before the Buddha, people placed offerings on a fire altar to ascend in the subtle form of smoke to the realms of the gods. The rite of cremation involves a similar transformation, reducing the physical body to ashes but—or so the ancient Indians believed— sending the subtle aspect of being, the "soul," to the moon or to the sun, to the world of the fathers or to the world of the gods. In Hin- duism the cremation ground is the domain of Shiva the Destroyer, who is the god not only of destruction but also of spiritual rebirth, because before you can build up you must break down. And the flames which surround the wrathful deities of Tibetan Buddhism also symbolize a transformation by fire—the fiery breaking through of the spirit of Enlightenment into the darkness and ignorance of the world.

But fire is a threat to the children in the mansion; in fact they are in danger of burning to death. Who do the children represent? Obvi- ously they represent living beings, especially human beings—that is to say, especially ourselves. In the context of the *Saddharma Pun- darika*, the *White Lotus Sutra* from which this story comes, they rep- resent disciples who are following lower spiritual ideals, but more generally speaking, we can say that they represent all those who have evolved only up to a certain point and have some distance—maybe a great distance—still to go.

The children in the parable are in danger of being burned to death. The implication is that human beings are in danger—*we* are in danger. What does this mean? It could mean that we are in danger of remain- ing within the world, within the process of conditioned existence, the cycle of birth, death, and rebirth as illustrated by the Tibetan Wheel of Life. The danger is that if we carry on turning round and round within the wheel we must inevitably suffer, at least sometimes. But the symbolism could also mean that we are in danger of getting stuck at a lower level of development. Unfortunately this happens to very many people, and it isn't always entirely their own fault. The human organism, biologically, psychologically, and even spiritually speaking, has a natural tendency to grow. In fact, to grow is the nature of life itself. Life in all its forms wants to unfold its inner potentialities, and if any living thing cannot do this it feels miserable, or at least uneasy and dissatisfied. People are often so restricted by their circumstances that they simply cannot grow—indeed, they sometimes feel that they cannot even breathe. All sorts of unpleasant and uncontrollable factors press in on them from all sides. They strangle them, stifle them, and make them feel that they are not developing as they should and could, so that they feel not only frustrated and restricted, but miserable, resentful, and unhappy in every way.

In the parable, of course, the person trying to rescue the children from danger is their father. If the "father" here meant the begetter of the children, this might seem to imply that the Buddha is a kind of creator god, the creator of the world, of men and women, and all living beings. But this "father" simply stands for someone older, more experienced, and more highly evolved. He is like the "cultural father" of some cultures where you have both a biological father, who begot you, and a cultural father—usually your mother's brother—who is responsible for educating you and bringing you up. (In modern societies the biological father fulfills both roles, but this is not an invariable rule.) So there is no implication of theism here.

The elder's first impulse when the fire starts is to rush into the house and carry the children out—he would be strong enough to do that—but on reflection he dismisses the idea. This goes to show that however willing and able you may be, you just cannot save people, spiritually speaking, by force. You could conceivably drag them out of a burning building against their will, but it is impossible to make anybody evolve against their will. Yes, you can drag them to meditation classes; you can drag them into church. You can force them to recite the Creed and read the Bible. You can intimidate them into not doing this or not doing that. But you cannot make them evolve against their will. By its very nature the Higher Evolution is a voluntary process, something *you* do because *you* want to do it.

Unfortunately, this is sometimes forgotten. Some religious teachers hold the view that what people really need to make them grow spiritually is discipline—and these teachers are only too willing to dish it out, and give their disciples a very tough time indeed. Of course, there is no shortage of people who are ready to accept this sort of discipline. It is not difficult to find ways of conditioning people along certain lines. This kind of conditioning, however, is a very different thing from real spiritual development. Buddhist teachers, therefore, do not force, do not compel, do not intimidate, and do not have recourse to discipline in this almost military sense of the term, because trying to force people to develop is self-defeating. Throughout the history of Buddhism, Buddhist teachers have been very tolerant. In fact, Buddhism has never tried to force anybody to do anything.

So in the end the elder gives up the idea of rescuing the children and instead tries calling out to them. Now this call is full of meaning. It represents the call of Truth, the call, if you like, of the divine. Turning to the Hindu tradition again, we find the symbolism of the call beautifully expressed in the medieval Hindu story of Krishna and his flute. Krishna is one of the great spiritual figures of Hinduism, a demigod said to be an incarnation of Vishnu the Preserver, and he is surrounded by all sorts of myths and legends. The story of Krishna's flute is set in an Indian village called Vrindavana where the people live by herding cows. Just imagine the scene. It is a dark night with no moon and the whole village is sound asleep. The cows are all shut in their stalls for the night and everywhere—the little thatched mud-walled huts, the fields, and the forest—is absolutely still. Then, suddenly, in the midst of the darkness, in the midst of the silence, from the depths of the forest there comes a sound, faint but sweet and shrill, a sound that seems to come from an infinitely remote distance—the sound of a flute. Even now in India you can sometimes have this experience. You can be all by yourself in the midst of the countryside, with no one for miles around, and all of a sudden, out of the dark and the silence, there comes the sound of a flute.

Now although the sound of the flute is very faint and distant, it does not go unheard in the village of Vrindavana. Almost as though they have been expecting to hear it, the wives of the cowherds—the *gopis*—wake up, and know at once that Krishna is calling them. Without making a sound, without telling anybody, they get up and steal out of their houses, along the streets of the village and into the forest. Leaving their husbands and their children, their pots and their pans, their cows and their goats, they all go stealing away, rushing away as soon as they are at a safe distance, to dance with Krishna in the heart of the forest.[87]

In this story Krishna is a symbol of the divine, and the gopis represent the human heart, or the human soul if you like; and the sound of Krishna's flute is the call of the divine, sounding from the very depths of existence. In fact, most of us hear such a call at some time in our lives. It may come in a moment of quietness when we are out in the country, or through an experience of great art, literature, or music. Perhaps we may hear it after some tragic event, or perhaps when we are just rather weary of life. At such a time we may hear the call, the call which is sometimes termed the voice of the silence, the voice of something beyond. But even if we have heard this call very clearly, what usually happens is that we ignore it. Indeed, the very idea that there might have been a voice vaguely worries us. We don't know where it came from, or what mysterious region it might be calling us to. And if we follow it into unknown territory, we are afraid that we will have to give up all sorts of things that we are attached to. So we tell ourselves that we were imagining things, or that it was just a dream, and go on living and working and enjoying ourselves as though we had never heard anything at all.

Quite often, of course, we are much too busy enjoying ourselves even to hear the call, like the children in the parable. They almost completely ignore their father's calls because, the Buddha says—and we can imagine him saying this with a smile—they are absorbed in their games. We are absorbed in our games—the psychological games, spiritual games, and cultural games that we play almost all the time. We are so fascinated by our little games of success, prestige, popularity, ego-tripping dressed up as self-fulfillment, and so on, that even though we hear the call of the divine, the voice of the Buddha, we just go on playing.

And like the children in the burning house, we are not only playing our games, but running to and fro from one game to another. We are restless, anxious, incapable of staying anywhere for long. We constantly want to change the game we are playing or to change our partner—in more ways than one—so we end up running backward and forward in desperation. Just one thing occasionally stops us in our tracks. In the story, you may remember, the children just occasionally glance at their father as they run past. Similarly, as we run to and fro playing our little games, we do give the odd glance in the direction of religion.

So what is the elder to do? Force is out of the question and the children will not respond to a direct appeal. In the end his only alternative is to have recourse to a stratagem—in plain words, to play a trick. This kind of "trick," which benefits the person on which it is played, is known in Buddhism as *upaya kausalya*—"skillful means." The elder knows that the children are very fond of toys, so he decides to persuade them to come out of the burning house by promising them carts of different kinds to play with: deer carts, goat carts, and bullock carts. These three different kinds of cart represent, technically speaking, the three "vehicles," the three *yanas*—the *sravakayana*, the *pratyekabuddhayana*, and the *Bodhisattvayana*—that is, the Arahant Ideal, the ideal of private Enlightenment, and the Bodhisattva Ideal.[88] Less technically the carts stand for different formulations of the Buddha's teaching, or even different sectarian forms of Buddhism adapted to the needs of different temperaments.

Although the children take no notice of their father's warnings of danger, as soon as he promises them all these marvelous toys, out they come rushing. Their eager response to being promised their favorite kind of toy says something very perceptive about how religions appeal to people. It seems to suggest—bearing in mind what the toys represent—that a subjective and sectarian approach to the truth is much more attractive for many people than a more objective, universal approach. And this does seem to be the case in practice. It is certainly the more exclusive forms of religion that exert the most powerful emotional appeal. If your opening gambit is "Well, look, this is how I see it. Other people see things differently, but perhaps we're all right from our own point of view. Let's go forward together," that is no way to convince the average person. The way to get a following is to put it about that yours is the only true religion and all the others are just plain wrong. This explains why it is that the forms of Buddhism which in the course of history have become the most exclusive—that is, exclusive by Buddhist standards—have become the most popular in the West.

A sectarian approach may be more popular, but does this mean that it is necessary? Do we have to follow a particular path believing it to be the only true way, and only later on in our spiritual experience come to a broader outlook, like the Arahants in the sutra? If we look at our situation it is really questionable whether this is actually possible for us. In the Buddha's day no doubt it *was* possible. His disciples would have been able to learn and practice one teaching at a time. There was no writing in those days, at least not for religious purposes, so the Buddha did all his teaching orally. The disciples couldn't just pick up books about religion, and they certainly didn't go to other teachers, so they knew only what the Buddha taught them.

Even in more recent times, different forms of religion existed independently in different parts of the world—even in different parts of the same country—so it was perfectly possible to stick to one teaching or sect and ignore all the others completely. Until comparatively recently you could be a Christian in the West and never have heard of Buddhism or Hinduism, and you could be a Buddhist in the East and never hear the name of Christianity from one year to the next.

The world is now a very different place. Nowadays, everybody can study everything. All the spiritual teachings are available in written form—"Who runs, may read," as John Keble said—so it is no longer possible to keep people away from a teaching for which they are not ready. This means that people get hold of all sorts of teachings which, because they are not spiritually developed enough, they can only misunderstand and misinterpret. This just can't be helped. With improved communication and transport, the world is becoming a smaller place all the time. All religions, even all sects, are increasingly to be found everywhere, so it is no longer possible to follow one and ignore all the others—at the very least we will know about them from books or hearsay.

In this situation, the only thing to be done is for religions to try to see the parable of the burning house in its universal perspective. We all need to try to recognize that all the ways are different aspects of one and the same path, the path to perfect Buddhahood, the path to Enlightenment. Of course differences of temperament still exist, but sectarianism is no longer needed to cater for them. It is quite enough to choose a method of spiritual practice appropriate to our needs— for example, an appropriate method of meditation. We don't need to belong to a sectarian organization that excludes all the others. We don't need to be "Theravadin" or "Zen" or "Mahayanist"—why not just be Buddhist? And Buddhism itself can be interpreted very broadly. According to the Buddha's own criterion, Buddhism is whatever conduces to the Enlightenment of the individual. The Buddha alone among religious teachers seems to have understood that religion is really the process of the evolution and development of the individual. Sectarian organizations tend to lose sight of this, and in fact many of them express for the most part merely negative emotions, and we would be better off without their exclusivity and intolerance.

You notice that, in their eagerness to get their own particular carts, the children come out of the house pushing and shoving one another. In the same way, in our rush to get out of the house and grab the toy we want, instead of going out side by side or hand in hand, we jostle and shove all the others who are doing the same thing. We may not actually persecute anybody—at least not if we are Buddhists—but at the same time we may not exactly radiate positive feelings toward other people following other paths. This, as we have seen, needs to change, and in fact the parable goes on to show that as you progress on your chosen path it does change. Once the children are all outside, the elder gives each of them the very best kind of cart—or even one and the same cart—bigger and better than anything they could ever have imagined. Here is the indication that the closer people come to the goal, the more their paths converge.

People get into the spiritual life in different ways—some through music, art, or poetry, some through social service, some through meditation, some through the desire to resolve pressing psychological problems. Some people are attracted to Zen, others to the Theravada. We all have our own personal idiosyncrasies, so we are naturally attracted by different things in the beginning. But as we get more and more deeply into our chosen approach, we realize that it is changing us. We begin to notice that our idiosyncrasies of temperament—even those which led us to this particular approach—are being resolved. In the end we come to realize through our own experience that all forms of art, all forms of religion, are means for the higher evolution of humanity. By participating in any of them we ourselves are evolving, and other people are also evolving, even though their interests and preoccupations are different from our own. We are all evolving together, all participating in the same process of the Higher Evolution, the process—in Buddhist terms—of cosmic Enlightenment; this is really the message of the parable of the burning house.

So does this mean that the parable is teaching universalism? It is, after all, saying that the distinction between the different *yanas* is illusory, that in reality there is only one *yana.* But is this universalism? Well, I understand universalism as saying that all religions teach the same thing and that there is therefore no difference between them.[89] The doctrines may appear to differ, but universalists would say that this is only a matter of words—the substance is the same—and they would back this up by trying to equate doctrines from different religions. For example, they would say that the Christian Trinity—

Father, Son, and Holy Ghost—corresponds to the Buddhist *trikaya* (*dharmakaya, sambhogakaya, nirmanakaya*) and the Hindu *trimurti* (Brahma, Vishnu, Mahesvara). This kind of wholesale system of equations—the very substance of universalism—often leads to very forced interpretations.

It is clear enough that the parable of the burning house does not teach universalism in this sense. It doesn't say that all religions teach the same thing; they obviously teach different things. The parable is not even saying that all the *yanas* of Buddhism teach the same thing. What it does maintain very definitely is that all the different ways are part of the same "stream of tendency," to use an expression of Matthew Arnold's. Everyone is trying to get out of the same burning house. Indeed the parable emphasizes movement, escape; it is dynamic, unlike the static teaching of universalism. The universalist fixes systems of belief into patterns which have to rely heavily on intellectual resemblances, whereas the parable of the burning house can rely on the unity of the evolutionary process.

Another general consideration arising out of this parable, and one which must be addressed as it constitutes the main theme, is the idea of escape as a model for the spiritual life. The elder's sole concern is that the children should escape from the burning house. Does this mean that the parable is teaching escapism? Well, obviously enough, it does—in a sense. A lot of people would say that this is typical of the way religions encourage us to run away from the problems of the world and even from our own problems. And, they would say, this is particularly true of Buddhism. After all, look at the Buddha—leaving his wife and child like that, ducking out of his responsibilities and obligations! Some would say that Christians stay in the world and try to make it into a better place, try to help the sick and care for the needy, whereas Buddhists just sit around meditating, ignoring the sins and sufferings all around them. Pure escapism!

But is escape morally wrong? Suppose you were literally trapped in a burning house. There you would be, standing at the upstairs window, surrounded by smoke and flames. Along would come the fire brigade and you would escape, either by jumping into a net or by being carried down a ladder. Would your friends say afterward, "You shouldn't have done that. That was sheer escapism"? Buddhism simply sees that our situation is one of pain and suffering—or at least limitation, imperfection, frustration—and says "Get out of it." This is just acting realistically, like escaping from that burning house.

Perhaps the word "escape" is the wrong one. The word traditionally means "to gain one's liberty by flight," "to get safely out of," and so on, but in the nineteenth century it gained a new usage—"mental or emotional distraction from the realities of life"—and it is this which has given birth to the notion of escap*ism:* "the tendency to seek or the practice of seeking such distraction." The burning house in the parable represents the predicament in which we find ourselves as human beings. Given the connotations of the language of escape, it would perhaps be better to speak of *transcending* this human predicament rather than escaping from it. The parable is showing us how we can transcend our present state, how we can grow from a lower, less satisfactory state of existence to a higher, more satisfactory state.

This is not to say, of course, that there is no such thing as escapism, but we need to understand what escapism really is. Not everybody is prepared to make the kind of effort that the process of growth and development requires—*that* is what we try to escape from. When we try to avoid situations which demand that we go beyond ourselves, when we try to forget our human predicament, when we try to secure an easy life—these are the times when we are really being "escapist." Escapism is stagnation, even regression. Sometimes, it is true, religious activity—of the kind which involves lip service but no effort toward personal change—is escapism, though there is less of this these days simply because fewer people are involved in religion of any kind. Nowadays it is more usually non-religious activities that provide outlets for escapism. For many people work is escapism, politics are escapism, even the arts are escapism. Reading is escapism. Watching television is escapism. Sex is escapism. In short, any kind of life that involves no positive, deliberate effort to evolve is escapism—which means, if you think about it, that escapism is the rule rather than the exception. And of course, escapism of this kind is the last thing that the parable of the burning house teaches. It is concerned above all with growth, development, evolution.

Today the burning house is burning more merrily than ever; we only have to open our newspapers or turn on the television any day of the week to know that. So the whole question of escape—or rather the whole question of transcendence, growth, and development into a higher state—becomes more urgent than ever, both for the individual alone and for the individual as part of a spiritual community.

But we need not despair. If we take heed of the message of the parable of the burning house, even here, even now, we can transcend the human predicament.

8. The Myth of the Return Journey

Religion, when properly understood, is not remote from life, not just a dull, churchy little backwater, but life become conscious of its own upward tendency, its own tendency to grow and develop. And whether we know it or not, we are all involved, directly or indirectly, in this upward tendency of life.

THE PARABLE of the burning house gives us the metaphor of life as predicament, or even as trap, but this is of course only one way of looking at it. Human existence is multi-faceted, deep and mysterious, difficult to understand. "Wonders are many, and none is more wonderful than man" chants the chorus of Sophocles's play *Antigone*. Throughout history, facets of the nature and purpose of human life have been reflected by symbols and similes from which have arisen myths, legends, and stories—and these in turn have crystallized into epic poems, novels, dramas, and parables. The mystery of human life always having been the compelling preoccupation of humanity, the great works of ancient and modern literature which concern some

368 ~ THE ESSENTIAL SANGHARAKSHITA

aspect of human existence are read and reread, even after hundreds and thousands of years.

Some of these great works see human life in terms of conflict, or even warfare. Homer's *Iliad*, for example, tells the story of the battle between the Greeks and the Trojans over Helen of Troy, a battle involving not just men and women but even gods and goddesses. Two or three hundred years after the *Iliad* another epic was written, perhaps not so eminent from a literary point of view, but very, very much longer: the *Mahabharata*. This was composed by the Indian poet and sage Vyasa, and gives an account of the battle between the Kauravas and their cousins the Pandavas for possession of their ancestral kingdom. Northern Europe produced the anonymous eighth century Anglo-Saxon epic *Beowulf*, which recounts the battles of the hero Beowulf against three terrible adversaries: the fiendish monster Grendel, Grendel's still more fiendish mother, and the dragon. Even from comparatively modern times we have one of the very greatest of all epic poems, Milton's *Paradise Lost*, whose main theme is the War in Heaven, the battle between Satan and the Messiah. In all these works life is seen in terms of conflict. Life is a battle—between right and wrong, between light and darkness, between heaven and hell, between conscious and unconscious—and the battleground is the human heart.

But human existence can also be seen as a riddle, a mystery, or even a problem, and this is how the book of Job in the Bible sees it. Job has been brought up to believe that God rewards the good for their virtue—and punishes the wicked—here in this very life. But although Job is conscious of no evil in himself, he suffers, and it seems that his suffering is the punishment of God. Why should the just man be ground into dust while the unjust man "flourishes like the green bay tree"? To make sense of life Job needs to know the answer. The same kind of question plagues Shakespeare's Hamlet, confronted with the murder of his innocent father by his villainous uncle. When Hamlet asks his famous question, "To be or not to be?," life itself has become a problem.

There are many other ways of viewing human existence. However, of all the symbols and similes for life, perhaps the most popular and significant is that of the journey or pilgrimage. Life is not only a battle, not only a problem. It is a journey: a journey from the cradle to the grave, from innocence to experience, from the depths of existence to the heights, from darkness to light, from death to immortality. We find life seen as a journey in a great number of works: the *Odyssey*, the *Divine Comedy*, *Monkey*, *Pilgrim's Progress*, *Wilhelm Meister*, *Peer Gynt*, and countless others.

The *White Lotus Sutra* gives its own account of human life as a journey. The parable of the return journey, which occurs in chapter 4 of the sutra, is related not by the Buddha but by four great elders. They have heard the Buddha tell the assembly that Sariputra is now so far advanced on the path that he is sure to reach the highest goal of all—not just emancipation from his own individual sin and suffering but Buddhahood itself. Amazed and delighted to learn that the spiritual life has a higher aim, the existence of which they had not hitherto suspected, the four great elders say they feel as though they have quite unexpectedly acquired a priceless jewel, and in chorus they give expression to their feelings in a parable.[90]

They say that once upon a time there was a man who left his father and went away into a distant country. He lived there for a long time—for many years—and during all that time he was miserably poor. Roaming around, doing a job here and a job there, he lived from hand to mouth, and all he ever possessed were the clothes he stood up in.

Meanwhile, his father was leading a very different kind of life. He was a businessman, and he met with such success in his various trading ventures that he became extremely rich. His trade took him from place to place until he finally settled in another country, where he continued to heap up riches—gold, silver, jewels, and grain. He had slaves and workmen and journeymen, horses and carriages, cows and sheep. He even had elephants—and in the East if you possess elephants you really are rich. He also, inevitably, had dozens of dependants and followers clustering around him in the hope of some reward. His influence in business—money-lending, agriculture, commerce—spread far and wide, and he lived the life of a merchant prince.

But despite his growing wealth and all his business activities, the rich man never stopped missing his son. How was the boy? Would they ever meet again? Sorrowful at their long separation, his one hope was that one day his son would come home to inherit the wealth due to him. "After all," the rich man thought, "I am getting old, and one day I must surely die."

All this time the son continued to roam from one town to the next, from one kingdom to the next, until one day, quite by chance, he came to the place where his father was living—although of course he had no idea that he was anywhere near his father. As he was passing, or rather skulking, through the streets keeping a lookout for odd jobs which would earn him a few coppers for food, he saw an enormous house, and sitting in the doorway he saw what seemed to be a very rich man. He was surrounded by an enormous company of people, all waiting on him, or waiting for him. Some had bills in their hands and others had great bundles of money that they wanted to give him. Others had presents, and maybe some had bribes.

The rich man was sitting in the gateway on a magnificent throne—even his footstool was ornamented with gold and silver. He was handling scores of gold pieces, just running his fingers through them, and someone was standing behind him fanning him with a yak's tail. In India a yak's tail is one of the symbols of royalty and divinity, so you would only be fanned with one if you were very, very rich indeed, and had been exalted almost to the plane of divinity. Not only that, he was sitting under a magnificent silk canopy which was inlaid with pearls and flowers, and hung all round with garlands of jewels. He really was a magnificent sight.

When the poor man saw this rich man seated there on his throne, he was absolutely terrified. He thought he must have come upon the king, or at the very least some great nobleman. "I'd better be off," he said to himself. "I'm much more likely to get work in the streets of the poor. If I stay here they might make me into a slave." And he hurried away, without the faintest idea that the rich man was his own father.

But the rich merchant no sooner saw that wretchedly poor man at the edge of the crowd of followers than he knew that this was his son, come back after all these years. What a relief! Now he would be able to hand over his wealth to its rightful inheritor and die happy. Joyfully he called a couple of servants and told them to run after the poor man and bring him back. But when they caught up with the poor fellow he was more terrified than ever. "They've been sent to arrest me. I'm probably going to have my head cut off!" he thought—and he was so afraid that he fell to the earth in a dead faint.

His father was rather surprised at this, but he began to see that all those years he had been living in riches, his son had been living in poverty, and this had created a great psychological difference between them. The boy was obviously not used to being in contact with the rich and powerful. But the faithful father thought, "Never mind. However low he may have sunk, he is still my son"—and he resolved to find a way of restoring their relationship. In the meantime, things being as they were, he decided that it would be better to keep his son's identity secret. He therefore called another servant and instructed him to tell the poor man that he was free to go. Hardly believing his luck, the poor man went off with all speed to seek work in the poorest quarter of the town.

But he was followed by two of his father's men, chosen for their humble appearance. When they caught up with him, the men offered him work, as the rich man had instructed them to do. The job would be to clear away a huge heap of dirt that had accumulated at the back of the mansion, and the wages would be double the normal rate. The poor man accepted this proposal at once, and went off to work with the two men. Day after day he shovelled the heap of dirt and removed it in baskets to a distant place. He found lodging in a straw hovel right next to the mansion, so close that the rich man could see it from his window. The rich man would often look out and think how strange it was that he should be living in a beautiful mansion while his son lived in squalor so near by.

One day, when the poor man had been working at the mansion for quite some time, the rich man put on dirty old clothes and, taking a basket in his hands, managed to have a talk with his son. "Don't think of working anywhere else," he said, "I'll make sure you've got plenty of money. If there's anything you need—a pot, a jug, some extra grain, anything like that—just ask me. I've got an old cloak in the cupboard; you can have that if you like. Just don't worry about a thing. You've been working well and I'm pleased with you. You seem honest and sincere, not like some of the rogues I've got working for me. In fact— well, I'm an old man—you look to me as your own father, and I'll treat you just like my own son."

So for a number of years the poor man carried on clearing away the heap of dirt, and he got into the habit of going in and out of the mansion without thinking twice, although he continued to live in his old straw hovel. Then it happened that the old man became ill, and knew that he was soon going to die. He called the poor man and said, "I feel that I can trust you completely now, just as I would my own son, so I'm going to hand over to you the management of all my affairs. You'll do everything on my behalf." And from that day onward the poor man was the rich man's steward, and looked after all his investments and transactions. As before, he went freely in and out of the mansion but continued to live in his old hovel. Even though he was handling all this wealth, he continued to think that he was poor, for as far as he knew the money was not his, but his master's.

But as time went on, the poor man changed. His father, who watched him constantly, saw that he was gradually becoming accustomed to handling riches, and feeling ashamed that in the past he had lived so miserably. It became obvious that the poor man had begun to want to be rich himself. By this time the rich man was very old and weak indeed, and he knew that his death was near. So he sent for all the people in the city—the king's representative, the merchants, his friends, his distant relations, ordinary citizens, and country folk from round about—and when they were all gathered, he presented his son to them and told them the whole story. When he had finished, he handed over all his wealth to his son, who, of course, could hardly believe his good fortune.

In the context of the *White Lotus Sutra,* this parable has a specific meaning which the four elders explain as soon as they have finished telling the story. Until now, they confess, they have been contented with an inferior spiritual ideal. Now, in his kindness and generosity, the Buddha has revealed to them the ideal of attaining supreme Enlightenment not for themselves alone but for the benefit of all sentient beings, and in this way has made them heirs to all his spiritual treasures. Like the son in the parable, the four elders feel overjoyed at the wealth which they have so unexpectedly gained.

The four elders' explanation takes us quite a long way, but with a little imagination we can go much further, even much deeper. We can start by reflecting on the strangely familiar ring of this story. You may well be thinking, "I'm sure I've heard that story somewhere before." Thinking back, you may be pretty sure that you haven't read the *White Lotus Sutra*—it isn't the sort of thing you can read one weekend and then forget about—so why does the parable of the return journey seem so familiar? The reason, as you may have realized, is that it resembles a much more widely known parable: Jesus's parable of the prodigal son. This parable is told by Jesus of Nazareth to elucidate a different point, and it has a different ending, but in general outline the two stories are the same. In both parables there is an affectionate father and a son who runs away; in both parables the runaway son lives miserably for a while before returning to the bosom of his father; and in both parables the position of servant is contrasted with the position of son.

These are the similarities between the parables; there are also significant differences between them. Perhaps the most important of these differences is that in the Gospel parable the prodigal son appears to be guilty of willful disobedience, whereas in the *White Lotus Sutra* the son seems to go astray just through carelessness and forgetfulness. This illustrates a crucial difference between Buddhism and Christianity, Christianity seeing the human condition in terms of sin, disobedience, and guilt while Buddhism sees it more in terms of forgetfulness, unmindfulness, and ignorance.

Another parable about a father and a son, belonging to roughly the same period as the parable of the return journey, constitutes an even more interesting parallel. It occurs in the apocryphal Acts of the Apostle Thomas, an essentially Gnostic work extant in Greek translation as well as in the original Syriac. Modern translators call the story the "Hymn of the Pearl," but the text gives it the title "Song of the Apostle Judas Thomas in the Land of the Indians."[91] Saint Thomas, one of the twelve Apostles, is traditionally known as the Apostle to India because he is supposed to have visited India soon after the death of Jesus, and this parable is said to have been composed while he was imprisoned there. Whether he had much contact with Buddhism, and whether the "Hymn of the Pearl" owes anything to the parable of the return journey, we can only speculate.

The parable says that in the East there live a father and his son. The son is quite happy living in the wealth and splendor of "the kingdom of his father's house," but one day his father sends him on a mission to the land of Egypt, to bring back the one pearl which lies, encircled by a great dragon, in the midst of the sea. When he reaches Egypt, the son finds the dragon and waits for him to go to sleep so that he can take the pearl. But the Egyptians become suspicious of this stranger, even though he is disguised in Egyptian garments, and they give him a drugged drink which causes him to lose his memory. Forgetting that he is the son of a king, forgetting all about the pearl, he enters the service of the king of Egypt. And eventually, living with the Egyptians, eating their food and drinking their drink, he becomes more and more like them. In the end, we are told, he falls into a deep sleep. His father in the East, who knows what is happening, becomes anxious, and sends his son a letter—in the form of a bird—reminding him of his mission. And as soon as he receives the letter, the son comes to his senses, enchants the dragon and seizes the pearl. He returns home in triumph, and his father receives him with great joy.

Each of these parables, the return journey, the prodigal son, and the "Hymn of the Pearl," has its own wealth of symbolism, but they all share the same central symbol. They all begin with a separation between a father and a son; this is the event from which everything else follows. So what is meant by this separation of father and son? Who or what are the father and the son?

Well, we could say that the father represents what may be called the higher self (although we need to be careful not to take the expression too literally), and the son is the lower self. And just as the son is separated from his father, the lower self is separated—or, in more contemporary language, *alienated*—from the higher self. Here, by the way, is another metaphor for the human condition: alienation. We are alienated from our own higher selves, our own better natures, our own highest potentialities. We are alienated from Truth, from Reality. And just as the son went not just a short distance away from his father, but to an altogether different part of the world, so the alienation between the higher self and the lower self is severe. Indeed, the schism between the two is complete; there is no contact of any kind between them.

We may say that the condition of the human race is one of alienation from Truth, but when did this condition begin? The son lives in a distant country for many years, which suggests that the alienation is of long standing. But if we take the parable literally, the implication is that although it may have happened a long time ago, it did happen at a certain point in time. This is the view of orthodox Christianity, which teaches that Adam and Eve lived happily in the Garden of Eden, in harmony with God and in obedience to his commands, until Adam took a bite of the apple, at which point mankind fell from grace and became alienated from God.

Buddhism holds a different view. According to the Buddha you can go back and back in time for millions of years, millions of ages, but you will never come to an absolute first beginning of things. However far back you go, you can still go further. You will never get back to a point before the point at which time begins. So the beginning of the parable is not in time at all, but completely outside time. This means that the

376 ~ THE ESSENTIAL SANGHARAKSHITA

"return journey" is not a journey back into the past, but a journey out of time altogether, a journey which transcends time. It is very important to understand this.

In the books about Zen which people are so fond of reading, there are all kinds of strange and wonderful—and apparently meaningful—expressions, all kinds of appealingly snappy little mondos and koans. One of these Zen sayings—which is of course absolutely true—speaks of "your original face before you were born." The Zen masters are apparently rather fond of asking their disciples, at a moment's notice, to show them their original face before they were born. "Come on!" they demand, "Show it to me. I want to see it." Of course the hapless disciple usually fails miserably, as hapless disciples tend to in these stories, written as they apparently are by the masters. The disciple tends to tackle the problem by sitting down and thinking about yesterday, the day before, the week before, a month ago, two months ago, a year ago, two years ago, twenty years ago, thirty years ago—until they get back to the day they were born. If they can get back past *that,* they think, they will encounter their original face.

This is all wrong. To think that before a certain point in time there was the original face and after that there was no original face is a complete misunderstanding. The expression may seem to mean this, but if we go trying to track down the original face in the past, if we take this expression "original" or the word "before" literally, we are not really practicing Zen, but just regressing in the psychoanalytical sense. The past is no nearer to Enlightenment than the present or the future, because time has nothing to do with Enlightenment. We are "born," in the Zen sense, out of time, and our original face also exists out of time, so the Zen expression "seeing your original face" has nothing to do with going back in time, or with going forward in time, or with standing still at the present moment of time. When Zen speaks of seeing your original face before you were born, it means going outside time altogether, rocketing through time and coming up on the other side in a dimension where there is no time at all, no past, present, or future. That is where the original face is to be seen, and nowhere else. That's where it "is" all the time.

So there is no question of going back in time to enquire into the beginning of our state of alienation. We are alienated from reality here and now, and all we have to do is overcome this alienation from reality. And we can't do that just by going back and back into the past because we are still running on the rails of the alienation itself. We have to take a leap, a crosswise leap—a jump from the top of the pole, to use another Zen expression—to land, if we're lucky, in the absolute.

This is the point of the Buddha's famous parable of the poisoned arrow—another parable connected with war—which is told in the Pali Canon.[92] The Buddha says that a soldier was wounded in battle by a poisoned arrow. Fortunately there is a surgeon on hand, but when he tries to take the arrow out, the wounded man says, "Just a minute! Before I let you take out that arrow I want to ask a few questions. Who shot this arrow? Was he a brahmin, a ksatriya, or a vaisya? Was he dark or fair? Was he young or old? What sort of bow was he using? And what sort of arrow is it?—A wooden one? An iron one? If it's wood, what sort of wood is it made from?—Oak? Cedar? Where does the feather come from? Is it a goose feather or a peacock feather? Answer all these questions, and then you can take out the arrow."

Long before his questions were answered, of course, the soldier would be dead from the poison in the arrow. The important thing is to get rid of the arrow, not to enquire where it came from. In the same way, if we try to go back and back all the time—"How did the world begin? How did we get into such a mess? What was I in my last birth? What are the roots of my neurosis?"—there is no end to it. We could go step by step back into the past and still be walking in millions of years. What we need to do is just see our present alienated, neurotic, conditioned, negative state, and rise above it, go soaring up into eternity, into a spiritual dimension. This is the message of the poisoned arrow. Likewise, the "return journey" of the son is not about going back in time, but about going beyond time.

The son, who represents the lower self, wanders from place to place looking for work, for the simple reason that he needs food and clothing.

He has no higher ideals. He has none of his father's ambitions of succeeding in trade and commerce. Translating this into modern terms (borrowed from Abraham Maslow's book *Toward a Psychology of Being*), the lower self is "need-motivated." Everything the son does is out of his subjective need, out of his craving. By contrast, the father — the higher self—is "growth-motivated." The parable expresses this in terms of his accumulation of riches, but this is in no way to imply that it is glorifying capitalism or anything like that; as a parable, its meaning is symbolic. The father, the higher self, accumulates wealth until he possesses all conceivable spiritual riches and qualities.

Although he is so rich, the father is not happy because he is thinking of his son all the time. What can we infer from this? It tells us that the higher self never loses its awareness. It is conscious *all the time.* Although we may completely forget the higher self, the higher self never forgets us. But at the same time—this is the mystery—we are it. An image may help to make this clear. Imagine an enormous subterranean chamber all lit up from within. We are living in a tiny chamber next to—indeed part of—the big one. A pane of glass which is transparent only from one side separates the two chambers, so that although someone in the large illuminated chamber could see everything going on in the little chamber, from the little chamber we can see nothing at all of what is going on in the large chamber. In fact, we have no idea that there is a large chamber. But although cramped in our little chamber we may forget, even be oblivious to, the existence of the large chamber, the large chamber always has a window onto the little chamber. Even though the lower self forgets the higher self, the higher self is the higher self *of* the lower self.

The parable says that the poor man roams from one town to another and one country to another until he eventually reaches the place where his father is living. So he is already on his way back to his father, although he does not know it. It is his need for food and clothing, his craving, which drives him from place to place and brings him almost to his father's door. What are we to make of this?

Let's look at an example. A man has a certain psychological problem.

He's so worried about it that he just can't sleep, and sleeping tablets don't help. He is really getting desperate for some peace of mind. One day he meets a friend who says, "I know what will help you. You need to meditate." By this stage the man is ready to try anything, so he asks where he can learn to meditate and goes along to a class. His only concern is to get rid of the problem and get some sleep. But at the meditation classes he starts to hear about something new: Buddhism. At first he is not particularly interested, but after a few months—rather to his surprise—he finds himself not just trying to get peace of mind but trying to follow the spiritual path. After a while he even starts thinking in terms of Enlightenment. So when did he take the first step in that direction? It was when, driven by his need for peace of mind, he joined the meditation class. In the same way the poor man, driven by his basic needs, made his way to his father's door without knowing it. This is the first stage of the return journey.

When the poor man eventually arrives at his father's door, his father is sitting outside surrounded by gold, jewels, and flowers. The poetic description of the rich man—who represents the higher self—is highly significant. He is a glorious archetypal figure, a god, even a Buddha, so he is described with light and color, jewels and brilliance. But how does the poor man react? He is so terrified at the sight that he wants to run away. He thinks that he has come upon a king or nobleman, not recognizing in this glorious figure his own father. This goes to show that the alienation between the lower self and the higher self is quite severe. Even when the two confront each other, the lower self does not recognize the higher self as its own higher self, but thinks it is something strange and foreign. Such a confrontation occurs when we come face to face with an embodiment of the spiritual ideal. Whenever we read a description or see an image of the Buddha—or some god or saint—we think, or our lower self thinks, "This has nothing to do with me. I'm down here, poor and humble. I'm not like that. I don't have those qualities." The theistic systems which believe in a personal creator god, and indeed all dualistic systems, encourage this attitude.

We could call this the stage of religious projection. We project outward all the qualities which are buried deep down in the depths of our
own nature, not realizing that they are our own. As we see it, these glorious external figures are endowed with all the qualities which we lack.
We are poor and they are rich. This religious projection is a step in the
right direction; indeed, it is the next stage of the journey. It is a positive thing because it enables us to see spiritual qualities in a concrete
way. But the projection must be resolved. These qualities belong to
us—not to our ego, but to the deepest and truest depths of our
being—and we must claim them as our own.

As yet, however, the son does not recognize his father, although his
father immediately recognizes him and sends messengers to bring
him back. But the poor man is terrified, thinks he is going to be
arrested, and faints away. This reminds me of the account of the death
experience given in the *Tibetan Book of the Dead.* At the time of death,
so the text says, the Clear Light, a white light of absolutely unbearable
brilliance, like a million suns, suddenly bursts on the vision of the
dying person. This light is the light of Reality, the light of Truth, the
light of the Void. If we recognize that this is no light bursting upon us
from without, but the light of our own intrinsic mind, our own true
self, unfolding from deep within, if we can realize our oneness with
that light, then we gain Enlightenment on the spot. But what happens? The light comes—blinding, terrible, overpowering—and most
dying people shrink back in fear. "Human kind cannot bear very much
reality'—so T.S. Eliot wrote in his *Four Quartets,* and it is true not
only at the moment of death, but at all those moments when we
encounter a truth that seems more than we can possibly bear.

The poor man, you notice, is not just terrified. His imagination is
working overtime. He thinks that he is being arrested: already in his
mind's eye he can see the block and the executioner's axe. His first
thoughts are of imprisonment, slavery, violent death. Only too often
when we come in contact with the Truth, it seems not liberating but
an imprisonment, a limitation, or at least a nuisance. We do not want
to change our ideas, or to change ourselves, and in that diseased state

the liberating truth seems to us confining and narrow. Not only that, like the poor man in the parable we are afraid of dying. When the lower self—the I, the ego—comes in contact with Reality, it thinks, as it were, "I'm for the chop. I'm finished; this is the end of me," and so it shrinks back.

So the rich man lets his son slope off, but of course he has not given up hope, and by some clever planning he manages to get his son clearing away the heap of dirt at the back of his mansion. Now according to the interpretation of the parable which the four elders give, the son's clearing away dirt represents the narrow, selfish type of religious life which is aimed at individual development to the exclusion of any concern for others. The four elders identify this sort of approach with the lesser teaching which until so recently had been all they had known, but a better—or at least more contemporary—interpretation would suggest that the clearing away of the dirt represents the process of psychoanalysis, the heap of dirt representing all the repressions which the alienated person uncovers during analysis. The sutra mentions that it takes twenty years to clear away the dirt, which seems rather a long time, but resolving repressions, negative emotions, complexes, and all the rest of it is rather time-consuming, so analysis does sometimes take as long as that.

And eventually, while the process of removing the dirt-heap continues, the father manages to speak to his son, and confidence springs up between them. As this trust develops, the poor man begins to enter the rich man's mansion without hesitation, but he continues to live in his own hovel. So what does this mean? On one level it refers to the scholar, the academic specialist in comparative religion. He knows the texts, sometimes in the original languages, and he knows the teachings, even the higher teachings. Sometimes he even claims to know the esoteric teachings. In other words, he goes in and out of the mansion without hesitation, knowing exactly what is there—but he does not live there himself. He still lives in the straw hovel which represents all the things he is really interested in as an academic: promotion within his department; his annual increment; prestige within his profession; controversy and brisk exchange of articles and opinions with other scholars.

On a higher level, the poor man's going in and out of the mansion without hesitation refers to the average follower of religion. Such people are undoubtedly sincere and have perhaps had genuine religious experience—they go in and out of the mansion, as it were—but their home is elsewhere. Even though they have some spiritual experience, maybe during the weekly meditation class, they are preoccupied most of the time with mundane things. In one of his books, William James, the great psychologist and author of *The Varieties of Religious Experience,* discusses the question "What is a religious person?" He says that a religious person is not one who has religious experiences—anybody can have those—but one who makes religious experiences the center of their existence. It is not important where we visit; what is important is where we permanently live, or at least where we live most of the time—in other words, where our real center of interest lies. As the Gospel says, "Where your treasure is, there will your heart be also."

When the rich man falls sick, he hands the management of his affairs over to the poor man, who thus becomes familiar with riches but still continues to live in the hovel. This element of the parable represents the theist, or the theistically inclined mystic, and the dualistic approach in general. Such a person may have great, overwhelming, uplifting spiritual experiences, but they all seem to come from outside, not from within. The mystic says "These experiences are not mine; they are the gifts of God."

Once you reach this stage of the journey, only time is required. The rich man sees that his son is becoming used to riches and ashamed of his poverty, and that he aspires to be rich himself. In other words, the alienation of lower self from higher self is becoming less and less. When the rich man is at the point of death, the alienation is practically over, with just a thin thread remaining; the lower self and the higher self are almost one. And when at last the rich man acknowledges the poor man as his son, he dies, and there are no longer two—father and son, rich man and poor man—but only one, a rich man who was once a poor man. In other words, unity between the lower self and the higher self has been completely restored. The return journey has been accomplished.

Our journey also is nearly accomplished. The four elders who have told the parable compare themselves to the son—and the Buddha, of course, is the father. Formerly, they say, they had not dared to think in terms of becoming like the Buddha, thinking only of following his verbal teaching, which had seemed to indicate a lesser goal, the goal of individual emancipation, the goal of the destruction of negative emotions. But they now realize, they say, that that is not enough, for there are all sorts of positive qualities to be developed. It is not enough to have Wisdom; you need Compassion too. It is not enough to be an Arahant; you can become like the Buddha himself. You can follow the Bodhisattva Path; you can aspire to supreme Enlightenment.

In other words, the four elders wake up to the truth of the Higher Evolution of humanity. They realize that the Buddha is not something unique and unrepeatable, but a forerunner, an example of what others too can become if only they make the effort. They realize that the religious life is not just a personal affair in a negative limited sense, but part of a cosmic adventure—and this is what we too have to try to realize. Religion, when properly understood, is not remote from life, not just a dull, churchy little backwater, but life become conscious of its own upward tendency, its own tendency to grow and develop. And whether we know it or not, we are all involved, directly or indirectly, in this upward tendency of life. Each one of us is the poor man in the parable, the son who has run away; but each one of us also, if we only knew it, is the rich man, the father. And each one of us is making, even at this very moment, the return journey.

PART FOUR

Buddhism and the Heart

1 ← Buddhism and Emotional Life

1. INVOLVING THE EMOTIONS IN SPIRITUAL LIFE

For most of us the central problem of the spiritual life is to find emotional equivalents for our intellectual understanding.

IT APPEARS that in ancient times Indian monks used to go from India to China in large numbers to preach the Doctrine, and that at one period of Chinese history there was a very pious Chinese emperor who was always eager to welcome great sages and teachers from India. Now one day it so happened that one of the greatest of the Indian teachers turned up in the Chinese capital. The emperor was delighted to hear the news, thinking that he would have a wonderful philosophical discussion with this newly-arrived teacher. So the teacher was invited to the palace, where he was received with due pomp and ceremony. When all the formalities were over and the teacher and the emperor had taken their seats, the emperor put his first question. "Tell me," he said, "what is the fundamental principle of Buddhism?" Then he sat back, waiting to get the answer straight from the horse's mouth, as it were. The teacher replied, "Ceasing to do evil; learning to do good; purifying the heart—this is the fundamental principle of Buddhism." The emperor was rather taken aback. He had heard all that before. (We have usually heard it all before!) So he said, "Is that all? Is *that* the fundamental principle of Buddhism?' "Yes," replied the sage,

"That's all. Cease to do evil; learn to do good; purify the heart. That is indeed the fundamental principle of Buddhism." "But this is so simple that even a child of three could understand it," protested the emperor. "Yes, your majesty," said the teacher, "that is quite true. It is so simple that even a child of three can understand it. But it is so difficult that even an old man of eighty cannot put it into practice."

This story illustrates the great difference between understanding and practice. We find it easy simply to *understand.* We can understand the Abhidharma; we can understand the Madhyamika; we can understand the Yogacara; we can understand Plato; we can understand Aristotle; we can understand the Four Gospels; we can understand everything. But to put into practice even a little of all this knowledge and make it operative in our lives, this we find very difficult indeed. In the famous words of St. Paul, "The good that I would I do not: but the evil which I would not, that I do."[93] He knows what he ought to do but cannot do it; and he cannot help doing that which he knows he should not do. Again we see this tremendous, this terrible disparity between understanding and practice.

This state of affairs is not exceptional. It is not the Chinese emperor and Saint Paul who ran into this difficulty: all religious people find themselves at some time or other, sometimes for years together, in this terrible and tragic predicament. They know the truth intellectually; they know it from A to Z and from Z back to A. They can talk about it, write about it, give lectures about it. But they are unable to put it into practice. For those who are sincere this can be a source of great suffering. They may feel, "I know this very well, and see it so clearly; but I just can't do it." It is as though there is a blind spot, an "x-factor" which obstructs our efforts all the time. No sooner do we lift ourselves up a few inches than we slip back what sometimes feels like a mile.

Why does this happen? Why is there this terrible gulf between theory and practice, understanding and action? Why are most of us unable to act most of the time in accordance with what we *know* is true, what we *know* is right? Why do we fail so miserably again and again? The answer to this question is to be sought in the very depths of human nature. We may say that we "know" something, but we know it only with the conscious mind, with the rational part of ourselves. We know it theoretically, intellectually, abstractly. But we must recollect that we are not just our conscious minds. We are not all reason—though we may like to think we are. There is another part of us, a much larger part than we care to admit, which is no less important than our reason. This part is made up of instinct, of emotion, of volition, and is more unconscious than conscious. And this wider, deeper, and no less important part of us is not touched at all by our rational or intellectual knowledge, but goes its own way, as it were dragging the mental part, protesting, along with it.

Thus we see that we cannot go against the emotions. The emotions are stronger than reason. If we want to put into practice what we know to be right, what we know to be true, we have to enlist, in one way or another, the cooperation of the emotions. We have to be able to tap those deeper sources within ourselves and harness them to our spiritual life. For most of us the central problem of the spiritual life is to find emotional equivalents for our intellectual understanding. Until we have done this no further spiritual progress is possible. This is why Perfect Emotion is the second stage, or second aspect, of the Noble Eightfold Path, immediately after Perfect Vision.

2. Being Moved by the Dharma

It is as though the Dharma touches some spring in you, opens something up that was hitherto blocked, melts something that was congealed, frees up energy that was imprisoned.

> Thereupon the impact of Dharma moved the Venerable Subhuti to tears. Having wiped away his tears, he thus spoke to the Lord: It is wonderful, O Lord, it is exceedingly wonderful, O Well-Gone, how well the Tathagata has taught this

discourse on Dharma. Through it cognition has been produced in me. Never have I before heard such a discourse on
Dharma. Most wonderfully blest will be those who, when
this Sutra is being taught, will produce a true perception.

THE TEACHING put forth in the *Diamond Sutra* may seem quite
abstract in form, but for Subhuti it is not abstract at all. His emotional
response demonstrates a distinctive emphasis of the Mahayana. It is
well known that when the Buddha died, the Arahants that were
there—and Subhuti is, according to this text, an Arahant—exhibited
no particular emotion. Only those who were relatively unenlightened
felt any separation or loss at the removal of the Buddha's physical
body. Thus arose the view of Arahants as cool, impassive figures. The
Mahayana, however, recognized that there were appropriate objects
for the expression of powerful emotion—even, and indeed all the
more so, at the highest levels of spiritual development. In the *Astasa-
hasrika Sutra,* the "Perfection of Wisdom in 8,000 Lines," for example,
there is a Bodhisattva called Sadaprarudita—*sada* meaning "always,"
and *prarudita,* "weeping"—and he is always weeping because he is
constantly moved by the Dharma.

Subhuti is of course only an Arahant, so he just sheds a few tears—
but the important thing is that he is deeply moved by the Dharma. It
is essential that we feel strongly and deeply about the Three Jewels,
and also about the particular context within which we practice, our
Sangha, and the local spiritual community within which we live or
work. It comes down to fidelity, staying true to your friends and keeping faith with the Dharma. It is quite significant that in Tibet the
Bodhisattva Tara is known as "the faithful Tara."

In the modern West, our social mobility gives us a kind of freedom,
but at the same time it tends to limit our ability to develop close, deep,
and strong relationships. The ease with which we can move on to new
pastures tends to blunt our appreciation of our experience. We can
always go off and make new friends when a situation or a relationship
begins to make deeper demands upon our emotions, and this means

that we seldom expose ourselves to any experience deeply and lastingly enough for it to move us. But to be strong and healthy, emotions need to be rooted in loyalty and commitment. When people are moving from one place to another, from one relationship to another, from one religion to another, and when the idea of not being tied down, of not limiting our options, of not identifying with a particular set of values, is understood as freedom—when it no longer seems clear at what to weep and at what to rejoice—then a situation develops in which there is no longer any outlet for the natural expression of strong emotion.

Of course, this has not always been the case in our society. We have only to go back to the nineteenth century to find the whole country, even hard-boiled politicians, awash with tears over the death of Little Nell or Paul Dombey. Dickens himself apparently used to laugh and cry and behave rather like a madman when he was writing, quite carried away by the events his imagination was conjuring up. Even fifty years ago, my mother and her friend would come back from the cinema on a Thursday night saying how much they'd enjoyed it—"We had a really good cry." Perhaps these days we are afraid of seeming sentimental. We are increasingly uneasy about responding naturally to what may seem to our social consciences rather less than worthy demands upon our emotions. Also, perhaps, the emotions gradually become constrained within a social context of increasing control and security.

But Subhuti does weep. He weeps because the Dharma has touched something in him that has not been touched before. Weeping when you hear the Dharma is a sign that something has got through to you. It is as though the Dharma touches some spring in you, opens something up that was hitherto blocked, melts something that was congealed, frees up energy that was imprisoned. And you are touched, you are moved, you are stirred. There is a powerful expression for this sort of state in Pali: *samvega*—to be shaken by the Dharma. There is even quite a powerful word in English which gives some idea of the sort of emotional response we need to discover in ourselves before we can claim to have taken in even a little of this

392 ~ THE ESSENTIAL SANGHARAKSHITA

teaching—and that is the adjective "sublime." We begin to understand the *Diamond Sutra* not when we imagine that we have worked out what it means, but when, as we contemplate it, we are moved—even to tears—by a sense of the sublime.

What the sublime represents is something vast and grand and overwhelmingly powerful which gives us a terrifying sense of our own smallness, but which at the same time—and this is what moves us, even exhilarates us—allows us the realization that on another level it is no greater than us, that there is that within us which resonates with that grandeur. The sublime moves us in a way that the simply beautiful cannot. It is there in the works of Michelangelo and Beethoven; among the ragas of traditional Indian music it is expressed in the *bhairava,* the "terrible" mode; and in the *Tibetan Book of the Dead* it is embodied in the wrathful deities, who are not beautiful like the peaceful forms, but sublime and awesome.

Subhuti is shaken by a revelation of something even more sublime than the nirvana that he has, presumably, so far attained. It is as though he were standing on a mountain peak imagining that it was the highest peak of all, and then, the mist clearing, he looked up, and there was another peak still, towering above him. As the Buddha carefully removes the Dharma beyond the reckoning of the most extravagant scale of values, it is the sublimity of the perspective revealed to him that moves Subhuti to tears.

3. The Difference between Feelings and Emotions

Being able to identify feelings is what makes it possible for us to follow the Buddhist path.

JUDGING FROM what one reads about them, one gets the impression that the people of previous times experienced their feelings in a much more full-blooded way than we do in the urbanized modern world. What stands out in the accounts of ancient and traditional societies is their sheer emotional energy. Take the ancient Greeks, for example. In the days of Plato and Socrates, it seems that people took their friendships very seriously indeed. If they loved you, they would love you without reservation and do anything for you. But they hated unreservedly too, and made fearsome, even ruthless, adversaries. Life today might be more comfortable, but in comparison with the people of earlier times, we seem to live it in a very flat, lifeless emotional state. Going to work on the bus, or packed into a crowded train, our emotions are for the most part disengaged as we simply try to get through the day. One might well say that in this tepid, unresponsive state, we are "out of touch with our feelings."

Why is this? One obvious fact of life these days is that it is very complicated. The traditional society, in which one was born, lived, and died in the same place among the same people, is a thing of the past. Many people move every few years, and have to build up a new social network time after time. In these circumstances they have little chance to build up strong friendships outside the nuclear family, and the weakness of their connections with others makes it difficult for them to respond emotionally to the people around them.

However, as Western psychology tells us, those strong feelings do not go away, but remain repressed on a subconscious level. One of the aims of psychotherapy is to bring them to the surface and restore a full awareness of oneself as a whole personality. When Buddhist psychology refers to developing mindfulness of feelings, however, something rather different is meant from the "getting in touch with one's feelings" with which psychotherapy is concerned—something less complex, though perhaps more useful. Indeed, being able to identify feelings (in the sense of *vedana* as defined by Buddhist tradition and explained below) is what makes it possible for us to follow the Buddhist path.

The Pali term *vedana* refers to feeling not in the sense of the emotions, but in terms of sensation. *Vedana* is whatever pleasantness or unpleasantness we might experience in our contact with any physical or mental stimulus. To understand what we would call emotion, Buddhism looks at the way in which that pleasant or painful feeling is interwoven with our reactions and responses to it. In Buddhist psychology, *vedana* is said to combine with *samkhara,* a volitional quality involving a tendency toward action. It is this combination of sensation with volition that approaches what we would recognize as fully developed emotion.

Feeling—whether pleasure or pain—is passive: that is, it arises as a result of all sorts of conditions. We can change feelings that arise in various ways by changing the conditions that give rise to them—opening the window when we're hot, to take the simplest of examples. But there is a certain kind of painful feeling against which we can do nothing to protect ourselves: the feelings that arise as a result of our past unskillful karma. These must simply be borne, although of course we can protect ourselves from future pain by making the effort to create fresh positive karma, even while we are experiencing pain.

It is very important that we learn to do this. Feelings of pleasure and pain are not themselves productive of fresh karma, but when we allow ourselves to react to them in the form of some emotion, and when that emotional reaction is negative, negative karmic consequences will follow. The practice of recollecting feelings is intended to help us be aware of our feelings before an emotional reaction to them sets in. If we can distinguish between the feelings we receive as impressions and what we then make of them, we will be able to take more responsibility for our emotions, while not suppressing our feelings. We need to know what we feel if we are to direct the flow of our emotional life in a positive way.

This is quite difficult because most of the time our feelings get lost in our emotional reactions to them. If you are meditating, for example, and you feel an itch or hear an ugly sound, the simple experience of feeling tends swiftly to be overlaid with an emotional reaction—in this case, of aversion. Our natural tendency is to want to get away from a feeling if it is painful and to want more of it if it is pleasant.

Before we know where we are, we have thus shifted from the simple experience of pleasure or pain into some form of craving or hatred. The practice, therefore, is to keep returning to the bare feeling, allowing no space for these habitual reactions to establish themselves.

4. Cultivating Positive Emotions

If spiritual practice is to transform your life, you need to think of it as something you can enjoy, not just a hard grind, and this means making sure that there is not too much of a contradiction between "spiritual" activities and the activities of daily life—and looking for enjoyment in both.

Modern living seems almost designed to drain away energy and dissipate positivity. Continual contact with the day-to-day stress of ordinary life tends to damp down one's responses: walking through the city, you pass many people in quite negative mental states and you can feel your energy being drained away just through warding off those influences and keeping all the noise at bay. City life seems to draw out energy and waste it senselessly, not just through noise and worry, but also through the mechanical and electronic devices that dictate the pace of life. Our senses are bombarded by all manner of powerful messages, both crude and subtle, and all demanding our attention. Another feature of modern life is the extraordinary range of superficial enjoyments available to us. Although many of these little outlets of energy are not harmful or unethical in themselves, if our attention is spread thinly across all of them, we will be unable to have any single experience of real depth.

If we are to make any progress spiritually we therefore need to intervene positively in the way we feel and the way we experience the world. In our own interests, we need to shield ourselves from negative influences. Feelings do not arise of their own accord; they come about in dependence on conditions and disappear when those conditions are removed. By being aware of how we are liable to be influenced by our environment and activities, we can manage the feelings that are likely to arise and cultivate a reserve of positive energy upon which to draw in the pursuit of stronger, brighter states of awareness.

This is all common sense, and easily verifiable in our own experience. If you are feeling depressed, for example, you might decide to spend a day in the country to put you in a more positive mood. If you feel uninspired, making contact with someone who shares your ideals and aspirations will give life a much more positive aspect. By taking a more active role in handling our sense impressions we can bring our feelings more effectively under our control. One might say that this is the purpose of going on retreat. A retreat center is an environment dedicated to concentrating one's energies and directing them toward the attainment of higher states of awareness and more positive and refined emotion. It might take a little time to adjust to the absence of distractions to which you are accustomed in everyday life, but as you get used to it, your state of mind becomes much more contented, even blissful, just through simplifying your sensory impressions and cutting down on the activities through which your energy is usually frittered away. Sometimes on retreat one is asked to observe regular periods of silence, and people are often amazed to find that as a result they have much more energy than usual, with, strange to say, no diminution of their level of communication with others—a good basis from which to tap deeper sources of inspiration through meditation. One invariably comes back from retreat charged with energy. (Incidentally, this is also one reason for observing celibacy. Even athletes are said to conserve their energy in this way and some would say that it is essential if one intends to explore the deeper levels of meditative experience.) The stillness and simplicity of a retreat provides the ideal basis for a heightened and consistent emotional positivity. When you are not on retreat, one of the most effective ways of banking up your energies and preventing them from leaking away is a regular lifestyle which keeps energy flowing continuously through the same channels. Regular sleep, diet, working hours, and meditation all help to clarify and concentrate one's energies, harmonizing them in the service of one's higher aspirations.

But external conditions are not everything. Even if you went on solitary retreat and placed yourself in ideal conditions, free from any external factors that might dissipate your energies, even if you had plenty of time in which to meditate and reflect, you might still lack the inspiration to do it. Obviously you couldn't blame your surroundings; the reason would have to be subjective. You might look for a clue by investigating what does seem to stimulate an emotional response. You might discover that while higher thoughts and aspirations leave you cold, when your mind wanders toward visions of a succulent meal or some beautiful sexual partner, you are much more interested. Food and sex, after all, are likely to arouse almost everyone's interest, and the energy to pursue them is more or less ever-present.

So it is inaccurate to talk about having or not having energy in absolute terms. Emotional energy can't be measured in terms of a fixed quantity like water or heat or even the capacity to perform physical work. It is all about one's level of inspiration. The question is not how much energy you can muster, but how refined that energy is. Energy arises in connection with objects of pleasure and interest, and your relationship to those objects says a great deal about the kind of person you are. One way of thinking of the spiritual life is that it is about shifting the focus of your emotional energy from, say, food or sex, or watching football or boxing, to the more refined pleasures of art, music, friendship, and meditation.

Sometimes it is only when we are on retreat and our everyday supports and pleasures are removed that we find out what is really keeping us going from day to day. We may have an idea or even a conviction that higher pleasures are the most fulfilling, but our ability to enjoy them is unlikely to be as fully developed as our intellectual understanding that they are a good thing. In other words, our spiritual ideals may not have filtered very far into our deeper emotions and volitions, so that we continue to seek pleasure in the same old places. This is the usual pattern of spiritual life: our intellectual understanding will always be some way ahead of our emotional involvement. It is quite usual to find oneself oscillating between relatively crude pleasures and a rigid determination to engage with spiritual practice which has little of the warmth and ease characteristic of truly positive emotion.

But in the end this is not sustainable. If spiritual practice is to transform your life, you need to think of it as something you can enjoy, not just a hard grind, and this means making sure that there is not too much of a contradiction between "spiritual" activities and the activities of daily life—and looking for enjoyment in both. If there is at least an element of enjoyment in our daily lives, we will be able to bring that positive attitude to puja, our study of the Dharma, and our meditation. The alternative—a dreary day followed by a meditation that is nothing short of a struggle—is hardly an inspiring prospect.

5. Dealing with Desire

It cannot give you real satisfaction—but it's difficult to give up hoping that it might be able to, and trying just once more.

OFTEN WE FEEL desires for all sorts of things we think we want, but even if we get what we thought we wanted, our desires remain unsatisfied. We experience this, of course, because we are so busy going after things we don't really want. Only too often when we have had it and enjoyed it—if it was enjoyable—we realize that we didn't really want it after all. We are not really satisfied; we have just been distracted or amused for a while, no more than that. When we think about it, we realize that we could easily have done without it—even have been better off without it.

But when you are in the grip of desire, it's hard to remember all this. When you think you want something, well, you think you want it. You may need to go through the same procedure time and time again, maybe hundreds of times, before you learn your lesson and accept that you're not going to get what you really want from that thing. It cannot give you real satisfaction—but it's difficult to give up hoping that it might be able to, and trying just once more. "I'll give it another chance before trying nirvana!" You have to really wallow in it before you know it's muck.

Even if somebody tells you that the object of your desire will be a disappointment, and on a rational level you can see that he is right, this won't help if deep down you remain unconvinced. However rational and reasonable the arguments against doing it are, you may well feel compelled to do whatever it is anyway, just to see for yourself.

But, of course, there is really no need to try out everything personally. If somebody tells you that if you put your finger in the fire it will burn, you don't have to test it to see. You might put your finger near enough to get warm, and a bit nearer to get warmer, but that should be enough to convince you. It's a delusion to think that we have to experience personally everything that the Buddha has warned us does not lead in the direction of nirvana. We just have to take the Buddha's word for it in at least certain areas, and not insist on a personal confirmation of the unsatisfactoriness of every vice.

It isn't even really necessary to experience something of every kind or category of vice. You can group them into one big group called "worldly pleasures"; if you have had even a taste of one of them, that should be enough to disillusion you about them all. They all come under the same heading; they're all conditioned things, so they don't really differ in any essential respect from one another.

On the other hand, it could be quite dangerous to deprive yourself of all comforts on the basis of a purely rational understanding of the truth, before you have started to get any real satisfaction from practicing Buddhism. If you did that, you could well feel so bored and frustrated, and find life so blank and meaningless, that you would be tempted to go to the opposite extreme. You must begin to enjoy being a Buddhist before you give up too much, otherwise you will associate being a Buddhist with a dull, dry, painful, difficult, joyless sort of existence.

This should not, of course, be used as a rationalization for not giving up anything at all. In fact, if you haven't got any enjoyment at all from the Dharma, it might be best to give up a few things and make things really uncomfortable for yourself. That might force the issue. Otherwise you could remain stuck indefinitely, just being mentally occupied with the Dharma, getting no real pleasure from it, and not being willing to give up even small things because you haven't yet started to enjoy the spiritual life. You could stay like that all your life. You might have to do something drastic, take a risk, make yourself really uncomfortable, thoroughly bored and frustrated. Then you would have to get pleasure from the Dharma because you weren't getting it from anywhere else.

It is tempting to think that the golden light might be somehow reflected in the more refined worldly pleasures, but this is not so. It is true that in the case of aesthetic experiences at their very highest, like the music of Bach at its most sublime, you get distant reflections—or perhaps we should say echoes—of the golden light. But it's not enough just to have a glimpse in the distance in an indirect, remote way. We have to make the experience our own, and this involves a regular, disciplined way of life directed to that end.

In modern times we have got into the habit of sampling experience with no corresponding commitment to what the experience is meant to represent. To take the example of music, we don't usually think of it very seriously. It doesn't involve us in any responsibility toward it; it's just available for us to use and enjoy. We go along to concerts because it's a pleasant sensation. But we could experience them as a revelation which would make a real difference to our lives. It is the nature of the aesthetic experience that you are lifted out of yourself a bit—that's part of its value—but most of us are then dropped right back into ourselves, virtually the same as we were before. Probably only a musician could listen to music with commitment. The rest of us are more like the so-called religious person who sits at home in the evening with a box of chocolates leafing through the life of Milarepa or the *Mahaparinibbana Sutta.* It's just an experience in a very superficial, untransforming sense.

We might have a taste of what Bach was trying to convey, but most of us can't become a musician like Bach. In the case of spiritual experience, however, it's different. Something is pointed out to us, or we experience something fleetingly, and then within the spiritual tradition we can make an effort, reproduce that experience within ourselves, and experience it fully. You might never become a Bach, but you can become a Buddha.

6. DESIRE FOR THE ETERNAL

All unillumined desire is really a groping in the dark for Enlightenment, a looking for Buddhahood in the wrong direction.

DESIRE FOR the transitory is doomed, sooner or later, to disappointment. Even if it is possible to strive after and obtain such an object of desire, it is not possible to grasp hold of it forever. Only in the desire for the Eternal resides the possibility of permanent satisfaction and everlasting joy, for the Eternal gives itself freely to those who freely give themselves to it. All unillumined desire is really a groping in the dark for Enlightenment, a looking for Buddhahood in the wrong direction, as it were, so that even when we succeed in gaining the object of an unillumined desire we do not feel satisfied, because we were really not looking for that at all, but for something else. For this reason, also, when the desire for the eternal is satisfied, all other desires are satisfied simultaneously, since they were nothing but deformations of it. This is the meaning of the saying that if we seek first the Kingdom of Heaven, all things will be added unto us; although we should, of course, seek the Kingdom of Heaven for its own sake, and not for the sake of what, it is promised, will be added unto us if we do so. Otherwise we shall succeed in gaining neither the Kingdom of Heaven nor anything else. In the modern West we must once again recognize ourselves as essentially spiritual beings, and acknowledge the attainment of Enlightenment as the Supreme End of human life. Otherwise we will continue to whirl round and round in the vortex of existence, ignorant, frustrated, and miserable.

7. RENUNCIATION: NOT GIVING UP BUT GROWING UP

If we really have some degree of vision of the true nature of existence, and have really to some extent seen the inadequacy of material things, then our hold on them will be relaxed, and we will be quite willing and happy to let at least some of them go.

THERE IS NO single uniform pattern of renunciation. No one has the right to say that because someone has not given up this or that particular thing they are therefore not a practicing Buddhist. Different people will give up different things first. But the net result must be the same: to make life simpler and less cluttered. Most of us have so many things we do not really need. If here and now you were to take a piece of paper and write down all the unnecessary things you possess it would probably be a very long list. But you would probably think a long time before giving any of them away.

Sometimes people think of giving things up in terms of sacrifice, parting with things with a painful wrench, but it should not be like that. In Buddhism there is really no such thing as "giving up" in this way. From the Buddhist point of view what is required is not so much *giving* up as *growing* up. It is no sacrifice to the adolescent to give up the toys of childhood; and in the same way it should not be a sacrifice for the spiritually mature person, or for a person who is at least verging on spiritual maturity, to give up the toys with which people usually amuse themselves. I do not suggest that we do this in a dramatic or violent fashion; not like the gentleman I heard about on the radio the other day who climbed up the Eiffel Tower and threw his television set from the viewing platform. (He was protesting against the quality of French television programs, but at least his action indicated a certain degree of detachment from his television set!) The point to be made is that if we really have some degree of vision of the true nature of existence, and have really to some extent seen the inadequacy of material things, then our hold on them will be relaxed, and we will be quite willing and happy to let at least some of them go—to have just *one* car perhaps!

8. REMEMBERING THE RETREAT

> At the wood's edge, a solitary hut;
> Sharing my quiet room, a single friend.
> Here on the table, two or three books of verse;
> There on the shelf, half a dozen frost-blackened violets.
> Hour after hour, we exchange only a few words;
> Day after day, I polish a single poem.
> Who would have thought it? A whole world of content
> Found in these things!

9. THE PRACTICE OF FORBEARANCE

It is possible to learn to respond differently.

KSANTI—to be distinguished from *santi*, which means peace—is one of the most beautiful words in the whole vocabulary of Buddhism. It links a number of associated meanings, so there is no one English word which can do it full justice. It literally means patience or forbearance, and it is the antidote to anger (as dana, generosity, is to craving). As well as the absence of anger, and the absence of the desire for revenge, ksanti has overtones of love, compassion, tolerance, acceptance, and receptivity. It also includes gentleness and docility. There is even a suggestion in it of humility—though not in any artificial self-conscious sense. When Mahatma Gandhi founded one of his ashrams in India he apparently drew up a list of virtues to be practiced by the ashramites. It was a long list, and at the top he put "humility." But someone pointed out that if you practice humility deliberately, self-consciously, it becomes not humility but hypocrisy. So the Mahatma crossed out "humility" and wrote at the bottom of the list, "All the virtues are to be practiced in a spirit of humility"—a rather different thing.

Ksanti as forbearance can be illustrated by a story from the life of the Buddha, a story found in the *Sutra of Forty-two Sections*—which, incidentally, was the first Buddhist text to be translated into Chinese. The original version—we don't know whether it was in Pali or Sanskrit—no longer exists, but historically the sutra is of considerable importance. Anyway, apparently the Buddha was walking along one day when he happened to encounter somebody—probably a brahmin, but we don't know—who for some reason wasn't very pleased with the Buddha and immediately started to call him all sorts of names. This sort of thing often happens in the Pali scriptures; the Buddha was by no means universally popular in his own day. Some people resented the fact that he seemed to be enticing people away from their families and encouraging them to think of nirvana instead of thinking about making money.

So the man stood there for a while, abusing the Buddha with all the offensive words in his vocabulary. But the Buddha didn't say anything. He just waited for the man to stop speaking. And eventually the man did dry up—perhaps he ran out of breath. The Buddha quietly said, "Is that all?" Rather taken aback, the man said, "Yes, that's all." The Buddha then said, "Let me ask you a question. Suppose one day a friend brings you a present, but you don't want to accept it. If you don't accept it, to whom does it belong?" The man said, "Well, if I won't accept it, it belongs to the person who is trying to give it to me."

So the Buddha said, "Well, you have tried to make me a present of your abuse, but I decline to accept it. Take it; it belongs to you."[94]

Of course, few of us would be capable of such a measured response. If someone verbally abuses us, we tend to come up with a stinging retort, or keep the insult burning in our mind and find a way of getting our own back later on. But it is possible to learn to respond differently. How? The great teacher Shantideva gives some hints. He says, for example, suppose someone comes along and beats you with a stick. That's a painful experience, but it doesn't justify your flying into a rage. Instead, you need to try to understand what has happened. If you analyze it, he says, it is simply that two things have come together: the stick and your body. And who is responsible for this coming together? The other person has admittedly taken the stick to you, so he is partly responsible. But you have provided the body—and where did that body come from? It came from your previous samskaras: your ignorance and the things you did based on your ignorance in your previous lives. Why should you get angry with your enemy for bringing his stick, and not with yourself for bringing your body?[95] In his *Bodhicaryavatara* Shantideva produces a number of reflections of this kind designed to help us practice forbearance.

Of course, it isn't just a question of practicing forbearance toward people who assail us with harsh words or sticks. In Buddhist literature the contexts in which forbearance is to be practiced are classified into three groups.[96] First of all, there is nature: the material universe which surrounds us, especially in the form of the weather. It is generally either too hot or too cold, or there's too much wind or too much rain or not enough sunshine. All these climatic changes demand a certain degree of forbearance. Then there are what are known in law as acts of God—natural disasters beyond human control, like fire and flood, earthquake and lightning. Occasionally we may need to practice forbearance in the face of such events as these.

Secondly, we need to be forbearing toward our own body, especially when it is sick or suffering. We shouldn't get angry with the body and all its aches and pains; we shouldn't start beating "brother ass," as

Saint Francis would say. After all, we have brought the body here; it is our responsibility. While we should always try to alleviate suffering, whether our own or that of other people, as best we can, we need to realize that there is a residue which cannot be relieved and must simply be borne with patience.

Even if we stay well, sooner or later old age and death will come. In the modern West many people refuse to grow old gracefully, with sometimes quite tragic consequences. In the East, and perhaps in traditional societies generally, by contrast, people often look forward to old age, and indeed tend to see it as the happiest time of life. All the passions and emotional turbulence of youth have subsided. One has gained experience, and with experience perhaps just a little wisdom. And having handed everything over to the younger generation, one has fewer responsibilities and plenty of time for reflection, even meditation. Death is another matter, though; for most people everywhere it is a sobering consideration. But whether we like it or not, death will come, and we are well advised to practice forbearance toward the idea.

Thirdly, one should practice forbearance toward other people. This is, of course, far more difficult than being forbearing toward the weather, or even one's own aches and pains. Other people can be very difficult indeed. As a character in Jean-Paul Sartre's play *Huis Clos* famously puts it, "Hell is other people." One might add that heaven is other people too, but that's another story.

10. THE IMPORTANCE OF FEELING ALIVE

When you come in contact with the truth, with the Buddha's teaching, do you feel as though you are being refreshed by a great shower of rain?

THE BUDDHA SAYS that wherever you go in the great ocean, you can scoop a handful of water and it will have the same taste: the taste of salt. Likewise, whatsoever part of his teaching you take up, it will have one taste: the taste of freedom. In other words, whatever aspect of the Buddha's teaching you practice, it has one essence, one purpose, one effect—to help you to get free from your conditioning. There are many different presentations of the Buddha's teaching. There are the lists: the Eightfold Path, the Five Spiritual Faculties, the Three Refuges. There are the teachings about suffering, impermanence, and no-self. And there are all sorts of methods of practice: the mindfulness of breathing, the metta bhavana, the contemplation of the impurities, the *brahma viharas*. But all these many teachings, traditions, and practices have just one aim: to help individual human beings to become free from their conditioning.

From this the important corollary follows that the Buddha's teaching is not to be identified with any one formulation. It is not possible to say that the Buddha's teaching is the Noble Eightfold Path and just that, or the contents of the Pali Canon and just that. The Buddha's teaching is not just Zen, or just Theravada, or just what Professor so-and-so says it is. Buddhism cannot be identified with any one formulation, much less with any one school or sect. The Buddha's teaching or message can only be identified with that spirit of liberation, of freedom from conditionedness, that pervades all these formulations, just as the taste of salt pervades all the waters of the ocean. Whether it is the teaching of the Eightfold Path or the teaching of the Bodhisattva Ideal, whether it is this meditation practice or that, if it helps us to become free from our conditioning, it is part and parcel of the Buddha's teaching.

When we read about Buddhism, it is very important not only to remember this but to try really to feel it; otherwise all our studies and knowledge will be in vain. When we read the scriptures or hear about the Buddha's teaching, it is not enough just to pay attention to the words, the ideas and concepts. What really matters is to feel, through the concepts, through the images and symbolism, that which informs and gives life to them all—the experience of emancipation from all conditions whatsoever. In other words, we are trying to feel at least to some degree the absolute consciousness of the Buddha, the Enlightened consciousness from which all the teachings originally came.

To translate this into more simple terms, we must be nourished through both emotion and reason. Presentations of Buddhism in the West sometimes emphasize the rational aspect, or even give the impression that Buddhism is exclusively rational. We are told about Buddhist thought and philosophy, Buddhist metaphysics, psychology and logic; and sometimes it all seems very dry and academic. The other side, however, the side represented by myth, symbol, and the imagination, the emotions and vision, is no less important, and for many people perhaps even more important. This is why we need to absorb texts which appeal to our emotions, like the parables, myths, and symbols of the Mahayana in the *White Lotus Sutra.*

It is not enough to understand the Buddha's teaching intellectually. Anybody who has the ability to read—and a moderate intelligence— can do that. We have to ask ourselves again and again not just "Do I know? Do I understand?" but "Do I feel? Do I vibrate with this?" We might even ask ourselves, borrowing a simile from the *White Lotus Sutra*'s parable of the rain-cloud, "Do I really feel like a plant at the end of the hot season? Is this how I feel after a day's work or after I've been immersed in the ordinary daily round? Do I feel all dry and withered? Do I feel in need of nourishment? Do I really feel ready to take something in?" When you come in contact with the truth, with the Buddha's teaching, do you feel as though you are being refreshed by a great shower of rain? Do you really feel that you are going to drink something in after having been dry and thirsty for a long time?

Again, when you come in contact with the Dharma, do you really feel that the sun has come out? During the months of winter it is not unusual to feel dull and tired, and even miserable, because the sky is grey with fog and mist, and you are cold. You look forward to the spring sunshine, to your summer holiday, to the first beautiful, warm, bright weekend when you feel that spring is really on the way. When you see the buds begin to open and the flowers blooming in the parks and gardens, you can hardly help but feel a lifting of the heart. You feel as though a new spirit were rising within you.

But do you feel like this when you come into contact with the Buddha's teaching? Do you feel as though you are drinking in spiritual sunshine? If you do not respond in this way, your approach is still just intellectual. It is important that we should actually feel ourselves living, feel ourselves growing just like the plant when the rain falls and the sun shines.

2 ← Meditation

1. MEDITATION

Here perpetual incense burns;
The heart to meditation turns,
And all delights and passions spurns.
A thousand brilliant hues arise,
More lovely than the evening skies,
And pictures paint before our eyes.
All the spirit's storm and stress
Is stilled into a nothingness,
And healing powers descend and bless.
Refreshed, we rise and turn again
To mingle with this world of pain,
As on roses falls the rain.

2. RAINY SEASON RETREAT

IN JUNE the rainy season began. The grey clouds came rolling up
from the plains, first of all infiltrating the valley of the Teesta in loose,
detached masses, then moving in across the hills in a solid wall of rain
that at times blotted out the entire landscape. For days on end Mount

Kanchenjunga could not be seen. Instead, even when the sky cleared, there was only thick white cloud piled up against the horizon. Though the rain fell heavily enough at times, the rainy season was much less severe in the hills than in the plains. In between the downpours the sun was hot and bright, and the sky intensely blue, though the thick white cloud hardly ever moved—hardly ever moved aside to reveal the snows of Mount Kanchenjunga sparkling through the rain-washed air. It was my fourth year in India. Already I had learned to love the rainy season. I loved the heavy drumming sound of the rain on the roof. I loved the sense of green things thirstily drinking up the rain and growing as they did so. Above all, I loved the way in which the rain insulated one from the rest of the world, weaving around one a silver-grey cocoon of silence within which one could sit, hour after hour, and quietly muse. No wonder the Buddha had advised his monks not to wander about during the rainy season but to remain in one place, whether in a mountain cave, a woodland shrine, or a shed at the bottom of somebody's garden! No wonder the rainy season had come to be regarded, in the course of centuries, as a time of spiritual retreat—a time of more intensive study of the scriptures and more intensive practice of meditation!

3. The Five Basic Methods of Meditation

Meditation is not so much a science as an art, and in this art, as in all others, it is the inner experience rather than the technique that is all-important.

HERE I WANT to focus on five methods of meditation which correspond to the five "mental poisons" that stand between us and our own innate Buddhahood.[97] Enlightenment is within us all, but it is shrouded in spiritual ignorance or *avidya*—as the vast azure vault of the sky may be obscured from horizon to horizon by dark clouds. This obscuring factor of *avidya,* when it is analyzed, is found to consist of the aforesaid five mental poisons.

The first poison is distractedness, inability to control wandering thoughts, mental confusion; and the meditation practice that acts as its antidote is the mindfulness of breathing. Then the second poison is anger, aversion, or hatred; and its antidote is the meditation practice called in Pali the *metta bhavana,* the cultivation of loving-kindness. The third poison is craving or lust, and it is countered by the "contemplation of decay." Ignorance, in the sense of ignorance of our own conditionality, is the fourth poison; and it can be tackled by the contemplation of the twelve links of conditioned co-production. Finally, the fifth poison is conceit, pride, or ego-sense, whose antidote is the analysis of the six elements.

The Mindfulness of Breathing

The mindfulness of breathing is the antidote to the mental poison of distractedness because it eliminates wandering thoughts. This is one of the reasons why it is generally the first meditation practice to be taught to beginners; no other method can be practiced successfully until some degree of concentration has been mastered.

The mindfulness of breathing is not about concentration in the sense of a narrow, willed application of the attention to an object. It involves gradually unifying the attention around one's own natural breathing process, integrating all one's mental, emotional, and physical faculties by means of gently but persistently bringing the attention back to the experience of the breath, again and again. The point is not to *think* about the breath, or do anything about it at all, but simply to be aware of it. There are four stages to the practice. For beginners, five minutes to each stage is about right.

Sitting still and relaxed, with the eyes closed, we begin by bringing our attention to the breathing. Then we start mentally to count off each breath to ourselves, after the out-breath, one to ten, over and over again. There is no particular significance to the counting. It is just to keep the attention occupied with the breathing during the early stages of the practice while the mind is still fairly scattered. The object of our developing concentration is still the breath (rather than the numbers).

In the second stage we continue to mark the breaths by counting them, but instead of counting after the out-breath we now count before the in-breath. Ostensibly there may not seem to be any great difference between these first two stages, but the idea of the second is that we are attentive right from the start of each breath, so that there is a quiet sharpening of the concentration taking place. There is a sense of anticipation; we are being aware before anything has happened, rather than being aware only afterward.

In the third stage we drop the support of the counting and move to a general and continuous (at least, as continuous as we can manage) awareness of the whole process of the breathing, and all the sensations associated with it. Again, we are not investigating or analyzing or doing anything special with the breath, but just gently nudging the attention to a closer engagement with it. As our concentration deepens, it becomes easier to maintain that engagement, and the whole experience of the breath becomes more and more pleasurable.

In the fourth and final stage we bring the attention to a sharper focus by applying it to a single point in our experience of the breath. The point we focus on is the subtle play of sensation where we feel the breath entering and leaving the body, somewhere round about the nostrils. The attention here needs to be refined and quiet, very smoothly and intensely concentrated in order to keep continuous contact with the ever-changing sensation of the breath at this point. The practice is brought to an end by broadening our awareness again to include the experience of the whole of the breath, and then the whole of the body. Then, slowly, we bring the meditation to a close and open our eyes.[98]

The Metta Bhavana

The cultivation of universal love, or *metta bhavana,* is the antidote to anger or hatred. Metta, *maitri* in Sanskrit, is a response of care and

warmth and kindness and love to all that lives, a totally undiscriminating well-wishing that arises whenever and wherever we come into
contact with, or even think about, another living being. The practice
is divided into five stages.

In the first stage we develop love toward ourselves, something that
many people find very difficult indeed. But if one can't love oneself
one will find it very difficult to love other people; one will only project
onto them one's dissatisfaction with—or even hatred of—oneself. So
we try to appreciate or enjoy what we can about ourselves. We think
of a time when we were happy and content, or we imagine being in a
situation where we would feel quite deeply happy being ourselves,
and then we try to tune in to that feeling. We look for and bring awareness to elements in our experience of ourselves that are positive and
enjoyable.

Then, in the second stage, we develop metta or love toward a near
and dear friend. This should be someone of the same sex, to reduce
the possibility of emotional projections—and it should be someone
toward whom we have no erotic feelings, because the point of the
practice is gradually to develop a focus on a very specific positive emotion that is closer to friendship than to erotic love. For the same sorts
of reasons, this person should be still living and approximately the
same age as oneself. So we visualize, or at least we get a sense of, this
person, and we tune into the feeling they evoke in us, looking for the
same response of benevolence that we have been developing toward
ourselves. Usually this second stage is the easiest, for obvious reasons.

In the third stage, while maintaining the sense of an inner warmth,
the glow that we have generated toward ourselves and our good
friend, we bring to mind in their stead a "neutral" person. This is
someone whose face we know well, whom we see quite often, but
whom we neither particularly like nor dislike. It may well be someone who plays a more or less functional role in our life, like a post-
man, a shopkeeper, or a bank-clerk, or it may be someone we see
regularly on the bus. We apply to this neutral person the same
benevolence and care that we naturally feel for our friend. It must be

emphasized that what we are trying to develop in this type of practice is not a thought—not an *idea*—about developing a feeling, but the actual feeling itself. Some people may find this quite difficult to achieve—they feel dry and numb when they try to be aware of their emotions. It is as if their emotional life is so unconscious that it is simply unavailable to them to begin with. However, with time and practice it all starts to flow more easily.

In the fourth stage, we think of someone we dislike, even someone we hate—an enemy, someone who has perhaps done us harm or an injury—though to begin with it may be best to think of someone with whom we just don't get on. At the same time we deliberately leave our heart open to them. We resist the urge to indulge in feelings of hatred or animosity or resentment. It is not that we necessarily condone their behavior; we may well need to criticize and even condemn it; but we stay in touch with a fundamental care for their welfare. In this way, by continuing to experience our friendly attitude even in relation to an enemy, our emotion starts to develop from simple friendliness into real metta.

These first four stages are introductory. At the beginning of the fifth and last stage, we bring together in our mind all these four persons—self, friend, neutral person, enemy—and we cultivate the same love equally toward them all. Then we go a little further, we spread our vision a little wider, to direct this metta toward all beings everywhere, starting with those close to us, either emotionally or geographically, and then expanding outward to include more and more people, and excluding no one at all. We think of all men, all women, all ages, nationalities, races, religions; even animals, even beings, maybe, who are higher than human beings—angels and gods—and even beings higher than that: Bodhisattvas and spiritual teachers, whether Buddhist or non-Buddhist; whoever is eminent in good qualities. We may also expand out beyond our own planet, sending metta to whatever beings may live in other parts of the universe, or in other universes. We develop the same love toward all living beings.[99]

In this way we feel as though we are being carried out of ourselves

in ever expanding circles; we forget ourselves, sometimes quite literally, becoming enfolded in an ever-expanding circle of love. This can
be a very tangible experience for those who practice the metta bhavana, even after a comparatively short time. Not for everyone, of
course: it is very much a matter of temperament. Some people take
to it like ducks to water and enjoy it immensely within a matter of
minutes. For others it is a struggle to get a fitful spark of metta going,
and the idea of radiating it seems a joke—they don't see how they
are ever going to do it. But they can, and they do. In the end, with a
bit of practice, a bit of perseverance, it happens, it arises. If the potential for Buddhahood is within all of us, then the potential for metta
certainly is.

The Contemplation of Decay

The contemplation of decay or impurity, which counteracts lust or
craving or attachment, is not a practice that many people care to take
up, though it is popular in some quarters in the East. There are three
different forms of it. The first, and the most radical, is to go to a charnel ground and sit there among the corpses and charred remains. It
may sound a drastic course of action, but it has to be so, in order to
counteract the fierce power of craving. You look closely at what death
does to the human body and you think, "This is what will happen to
me one day."[100]

There is no special teaching here, nothing esoteric or difficult to
understand. There is no big secret in this practice. You simply recognize that one day your own body will be swollen and stinking with
putrefaction like this one, your own head will be hanging off, and your
own arm lying there on its own, like that one, or that you too will be a
heap of ashes in an urn (cherished somewhere, we hope).

These are all clear models of our own end, so why not admit it?
Why not face the fact? And why not change the direction of our life to
take account of this fact? It is in order to bring out such a vein of self-
questioning that monks in the East make their way—often quite light-
heartedly—to the charnel ground and sit looking at one corpse after

another: this one quite fresh, recently alive; that one a bit swollen; and that one over there—well, rather a mess. They go on until they get to a skeleton, and then a heap of bones, and finally a handful of dust. And all the time a single thought is being turned over in the mind: "One day, I too shall be like this." It is a very salutary practice which certainly succeeds in cutting down attachment to the body, to the objects of the senses, the pleasures of the flesh.

If this practice seems too drastic, or even just rather impractical, there is another way of doing it. Rather than literally going to the cremation ground, you can go there in your imagination and simply visualize the various stages of the decomposition of a corpse. Or even more simply, you can just remind yourself, you can just reflect on the fact, that one day you must die, one day your consciousness must be separated from this physical organism. One day you will no longer see, you will no longer hear, you will no longer taste or feel. Your senses will not function because your body will not be there. You will be a consciousness on its own—you don't know where—spinning, perhaps bewildered, in a sort of void; you just don't know.

If even this sort of train of reflection seems a bit too harsh and raw, a bit too close to the bone, we can reflect on impermanence in general. Every season that passes carries its own intimations of impermanence. The sweetness of spring is all the more intense, all the more poignant, for its brevity, for no sooner are the blossoms on the trees in full bloom than they start to fade. And of course in autumn we can contemplate the decay and end of all things as we see the leaves turning yellow and falling, and our gardens dying back into the earth. This kind of gentle, melancholic contemplation, so often evoked in English poetry, particularly the odes of John Keats, and in the poetic tradition of Japan—this too can have a positive effect in freeing us to some extent from our unrealistic perception of the solidity and permanence of things.

But really there is no need to approach even the most drastic of these practices in a mournful or depressed spirit, because they are all about freeing ourselves from a delusion that just brings suffering in its wake. It should be exhilarating—if you take up this practice at the right time—to remind yourself that one day you will be free of the body.

I did the cremation ground practice myself once when I was a young monk in India. I went along to a cremation ground at night and sat there on the banks of the river Ganges. There was a great stretch of silver sand, and at intervals funeral pyres had been lit and bodies had been burned, and there was a skull here and a bone there and a heap of ashes somewhere else. . . . But it was very beautiful, all silvered over by a tropical moon, with the Ganges flowing gently by. The mood the whole scene evoked was not only one of serious contemplation, but also one of freedom and even exhilaration.

This sort of mood probably reflects the fact that the practice overcomes fear. It is said that the Buddha himself used it for this purpose. If you can stay alone in a graveyard full of corpses at night, you are unlikely ever to be afraid of anything again, because all fear, basically, is fear of losing the body, losing the self. If you can look death—your own death—in the eye, if you can absorb the full reality of it and go beyond it, then you'll never be afraid of anything again.

However, the more challenging forms of this practice are not for beginners. Even in the Buddha's day, we are told, some monks who practiced it without proper preparation and supervision became so depressed by contemplating the impurity and decay of the human body that they committed suicide.[101] So normally one is advised to practice the mindfulness of breathing first, then the metta bhavana, and go on to contemplate corpses only on the basis of a strong experience of metta. But all of us can at least recall the impermanence of all things around us, and remember that one day we too will grow old and sicken, that we too must die, even as the flowers fade from the field and the birds of the air perish, to rot and return to the ground.

The Nidana Chain

The contemplation of the twelve links of conditioned co-production is the antidote to ignorance. In this meditation practice one consciously reflects on it, by means of the images that depict it in the outermost circle of the Tibetan Wheel of Life, as follows:

(1) Ignorance, *avidya:* represented by a blind man with a stick; (2) volitions or karma formations, *samskaras:* a potter with a wheel and pots; (3) consciousness, *vijnana:* a monkey climbing a flowering tree (we climb up into the branches of this world and reach out for its flowers and fruit); (4) mind and body, *nama-rupa* (name and form): a boat with four passengers, one of whom, representing consciousness, is steering; (5) the six sense-organs, *sadayatana:* a house with five windows and a door; (6) sense-contact, *sparsa:* a man and woman embracing; (7) feeling, *vedana:* a man with an arrow in his eye; (8) craving, *trsna:* a woman offering a drink to a seated man; (9) grasping, *upadana:* a man or woman gathering fruit from a tree; (10) becoming or coming-to-be, development, *bhava:* a man and a woman copulating; (11) birth, *jati:* a woman giving birth; (12) old age and death, *jaramarana:* a corpse being carried to the cremation ground.

Here is the whole process of birth, life, death, and rebirth according to the principle of conditioned co-production. As a result of our ignorance, and of the volitions based upon our ignorance in previous lives, we are precipitated again into this world with a consciousness endowed with a psychophysical organism, and thus six senses, which come into contact with the external universe and give rise to feelings—pleasant, painful, and neutral. We develop craving for the pleasant feelings, and thus condition ourselves in such a way that inevitably we have to be born again and die again.

These twelve links are distributed over three lives, but at the same time they are also all contained in one life—even in one moment. They illustrate—whether spread over three lives or a day or an hour or a minute—the whole way in which we condition ourselves; how we make ourselves what we are by our own reactions to what we experience.

When we look at the Wheel of Life we are looking in a mirror. In all its circles and all its details, we find ourselves. When I contemplate anger, in the image of a snake at the center of the Wheel of Life, it is not anger in general I am concerned with. When I contemplate greed, in the likeness of a cock, I am not considering the universal psychological phenomenon of greed. When I contemplate igno-rance, in the form of a pig, I am not studying some category of Bud-dhist thought. It is me there, just me: the anger, the greed, and the ignorance—they're all mine.

Seeing, next, a circle of people either going from a lower to a higher state or slipping from a higher to a lower state, I recognize myself in them. I am never standing apart from that wheel: at any one time I am going either one way or the other, up or down.

Looking beyond these figures I may imagine that at last I am exam-ining a representation of six different and separate realms of exis-tence—which in a sense they are. The human realm is clearly my own, where people are communicating, learning, creating. But when I look at the realm of the gods I find there my own moments and dreams of bliss and joy, and in the realm of the titans, my own ambition and competitiveness. Grazing and snuffling with the animals is my own lack of vision, my own consumerism, my own dullness. In the realm of the hungry ghosts is my own desolate yearning for some solid satis-faction from the objects of my craving. And in hell are my own night-mares, my own moments of burning anger and cool malice, my own brief seasons of hatred and revenge.

Finally, in contemplating the twelve nidanas of the outermost cir-cle we get a picture of how the whole process goes on, the mechanism of the whole thing. We see ourselves as a piece of clockwork, as indeed we are most of the time. Much of the time we are really no freer, no more spontaneous, no more alive, than a well-programmed com-puter. Because we are unaware, we are conditioned and therefore fet-tered. So in this practice we become aware of our conditionality, the mechanical, programmed nature of our lives, our tendency to react, our self-imprisonment, our lack of spontaneity or creativity—our own death, our spiritual death. Almost everything we do is just tight-ening our bonds, chaining us more securely to the Wheel of Life. The contemplation of the twelve nidanas provides a traditional support for this kind of awareness.[102]

The Six Element Practice[103]

The analysis of the six elements is the antidote to conceit or pride or ego-sense: that is, the antidote to the feeling that I am I, this is me, this is mine. In this method of practice we try to realize that nothing really belongs to us, that we are, in fact, spiritually (though not empirically) just nothing. We attempt to see for ourselves that what we think of as "I" is ultimately (though not relatively) an illusion; it doesn't exist in absolute reality (even though clearly it does exist at its own level).

Before starting, we develop a degree of meditative concentration, and establish a healthy emotional basis for the practice to follow with perhaps a preliminary session of the metta bhavana. Then we contemplate the six elements in an ascending order of subtlety: earth, water, fire, air, ether or space, and consciousness.

So first of all, earth—the earth upon which we are standing or sitting, and the earth in the form of trees and houses and flowers and people, and our own physical body. In the first stage of the practice we consider this element of earth: "My own physical body is made up of certain solid elements—bone, flesh, and so on—but where did these elements come from? Yes, they came from food—but where did the food come from? Basically, the food from which my body is substantially made came in the first place from the earth. I have incorporated a portion of the earth into my physical body. It doesn't belong to me. I have just borrowed it—or rather, it is temporarily appearing in this form of myself. To claim that it is mine is, in a sense, theft, because it does not belong to me at all. One day I will have to give it back. This piece of earth that is my body is not me, not mine. All the time it is returning to the earth." When we see this clearly enough we relinquish hold on the solid element in our physical body. In this way the sense of "I" starts to lose its firm outlines.

Then we take the element of water, and we consider: "So much of this world is water: great oceans and rivers, streams and lakes and rain. So much of my body, too, is water: blood, bile, spittle, and so on. This liquid element in me—where have I got it from? What I assume to be mine I have only taken on loan from the world's store of water. I will have to give it back one day. This too is not me, not mine." In this way the "I" dissolves further.

Now we come to a still subtler element: fire. In this stage we consider the one single source of light and heat for the whole solar system—the sun. We reflect that whatever warmth there is in our own physical body, whatever degree of temperature we can feel within us, all of it derives ultimately from the sun. When we die, when the body lies cold and still and rigid, all the warmth that we think of as our own will have gone from it. All the heat will have been given back, not to the sun of course, but to the universe. And as we do this the passion of being "I" cools a little more.

Then, air: we reflect on the breath of life, on the fact that our life is dependent upon air. But when we breathe in, that breath in our lungs is not ours; it belongs to the atmosphere around us. It will sustain us for a while, but eventually the air we make use of so freely will no longer be available to us. When the last breath passes from the body we will give up our claim on the oxygen in the air, but in fact it was never ours to begin with. So we cease to identify ourselves with the air we are, even now, taking in; we cease to think, even tacitly: "This is *my* breath." And thus the "I" gradually begins to evaporate.

The next element is called in Sanskrit *akasha,* a term translated either as "space" or as "ether." It isn't space in the scientific sense, but rather the "living space" within which everything lives and moves and has its being. We reflect that our physical body—made up of earth, water, fire, and air—occupies a certain space, and that when those constituent elements have gone their separate ways again, that space will be empty of the body that formerly occupied it. This empty space will merge back into universal space. In the end we see that there is literally no room for the sense of "I."

At this point we should, at least in principle, be dissociated altogether from the physical body. So sixthly and lastly we come to the element of consciousness. As we are at present, our consciousness is associated with the physical body through the five gross physical senses and through the mind. But when we die we are no longer conscious of the body; consciousness is no longer bound up with the material elements, or with physical existence at all. Then consciousness dissolves, or *re*solves itself, into a higher and a wider consciousness, a consciousness that is not identified with the physical body.

This higher and wider consciousness may be realized at many different levels. The individual consciousness, free from the body, may be expanded to a more universal, even collective, consciousness; from that to the *alaya-vijnana,* the repository or store-consciousness;[104] and from that we may even break through to the fringes of Absolute Mind. In this way our own petty individual mind is dissolved or resolved into the ocean of universal consciousness, so that we go completely beyond the sense of "I," and become completely free from the sense of "mine."

The five basic methods of meditation fall quite naturally into two important groupings (though there is some overlap between them). The mindfulness of breathing and the metta bhavana are primarily concerned with developing *samatha,* that is, tranquillity, calm, and expansion of mind or consciousness. Any technique of concentration on a simple object or developing a fundamental basis of positive emotion will fall into this category. And it should be said that some effective acquaintance with such techniques is essential before one attempts any more complex or advanced ones.

The other three basic practices are *vipasyana* practices—that is, they are concerned primarily with the development of insight, a deep, supra-rational understanding of reality. Any visualization or devotional practice or mantra recitation will also be concerned fundamentally with this goal.

The sheer wealth of different meditation techniques that one may attempt to master may seem bewildering—or enticing. But in a way one needs to be wary of the very idea of a meditation "technique." All the five basic methods of meditation involve following certain tried and trusted procedures, and we need to be thoroughly familiar with these if we are to make progress in meditation. But this is not to say that the practice of meditation consists simply in the application of particular techniques. Meditation is not so much a science as an art, and in this art, as in all others, it is the inner experience rather than the technique that is all-important. It is even possible to master the techniques of meditative concentration and yet realize nothing of the real spirit of meditation. It is far better to master the spirit—as well as the technique—of just one practice than to manage the empty manipulation of a dozen of them.

4. FINDING A PLACE TO MEDITATE

The Westerner learning to meditate is quite likely to do so alone, buying a book on the subject and beginning the practice in the comfort of his or her own home, but this is not to be recommended.

IN THE SATIPATTHANA SUTTA of the Pali Canon, having laid down the four foundations of mindfulness (mindfulness of the body, of the feelings, of thoughts, and of Reality), the Buddha goes on to recommend a particularly accessible method of developing mindfulness: the mindfulness of breathing. The fact that it is *accessible* is very important. The plain truth is—and we had better face this squarely—that awareness of any kind is not easy to develop. The Buddha's method is therefore to start by encouraging us to develop awareness of the aspect of our experience that is closest to us: the body. Even this is not as easy as one might think. The first of the four foundations may be "mindfulness of the body," but it is hard to focus on "the body" as a whole; it is such a complex thing, within which all sorts of processes are going on at the same time. To lead your awareness toward a broader experience of the body, it is therefore best to begin by focusing on the breath. Breathing is a simple bodily activity, providing a relatively stable object of attention that is both calming and capable of sustaining one's interest. On this basis, you can go on to become aware of your bodily sensations and even of your feelings and thoughts, which are still more subtle and difficult to follow.

The breath is available to us at every moment of our lives, and becoming aware of it has a calming effect at stressful times, as we know from the received wisdom of our own culture: "Take a deep breath." But it is possible to cultivate a more systematic awareness of the breathing through a meditation which is widely practiced throughout the Buddhist world: the mindfulness of breathing (*anapana-sati* in Pali), which some say was the meditation the Buddha was practicing when he gained Enlightenment. In the *Satipatthana Sutta* the Buddha launches straight into a description of how the bhikkhu should go about this practice. He is directed to go into the depths of the forest, or to the foot of a tree, or just to an empty place. Then, sitting down with his legs crossed, he is to keep his body erect and his mindfulness alert or "established in front of him," and start to become aware of his breathing. Thus we learn straightaway that the right place, the right time, and the right posture are all important for successful meditation.

The right place, we gather, is a place of solitude. In the Buddha's time, of course, there was plenty of space in the depths of the forest for meditators to sit there for long periods without being disturbed, but I think the Buddha's instruction here means something more. We need to imagine what it would be like to take up this practice if you had always lived in the traditional Indian family, which was the core of brahminical society in the Buddha's day. An Indian village, with all its noise and bustle, was hardly conducive to the development of mental calm, and the psychological and moral pull of the family group would have been just as inimical to spiritual practice. Even today in India, if you live in a traditional extended family it can be very difficult to steer your life in a direction not dictated by your family. For anyone seeking an awakening to truth, simply going forth to the undisturbed solitude of the forest, abandoning anything to do with home and family life, at least for a while, was—and continues to be—a major step.

Finding solitude is just as much of a challenge for us in the West today, although for us "solitude" might mean getting a respite from the world and worldly concerns rather than literally getting away from other people. Indeed, the companionship of other people following the same spiritual tradition as yourself can be a great source of encouragement, especially when you are just starting out. To meditate in isolation, you need to know what you are doing and be very determined. It is all too easy for discouraging doubts to arise about whether you are doing the practice properly, and in the absence of an experienced guide you might lose interest in meditation altogether. While the Buddha's instruction to seek out the foot of a tree certainly suggests finding a place where you are likely to be undisturbed for a while, it does not necessarily mean going off into the depths of the forest or isolating yourself from other meditators.

People didn't always meditate alone even in the Buddha's day. The Pali suttas contain striking descriptions of the Buddha and his disciples sitting and meditating together, sometimes in very large numbers. We come upon such a scene at the beginning of the *Samannaphala Sutta*. On a full-moon night, King Ajatasattu decides to have his elephants saddled up (five hundred of them) and ride with his entourage deep into the forest in search of the Buddha. It is quite a long way, and the king (who has a guilty conscience) is beset by all sorts of fears as they journey through the darkness. But at last they come upon the Buddha, seated in meditation with twelve hundred and fifty monks, all of them perfectly concentrated and spread out before him like a vast, clear lake. The silence, says the sutta, fills the guilty king—he has murdered his own father to gain the throne—with a nameless dread, making the hairs on his body stand on end. But he is sufficiently moved to ask to become a lay disciple of the Buddha on the spot.[105]

Since those early times, Buddhists throughout the tradition—especially in the Zen schools, which place a particular emphasis on meditation—have well understood the benefits of collective practice. The Westerner learning to meditate is quite likely to do so alone, buying a book on the subject and beginning the practice in the comfort of his or her own home, but this is not to be recommended.

It is hard to tell from the printed page how much experience the author has, and in any case no book can cover every contingency. There is also the danger that you will end up just reading about Buddhist meditation and never getting round to doing any. It is certainly possible to learn the basic techniques from a book, but if you can, it is worth seeking out a meditation teacher and other meditators with whom to practice.

As for the Buddha's instruction that the bhikkhu should sit cross-legged, this posture is recommended because it spreads the weight of the body more broadly and evenly than any other sitting position, and thus gives stability and enables you to sit comfortably for a long time. However, while it would have come naturally to the people of the Buddha's time and culture to sit cross-legged on the floor, we might find it more difficult. In fact, any posture can be adopted, whether on the floor or on a chair, as long as it is stable and comfortable. Incidentally, this is another reason to go along to a meditation class—to get some help with working out a suitable meditation posture.

5. HAPPINESS AND CONCENTRATION

Meditation is not about pushing parts of yourself away in order to force yourself into a superficially positive mental state.

A LOT OF Buddhist practice can seem very self-absorbed and in a way it is, especially at the stage of the path called *samadhi,* which means "one-pointed concentration." But there is no healthy alternative, if one is to be effective in the world. Buddhist meditation is a clearing of the decks for action, a transforming of unskillful and unexamined mental states into integrated and refined energy, for a purpose beyond self-absorption.

As the Buddha states in the Pali Canon, concentration is the natural outcome of spiritual bliss. It increases with pleasure, and as pleasure turns into rapture and then bliss, this process of deepening and refining pleasure has the effect of deepening one's concentration even more. . . . *Samadhi* is what arises naturally when you are perfectly happy; when you are not, you go looking for something to make you happy. In other words, to the extent you are happy, to that extent you are concentrated. This is a very important characteristic of *samadhi,* and should be clearly distinguished from the forcible fixing of attention that is often understood by the term meditation.

It is a question of motivation. If you are looking for an experience of pleasure or excitement or bliss in meditation, the result is going to be as superficial as the motive. It is rather like the difference motivation makes to sexual relationships. There is a famous passage in Malory's medieval romance *Morte d'Arthur* in which the author bewails how times have changed: once upon a time, he says, a lover and his beloved would be faithful to each other for seven years with no "likerous lust" between them, whereas now all a lover wants is to whisk his beloved into bed. Clearly not much has changed on that front since the fourteenth century. And something quite similar can happen in the case of meditation: people grab at the end result they want without working through the whole process—and so, of course, never get the desired result at all.

Probably this was what the Buddha realized when, recollecting his childhood experience of spontaneously entering the first *dhyana,* he came to understand that this was the key to Enlightenment. This is a turning point in the story of his quest. Having tried all kinds of methods and practices, having meditated and fasted and performed austerities, the Buddha-to-be remembered an experience he had as a boy. He had been sitting under a rose-apple tree out in the fields when he had spontaneously entered a state of meditative concentration. He sat there all day, absorbed and happy. And it was the recollection of this when he was on the very threshold of Enlightenment that gave him the clue he needed. One might wonder what such an elementary spiritual attainment might signify to one who had advanced in meditation even as far as the formless *dhyanas* under the guidance of his teachers.

But he knew that he had still not attained the goal to which he aspired, and now he understood why. What he realized was that his previous mastery of meditation had been forced, however subtly; this was why it was in the end useless. Progress had been made but only part of him had been involved in that progress, because it had been produced through sheer will-power. It was not so much the first *dhyana* itself that was the answer, but the natural manner in which he had entered into that state. The answer was to allow a natural unfolding of the whole being to take place, through the steady application of mindfulness.

We too can make use of this important insight. The states of mind we have produced through our actions during the day and during the course of our life in general, whatever they are, will be the states of mind we have to address in our meditation. Meditation is not about pushing parts of yourself away in order to force yourself into a superficially positive mental state. If you are distracted, unreflective, self-indulgent, and reactive in your everyday life, you might as a novice meditator force yourself in the opposite direction to some short-term effect, but in the long run meditation is about transforming mental states, not suppressing or ignoring them.

6. WHY ARE WE SO EASILY DISTRACTED?

Why is it that we are so easily distracted? How does it happen?

SUPPOSE YOU ARE writing a letter, an urgent letter that must go off by the next post. But, as so often happens in modern life, the telephone rings, and on the other end is a friend of yours who wants a little chat. Before you know where you are, you are involved in quite a lengthy conversation. You go on chatting perhaps for half an hour, and eventually, the conversation completed, you put down the phone. You have talked about so many things with your friend that you have quite forgotten about the letter, and you have talked for such a long while that you suddenly feel quite thirsty. So you wander into the kitchen and put the kettle on for a cup of tea. Waiting for the kettle to boil you hear a pleasant sound coming through the wall from next door, and realizing it is the radio, you think you might as well listen to it. You therefore nip into the next room, switch on the radio, and start listening to the tune that's playing. After that tune is finished there comes another, and you listen to that too. In this way more time passes, and of course you've forgotten all about your boiling kettle. While you are in the midst of this daze, or trance-like state, there is a knock at the door. A friend has called to see you. Since you are glad to see him, you make him welcome. The two of you sit down together for a chat, and in due course you offer him a cup of tea. You go into the kitchen and find it full of steam. *Then* you remember that you had put the kettle on some time ago, and *that* makes you remember your letter. But now it is too late. You have missed the post.

This is an example of unmindfulness in everyday life. Indeed everyday life consists, for the most part, of this sort of unmindfulness. We can all no doubt recognize ourselves in the portrait, and may have to admit that this is the chaotic, unmindful fashion in which, for the most part, we live our lives. Now let us analyze the situation, to give ourselves a better understanding of the nature of unmindfulness. First of all in our example we see the plain and simple fact of forgetfulness, which is a very important element of unmindfulness. We forget about the letter which we are writing when we are talking on the phone, and we forget the kettle which is boiling for tea when we are listening to the radio.

Why do we forget so easily? Why do we so often lose sight of something we ought to be bearing in mind? The reason is that we are very easily distracted; our minds are very easily turned aside. It often happens for instance that I am giving a lecture or talk of some kind. Everybody is paying close attention, and there is a pin-drop silence. But then the door opens, and someone comes in. And what happens? Half the heads swivel round as though they had all been pulled by the same string. People are as easily distracted as that. Sometimes it is a bluebottle buzzing against the window-pane, or the dropping of a sheet of my notes that distracts people. Such things show how easily we are distracted, which is why we tend to forget in the affairs of everyday life.

Why is it that we are so easily distracted? How does it happen? It is because our concentration is weak. Usually we attend to what we are doing or saying or thinking only in a half-hearted way. But why is our concentration so weak? Why are we so half-hearted? It is because we have no continuity of purpose. There is no one overriding purpose that remains unchanged in the midst of all the different things that we do. We switch from one thing to another, one wish to another, all the time, like the character in Dryden's famous satire who

> Was everything by starts, and nothing long;
> But in the course of one revolving moon
> Was chymist, fiddler, statesman, and buffoon.

Because we have no continuity of purpose, because we are not bent on one main thing all the time, we have no real individuality. We are a succession of different people, all of them rather embryonic. There is no regular growth, no real development, no true evolution.

Some of the main characteristics of unmindfulness should now be clear. Unmindfulness is a state of forgetfulness, of distraction, of poor concentration, of an absence of continuity of purpose, of drift, and of no real individuality. Mindfulness, of course, has just the opposite characteristics: it is a state of recollection, of undistractedness, of concentration, of continuity and steadfastness of purpose, and of continually developing individuality.

7. THE JAPANESE TEA CEREMONY

If the Japanese tea ceremony represents a certain level of awareness in everyday life and a certain type of spiritual culture—that of Far Eastern Buddhism, especially Zen—what analogous ceremony or institution is there which represents the attitude of the West today?

ON THE FACE of it the Japanese tea ceremony revolves around a very ordinary act which we do every day: the making and drinking of a cup of tea. This is something we have all done hundreds and thousands of times. But in the Japanese tea ceremony, it is done in a quite different way, because it is done with awareness. With awareness the kettle is filled with water. With awareness it is put on the charcoal fire. With awareness one sits and waits for the kettle to boil, listening to the humming and bubbling of the water and watching the flickering of the flames. Finally with awareness one pours the boiling water into the teapot, with awareness one pours out the tea, offers it, and drinks it, all the time observing complete silence. The whole act is an exercise in awareness. It represents the application of awareness to the affairs of everyday life.

This attitude should be brought into all our activities. We should do everything on the same principle as the Japanese tea ceremony, with mindfulness and awareness, and therefore with stillness, quietness, and beauty, as well as with dignity, harmony, and peace.

But if the Japanese tea ceremony represents a certain level of awareness in everyday life and a certain type of spiritual culture—that of Far Eastern Buddhism, especially Zen—what analogous ceremony or institution is there which represents the attitude of the West today? What do we have that breathes the whole spirit of our commercial culture? After turning this question over in my mind, I have come to think that what is characteristic of our culture is the business lunch. In the business lunch you are trying to do two things at the same time: trying to have a good meal, and trying to pull off a good deal. This sort of behavior, where one is trying to do two contradictory things at once, is quite incompatible with any true, real, or deep awareness. It is also very bad for the digestion.

Awareness of the body and its movements will, if practiced continually, have the effect of slowing these movements down. The pace of life will become more even and more rhythmical. Everything will be done more slowly and deliberately. But that does not mean that we will do less work. That is a fallacy. If you do everything slowly because you are doing it with awareness and deliberation, you may well accomplish more than someone who looks very busy, someone who is always dashing around and whose desk is piled high with papers and files, but who is in fact not busy but just confused. If you are really busy, you go about things quietly and methodically, and because you don't waste time in trivialities and fuss, and because you are aware, in the long run you get more done.

8. Mindfulness and Spontaneity

There's a certain energy in spontaneity which is refined and made more aware as you become more mindful.

You learn to draw the line between joy and intoxication when you are able to realize that you are losing your mindfulness. On the other hand, if you become stiff and self-conscious, that's not real mindfulness either. Your awareness has become "alienated." Most people tend to begin practicing Buddhism by being over-mindful (or rather, falsely mindful), because they usually start off by being completely unmindful. It's as though you have to go to the other extreme for a while and learn to be mindful, and then—not exactly forget about mindfulness, but let go and loosen up a bit. Of course, if you're not careful, you go to extremes again, and need to introduce more mindfulness and awareness. You just have to see which extreme you're tending toward at the moment, and correct the imbalance. The aim is to reach the middle ground where you've got lots of spontaneous, happy energy, but you're mindful at the same time.

Although mindfulness is certainly a key factor in the development of individuality, so is spontaneity. Even "animal" spontaneity can be turned into a more truly human or even spiritual spontaneity. It's as if there's a certain energy in spontaneity which is refined and made more aware as you become more mindful. Clearly some people need to check their exuberance and high spirits, but others need to get their energies flowing and express themselves more freely. It may be that they need to forget all about mindfulness for a while and let their hair down.

It isn't, of course, that you have spontaneity and mindfulness going on side by side; they are completely blended. It's like the deep absorption of creative activity. When you are painting a picture, for instance, your energy is freely flowing, but at the same time you are aware. You know just what you are doing, but you are not stiff—everything is flowing freely. This is the kind of state I'm talking about, but raised to a much higher pitch of intensity. Sometimes it happens in an emergency. When you've got to do something quickly, all your energy is mobilized, but at the same time you are very aware and alert—you know exactly what you are doing. In a dangerous situation you can act quickly and spontaneously, but very effectively, with full awareness of the total situation.

9. HOW TO SUCCEED AT MEDITATION

It is sometimes said in India that if people devoted the same energy and interest to the spiritual life that they devote to material things, success would be assured.

MEDITATION is like any other aspect of life: to succeed, you must want to succeed. Otherwise, you won't get far. A lot of people like the idea of making a lot of money, but they don't *really want* to make it; they are not prepared to go all out to make a million dollars by the time they're thirty. People who make money do it by sacrificing absolutely everything else. They think of nothing, day and night, except making that money; all their energies are bent in that direction. It's the same with someone who really wants to be a great writer or a great musician: they throw themselves into it, and in this way find out for sure whether they have it in them or not.

The only difference with meditation is that success is guaranteed. One can spend ten years producing an epic poem, and it may be a second *Paradise Lost* or a complete failure. But if you spend ten years meditating and you get into dhyana states, there is no question of those dhyana states not being the right ones. It is impossible to fail. It is sometimes said in India that if people devoted the same energy and interest to the spiritual life that they devote to material things, success would be assured, and one does see plenty of evidence that this is true. It is very noticeable how someone's energy seems to start flowing again if something they are really interested in doing comes up. Someone who professes to be too tired to go to a Dharma study class will suddenly perk up at the prospect of going to a film they have been wanting to see. If we are interested in something, we will find the energy to do it; and unless we really want to do it, we might just as well not bother.

But how do you transform a purely intellectual recognition of the rightness of something into an ardent desire to achieve it? The only way is to find some emotional connection; you have to want to want—which brings you straight back to the same problem. The only solution is to find out what you truly want. Then you can try to link your desire for that with whatever activity or interest or goal it is that as yet you only intellectually recognize as being of value.

For example, you might be passionately interested in sculpture. At the same time, intellectually you know that Buddhism makes sense. How are you going to bring head and heart together? To bridge the gap, you could perhaps make a special study of Buddhist sculpture:

Gandharan sculpture, Chinese and Japanese wooden sculpture, and so on. That interest could act as a bridge between what you have a strong feeling for and what you feel you ought to be doing. To put aside your interest in sculpture and try to study Buddhist philosophy instead would be very difficult. Some people can force themselves for a while to study things they are not interested in, or do things they don't want to do, but no one can do that for very long. At some point there will be a strong reaction from the part of oneself that hasn't been involved and doesn't want to be involved.

So first of all you have to ask yourself, "What do I really want to do? Do I really want to meditate? Do I really want to study the Dharma? If not, what *do* I want to do? If I had a completely free choice, what would I do?" The answer may come quite readily to mind; or you may find yourself quite thrown by the question. Sometimes you have to stop, not do anything, and allow your real desires, skillful or unskillful, to surface. Perhaps you have been so busy, so much swept along by the whirlwind of life, that you haven't even asked yourself what you really want to do.

Simply asking the question does not have to lead inexorably to indulging dark, unspoken desires. One tends to suspect that if one were to allow one's desires to surface, something dreadful would be sure to come up. Perhaps it will—maybe you will be shocked by what emerges—but why make that assumption? It is much more likely that what will surface will be some harmless, innocent yearning which you have never been able to fulfill. And even if your desires turn out to be unskillful, you may be able to establish some connection between them and something more healthy, skillful, or Dharmic. You might, for instance, discover that you dislike people, to the extent that you feel quite destructive toward them. Clearly that is unskillful, but it might be possible to transfer that animosity to certain ideas. You could think in terms of annihilating your own wrong views, fishing around for *miccha-ditthis* (that being the traditional Pali terms for wrong or false views) lodged deep in your psyche toward which one could direct your anger and hatred. Few desires are so irredeemably and utterly negative that they cannot possibly be connected with some aspect of the spiritual life.

10. Meditation Isn't the Only Way

It does seem as if, for most people, a positive change of environment leads quite naturally to a raising of their level of consciousness—even without any further effort.

SOME PEOPLE appear to think that meditation is the only way there is to raise the level of consciousness, as if to say that consciousness must be raised by working on the mind directly or not at all. Such people may even identify meditation with the spiritual life, and the spiritual life exclusively with meditation. If you are not meditating, you cannot possibly be leading a spiritual life, they would say. Sometimes they even identify the spiritual life with a particular kind of meditation, or a particular concentration technique. But this is far too narrow a view, and one that seems to forget what the spiritual life really is—and it is really the process of raising the level of one's consciousness—and what meditation itself really is. It is true, of course, that meditation is an especially effective and important way of raising one's level of consciousness. But other methods do exist, and to forget this is to run the risk of having a one-sided approach to the spiritual life and one that excludes certain kinds of people—people of certain temperaments, for example—who are not, perhaps, particularly interested in meditation. So let us briefly look at some of these indirect methods of raising the level of consciousness.

First of all there is change of environment. We quite consciously employ this as an indirect means of changing, and hopefully raising, our level of consciousness when we go away on retreat—perhaps into the country, to a retreat center. There we spend a few days, or even a few weeks, simply in more pleasant, more congenial surroundings, perhaps not even doing anything in particular. This is often more helpful than people realize, and it suggests that the environment in which we normally live and work is not very good for us. It does seem as if, for most people, a positive change of environment leads quite naturally to a raising of their level of consciousness—even without any further effort.

Another practical and simple indirect method of raising the level of consciousness is what in Buddhism is called Right Livelihood. Practically everybody has to work for a living, and quite a lot of us do the same kind of work every day, five days a week, fifty weeks of the year. We may do it for five, ten, fifteen, twenty, twenty-five, or thirty years, until we come to the age of retirement. All this has a continuous effect on one's state of mind, and if one's work is unhealthy in a mental, moral, or spiritual sense, the effect on one's mind will also be unhealthy. As Buddhists, we are therefore advised very strongly to practice Right Livelihood, which means earning our living in a way which does not lower our state of consciousness or prevent us raising it, and which does no harm to other living beings. In Buddhist tradition there is a list of occupations which are seen not to be very helpful: the work of a butcher, of a trader in arms, of a dealer in liquor, and so on. We may find that changing our means of livelihood (assuming that at present it is not quite right)—changing our environment, the sort of people we work with, the sort of thing that we have to do every day— will have a positive and helpful effect on our level of consciousness.

Something else that can have a strong effect is the leading of a regular and disciplined life, though this is a method which is apparently becoming less and less popular these days. It may consist in the observance and practice of certain moral precepts and principles, in having regular hours for meals, for work, for recreation, and for study, or in observing moderation in such things as eating, sleeping, and talking—perhaps even in fasting occasionally, or observing silence for a few days or weeks. In its fully developed form this more regular, disciplined life is what we call the monastic life. One can see quite clearly that those who lead such a regular, disciplined life over a period of years, even without meditating, experience a change in their state, their level, of consciousness.

There are other indirect methods, such as yoga and t'ai chi, which affect not only the body, but the mind as well. They affect the mind *through* the body, and even people who meditate regularly sometimes find them very helpful. Sometimes even an experienced meditator may be too tired at the end of a day's work, or too worried, to meditate properly. If this happens to you, you may prefer to practice a few yoga poses until your mind becomes calmer and more concentrated. Thus you lose your tiredness and feel refreshed, almost as though you had meditated.

Then again there are the various Japanese *do* or "ways"—like *ikebana,* flower arrangement. It might seem a very simple and ordinary thing, just to arrange a few flowers in a vase in a traditional way, but people who have engaged in this over a period of years definitely experience a change in their consciousness. Likewise, the enjoyment of great works of art—poetry, music, and painting—often helps to raise the level of consciousness, especially if the works of art issue from a higher state of consciousness in the artist himself.

On a more practical level, another method is simply helping other people. You might devote yourself to helping the sick, the destitute, or the mentally disturbed, or to visiting people in prison. You might do these things very willingly and cheerfully, disregarding your own comfort and convenience—might do them without any personal, selfish motive. This is what in the Hindu tradition is called *nishkama karma yoga,* or the yoga of disinterested action. This too is an indirect means of raising one's state of consciousness.

Then there is association with spiritually minded people, especially those who are more spiritually advanced than we are. Such association is regarded in some traditions, or by some teachers, as the most important of all the indirect methods. It is what is referred to again and again in Indian religious and spiritual literature as *satsangh. Sat* means true, real, authentic, genuine, spiritual—even Transcendental—while *sangh* means association, or communion, or fellowship.

Satsangh is therefore simply a getting together—often in a very happy, carefree spirit—with people who are on the spiritual path and whose predominant interest is in spiritual things. This rubs off on oneself, almost without any effort on one's own part. Thus *satsangh* too is an indirect means of raising the level of consciousness. It is what in Buddhism we call *kalyana mitrata*—spiritual friendship.

Then again, there is chanting and ritual worship. Ritual is very much looked down upon today, especially by more intelligent, or perhaps I should say "intellectual," people, but it is a time-honored method of raising the level of consciousness. Even if we simply offer a few flowers, or light a candle and place it in front of an image or picture, all this has an effect upon the mind, and sometimes we are surprised to find how much effect it does have. We might read lots of books about the spiritual life, we might even have tried to meditate— might even have succeeded in meditating—but sometimes we may find that the performance of a simple but meaningful and symbolic ritual action helps us far more.

11. TANTRIC MEDITATION: THE YIDAM

For you, your yidam is the whole Dharma, the whole teaching, distilled into a single figure with which you become spiritually intimate.

YIDAM IS A TIBETAN WORD which literally means "oath-bound." It is sometimes translated as "guarantor," that is, one who guarantees that the disciple will eventually gain Enlightenment, and it is equivalent to, though not an actual translation of, the Sanskrit term *ista devata*, which means "chosen or selected divinity." The yidam is thus that special aspect of the Dharma, that special aspect of reality, through which the disciple approaches the Enlightenment experience. The yidam is not an abstract concept or an idea but a figure—a figure of a Buddha or Bodhisattva, embodying a particular aspect or attribute of Enlightenment. Your yidam could be Amitabha, the red Buddha of infinite light and eternal life; or Manjughosa, the golden Bodhisattva of Wisdom with the flaming sword; or Tara, the savioress, usually white or green in color, carrying lotus flowers; or Vajrasattva, the embodiment of the innate purity of one's own mind. Whichever figure it is, as a disciple of the Tantra, the whole of the Dharma is contained, embodied, in your yidam, and you direct all your attention to that. You don't bother too much about scriptures, studies, teachings, doctrines. The center of your attention, spiritually speaking, is occupied by the figure of the yidam, and you devote yourself to becoming familiar with that figure.

You first make the acquaintance of the yidam in the course of Tantric initiation. In effect, in giving you the initiation of, say, Tara, the guru is introducing you to her, saying to her, "Tara, this is So-and-so," and to you, "This is Tara. Now I've introduced you to her, you know each other and there is a connection between you." Once you have made the acquaintance of a yidam in this way, your practice is to keep the yidam at the center of your attention. One way of doing this is to visualize the figure in meditation. With your inner eye you see the yidam before you, and you contemplate and become absorbed in that figure, and chant the yidam's mantra. Becoming absorbed in the yidam, you thereby absorb the spiritual qualities and principles and experiences which the yidam represents, which the yidam is. Eventually, you are absorbed into the yidam, or the yidam is absorbed into you, so that the two of you become one. If you have been focusing on Manjughosa, for example, you absorb the wisdom that Manjughosa represents, while if your yidam is Tara you develop the purity, the tenderness, the compassion, which is Tara, and if you have Vajrapani as your yidam, you acquire the energy, strength, courage, even spiritual ferocity he stands for. For you, your yidam is the whole Dharma, the whole teaching, distilled into a single figure with which you become spiritually intimate, and into whom, or into which, you are incorporated.

To give an idea of what this involves, I will say a little more about some of these figures. Avalokitesvara is among the most prominent of all of them. His name means "the Lord who looks down," and he is so called because he looks down on the world in compassion; he represents the compassionate aspect of Enlightenment. Imagine a vast blue sky, a sky which is completely empty, nothing but blueness stretching to infinity. Then, in that blue sky you see—not even a face, just the barely visible lineaments of a compassionate smile. This is the compassion aspect of reality; this is Avalokitesvara—though, of course, where there is compassion, there must be wisdom: it is Avalokitesvara who appears in the *Heart Sutra*, the heart of the Perfection of Wisdom.

Iconographically he is pure white in color and carries lotus flowers, symbolizing spiritual rebirth. His face is alive with a sweet, compassionate smile. In some depictions of him, one foot is tucked up in the posture of meditation, showing that he is deep in dhyana, while the other foot hangs loose, showing his readiness to step down at any moment into the turmoil of the world to help living beings. For the Bodhisattva inner tranquillity and external activity are not contradictory, but different aspects of the same thing.

Altogether there are 108 forms of Avalokitesvara. One of the most famous is the eleven-headed, thousand-armed form. To us this is perhaps going to seem grotesque, but the symbolism is very interesting. It is said that once Avalokitesvara was contemplating the sorrows of the world, the miseries of sentient beings, their suffering by fire, flood, famine, bereavement, separation, war, shipwreck, and so on. He was overwhelmed by such compassion that he wept, and went on weeping so violently, we are told, that his head shivered into eleven fragments, each of which became a face. There are eleven of them because there are eleven directions of space (north, south, east, west, the four intermediate points, up, down, and the center), and compassion looks in all directions simultaneously. Not only that; he has a thousand arms—at least iconographically he is supposed to have a thousand arms. In truth the Bodhisattva of compassion has millions of arms, each of which is stretched out to help living beings in one way or another. It wouldn't be possible for any one person in any historical situation to do everything that is needed, but each individual can imbibe the spirit of the Bodhisattva and express that in their own way within their own life. One can aspire to be one of the thousand arms of Avalokitesvara.

Another of the Bodhisattvas is Manjughosa, who represents the wisdom aspect of Enlightenment. He is a beautiful golden, orange, or tawny color—his is the golden wisdom of Enlightenment that dispels ignorance as the sun dispels the darkness—and he carries a sword and a book. The flaming sword in his right hand symbolizes his wisdom; he whirls it above his head, cutting asunder the bonds of ignorance and of karma, all the knotty tangles that keep tripping us up. And the book he holds in his other hand is the Perfection of Wisdom, which he holds close to his heart. His legs are crossed in the meditation posture, because wisdom springs, as the Dhammapada teaches us, from meditation.[106] Manjughosa is the patron deity of all the arts and sciences. If you want to write a book, paint a picture, or compose a piece of music, you traditionally invoke Manjughosa, and his mantra is repeated for retentive memory, understanding of the Dharma, eloquence, power of speech, and so on.

Then there is Vajrapani, who represents the power aspect of En-lightenment—not power in the political sense, or in the sense of power over other people, but spiritual power. Although he has a peaceful form too, Vajrapani is usually depicted in wrathful form, an image of furious energy to crush the forces of ignorance. The wrathful Vajra-pani is dark blue in color, and he is not slim, slender, or graceful, but has a stout body, protuberant belly, and thick, short limbs. His coun-tenance expresses extreme anger and he has long white teeth or tusks. He is more or less naked apart from ornaments of human bone and a tiger skin, and he carries in one hand a vajra, a thunderbolt, with which he destroys the forces of ignorance. This terrifying figure is crowned with five skulls, representing the five wisdoms. One foot is uplifted, to crush and trample all the forces of conditioned existence that separate us from the light of truth, and he is surrounded by a great halo of flames. This is the Bodhisattva Vajrapani, destroying and breaking up conditioned existence, rending the veil of ignorance and scattering all the forces of darkness through the power of his spiritual energy.

Then, by way of contrast, there is Tara, who appears in female form. Tara is the spiritual daughter of Avalokitesvara. She is usually either white or green in color, and according to another beautiful legend she was born from the tears of Avalokitesvara as he wept over the sorrows of existence. In the midst of a great pool of tears there appeared a white lotus. The lotus opened, and there was Tara, the very essence, indeed the quintessence, of compassion.

Often she bears a blue or white lotus flower, and in her white form she has seven eyes—two ordinary eyes, plus a third in the forehead, two in the palms of her hands, and two in the soles of her feet. All these eyes symbolize Tara's awareness. There is nothing blind, sentimental, or foolish about compassion—it is informed by awareness, mindfulness, and knowledge. Sometimes what passes for compassion is really no more than pity, and it just makes things worse.

If there is one more archetypal Bodhisattva to be mentioned here, it is Vajrasattva. He represents purity: not physical purity, moral purity, or even spiritual purity; not any purity that can be attained. Vajrasattva represents primeval purity, the original spotless purity of the mind, unsoiled and untouched from beginningless ages. We cannot purify the mind through spiritual practice. We may purify the lower mind, because the lower mind can become soiled, but we never purify the ultimate mind, because the ultimate mind never becomes impure. We purify ourselves truly by waking up to the fact that we have never been impure, that we were pure all the time. This ultimately inherent purity of the mind, above and beyond time, above and beyond the possibility of impurity, is represented by Vajrasattva.

Vajrasattva is pure, dazzling white, like sunlight reflecting from snow. He is sometimes depicted completely naked and sometimes as wearing the silks and jewels of a Bodhisattva. His mantra, which has one hundred syllables, is recited and meditated upon to purify one's faults, or rather, to purify oneself of the impurity of thinking that one is not intrinsically pure.

12. WHITE TARA

Appearing from the depth of heaven,
The white-robed goddess, calm and bright,
Sheds moon-like on this lower world
The blessing of her silver light.

Seven eyes she has, all open wide,
In face and forehead, hands and feet,
For she of Pure Awareness is
Embodiment and paraclete.

One hand, in teaching gesture raised,
Imparts a wisdom thrice-profound;
The other, open on her knee,
For endless giving is renowned.

A lotus at her shoulder grows,
Complete with flower, and bud, and fruit;
Her form is straight and still, for she
Is grounded on the Absolute.

"Awake! Arise!" she seems to say,
"Leave dreams, leave sloth, leave passions vile!"
Oh may we, seeing her, go forth
Encouraged by her perfect smile.

3 ⬥ Faith, Devotion, and Ritual

1. Visiting Ghoom Monastery with Lama Govinda

A S WE LIFTED the heavy felt curtain that screened the entrance I saw a colossal figure seated there in the semi-darkness, a golden face glimmering beneath the great jewelled tiara. Smaller figures gleamed from behind the glass doors of showcases and glowed with a subdued richness from the frescoed walls like reflections seen in deep water. Rosary in hand, Lama Govinda and Li Gotami moved clockwise round the chamber, pausing for a moment in front of each image or *thangka* and reciting the appropriate mantra, and I followed in their wake. Some of the mantras were new to me, and of these two in particular—the mantra of Shakyamuni and the mantra of Padmasambhava—not only sounded strangely familiar but also set up reverberations that made themselves felt in the remotest corners of my being. The whole experience affected me deeply. There was the rectangular chamber itself, dimly lit from above by the light that filtered in at a kind of skylight, there was the brooding presence of the images, with the colossal Maitreya silently dominating the rest, and there was the sound of the mantras as the two dark figures in *chubas* made their way with bowed heads round the chamber. What affected me most deeply, however, was the evident devotion with which Lama Govinda and Li Gotami recited the mantras and the way in which they seemed to feel, behind each image, the living spiritual presence of which the image was the representation or, indeed, the veritable embodiment.

It was therefore only natural, perhaps, that of all the discussions Lama Govinda and I had in Kalimpong and Ghoom the only one to leave a distinct and separate impression on my mind should have taken place after our visit to the Ghoom Monastery and should have related to meditation and, in particular, to meditation on the different Buddhas and Bodhisattvas. While I listened enthralled, Lama Govinda explained how one took up first one kind of spiritual practice, then another, in accordance with the various needs of one's developing spiritual life. It was not, however, that on taking up a new practice one discarded the old practice and put it behind one, so to speak. What one did was add the new practice to the old and incorporate both in a higher unity. In this way one's meditation or spiritual practice would, over the years, gradually become an ever richer and more complex thing. As Lama Govinda spoke, I had a vision of petal being added to petal, or facet to facet, until one had a thousand-petalled rose or a thousand-faceted crystal ball complete in all its glory. What Lama Govinda was doing, of course, was speaking of meditation or spiritual practice—indeed, of the spiritual life itself—in terms of the gradual building up of a mandala. In other words, he was speaking of it not only in terms of time but in terms of space. Hitherto I had thought of it as a progression from stage to stage, or level to level. Now I also saw it as an unfolding from an ever more truly central point into an ever increasing number of different aspects and dimensions.

2. THE NATURE OF BUDDHIST FAITH

If you leave out devotion you are closing the door on any emotional engagement with your spiritual ideal.

I HAVE KNOWN people who have been surprised to find that there is any such thing as faith in Buddhism. They have come into contact with Buddhism under the initial impression that it is essentially rational, that emotion is not really involved at all. This confusion arises out of two mistaken ideas: that emotion is essentially irrational, and that faith is the same thing as belief.

Belief—in the sense of accepting as true on authority something that one can never verify, or something that is even inherently absurd—is not faith, at least not in Buddhism. In Buddhism, *sraddha* or faith covers the entire devotional or feeling aspect of spiritual life. Faith in Buddhism could never be said to be contrary to reason—or even beyond reason. Faith is the emotional counterpart of reason. What you understand with your intelligence you must feel also with your emotions. The two go together, and cannot be separated.

Sraddha in Buddhism is faith in the Three Jewels: the Buddha, the Dharma, and the Sangha. But it is especially faith directed toward the Buddha himself, because—at least from our point of view—the Buddha comes first. Even though the Dharma represents immemorial Truth, we would know nothing of it without the Buddha, and there would certainly be no Sangha without him. In Buddhism faith is faith in the founder of Buddhism himself.

However, it's not just belief; it's not even just feeling. Faith in the Buddha is the emotional response that you have when you are confronted by the embodiment of Enlightenment. This confrontation can take place in various ways. You can of course be confronted personally by some living human being who is the embodiment of Enlightenment. Alternatively, you can be confronted through literature, by reading about someone who was such an embodiment—if not the life of the Buddha himself, then perhaps the biography of the great Tibetan yogi, Milarepa, or that of Hui Neng, the sixth patriarch of Ch'an—or Zen—Buddhism. With any of the great masters or teachers, there is the possibility of an immediate emotional response to accounts of their lives—whether historical or legendary—a response that is not just sentimental, but engaged, challenging, personal, real.

Then again, you can be confronted by an image, an artistic representation—a painting or a statue—of someone who was Enlightened. And here I am reminded of a French Buddhist nun whom I knew in Kalimpong in the 1950s. She told me that in her student days in Paris she used to like visiting museums and art galleries, which is how she found herself eventually in the Guimet museum of oriental art. She was a rather militant, aggressive woman; she told me that she used to go around with a pair of ice-skates with which to defend herself if she was attacked. "Well, I thought that if I carried these skates with me, if anyone tried to attack me I could slash the blades across his face."

But as she strode along the galleries of the Guimet—having left the skates in the cloakroom—looking to left and right rather fiercely as she usually did, suddenly she encountered an image of the Buddha. From her description I gather that it was an image from ancient Cambodia. She just turned a corner and there was the celebrated smile— faint and delicate and rather withdrawn—so characteristic of this Khmer style of sculpture. The whole expression of the face is intensely peaceful.

This image—the face of this image—stopped her in her tracks. She told me that she stood looking at it without moving, almost without blinking, for forty-five minutes. She couldn't take her eyes off it. The impression of peace, tranquillity, and wisdom that emanated, that streamed as it were, from those features, was so strong that she couldn't pull herself away. She hadn't yet studied anything about Buddhism, but as soon as she saw this image, she felt compelled to ask herself, "What is it that gives its expression to this image? What is it trying to tell me? What depths of experience does it come from? What could the sculptor have experienced, to be able to express something like this?"

Confronted by this embodiment of Enlightenment, she could not move away unchanged. In fact, it determined the whole subsequent course of her life. This is the kind of emotional response we can have to an embodiment of Enlightenment simply rendered in stone, let alone one in the form of a living person. And it is a response that amounts to faith.

What it is in fact is the response of our potential Enlightenment— our own deeply hidden capacity for Enlightenment—to the actual Enlightenment with which we find ourselves confronted. There is something deep down within us that has a sort of affinity with what is fully realized, fully expressed, fully achieved, in that embodiment of Enlightenment. There's a sort of kinship. It's like what happens when you have two stringed instruments side by side: if you sound the strings of one, the other starts softly vibrating too.

And what this response gives rise to is devotion. There are all sorts of different ways of expressing devotion, but traditionally it is done by means of prostration or worship, the offering of flowers, the lighting of candles and incense, and so on. Some people in the West are a little shy of Buddhist devotional practices. They would like to think that Buddhism had no truck with the kind of apparently superstitious activities that they were trying to get away from when they abandoned Christianity. They feel, perhaps, that these are practices for children, and that it is time to be grown-up and stop bowing and scraping and offering candles and the like.

However, if you leave out devotion you are closing the door on any emotional engagement with your spiritual ideal. A healthy spiritual life, just as much as a healthy psychological life, must include the expression of emotion. At the same time, there is a balance to be maintained. Faith and devotion can go to extremes, and when they do so they become superstition, fanaticism, or intolerance. It is for this reason that, according to this teaching of the five spiritual faculties, faith—the whole emotional and devotional side of the spiritual life—should be balanced by wisdom.

3. The Necessity of Dependence

To attain Enlightenment is not such a light undertaking that we can afford to make it more difficult for ourselves than it already is.

THERE ARE PEOPLE to whom the idea of dependence of any kind is extremely distasteful, and who maintain with great vehemence that a true Buddhist should be independent of all external aids. It must be observed of them that they have failed to understand the Dharma. One of the most important teachings of the Buddha is that nothing arises without at least two causes, a teaching which is no less true of the mental than of the material world. Each stage of the path arises not only as a result of direct individual volition but also in dependence upon the whole complex of conditions which constitute the stage preceding it. If we rely for the achievement of nirvana solely upon our own unaided efforts we shall be like the man who tried to lift himself from the ground by means of his own boot-straps. Whether we choose to recognize the fact or not, it is the presence of certain objective conditions which enable us to lead the holy life. To begin with, if the Dharma were not a law inherent in the very nature of things, if the universe were not so constituted that different causes produce different effects, a certain action an equivalent and equal reaction, and if everything depended instead upon chance, which is to say upon nothing, then it would no more be possible for a human being to progress spiritually than it would be for a bird to fly in a vacuum, or for a man to walk without the existence of gravity.

Again, if the sequence of conditions upon which the attainment of Enlightenment depends had not been revealed to the world by the

Buddha it is extremely doubtful whether any of us would have ever succeeded in discovering them for ourselves. The independent spirit of those who wish to be entirely free from all external assistance is certainly to be admired, but if they wish to be consistent they cannot be Buddhists, since a Buddhist is one who takes refuge in the Buddha, the Dharma, and the Sangha, and such refuge cannot be taken without surrendering at least a little of one's independence. Moreover, the leading of the holy life depends upon numerous other conditions which the spiritual individualist either overlooks or ignores. It depends, for example, upon the possession of a human body, upon the enjoyment of moderately good health, upon the vicissitudes of climate and weather, on social and political environment, upon whether one meets spiritual friends or not. All such aids must be relinquished if one intends to achieve nirvana by the pure unaided exercise of personal volition, in which case the desired achievement should take place instantaneously.

There is no doubt at all that if the thrust of our volition were sufficiently powerful nirvana could indeed be won within the twinkling of an eye. But it is weak, and instead of piercing the dense cloud of ignorance by which the sun of supernal wisdom is obscured, it beats feebly upon it, like a moth fluttering against the window pane. We are therefore compelled to bethink ourselves of how to remove ignorance; but this task also we find beyond our powers, and we are forced to enquire how to bring the oscillations of the mind to a point of perfect balance. In this way we are brought step by step down to dependence upon the simplest supports of the Dharma life, to dependence upon ethical observances, rites and ceremonies, recitation of prayers, telling of beads, and many other humble and homely religious observances upon which the spiritual individualist looks down with a smile of contempt, but which are nevertheless humanity's first faltering steps upon the Path that leads to Peace.

Some spiritual individualists do not, indeed, regard external supports to the religious life as being entirely without use, and admit that for some types of people they may be helpful, even necessary; but the

454 ~ THE ESSENTIAL SANGHARAKSHITA

admission is generally made in a patronizing and condescending spirit, with the ungracious reservation that supports of this kind are concessions to the deplorable infirmity of people too weak, childish, and spiritually undeveloped to be able to manage without them. Forgetting that it is impossible to tread the Path to Nirvana without some kind of external assistance, some strange perversity of thought constrains them to assert that the spiritual individualist alone is the true Buddhist, although the words of the Buddha himself afford no warrant whatever for the adoption of such an attitude. Whether one depends for the time being upon meditation, or whether one depends upon the turning of a prayer wheel, the fact of dependence is there, and since both practices are means to an end, which is Enlightenment, neither can be regarded as intrinsically "better" or "worse" than any other. It is simply a question of suitability, of the fitness of a particular means for a person of a particular temperament at a certain stage of his or her spiritual development.

Similarly, no method is intrinsically "harder" or "easier" than any other. Those who believe that they follow the path of self-reliance because it is more difficult than the alternative path simply delude themselves. In the spiritual life, as in any other, one naturally takes the line of least resistance. To attain Enlightenment is not such a light undertaking that we can afford to make it more difficult for ourselves than it already is, and if one path were in truth less arduous only pride of Luciferian dimensions could induce us to reject it in favor of another which was more arduous. Some people, it seems, would rather preserve their independence and remain in samsara than renounce it even for one moment and thereby win the bliss and peace of nirvana. In the spiritual life we have to depend not only upon our own will, our own strength, but also upon a greater or lesser number of external supports most, if not all, of which fall into one or other of the three stages into which the Path has been divided: *sila, samadhi,* and *prajna.* There is neither absolute dependence nor absolute independence, but a Middle Way which passes between these extremes by escaping into a third dimension wherein the opposition does not exist. For this reason the Buddha has advised us to take refuge in the Dharma, as well as in ourselves, and to regard the Dharma as our light (or island), and not simply to rely, with prideful independence, upon our own unaided efforts.

4. What Is Ritual Trying to Achieve?

It is unfortunate that in the West we like to think we have gone beyond ritual altogether.

THERE HAS BEEN in recent times a considerable reaction against anything that smacks of faith and devotion. This has been in part caused by the fact that popular faith has been divorced from what might be called the "higher thinking faculty" and so become unacceptable to the intellect, bringing the whole notion of faith and devotion into disrepute, and along with it the practice of ritual. But unfortunately it has to be said that the rejection of faith, devotion, and ritual is for most people not the result of their own earnest and searching intellectual endeavor. More often than not it is just a received view, a part of their conditioning which has no more intellectual legitimacy than the "blind faith" which they look down upon.

Before we reject ritual we should really think about what is meant by it. What does ritual really signify? What is it really trying to achieve? It tends to be taken for granted that ritual is a sort of outgrowth upon religion. Some people have a very simplified picture of the history of religion, imagining a pristine, simple, purely spiritual teaching at the outset which in the course of a few centuries has degenerated and become loaded down with a lot of unnecessary ritual and dogma, so that periodically it must be purified of these things. People who think in this way see ritual not as really belonging to the essence of religion, but as something added on afterward, something which they can very well do without—even something harmful.

Other people again regard ritual as a kind of socio-cultural habit surviving from primitive times. Vaguely imagining tribal communities dancing around a bonfire at night, perhaps waving their spears, they think that something of this kind represents the basic, primal form of ritual, and that remnants of this sort of thing survive even in modern life and in the higher religions. According to this view, dancing around the maypole and taking part in a mass are the same sort of thing.

These rather dismissive views of ritual are beginning to shift in some radical circles, but they remain prevalent even among Buddhists, especially in the West. Some Western Buddhists have even been under the strange impression that there is no ritual in Buddhism. Indeed this is one reason why some of them are attracted to Buddhism, or at least to what they think is Buddhism.

It is true that there are elevated states of consciousness in which the need for ritual is transcended, in which our spiritual aspiration is so intrinsic to our being and so refined that it expresses itself purely spiritually and mentally, leaving the physical plane behind. If those who avoid taking part in ritual have attained to such states, that is fine. But we must not confuse that sort of highly positive development with the far more common case of someone who is inhibited about ritual expression because of all sorts of fears and misunderstandings.

The traditional Eastern Buddhist approach starts with devotion. Buddhists who are unable even to observe the precepts, let alone meditate or reflect on the Dharma, are at least able to attend a puja and offer flowers to the Buddha. However, in the West we tend to have to work our way toward devotional practices through meditation and study. It is of course necessary to resist easy emotional tricks. It may even be necessary sometimes to withdraw from devotional ritual for a while if one has problems with it. But it is unfortunate that in the West we like to think we have gone beyond ritual altogether.

Ritual is an integral part of Buddhism, as it is of all other religions, and an integral part of every school of Buddhism, whether Tibetan, Zen, or Theravada. Some people like to contrast Theravadin Buddhism and, say, Tibetan Buddhism in this respect, implying that there is no ritual in Theravada whereas Tibetan Buddhism is full of it (with the assumption that ritual represents a degeneration). But this view is quite wrong. The Theravada, like any other form of Buddhism, is highly ritualistic. I remember, for instance, that when I visited the Tooth Relic Temple at Kandy in Sri Lanka many years ago, there were elaborate rituals going on all morning in front of what is believed to be the Buddha's tooth. Zen, in China and Japan, is also highly ritualistic. In a Zen monastery they don't spend all their time meditating. There are all sorts of rituals to engage in: chanting of sutras, recitation of mantras, and a good deal of bowing down. This might come as rather a shock to some Western Zen enthusiasts.

This is not of course to say that there are no differences between the schools as regards the significance accorded to ritual. I would say that, in Tibetan Buddhism especially, the ritual is much more symbolically and spiritually significant. In Theravadin countries it tends to be more of the nature of ceremony than ritual proper; it is not so well integrated into the doctrinal tradition.

My main point is that we cannot get away from ritual in Buddhism, nor should we try to do so. Instead we should try to understand ritual and see what it really is. Erich Fromm, who first introduced the psychoanalytical distinction between rational and irrational ritual, gives an excellent definition of rational ritual as "shared action, expressive of common strivings, rooted in common values." Every word of this definition is of import, and worth discussing in some detail.

First of all, ritual is "shared action." The fact that ritual is a kind of action is indicated by the traditional Buddhist word for ritual, *kriya*, which in fact means "action"—being etymologically connected with the word *karma*, which means action in a more ethical and psychological sense. So *kriya* or ritual is something done, it is an action, and this fact should, if nothing else, remind us that religion, the spiritual life, is not just a matter of thought and feeling, but also of action: both moral action and ritual action. According to Buddhist tradition, human nature is threefold: body, speech, and mind together make up our total personality. Religion, which is concerned with our total personality, must cater for all three—and in order to involve the body, it must entail action.

Only too often in the West our approach to Buddhism is too one-sided. We pick and choose what we feel suits us, and the result is that part of us is simply never engaged in our practice. We may meditate and study, but if we miss out devotion and ritual, part of us is not involved. We need a Buddhist tradition in the West which provides not only for the head, not only for the heart, but even for the body and speech.

Ritual is not only action, but action that is shared, done together with other people. Here we come to an important difference between irrational, obsessive-compulsive ritual, and rational ritual. Neurotic ritual tends to isolate people. Like washing your hands every ten minutes, it is something done alone which does not bring the person doing it closer to others—quite the reverse. Rational ritual, however, tends to bring people together, and not just physically so. The sense of togetherness can also be, indeed should also be, spiritual. The performance of ritual action in company with others should celebrate a common spiritual attitude. For this reason a feeling of fellowship is essential, which means that ritual implies a spirit of *metta* (loving-kindness) and solidarity. If this is present, a very powerful spiritual atmosphere can be created.

Fromm's definition goes on to say that rational ritual is "expressive of common strivings." Ritual expresses a striving. It is something we make the effort—certainly in Buddhism—to do ourselves. It is not something which is done for us, say by a priest. We don't just sit back and watch someone else conduct it for us. Meaningful ritual is a matter of striving and exertion. It is part of the Buddhist practitioner's *sadhana,* or spiritual practice, or spiritual *exertion.* Ritual is not for the lazy person. Anyone who believes that ritual is a comfortable substitute for the more demanding methods of spiritual practice has not experienced it as it should be performed.

To be a really good ritualist is at least as difficult as, say, giving a lecture, or meditating, if not more so. A good ritualist has to be very mindful. You have to say each phrase and do each action in the correct order, in the correct manner, and with the right emphasis, often doing several things at the same time. You need to have your wits about you.

Ritual also requires attention to detail—you need to see that there is water in the offering bowls, that there are incense sticks, that the candles are alight, that the flowers are properly arranged. For a complex ritual, an expert may be required. Once when I lived in Kalimpong, I invited Dhardo Rinpoche, my friend and teacher, to perform a rather complex ritual and, as the custom is, all the offerings were to be placed ready on the shrine before his arrival. Usually my own Tibetan students and disciples made the preparations themselves, but on this occasion they were not satisfied with that. They did set up the elaborate offerings—lots of little lamps, tormas, and so on—on lots of little tables, but they then called in a lama to check it all before the Rinpoche arrived. The lama came and cast his eye over the arrangements. "No. This should be there, that should be over here, these should be the other way round. . . ." In about five minutes he had made the necessary adjustments and satisfied himself that everything was in order. This is the kind of attention to detail required of a good ritualist.

Good ritual must not only be correctly done; it must also be beautiful. If it is not beautiful, it is not inspiring. So an aesthetic sense is essential. In a Buddhist temple or shrine-room everything is very beautifully arranged, clean and bright. This is true in Tibet, in Sri Lanka, indeed in all Buddhist countries.

Perhaps most important, a good ritualist must understand the meaning of it all. It is no use being able to do the ritual mechanically, to go through all the right actions, without understanding what is really going on. That would be empty ritual.

Finally, I would say that a good ritualist needs plenty of physical stamina. You may have to sit chanting for long periods, from time to time performing various ritual actions, and always maintaining graceful composure and appropriate hand-gestures or *mudras*. This takes considerable physical vigor.

Sometimes we in the West like to think that ritual is a sort of kindergarten stage of religion, something for beginners. But the Tibetans do not think like that. Tibetan tradition permits only the spiritually advanced to do lengthy and complex rituals. Certainly every Tibetan Buddhist has a form of ritual which he or she does. But it is only the Rinpoches and the more highly developed people in general who are sanctioned to enact very long and complicated rituals, because ordinary folk do not have the necessary mindfulness, understanding, and stamina.

Dhardo Rinpoche, who was well versed in Buddhist philosophy, an excellent organizer, and highly knowledgeable about Buddhist yoga, was also a very good ritualist. I often watched him for hours on end going through certain rituals, and I sometimes wondered how he was able to coordinate it all. He would be chanting maybe for half an hour or an hour, ringing his bell and making offerings. Sometimes as he was chanting and got toward the end of his text, he would start folding the silken cover in which the book was wrapped in a very elaborate way, to make a particular pattern. And I noticed that as the last tinkle of the bell died away, and the last word of the ritual was recited, the last flower thrown—at that very moment, the last fold of the cloth would be put in place. It was all synchronized, effortlessly, so it seemed. It was harmonized like a piece of music and all the elements ended together, just at the right moment, like a closing cadence. His gestures or mudras, like those of many lamas, were very beautiful to watch. He had been trained in these skills for many years and was a perfect master of them.

Most of us will not develop our capacity for ritual to that degree, but nonetheless the ritual we perform at our own level should be something which we work at, and make as harmonious and expressive as we possibly can. It should involve striving—and not only our own striving, but a common striving. The implication of this important point is that the practice of ritual is possible only within a spiritual community. If you are just doing it on your own, it will not be ritual in the full sense. It may be a striving, but it will not be a common striving.

Ritual in the full sense does not just presuppose a common striving; it also *expresses* that common striving. This is the most important point of all: that ritual is an expression. To quote a further definition of Fromm's, ritual is "a symbolic expression of thoughts and feelings by action." So what exactly is meant by "expression"? Essentially expression means bringing something out from within, even from the depths within. It is in order to express our depths that symbolic expression is necessary. Conceptual expression isn't enough. Conceptual expression brings something out only from the conscious level of our minds—and we have got to do more than that. We have got to plumb the depths beneath the conscious level, to contact the parts of our being to which myth and symbol speak. We could say, in fact, that ritual is like an acting out of symbol or myth. By expressing what is deep within our being, we externalize it, see it, make it something we can know. We can then begin to understand it and incorporate it into our conscious attitude. In this way our whole being will be enriched and integrated. Tension between the conscious and the unconscious will be reduced. We will become more whole.

Through ritual expression, not only do we externalize and make conscious our deep spiritual feelings; we also strengthen and intensify them. This touches on another reason why quite a lot of people feel hesitant about expressing themselves through ritual speech and action. They are simply not sure about the feelings themselves. Perhaps in the case of many of us our devotional feelings are still quite underdeveloped. It is a big step to put our trust in these feelings, to give them space to grow and to exert their influence on our conscious lives.

All of this is a matter of experience. By participating in ritual to any degree, we come to know it. It happens even within very simple devotional meetings when we recite the Sevenfold Puja—as long as we do it properly, with concentration. (The Sevenfold Puja is an expression of seven different devotional moods or aspirations, each of which is evoked by a few lines of a traditional text. The verses in the particular version of the Sevenfold Puja recited in the FWBO come from a Mahayana text called the Bodhicaryavatara.) In ritual we create a very specific atmosphere. Just as meditation has its own atmosphere, which is very beautiful, just as a talk on the Dharma has its own very positive and happy ambience, so the Sevenfold Puja also has a distinctive atmosphere of its own which derives from what is brought up from the depths, externalized, and made conscious.

This atmosphere can have a noticeable effect. At a Buddhist Society Summer School which I attended shortly after my return to England in 1964, I remember being rather surprised that, although there were many lectures on the program—and also a little meditation—there was no provision for any sort of puja. So one day I suggested that we might try out a little ritual in the evening. At first this suggestion was not very well received. I was told that English Buddhists had no interest in ritual; they preferred the rational approach. So I said, "Well, never mind. Even if only five or six people want to do it, let's try it." It was announced, therefore, that there would be a short and simple puja conducted by myself at nine o'clock that evening. In the event, instead of having five or six people, we had practically the whole Summer School, about a hundred and forty people. It was difficult to get them all into the room. They continued to come every night after that and seemed thoroughly to enjoy it. Many people remarked that a special atmosphere was created. Something special manifested, they knew not how, they knew not why—but it came from the depths, and it created an altogether more meaningful and harmonious atmosphere.

Sometimes people are starved of this sort of thing. They get just the intellectual, conceptual approach: books, talks, ideas, philosophy, theory. It is an imbalance which is even encouraged in some places in the East. I've known Theravadin bhikkhus apologize for pujas and say that they were only for lay people, unintellectual people. Intellectuals—and of course Westerners were supposed to be honorary intellectuals—didn't need them at all. What was important was the intellectual understanding of the Dharma. I've even heard Buddhist bhikkhus say, "Well, we bhikkhus don't do pujas ourselves." But although the intellectual approach is no less necessary than the devotional or the imaginal approaches, sooner or later we must begin to engage the depths, the vast resources of energy which lie in the unconscious mind. We must begin to speak the language of myth, symbol, and image, and in this way integrate the unconscious with the conscious. And this is what ritual, among other things, helps us to do.

Lastly, in terms of Fromm's definition, ritual is "rooted in common values." Ritual is never just ritual. It is not self-contained. It issues from a whole religious philosophy, a system of beliefs and values. Having studied Fromm's definition of ritual, let us apply it to a simple example drawn from Buddhism: the ritual of Going for Refuge, which is very basic but also very important. First of all, it is an action. We say *Buddham saranam gacchami, gacchami* meaning "I go." In the Pali and the Sanskrit, the verb comes out very powerfully because it comes at the end. It is often translated as "I go for refuge to the Buddha," but a far more powerful translation is "To the Buddha for refuge I go." This stresses the fact that Going for Refuge is an action, an action of the whole being. We go for Refuge with body, speech, and mind. In the Tantric tradition it is not felt to be enough to go for Refuge mentally and verbally. You also go for Refuge physically, literally prostrating in front of the image. It is a threefold practice which involves the whole being.

Not only is it an action; it is a shared action, because we repeat the verses of Refuge together, in unison. In traditional Buddhist countries, the bhikkhu or monk recites first and the others recite after him. What emerges is almost a dialogue; an almost dramatic element is introduced. This emphasizes the fact that we are not just doing something in the same way as other individuals who happen to be there. We do it *with* them, with heart and mind and body.

Next, the Going for Refuge expresses a common striving, which is that we aspire to realize the common goal of nirvana or Enlightenment. We all want to become like the Buddha. We all want to follow the path of the Dharma. We all want to help, and to receive help from, other members of the Sangha.

Finally, our strivings are rooted in common values, the values which permeate the whole body of the Buddha's teaching. The Going for Refuge is not isolated in itself. It grows out of the whole teaching and tradition. If one were to expound the meaning of the Three Jewels to which we go for Refuge in full detail, such an exposition would incorporate the whole of Buddhism.

So Fromm's definition of ritual is readily applicable to the fundamental Buddhist practice of Going for Refuge, and it helps to give us some understanding of the psychology of ritual and some appreciation of its value. But the real way to appreciate the value of ritual is to practice it.

5. Secret Wings

We cry that we are weak although
We will not stir our secret wings;
The world is dark—because we are
Blind to the starriness of things.

We pluck our rainbow-tinted plumes
And with their heaven-born beauty try
To fledge nocturnal shafts, and then
Complain "Alas! we cannot fly!"

We mutter "All is dust" or else
With mocking words accost the wise:
"Show us the Sun which shines beyond
The Veil"—and then we close our eyes.

To powers above and powers beneath
In quest of Truth men sue for aid,
Who stand athwart the Light and fear
The shadow that themselves have made.

Oh cry no more that you are weak
But stir and spread your secret wings,
And say "The world is bright, because
We glimpse the starriness of things."

Soar with your rainbow plumes and reach
That near-far land where all are one,
Where Beauty's face is aye unveiled
And every star shall be a sun.

6. The Importance of Spiritual Receptivity

As a Buddhist one need not be too scared of the idea of prayer.

SPIRITUAL RECEPTIVITY is of the utmost importance; without it, spiritual progress simply cannot be maintained. We need to hold ourselves open to the truth as the flower holds itself open to the sun. This is what spiritual receptivity means: holding ourselves open to the higher spiritual influences that are streaming through the universe, but with which we are not usually in contact, because we usually shut ourselves off from them. We should be ready if necessary to give up whatever we have learned so far, which isn't easy by any means, and to give up whatever we have *become* so far, which is still more difficult.

How does one become receptive in this way? For a start, one can pray. As a Buddhist one need not be too scared of the idea of prayer. It doesn't necessarily have theistic connotations. When a Tibetan Buddhist engages in an activity he calls "prayer," he is not praying to God in the sense of the creator of heaven and earth, because such a conception is not part of the Tibetan Buddhist system of belief. He is praying to the Buddha, the Bodhisattvas, or the dakinis.[107]

Prayer in its proper sense, anyway, is not for material things, but for blessings, higher understanding, wisdom, compassion. One's prayers simply express the fact that one doesn't have those qualities and would like to have them. If you want something in an ordinary sense, you just say to someone, "Please pass me the toast," "Please give me some money," or whatever it may be. In the case of the Buddhas and Bodhisattvas, they have got wisdom and compassion, which you haven't got but would like to have, so your aspiration to develop wisdom and compassion takes the form of a request to the Buddhas and Bodhisattvas to *give* you those qualities. As an informed Buddhist you know very well that wisdom and compassion cannot be handed over like a slice of toast. But nonetheless you continue to use the language of petition. Why?

The reason is that the nature of language almost compels us to think of wisdom and compassion as qualities that can be acquired or received. If we use the language of prayer, we do so because it has a certain emotive value, and expresses an openness and receptivity. It certainly doesn't reflect a literal belief that one can be given those qualities by Buddhas and Bodhisattvas. In any case, one understands that those Buddhas and Bodhisattvas are not really separate from oneself. They can be regarded as symbolizing unrealized states of one's own being that one is trying to activate through prayer.

Prayer, understood in this way, is not out of place in Buddhism. It is very different from meditation. And it isn't that one is thinking, "I'll make a pretense of asking, but I know I've really got to do it myself." When one is praying, one really *feels* that one hasn't got what one desires, and that one must therefore ask for it. One may have an intellectual understanding that it is all within oneself, but that is not one's experience when one is praying. If you experience the desire to pray, there is no need to stop yourself on the strength of a purely rational understanding that the Buddhas and Bodhisattvas are not really "out there."

Quite a few people over the years have told me that sometimes they feel like praying to the Buddha or to Bodhisattvas but that they tend consciously to inhibit the impulse, thinking that it is a weakness, and not a very Buddhistic one, to imagine that the Buddhas and Bodhisattvas can give one anything. Surely, they say, any truly spiritual goal can be achieved only by one's own efforts. My reply is always that if you feel like praying, you should go ahead and do it, and work out the "theology" later. If it is a genuine feeling, don't suppress it. At the very least, prayer is a means of concentrating your emotional energies. And in any case, it is as true to say that the Buddhas and Bodhisattvas are outside you as that they are within. Either way, you are still operating within the subject-object duality. It is no more valid to think of them as existing in the depths of your own being than to think of them as existing beyond anything you can experience or conceive of. Both are equally real—or equally unreal. Whether you think of that reality (which is neither subject nor object) as a sort of super-object outside you or a super-subject within you doesn't make any difference.

The experience of many poets is rather like this. Poetic inspiration can be experienced as welling up from within or as coming in from outside. Some poets genuinely experience being visited by the Muses, so to speak. But whether poetic inspiration is called up from within or called down from above amounts to the same thing. Language has severe limitations here. One is trying to introduce into one's experience within the subject-object duality something which is beyond it, and which can be thought of either as emerging from within the depths of one's own being or as something transcendentally aloof toward which one must direct one's prayers and aspirations.

7. "In the woods are many more"

Selling wild orchids at my door one day
A man said, "In the woods are many more . . .
Deep in the gloom, high on the thickset trees,
Wild orchids hang like clouds of butterflies,
Golden and white, spotted with red and black,
As huge as birds, or tiny as a bee,
Wild orchids which no eye has ever seen

Save ours, who wander in these rich green glooms
All day throughout the year." I bought his sprays,
Paid him, and bore them in; and as I went
My eyes by chance fell on a shelf of books—
The Buddha's Teachings—and thereafter glanced
Up to the Buddha's image as He smiled
Above them from the alcove. Strange it was
That, as my eyes from book to image passed,
Dwelling an instant on that calm, pure Face,
There, with the frail cold blossoms in my hands,
The words that man spoke at my door should ring
Through my stilled heart again and yet again
Like music—"In the woods are many more . . ."

8. EVERYTHING THAT LIVES IS HOLY

Religion is not confined to particular places, but saturates and sanctifies the whole of nature.

SOCIETY has unfortunately acquired the habit of regarding certain actions, such as attending a temple, church, or mosque, or visiting a place of pilgrimage, as religious in themselves, without reference to the background of consciousness which stands behind them. Similarly, certain occupations or avocations, such as those of the monk or priest, are regarded as possessing, in some almost magical fashion, a certain virtue or sanctity. Particular places, buildings, costumes, books, languages, countries, colors, and so on are, in exactly the same way, set apart as sacred from the mass of profane objects of the same class by which they are surrounded, and from which they are so sharply distinguished. The result of this dichotomization of things into sacred and profane is an unhealthy division of the collective or social consciousness analogous to the split produced in the individual consciousness by its arbitrary classification of actions as "good" and "bad." This is not to deny the power which is certainly possessed by certain places and objects of inducing corresponding states of consciousness internally. This is because we have, either by deliberate individual choice or by passive acceptance of the cultural or religious traditions into which we are born, come to regard some material thing as the symbol of a spiritual value. But the sacredness or profaneness of that thing nevertheless continues to depend upon the state of mind which it is capable of inspiring. If a "holy" object no longer inspires holy thoughts then it ceases to be a symbol and becomes a superstition. For the very essence of superstition consists in regarding things—whether particular persons, places, or practices—as holy in themselves, without reference to the state of mind which accompanies them. That thought, word, or deed alone is holy concerning which the idea that "I am the doer" does not arise.

The most unfortunate practical consequence of regarding things as in themselves sacred or profane is that the vast mass of people consider themselves to be totally excluded from participation in the practice of religion. Religion, they think, belongs to the temple or church, not to the home; to the priest, not to the layman. It can be found within the covers of some musty book, but not among the flowers that bloom so freshly in the fields, or in consort with the "lutes that whisper softness in chambers." Priests and ecclesiastical bodies of every religious denomination have not only deliberately encouraged, but even sedulously inculcated, this wrong attitude of mind, in order to strengthen their positions and swell their revenues. But the truth of the matter is that you cannot see anything as holy until you see everything as holy. Distinctions are useful, even necessary, at the beginning of one's spiritual career; but they should not be clung to. A flower is sacred, a tree holy, if you look at it with an illumined mind, just as a religious observance is profane if you do it with a greedy, malicious, or deluded consciousness. It is better to sweep a floor egolessly than to meditate with the prideful sense that "I am meditating."

Swinging thus the emphasis from the external to the internal, from the act to the thought, from the symbol to the thing symbolized, we can see that religion is not confined to particular places, but that it saturates and sanctifies the whole of nature; that it is, properly understood, not for the few only, but inevitably and inescapably for all; and that there is, to the Eye of Enlightenment, no division between sacred and profane but that, in the words of a great poet-seer, "Everything that lives is holy."

9. DEVOTION AT LUMBINI

THE ASHOKA PILLAR stood beneath the open sky behind a low iron railing. On its highly polished surface the ancient Brahmi letters were cut deep and clear, and we could still spell out the announcement "Here the Blessed One was born." For some reason or other, I felt even more deeply moved here than I had done either at Sarnath or Kusinara. The truncated stone shaft stood so calmly and so simply beneath the cloudless blue sky; it seemed so unpretentious, and yet to mean so much. Lingering behind when Buddharakshita and the others had moved on in the direction of the mounds, I gathered some small white flowers and with a full heart scattered them over the railing at the foot of the column. As I did so I heard Buddharakshita's voice. "What are you messing about with those flowers for?" he shouted roughly. "Come on, we can't wait for you all day!"

10. CALL FORTH AS MUCH AS YOU CAN

The love, the respect, and the faith are all there, latent within us: they are natural human endowments.

Call forth as much as you can of love, of respect, and of faith!
Remove the obstructing defilements, and clear away all
   your taints!

> Listen to the Perfect Wisdom of the gentle Buddhas,
> Taught for the weal of the world, for heroic spirits intended!

SO HERE we are given a cautionary word of advice. Reflect on the emotional attitude you are bringing to this sutra. If the Buddha's first aim is to awaken a joyous emotional response, then we need to think again about our whole approach to the Perfection of Wisdom. It is not good enough, if we do not understand it, to assume that we are just not up to it intellectually. The first thing the Buddha asks is not "I hope you have your wits about you," or "Do you have a degree in philosophy?" but "Are you emotionally positive? Are you receptive to the Dharma? And are you allowing this positivity and receptivity to develop without limitation?"

The expression "call forth," after all, suggests that we are to bring out something that is already there. The love, the respect, and the faith are all there, latent within us: they are natural human endowments. It is as though the Buddha is saying, "Let them express themselves, let them manifest themselves. They are there, and they are the appropriate emotions to bring to the Perfection of Wisdom. So don't place any limitation on them by imagining that you have to start laboriously manufacturing them. You are better than you think you are."

This idea, fundamental to Buddhism, is one that goes against the grain for those of us who imagine that our socialized selves are sitting on a lot of unattractive, basic animal urges, and that if we become less inhibited, all sorts of unpleasant negative emotions are going to come pouring out. But that is a one-sided view of things; there is a lot that is good and positive that also gets repressed. In a largely secular society this is perhaps especially true of devotional feelings. If you no longer believe in the Blessed Virgin Mary, for example, you cannot offer even so much as a candle in a church, and in this way your love and reverence and faith remain unused and stifled. You may even come to the conclusion that you simply have no devotional feelings. I have known a lot of apparently quite intellectual people who, while they used to find the devotional demands of religion quite suffocating, nevertheless discovered, when they eventually took up Buddhist devotional practices, that they enjoyed being devotional. They found—rather to their surprise—that they really rather enjoyed offering flowers and lighting candles; that it was, in fact, quite a relief to feel able to do so at last. So call forth as much as you can of love, of respect, and of faith!

4 ❧ Buddhism and the Natural World

1. ANIMISM AND SPIRITUAL LIFE

The universe we know and love in the form of our native land and folklore puts heart into our highest ideals, making them personal, something we can love.

> Hence, all ye spirits, hear attentively.
> Look lovingly upon the race of men,
> And, since they bring thee offerings day and night,
> Keep watch and ward about them heedfully.[108]

THIS VERSE clearly reflects an animistic attitude to nature. It is perhaps not easy for us, with our Christian conditioning, to imagine having such a strong feeling for nature and for the things of nature. The people of India are much closer to their pagan roots: if you give them half a chance to worship anything, village people especially will happily take it. This at least was the view of my teacher Bhikkhu Jagdish Kashyap, who told me once of a curious example of it that he observed as a boy in a village in a remote part of the Indian state of Bihar. A new road was being built and marked out with milestones, and one morning he saw a woman making her way from the village to the nearest milestone, carrying a tray upon which she had placed some vermilion, some flowers, and a few sticks of incense. On reaching the milestone she anointed it with the vermilion, scattered the flowers, and stuck the sticks of incense in the ground in front of it. She then bowed to the milestone with folded hands. She evidently thought it was a new kind of god.

The attitude behind such undiscriminating devotion is essentially animistic, and for all its primitiveness and simplicity, it is a healthy basis for spiritual life. You feel that everything is alive; you feel a rapport with the forces of nature, and you want to propitiate them, be on friendly terms with them. Mechanistic materialism suggests that everything is just dead matter, but it is surely much better to think that all things—trees, stones, streams, clouds—are alive, even if you personify them in a rather childish way.

Some western scholars are disturbed to find that in some traditional Buddhist cultures, the pure philosophical and ethical teachings of Buddhism have been corrupted, as they see it, by being mixed up with a lot of animism and spirit worship. I myself do not share their unease. At a certain level we *are* a part of nature; we are surrounded by all sorts of natural forces and energies that are also present within us, and we cannot help feeling and experiencing them, even in the form of spirits and gods of the earth and sky. And if you do experience them in that way, you naturally want to keep up a positive relationship with them: you give them offerings and in return they protect you.

In this verse from the *Ratana Sutta* the compiler of the sutta is taking up this archaic, pagan, animistic way of looking at things and giving it wider significance. He is saying, "Be on friendly terms with the universe. If you feel friendly toward the universe, the universe will feel friendly toward you." It's as though the universe (in the form of the gods) is prepared to strike a bargain with us. We agree to worship the gods and provide them with oblations, and in return they agree to protect us. Today it is considered more realistic to regard the universe as implacably hostile and threatening, but really this view is just more paranoid, the natural result of living in a universe conceived of as impersonal.

It is difficult to feel good will and love toward something you think of as impersonal. Before you can feel positive emotion toward it, you have to invest it with personal qualities, and you can see this in the way some people love their car or motorbike almost as though it were human. Making a living connection with something whose workings are ultimately perhaps a bit of a mystery involves personalizing it, calling it "he" or "she." You may end up saying things like, "She's not going very well today. I don't think she's very happy. Maybe she doesn't like the change in the weather." Similarly, to the extent that you feel positive toward life as a whole, you will start personalizing things, so that they are not just things but "spirits"—spirits at least in a poetic sense. If you want to enter into relationship with the universe, if you want to love it, you have to see it as personal.

Throughout the Buddhist tradition one finds this same sense of the importance of propitiating local spirits. For example, in one of his songs Milarepa sings:

> Ye local demons, ghosts, and gods,
> All friends of Milarepa,
> Drink the nectar of kindness and compassion,
> Then return to your abodes.[109]

These gods and goddesses and spirits can also be seen as representing aspects of oneself. The basic energies that find their expression in nature through the folklore of our indigenous culture also exist in us, and we cannot afford to ignore them or cut ourselves off from them. Instead, we can take notice of them, absorb, assimilate, and direct them, as Padmasambhava is said to have harnessed the demons of Tibet. And just as we must harness our inner drives, so we must harness the same forces as they express themselves through the indigenous culture. For example, rather than building an exact replica of a Tibetan or Japanese Buddhist temple in England, which might seem somewhat alien, one could build it in an English style. You would still want to center it upon a Buddha image, but you could introduce motifs or symbols with indigenous significance. Instead of bodhi leaves, for example, you could decorate the shrine with carvings of oak leaves, which have deep associations for the English. Druids worshipped the oak tree, and the mistletoe that grows upon it, and in more modern times the oak has developed associations of strength and stability—"hearts of oak"—based on the extraordinary success of the English ships that were built from it. All the energy bound up with these old associations would contribute to whatever was done in the temple.

In India, when Buddha images were first made, the principal gods of the indigenous tradition, Indra and Brahma, were not banished completely. You find for example, in images of the Buddha descending from the *devaloka,* that he comes escorted by these two deities. They are smaller than the Buddha—very much attendants—but they have not been excluded, they have been given their place. The ethnic, one might say, has been integrated with the universal, the lower ideal with the higher. The universe we know and love in the form of our native land and folklore puts heart into our highest ideals, making them personal, something we can love.

2. FEELING THAT THE UNIVERSE IS ALIVE

Concepts are vital—but they do not exhaust the whole of life's mystery.

IN OUR MODERN techno-scientific culture we are able to do all kinds of things with and to the natural world, but as a result we have lost our affinity with it. Alienated from nature, no longer experiencing it as a living presence, we sorely need to recapture the sense that to be human is to be part of nature.

This feeling, of course, came naturally to people in the early days of Buddhism. The Buddha and his disciples lived in the midst of nature, wandering on foot for eight or nine months of the year from one village to another through the jungles of northern India. Their days and nights were spent in forests, in parks, on mountains, or by rivers; out in the elements, sleeping under the stars. Theirs was a world populated not only by human beings and animals, but by gods and spirits of the hills and streams, trees and flowers. The sense of the physical environment experienced as a living presence is a significant theme in all the oldest texts of the Buddhist tradition. For all its factual content, the Pali Canon also reminds us that the supernatural world was a reality for the early Buddhists; and one might say that it was the continuous presence of nature that made it so.

All the episodes of major significance in the Buddha's life history unfolded in close contact with a natural world which actively responded to his presence. He was born in the open air, we are told, while his mother supported herself by holding a bough laden with flowers. He gained Enlightenment beneath the Bodhi tree, seated on a carpet of fresh grass. And in the end he passed away between twin *sal* trees which sprinkled his body in homage with blossoms out of season. This sense of nature as a vibrant and animated presence is often the part of the Pali Canon that is edited out of selected translations into English; the editors tend to leave intact the outline of the Buddha's teaching but include little of the world in which it is set. If some mythic strands are left, the modern reader is likely to skip over the accounts of nagas, yaksas, and other supernatural beings to concentrate on the "real" stuff, the doctrine. But the gods and goddesses, and all the various kinds of non-human beings, are not there simply as ornamentation. Their presence is itself part of the teaching. They provide glimpses of an ancient mode of human consciousness fully integrated into a universe of value, meaning, and purpose. To miss them is to miss the poetry, and the heart of the Buddha's message.

If we are really to understand the traditional Buddhist practice of the contemplation of the elements—earth, water, fire, air, and sometimes additionally space and consciousness—as taught by the Buddha and recorded in texts like the *Satipatthana Sutta,* therefore, we need to find ways of deepening our understanding of what this elemental imagery meant to the early Buddhists, how they knew those mythic figures and lived in relation to them. To help us do this, we can return to the term *mahabhuta,* whose meaning hints at the living, inherently ungraspable quality of the elements. *Mahabhuta,* "great ghost," means something that has somehow arisen, or has been conjured up—a mysterious, other-worldly apparition. To think of the four elements as "great ghosts" suggests that we are dealing not with concepts or inanimate matter, but with living forces. The universe is alive, magically so, and the haunting appearance within it of the four great elements makes that experience inherently mysterious and inaccessible to definitive knowledge. Rather than trying to pin down reality with technical and scientific thinking, the Buddhist conception of the four elements helps to bring about a fusion of objective and subjective knowledge, enabling us, like Shakespeare's King Lear, to "take upon's the mystery of things."

This does not mean that the Buddhist conception of the elements is vague or imprecise, nor that the rational faculty is no longer necessary. Concepts are vital—but they do not exhaust the whole of life's mystery. To understand the four elements as psychophysical states rather than as material substances or states of matter undermines the conventional idea of what the body is. It reminds us that the division between inner and outer worlds is a product of dualistic thinking. Rather than any division between a thing called matter and a thing called mind, or a thing called body and a thing called consciousness, there is a continuity running all the way through, a continuity of our awareness patterned in different ways. If we can really understand this, those inner and outer worlds become interfused in a deeper, more meaningful vision of what it is to be alive.

All this runs counter to the way we in the West have been conditioned to experience the body and the world of which it is a part. But it must surely be better—or at the very least more fun—to be an animist and feel that the whole world is animated by spirits, rather than gazing out at a world of non-living matter which occasionally and haphazardly comes to life, and in which even our own life is ultimately reducible to inanimate matter. All the same, it is not easy for us to develop a genuine feeling that the material elements are really living entities. Conversely, it is all too easy to generate a false and sentimental notion that "the hills are alive" by projecting all kinds of imaginary properties onto the world. We cannot generate a belief in, say, naiads and dryads by force of will; nor can we deny what we know scientifically about the way the universe operates. We have somehow to hunt for a real feeling for the life of things, even from our sophisticated viewpoint. It starts with intuitive knowledge, not a set of beliefs.

There is a hierarchy: rocks are not as alive as plants, and plants are not as alive as human beings. We have to draw the line somewhere—it would be hard to regard, say, stainless steel as a living substance; each of us will have a point at which we stop acknowledging and respecting the life of another being or "thing" and start simply using it for our own convenience. For some unfortunate people this line is drawn even at certain other human beings—of course this is also unfortunate for the people with whom they come into contact. At the other end of the spectrum, the Tibetans used to refuse to engage in mining for minerals: they would pan for gold but not, as the Chinese are now doing in Tibet, disturb the earth and the dragons that they believe guard the gold it conceals.

I would go so far as to say that a universe conceived of as dead cannot be a universe in which one stands any chance of attaining Enlightenment. (Whether you stand any chance in a living universe is of course up to you.) It may be difficult for us to get back to the view of the world that came naturally to our ancestors, but poets have persisted in seeing the universe as alive: surely no poet could have a totally Newtonian outlook, the kind of attitude that Blake termed "single vision" and "Newton's sleep." Milton, for example, traces the origin of mining to Hell itself: in *Paradise Lost* the devils start excavating minerals in order to manufacture artillery to use against heaven. One could even interpret the whole Romantic Movement as expressing a great protest against the Newtonian picture of nature and a reassertion of essentially pagan values.

3. THE TRADITIONAL SOCIETY

For modern men and women there is in the common things of life no hint of anything beyond.

IN A TRADITIONAL civilization every branch of knowledge and every kind of activity is integrated with conceptions of a metaphysical order. Every aspect of life, even the lowest and most mundane, is given a transcendental orientation that enables it to function, in a general way, as a support, if not for the actual living of the spiritual life, then at least for a more or less constant awareness of the existence of spiritual values. In such a civilization, religion (to use the narrow modern term) is not something from which you can escape, even if you want to; it encounters you at every step, with the familiar objects of home and the accustomed routine of daily life. Nurtured in such an environment, in which the whole of existence appears to be a great Smaragdine Tablet, constantly reminding us that "the things below are copies" and that the originals are above, sensitive hearts and minds become more subtle and sensitive still. To them "rocks and stones and trees," and other natural objects, are not simply lumps of matter of various shapes and sizes, but "huge cloudy symbols of a high romance" traced, not by the "magic hand of chance," but by the irresistible finger of omnipresent spiritual law. Nature is not dead, but alive with many voices, and to an eye accustomed to see and to hear things that point beyond themselves even

> An old pine tree is preaching wisdom,
> And a wild bird crying out truth.

Through the non-traditional civilization of the modern West, however, the sledgehammer blows of science have driven a wedge that threatens to split asunder the whole fabric. "Religious" and "secular," "sacred" and "profane" interests and activities are sharply distinguished and ruthlessly divided the one from the other. The sphere of "religion" has progressively shrunk, so that it now has little or no connection with, or influence over, the vast majority of the activities in which men at present engage. It may no longer be compared with the ocean bed which supports (*Dharma* is derived from a root meaning "to support") the mighty mass of waters rolling above, but to a small volcanic island reeling and shuddering beneath the relentless impact of the hostile element by which it is surrounded and well nigh overwhelmed. For modern men and women there is in the common things of life no hint of anything beyond; for them there falls, like moonlight upon shifting leaves, no steady radiance of the Eternal upon the flickerings of their days. They are the true descendant of Peter Bell, in whom Wordsworth, writing when the smoke of the Industrial Revolution had already begun to darken the skies of England, described a type of humanity now fast becoming universal:

A primrose by a river's brim
A yellow primrose was to him
And it was nothing more.

Religion, banished from the affairs of men, sits dark and solitary in the temple. Life goes on, or seems to go on, as before; but that which was "the life of life" is no longer there, and it is problematical how long the ghastly simulacrum will be able to continue its antics.

Such a displacement of civilization from its age-old foundations in spiritual values, and the consequent opening of a breach between the "religious" and "secular" aspects of life, will inevitably find a counterpart not only in the student's life but in his or her approach to the study of Buddhism. Brought up in a non-traditional environment, wherein few objects and activities have any significance beyond themselves, he or she will be naturally prone to think that the study of Buddhism is one activity among many to be pursued without the necessity of considering either what influence it may have on other activities or what effect they may have upon it. In a traditional society such negligence would not have very serious consequences; for, as already stated, in such a society everything receives, ultimately, a transcendental orientation, and few activities other than those which violate the moral law could be positively deleterious in their effect upon the study of Buddhism. The "spiritual" life and "religious" studies point in the same direction as the "worldly" life and its duties; but one points directly, the other indirectly.

In a non-traditional society, however, there is a constant tug-of-war between those departments of life which have been dissociated from their transcendental principles, on the one hand, and the isolated remnants of tradition on the other. Even the sincerest student cannot entirely withdraw himself or herself from activities which, being no longer traditional, are in principle, or rather because of their very lack of principle, at variance with the proper method of studying the Dharma. If you are in this situation, your life, lacking a common guiding principle for all its activities, will be to some extent disintegrated. You will be like a man who, clinging desperately to a rock in midstream, feels against his body the mighty rush of waters which seeks to tear him from his refuge and whirl him to destruction. In order to integrate your life and strengthen your hold upon the unshakable rock of the Dharma, you will have to withdraw yourself from as many profane activities as possible, and reinforce the traditional supports not only of your own life but, as far as you can, of society as well. You should take part, and encourage others to take part, in traditional observances of all kinds; taking care, first, to understand the meaning and value of each observance. Worship of the image of the Buddha with the traditional offerings of flowers, lights, and incense; paying homage to spiritual teachers, to sacred objects and buildings, and to elders and members of the Holy Order, in the manner traditionally prescribed; the wearing of the traditional costume (in societies that still have one); participating in celebrations such as those held in honor of the Lord Buddha's Enlightenment—in these and many other similar ways, by multiplying opportunities for contact with Tradition and consequent recollection of the Dharma, it is possible to effect at least a partial integration not only of your own life but also, albeit to a lesser extent, of the lives of your associates.

Abstention from participation in untraditional activities of all kinds, particularly from forms of entertainment which are calculated to excite the senses and stimulate the lower mind, is no less essential to the successful study of the Dharma. If your aim is to be a Dharma student but you think that if you devote an hour a day or two or three hours a week to the study of the Dharma it will be sufficient, and that when not so engaged you can spend your time playing games, or reading a trashy novel, or under the hypnotic influence of the latest popular film, with no effect on your state of mind, you are making a big mistake. It is no accident of language that the words "whole" and "holy" are etymologically connected, or that one of the definitions of "holy" should be "spiritually whole." The quest for holiness, which the study of the Dharma serves, is a quest for spiritual wholeness, for complete integration of the "personality" not with any subjective principle merely, but with Reality. The more faithfully the study of Buddhism is pursued, the more difficult will it be to allow even activities of minor importance to remain outside the circle of its influence. Only from the intellectual or dogmatic scientific point of view is it possible to regard Buddhism as being merely one among hundreds of other possible subjects for scholarly research and doctoral dissertation. To one who studies it with some attempt at approximation to the fully traditional method we have endeavored to describe, it can appear as nothing less than what it actually is, the dominating and controlling influence of the whole of life.

5 ↤ Friends and Teachers

1. WHY SHOULD A BUDDHA NEED A FRIEND?

In spiritual friendship we take delight in the spiritual *beauty of our friend.*

ALTHOUGH the Buddha had had some difficulty in finding a satisfactory personal attendant, Ananda was by no means in a hurry to take on the task. It is as though he realized that it would be no easy matter to be the constant companion of an Enlightened one. Ananda had made steady progress in the spiritual life. He was certainly a "Stream-entrant," so his progress toward full Enlightenment was assured. But he was not a Buddha. And even for someone like Ananda, even for a Stream-entrant, even for someone who had grown up with the Buddha, it was a rather awe-inspiring prospect to be the Buddha's constant companion, to be with him, by day and by night, in rain and in sun, year in and year out. Ananda therefore thought the matter over very carefully. He had seen some previous attendants come somewhat to grief, and was reluctant to give the Buddha any further trouble.

In the end, however, Ananda decided to accept the challenge, but laid down certain conditions, of which a couple are relevant here. One of these was that he should not be given any share in the various offerings and invitations that were given to the Buddha. He argued that, if people saw him benefiting from the offerings that were made to the Buddha—all the new robes and so on—then they might think that he was acting as the Buddha's companion just for the sake of what he could get out of it. He also realized that there would be times when he might have to be away from the Buddha, running errands, taking messages, and so on. While he was away, someone might come to see the Buddha and ask for a teaching. In consequence, the Buddha might give a discourse, might even give an important teaching, in his absence. So another condition he laid down was that the Buddha should repeat to him whatever teaching he had given during his absence.

The Buddha accepted these conditions, and Ananda became his constant companion for twenty years. How successful this arrangement was can be seen from an incident that occurred shortly before the Buddha's *parinibbana,* his final passing away. Ananda was very deeply upset by the prospect of losing the Buddha. Apparently he stood leaning against the door, weeping. As he wept, he said: "Alas, I am still a pupil with much to be done, and my Master will be passing utterly away, *he who was so kind to me.*" This was Ananda's impression of the Buddha after twenty years of constant, day to day, companionship. He did not say that the Buddha was wise, or energetic, but that he was kind.

Fortunately, we also know about the Buddha's impression of Ananda. When he was told that Ananda was weeping outside, he sent for him and spoke the following words of encouragement:

> For a long time, Ananda, you have been in the Tathagata's presence, showing loving-kindness in act of body, speech and mind, beneficially, blessedly, wholeheartedly and unstintingly.[110]

Thus the Buddha's predominant impression of Ananda was that he too was kind, that Ananda had served him with kindness of body, speech, and mind, that he had kept nothing back, that he had given himself totally. The relation between the Buddha and Ananda was essentially one of mutual kindness, even though the Buddha was spiritually by far the more developed of the two.

This may seem like a very small thing, but if we reflect we shall realize that it is actually a very big thing. Their kindness had never failed, had never been found wanting even for a moment on either side. When two people are constant companions, and when the relation between them is of unfailing mutual kindness, you can only say of them that they are *friends*. Indeed, you can only say that they are *spiritual friends,* because such unfailing mutual kindness over such a long period of time is possible only on a deeply spiritual basis.

To some, it may seem a little strange that the Buddha and Ananda were friends. It may seem strange, perhaps, that the Buddha should have had a friend. One may wonder whether a Buddha *needs* a friend. But this depends on one's conception of Enlightenment. In response, I can give only a hint.

The Enlightenment experience is not self-contained in a one-sided way. The Enlightenment experience contains an element of communication, and contains, therefore, an element of spiritual friendship, even transcendental friendship, or friendship of the highest conceivable level. This, perhaps, is the significance of the Buddha's having a constant companion. There is surely no question of the Buddha keeping up the "dignity" of a Buddha. Ananda is not a sort of spiritual valet-cum-private-secretary. The fact that he is in the Buddha's presence, as the translator has it, represents the fact that there exists within the Enlightenment experience, within the heart of Reality, an element of communication, an element of spiritual friendship, something that found expression in the later history of Buddhist thought as that rather mysterious concept of *sambhogakaya.*

We can see how the Buddha and Ananda worked together as friends in a story that is told of how they once came upon a monk who was sick. We will join them as they make their way around the lodgings of a group of monks.

488 ~ THE ESSENTIAL SANGHARAKSHITA

The Exalted One was going his rounds of the lodgings,
with the Venerable Ananda in attendance, and came to the
lodging of that brother.

A point to notice here is that the Buddha was going his rounds of
the *lodgings*. In the original, the word for "lodging" is *vihara*, and that
is all that *vihara* means. We must not imagine the Buddha going his
rounds of a large, palatial, well-furnished monastery. The lodgings in
question were probably just clusters of thatched huts scattered over
an area of parkland just a few miles outside the city gates.

The Buddha was making his *rounds* of these lodgings. In other
words, he was taking a personal interest in the monks. How were
they getting on? What were they doing? How were they passing their
time? There was of course no question of them sitting outside their
thatched huts reading newspapers, or listening to transistor radios, or
watching television, but they might possibly have been up to other
things that they should not have been up to. They might have needed
some encouragement, some teaching, or even a little correction. The
Buddha was seeing things for himself. In this way, he and Ananda
came to "the lodging of that brother."

Now the Exalted One saw that brother lying where he had
fallen in his own excrements, and seeing him He went to-
ward him, came to him, and said: "Brother, what ails you?"
"I have dysentery, Lord."
"But is there anyone taking care of you, brother?"
"No, Lord."
"Why is it, brother, that the brethren do not take care
of you?"
"I am useless to the brethren, Lord: therefore the bre-
thren do not care for me."[111]

There are a number of points to be noted here. The Buddha goes
toward the sick monk, asks him what is wrong with him, and gets very

quickly to the heart of the matter, especially in the sick monk's last reply: "I am useless to the brethren, Lord: therefore the brethren do not care for me."

This is a very significant statement indeed. It is a shocking, terrible statement. Of course, we have only the bare words of the printed page to go by. We do not know how those words were spoken—and this of course makes a difference. Did the Buddha say, "Why is it, brother, that the brethren do not take care of you?" indignantly, or with concern, or sadly? And did the sick monk reply with dignity, with resignation, with weariness, or with bitterness and anger? We do not know. All we have is the bleak, shocking statement itself, "I am useless to the brethren, Lord: therefore the brethren do not care for me."

However the words were spoken, they must imply, sadly, that people are interested in you only so long as you are useful to them, only so long as they can get something out of you. It implies that they see you not as a person but as a thing. To treat a person as a thing is to treat them unethically. And this, apparently, is how the other monks were treating the sick monk. He was not useful to them, and so they were not interested in him. He was left lying in his own excrement. No one took care of him. There was no kindness between the sick monk and the other monks as there was between the Buddha and Ananda. There was no ordinary human friendship—not to speak of spiritual friendship; neither was there any sympathy or sensitivity or awareness. There could not be, because these are qualities that you can experience only in relation to a person whom you actually see as a person. The other monks did not see the sick monk as a person. To them he was like an old worn out broom, or a broken pot. He was useless to them so they did not care for him.

Only too often we ourselves can behave like this. We often consider people primarily in terms of their usefulness. We do this even within the spiritual community. Sometimes we are more interested in someone's talents and capacities—as a bricklayer, accountant, or lecturer—than in who they are in themselves. If you are treated in this way, then, when you are no longer able or willing to employ your talents, you may have the disappointing and disillusioning experience of finding that nobody wants to know you, nobody wants to be "friends" with you any more. We must therefore learn to see persons as persons. There must be kindness between us, there must be spiritual friendship, as there was between the Buddha and Ananda. There must be sympathy, sensitivity, and awareness.

There are two principal aspects to persons treating each other as persons. These are communication and taking delight, and these two qualities are of the essence of friendship. Even in the case of ordinary friendship there is the great benefit and blessing of being able to share our thoughts and feelings with another human being. It has been said that self-disclosure, the making of oneself known to another human being—being known by that person and knowing that you are known by that person—is essential to human health and happiness. If you are shut up in yourself, without any possibility of communication with another person, you don't stay healthy or happy for long. In the case of spiritual friendship, we share our experience of the Dharma itself. We share our enthusiasm, our inspiration, and our understanding. We even share our mistakes—in which case communication takes the form of confession.

The aspect of "taking delight" means that we not only see a person as a person, but also like what we see, enjoy and take delight in what we see, just as we do with a beautiful painting or poem—except that here the painting or poem is alive: the painting can speak to you, and the beautiful poem can answer back! This makes it very exciting and stimulating indeed. Here we see, we like, we love and appreciate a person entirely for his or her own sake, and not for the sake of anything useful that we can get out of that person. This also happens in ordinary friendship to some extent, but it happens to a far greater extent in spiritual friendship—*kalyana mitrata*. The primary meaning of *kalyana* is "beautiful." In spiritual friendship we take delight in the *spiritual* beauty of our friend; we rejoice in his or her merits.

2. The Network of Relationships

However calm, kind, and wise we may feel in the privacy of our own hearts or shrine-rooms, the true test of how fully we have developed these qualities comes when we are faced with the realities of life as represented by the challenges offered by "other people."

SOME VERSES I once composed for the dedication of a Buddhist shrine-room include the aspiration: "May our communication with one another be Sangha." This reflects the very great importance that has always been given in Buddhism to the quality of communication both between members of the Sangha and in the context of all the relationships an individual Buddhist has with other people. The Buddha had a great deal to say about communication—about the importance of truthful, kindly, meaningful, and harmonious speech, and about the necessity to pay attention to one's relationships in general, making sure that one is relating in ways that accord with one's Buddhist principles.

The reasons for this are quite obvious. To be human is to be related to other human beings. We cannot live our lives in isolation; whatever efforts we make to develop as individuals are continually tested in the fires of our relationships with other people. However calm, kind, and wise we may feel in the privacy of our own hearts or shrine-rooms, the true test of how fully we have developed these qualities comes when we are faced with the realities of life as represented by the challenges offered by "other people."

The first human being to whom we are related is of course our mother. That relationship is very intimate, and it affects us for the whole of our lives. After that, our father comes into view, and perhaps brothers and sisters as well, together with grandparents, if we are fortunate. A little later we may also become aware of aunts, uncles, and cousins. This is usually the extent of our family circle. But then there are neighbors—next door, up the street, over the way—and from the age of four or five there are teachers, schoolfellows, and friends. Later, there may be a husband or wife, and perhaps children. On top of these relationships we will probably have connections with employers and workmates, perhaps even employees. And we will also, sooner or later, have to have relationships of a kind with government officials, bureaucrats, even rulers, whether in our own country or abroad. By the time we reach maturity, we will find ourselves in the midst of a whole network of relationships with scores, perhaps hundreds, of people, and connected indirectly or distantly to very many more.

This network of relationships is the subject-matter of a Buddhist text known as the *Sigalaka Sutta,* which is to be found in the *Digha Nikaya,* the "Collection of Long Discourses," in the Pali Canon.[112] It is a comparatively early text, the substance of which, we can be reasonably certain, goes back to the Buddha himself. It is called the *Sigalaka Sutta* because it is a discourse given by the Buddha to a young man called Sigalaka. One translator describes the sutta as "Advice to Lay People." In it the Buddha lays down a pattern for different kinds of relationships, explaining how each should be conducted. All this is set forth with such clarity and succinctness that it remains of considerable interest today.

Sigalaka is a young brahmin, which means that he belongs to the priestly caste, the highest and most influential caste of Indian society. The introduction to the sutta reports that the Buddha happens to meet Sigalaka early one morning. Sigalaka's clothes and hair are still dripping wet from his purificatory ritual bath. (This is something you can still see today—brahmins standing in the holy River Ganges at Varanasi, dipping into the water and reciting mantras.) Having taken his bath, Sigalaka is engaged in worshipping the six directions: north, south, east, west, the zenith, and the nadir.

He is doing this, so he informs the Buddha, in obedience to his father's dying injunction, in order to protect himself from any harm that might come from any of the six directions. The Buddha thereupon tells Sigalaka that although worshipping the six directions is right and proper he is not going about it in the right way, if he wants such worship to protect him effectively. He then proceeds to explain what the six directions really represent.

The east, he says, means mother and father (in Indian languages mother comes before father) because one originates from them just as the sun—or at least the day—originates in the east. So the first relationship the Buddha refers to is that between parent and child. As for the other directions, they refer to the other key relationships in life: the south to the relationship between pupil and teacher; the west to that between husband and wife; the north to friends and companions; the nadir to the relationship between "master and servant" (employer and employee, in modern terms); and the zenith to the relationship between lay people and "ascetics and brahmins."

True worship of the six directions, the Buddha explains, consists in carrying out one's duties with regard to these six kinds of relationship. Such ethical activity is naturally productive of happiness, and it is in this sense that one protects oneself through this kind of "worship." Here the Buddha envisages the individual as being at the center of a network of relationships, out of which he enumerates just six. The Buddha seems to give equal emphasis to these six primary relationships, which represent a fairly wide spread of human interaction, and in this respect he is characteristic of his culture, that of northeast India in the sixth century BCE.

But most other cultures emphasize one kind of human relationship rather more than the others. For example, a similar list to the one the Buddha gave Sigalaka can be found in Confucianism, according to which there are five standard relationships: between ruler and subject (sometimes described as prince and minister), between parent and child, between husband and wife, between brother and brother, and between friend and friend. But in ancient China particular emphasis was always placed on the relationship between parents and children, and especially on the duties of children toward parents. According to some Confucian writers, filial piety is the greatest of all virtues, and in classical times sons and daughters who were conspicuous examples of it were officially honored by the government with a title, or a grant of a large piece of land, or a monument erected in their honor. The whole idea can only seem rather strange to us now, living as we do in very different times, when independence from one's parents is the goal as far as most people are concerned.

Turning to the ancient Greeks, we find no particular list of significant relationships. However, if we take Plato's account of the teachings of Socrates as representative of the highest Greek ideals, it is clear that for them the relationship between friend and friend was the most significant. The moving description of Socrates' death puts this emphasis into stark perspective. Some time before his death we find him bidding a rather formal farewell to his wife and children, who are nevertheless described as sobbing bitterly. He then dismisses them, and devotes his last hours to philosophical discussion with his friends.

In medieval Europe, on the other hand, the emphasis was placed on the relationship between master and servant, particularly that between the feudal lord and the vassal. Such was the centrality of this relationship that a whole social system was built around it. In the feudal system the great virtue was loyalty, especially to the person directly above you in the social pecking order. If you were a great lord it would be the king; if you were a small landowner it would be the local lord; if you were an ordinary servant or serf it would be your knight. And you would be prepared and willing to die for your feudal superior.

In the modern West, of course, we find the main emphasis placed upon the sexual or romantic relationship. One may move from one such relationship to another, but through all these ups and downs, their current sexual relationship nevertheless remains the central relationship for most people, giving meaning and color to their lives. The romantic relationship is the principal subject-matter of films, novels, plays, and poems, and as an ideal it is all-consuming—lovers commonly declare that they cannot live without each other, even that they are prepared to die for each other. Thus for most people in our culture, the sexual/romantic relationship is the central and most important one—an idea which people of the ancient civilizations would

FRIENDS AND TEACHERS ~ 495

probably have found ridiculous. This is not to say that they would necessarily have been right, but we can at least remind ourselves that people have not always felt as we feel today.

In the modern West other relationships often tend to be superficial because they are simply not given the same weight. We tend to neglect our relationships with our parents and with our friends, rarely taking these relationships as seriously as we do our romantic liaisons. That, we think, is the way things are meant to be. We tend to think that the tremendous value we give to this particular relationship compared with the lesser value we accord to others is perfectly normal; indeed, we are apt to assume that it has always been like that everywhere in the world. But that, as we have seen, is not really the case. On the contrary, our position is a distinctly abnormal one—no other society has raised the sexual relationship so high above all others.

Quite apart from the neglect of other relationships, our attitude has the unfortunate result of overloading the romantic relationship. We come to expect from our sexual partner far more than he or she is able to give. If we are not careful we expect him or her to be everything for us: sexual partner, friend, companion, mother, father, adviser, counsellor, source of security—everything. We expect this relationship to give us love, security, happiness, fulfillment, and the rest. We expect it to give meaning to our lives, and in this way it becomes like an electrical cable carrying a current that is too much for it. The result is that the poor, unfortunate sexual relationship very often blows a fuse—it breaks down under the strain. The obvious solution is to work at the development of a greater spread of relationships, all of which are important to us, and to all of which we give great care and attention.

But one can see it the other way round too. As well as contributing to the decline of other relationships, the present-day centrality of the sexual or marital relationship also reflects the fact that other relationships have become more difficult or have tended to fall into abeyance. Teacher-pupil, employer-employee, and ruler-subject relationships have all been seriously depersonalized—indeed, often they are not seen as relations that should involve a personal element at all. But this was not the case in older societies. Centuries ago—as little as a hundred and fifty years ago in some areas of Europe—if you were a servant or an apprentice, you would probably have lived with your master under the same roof. You would have shared in his day-to-day existence, eating the same food at the same table, just as though you were a member of the family, albeit one who knew his or her place. Under the traditional apprenticeship system, a very close personal relationship could grow up between master and apprentice or servant, or in modern terms, between employer and employee.

The novels of Dickens, which date from the 1840s, by which time the industrial age was well under way, could still portray the relation between master and servant in distinctly feudal terms, because those terms were still a reality for many people. When in *The Pickwick Papers* Sam Weller, Mr. Pickwick's faithful servant, wants to get married, Mr. Pickwick naturally offers to release Sam from his service. Sam declares his intention to stay with Mr. Pickwick, who says, "My good fellow, you are bound to consider the young woman also." But Sam says that she will be happy to wait for him. "If she don't, she's not the young woman I took her to be, and I give her up with readiness." His duty, he says, is to serve Mr. Pickwick.

In this way he was harking back to the situation where you served a feudal chief who led you in battle, who was more powerful than you, who protected you, and to whom you were unconditionally loyal. This commitment made it a truly personal relationship, and very often the most important relationship in a man's life, even emotionally, and one for which other relationships would be sacrificed if necessary.

This attitude was still around to some extent in the East when I was there in the 1950s. In Kalimpong I sometimes had to engage Tibetan or Nepalese cooks, handymen, or gardeners, and it was noticeable that they quickly became very loyal. They weren't interested in just getting the money at the end of the month. Some of them didn't even want to work for money at all. They were much more concerned to have a decent relationship with a good master.

Nowadays, for better or worse, all this is on the way out, with the steady incursion of Western values. The very word "master" makes people today feel slightly uneasy. The result is that you cannot generally have any truly personal relationship with your employer. You work not for a master but for a department in a company, and your work is overseen by people who have more power than you, but no loyalty or commitment to you. Only in truly archaic situations, like an army regiment, in which loyalty and devotion to duty is the key to success, do you still find anything like this sort of relationship. Likewise, we have a very remote, impersonal relationship with those who are meant to protect our interests, and we certainly don't think in terms of serving them. You may, once or twice in your lifetime, get round to shaking hands with your local Member of Parliament or Congressman, but usually that's about as close to them as you are likely to get.

One might think that the relation between teacher and pupil would be a naturally personal one; it certainly can be so in the tutorial system of some universities. However, in general, teaching these days is a businesslike process of passing pupils from one teacher to another in the hope that a balanced ingestion of facts will result. Under the usual classroom system, one teacher sometimes has to address as many as forty pupils, and then moves on to teach another large group. A relationship is necessarily an individual thing, and it is virtually impossible to develop such relationships with every pupil in your care in such circumstances. Nor can you have favorites, as this will lead to resentment.

Anyway, most of us come in contact with teachers only when we are comparatively young, so that any relationship we might have with a teacher never gets a chance to mature. We don't generally think in terms of learning anything beyond the point at which we stop accumulating qualifications; that is the end of the teacher-pupil relationship for us, although certain relationships later on may involve an unofficial mentoring element which can have a profound effect on our development.

In modern life, relationships between friends are not, in the case of men anyway, meant to go deep enough to produce problems. We tend to keep such relationships at an easygoing, undemanding level, probably because in many people's minds there is a fear of homosexuality. Any strong emotional relationship between two people of the same sex, especially between two men, tends in our times to be rather suspect.

We can also say that relationships among brothers and sisters are much less important than formerly. One obvious reason for this is that some of us don't have brothers and sisters. It is all too common to find oneself an only child—very different from the large families of earlier times, when (especially before the advent of the Welfare State) members of the family would be expected to care for one another.

The fact that these various kinds of relationship have become more superficial means that we are left with only two effective personal relationships in our lives nowadays. The ancient Indians had six, the ancient Chinese had five, but we, for all practical purposes, have two: the parent-child relationship, and the husband-wife or boyfriend-girlfriend relationship. And of these two, it is the second that is for many people by far the more important.

Of course, there are various complicating factors in sexual relationships, the most obvious one being sex itself. Under the conditions of modern life, sexual needs are not only biological but also psychological. For example, a man will tend nowadays to associate the expression of his manhood less with his activity in the world than with his sexual activity, particularly if his work is fairly meaningless and undemanding.

Another complicating factor is that, as in most civilizations, the man-woman relationship is institutionalized—whether as marriage or as cohabitation. Apart from the parent-child relationship (which is on a rather different basis), marriage is the only one of our relationships that we legalize and institutionalize in this way. It is not just a personal understanding between two people; it involves a legal obligation, which under certain circumstances is even enforceable in a court of law. It is not always easy to make changes in such a relationship, and this can lead to difficulties.

When a conflict arises between our need to develop as an individual on the one hand and our sexual relationship on the other, the psychological pressure can build up to create intense distress. Indeed, any personal relationship has the potential to get in the way of our attempts to grow spiritually. There is something of a paradox here. On the one hand, personal relationships are absolutely necessary for human development. On the other hand, if we are committed to spiritual development, it is much easier to sustain a personal relationship with another person who is also trying to lead a spiritual life. Problems are likely to arise—especially in the context of a sexual relationship—when one of the two people wishes to engage in spiritual practice and the other does not, and such problems are difficult to resolve because we are unlikely to be completely wholehearted in our commitment to the spiritual life anyway. Part of us, so to speak, is likely to side with the other person against our spiritual aspiration, so that we may find ourselves agreeing that setting aside time to meditate, for example, is simply selfish.

Some people find that as they get involved with spiritual practice, the importance to them of their old personal relationships diminishes, at least for a time. This can be very difficult to accept. It sounds unbearably harsh to say that as you grow, you just have to leave family and friends behind in some sense. But in a way this is only to be expected. Spiritual life does involve an element of going forth. And if you are interested in things that your friends and family have little or no knowledge of or interest in, you can't help losing contact with them to some extent.

However, many people find that as they mature in their spiritual practice, their increased positivity, sensitivity, and sense of gratitude brings them into much deeper and closer relationship, especially with their families, and this is very much to be welcomed, and indeed consciously worked on. After all, as the Buddha reminded Sigalaka, our parents gave us this life, which we increasingly feel to be very meaningful and precious; great love and respect is due to them for that, whatever has happened since. At the same time, as we move more deeply into spiritual practice, we will be forming new personal relationships with other people who are trying to live a spiritual life—in other words, we are likely to join or help form a spiritual community.

3. The Importance of Spiritual Friendship

The real significance of the deep individual-to-individual contact that Going for Refuge to the Sangha involves lies in a simple psychological fact: we get to know ourselves best in relation to other people.

It has been said that the history of Buddhist philosophy can be summed up as the struggle between Buddhism and the abstract noun. So—to guard against the ubiquitous enemy, abstraction—I should be clear that when I speak of the spiritual community, I am not referring to some ethereal entity apart from the people who comprise it. Membership of a spiritual community means relationship with people within that community. But how is it that entering into relationship with other people who hold a common ideal and follow a common path should help us in our spiritual life?

In a sense, it comes down to the simple saying: "Birds of a feather flock together." That is how they survive. There was an occasion when the Buddha addressed the Vajjians, a tribe from the Vaisali area who had come under some threat. Among other things, he told them that they would prosper as long as they continued to meet regularly, in full and frequent assemblies, conducting their business in harmony and dispersing in harmony. Afterward he went on to apply the same criteria to the spiritual survival of the Sangha.[113]

The heart of the Sangha is *kalyana mitrata*, a very beautiful phrase; in fact, it is less a philosophical term than a poetic one. *Kalyana* means beautiful, charming, auspicious, helpful, morally good. Thus the connotations are aesthetic, moral, and religious. The term covers much the same ground as the Greek expression *kalon kai agathos,* which means "good and beautiful." *Mitrata* means simply friendship or companionship. *Kalyana mitrata* therefore means something like "beautiful friendship," or "morally good companionship," or—as I have translated it—"spiritual friendship." There is a well-known exchange between the Buddha and his disciple Ananda which spells out its importance to the Buddha himself. Ananda was the Buddha's cousin and became his attendant for the last twenty years of the Buddha's life. He accompanied the Buddha wherever he went, and they had an understanding that if by any chance Ananda was not present when the Buddha delivered a discourse, or discussed the Dharma with anyone, when they were alone together the Buddha would repeat to Ananda everything he had said. Ananda had an astonishingly retentive memory; he was apparently the human equivalent of a tape-recorder. Indeed, it is said that we owe our knowledge of the Buddha's teachings to him. Because he made a point of listening to everything the Buddha said, storing it away in his memory so that he could repeat it later on for the benefit of others, his testimony was used to authenticate the teachings that were preserved after the Buddha's death.

But on this particular occasion the Buddha and Ananda were on their own, just sitting quietly together, when Ananda suddenly came out with something to which he had obviously given a bit of thought. He said, "Lord, I think that kalyana mitrata is half the spiritual life." And then one presumes that he sat back and waited for some kind of appreciative affirmation from the Buddha. It seemed to Ananda that what he had said was incontrovertible: having like-minded people around you who are also trying to grow and develop must be half the battle won. But the Buddha said, "Ananda, you're wrong. Kalyana mitrata is not half the spiritual life; it's the whole of it."[114]

Why is this? Of course we learn from those we associate with, especially those who are more mature than we are, and learning will clearly be important if we are to make progress in the spiritual life. But in what does "progress in the spiritual life" really consist? What are we really learning? The knowledge we need, in the end, is self-knowledge. And the real significance of the deep individual-to-individual contact that

Going for Refuge to the Sangha involves lies in a simple psychological fact: we get to know ourselves best in relation to other people. If you spent your whole life alone on a desert island, in a sense you would never really know yourself. As it is, though, we have all had the experience of clarifying our ideas through discussion—and even of discovering that we knew more than we thought we did—simply through trying to communicate with another person. It is as though trying to communicate activates an understanding that is already there but has never manifested until now, and even brings forth new aspects of oneself—aspects which one only ever discovers as a result of contact with another person. Through meeting the challenge of real communication, one comes to know oneself better.

It is not only a matter of activating our understanding. Meeting certain people can disturb aspects of us which had been rather deeply buried. We say that particular people "bring out the worst in us." Perhaps nothing is said, but they somehow touch a raw nerve. It can be a shock to realize what that individual has evoked in us, to find ourselves behaving in a way that we like to think is uncharacteristic of us, even expressing hatred or contempt toward the person who has triggered off this uncharacteristic behavior. Of course, that unpleasant side of us was always there, but it needed that person to bring it to the surface. In this apparently negative—but highly spiritually beneficial—way too, other people can introduce us to ourselves. We cannot transform ourselves unless we have a full sense of what lies within us.

Conversely, certain people seem to "bring out the best in us." Again, nothing necessarily needs to be said, but just being with them makes us feel lighter, more cheerful, more energetic, more positive. Other people can also sometimes activate resources of kindness and decency that we didn't know we had. And in a specifically Buddhist context, there will be certain people who activate a quality of faith in us simply through contact with their own faith. Something that was not active before is stirred up.

The Sangha is necessary, in short, because personal relationships are necessary for human development. This applies at all levels—cultural, psychological, and spiritual. The vast majority of people undoubtedly develop most rapidly, and even most easily, in the company of others—or at least in contact with others. Not that it is impossible to develop entirely on one's own; indeed, there is a Buddhist term for those who do so: *pratyekabuddhas,* private or solitary Buddhas. However, although there are a number of canonical references to them, it is significant that all these solitary Buddhas are located in the remote and legendary past. There appear to be no historical examples.[115]

We generally need the stimulation, reassurance, and enthusiasm of others who are going in the same direction as we are. We are naturally stimulated by someone who shares our special interest in something. Even though we still have to put in the effort ourselves, at least we see the point of it more clearly—we are less undermined by doubts. Membership of the Sangha also gives us the opportunity to serve others, to express our generosity and helpfulness. Even in such a simple activity as providing tea and biscuits at a Buddhist festival, we can discover in ourselves the capacity for generosity, altruism, and general positivity.

Thus the Sangha is there to help us know ourselves and express ourselves better. It is able to do this because everyone who participates in it is committed to the Buddha as the ideal of self-knowledge in the highest and deepest sense, and to the Dharma, the various principles and practices by which that self-knowledge may be achieved. A common allegiance to the first two Refuges constitutes the bond of unity between the members of the spiritual community. We are all following—albeit at different stages—the same path to the same ultimate goal.

By the same token, if one is not really aiming for Enlightenment, and not really trying to practice the Dharma, then one may say that one is committed to these ideals, but whatever one may say, one is no more a member of the Sangha than a donkey following a herd of cows can be a member of that herd. This is the image used by the Buddha in the *Samyutta Nikaya:* as he puts it, "The donkey may say, 'I am a cow too, I am a cow too'... but neither in his horns nor in his hoofs is he anything like a cow, whatever he may say." Likewise, simply reciting the Refuges does not make one a member of the Sangha. The bond is inner and spiritual.[116]

At a certain point in our development, however much we may meditate and read books about spiritual practice, we have to recognize that these are not enough. There is no doubt that we can learn a lot on our own. But if we are to grow spiritually in a fully rounded way, we eventually have to experience the vital part that communication has to play in our spiritual life. The following verse comes from the *Dhammapada,* a very early collection of the Buddha's teachings, here quoted in the original Pali:

> *Sukho buddhanamuppado,*
> *sukha saddhammadesana.*
> *Sukha sanghassa samaggi,*
> *samagganam tapo sukho.*[117]

The first line means "happy—or blissful, or blessed (*sukho*)—is the arising of the Buddhas." When someone becomes a Buddha, this is a happy thing for all humanity. The second line may be translated "Happy is the preaching of the true doctrine." The teaching of the Dharma is a blessing for the whole world. The third line is "Happy is the spiritual community in following a common path." In the fourth line *tapo* means "heat" and refers to spiritual practices which are like a fire burning up all impurities. The line therefore runs, "The blaze of spiritual practice of those on the same path is happy or blessed."

So, it is not enough to have a distant idea of Enlightenment, the theory of the Buddha's teaching, or a Buddhist organization. There is no future for Buddhism without a truly united and committed spiritual community, dedicated to practicing together. And when Buddhists do come together in the true spirit of the Sangha, there is then the possibility of inhabiting, for a while at least, the *dharmadhatu,* the realm of the Dharma. In this realm, all we do is practice the Dharma, all we talk about is the Dharma, and when we are still and silent, we enjoy the Dharma in stillness and silence together. The clouds of stress and anxiety that so often hang over mundane life are dispersed, and the fountains of inspiration within our hearts are renewed.

4. Friendship: the Whole of the Spiritual Life?

No one else can practice the Dharma for us; we have to practice it ourselves. But we do not have to practice it *by* ourselves.

IN THE MODERN WORLD, friendship is arguably the most neglected of all the primary human relationships. But as we have seen, according to the Buddha himself, friendship has a direct connection with the spiritual life. Speaking to Sigalaka on the subject, he says that friends and companions are to be served and looked after in five ways.[118] In other words, we have five duties toward our friends, and if we perform these, our friendships will flourish.

First of all, it is our duty to be generous. We should share with our friends whatever we have. This should ideally be taken quite literally. Some Buddhist residential communities live on the basis of a common purse, pooling all their resources. This isn't easy to do, of course—some people find it difficult even to share a book—but it reflects the ideal relationship between friends. Ideally, your friend should not even have to *ask* you for money. If you take the principle of sharing seriously, you share everything: time, money, resources, interest, energy, everything. You keep nothing back for yourself.

The second duty is never to speak harshly or bitterly or sarcastically to our friends, but always kindly and compassionately. Speech is taken very seriously in Buddhism. The five basic Buddhist precepts include just one speech precept—to refrain from false speech—but it is not enough just to speak truthfully, and this is reflected in the ten precepts taken by some Buddhists. These include no less than four speech precepts, because it is so easy to fall into harmful, destructive speech, to speak in an indifferent, careless, or even callous way.

Our third duty to our friends is to look after their welfare, especially their spiritual welfare. As well as seeing that they are all right in terms of their health and economic well-being, and helping them with any difficulties they have, we should help them in whatever way we can to grow and develop as human beings.

Fourthly, we should treat our friends in the same way that we treat ourselves. This is a very big thing indeed, because it means breaking down the barrier between oneself and others. One of the most important Mahayana texts, the *Bodhicaryavatara* of Santideva, deals with this topic in great depth and considerable detail.[119]

And fifthly, we should keep the promises we make to our friends. We should keep our word. If we say we will do something for a friend, we just do it, come what may. If we are careless about fulfilling our promises, it is usually because we make them carelessly. We therefore have a duty to make our promises so mindfully that we treat them as serious obligations. Once we have given our word, that should be that.

Just as we have these five duties toward our friends, they have the same duties toward us; it's a two-way thing. Our friends and companions minister to us, serve us, reciprocate our friendship. Having listed our duties toward our friends, the *Sigalaka Sutta* therefore gives a list of five ways in which our good friends look after us. Firstly, according to the sutta, they take care of us when we are sick. Secondly, they watch over our property when we are neglectful; in other words they take more care of our possessions than we do ourselves—that is a sure sign of friendship. Thirdly, they are our refuge in time of fear: they can allay our anxiety, and if we have genuine cause for fear they help us deal with the situation. Fourthly, they do not forsake us when we are in trouble; as the proverb says, "A friend in need is a friend indeed." And lastly, they show concern for our dependants. If we have children, our friends are just as concerned for their welfare as we are ourselves, and the same goes for the welfare of our disciples, if we happen to have disciples.

These, in brief, are the duties of a friend. Clearly they represent a very high ideal of friendship, and they repay careful reflection. Here I will just point out one or two salient features. It is interesting, for example, that the first four duties are identical with another well-known list that occupies an important place in Mahayana Buddhism: the four samgrahavastus, usually translated as the four elements of conversion.[120] These form part of the seventh *paramita,* the seventh of the ten Perfections to be practiced by the Bodhisattva: *upaya-paramita,* the perfection of *upaya* or skillful means. The four *samgra-havastus* are thus an aspect of the Bodhisattva's skillful means.

The fact that these elements of conversion are the same as the first four duties of a friend says something deeply significant about how the Sangha operates at its best. It suggests that the best way of converting people is simply by being friends with them. Some people try to convert others to their point of view or their religion almost forcibly, but this is not the Buddhist way. Buddhists should convert people—if that is really the right word—simply by being friendly. We make friends and that's an end of it. There is no need to preach to people, to knock on their doors and say, "Have you heard the word of the Buddha?"

As a Buddhist one should not be thinking about "converting" people, or in any way maneuvering them onto the path that one follows oneself. One's business is just to be a friend, to be generous, to share whatever one has, to speak kindly and affectionately, to show concern for one's friends' welfare, especially their spiritual welfare, to treat them in the same way that one treats oneself, and to keep one's word to them.

However, the fact that these four things are elements of conversion means that in themselves they constitute a communication of the Dharma. You communicate the Dharma itself by practicing friendship in this way. One could even go so far as to say that friendship *is* the Dharma. William Blake, the great English poet, artist and mystic,

508 ~ THE ESSENTIAL SANGHARAKSHITA

said, "Religion is politics." But he went on to say: "Politics is brother-hood."[121] Religion, therefore, is brotherhood. We can say, following him, that the Dharma is friendship. If you are practicing friendliness you are not only practicing the Dharma, but communicating it.

One further issue raised by the duties of friendship has particularly important implications. It concerns the fourth duty: treating our friends and companions like our own self. The Sanskrit term, here, is *samanarthata*—*saman* meaning equal. A friend is one whom you treat equally. But what does this mean? A clue is to be found in the etymology of the word friend, which is apparently cognate with the word free. Friendship is a relationship that can exist only between two or more free people—that is to say, people who are equals. Understanding this, the ancient Greeks maintained that there could be no friendship between a free man and a slave.

We can take this metaphorically as well as literally. Friendship, we can conclude, can never involve any kind of power relationship. The relation between master and slave is based upon power, and where one person has any kind of power over another, there can be no friendship, because friendship is based upon love—to use the word love in the sense of the Pali term *metta* rather than in the sharply dif-ferentiated sense of the term *pema,* which is love as sticky attachment or possessiveness. *Pema* is fundamentally selfish, and it can easily turn into hatred; sexual love, of course, is often of this kind. But metta is unselfish or non-attached, concerned only with the happiness and well-being of others.

The Pali word for friend, *mitta* (Sanskrit *mitra*), is closely related to the term *metta* (Sanskrit *maitri*). With the help of the metta bhavana meditation practice we can develop a friendly attitude. In other words, we can shift from operating in the power mode to operating in the love mode. There are many ways of operating in the power mode—that is, focusing on getting what we want in a situation that involves other people. Usually, if we are clever enough, we don't have to use force. Subtly and indirectly we manipulate other people into doing what we want them to do, not for their good but for our own purposes. Some people are very good at this. They are so subtle, they seem so unselfish and so frank, that you hardly know that you are being manipulated, and it's so indirect that they may not even realize they're doing it. But in one way or another we deceive people, and ourselves, as to our real motives. We cheat, we lie, we commit emotional blackmail. But in metta, in friendship, there is none of this, but only mutual concern for each other's happiness and well-being.

Thus, friendship has a definitely spiritual dimension. We see this in chapter four of the *Udana*, in which we find the Buddha staying at a place called Calika, accompanied by his attendant, who is at this time a monk called Meghiya. The two of them are alone together one day when Meghiya, who seems to be quite a young monk, happens to see a lovely grove of mango trees. In India you often get these on the outskirts of a village; the trees are very beautiful, with an abundance of dark green leaves, and they grow close together, so that as well as producing mangoes, they provide cool shade in the hot Indian summer.

Meghiya thinks to himself, "What a beautiful grove of mango trees! And what a very fine place in which to sit and meditate—so cool and refreshing!" He therefore asks the Buddha if he may go and spend some time there. The Buddha, however, asks him to wait a while until some other monk arrives, because, for one reason or another, the Buddha needs someone to be with him. But Meghiya is not concerned with what the Buddha needs. Instead, he comes up with a clever and apparently unanswerable argument. He says, "It's all very well for you—you've reached the goal of Enlightenment—but I have a long way to go in my practice. It's such a beautiful mango grove, I really want to go there and meditate." In the end the Buddha has to agree, and off Meghiya goes, leaving the Buddha on his own. However, although Meghiya has got what he wanted, and the mango grove turns out to be just the fine, peaceful place he thought it was going to be, he finds that he can't settle into his meditation at all. Despite his enthusiasm and energy, as soon as he sits down his mind is overwhelmed with greed, jealousy, anger, lust, false views—the lot. He just doesn't know what to do.

In the end he trudges back to the Buddha and reports on his abject failure. The Buddha doesn't scold him, but he gives him a teaching. He says, "Meghiya, when you are spiritually immature there are five things that conduce to spiritual maturity. And the first of these is spiritual friendship. The second thing is the practice of ethics; and the third is serious discussion of the Dharma. Fourthly, you need to direct energy toward eliminating negative mental states and developing positive ones. And fifthly, you must cultivate insight in the sense of a deep understanding of universal impermanence."[122]

In marking out these five things as necessary for the spiritually undeveloped, of course the Buddha was implying that Meghiya should put spiritual friendship first. If you have a spiritual friend, whether the Buddha or someone much less eminent, that one cannot be disregarded in the careless way that Meghiya has brushed off the Buddha. But like Meghiya, we are often unaware of the extent to which we are dependent spiritually on having personal contact with our spiritual friends, particularly those who are more developed than we are. It is very difficult to make any spiritual progress without them. The Buddha himself is no longer around, but most of us, like Meghiya, would not be ready for such a friend anyway. We would probably act in one way or another rather as Meghiya did.

We may not have the Buddha, but we do have one another. We can help one another and encourage one another in our practice of the Dharma. We can confess our faults and weaknesses to one another. We can share our understanding with one another. We can rejoice in one another's merits. In these ways we can make a practice of spiritual friendship.

No one else can practice the Dharma for us; we have to practice it ourselves. But we do not have to practice it *by* ourselves. We can practice it in the company of other like-minded people who are trying to do the same, and this is the best way—in fact, the only effective way— to practice.

As the Buddha was to say to his disciple and cousin Ananda, some years later at a place called Sakka, "Spiritual friendship is the whole of the spiritual life." But how are we to take this? We can understand that friendship is important, but the idea that friendship, even spiritual friendship, should be the whole of the spiritual life, does seem hard to swallow. But let us look a little more closely at what is being said here.

The Pali word I have translated as "spiritual life" is *brahmacariya*, which sometimes means celibacy or chastity—that is to say abstention from sexual activity—but in this context it has a much wider meaning. It consists of two parts. *Brahma* means high, noble, best, sublime, and real; it also means divine, not in the theistic sense but in the sense of the embodiment of the best and noblest qualities and virtues. And *cariya* means walking, faring, practicing, experiencing, even living. Hence *brahmacariya* means something like "practicing the best" or "experiencing the ideal"; we could even render it "the divine life," or just "spiritual life."

There is a further aspect to the term *brahmacariya* that brings us to a deeper understanding of what it means in this context. In early Buddhism there is a whole series of terms beginning with *brahma*, and one of these is *brahmaloka*, which means the sublime realm, the divine world, or simply the spiritual world in the highest sense. So the *brahmacariya* or spiritual life is that way of life that leads to the *brahmaloka* or spiritual world. But how is it able to do this? For the answer, we must turn to yet another early Buddhist text: the *Mahagovinda Sutta*. Without going into the background to this sutta—it's a long story—we find in it this very question being asked: "How does a mortal reach the immortal brahma world?" In other words, how can one pass from the transient to the eternal? And the answer given is short and simple. "One reaches the brahma world by giving up all possessive thoughts, all thoughts of me and mine." In other words, one reaches the brahmaloka by giving up egoism and selfishness, by giving up all sense of "I."[123]

Thus the intimate connection between spiritual friendship and spiritual life starts to come into focus. Spiritual friendship is a training in unselfishness, in egolessness. You share everything with your friend or friends. You speak to them kindly and affectionately, and show concern for their welfare, especially their spiritual welfare. You treat them in the same way you treat yourself—that is, you treat them as being equal with yourself. You relate to them with an attitude of metta, not according to where the power between you lies. Of course this is very difficult; it goes against the grain, because we are naturally selfish. The development of spiritual friendship is very difficult. Leading the spiritual life is very difficult. Being a Buddhist—a real Buddhist—is very difficult. We need help.

And we get that help not only from our teachers but also from one another. We can't be with our spiritual teacher all the time, but we can be with our spiritual friends all the time, or at least much of the time. We can see them regularly, perhaps live with them, perhaps even work with them. If we spend time with spiritual friends in this way, we will get to know them better, and they will get to know us better. We will learn to be more open and honest, we will be brought up against our weaknesses, and in particular we will be brought up against our natural tendency to operate in accordance with the power mode. If we have spiritual friends, they will try not to relate to us in this way and they will expect us to operate in the love mode as well, to relate to them with metta. Learning to relate to our friends in this way, we will gradually learn to respond to the whole world with metta, with unselfishness. It is in this way that spiritual friendship is indeed the whole of the spiritual life.

5. Is a Guru Necessary?

One could say that there are many misconceptions about the guru, but only one true conception.

Is a guru necessary? This is not a question that is likely ever to have occurred to anyone at the time of the Buddha; then, the first question anyone would have asked you would have been, "Who is your teacher?," not "Do you think a teacher is necessary?" But this question will inevitably arise sooner or later for anyone today who is genuinely trying to develop as an individual, trying to be authentically himself or herself. In particular, it is likely to arise if one attempts quite specifically and consciously to follow what we usually refer to as the spiritual path, and it will demand an answer all the more imperatively when one tries to follow that spiritual path in one or another of its oriental forms.

However, before we address the question itself, we must banish the haze of imaginative associations that gather around the magic word "guru." We must, unfortunately, dispel the vision of brilliant blue skies, beautiful white snow peaks, and, just above the snow line, the snug little caves which are in the popular imagination the natural habitat of that rare creature, the guru. We must come down to earth from those inaccessible valleys of Shangri-la in which benign and wise old men with long white beards and starry eyes pass on the secret of the very highest teaching to a very few devoted disciples. We must ruthlessly dismiss any notion of those lucky disciples effortlessly floating up to nirvana on the strength of having secured the most advanced techniques from the most esoteric lineage holder.

We need to consider the whole question of the guru in as sober and matter-of-fact a fashion as possible, and try to understand what a guru is, and what a guru is not. On that basis, it should become clear to what extent and in what way a guru is necessary, if at all. We can also consider the attitudes it may be appropriate to adopt in relation to the guru.

Let us begin by seeing what a guru is not. First of all, a guru is not the head of a religious group. By a religious group I do not mean a spiritual community, but rather a number of non-individuals organized into a power structure around the forms or conventions of some kind of religious practice. Religious groups are of many kinds—sects, churches, monasteries, and so on—and they each have someone at their head. Such heads are regarded with great veneration by other members of the group, but there is likely to be something unfocused or off-key about this devotion. They are venerated not for what they are in themselves, as individuals, but for what they represent, what they stand for, even what they symbolize.

It might seem obvious that they should stand for or symbolize something spiritual; and in a superficial sense they do. But in fact they represent the group itself. That they are the head of a group is their principal significance. It is easy to see when this is the case; you just have to wait for the head of a group to be criticized or even vilified, as in course of time will inevitably happen. Members of groups usually feel that an attack on the head of their group is an attack on them. Any disrespect shown to the head of the group by those outside the group is interpreted by group members as lack of respect for the group itself.

The Buddha refused to countenance any such attitude among his followers. The *Brahmajala Sutta* of the *Digha Nikaya* tells the story of how the Buddha and a great crowd of his followers were once traveling on foot between Rajagaha and Nalanda, and found themselves in company with a wanderer called Suppiya and a follower of his, a young man called Brahmadatta. These two, in the hearing of the Buddha and his followers, began to argue, and kept arguing as they walked. And the subject of their argument, one can imagine, must have upset some of the Buddha's disciples considerably. For Suppiya, the text tells us, was finding fault in all sorts of ways with the Buddha, the Dharma, and the Sangha—though Brahmadatta was praising them just as strongly. All the travelers found themselves staying in the same place overnight, and still Suppiya and Brahmadatta kept on arguing.

Not surprisingly, when dawn came, the Buddha's followers gathered together and started talking among themselves about this disconcerting behavior on the part of their fellow travelers. Coming to join them, the Buddha asked them what they had just been talking about, and they told him. Reading between the lines here, we can gather that they were somewhat upset, even angry, at what had happened. But the Buddha said: "Monks, if anyone should speak in disparagement of me, of the Dhamma, or of the Sangha, you should not be angry or displeased at such disparagement; that would only be a hindrance to you."

Nor did the Buddha let the matter rest there. He said: "If others disparage me, the Dhamma or the Sangha, and you are angry or displeased, can you recognize whether what they say is right or not?" And the monks had to admit that, in those circumstances, they would be in no state to think about things objectively.

So the Buddha said, "If others disparage me, the Dhamma or the Sangha, then you must explain what is incorrect as being incorrect, saying: 'That is incorrect, that is false, that is not our way, that is not found among us.'"[124]

If one reflects on this episode, one realizes that the Buddha is pointing out to his disciples a tendency that is all too human. If they had become angry, they might have thought that their anger had arisen because the Buddha was being criticized, but in fact it was probably because the group to which they belonged was being criticized, and so, in effect, *they* were being criticized. A disciple in that position might well feel that his wisdom in being a member of that group, and a follower of the person being criticized, was being called into question.

Examples of such sensitivity are not confined to the Pali Canon. I have come across Buddhists who would hunt through books on comparative religion, dictionaries of religion and philosophy, and the like, to see if they could find unfavorable references to Buddhism. When they found them, they would write to the publishers, call public meetings, and organize protests and demonstrations. It seemed that little short of stringing up the unfortunate person responsible for the offending comments could pacify them. The most interesting aspect of the whole business was that the Buddhists who thus spluttered and seethed with rage were invariably convinced that they were thereby demonstrating their devotion to the Dharma. What they were exhibiting, however, was their group spirit—a thing that has nothing to do with the spiritual life or the Buddha's teaching.

Hence a guru is not the head of a religious group. Nor is he an ecclesiastical superior, someone high up in the power structure of a religious group. When prominent religious personalities come from the East, they are sometimes heralded by advance publicity in which one is told that this particular personality is in charge of an important group of monasteries, or that he is second-in-command of an ancient and historic temple. Sometimes in India one is told simply that he is very wealthy. I was once in Calcutta [Kolkata] at a time when preparations were being made for the arrival of a monk from a famous temple in Sri Lanka, and I was told by the head monk of the temple where I was staying that I ought to go and see him, as he was very important and influential. Naturally I asked, "In what way is he important?" The head monk replied, "He's the richest monk in Sri Lanka." It was on that basis that I was expected to go and pay my respects to him.

This is an extreme example, but it is representative of a general expectation that one should be impressed by people who are higher up in the ecclesiastical structure, and regard them as gurus. But a guru is not this sort of figure at all. Someone who is organizationally important or influential is not thereby a guru.

A guru is not a teacher either—a statement that may come as something of a surprise. It is comparatively easy to understand that a guru is not the head of a religious group, but it is quite usual to think that a spiritual teacher is just what a guru is supposed to be. But what is meant by a teacher? A teacher is one who communicates information. A geography teacher teaches facts and figures about the earth; a psychology teacher teaches facts and figures about the human mind. In the same way, a teacher of religion may teach the general history of all the different religions of the world, or the theology or doctrinal system of a particular tradition. But a guru, as such, doesn't teach religion. In fact, he or she doesn't necessarily teach anything at all.

People may ask questions, and he may answer those questions—whether or not he does so is up to him. But he has no vested interest in teaching. If nobody asked him any questions, he probably wouldn't bother to say anything. The Buddha himself made this perfectly clear. In several places in the Pali scriptures he is reported as saying that he has no *ditthi*—no view, no philosophy, no system of thought. "There are lots of other teachers," he says, "who have this system of thought to expound, or that philosophy to teach; but I have none. I have no 'view' to communicate. The Tathagata (Buddha) is free from views, liberated from doctrines, emancipated from philosophy."[125]

Outside the Pali Canon the Buddha is further reported as saying that he has no Dharma to impart. The great *Diamond Sutra* describes innumerable Bodhisattvas and disciples sitting and waiting for the Buddha to teach them the Dharma. But the Buddha tells them, "I have nothing to teach."[126] In another celebrated Mahayana text, the *Lankavatara Sutra,* the Buddha goes so far as to say that he has never taught anything. "Whether you have heard me speaking or not, the truth is that from the night of my Enlightenment, all through the forty-five years until the night of my parinirvana, the night of my passing from the world, I have not uttered a single word."[127] So the Buddha, the ultimate Buddhist guru, has no view, no teaching to impart. He is not a teacher.

Something else that the guru is not relates to one of the most striking facts about the human race as a whole, which is that the majority of its members do not grow up. People develop physically, of course, and they also develop intellectually in the sense that they learn how to organize their knowledge more and more coherently. But they don't grow up spiritually, or even emotionally. Many people remain emotionally immature, even infantile. They want to depend on someone stronger than themselves, someone who is prepared to love and protect them absolutely and unconditionally. They don't really want to be responsible for themselves. They want some authority or system to make their decisions for them.

When one is young, one depends on one's parents, but as one grows older, one is usually obliged to find substitutes for them. Many people find such a substitute in a romantic relationship, which is one of the reasons marriage is so popular, and also, often, so difficult. Others find their parent-surrogate in a concept of a personal God. One might even follow Freud in saying that God is a father-substitute on a cosmic scale. The believer expects from God the kind of love and protection that a child expects from his or her parents. It is highly significant that in Christianity, God is addressed as "our Father."

The role of father-substitute is often played by a guru—or rather a pseudo-guru. Mahatma Gandhi, for instance, was a great Indian politician, thinker, activist, even revolutionary, but it is rather significant that as a religious figure for much of his life he was addressed by his disciples as Bapu, "Father." Nor was this sort of title at all unusual in India. When I lived there I was in contact with quite a number of religious groups and their gurus, many of whom liked to be addressed as Dadaji, or "Grandfather." Their disciples, it seemed, were only too happy to fall in with their wishes in this respect.

This rather amused me, and when I was in Kalimpong and had some pupils of my own—most of them Nepalese rather than Indian—I asked them out of curiosity how they regarded me. At that time I was about thirty, and they were in their late teens and early twenties, so when they clasped their hands together and said with great fervor, "Oh sir, you are just like our grandfather," I was taken rather by surprise.

In India I also met a number of female gurus, and they were invariably addressed as Mataji, "Mother," or even Ma, which means "Mommy." One of these gurus, who was well into middle-age when I first got to know her, was surrounded by young male followers, most of whom, as I discovered later, had lost their mothers. In the evenings they would gather in the meeting-hall to sit gazing up at "Mommy" and singing in chorus the word Ma—nothing else, just that word, "Mommy"—to the accompaniment of drums and cymbals. They would keep it up for two or three hours at a time: "Ma, Ma, Ma, Ma, Ma." They believed that what they called "Ma-ism" was a radical new development in religious history, and that the worship of Mother—this particular mother, anyway—would be the future religion of humanity. I was not at all surprised to find that there was intense competitiveness and jealousy among her disciples, as if they were all vying with one another to be the favorite, if not the only, son. It was also noticeable that they tended to disparage other groups. In the same way that children will say, "My daddy is much stronger/richer than your daddy" or "Our house is bigger than your house," they would maintain that in comparison with their own guru, other gurus were insignificant.[128]

Fortunately, I have known gurus who knew how to manage their followers in a much healthier manner—particularly certain Tibetan gurus. A story about three great lamas I knew personally in Kalimpong will illustrate this. All three were eminent lamas of deep and genuine spiritual experience, and they all had many disciples. Though they all belonged to the predominantly "Red Hat" tradition, their characters were very different. One wore a sheepskin robe, dyed red, and was always on the move, so that it was difficult to catch him. Another lived with his wife and son, and gave initiation to thousands of people—initiations that were said to be particularly powerful. The third was the scholarly head of an important monastery.

The story I was told by one of their disciples—and they had a number of disciples in common—was that a discussion had once arisen among the disciples as to which of the three gurus was the greatest. In the end, one of the bolder spirits plucked up courage and approached one of the gurus. He said, "Look, there's been a lot of discussion as to how the three of you would place yourselves with respect to each other. We all have immense veneration for all three of you, but we would appreciate it if you could clear up this point: Which of you is the greatest? Who has gone furthest? Who is nearest to nirvana?" So the guru smiled and said, "All right, I'll tell you. It is true that among us three there is one who is much more highly developed than the other two. But none of you will ever know which one that is."

A real guru does not fall into the role of a father figure. This is not to say that people do not need father-substitutes, at least for a while. Such a projection may be necessary for their psychological development. One must also allow that the function of the guru is analogous to that of the true father: the guru fulfills the same function on a spiritual level that the true father fulfills on the ordinary human level. But the guru is not a substitute for a father where the father has been lack-ing, or where he is still required.

Neither should a guru be taken for a problem-solver. This brings us to a distinction that I find it helpful to draw between a problem and a difficulty. The difference is that a difficulty can be overcome or resolved with effort, whereas a problem cannot. If you put a lot of effort into what I call a problem, you only make it more problematic. It's like finding a knot in a piece of string and pulling on the two ends in order to untie it. You can pull as hard as you like, but you'll only suc-ceed in tightening the knot. The genuine guru may help people over-come their difficulties, but he will not attempt to grapple with their problems.

There are fundamentally two kinds of problem: doctrinal prob-lems and personal, usually psychological, problems. The problems of Westerners tend to be of the second type, whereas in the East people's problems are often doctrinal—they want to resolve technical ques-tions to do with nirvana, the *skandhas,* the *samskaras,* and so on. How-ever, even such doctrinal problems are very often psychologically motivated, or at least psychologically oriented. One asks even the most abstract theoretical question ultimately for personal psycholog-ical reasons, though usually one is not conscious of this.

If you have a problem, it embodies a self-contradictory situation; it cannot be solved on its own terms. But if you bring it to your guru, you are in effect asking him or her to solve the problem on its own terms. For instance, a woman comes along in great distress, so upset that she can hardly speak. Eventually she tells her guru that she just can't live with her husband any longer. She's had enough. If she has to put up with any more, she'll go stark staring mad. She's just got to leave him. But her problem is that if she leaves her husband, she will have to leave her children too—because the children cannot be taken away from their father—and leaving her children is no less impossible than con-tinuing to live with her husband. She will go mad if she has to stay with her husband, but she will also go mad if she has to leave her children. "What am I to do?" she asks her guru expectantly.

Then somebody else comes along and complains of lack of energy: "I'm always tired," he says. "I feel exhausted all the time, constantly at a low ebb, totally depleted. I can't do a thing. I don't seem able to work up any interest in anything; I just lie around all day like a limp, wet rag. I can watch a bit of television or listen to the radio, but that's it. I feel utterly drained all the time. There's just one thing that I know will help: meditation. I can get energy through meditation—I'm convinced of that." So the guru says, "Well, why don't you meditate?" And the unfortunate disciple replies wearily, "I just don't have the energy."

But if the guru has to send this person away with his problem still unresolved, there are still more problems waiting in the wings. To take yet another example, someone comes along and says that he just wants to be happy. That's all he asks from life. And he feels that he could be perfectly happy if only someone would give him a satisfactory reason for being happy. He has examined all the reasons offered by religions, philosophies, and friends, but none of them has proved truly convincing. Can the guru do better? If anyone has the answer, surely the guru will. Surely a guru is there to provide the answers to the big problems. Of course, the guru knows quite well that every reason he can produce will be rejected as unsatisfactory. But still the man demands a reason.

If you asked any of these people what they are really looking for, all of them would say that they want to find a solution to their problem. That is why they have come to the guru. They firmly believe he can solve their problems if he chooses to do so. But, in fact, this is not the situation at all. What these people really want to do is defeat the guru. They present their problem in such a way that the guru cannot solve it without their consent or cooperation—which they have no intention of giving.

Such people are sometimes very cunning. Especially in the East they will very often approach the guru with a great show of devotion and humility, bearing presents, making offerings, bowing, and declaring their unshakable faith in the guru. They say, "I've taken this problem of mine to lots of other gurus, to all the most famous teachers and masters, and not one of them could solve it. But I've heard so much about you, and I'm sure that you are the one person who can."

Only a guru who lacks experience, or isn't a true guru, will be taken in by all this. The true guru will see what is going on at once, and will refuse to play the role of problem-solver, even if, as is very likely, the person with the problem goes away disgruntled, and starts saying that the guru cannot be a true guru because he hasn't got the down-to-earth compassion to deal with his disciples' problems. Some gurus are rewarded with quite damaged reputations for refusing to play this sort of game.

So a guru is not the head of a religious group, or a teacher, or a father-substitute, or a problem-solver. This does not mean that he or she may not, from time to time, function in these ways, and in many others. A guru can function, for instance, as a physician, a psychotherapist, an artist, a poet, a musician, or even just a friend. But he or she will not identify with any of these roles.

The guru may be the head of a religious group, although this rarely happens, because the qualities that make a guru are not those that assist promotion within an ecclesiastical system. Much more often, particularly within the Buddhist Sangha, the guru may be a teacher—that is, he or she may function outwardly as a teacher. But it remains important to distinguish the teacher from the guru as such. Some gurus may be teachers, but by no means all teachers are gurus. A guru may even function as a provisional father-substitute or problem-solver, but the emphasis is on "provisional." As soon as possible, he or she will discard this role and function as a guru.

But if the guru is none of these things, what is a guru? It has been said that there are many different ways of being wicked, but only one way of being good (which in the eyes of some people makes goodness seem rather dull). One could also say that there are many misconceptions about the guru, but only one true conception. There is therefore much that can be said about what a guru is not, but comparatively little to be said about what he or she positively is. Of course, this doesn't mean that it is any less important. Indeed, from a spiritual point of view, the more important a thing is, the less there is to be said about it.

Perhaps, above all, the guru is one who stands on a higher level of being and consciousness than ourselves, who is more evolved, more developed, more—in a word—aware. Also, a guru is someone with whom we are in regular contact. This contact may take place at different levels. It may take place on a higher spiritual plane—that is, telepathically—as the direct contact of mind with mind. There may be contact between the guru and the disciple in dreams or during meditation. But for the ordinary disciple it generally takes place on the physical plane—that is, on the ordinary social plane, in the ordinary way. The relatively undeveloped disciple will need regular and frequent physical contact with the guru. According to Eastern tradition, ideally he or she would be in day-to-day contact with the guru, even living under the same roof.

Contact between the guru and the disciple should be "existential"—that is, there should be real communication between them— not just the sharing of thoughts or ideas or feelings or experiences, even spiritual experiences, but communication of being, or, if you like, action and interaction of being. The guru and the disciple need to be themselves as fully as possible in relation to each other. The guru's business is not to teach the disciple anything, but simply to be himself in relation to the disciple. Nor, as the disciple, is it your business to learn. You simply have to expose yourself to the being—and to the effect of the being—of the guru, and at the same time, be yourself in relation to him.

Spiritual communication, like integration, can be thought of as being of two kinds: "horizontal" and "vertical." Horizontal communication takes place between two people who are on more or less the same level of being and consciousness. Because their states of mind fluctuate from day to day, sometimes one of them will be in a better state of mind than the other, but the next day it may be the other way round. Vertical communication, on the other hand, takes place between people one of whom is on a consistently higher level than the other, quite apart from any ups and downs. It is such vertical communication that takes place between guru and disciple.

In all communication, whether horizontal or vertical, there is mutual modification of being. In the case of horizontal communication, in the course of communication anything one-sided or unbalanced in one's nature is corrected. People who really communicate gradually develop a similarity of outlook, responding to things in the same spirit; they have progressively more in common. At the same time, paradoxical as it may seem, they become more truly themselves.

Suppose, for example, a very rational person engages in true communication with a very emotional person. If they sustain this communication long enough, the emotional person will become more rational and the rational person will become more emotional. At the same time, if you are the rational person (to take that example) you do not just have emotionality added to you from outside. Through communicating with the emotional person, you are enabled to develop your own undeveloped emotionality which has been there all the time (as it were) beneath the surface. A quality emerges that was there, but not active. The communication has simply enabled you to become more yourself, more whole, more complete. And it's the same, obviously, if you are the emotional one of the two.

Vertical communication is different. The disciple grows in the direction of the guru's higher level of being and consciousness, but the guru does not become correspondingly more like the disciple. The principle of mutual modification of being does not mean that the guru slips back in his development as a result of his communication with someone less developed. He does not meet the disciple halfway, as it were. In the intensity of his or her communication with the guru, the disciple is in a sense compelled to evolve. He or she has no choice, except to break off the relationship altogether, and a real disciple cannot even do that. It is said that the true disciple is like a bulldog puppy. When offered a towel, the puppy will snap at it and not let go, even if he is lifted off the ground with his jaws still attached to it. The true disciple has that sort of tenacity.

As a result of his vertical communication with the disciple, the guru also grows spiritually. The only guru who doesn't do this is a Buddha, a fully and perfectly Enlightened one, and even among gurus a Buddha is extremely rare. It is sometimes said in Tantric circles that disciples are necessary to a guru's further development, that nothing helps a guru so much as having a really good disciple—not an obedient, docile disciple, but one who really engages in communication, one who is really trying to grow. A good disciple may give the guru quite a lot of trouble, sometimes more trouble than all the other disciples put together. It also occasionally happens that the disciple overtakes the guru, and a reversal of roles takes place. This situation is less problematic than it might seem from the outside, because the relationship is not one of authority or power, but of love and friendship.

So is a guru necessary? Well, to grow spiritually without any contact with a guru is extremely difficult. Generalizing, one might say that for most people spiritual growth does not take place without at least two factors being present: the experience of suffering, and contact with a more highly developed person or persons. Why?—because personal relationships and real communication are necessary to human development. Not only that—we need real communication that includes a vertical element. Through communication with our friends we develop horizontally—we become more whole, more ourselves. But most people seem to need communication with a guru to enable them to rise to a higher level of being and consciousness. Just as a child develops into an adult mainly through contact with his or her parents, regular contact with at least one person who is more highly developed than we are is necessary for our spiritual development. Not that it is absolutely impossible to make progress without being in contact with such a person, but that kind of contact certainly speeds up and intensifies the whole process.

But if a guru is necessary, how do you go about choosing one? How do you know whether someone is more highly evolved than you are? Obviously, it is important not to make any mistake in this matter. The problem is that it is very difficult indeed to know if someone is really more advanced—perhaps impossible—without prolonged contact. Some gurus in the East say not only that it is impossible for the disciple to choose the guru, but that it is quite presumptuous for the disciple to think that he can do so, or that he can know whether someone is more developed than himself. What actually happens, they say, is that the guru chooses the disciple. You may think that you are choosing a guru, but in fact the only choice you are capable of making is of a religious group (with the guru as its head), or a religious teacher, or a father-substitute or problem-solver. You are not choosing a guru as such, because you are not equipped to see who has greater spiritual attainment.

So as a would-be disciple, what are you to do? All you can do is make as much progress as possible by yourself so that you can recognize and make contact with a spiritual community (as distinct from a religious group). Then you must hope that some member of that community will take you on as a friend, or refer you to somebody else who can. In any case, you should always be ready and receptive for the advent of the guru.

In a way, the guru cannot be overvalued. Nothing can be more valuable than the person who helps you to develop spiritually. All the same, it is true to say that in the East the guru often tends in a sense to be overvalued, while in the West he is usually undervalued. What can happen in the East is that a false and inflated value is attached to the guru. People in India sometimes say that the guru is God. This is asserted not just as a figure of speech, but quite literally. If you are sitting in front of the guru, you are not just looking at a human being, seated on a cushion on the floor. You're sitting in front of God—in fact, all the gods rolled into one, the all-powerful, the all-knowing himself. He may look just like an ordinary human being, but he knows everything that is going on in the whole universe, including everything going on in your mind. He can read your thoughts like an open book. If you've got a problem, you don't have to tell him—he knows already. He can do anything he likes. He can bless you, give you riches, promotion, fame, children, all with just a word of blessing. He can give you Enlightenment if he wants to. It is all in his hands—it's all the "grace of the guru," as they say.

All the disciple has to offer is faith in the guru, faith that the guru is God. If the disciple only has enough of this kind of faith, the guru can work miracles on his behalf. Such faith is therefore regarded as of the very greatest importance. There are, of course, little difficulties. It sometimes happens that the guru appears not to know something, or to forget something you have told him, and you may get a bit upset by this. But the true disciple isn't bothered at all because he knows that these apparently human limitations and failings are tests of faith. The guru is only pretending to have slips of the mind to see if your faith is still firm and sound, just as a potter taps a pot after it's been baked, to see whether or not there's a crack in it.

It is no wonder that over the years the disciple comes to inhabit a fantasy world in which whatever happens is seen to do so on account of the guru's "grace" and the guru's will. If the guru isn't careful, he may come to inhabit this fantasy world too, especially if he isn't a real guru. After all, it isn't easy to escape such a fantasy world if you your-self are at the center of it. If someone comes and tells you that their child was sick and has now recovered due to your blessing, you may not be inclined to dispute that interpretation, even if you hadn't given the child a moment's thought.

The problem from the guru's point of view is that sooner or later it will dawn on certain of his more perceptive disciples that he isn't really God. While he may have a deep level of insight and spiritual experience, he also has some quite human limitations. Perceiving this, they are likely to conclude that he isn't a true guru, and go off to look for someone else, someone who is a true guru, someone who *is* God. If they do that, the same thing will inevitably happen all over again. They will start noticing little discrepancies, get disillusioned, and see that this guru too is "only" a human being after all. And so the merry-go-round continues.

This happens among Buddhists as well to some extent. A Tibetan friend of mine, a lama and guru living in Kalimpong, recalled that when he first arrived there, the local Nepalese Buddhists used to flock to see him, bringing him wonderful offerings and eager to take initiations from him. But after a few years they got a bit tired of him. They continued to come to pay their respects, but he was amused to observe that they didn't bring quite such big offerings as before. Then a new lama arrived on the scene (he was a friend of the first one) and everybody abandoned my friend to get their new initiations from the new lama—to the amusement of both lamas. Eventually, as the Chinese communists seized power in Tibet, more and more gurus started to arrive in town, which was very bewildering for the local community. No sooner had they identified a supremely powerful guru and rushed to make him offerings, than another one arrived, who—according to some people—was even more eminent and accomplished. In the end they must have run through perhaps twenty gurus, looking for the "real" one.

Clearly, the guru is overvalued in this manner in the East because he is regarded as an idealized parent figure: all-knowing, all-powerful, infinitely loving and tolerant. The disciple in such cases wants to adopt an attitude of infantile dependence. Gurus are usually very popular in India, but there is one thing demanded of them, regardless of almost anything else: they must always be kind and affectionate, soft-spoken and gentle. What they teach and how they live are side-issues by comparison.

In the West we have traditionally gone to the opposite extreme. Here, far from overvaluing the guru, we have hardly any concept of the guru at all. This is no doubt largely due to the influence of Christianity. On the one hand you have belief in God with all his various attributes, and on the other you have submission to the head of the particular religious group to which you belong, your ecclesiastical superior, but there seems to be no room for the guru in the true sense.

The gurus who do appear—who may eventually be identified as saints—are usually subject to the rule of the ecclesiastical authorities. In medieval times, even a great saint sometimes had to submit to a bad Pope. Perhaps that didn't do the saint much harm, but it was bad for the Pope, and for the Church as a whole. However, we must not imagine that the Christian tradition is the only spiritual tradition the West has ever known. Nor should we accept the assumption that the concept of the guru in the Eastern sense is alien to the Western mentality. There were certainly gurus in ancient Greece and Rome—for example Plato, who maintained a sort of school or academy, Pythagoras, who founded spiritual communities, Apollonius of Tyana, and above all perhaps, Plotinus. From Porphyry's life of Plotinus, especially the description of his later life in Rome, one gets the definite impression of a sort of spiritual community, set up more along the lines of an Indian ashram than in a manner typical of the kind of institution one might think of as characteristic of the later Roman Empire.[129]

Such great figures of classical times were gurus in the true sense of the term. And in modern post-Christian times there are signs that the importance of the guru is again beginning to be appreciated in the West, despite our democratic and egalitarian prejudices, our modern belief that no one should be seen as better than anybody else. Even in modern cultures so apparently hostile to the possibility of spiritual development, there are signs that people are beginning to appreciate the significance of those who are more highly developed than the average person.

As Buddhists, we have to follow a middle way. We have to recognize above all that we are capable of evolving from our present state of being and consciousness to a more fully developed degree of self-consciousness and even to a realization of transcendental consciousness, leading to what, without really being able to understand it, we can only call absolute consciousness. In order to do this, we have also to recognize that different human beings are at different stages of this great process of spiritual development. Some are lower down than we are, while others are higher up, even a great deal higher up. We have to recognize that those who are higher up in the scale of the evolution of humanity are in a position to help us, and that we will develop through communication with them. It is gurus in this sense whom we need to recognize as being superior. The kind of guru we don't need is one to whom we give an unrealistically inflated value and onto whom we project our desire for an idealized father-figure. It is a great mistake to expect from a guru what we can only get, ultimately, from ourselves.

The Buddha did not ask anybody to regard him as a god or as God. He never asked anybody to have faith—much less to have absolute faith—in him. In fact, this is a very important aspect of Buddhism. The Buddha never said, "You must believe in me, and believe what I say, if you want to be saved, or if you want to realize your own true nature." Again and again in the Buddhist scriptures he is presented as saying, "Let any reasonable man come to me, one who is willing to learn; I will teach him the Dharma."[130] All he asks is that we should be rational and open-minded. All he requires is reasonable and receptive human contact. He seems to have been quite convinced that he could introduce anyone to the spiritual life without making any appeal for absolute faith and devotion, but purely by rational and empirical means. On this basis alone he could awaken anyone to the truth that the path to Enlightenment is the most worthwhile thing to which as human beings we can possibly devote ourselves.

6. Spiritual Hierarchy

It is this kind of spontaneous emotion that creates the spiritual hierarchy: a spontaneous feeling of devotion when one encounters something higher; a spontaneous overflowing of compassion when one is confronted by other people's distress or difficulty; and a spontaneous welling up of love and sympathy when one is among one's peers.

According to the Pali Canon, just after the Buddha became Enlightened—or rather, while he was still exploring the different facets of that experience which we usually refer to as though it were a single undifferentiated occurrence—he became aware of a very powerful aspiration. He knew that he had to find somebody or something that he could revere and respect. His fundamental impulse, it seems, so soon after his experience of Enlightenment, was to reverence: to look up, not down. After some reflection he realized that, having attained Enlightenment, there was now no person he could look up to, because no one else had attained what he had attained. But he saw that he could look up to the Dharma, the great spiritual law by virtue of which he had attained Enlightenment. He therefore decided to devote himself to reverencing the Dharma.[131]

This episode cannot be called to mind too often, especially because it is so contrary to the modern spirit of not wanting to honor or be indebted to anybody or anything. We are sometimes only too willing to look down on others, but we are unwilling to look up, and even feel resentful if others appear to be superior to us in any way. We are generally happy enough to admire and even venerate the superior physical strength, quickness of eye, and will to win of the athlete, but very often we are unwilling to respect or reverence qualities that are superior from a spiritual point of view.

Someone once made the point that in any culture where a particular principle is of such fundamental importance that it is taken for granted, no word for that principle exists in the local language. One quite interesting reflection of this is to be found in the fact that in Buddhism there is no traditional term that corresponds to "tolerance." It's as though in order to appreciate the tolerance of Buddhism you have to be able to look at it from the standpoint of a tradition or culture that is *not* tolerant. Buddhism traditionally does not think of itself as tolerant. It doesn't promote that concept, doesn't recommend itself as being a tolerant religion; it has never attained that sort of self-consciousness with regard to its own nature.

It is the same with hierarchy. Buddhism is traditionally saturated in it, to the extent that Buddhists are almost unable to step aside and see Buddhism as hierarchical. The very fact that the spiritual path consists of a series of steps or stages shows how deeply the hierarchical principle is embedded within Buddhism. In fact, the spiritual life itself is inseparable from the hierarchical principle. There is a hierarchy of wisdoms: the wisdom you hear or read about (*sruta-mayi-prajna*), the wisdom you cultivate through reflection (*cinta-mayi-prajna*) and, as the highest form, the wisdom cultivated in meditation (*bhavana-mayi-prajna*).[132] There is a hierarchy of the different levels of the cosmos, from the *kamaloka* up to the *rupaloka* and the *arupaloka*.[133] And of course there is a hierarchy of persons: both the *ariya-puggalas*[134] of the Theravada and the Bodhisattvas of the Mahayana are organized into hierarchies. It would seem that the concept of hierarchy is absolutely fundamental to Buddhism; without it, Buddhism as we know it can hardly exist. And for that very reason, perhaps, there is no traditional word or concept for hierarchy. There are certain words that express the idea of a sequence of increasing value within a particular context, but there is no overall, generalized term covering all the different, more specific hierarchies.

But when as Westerners we approach Buddhism from the outside, as it were, its hierarchical nature certainly strikes us, and some people have to struggle with this in a way that Eastern Buddhists, with different cultural and psychological conditioning, do not. After many years as a Buddhist myself, however, my own difficulty lies in trying to sympathize with the non- or anti-hierarchical concept of equality, which seems very limited and restricting. It would seem to me that inequality is one of the most obvious things about life.

Of course, there are true hierarchies and false ones. In Europe in the eighteenth century, especially in France, the social and ecclesiastical hierarchy was completely false; it did not correspond to any facts or realities. For example, court favorites with barely the faintest pretense to piety were appointed to bishoprics. When the name of a certain courtier was proposed to Louis XV for Archbishop of Paris, he demurred: "No, no, the Archbishop of Paris should at least believe in God!"—which shows how far things had gone. In the case of poor Louis XVI, who was guillotined, his real interest was in making locks, and that is what he spent most of his time doing. He had no idea about government; in other words, he wasn't really a king in the true sense of the word.

Eventually there was the great upheaval of the French Revolution and the false hierarchy was overthrown in both church and state. But in negating the false hierarchy people asserted not true hierarchy but no hierarchy, or anti-hierarchy: hence the famous slogan "Liberty, Equality, Fraternity." We have inherited a great deal from that period, politically, socially, intellectually, and spiritually. In particular, we have inherited an anti-hierarchical tendency—opposition not just to false hierarchies but to hierarchies as such. That is unfortunate. One can understand people in revolutionary France being unable or unwilling to distinguish between genuine hierarchy and false hierarchy. They didn't want to give a false hierarchy any reason for existing at all. But in calmer times we shouldn't have to reject the very idea of hierarchy in that way.

It is sometimes said that everybody is as good as everybody else "as a person." But this assumption is questionable. It is not as though the terms "person" and "individual" refer to something static; they suggest a degree of development. And some people are more developed than others; that is to say, some are better as persons or individuals than others.

The point of such an assertion of hierarchy is not to put people in their place. Quite the opposite is true, because this hierarchy is not fixed. All that matters is that everybody should be encouraged to grow, and that none of us should accept some fixed idea of our value as individuals. Our value consists in the effort we make at the level we are at rather than in some fixed position we hold in the hierarchy. If we have done our best, there can be no criticism of us.

It does seem that competition helps people to give of their best, achieve their best, be their best. In one of his discourses, the Buddha spoke of each of his more intimate disciples in turn, declaring who was best at what. And, it seems, each of them could indeed be found to be the best at something or other. One was the best at giving talks, another was the best meditator, another was the best at going for alms. Everybody excelled at something.[135]

Still, the word hierarchy is very unpopular these days, and the dictionary definition—"a body of ecclesiastical rulers"—does nothing to make the term more appealing. But in its original sense, hierarchy meant something like an embodiment, in a number of different people, of different degrees of manifestation of reality. One can speak, for instance, of a hierarchy of living forms—some lower, expressing or manifesting less reality, others higher, expressing or manifesting more reality. There is a continuous hierarchy of living forms from amoebas right up to human beings—the higher the level, the greater the degree of reality.

And there is another hierarchy of living forms: the hierarchy from the unenlightened human being right up to the Enlightened Buddha. This corresponds to what in other contexts I have described as the Higher Evolution. Just as the unenlightened human being embodies or manifests more reality, more truth, than the amoeba, in the same way the Enlightened human being embodies or manifests more reality in his or her life and work, and even speech, than does the unenlightened person. The Enlightened person is like a clear window through which the light of reality shines, through which that light can be seen almost as it is. Or one can say that he or she is like a crystal or diamond concentrating and reflecting that light.

Between the unenlightened human being and the Enlightened one, the Buddha, there are a number of intermediate degrees, embodied in different people at different stages of spiritual development. Most people are still short of Enlightenment, to a greater or lesser extent, but at the same time they are not wholly unenlightened. They stand somewhere between the unenlightened state and the state of full Enlightenment, and thus make up the spiritual hierarchy, the higher reaches of which can be referred to as the Bodhisattva hierarchy. We may have an appreciation of the intensity of Bodhisattvas' aspiration and commitment to the spiritual life, but even among Bodhisattvas there are degrees of spiritual attainment.

The principle of spiritual hierarchy is very important. As human beings we are related to ultimate reality both directly and indirectly. We are related to reality directly in the sense that in the very depths of our being is something which all the time connects us with reality, a kind of golden thread which, though it may be gossamer thin, is always there. In some people that thread has become a little thicker, a little stronger, in others it has strengthened almost into a rope, while in those who are Enlightened there is no need for a connecting thread at all, because there is no difference between the depth of their being and the depth of reality itself. We are all directly connected in the depth of our being with reality, although most of us don't realize it. But although we don't see that thin golden thread shining in the midst of the darkness within us, nevertheless, it is there.

We are related *in*directly to reality in two ways. In the first place, we are related to those things that represent a lower degree of manifestation of reality than ourselves. We are related to nature: rocks, water, fire, the different forms of vegetable life, and the forms of animal life that are lower in the scale of evolution than ourselves. This relationship may be compared with seeing a light through a thick veil; sometimes the veil seems to be so thick—especially in the case of material forms—that we are unable to see the light at all.

We are indirectly related to reality also through those forms that represent a higher degree of manifestation of reality than ourselves. This is like seeing a light through a thin veil—a veil that seems at times as fine as gossamer, and even, just occasionally, parts and falls away to allow the light of reality to be seen directly, as it is, without any mediation at all. We could say that this thin veil, through which we see the light of reality, is the spiritual hierarchy, especially the Bodhisattva hierarchy.

It is of the utmost importance for us to be in contact with people who are at least a little more spiritually advanced than we are ourselves, through whom the light of reality shines a little more clearly than it shines through us. Such people are known traditionally in Buddhism as our spiritual friends, our kalyana mitras, and they are more important to us than even a Buddha would be. If we happened to have the opportunity to meet a Buddha, we probably wouldn't be able to make much of the encounter, or even realize the nature of the person in front of us. We are likely to benefit much more from contact with those who are just a little more spiritually developed than we are.

In this connection there is a beautiful passage in that great Tibetan spiritual classic, *The Jewel Ornament of Liberation* of Gampopa. Speaking of spiritual friends, Gampopa says:

> Since at the beginning of our career it is impossible to be in touch with the Buddhas or with Bodhisattvas living on a high level of spirituality, we have to meet with ordinary human beings as spiritual friends. As soon as the darkness caused by our deeds has lightened, we can find Bodhisattvas on a high level of spirituality. Then when we have risen above the Great Preparatory Path we can find the nirmanakaya of the Buddha. Finally, as soon as we live on a high spiritual level we can meet with the sambhogakaya as a spiritual friend.
>
> Should you ask, who among these four is our greatest benefactor, the reply is that in the beginning of our career when we are still living imprisoned by our deeds and emotions, we will not even see so much as the face of a superior spiritual friend. Instead we will have to seek an ordinary human being who can illumine the path we have to follow with the light of his counsel, whereafter we shall meet superior ones. Therefore the greatest benefactor is a spiritual friend in the form of an ordinary human being.[136]

We can't get far on our own. If week after week, year after year, we had no meditation classes to go to, if we never met another person who was interested in Buddhism, if we couldn't even get any books— because reading books of the right kind is also a sort of spiritual communication—if we were entirely on our own, we wouldn't get far, however great our initial enthusiasm and sincerity. We get encouragement, inspiration, and moral support from associating with others who have similar ideals and who are following a similar way of life. This is especially the case when we associate with those who are a bit more spiritually advanced than we are, or, to put it more simply, who are just a bit more human than most people are—a bit more aware, a bit kinder, a bit more faithful, and so on.

In practice, this means that we should try to be open and receptive toward those whom we recognize to be above us in the spiritual hierarchy, those who clearly have greater insight, understanding, sympathy, compassion, and so on. We should be ready to receive from them, just as a flower opens its petals to receive the light and warmth of the sun. As for those who are, as far as we can tell (and bearing in mind we might be mistaken), below us in the spiritual hierarchy, our attitude should be one of generosity, kindliness, and helpfulness—giving them encouragement, making them feel welcome, and so on. And with regard to those who seem to be roughly on the same level as ourselves, our attitude should be one of mutuality, sharing, reciprocity.

These three attitudes correspond to the three great positive emotions of the Buddhist spiritual life. First of all there is *sraddha*. This is often translated as "faith" or "belief," but it really means a sort of devotion, a receptivity to the light streaming down—as it were—from above. Secondly there is compassion, which is a giving out of what we have received from above to those who are lower in the spiritual hierarchy. And thirdly there is love or metta, which we share with all those who are on the same level as ourselves.

In *The Jewel Ornament of Liberation,* Gampopa goes on to say: "The Enlightenment of a Buddha is obtained by serving spiritual friends"— a strong statement, to say the least, and possibly not a palatable one. The whole idea of service is rather alien to us. We are familiar with the idea of devoting ourselves to caring for our children, perhaps, or looking after our parents when they are old, but it is not always easy for us to transpose that feeling to other situations. This is very much connected with the collapse of the idea of spiritual hierarchy, or any kind of hierarchy. If we are all equal, why should you do something for someone else? Why shouldn't he or she do it for you? Or why can't you do it on an exchange basis? "I'll do it for you today, if you'll do it for me tomorrow."

To put oneself in the position of serving someone is to acknowledge that the person one is serving is better than oneself in some respects. It is this that many people are unwilling to do. But unless one can make that acknowledgement, one cannot grow spiritually. In "serving spiritual friends" one grows to become more like them—and then one finds that there are other spiritual friends to be served. Even when one becomes an advanced Bodhisattva, one finds that the universe is full of Buddhas to whom one can give devoted service. There is always someone whom one can serve.

Gampopa also says that one should "think of a spiritual friend as the Buddha." The idea of this is not to burden your friend—as an ordinary human being—with the idea that he or she is a Buddha, or to try to convince yourself that they are a Buddha when your reason tells you that they are not. You need not regard everything they do or say as the action of a Buddha. What is important is that, while your spiritual friend may be very far from being a Buddha, he or she is at least a little more spiritually developed than you are yourself. It's as though behind your friend stands his or her own teacher, and behind that teacher another one, back and back until, behind them all, stands the Buddha. So the Buddha is shining, as it were, through all these people, who are of varying degrees of translucency.

At least, this is one way of interpreting the advice to "think of a spiritual friend as the Buddha." However, Gampopa, who belonged primarily to the Tantric tradition, being a guru of the Kagyu school of Tibet, as well as one of Milarepa's main disciples, might well have intended this statement to be taken quite literally. Fundamental to the Vajrayana is the idea that each of the Three Jewels has its esoteric aspect. Esoteric as it is, this notion is a profoundly practical one. The Vajrayanists said, in effect, that the Buddha's Enlightenment, his teaching of the truth he had discovered, and the growth of the circle of his Enlightened followers—these Three Jewels which have been revered down the ages of Buddhist tradition—all happened a very long time ago. We ourselves can have no direct contact with them, and cannot benefit from their direct influence. We have to find, in effect, our own Three Jewels. The question is where to find them. The answer the Vajrayana came up with was that one should regard one's Dharma teacher, one's guru, as the Buddha, the exemplar of Enlightenment as far as one is personally concerned. Similarly, one should see one's yidam, the Buddha or Bodhisattva upon whom one meditates, as the embodiment of the truth itself. And the esoteric Sangha Refuge is the company of dakinis, with whom, according to Vajrayana tradition, one can be in living contact. In one's own particular context the guru or teacher stands for the Buddha, and even—in the Tantric context—*is* the Buddha.

Another way of approaching Gampopa's maxim is to reflect on the teaching that every human being is potentially a Buddha. According to some Buddhist schools, if one could only look hard enough, one would see that every human being *is* in fact a Buddha, whether they realize it or not. In the case of a spiritual friend, since he or she has become at least a little Buddha-like, it is easier to see in him or her the fundamental Buddha-nature that we all possess.

Gampopa goes on to recommend not just that we should serve our spiritual friends, but that we should please them. That is, we should give them cause to rejoice in the qualities they perceive developing in us. If you please a spiritual friend and he or she pleases you, both of you will be in this state of sympathetic joy (*mudita*), and communication will be established and will flow. Your friend will be able to teach, and you to learn.

In an interesting passage in the Great Chapter of the *Sutta-Nipata*, a certain brahmin is not sure whether the Buddha is in fact the Buddha, the Enlightened One, or whether he is just a great man, a "superman" or *mahapurisa*. But it seems that this brahmin has heard of a way to find out. He has heard that the Buddhas reveal their true self, their true nature, if they are praised.[137] Praising is related to pleasing—a sort of pleasing in words. If you praise a Buddha, he cannot but show his true nature. And conversely, even a Buddha cannot show his true nature unless the situation is positive enough to allow him to do so.

It is much the same, on another level, with a spiritual friend. To please him or her is to make communication more effective, whereas to displease him or her is to set up a barrier to communication. "Pleasing" here doesn't mean gratifying someone's ego, but relating to them in an open, free, sincere, genuine, and warm way, showing metta, "sympathetic joy"—that is, joy in the virtues of others—and equanimity. If you please a spiritual friend, it makes it easier for your friend to communicate with you, for his or her true nature to emerge. And you are the one who benefits from that; it is you who gains in the long run.

Although I have referred to those who are "higher up" and those who are "lower down," there is no question of any official grading. If we start even thinking in terms of being higher or lower than other people, we have failed to grasp the nature of spiritual hierarchy. Everything should be natural and spontaneous; the appropriate emotion, whether of devotion, compassion, or love, should flow forth unselfconsciously and spontaneously in response to whomsoever we meet.

I used to go with Tibetan friends, both lamas and lay people, to visit monasteries and temples, and it was interesting to see their responses when they entered such places. When we in the West go to a place of worship, a great cathedral or something like that, we may not know quite what to do, how to respond, what to feel. But when I used to visit temples with my Tibetan friends, there was none of that sort of confusion or inner conflict. As soon as they saw an image of the Buddha, one could almost see the feelings of devotion and faith and reverence welling up within them. They put their hands to their foreheads and often prostrated themselves flat on the ground three times. They did this completely unselfconsciously; it was natural to them because of the context in which they had grown up (a context which has now, of course, largely been shattered).

It is this kind of spontaneous emotion that creates the spiritual hierarchy: a spontaneous feeling of devotion when one encounters something higher; a spontaneous overflowing of compassion when one is confronted by other people's distress or difficulty; and a spontaneous welling up of love and sympathy when one is among one's peers. These are the emotions that should influence the whole Buddhist community. People in such a community are like roses in different stages of growth all blooming on a single bush, or like a spiritual family of which the Buddha is the head and the great Bodhisattvas the elder brothers and sisters. In such a family, everybody gets what they need; the younger people are cared for by the older ones, everybody gives what they can, and the whole family is pervaded by a spirit of joy, freedom, warmth, and light.

The Bodhisattva hierarchy concentrates all this into a single focal point of dazzling intensity. It has its own degrees, its own radiant figures, at higher and ever higher stages of spiritual development, right up to Buddhahood itself.

7. GRATITUDE

The newly Enlightened Buddha was a *grateful* Buddha, an idea which is perhaps unfamiliar to us.

USUALLY, influenced by books or even Buddhist scriptures, we think of the Buddha's Enlightenment as having taken place at a particular time, roughly two thousand five hundred years ago—which, of course, in a sense, it did. We also tend to think of it as having taken place on a particular day, at a particular hour, even at a particular minute, at the instant when the Buddha broke through from the conditioned to the Unconditioned.

But a little reflection, and a little further study of the scriptures, will show us that it didn't happen quite like that. Here we can consider the distinction between the path of vision and the path of transformation—a distinction usually made in connection with the Noble Eightfold Path. On the path of vision one has an experience of the transcendental, a profound insight into the true nature of Reality which goes far beyond any merely intellectual understanding. This insight comes gradually to pervade and transform every aspect of one's being—one's body, speech, and mind, to use the traditional Buddhist classification. It transforms all our activities. It transforms one, in fact, into a very different kind of person—a wiser and more compassionate person. This process is known as the path of transformation.

Something like this takes place in the spiritual life of each and every one of us. And we see the same sort of thing happening, on a much more exalted plane, in the case of the Buddha. The Buddha's vision is unlimited, absolute, and all-embracing, and his transformation of body, speech, and mind can therefore be described as total, even infinite. But all the same, it did take a little time for this final transformation to take place. Buddhist tradition speaks of the Buddha as spending seven—or nine (accounts vary)—weeks in the vicinity of the Bodhi tree, the tree beneath which he attained Enlightenment. In the course of each of those weeks something of importance happened. We could say that the Buddha's experience of Enlightenment started percolating through his being, until by the end of the last week (whether the seventh or the ninth) the process of transformation was at last complete.

One week a great storm arose, and the Buddha was sheltered from the rain, so the story goes, by the serpent king Mucalinda, who spread his sevenfold hood over the Buddha's head as he meditated. Another week, Brahma Sahampati, the ruler of a thousand worlds, requested the Buddha to teach the Dharma, saying that at least some of the beings in the world would be capable of understanding it, their eyes being covered with only a little dust. And the Buddha, out of compassion, agreed to teach.

But here I want to focus on another episode, one that occurred quite early in the period after the Buddha's attainment of Enlightenment—during the second week, according to one source. According to this tradition, the Buddha stood at a distance to the northeast of the Bodhi tree and remained for one week gazing at the tree with unblinking eyes.[138]

Centuries later, a stupa was erected on that very spot, to mark the place where the Buddha had gazed at the Bodhi tree. It was known as "the stupa of unblinking eyes," and Hsuan Tsang, the great Chinese pilgrim, saw it when he visited India in the seventh century CE. In the memoirs he dictated to his disciples in his old age back in China, he described it thus: "On the left side of the road, to the north of the place where the Buddha walked, is a large stone on the top of which, as it stands in a great vihara, is a figure of the Buddha with his eyes raised and looking up. Here in former times the Buddha sat [he says "sat" but the source text says "stood"] for seven days contemplating the Bodhi tree."[139]

Perhaps the Buddha didn't literally stand or sit there for a whole week, but we may take it that he gazed at the Bodhi tree for a very long time. And the source text makes it clear why. He did it because he was grateful to the tree for having sheltered him at the time of his attainment of Enlightenment. According to the scriptures, the Buddha demonstrated gratitude in other ways too. After Brahma Sahampati had made his request that the Buddha should teach the Dharma, and the Buddha had decided to do so, he then wondered to whom he should teach it. He thought first of his two old teachers, from whom he had learned to meditate not long after he left home. Finding their teaching insufficient, he had left them, but they had been helpful to him at a particular stage of his career, and after his Enlightenment he remembered that. It's as though he had a spiritual debt to them that he wanted to repay. But he quickly realized that his old teachers were dead.

He then thought of his five former companions. They too were people he knew from an earlier period of his spiritual quest, from the time of his experiments in asceticism. After leaving his first two teachers, he started practicing extreme self-mortification in the company of five friends who became disciples of his, and admired him greatly because he had gone further in his self-mortification than anybody else at that time. But eventually the Buddha-to-be saw the futility of asceticism, realized that that was not the way to Enlightenment, and gave it up. When he started taking solid food again, just a few handfuls of rice to sustain himself, the five ascetics left him in disgust, saying, "The sramana Gautama has returned to luxurious living." But this parting was not what remained in the Buddha's mind. Having realized that his two old teachers were dead, he reflected, "The five ascetics were of great help to me when I was practicing the penances. I would like to preach the Dharma to them." So this is what he did. He went to them, he taught them, and eventually they too realized the Truth that he had realized. And he did this out of gratitude.

So the newly Enlightened Buddha was a *grateful* Buddha, an idea which is perhaps unfamiliar to us. We think of the all-wise Buddha, the compassionate Buddha, the resourceful Buddha, but we don't usually think of the grateful Buddha. But one of the very first things the Buddha did after his attainment of Enlightenment was to show his gratitude to those who had helped him. He was even grateful to a tree.

This incident alone gives us food for thought. The Buddhist scriptures contain a number of references that show that the Buddha and his disciples didn't regard trees and stones as inanimate dead matter. They regarded them as living things. They would even have a relationship with them; they would talk to a tree or a flower, or rather to the spirit—the devata, as they called it—inhabiting it. It is surely much better to have this attitude, to be an animist, than to think that trees and flowers and rocks and stones are just dead matter. The Buddha certainly didn't think in that way, and it was therefore possible for him to be grateful even to a tree.

It is not surprising, given that this was the Buddha's attitude, that gratitude finds a place in his ethical and spiritual teaching. It is found, for example, in the *Mangala Sutta,* the "Sutta of Blessings or Auspicious Signs." This sutta, which is very short and is found in the Pali Canon, is often regarded as summarizing the whole duty, as we may call it, of the serious-minded Buddhist, and it enumerates gratitude as one of the auspicious signs. According to the *Mangala Sutta,* it is a sign that you are making spiritual progress.[140]

But what is gratitude? What do we mean when we use this term?

To find this out, we can turn to the dictionaries—and, of course, we should be very grateful to the makers of dictionaries. I am personally very grateful to Doctor Samuel Johnson. His historic dictionary is always at my elbow in my study, and when I am writing I sometimes consult it several times a day. Doctor Johnson defines gratitude as "duty to benefactors" and as "desire to return benefits." Coming to more modern dictionaries the *Concise Oxford* says, "being thankful; readiness to show appreciation for and to return kindness," while *Collins* has "a feeling of thankfulness or appreciation, as for gifts or favors."

Such are the definitions of the English word, and they do give us some understanding of what gratitude is. But from a Buddhist point of view we need to go further, and look at the Pali word being translated as gratitude: *katannuta. Kata* means that which has been done, especially that which has been done to oneself; and *annuta* means knowing or recognizing; so *katannuta* means knowing and recognizing what has been done to one for one's benefit. These definitions indicate that the connotation of the Pali word is rather different from that of its English translation. The connotation of the English word gratitude is emotional—we speak of *feeling* grateful. But the connotation of *katannuta* is rather more intellectual, more cognitive. It makes it clear that what we call gratitude involves an element of *knowledge:* knowledge of what has been done to us or for us for our benefit. If we do not know that something has benefited us, we will not feel grateful.

The Buddha knew that the Bodhi tree had sheltered him, and he knew that his five former companions had been helpful to him, so he felt gratitude toward them. Not only that: he gave expression to that feeling. He acted upon it by spending a whole week simply gazing at the Bodhi tree, and then by going in search of his five former companions so that he could communicate to them the truth that he had discovered. The important implication is that it is a perfectly natural thing to feel grateful for benefits we have received.

But the benefit has to be recognized as a benefit. If we don't feel that someone or something has benefited us, we won't feel grateful to them or to it. This suggests that we have to understand what is truly beneficial, what has really helped us to grow and develop as human beings. We also have to know who or what has benefited us, and remember that they have done so—otherwise no feeling of gratitude is possible.

In Buddhism there are traditionally three principal objects of gratitude: our parents, our teachers, and our spiritual friends. Here I want to reflect a little on gratitude in relation to each of them.

I came back to England after spending twenty years uninterruptedly in the East studying, practicing, and teaching the Dharma. When I came back, I found that much had changed. Quite a few things struck me as unusual—I hadn't encountered them in India, or at least not to the same extent. One thing that definitely surprised me was finding out how many people, at least among those I knew, were on bad terms with their parents. Perhaps I noticed this especially because I was in contact with people who were concerned about their spiritual development, and wanted to straighten themselves out psychologically and emotionally.

If one is on bad terms with one's parents, something is quite seriously wrong. Perhaps it wouldn't even be an exaggeration to say that one's whole emotional life is likely to be affected, indirectly at least, by this state of affairs. I therefore generally encourage people to get back into positive contact with their parents, if it happens that they are estranged from them for any reason. I encourage people to be more open with their parents and to develop positive feelings toward them. This is especially necessary in connection with the practice of the metta bhavana, the development of loving-kindness. People have to learn to develop metta even toward their parents, and for those who have had difficult childhoods, or have even suffered at the hands of their parents in some way, this is not easy. But even so, it is necessary in the interests of their own emotional, psychological, and spiritual development to get over whatever feelings of bitterness or resentment they are harboring.

Some people, I have discovered, blame their parents in all sorts of ways for all sorts of things—an attitude which is reflected in a well-known little poem by Philip Larkin called "This Be The Verse." In this poem, Larkin gives expression in rather crude language to what he thinks your parents have done to you, and he draws a rather depressing conclusion from that. The last verse of the poem reads:

Man hands on misery to man,
It deepens like a coastal shelf;
Get out as early as you can,
And don't have any kids yourself.

What a grim, nasty little poem! In 1995, however, it was voted one of Britain's favorite poems, coming in between Thomas Hood's "I remember, I remember" and D.H. Lawrence's "The Snake." The fact that Larkin's poem should be so popular among intelligent poetry readers gives food for thought, suggesting as it does that negative attitudes toward parents are fairly widespread in British society.

The Buddha himself had quite a lot to say about our relation to our parents. In the *Sigalaka Sutta* he is represented as saying that there are five ways in which a son or daughter should minister to his or her mother and father as the eastern direction. He or she should think, "Having been supported by them, I will support them, I will perform their duties for them. I will keep up the family tradition. I will be worthy of my heritage. After my parents' deaths I will distribute gifts on their behalf."[141] There is a lot that could be said about the five ways in which one should minister to one's parents. Here, though, I want to touch on something even more fundamental—so fundamental that in this sutta the Buddha seems to take it for granted. It is hinted at, however, in the imagery of the sutta. The Buddha explains to Sigala that one pays homage to the east by ministering to one's parents in five ways. But why the east?

The reason is perhaps obvious. The sun rises in the east, it has its origin in the east, so to speak, and similarly we owe our origin to our parents—leaving aside questions of karma, of which perhaps parents are only instruments. If it were not for our parents, we would not be here now. They have given us life, they have given us a human body, and in Buddhism the human body is regarded as a very precious thing. It is precious because it is only in a human body that one is able to attain Enlightenment. In giving us a human body, our parents are therefore giving us the possibility of attaining Enlightenment and we should be intensely grateful to them for that, especially if we are actually practicing the Dharma.

Not only do our parents give us a human body; despite Larkin, they bring us up as best they can. They enable us to survive, they educate us. They may not always be able to send us to university and all that, but they teach us to speak, and this is the basis of most of the things we subsequently learn. Usually it is our mother who teaches us our first words, and this gives us the expression "mother tongue." It is through our mother tongue that we have access to all the literature that has been written in the language we learn in our earliest days, and we can enjoy that literature fully because it is in our mother tongue, rather than in a language we learn in later life.

Of course, not everybody cares to acknowledge their debt to their parents. We will consider the question of why people are so ungrateful later on. First, though, let us turn to the second of the principal objects of gratitude in Buddhism: our teachers. By teachers here I mean not Dharma teachers, but all those from whom we derive our secular education and culture. Here our school teachers obviously have an important place. From them we derive the rudiments of such learning as we have, and we therefore have to be grateful to them. The fact is that we have found out very little of what we know, or what we think we know, as a result of our own efforts. Practically everything we know has been taught to us in one way or another. If we think of our knowledge of science or history, for example, few of us have even performed a single scientific experiment, or discovered a single historical fact, which no one else had performed, or discovered, before. All our work in this field has been done for us by others. We have benefited from their efforts, and our knowledge is little more than the echo of theirs.

As well as learning from living teachers, we also learn from people who have been dead for hundreds of years, from the writings they have left and the records of the words they spoke. It is not just a question of learning from them in a purely intellectual sense, acquiring information. Among those books are works of the imagination—poems, novels, dramas—and these works are a source of infinite enrichment, without which we would be immeasurably poorer. They help us deepen and enlarge our vision. We should therefore be grateful to the great men and women who have produced them. We should be grateful to Homer and Virgil, Dante and Milton, Aeschylus and Kalidasa, Shakespeare and Goethe. We should be grateful to Murasaki Shikibu, Cervantes, Jane Austen, Dickens, Dostoyevsky, and hundreds of others, who have influenced us more than we can possibly realize. The American critic Harold Bloom has gone so far as to claim that Shakespeare is the creator of human nature as we know it, which is a very big claim indeed (though he gives his reasons for it).

Of course, our experience is also deepened, and our vision enlarged, by the visual arts and by music. The great painters, sculptors, and composers are also among our teachers. They too have enriched our lives, and to them too we should be grateful. I won't mention any names in this connection because there are simply too many to choose from—both ancient and modern, Eastern and Western—certainly not because I think that the great artists and composers are any less important than the great poets, novelists, and dramatists.

Thus by "teachers" I mean all those who between them have created our collective cultural heritage, without which we would not be fully human. Remembering what we owe them, and feeling grateful to the great artists, poets, and composers, we should not only enjoy their work but also celebrate their memory and share our enthusiasm for them with our friends.

Before we go on to consider the third principal object of gratitude, our spiritual friends, I want to make the general point that we need not think of these three objects of gratitude as being completely separate and distinct from one another. There is a certain amount of overlap between the first and second, and between the second and third. Our parents are also our teachers to an extent. In Buddhist tradition parents are called *poranacariyas,* which means "former (or ancient) teachers." They are called this because they are the first teachers we ever had, even if they only taught us to speak a few words. We can be grateful to our parents not only for giving us life but also for giving us at least the rudiments of knowledge, and initiating us into the beginnings of our cultural heritage.

Similarly there is some overlap between teachers and spiritual friends. The very greatest poets, artists, and composers can inspire us with spiritual values and help us rise to spiritual heights. In the course of the last few hundred years, great changes have taken place, at least in the West. Previously, Christianity as represented by the Church was the great, even the sole, bearer of spiritual values. But now many people look elsewhere to find meaning and values, and they find them in great works of art: in the plays of Shakespeare, the poetry of Wordsworth, Baudelaire, and Rilke, the music of Bach, Beethoven, and Mozart, the great painters and sculptors of the Italian Renaissance. These great masters become, as it were, our spiritual friends, especially if we remain in contact with them and with their work over many years. Learning to admire and love them, we feel intensely grateful to them for what they have given us. They are among our spiritual friends in the broadest sense.

But now let us come to our spiritual friends "proper." Here, as with the word gratitude, we have to go back to the Sanskrit words behind the English equivalent. As we have already seen, the Sanskrit phrase translated as "spiritual friend" is *kalyana mitra. Mitra* comes from the word *maitri* (Pali *metta*), and *maitri* is strong, unselfish, active love, sharply distinguished in Buddhist tradition from *prema* (Pali *pema*), in the sense of sexual love or attachment. A mitra or friend is therefore one who feels a strong unselfish active love toward one. And *kalyana* means firstly "beautiful, charming," and secondly "auspicious, helpful, morally good." Thus kalyana mitra has a much richer connotation than the English phrase "spiritual friend."

Our spiritual friends are all those who are spiritually more experienced than we are. The Buddhas are our spiritual friends. The Arahants and the Bodhisattvas are our spiritual friends. The great Buddhist teachers of India and China, Tibet and Japan, are our spiritual friends. Those who teach us meditation are our spiritual friends. Those with whom we study the scriptures are our spiritual friends. Those who ordain us are our spiritual friends. And all these spiritual friends should be the objects of our intense, heartfelt gratitude. We should be even more grateful to them than we are to our teachers.

Why? Because from our spiritual friends we receive the Dharma. We have not discovered or invented the Dharma. We have received it as a free gift from our spiritual friends, from the Buddha downward. In the *Dhammapada* the Buddha says, "The greatest of all gifts is the gift of the Dharma."[142] The greater the gift, the greater the gratitude we should feel. We should not only feel that gratitude in our hearts; we should give expression to it in words and deeds. We can do this in three ways: by singing the praises of our spiritual friends, by practicing the Dharma they have given us, and by passing on that Dharma to others to the best of our ability.

The greatest of our spiritual friends is the Buddha Shakyamuni, who discovered—or *re*-discovered—the path that we as Buddhists follow today. It is to him that we go for Refuge, it is the Dharma he taught that we try to practice, and it is with the support of the Sangha he founded that we are able to practice the Dharma. We therefore have reason to be intensely grateful to him—more grateful, in principle, than we are to anyone else. Our parents have indeed given us life, but what is life without the gift of the Dharma? Our teachers have given us knowledge, education, and culture, but what value do even these things have without the Dharma? It is because they are so intensely grateful to the Buddha that Buddhists perform pujas in devotion to him, and celebrate his life in the context of the various Buddhist festivals.

But people don't always find it easy to be grateful to their parents, or their teachers, or even their spiritual friends. Why is this? It is important to understand the nature of the difficulty. After all, gratitude is an important spiritual quality, a virtue exemplified and taught by the Buddha and many others. Cicero, the great Roman orator and philosopher, said that gratitude is not just the greatest virtue, but the mother of all the rest. Ingratitude therefore represents a very serious defect. On one occasion the Buddha said that ingratitude was one of the four great offenses which bring about *niraya* in the sense of rebirth in a state of suffering—a very serious and weighty statement.[143]

But why are we ungrateful to our parents, our teachers, our spiritual friends? One would have thought that as Buddhists we would be simply bubbling over with gratitude to all these people. A clue is to be found in the Pali word which we render as gratitude, *katannuta*. As we have seen, it means knowing or recognizing what has been done for one's benefit. Similarly, *akatannuta* (*a* being the negative prefix), ingratitude, means not knowing or recognizing what has been done for one's benefit.

There are a number of reasons for ingratitude. Firstly, one may fail to recognize a benefit as a benefit. There are some people who do not regard life itself as a benefit, and hence do not feel grateful to their parents for bringing them into the world. Sometimes people say things like, "Well I didn't ask to be brought into this world." If you believe in karma and rebirth, of course, this isn't quite true—but anyway, it is what people say. In a few cases, they may not regard life as a benefit because they experience it as painful, even predominantly painful, and therefore don't appreciate its value, don't realize the immense potential of human life. In Buddhist terms, they don't realize that it is possible for a human being, and only for a human being, to attain Enlightenment, or at least to make some progress in that direction.

Similarly, there are people who don't regard knowledge or education or culture as benefits. They feel no gratitude toward their teachers, or toward those who at least try to teach them something. They may even feel resentment. They may feel that education or culture is being imposed upon them. Such people are unlikely to come into contact with spiritual values, with the Dharma, or with spiritual friends, and even if they do, such contact will be external and superficial. They will not be able to recognize it for what it is. They may even see those who try to be their spiritual friends as enemies, and therefore the question of gratitude will not arise.

This was true of some people's responses to the Buddha himself. Not all those who heard him speak or teach felt grateful to him, by any means. There were many people in his day who saw him as a rather eccentric, unorthodox teacher. They certainly didn't feel any gratitude toward him for the gift of the Dharma. Sometimes people slandered him, and some people even tried to kill him.

On the other hand, we may recognize benefits as benefits, and even recognize that they have been given to us by other people, but we may take those benefits for granted. Not realizing that they are a free gift, we may think that they are owed to us, that we have a right to them, and that therefore in a sense they belong to us already, so that we have no need to be grateful for them.

This attitude is widespread in society today. People tend to think that everything is due to them, that they have a right to everything. Parents, teachers, or the state have a duty to provide them with whatever they want. Even spiritual friends, they may think, have a duty to provide them with what they want. If they don't get what they want from one spiritual friend, or teacher, or guru, and get it quickly, in the way they want it, off they will go, to try to get it from someone else. Once again, the question of gratitude doesn't arise. Of course, parents, teachers, and friends have a duty to bestow benefits to the best of their ability. But it should be recognized that those benefits have been *given,* and that the response to them should therefore be one of gratitude.

Another reason for ingratitude is egoism. Egoism takes many forms, and has many aspects. Here I mean by it an attitude of chronic individualism: the belief that one is separate from others, not dependent on others in any way, and that one therefore does not owe anything to others. One feels that one is not obliged to them, because one can do everything oneself. Examples of this sort of attitude abound in literature: Mr. Bounderby in Dickens' *Hard Times,* Satan in Milton's *Paradise Lost,* and "Black Salvation" in *The Life and Liberation of Padmasambhava.* People who are egoistical in this sense are incapable of feeling gratitude, and cannot admit that they have been benefited by others. They may not actually say so in the way Mr. Bounderby does, but this is their underlying attitude.

This attitude sometimes finds expression in the sphere of the arts. Some writers and artists don't like to think that they owe anything to their predecessors. Wanting to be original, to strike out on a completely new path, they don't like to think that there is such a thing as cultural heritage, or a literary canon. In some circles this attitude has taken an extreme, even a virulent form, and has resulted in an attempt to repudiate the greater part of our literary and artistic heritage on ideological grounds. This is an extremely unfortunate, even potentially disastrous development, and it is to be resisted wherever possible.

Egoism in the sense in which I am using the word also finds expression in the sphere of religion. It happens when we don't acknowledge the sources of our inspiration, or when we try to pass off as our own a teaching or practice that we have in fact learned from our spiritual friends.

The fourth and last reason for ingratitude that I want to mention here is forgetfulness. There are two main reasons for forgetfulness of benefits received. First, there is simply the passage of time. Perhaps the benefits were given to us a long time ago—so long ago that we have no distinct recollection of them, and no longer feel grateful to whoever bestowed them upon us, even if we did originally feel grateful. This is perhaps the principal reason for our not feeling actively grateful toward our parents. Over the years so much has happened in our life: early memories have been overlaid by later ones, other relationships have assumed importance, and perhaps we have moved away from our parents, geographically, socially, or culturally. The result is that—practically speaking—we forget them. We forget the numerous ways in which they benefited us when we were young, and we cease therefore to feel grateful. The other possible reason for our "forgetting" to be grateful is that we did not feel the positive effects of the benefits very strongly in the first place, and therefore did not feel much gratitude. In such circumstances, it is easy for the gratitude to fade away and be forgotten altogether.

These, then, are the four most important general reasons for ingratitude: failure to recognize a benefit as a benefit, taking benefits for granted, egoism, and forgetfulness. Ingratitude is unfortunately liable to crop up in various ways in the context of the life of a practicing Buddhist. Of course, beyond a certain point of spiritual progress, it is simply impossible to feel ungrateful. A Stream-entrant is incapable of it, and in fact will be overflowing with gratitude to parents, teachers, and spiritual friends. But until we have reached that point, we are in danger of forgetting to be grateful.

Over the years—more than thirty, at the time of writing—since I myself founded a Buddhist movement, I have received many, many letters, perhaps thousands, from people who have recently discovered the Dharma through one of the centers of the movement I founded, or through contact with individual members of the Order. Every year I receive more and more of these letters. They come from young people and old people, from people in many different walks of life, from many different cultural backgrounds and nationalities. And all these letters say, among other things, one and the same thing. They say how glad the writers are to have discovered the Dharma. Not only that: the writers of the letters want to express their gratitude to the Three Jewels and to this Buddhist movement, and to me personally for having founded it. Some people express their feeling of gratitude very strongly indeed. They say that the Dharma has changed their lives, given their lives meaning, saved them from despair, even saved them from suicide.

Such letters of gratitude reach me nearly every week, and they make me think that I have not altogether wasted my time all these years. But over the years I have also noticed that while some people, perhaps the majority, stay grateful, and even become more and more grateful, in the cases of a few people, unfortunately, the feeling of gratitude weakens. They start forgetting the benefits they have received, and even start questioning whether they really were benefits at all. No longer knowing or recognizing what has been done for them, they become ungrateful. Feeling ungrateful to their spiritual friends, they may even start finding fault with them. This is a very sad state of affairs indeed, and in recent years I have given some thought to it and have come to certain conclusions about how it happens.

It seems to me that people forget the benefits they have received because they no longer feel them. And they no longer feel them because for one reason or another they have put themselves in a position where they cannot receive them. Let me give a concrete example. Suppose you have started attending a meditation class. You learn to meditate, and you achieve some success. You start practicing at home. But one day, for one reason or another, you stop attending the class and then you gradually stop practicing at home. You cease to meditate. Eventually you forget what meditative experience was like. You forget the peace and the joy you felt. You forget the benefits of meditation. So you cease to feel grateful to those who introduced you to the practice. The same thing can happen with regard to retreats, Dharma study, spending time with spiritual friends, taking part in pujas, and attending Buddhist celebrations. People can get out of touch. They can forget how much they did, once upon a time, benefit from those activities, and therefore they can cease to feel grateful to those who made the activities possible.

Sometimes people reconnect after a while; they start attending the meditation class again, or go on retreat again, perhaps after many years. I have known people who have re-established contact after anything up to twenty-two years—rather a long time in anybody's life. When this happens, they nearly always say the same thing: "I had forgotten how good it was." And therefore they feel renewed gratitude.

This is entirely appropriate. It is appropriate that we should be grateful, that we should recognize the benefits we have received. It is appropriate that we should be grateful to our parents, with all their admitted imperfections—parents are not perfect any more than children are. It is appropriate that we should be grateful to our teachers, to our spiritual friends, and to the Buddhist tradition. Above all, it is appropriate that we should be grateful to the Buddha, who, as we have seen, was himself utterly and instinctively full of gratitude.

PART FIVE

Buddhism and the World

1 ← Compassionate Activity

1. The Bodhisattva's Reply

What will you say to those
Whose lives spring up between
Custom and circumstance
As weeds between wet stones,
Whose lives corruptly flower
Warped from the beautiful,
Refuse and sediment
Their means of sustenance—
What will you say to them?

That woman, night after night,
Must sell her body for bread;
This boy with the well-oiled hair
And the innocence dead in his face
Must lubricate the obscene
Bodies of gross old men;
And both must be merry all day,
For thinking would make them mad—
What will you say to them?

Those dull-eyed men must tend
Machines till they become
Machines, or till they are
Cogs in the giant wheel
Of industry, producing
The clothes that they cannot wear
And the cellophaned luxury goods
They can never hope to buy—
What will you say to them?

Or these dim shadows which
Through the pale gold tropic dawn
From the outcaste village flit
Balancing on their heads
Baskets to bear away
Garbage and excrement,
Hugging the wall for fear
Of the scorn of their fellow-men—
What will you say to them?

And wasted lives that litter
The streets of modern cities,
Souls like butt-ends trampled on,
Human refuse dumped
At the crossroads where civilization
And civilization meet
To breed the unbeautiful—
What will you say to them?

"I shall say nothing, but only
Fold in Compassion's arms
Their frailty till it becomes
Strong with my strength, their limbs
Bright with my beauty, their souls

With my wisdom luminous, or
Till I have become like them
A seed between wet stones
Of custom and circumstance."

2. COMPASSION: THE MOST IMPORTANT VIRTUE

"Since you have learned compassion—you'll do!"

IN THE MAHAYANA form of Buddhism, that is to say in the teaching of the "Great Way," the highest possible importance is attached to compassion. In one of the Mahayana sutras, in fact, the Buddha is represented as saying that the Bodhisattva—the one who aspires to be a Buddha—should not be taught too many things. If he is taught only compassion, learns only compassion, that is quite enough. No need for him to know about conditioned co-production, or about the Madhyamika, or the Yogacara, or the Abhidharma—or even the Eightfold Path. If the Bodhisattva knows only compassion, has a heart filled with nothing but compassion, that is enough. In other texts the Buddha says that if one has only compassion for the sufferings of other living beings, then in due course all other virtues, all other spiritual qualities and attainments, even Enlightenment itself, will follow.

This is illustrated by a very moving story from Japan. We are told there was a young man who was a great wastrel. After running through all his money and having a good time, he became thoroughly disgusted with everything, including himself. In this mood he decided that there was only one thing he could do, and that was to enter the Zen monastery and become a monk. This was his last resort. He didn't really *want* to become a monk, but there was nothing else left for him. So along to the Zen monastery he went. I suppose he knelt outside in the snow for three days, in the way we are told applicants have to kneel. But in the end the abbot agreed to see him. The abbot was a grim old soul. He listened to what the young man had to say, himself not saying very much, but when the young man had told him everything, he said, "Hmm, well . . . is there *anything* you are good at?" The young man thought, and finally said, "Yes. I'm not so bad at chess." So the abbot called his attendant and told him to fetch a certain monk.

The monk came. He was an old man, and had been a monk for many years. Then the abbot said to the attendant, "Bring my sword." So the sword was brought and placed before the abbot. The abbot then said to the young man and the old monk, "You two will now play a game of chess. Whoever loses, I will cut off his head with this sword!" They looked at him, and they saw that he meant it. So the young man made his first move. The old monk, who was not a bad player, made his. The young man made his next move. The old monk made his. After a little while the young man felt the perspiration pouring down his back and trickling over his heels. So he concentrated: he put everything he had into that game, and managed to beat back the old monk's attack. Then he drew a great breath of relief, "Ah, the game isn't going too badly!" But just then, when he was sure he would win, he looked up, and he saw the face of that old monk. As I have said, he was an old man, and had been a monk many years—maybe twenty or thirty, or even forty years. He had undergone much suffering, had performed many austerities, and had meditated for many, many hours. His face was thin and worn and austere.

The young man suddenly thought, "I have been an absolute wastrel! My life is no use to anybody. This monk has led such a good life, and now he is going to have to die." A great wave of compassion came over him. He felt intensely sorry for the old monk, just sitting there and playing this game in obedience to the abbot's command, and now being beaten, soon to have to die. A tremendous compassion welled up in the young man's heart, and he thought, "I can't allow this." So he deliberately made a false move. The monk made a move. The young man deliberately made another false move, and it was clear that he was losing, and was unable to retrieve his position. But suddenly the abbot upset the board, saying, "No one has won, and no one has lost." Then to the young man he said, "You have learned two things today: concentration and compassion. Since you have learned compassion—you'll do!"

3. Responding to the Needs of Others

Caring for others on the basis of a spiritual motivation is much more diffi-cult than caring for them out of a sexual or family interest.

It is not often that we see people just as themselves rather than as instruments of our own needs, and very rare indeed for us to put our-selves out for other people in a completely disinterested way. We might do it for our own mother or father, friend, lover, or child, but mostly we look after number one. For monks or nuns there is a partic-ular danger in this regard, inasmuch as they have left behind the natu-ral and biological attachments that will draw the ordinary lay-person out of complete selfishness. The danger of the monastic life is well illustrated in the *Mahavagga* section of the Vinaya, which recounts how the Buddha finds a monk suffering from dysentery and who is neglected by the other monks.[144] When the Buddha asks why the poor fellow is not being looked after, the monks reply, "Lord, he is not use-ful to us": a dreadful admission. They are duly reprimanded, and even though in the Pali Canon there is no mention of the Bodhisattva Ideal as such, something like it, or the seeds of it, is clearly implied. "You have no father and mother to look after you," the Buddha says. As a member of a spiritual community you do not belong to any natural group to the members of which you may look for help simply on account of the ties of blood. The help you give one another can only be motivated by a purely spiritual impulse, a feeling of common mem-bership of a purely spiritual body.

Caring for others on the basis of a spiritual motivation is much more difficult than caring for them out of a sexual or family interest. If your son needs a new pair of shoes, you may well be willing to put off getting yourself a new shirt—and this sort of thing has a maturing effect. So the danger of falling into selfishness and self-preoccupation is much greater for the monastic community than it is for lay people with all their kith and kin to care for. The advantage of being a monk or nun is of course that you are able to avoid the often unconscious mutual exploitation that so often disguises itself as the caring and meaningful sexual relationship.

There is in fact only one need of one's own that has to be fulfilled before one can preoccupy oneself effectively with the needs of others, and it is not a physical or material need, but simply a matter of emotional positivity and security. We need to appreciate our own worth and feel that it is appreciated by others, to love ourselves and feel that we are loved by others. On this basis we can begin to develop the sensitivity and awareness to appreciate the real needs of others—not only their material needs, or even their educational needs, but their need for an ideal to which they can devote themselves, a spiritual path they can follow. At the same time, the group of others to whom our concern extends can grow to include not only our own family and friends, but people beyond our own kind, race, gender, and even views. It can even include quite different classes of beings.

4. WITHDRAWAL AND INVOLVEMENT

There is a conflict, if you are big enough and rich enough in your nature to embrace the possibilities of such a conflict.

THE WILL TO ENLIGHTENMENT (*bodhicitta*) is said to arise as a result of the coalescence of two trends of experience which are generally considered to be contradictory, since in ordinary experience they can-

COMPASSIONATE ACTIVITY ~ 567

not both be pursued simultaneously. We might call these the trend of withdrawal from the world and the trend of involvement in the world.

The first of these trends represents renunciation in the extreme sense, a withdrawal from worldly activities, worldly thoughts, and secular associations. This withdrawal is aided by a particular practice, that of reflection on the faults or imperfections of conditioned existence. You reflect that life in this world, whirling round and round in the Wheel of Life, is profoundly unsatisfactory, involving as it does all sorts of disagreeable experiences. You experience physical pain and discomfort, you don't get what you want, you're separated from people you like, you have to do things you don't want to do. There's the whole wretched business of having to earn a living, doing your daily chores, taking care of your body—feeding it, clothing it, housing it, looking after it when it gets sick—not to mention taking responsibility for looking after your dependants. It all seems too much. All you want to do is get away from it all, away from the fluctuations, vicissitudes, and distractions of mundane life into the peace of the perfection of the Unconditioned, the unchanging rest of nirvana.

The second trend in our experience—involvement—is concern for living beings. You reflect: "Well, it would be all right for me to opt out and withdraw from it all—I'd like that—but what about other people? What will happen to *them?* There are people who have a much harder time in this world than I do, who can stand it even less than I can. How will they ever get free if I abandon them?" This trend of involvement is aided by the practice of reflection on the sufferings of sentient beings. In the trend of withdrawal, you reflect on the sufferings and imperfections of conditioned existence only in so far as they affect you, but here you reflect on them as they affect other living beings. You just look around at all the people you know, your friends and acquaintances, all the people you meet, and you reflect on all their troubles and difficulties. Perhaps one or two have lost their jobs, another's marriage has broken up, yet another may have had a nervous breakdown, and there may well be someone who has recently been bereaved. If you think it over, there is not a single person you know who is not suffering in some way. Even if they seem comparatively happy in the ordinary sense, there are still things that they will have to bear: separation or illness, the weakness and tiredness of old age, and finally death, which they almost certainly don't want.

Then, when you cast your gaze further afield, there is so much suffering in so many parts of the world: wars, catastrophes of various kinds, floods and famines, people dying in horrible ways. You can even think of animals and how they suffer, not only at the teeth and claws of other animals but at the hands of human beings. The whole world of living beings is involved in suffering. And when you reflect on this, you ask yourself: "How can I possibly think simply in terms of getting out of it all on my own? How can I possibly think of getting away by myself to some private nirvana, some private spiritual experience, which may be very satisfactory to me but is of no help to others?"

So there is a conflict, if you are big enough and rich enough in your nature to embrace the possibilities of such a conflict. On one hand you want to get out; on the other you want to stay here. Of course, the easy solution is simply to choose between them. There are some people who withdraw into spiritual individualism, private spiritual experience, while others remain in the world without much of a spiritual outlook at all. But although these trends are contradictory, both of them must be developed in the course of the spiritual life. The trend of withdrawal may be said to embody the wisdom aspect of the spiritual life, while the trend of involvement embodies the compassion aspect.

These two practices—reflecting on the faults of conditioned existence and reflecting on the sufferings of sentient beings—form part of a traditional method of creating the conditions in dependence upon which the bodhicitta can arise. This is the method taught by a great Indian master of the Mahayana, Vasubandhu, who lived, so the Mahayana tradition says, in the latter half of the fifth century CE. Vasubandhu enumerated four practices which would provide a basis for the arising of the bodhicitta; they are known as Vasubandhu's Four Factors. The first two are "seeing the faults of conditioned existence" and "reflecting on the sufferings of living beings"—the trends of withdrawal and involvement we have just discussed—and the third and fourth are "the recollection of the Buddhas" and "the contemplation of the virtues of the Tathagatas" ("Tathagata" being another word for Buddha).

In recollecting the Buddhas, one brings to mind the historical Buddha Shakyamuni, who lived in India about two thousand five hundred years ago, and the lineage of his great predecessors of which the Buddhist tradition speaks. In particular, one reflects that these Buddhas started their spiritual careers as human beings, with their weaknesses and limitations, just as we do. Just as they managed to transcend all limitations to become Enlightened, so can we, if only we make the effort.

There are several ways of approaching the fourth practice, the contemplation of the virtues of the Tathagatas. One can dwell on the life of an Enlightened One—the spiritual biography of the Buddha or Milarepa, for example. One can perform pujas in front of a shrine, or perhaps just sit and look at a Buddha image, really trying to get a feeling for what the image represents. Then again, one can do a visualization practice in which—to be very brief indeed—one conjures up a vivid mental picture of a particular Buddha or Bodhisattva, an embodiment of an aspect of Enlightenment such as wisdom, compassion, energy, or purity.

We can think of these Four Factors as forming a kind of sequence. First, through recollecting the Buddhas, we become convinced that Enlightenment is possible for us. Then, on seeing the faults of conditioned existence, we become detached from it, and the trend of our being is set in the direction of the Unconditioned. Thirdly, through observing the suffering of sentient beings—whether in imagination or close at hand—compassion arises, and we want to rescue not only ourselves but other beings from suffering. Then, as we contemplate the virtues of the Tathagatas, we gradually become assimilated to them, and approach Enlightenment itself.

However, although we can think of the Four Factors sequentially in this way, the bodhicitta in fact arises in dependence on all four simultaneously. This means—returning to the tension between withdrawal and involvement—that we must not allow the tension between these two trends to relax. If we do that, we are lost. Even though they are contradictory, we have to follow both trends simultaneously, seeing the faults of conditioned existence and at the same time feeling the sufferings of sentient beings, developing both wisdom and compassion. As we develop and pursue both of these, the tension—and this tension is not psychological but spiritual—builds up and up until we simply can't go any further.

At that point, something happens. It is very difficult to describe exactly what does happen, but we can think of it provisionally as an explosion. The tension which has been generated through following these two contradictory trends simultaneously results in a breakthrough into a higher dimension of spiritual consciousness. Withdrawal and involvement are no longer two separate trends, not because they have been artificially amalgamated into one, but because the plane or level on which their duality existed, or on which it was possible for them to be two things, has been transcended. When that explosion occurs, one has the experience of being simultaneously withdrawn and involved, simultaneously out of the world and in the world. Wisdom and compassion become non-dual, not separate, not-two—without, at the same time, being simply numerically one. When this breakthrough occurs, when for the first time one is both withdrawn and involved, when wisdom and compassion are not two things side by side but one thing, then the bodhicitta has arisen. There has occurred a conversion from spiritual individualism to a life of complete selflessness—or at least such a life has been initiated.

5. Giving: The Basic Buddhist Virtue

According to Buddhist teaching we should be giving in some way or other, on some level or other, all the time.

IN A SENSE *dana* or giving is the basic Buddhist virtue, without which you can hardly call yourself a Buddhist. Dana consists not so much in the act of giving as in the feeling of wanting to give, of wanting to share what you have with other people. This feeling of wanting to give or share is often the first manifestation of the spiritual life—the first sign that craving and attachment have decreased to some extent. Dana is discussed at great length in Buddhist literature, and many different forms are enumerated.

First, there is *the giving of material things,* or sharing what you have of the good things of life: food, clothing, and so on. Some people in the East make it a practice to try to give something of a material nature every day, be it food to a beggar, a small sum of money, or just a cup of tea, so that every day something is given, or something shared, on the material plane.

Secondly there is *the giving of time, energy, and thought.* Time is a very precious thing, and if we give some of it to help other people this is also a form of dana.

There is also *the giving of knowledge,* in the sense of the giving of culture and education. This has always ranked very highly in Buddhist countries. Intellectual acquisitions should not be kept to oneself, but should be shared with all. All should be able to benefit from them. This was particularly emphasized in Buddhist India, because the Brahmin caste, the priestly caste of Hinduism, invariably sought to monopolize knowledge and keep other castes in a state of ignorance and subservience. Buddhism has always stressed that knowledge, even secular knowledge and secular culture, should not be a monopoly of any particular caste or class of people, but should be disseminated among the whole community.

Another important kind of giving mentioned in Buddhist literature is *the giving of fearlessness.* This might seem a rather strange kind of gift. You cannot hand anyone fearlessness on a plate, or wrapped up in a little parcel tied with ribbon. But you can share your own confidence with other people. You can create among people a feeling of fearlessness or security by your very presence, your very attitude. Buddhism attaches great importance to this ability to reassure people by your mere presence. According to Buddhism this form of dana is an important contribution to the life of the community.

Yet another form of dana which is mentioned in Buddhist literature is *the giving of life and limb.* For the sake of other people, or for the sake of the Dharma, the Teaching, one should be prepared to sacrifice one's own limbs, even one's own life. *Dana* can go as far as this.

Finally, surpassing even the giving of one's own life, there is what is called in Buddhism *the giving of the gift of the Dharma:* the gift of truth itself; the gift of the knowledge, or understanding, of the way to Enlightenment, Emancipation, Buddhahood, or Nirvana. The gift of this sort of knowledge surpasses all other gifts whatever.

These are just some of the things which one can give, and looking at them we begin to see how vast and comprehensive the practice of giving can be. According to Buddhist teaching we should be giving in some way or other, on some level or other, all the time. In the Buddhist East dana or giving penetrates and permeates all aspects of social and religious life. If you are going to a temple, for instance, you don't go empty-handed: you take flowers, candles, and incense to offer. In the same way if you go to see a friend, even if the visit is only a casual one, you always take a present. When I was staying in Kalimpong, and mixing a great deal with Tibetans, I found that this was absolutely *de rigueur.* A friend would not think of appearing on your doorstep without a tin of biscuits or some other gift under his arm. In this way the spirit of giving permeates all aspects of life in many Buddhist countries. No doubt all this does sometimes become just a custom, and often there might not be much feeling attached to it. But nonetheless when you are giving all the time in one form or another it does have some influence upon the mind—even if you are doing it only because you are expected to. You get into the habit of giving and sharing, and of thinking a little bit about others, instead of all the time about yourself.

6. THE ALTRUISTIC DIMENSION OF GOING FOR REFUGE

If you are even a little bit open-handed, then whatever else you may be, there is some hope for you, from a spiritual point of view.

DANA—literally giving or generosity—is the practical, altruistic aspect of the Bodhisattva's life and activity, and the first of the six *paramitas*, the six perfections or transcendental virtues. Dana is right at the top of the list of perfections for a very good reason, which is that our natural tendency is not to give, but to take. If any new proposition comes up, whether in connection with work or home, professional activity, sport, or entertainment, our usual reaction, at least half-consciously, is "What's in it for me?" There is always this self-referential tendency, this grasping. The fact that it is put right at the hub of the Wheel of Life is a recognition of the fact that craving—not just ordinary healthy desire, but craving—occupies a very important place in our life and activity. In fact it dominates our life, at least unconsciously. We are all in the grip of craving, swept along, impelled, by this thirst. Everything we do, everything we are interested in, has an element of self-reference.

If we are to get anywhere near Enlightenment, we have to reverse this tendency. Giving is the first *paramita* because giving is the direct opposite of grasping. It's as if the teaching is saying, "You may not be morally scrupulous. You may not be able to meditate even for five minutes at a time. You may not dip into the scriptures from one year to the next. But if you aspire to lead any sort of higher life, then at the very least you will give." If you find it difficult to part with things, difficult to look to the needs of others, you aren't going to get very far, spiritually speaking. On the other hand, if you are even a little bit open-handed, then whatever else you may be, there is some hope for you, from a spiritual point of view. This is the message of the Mahayana.

It isn't just a question of handing over one's possessions. Generosity is above all an attitude of heart and mind, indeed, of one's whole being. Walt Whitman says, "When I give, I give myself,"[145] and this is very much the Bodhisattva's attitude. To forget about traditional definitions for a moment, perhaps we could simply define a Bodhisattva as someone who gives himself or herself all the time, to everybody.

The Bodhisattva may, upon occasions, need to give his or her very life. This form of giving is the subject of many a Jataka story (the Jatakas being stories about the Buddha's previous lives). Some of these stories may seem lurid, melodramatic, or simply weird. The story of Prince Vessantara, for example, describes the Bodhisattva ("Bodhisattva" in this context referring to the Buddha-to-be) giving away his wife and children.[146] We may be inclined, perhaps thinking of incidents from our own society, to feel upset or even outraged at the very idea. Were his wife and children the property of the Bodhisattva that he should give them away like so many goods and chattels? And, of course, in our society men—and sometimes women—have been known to give up their families not for any noble or altruistic reason, but simply in pursuit of their own happiness.

But the story of Prince Vessantara (which is after all from a cultural context very different from our own) is intended to illustrate how Bodhisattvas may need to give up even those who are naturally nearest and dearest to them. For some, this will seem an even harder sacrifice than that of their own life—a sacrifice which the Bodhisattva hero of many Jatakas also makes, on one occasion, for example, sacrificing his body to a starving tigress so that she could feed her cubs.[147]

We are unlikely ever to find ourselves in a situation anything like that, but we should never forget that if we take Buddhism seriously, we may be required under certain circumstances to make great sacrifices for our ideals. In the West at present, if we want to practice Buddhism, nobody can stop us. We can study texts, we can meditate, we can practice dana, we can perform devotional ceremonies, we can do whatever we like, and we are fortunate that this should be so. But it isn't the case in all parts of the world, even now. We need to recognize how fortunate we are to have religious freedom.

We might even have to be prepared to sacrifice our lives for the sake of our principles. In present circumstances it may be easy enough to go along to a meditation class; but suppose you had to make your way to it under cover of darkness, watching out for the police or the informer? If you meditated in peril of your life, or read a book on Buddhism in peril of your life, or stood up and spoke about the Dharma in peril of your life—as would be the case in some countries in the world today—would you do it? Or would you think, "Well, I'll be a Buddhist in my next life; it's too difficult in this one"? One just doesn't know. All this is not to suggest that there is any virtue in throwing away one's life in a reckless or showy manner; but we must ask ourselves whether, if the sacrifice were necessary, we would be prepared to make it.

7. Is the Bodhisattva Ideal Realistic?

How can we take this as a workable aspiration for a real live human being? We find it difficult enough to help with washing the dishes sometimes.

As ordinary individuals we can perhaps allow ourselves to think in terms of rebirth—even in terms of a series of rebirths extending over quite a long period of time. We can perhaps imagine ourselves as continuing our spiritual life through a succession of lives. But can we think in terms of a Bodhisattva career literally extending over three *kalpas?* A kalpa is a very long time. The traditional description of a kalpa asks us to imagine a rock a mile high, a mile wide, and a mile long. Then we imagine that once every hundred years someone comes and strokes a piece of Benares [Varanasi] silk, just once, along the top of the rock. A kalpa is the amount of time it would take to wear down the whole rock, at that rate.[148] It is a truly immense period of time.

Gampopa, the great Tibetan Kagyu teacher who lived at about the time of the Norman Conquest in Britain, quotes the *Bodhisattva-bhumi* in his *Jewel Ornament of Liberation*:

> I shall rejoice at staying in hell for thousands of aeons if only to save one single being from misery, to say nothing of still longer periods and of still greater miseries. Such is a Bodhisattva's armor of strenuousness.[149]

So apparently the Bodhisattva volunteers for sojourns of millions of years in various hells for the sake of helping just one living being. But can we really imagine ourselves doing that? Surely it would be impossible for any human being to say that and sincerely believe it. If we try to imagine what the pains of hell would be like, we realize we wouldn't be able to stand even a hundredth part of that sort of pain. How can we take this as a workable aspiration for a real live human being? We find it difficult enough to help with washing the dishes sometimes. When the texts speak of the Bodhisattva in this way, it makes most sense to think that they are referring to a sort of cosmic trend, or recognizing the existence of a potentiality for Enlightenment even under the most unfavorable circumstances.

We find a similarly formidable prospect in *The Precious Garland,* in which Nagarjuna says:

> (A Bodhisattva) stays for a limitless time [in the world],
> For limitless embodied beings he seeks
> The limitless (qualities of) enlightenment
> And performs virtuous actions without limit.[150]

So here again we find a Mahayana text describing the Bodhisattva, the embodiment of the ideal we are exhorted to fulfill, but it doesn't seem at all practicable for us. Indeed, to judge from this description, the Bodhisattva hardly seems like a person at all. The impression one gets is that the Bodhisattva is beyond individuality as we usually understand it, a disembodied impersonal spiritual energy.

This being the case, we can gather that the Mahayana isn't expecting us to behave in literally the manner described. We don't have to imagine ourselves performing infinite good deeds, establishing Buddhafields, liberating infinite numbers of beings. . . . It is more practical to take the Bodhisattva as representing a universal, even omnipresent spiritual energy at work in the universe—an energy we get a sense of every now and then. We can't literally think of being a Bodhisattva, but we can be open to the ideal, aspiring to be a channel for that energy within our own particular sphere. That is the most realistic, even the most honest way to see it. We have to stick very close to our actual situation; otherwise we can get lost in unrealistic aspirations. It can all become a bit theatrical; and this does sometimes happen in the Mahayana countries of the Buddhist East. The Theravada is much more sober, much closer to the facts of the situation.

But the Mahayana conveys very well the spirit of the whole process: the fact that this process takes place within a much wider, even a cosmic context. In *The Precious Garland* Nagarjuna says:

> Through faith in the Mahayana
> And through the practices explained therein
> The highest enlightenment is attained
> And along the way all pleasures.[151]

Why should there be "all pleasures" along the way on the Mahayana—as distinct from the "Hinayana"—path? The difference, one can say simply, is the Bodhisattva ideal. The "Hinayana" speaks more in terms of giving things up, disciplining oneself, getting rid of craving, and so on. If the goal is mentioned at all, it is usually referred to in terms of the cessation of suffering or the cessation of craving—not, for most people, a very inspiring prospect, not in the early stages of their spiritual life anyway. The Mahayana's ideal of the Bodhisattva is quite simply more inspiring.

During the Buddha's lifetime, when the ideal was visibly present in the form of the Buddha himself, there was presumably no need to talk about it very much. But when the Buddha was no longer around, the ideal he represented had to be formulated somehow. Something had to be created to take the place of the actual presence of the Buddha. With the emergence of the Bodhisattva ideal, the Bodhisattva came to represent the sort of person you had to become if you wanted to be like the Buddha.

It's all about vision. If one is to be inspired to build a Buddhist center, to take that example, one will need to be given a vision of what one is creating. If one has a picture in one's mind of beautiful Buddha images, spacious, peaceful rooms, and a wonderful community of people, even if what one is doing is plastering a ceiling or knocking down a wall, one will be inspired to do it. If someone just came along and said, "Knock down that wall," that would feel entirely different. If one is doing what one is doing for the sake of a positive goal, one can work much more happily. Indeed, it becomes pleasure all the way.

So we need to find a balance between vision and pragmatism. Perhaps the best solution is to take the two together: take the smaller view for here and now, for daily practice, and the cosmic view as a guide to the ideal as it exists outside space and time, independent of one's own small efforts.

All one really needs is a faith in the conservation of spiritual values beyond death. If one has that, one can be sure that if one practices the Dharma here and now, the future—how and where one will be reborn, whether or not one will become a Buddha in some distant world system and so on—will look after itself. Perhaps one can't realistically make one's future Buddhahood the object of an aspiration. We need not take the Mahayana sutras literally; they can be regarded as giving an inspiring glimpse of an archetypal world, but not as providing a pattern for Buddhist living in a detailed sense. One gets a much stronger sense of such a pattern from the Pali Canon.

8. WAYS OF HELPING

There is so much that can be done if we have the will and the heart to do it.

ONE CAN'T DO ANYTHING with or for other people without at least a touch of the Bodhisattva ideal to keep one going. Otherwise, there will be a reaction sooner or later. Resentment will set in the moment one feels taken for granted. One can even start hating the people one is trying to help; at the very least it will feel a strain. But the Bodhisattva feels no tension or strain, because he or she is acting on the basis of the arisen bodhicitta.

The *Bodhicittavivarana* says, "One who understands the nature of the bodhicitta sees everything with a loving heart, for love is the essence of the bodhicitta. . . . All Bodhisattvas find their *raison d'être* . . . in this great loving heart."[152] It's the bodhicitta that makes the Bodhisattva. However altruistic one is, or tries to be, one is not a Bodhisattva if that transcendental dimension hasn't entered one's being. It could even be said that only when the bodhicitta has arisen is one really on the spiritual path; until then one is just preparing the ground.

But whether or not the bodhicitta has arisen, there are certainly a great many people in need of help, and we should not delay in helping where we can. There are certain groups of people who are perhaps especially in need of whatever help we can give them. First of all, old people are often in need of help. Many of them have to live alone, and they often, not unnaturally, feel lonely and neglected. If one can offer a few old people in one's neighborhood a bit of warm human contact on a regular basis, it may make a great deal of difference to their lives.

Then there are the sick: not just those who are down with flu for a couple of days—though they need help too—but especially those who are confined to the hospital, sometimes with serious, painful diseases, for long periods of time. It sometimes happens that after a while even their closest relations begin to neglect them, thinking, "Ah well, I can go next week or the week after. After all, old so-and-so's there all the time; they don't go away." In the end they may stop visiting altogether. And many hospital patients, especially those who have been there a long time and those who are old, have no relations or friends to visit them. So this is something very practical we can do.

Then what about those confined to prison for one reason or another? We may not be able to visit them, but we could write. A lot of prisoners get a great deal of support from people writing to them and helping them to keep in touch with what is happening outside, helping them to feel that they still belong to the world to which one day they will have to return.

Also, those who are suffering mentally in one way or another need help and support. Many people whose psychological balance is disturbed need expert help—we certainly shouldn't try to do more than we are qualified to do—but it may be that simple friendliness will help someone a great deal. Much mental distress is due to a lack of communication with other people, a lack of any opportunity to disclose oneself. In such cases befriending people and making it possible for them to talk about what's on their mind can be very helpful.

I once read about a catatonic patient in a mental hospital who didn't respond at all, ever, to anybody or anything. But there was a young nurse in the ward who became convinced that he could be brought to respond. So every day she simply took his hand and held it for half an hour. She did this for six months without any response at all, but then one day the patient squeezed her hand in return, and that was the turning point. Over a period of a few months she was able to open up some sort of communication with him, and in the end he came out of his catatonic state. Such things are possible. In psychotherapy, one of the main factors that contributes to helping the patient is that the analyst is listening to them. Ordinary doctors are sometimes put in this position—the person who comes ostensibly as a patient is just desperate for somebody to talk to. We shouldn't underestimate the value of simple communication.

And sometimes expert help doesn't help. Psychotherapy can help people in many ways, but in cases where there are symptoms of some deeper existential disturbance, psychotherapy in the ordinary medical sense may not help much. The effectiveness of a system of psychotherapy depends very much on the ideas it is based on, especially its idea of what it is to be a human being. If you have a limited view of human beings, you cannot help having a limited view of mental illness, and therefore a limited view of psychotherapy. There is a great difference between somebody who sees a human being as a potential Buddha and somebody who sees a human being merely as a rational animal, or even an irrational one.

Today schools of psychotherapy are increasingly aware of the need to help people confront existential problems. We are ultimately spiritual beings, and if our need for spiritual life is frustrated, that may result in mental distress. There will always be people whose psychological problems call for therapy rather than meditation. But ultimately there is no such thing as a psychological solution. In the long run the key to mental health is not psychological but spiritual. In any case, communication is always the key factor, and whenever our friendship may help someone in psychological difficulties, we should not hesitate to offer it.

There are, of course, many other kinds of people to whom we can offer help: refugees, the homeless, the starving, the under-privileged all over the world. It is difficult to help directly—not everybody can just go off to Africa or India—but we may be able to help indirectly through a charity. There is so much that can be done if we have the will and the heart to do it. And this is the first thing that the Bodhisattva sets out to do: to help living beings—human beings and animals—out of their immediate, practical, material difficulties. At this stage one doesn't presume to think of leading anybody to Enlightenment. To begin with it's enough to give someone a helping hand in the affairs of everyday life according to one's capacities.

However, whether or not we are qualified to give spiritual help and guidance, this is what many people need more than anything else. If we ourselves are not in a position to give that sort of help directly, we can give it indirectly, by helping those who *can* give it, perhaps by freeing them from other responsibilities or providing facilities of some kind. For example, a good writer, or a good meditation or Dharma teacher, will very often need financial support if they are to put their valuable gifts to best use.

One should be careful to avoid the feeling that the way of helping one has found is the only way. Years ago, when I was working among the most socially deprived Buddhists in India, often treated as untouchables, I met a man on a train who, in no uncertain terms, expressed the opinion that I was wasting my time. According to him the people who needed help were the lepers, and I ought to be devoting my time to them. Well, I could see his point, but he couldn't see mine. I certainly didn't feel that it was wrong for him to be working among the lepers, or that he should be working among the neo-Buddhists instead. But he could not see that working for the neo-Buddhists might be just as valid as working for the lepers. Indeed, the only way we can extend the relief of suffering in the world is by taking an interest where others have not yet done so.

2 ☙ Buddhist Ethics

1. Before Dawn

> Cut off from what I really think and feel,
> The substance of my life becomes ideal.
> A whited sepulchre, a plaster saint,
> Is not much use, however bright its paint.
> Dreaming, awake, I must do all I can
> To join the inward and the outward man.
> Death stares me in the face: I watch and pray.
> So near the goal, and yet so far away!

2. The Basis of Buddhist Ethics

We can perhaps summarize the position of traditional ethics today by saying that it consists in not doing what we want to do, and doing what we do not want to do, because—for reasons we do not understand—we have been told to by someone in whose existence we no longer believe. No wonder we are confused.

CHURCHMEN AND OTHERS are fond of lamenting what they call the decline of morals. In the course of the last few decades everybody is supposed to have become progressively more immoral, and I gather we are now in a pretty bad state. The decline of morals is usually linked very firmly with the decline of religion, especially orthodox religion. Having turned our back on the Church, we are told, we have at once plunged into the pit, the mire, of immorality. Indeed we may argue that traditional ethics have to a very great extent collapsed. Many people are no longer convinced that there are any fixed standards of right and wrong. In the seventeenth century one of the Cambridge Platonists, Ralph Cudworth, wrote a book which he called *A Treatise on Eternal and Immutable Morality*. If anyone, even the Archbishop of Canterbury or the Pope, were to write a book with this title nowadays it would seem quite ridiculous. Even the great humanists and freethinkers of the nineteenth century, widely as they might range in their intellectual questioning, continued to conform to Christian ethics. Apart from one or two slips, when it came to their "home life," as the Victorians called it, people like Darwin, Huxley, and even Marx were models of morality. But that is all changed now. A young lady said to me the other day, "If you do something and it makes you feel good, then that thing is right, at least for you." This is a very widely held view. It may not always be held as explicitly, openly, and frankly as this; but it is, in fact, what many people think.

This development is not necessarily a bad thing. In the long run it might even be a good thing that morals should be thrown—temporarily we hope—into the melting-pot, and that we should have to re-think and re-feel, even re-imagine, our morality. It is good that, ultimately, as I hope, a new ethic should emerge from the ruins of the old.

Judeo-Christian Ethics

The Western ethical tradition is a composite thing. There are elements deriving from the classical Greek and Roman tradition; there are Judeo-Christian elements; and, especially in some of the northern European countries, there are elements of Germanic paganism. But though our Western ethical tradition is made up of many interwoven strands, it is the Judeo-Christian element which predominates.

This is the "official" ethic to which, at least in the past, everybody paid lip-service, whatever their private practice or preference may have been.

In this Judeo-Christian ethic, morality is traditionally conceived very much in terms of Law. A moral obligation or moral rule is something laid upon man by God. This is well illustrated by the biblical account of the origin of the Ten Commandments. Moses goes up Mount Sinai and there, amid thunder and lightning, he receives the Ten Commandments from God. On coming down from Mount Sinai with—according to Christian art—the two stone tablets on which they were inscribed tucked under his arm, Moses in turn gives the Ten Commandments to the Children of Israel. This illustrates the idea of ethics as something imposed on man, almost against his will, by a power or authority external to himself. According to the Old Testament God has created man, has formed him out of the dust of the earth and breathed life into his nostrils. So man is God's creature, almost God's slave, and his duty is to obey. To disobey is a sin.

This attitude is again illustrated by the story of the Fall. Adam and Eve were punished, as we all know, for disobeying an apparently arbitrary order. God said, ". . . of the tree of knowledge of good and evil, thou shalt not eat." But he did not give them any reason for the prohibition. Although few people today believe such stories to be literally true, the attitudes which they represent still persist. The word *commandment* is itself significant. It is significant that a moral law or rule should be a *commandment*—something you are commanded to do, obliged to do, almost coerced into doing, by some power or authority external to yourself.

Christianity certainly goes beyond this conception of ethics; but it does not go very far beyond it. The sources of specifically Christian ethics are, of course, to be found in Jesus's teaching as contained in the four Gospels; but according to Christian tradition Jesus is God, so when God himself tells you to do something the order obviously comes with a tremendous weight of authority behind it. Thus one does something not so much because it is good to do it but because

586 ~ THE ESSENTIAL SANGHARAKSHITA

one is asked to do it, even commanded to do it, by one in whom reposes all power and all authority in heaven and upon earth. Even within the context of Christian ethics, therefore, there is, generally speaking, this same idea of ethics as something obligatory, as something imposed upon one from without to which one must conform. This is our traditional heritage. This is the mode of thought by which, consciously or unconsciously, we are all influenced when we think in terms of ethics.

Nowadays the majority of people in Britain, for example, are not Christian in any meaningful sense, but nevertheless they still tend to think of morality, of ethics, in this way: as an obligation laid upon them from without, a command which they are obliged to obey. We can perhaps summarize the position of traditional ethics today by saying that it consists in not doing what we want to do, and doing what we do not want to do, because—for reasons we do not understand— we have been told to by someone in whose existence we no longer believe. No wonder we are confused. No wonder we have no ethical signposts, and therefore have to try to muddle through somehow or other. But though we try to make some sort of sense of our lives, try to discover some sort of pattern in events, where ethics is concerned the picture is mostly one of chaos.

The Buddhist Criterion

Now I do not want to exaggerate, or to make the contrast seem too abrupt or dramatic, as between black and white, but in the Buddhist tradition the attitude to ethics is quite different from the one I have described. In fact this is true of the whole Eastern, especially Far Eastern, tradition. According to the Buddha's teaching, as preserved in the traditions of whatsoever sect or school, actions are right or wrong, perfect or imperfect, according to the state of mind with which they are performed. In other words the criterion of ethics is not theological but psychological. It is true that in the West we are not unacquainted with this idea, even within the context of Christianity; but so far as Buddhist ethics is concerned—indeed so far as Far Eastern ethics is concerned, whether Buddhist, Taoist, or Confucian—this criterion is the only one. It is a criterion which is universally applied and rigorously carried through to the very end.

According to Buddhist tradition there are two kinds of action, skillful (Sanskrit *kausalya,* Pali *kusala*) and unskillful (Sanskrit *akausalya,* Pali *akusala*). This is significant, because the terms skillful and unskillful, unlike the terms good and bad, suggest that morality is very much a matter of intelligence. You cannot be skillful unless you can understand things, unless you can see possibilities and explore them. Hence morality, according to Buddhism, is as much a matter of intelligence and insight as one of good intentions and good feelings. After all, we have been told that the path to hell is paved with good intentions; but you could hardly say that the path to hell is paved with skillfulness.

Unskillful actions are defined as those which are rooted in craving or selfish desire; in hatred or aversion; and in mental confusion, bewilderment, spiritual obfuscation, or ignorance. Skillful actions are those which are free from craving, free from hatred, free from mental confusion; positively speaking they are motivated instead by generosity, or the impulse to share and to give, by love and compassion, and by understanding. This simple distinction at once places the whole question of morality in a very different light. The moral life becomes a question of acting from what is best within us: acting from our deepest understanding and insight, our widest and most comprehensive love and compassion.

3. The Five Precepts

One must be quite honest with oneself, and not pretend that one is mindful when one is merely merry.

THE BEST-KNOWN pattern of ethical behavior in Buddhism is that of the "Five *Silas,*" generally known as the Five Precepts. The Five

Precepts, as usually transmitted, are negative in form. They tell us what not to do. In the case of each Precept, however, there is a positive counterpart. It is significant that in modern Buddhist teaching the positive counterpart is far less widely known than the negative formulation. Many who have heard of the Five *Silas* will never have heard of the "Five *Dharmas*," as the five positive counterparts are called. In this context, the Five *Dharmas* may be translated as the "Five Ethical Principles." We shall briefly consider both the Five Precepts and the Five *Dharmas,* one by one, examining first the negative and then the positive formulation. This will give us a balanced picture of this particular pattern of Buddhist ethics.

The first of the Five Precepts is abstention from harming living beings. This is the literal translation. Although sometimes rendered as "not to kill," it is really abstention not only from killing but from harming in any way. It conveys the meaning of abstention from all forms of violence, all forms of oppression, all forms of injury. Violence is wrong because ultimately it is based, directly or indirectly, on an unskillful mental state—the state of hatred or aversion—and if we indulge in violence this unskillful mental state, of which violence is the natural expression, will become stronger and more powerful than it is already.

The positive counterpart of abstention from violence is, of course, the practice of *maitri* (Pali *metta*), love or friendliness. Here, *maitri* is not just an emotion or a feeling, but *maitri* as embodied in deeds—as put into actual practice. It is not enough simply to *feel* goodwill toward others. It must be expressed in action. If we simply gloat over it in our own mind, thinking how much we love everybody and how kind we are, it becomes a sort of emotional self-indulgence—or even something worse. So we should watch ourselves in this respect. We often consider that we love other people. At least, we consider we love *some* other people. But if we examine ourselves, we find we seldom express our love: we take it for granted that it is understood.

A familiar example is that of the couple who have been married for twenty or thirty years, and the husband never bothers to give his wife so much as a bunch of flowers or a box of chocolates. If someone were to ask him, "Don't you love your wife? You never give her so much as a bunch of flowers or a box of chocolates," the average husband would reply, "What's the need? Of course I love her, but she should know that after all these years!" This is very bad psychology. People should not have to take it for granted, or just imagine, that we have feelings toward them. It should be quite obvious from our words and actions. Indeed, we should take steps to keep alive the spirit of love and friendship. That is why in all social life, and in Buddhist social life especially, such things as the exchanging of gifts and the extending of invitations are very much emphasized. It is not enough to sit in your own room, or even in your own cell, radiating thoughts of love. Good and wonderful though that may be, it must come down to some concrete expression. Only then will such thoughts be reciprocated in a tangible way by other people.

The second of the Five Precepts is abstention from taking the not-given. This, again, is a literal translation. It is not just abstention from theft. *That* would be too easy to evade or to circumvent. The second Precept involves abstention from any kind of dishonesty, any kind of misappropriation or exploitation, because all these things are expressions of craving, or selfish desire. The positive counterpart of abstention from taking the not-given is, of course, *dana,* or generosity. Here, again, it is not simply the generous feeling, the will to give, that is meant, but the generous act itself. *Dana* is something which all those who have contact with living Buddhism for any length of time quickly come to understand.

The third Precept is abstention from sexual misconduct. In the sutras the Buddha makes it clear that, in the context of the Five Precepts, sexual misconduct comprises rape, abduction, and adultery. All three are unskillful because they are expressions, simultaneously, of both craving and violence. In the case of rape and abduction, which in the comparatively unorganized society of the Buddha's day seem to have been fairly common, violence is committed not only against the woman herself but also, if she happens to be a minor, against her parents or guardians. In the case of adultery, the violence is committed against the woman's husband, inasmuch as his domestic life is deliberately disrupted. It should also be noted that in Buddhism marriage is a purely civil contract, not a sacrament. Moreover, divorce is permitted and from a religious point of view monogamy is not compulsory. In some parts of the Buddhist world there are communities which practice polygamy and this is not considered as amounting to sexual misconduct.

The positive counterpart of abstention from sexual misconduct is *samtushti* (Pali *santutthi*), or contentment. In the case of the unmarried, contentment means contentment with the single state; in the case of the married, it means contentment with one's recognized, socially accepted sexual partner. Here contentment is not just passive acceptance of the status quo. In modern psychological terms, it means a positive state of freedom from using sex to satisfy neurotic needs in general and, in particular, using it to satisfy the neurotic need for change.

The fourth Precept is abstention from false speech. False speech is speech which is rooted in craving, hatred, or fear. If you tell a lie, it is either because you want something, or because you wish to harm or hurt someone, or because for one reason or another you are afraid of telling the truth. Untruthfulness, therefore, is rooted in unskillful mental states. This requires no demonstration. The positive counterpart of abstention from false speech is *satya* (Pali *sacca*), or truthfulness.

The fifth Precept is abstention from drink and drugs the taking of which results in loss of awareness. There is a certain amount of disagreement about the interpretation of this precept. In some Buddhist countries it is interpreted as requiring strict teetotalism—that is, total abstinence; in other Buddhist countries it is interpreted as requiring moderation in the use of anything which, taken in excess, is likely to result in intoxication. One is free to take one's choice between these two interpretations. The positive counterpart of the Precept is, of course, *smrti* (Pali *sati*), mindfulness or awareness. This is the real criterion. If you can drink without impairing your mindfulness (it might be said), then drink; but if you can't, then don't. However, one must be quite honest with oneself, and not pretend that one is mindful when one is merely merry. Thus even if the fifth Precept is interpreted as requiring simply moderation, in the light of its positive counterpart total abstinence will still be required in the vast majority of cases.

4. NATURAL MORALITY AND CONVENTIONAL MORALITY

It is quite important to be sure within oneself whether one is really leading a moral life or just respecting the prejudices of the group within which one happens to be.

NATURAL MORALITY refers to behavior that is directly related to mental states, while conventional moral behavior is a matter of custom and tradition, and has no basis in psychology, not being related to a specific mental state. For instance, that one should try not to do things based on a mental state of craving, especially in its more neurotic forms, is a matter of natural morality; but whether one has one spouse or two, or four, is a matter of conventional morality.

Conventional morality also includes matters of etiquette and behavior such as whether you take off your hat in a holy place or keep it on. There isn't necessarily any connection between whether you are wearing your hat or not and the degree of reverence you feel; it is simply customary in one society or culture to show reverence by keeping one's hat on, while in another culture one shows reverence by taking one's hat off. The feeling of reverence is a matter of natural morality, but how it is shown is a matter of conventional morality in most cases, although it could be said that there is a psychological connection between certain mental states and certain bodily attitudes.

Within Buddhist tradition there are some precepts, especially precepts to be practiced by monks, which have nothing to do with natural morality. That a monk wears yellow robes, shaves his head, and so on is simply a matter of convention. This is clearly recognized in Theravada tradition in theory, though often in practice, and certainly as far as public opinion is concerned, very great importance is attached to matters of conventional morality—as much as to even the most important precepts of natural morality—and this is rather unfortunate.

Unfortunately also, sometimes people feel very guilty about not observing matters of conventional morality, especially if the society to which they belong attaches great importance to those matters, virtually as though they were matters of natural morality. For instance, in some societies it is regarded as moral to work, and therefore immoral not to work; so people who don't work in the sense of being gainfully employed are looked down upon, regarded as slightly immoral, even made to feel guilty. Indeed, they themselves may feel guilty, as though they have done something wrong, when they have not offended against natural morality, but only gone against custom and convention. In a sense this is the difference between virtue and respectability. Sometimes the two coincide, but often they don't. One may be both virtuous and respectable, but it is also possible to be very respectable and not at all virtuous, or highly virtuous and not at all respectable.

Only matters of natural morality have any direct connection with the question of karma. One should not entangle a matter of real, substantial virtue, a matter of natural morality, with one's prejudices about what is right and wrong, which may be based merely on local custom, and have nothing to do with skillful or unskillful mental states.

It is quite important to be sure within oneself whether one is really leading a moral life or just respecting the prejudices of the group within which one happens to be. Moral life is essentially a matter of skillful mental states expressed in skillful behavior and skillful speech. The precepts of natural morality are those precepts which prevent one from committing unskillful actions—that is to say, actions based upon craving, aversion, and ignorance—and help one to perform actions based on skillful states of mind such as generosity, love, and wisdom.

And this is the nature of the traditional precepts of Buddhism, which guide the application of ethical principles to all aspects of life. There is a set of five precepts: one "undertakes the training principles," as the traditional wording has it, not to take life, not to take what is not given, not to engage in sexual misconduct, not to lie, and not to take intoxicants. A set of ten precepts—an elaboration of the five—involves a threefold purification of body, speech, and mind, and there are sixty-four special precepts for Bodhisattvas. There is much that could be said about the practice of these precepts, but here I want to concentrate on Buddhist ethics as applied to three basic spheres of human life: food, work, and marriage.

The most basic of these is, of course, food. You had some not long ago, and so did I; eating is just part of everyday life. Some people in some places can only afford to eat once a day, or even every other day, but most of us eat several times a day; food occupies a very important place in our lives, and takes many hours of our lifetime. An activity to which we devote so much time, energy, and money, and for which we require special provision in our houses in the form of kitchens and dining rooms and utensils, very definitely needs to be brought within the influence of our Buddhist principles.

The most important principle here is non-violence, reverence for life. This means, among many other things, vegetarianism. Some of the Mahayana sutras say that the Bodhisattva can no more think of eating the flesh of living beings than a mother can think of eating the flesh of her child. If one is to practice the first precept, therefore, one needs to make a definite move in the direction of vegetarianism. Sometimes circumstances at home may be difficult—it may be impossible to be strictly vegetarian—but at least one can move toward it, perhaps by giving up meat and fish on certain days of the week, or on certain occasions. No one is perfectly non-violent; it is always a matter of degree. But we should reverence life as much as possible. Vegetarianism, practiced to any degree, is a direct application of the principle that guides the life of the Bodhisattva: the principle of compassion.

It should be said that the Buddha himself did not insist on vegetarianism. He considered it more important for mendicants to practice not picking and choosing what they ate, but accepting what they were given (provided they were sure that any meat they were offered had not been killed especially for their benefit). However, it seems surprising that so few Buddhists in the East have subsequently made any attempt to encourage, where they could, this most basic application of a basic Buddhist principle. In the harsh climate of Tibet vegetarian foodstuffs are certainly scarce, but many Tibetan Buddhists living in India continue to eat meat although they no longer need to do so. It isn't just the Tibetans; Thai and Burmese Buddhists are, if anything, even greater meat-eaters, and the majority of Sinhalese monks and laymen are non-vegetarian too. But perhaps non-vegetarianism is especially strange among Mahayana Buddhists like the Tibetans, given the Mahayana's special emphasis on compassion. The *Lankavatara Sutra* contains a whole chapter about the unskillfulness of eating meat,[153] but people don't seem to take that very seriously.

In this connection Tantric teachings, misunderstood, play a part. Tibetan lamas sometimes say that when an animal is slaughtered, if certain mantras are recited over it, its consciousness is at once released and goes to a sort of heaven. Some even go so far as to say that the fact that the flesh of an animal passes through their system ensures the salvation of that animal. It isn't possible to prove or disprove such a statement, of course, but it has all the hallmarks of a rationalization.

The Thai bhikkhus I knew in India used to say that the lay people gave them meat and therefore they couldn't refuse it—it was just dropped into their bowls. But the lay people were Buddhists and had been so for hundreds of years, and the bhikkhus had taught them to do all sorts of things, for example devising elaborate ways for women to make offerings without coming into physical contact with the bhikkhus. If they could teach the lay people things like that, why couldn't they teach them not to offer them meat? After all, they were able to explain that certain kinds of meat were prohibited and should not be offered according to the Theravada Vinaya: human flesh, tiger flesh, and so on.[154] Could they not ask them to refrain from offering any flesh at all?

When I stayed with some of my Thai bhikkhu friends—in the place of the Buddha's Enlightenment, Bodh Gaya, of all places—every single dish they ate was mixed with meat. Sometimes when I had a meal with them, all I could eat was rice. They weren't very sympathetic, though; they clearly felt that I was just being awkward and that they were under no obligation to help me out of the difficulty I had created for myself.

The Sinhalese were much more sympathetic. Some Sinhalese bhikkhus are vegetarians, and Sinhalese lay Buddhists are very cooperative about that. Tibetans, when challenged about it, will often say, "Yes, we know we should be vegetarian, but it's difficult in Tibet." They do make an exception when they are engaged in any kind of puja or spiritual practice connected with the Bodhisattvas Tara and Avalokitesvara. Then they do observe vegetarianism, even if the pujas last for as long as ten days, because Avalokitesvara and Tara are especially associated with compassion.

As well as being vegetarian, one should practice loving-kindness toward oneself by eating pure and wholesome food. ("Pure" here does not mean refined to such an extent that there is no goodness left in it.) At the same time, one should eat only as much as is necessary for maintaining good health. Sometimes we forget that the purpose of eating is just to keep the body going. If one is down to a subsistence-level diet, as people are in so many parts of the world, one knows this very well, but it isn't so obvious in the West, where we have an optimum diet, to say the least.

Also, one shouldn't eat neurotically; one shouldn't use food in an attempt to satisfy some other need. And one should eat quietly and peacefully. These days many people have business lunches, during which they try to do business and eat at the same time. This is grossly uncivilized conduct. Eating should be quiet, peaceful, even meditative. To eat in a public restaurant or coffee bar, where there is a lot of noise and clatter, and loud conversations going on, is not good for any sensitive, mindful person. The principle here is that one should eat mindfully, with full awareness of what one is doing. One shouldn't eat while reading a newspaper at breakfast time, or having a family argument, or even discussing some practical matter.

For an example of mindfulness in this respect, there is nothing more beautiful than the Japanese tea ceremony. A small group of people gather together in some quiet corner, a little rustic hut in the garden perhaps, and they sit around a charcoal stove and listen to the kettle simmering away. Then, with slow, graceful, delicate, mindful movements, the tea is poured out and handed round to the guests. And people sip it, just sitting peacefully together, engaging in the ordinary, everyday activity of drinking tea.

The Japanese tea ceremony shows to what a pitch of perfection even everyday activities can be raised if we apply mindfulness. Indeed, although this statement could easily be misunderstood, one might almost say that it is better to eat steak and onions mindfully than to eat veggie burgers unmindfully. The main point is that even eating, this ordinary activity, can be made into a sort of art, a way—a *do,* to use the Japanese word. Someone who ate and drank mindfully every day, year after year, might even gain as much spiritually as they would get from a sustained practice of meditation. To encourage oneself to be mindful in this way, one could perhaps bring to mind a little verse or saying, reflecting, perhaps, on the source of the food one is eating.

Another area of ethics that is particularly important in the West has to do with work. We tend to think that everybody should work—that is, for money; we think it is wrong, sinful even, not to be gainfully employed. This is undoubtedly a legacy from Protestantism. Some people can't take a few days off, or even spend a few extra hours in bed in the morning, without feeling horribly guilty about it. We usually feel that we ought to be doing something. Sometimes if we see someone else just sitting around not doing anything, we feel all fidgety and uncomfortable and want to get them moving, as though the very fact of their sitting there quietly while we are so busy is a threat to us.

This is not a new thing. It is to be found, for example, in the Gospels, in the story of Martha and Mary—Martha bustling around getting everything ready, while Mary just sat at the feet of Jesus listening, when there was food to be prepared and served, and washing-up to be done. Martha was most indignant. Jesus, however, said that Mary had chosen the better part. In the West we tend to be Marthas rather than Marys; this feeling that we ought to be doing something is a sort of disease.

The Buddha never worked for his living, as far as we know. He was born into a wealthy, aristocratic family. He had lots of servants. According to all the accounts he spent most of his time in palaces with singing girls, dancing girls, and musicians. Then, after he left home as a mendicant, other people gave him food and clothing. He never did anything to earn his keep. Of course he taught the Dharma, but he would have done that anyway; it was his nature, just as the nature of the sun is to shine. He never worked for money; he never did a day's work in his life.

I have so far been referring to work in the sense of employment; but there is such a thing as creative work. Indeed, creative work is a psychological necessity. It may be in the form of bringing up and educating children. It may be in the form of writing or painting or cooking, or engaging in some constructive social venture. To produce, to create, is a human need. But it need not be linked with employment. In an ideal society, no one would have to work for wages. One would give to the community whatever one could, and the community would give to each person whatever they needed.

However, such an ideal state of affairs is no doubt a long way off, and in the meantime we do have to be gainfully employed in the ordinary sense—and so we have to apply the principle of right livelihood. In brief, this is that our means of livelihood should involve no exploitation of others and no degradation of oneself. And however one is employed, there should always be time for study, meditation, contact with friends, and other positive and creative activities.

Another aspect of life that affects practically everybody in one way or another, formally or informally, is marriage. The Buddhist conception of marriage is very different from the traditional Western one. In the first place, in Buddhism marriage is regarded neither as a religious sacrament nor as a legally binding contract. According to Buddhist tradition, marriage is simply a human relationship which is recognized by society in the form of one's family and friends.

Even in the West the white dress, the orange blossom, the church bells ringing, and all that sort of thing are not *de rigueur* in the way they used to be, but in the Buddhist East there has never been any marriage ceremony of that kind. If anything at all is done to mark the event, the couple concerned will give a feast for their friends and relations, and just make an announcement that they are living together. A Sikkimese friend of mine and his wife didn't give their feast until they had been together for twenty years and their children had grown up. But they were not regarded as "living in sin" in the interval. If a man and woman are living together, they *are* married. This is the Buddhist view. Marriage consists in living together, not in a legal contract, a social convention, or even an official announcement. The marriage is primarily the relationship itself. After the feast held to initiate it or celebrate it, the couple may go along to the temple or monastery and ask for a blessing, but this isn't a wedding ceremony. The monks may bless the relationship, but they don't create it—they just recognize it and give their blessing that the couple concerned may live together happily in accordance with the spirit of the Dharma, helping each other to practice the Buddha's teaching.

With that background, it is not surprising that in all Buddhist countries, from ancient times, there has never been any difficulty about dissolving a marriage, if the people concerned wish it. Also, after marriage the woman retains her own name. This practice is now increasingly common in the West, but here it is quite a new thing, whereas in the East it has never been any other way. In the Buddhist countries of the East there is no one pattern of marriage relationship; nowhere does Buddhism say that monogamy is the only possible form of marriage. Monogamy, polygamy, and even polyandry are all to be found in Buddhist countries, and are recognized as perfectly respectable. Buddhists direct their attention entirely upon the quality of the human relationships involved.

5. Beyond "Buddhist Respectability"

It is easy to forget that the Buddhist message is a subversive one, that its values run counter to mundane or worldly norms, and that your commitment to its ethical principles may lead you on occasion to offend conventional notions of morality.

I REMEMBER that when I was a small child, most children were not allowed to run about and play when they were dressed in their Sunday best. They were made to sit at home so that they would stay neat and tidy. This had nothing to do with religion; it was all about social niceties. Even during my youth, if a man didn't wear a tie or a hat, he was considered not to be fully dressed, while wearing a colored shirt was an act of flagrant recklessness. Those particular signs of respectability have changed, but the concern to display the appropriate marks of submission to group norms is still very apparent. In an age of consumerism, respectability is less a matter of a rigid dress code and more about a carefully maintained range of purchases and recreational activities that will ensure peer acceptance. You need to have the right sort of job and live in the right part of town, go on vacation to the right ski resort, drive the right kind of car, and even follow the right religion.

The perception of things as all-important when they are nothing of the kind is reinforced by vulnerability to group disapproval, and also by lack of imagination, an inability to contemplate stepping outside the range of possibilities that society thinks acceptable. Unfortunately, Buddhists have all too often succumbed to this kind of failure of nerve and vision. When you get a narrow and rigid monasticism, when the monastic rules and even the way you dress and shave your head have turned into a kind of Buddhist respectability, or when it becomes all-important to spend the right number of years studying Buddhist philosophy in the right monastic universities, then what is really all-important is to re-emphasize what is really all-important. It was for this reason that some Tantric yogis originally set out to flout convention, to challenge what other people considered important, even within the Buddhist world.

When I first came back to England in the early 1960s, after some twenty years in Asia, it was impressed upon me as all-important that Buddhism should be respectable. I soon realized that what the people who were trying to influence me meant by this was that Buddhism should be made as acceptable as possible to the values of the English middle classes. But if Buddhists agree to such a thing, Buddhism ceases to be Buddhism. The same may be said for the versions of Buddhism that are peddled to the consumer society these days, and the way that Buddhism is profiled to appeal to different niche markets, to fit in with whatever that society considers to be all-important. It may well find acceptance in this way, but it ceases to be Buddhism.

Of course, if you want to communicate the Dharma to a lot of people, you cannot afford to alienate them by causing offense, especially by breaking their taboos. At the same time, you need to be careful not to lose sight of what you are trying to communicate. It is easy to forget that the Buddhist message is a subversive one, that its values run counter to mundane or worldly norms, and that your commitment to its ethical principles may lead you on occasion to offend conventional notions of morality. If the Buddha "discreetly followed worldly customs," he did so only insofar as these did not compromise the ideals of the Dharma and the integrity of the lifestyle he had chosen through which to express those ideals.

It is normal to be ashamed of anything that excludes one from the group, and social inclusion is fundamentally predicated on the respect given to taboos, whether one observes them or breaks them. Milarepa, the Tibetan yogi of the eleventh century CE, speaks from a position that is not in opposition to social convention, but simply beyond it. That is to say, it is not a position at all. He avoids any fixed position, whether of conformity or individualism. He is not a conformist or an individualist, but an individual. He does not define himself in relation to the group, whether by joining it or by setting himself apart from it.

A true individual is someone who has developed self-awareness, through one discipline or another, and on that basis has a confidence and self-respect that does not depend upon convention or fashion. If you are a true individual, your sense of identity and purpose in life does not rely on your social identity—whether you are a citizen, family member, worker, rebel, or iconoclast. As a mature human being, your self-awareness transcends human social groups of all kinds. Your defining relationship is an inner relationship with the deeper reality of things, the truth behind appearances. One might even say that the true individual is one through whom that deeper reality of things functions and is present in the world. If you are a true individual you can stand on your own two feet and at the same time maintain a harmony with the way things really are.

Milarepa is an individual in the true sense because he is free of the power of social conventions. He doesn't need to conform to other people's expectations of how a spiritual practitioner should look; it doesn't matter to him how he is seen. We tend to be most ashamed of matters over which we have no control, like our social background or what we look like. Milarepa, by contrast, is ashamed only of "sinful, evil, and meaningless deeds." The things that preoccupy the vast majority of people are quite simply of no concern to him at all; and conversely, he sees how important it is to feel real shame about deeds and activities about which most people would feel no compunction.

6. THE ETHICS OF SPEECH

Speaking the truth really means being ourselves. Not in the conventional, social sense, as when we are said to "be ourselves" at a party, which usually means not being ourselves at all; but in the sense of giving expression in terms of speech to what we really and truly are and know we are.

IF WE REFLECT, we shall see that a great part of our culture depends, directly or indirectly, on speech. Through speech the parent and the teacher educate the child. Through books, which are, as it were, frozen, crystallized speech, we get information, we get knowledge; we may even get Enlightenment. All our culture, all knowledge, even our spiritual insight, is to a great extent derived directly or indirectly from the *word*—from speech, from utterance. It is therefore natural, even inevitable, that in the moral and spiritual life we should give as much consideration to speech as we do to thought and action.

In Buddhist texts Perfect Speech is usually described as speech which is truthful, which is affectionate, which is helpful, and which promotes concord, harmony, and unity. Similarly wrong or imperfect speech is described in precisely opposite terms, as speech which is untruthful, harsh, harmful, and which promotes discord, disharmony, and disunity.

1. The Level of Truthfulness

First of all Perfect Speech, or ideal communication, is truthful. We all think we know exactly what is meant when it is said that all speech should be truthful. We have been told since we were two years old not to tell a lie, like George Washington. But do we really know what is meant by speaking the truth? Have we considered all the implications? Speaking the truth does not mean just adhering to factual accuracy, saying that this cloth is yellow and that *that* is a microphone. The concept of truthfulness is not exhausted in this way. Factual accuracy is of course important. It is one of the elements of truthfulness, and we cannot dismiss it. But it is not the whole.

Anyone who knows Boswell's classic biography of Samuel Johnson will remember the famous remark of Dr. Johnson about factual truthfulness. He remarks that if your children say that something happened at one window, when in fact it happened at another, they should be instantly corrected, because once it begins you do not know where deviation from the truth will end. Thus factual truthfulness is important. It is the basis or foundation of Perfect Speech. Recognizing this, we should accustom ourselves to what Johnson calls "accuracy of narration," which is a sort of training ground for us in the higher, more refined kinds of truthfulness. Usually we are shaky and shoddy even on this level. Few people really practice accuracy of narration. We usually like to make things a little bit different. We like to pad out, we like to exaggerate, or to minimize, or to embroider. It may just be a poetic streak in us which makes us do this, but we do it even in the best of circles, even at the best of times.

We all tend to twist, or distort, or at least slightly bend facts, in the direction in which we would like them to go, so we have to be extremely careful here. If we say for instance that it was a lovely day, it must have been a lovely day. We must neither exaggerate nor minimize. If we say that there were ten people at the meeting, let us be sure that there were ten. If there were a thousand, let us say that there were a thousand. But if there were only fifty, let us not make it one-hundred-and-fifty. Or in the case of somebody else's meeting, if there were a thousand, let us not make it one-hundred-and-fifty! We must pay strict attention to factual accuracy, though it must again be emphasized that truthfulness in the real sense, in the deepest, the fullest, the most spiritual sense, is something very much more than mere factual accuracy, important as this is.

Truthfulness is also psychological, also spiritual. Besides factual accuracy, speaking the truth also involves an attitude of honesty and sincerity. It involves saying what we *really* think. You are not speaking the truth unless you speak the whole truth, and say what is really in your heart and mind—say what you really think, even what you really feel. If you do not do that you are not being truthful, you are not really communicating.

But then another question arises: do we really even know what we think? Do we really know what we feel? Most of us live or exist in a state of chronic mental confusion, bewilderment, chaos, disorder. We may repeat, as the occasion arises, what we have heard, what we have read. We may regurgitate it when we are required to do so, whether at the time of examinations in the case of students, or on social occasions in the case of other people. But we do all this without really knowing what we say. How can we, therefore, really speak the truth? Since we do not really know what we think, how can we be truthful?

If we want to speak the truth in the full sense, or at least in a fuller sense than is usually understood, we must clarify our ideas. We must introduce some sort of order into this intellectual chaos of ours. We must know quite clearly, quite definitely, what we think, what we do not think, what we feel, what we do not feel. And we must be intensely aware. We must know what is within us, what are our motivations, what are our drives and our ideals. This means that we have to be completely honest with ourselves. It means that we have to know ourselves. If we do not know ourselves, in the depths as well as on the heights, if we cannot penetrate into the depths of our own being and be really transparent to ourselves, if there is not any clarity or illumination within—then we cannot speak the truth.

This is something we all have to realize. If we do realize it we shall see that speaking the truth is no easy matter. We might even go so far as to say—and I do not think this is an exaggeration—that most of us, most of the time, do not speak the truth. If we wanted to put it forcibly, not to say paradoxically, we might even say that most of us, nearly all the time, speak what is in fact a lie, and that our communication is in fact most of the time a lie, because we are not capable of speaking anything else. We are incapable of speaking the truth in the fullest sense. If we reflect we might have to admit that most of us go through life, year after year, from childhood or at least adolescence into old age, without perhaps being able even once to speak the truth in the fullest and clearest sense of that much abused term.

We do know that if ever we are in a position to speak the truth, it is a great relief to be able to do so. Often we do not realize how many lies we have been telling until we have an opportunity, once in a while perhaps, of speaking the truth. We all know that if something has been weighing on our mind or on our heart, something about which we have been very worried or concerned, if we can only speak out—or tell somebody the truth of the matter, without holding back—then it is a great relief. Unfortunately for most people this is something that happens very rarely in their lives, if indeed at all.

Speaking the truth really means being ourselves. Not in the conventional, social sense, as when we are said to "be ourselves" at a party, which usually means not being ourselves at all; but in the sense of giving expression in terms of speech to what we really and truly are and know we are. Speaking the truth, however, even in this more rarefied, fuller, deeper, and more spiritual sense, is not done in a vacuum. You do not just go up to the top of the Empire State Building and speak the truth to the stars. The truth is always spoken to someone—another person, another human being. This brings us to the second level of Perfect Speech, or the second stage of communication.

2. The Level of Affectionateness

Perfect Speech is not only truthful, even in the fullest sense; it is also affectionate and loving. It is the truth spoken in or with love. This does not mean just using terms of endearment, or anything of that sort. Speaking with affection or love in this context means speaking the truth in its fullness, with complete awareness of the person to whom you are speaking. How many of us can do this? If we think about it we will realize that when we speak to people we do not usually look at them. Have you ever noticed this? It is probably true in your case, and in the case of people who speak to you. When they speak to you, or when you speak to them, you do not look at them. You look over their shoulder, you look at their forehead, up at the ceiling, down at the ground—anywhere, almost, except at the person to whom you are speaking. And if you do not look at others, you cannot be aware of them.

We can say that love, in the sense in which I am using the term at present, means awareness of the being of another person. But if you do not *know* the other person, how can you speak affectionately to him or her? It is not possible. We like to think, of course, that we have love for people, that we are affectionate, but this is very rarely so. We usually see other people in terms of our own emotional reactions to them. We react emotionally to them in a certain way, and then we attribute that emotional reaction *to* them as a quality of theirs. If, for instance, people do what we would like them to do, then we say that they are good, kind, helpful, and so on. We are not really communicating with that particular person. What really happens, most of the time is that we are communicating, or trying to communicate, or pretending to communicate, with our own mental projections.

This is especially so in the case of those who are—allegedly—near and dear to us. Parents and children, brothers and sisters, husbands and wives, very rarely know one another. They might have lived together for twenty, or thirty, or forty years, but they do not know one another. They know their own reactions to one another, and those reactions they attribute to the other person. They think, therefore, that they know them; but they do not really know them at all. They know only their own projected mental and emotional states.

This is a sobering thought. There used to be a saying, "It is a wise father that knows his own child." Well, it is a wise child that knows his own father; it is a very wise wife that knows her own husband; it is a very wise husband that knows his own wife: because the more you live with people, especially those to whom you are related by blood or by strong emotional ties, the less, in the real spiritual sense, do you know them. After all, to the baby, what is mother? Mother is just a wonderful sensation of warmth and comfort, security and well-being: *that* is what mother is. The child does not know mother as a person. The same is true with other relations. And it usually remains like that for most of our lives, with a bit of refinement and rationalization here and there. This is true for most of us, most of the time.

This is why there is so much misunderstanding between people, so much failure to communicate, so many disappointments, especially in the more intimate relationships of life. People are at cross-purposes because one person does not know another and therefore cannot love another. There is just pseudo-communication between projections, and nothing more. I know this sounds drastic and perhaps rather horrifying, but it is true; and I think it is best and most salutary if we face up to the truth about ourselves and other people as quickly as possible, and realize that, in most cases, our so-called relationships are just a maze of such mutual projections, with no mutual knowledge and understanding at all—not to speak of mutual love.

But if there *is* such a thing as mutual awareness and mutual love, and if we *are* able to speak the truth to another person, being aware of that other person—which means, of course, loving that other person, love being awareness of the person's being—we shall also know what he or she needs. If we really know the other person we shall know what he or she needs—as distinct from what we think the person ought to have because it would be good for us if they had it, which is what most people mean by "knowing what is good for others." Knowing what people need means knowing what is good for them quite objectively, without reference to ourselves. We will then know what has to be provided, what given, how they can be helped, and so on. This brings us to the third level of Perfect Speech, or the third stage of communication.

3. The Level of Helpfulness

According to the Buddha we should say that which is useful, in the sense of speaking in such a way as to promote the growth, especially the spiritual growth, of the person to whom we are speaking. This need not involve anything as formal as specifically religious instruction, although this too is very useful. Broadly speaking this aspect of Perfect Speech—speaking that which is useful—consists in speaking in a way that raises, and does not lower, the person or people to whom we are speaking in the scale of being and consciousness. At least we can be positive and appreciative. Most people are so negative. You tell them about something good, something happy, and they either pull a long face, or depreciate it, or try to undermine you. In the end you may feel quite guilty about having enjoyed that particular thing, or having liked and appreciated it. So we must at least be positive and appreciative, realizing that when we have this kind of attitude the other person is helped to grow—not when we are negative, critical, or destructive. Constructive criticism, based on emotional positivity and genuine concern for the other person, is not of course excluded. Such criticism—which may be mutual—promotes spiritual growth. It is therefore useful in the best sense of the term, and to be included under Perfect Speech.

There is a time, of course, even for destructive criticism: that is a legitimate activity. But most of us take to it far too readily and easily, to the neglect of the more positive side. Even if we are not in a position to give specifically spiritual instruction or to enlighten people—and very few of us can do that in any way, or to any extent—we can at least be helpful. We can at least be positive, and appreciative of whatever good we see growing in, or emerging from, that other person. If we do on occasion give some sort of instruction, this will only be effective if given in a helpful, positive, and constructive spirit.

If we communicate in the way I have described: if we speak the truth, the whole truth, and nothing but the truth; if we speak with love, that is, with awareness of the other person's being; if we speak in such a way as to promote the other's growth, to have a healthy, positive effect on him or her; if we are more concerned about that person's needs than about our own; if we are not projecting our own emotional states, or using or exploiting the other person; then the result will be that in speaking to, or communicating with, another person we will forget all about ourselves. This brings us to the fourth and highest level of Perfect Speech, or the fourth and final stage of communication.

4. The Level of Promoting Concord, Harmony, and Unity

As well as all the qualities already described, Perfect Speech is speech which promotes concord, harmony, and unity. This does not just mean verbal agreement. It does not mean saying "Yes, yes" all the time. It does not even mean sharing the same ideas—it is not a matter of "You believe in Buddhism, I believe in Buddhism." This is not what is meant here. What "speech which promotes concord, harmony, and unity" really means is mutual helpfulness, based on truthfulness and awareness of each other's being and each other's needs, leading to mutual self-transcendence. This mutual self-transcendence is Perfect Speech *par excellence.* It is not only Perfect Speech, but also the perfection of communication. When this sort of concord, harmony, and unity, this sort of understanding, is complete, is perfect, nothing more need be said. Even on the ordinary level, when you get to know someone for the first time, for a while you do a lot of talking, exchange ideas, get to know one another; but the more you get to know each other, in a sense the less there is to say. When Perfect Speech culminates in harmony, in oneness and mutual self-transcendence, at the same time it also culminates in silence.

We should not think that silence is mere absence of sound. When all sound dies away—when the sound of the traffic in the street or the creaking of the chairs in the room, the sound of our own breath, and even the "sound" of our thoughts, is utterly stilled—what is left is not just something negative or dead, not just a vacuum. What is left is a living silence.

In this connection I remember the very great example of the Indian sage and teacher Ramana Maharshi, who died in 1950. I had the good fortune to be with him for some time, about a year before he died, and he perfectly exemplified this attitude. He just sat there on a dais in the hall of the ashram, on a kind of settee with a tiger skin spread on it, and most of the time he said nothing at all. He had sat there for forty years, I think, and although the hall was usually full of people, when you entered there was a strangely vibrant quality to that silence. It quite literally seemed as though the silence flowed from him. You could almost see waves of silence flowing from him, flowing over all those people, flowing into their hearts and minds and calming them down. As you sat down yourself you quite literally felt the silence flowing over you, calming and quieting you, washing away all your thoughts. I am not speaking poetically or imaginatively—you felt it quite literally. You felt it as a sort of positive wave-like power flowing over you all the time. *This* was the silence—the real silence, the true silence—that Ramana Maharshi so beautifully exemplified.

Silence of this quality is very rare. Even ordinary silence, the lowest form of silence, is only too rare in modern life. Certainly in most of our lives there is far too much noise, and usually far too much talking. By talking I do not mean real communication through speech, but mere verbalization, the multiplication of words without much meaning. One cannot help thinking that speech, which is so precious and so wonderful, so expressive and such a treasure, should be something exceptional. At least it should be something, like eating, that you do occasionally, after thought and preparation; but all too often speech precedes thought, while talking is the rule and silence is the exception.

But perhaps there is hope for us all, as there was for the young Macaulay, about whom the great wit Sydney Smith remarked, "Macaulay is improving. He has flashes of silence." Most of us are in this position. Maybe we *are* improving. Maybe we *do* have, occasionally, even quite brilliant flashes of silence. We should therefore perhaps try to make more time for silence in our lives: make more time just to be quiet, just to be alone, by ourselves. Unless we do this from time to time, at least for an hour or two every day, we shall find the practice of meditation rather difficult.

7. Rights and Duties

Peace springs naturally and spontaneously from duties quietly and unobtrusively done, just as from the rose tree comes the rose, or as the lotus rises from the lotus lake.

DUTIES CONSIST in what is due from us to others, and are based upon giving, whereas rights consist in what is due from others to us, and are based (from the subjective point of view) upon grasping and getting. The performance of one's duty does not mean merely the grudging recognition and half-hearted rendering of what is legally or even morally due to one's family and friends, social or national group, political party, or religious organization, but in the unobstructed outward flow of one's love and compassion over the whole world. Duty is not, as the poet calls her, the "Stern daughter of the Voice of God,"[155] but the sweet child of the realization of emptiness—*sunyata*—within the depths of our own heart. The conscientious performance of one's duties to mother and father, child and wife, friends and acquaintances, masters and disciples, and to the complementary halves of all the other human relationships in which we are inevitably involved, results in the gradual loosening of the bonds of selfishness and egotism. The word for duty and the word for religion (which consists at bottom in the eradication of the ego-sense) are, in the language of India, one word: Dharma. But the clamorous insistence upon our rights, upon what is legally, morally, or even spiritually due from others to us, only strengthens greed, strengthens desire, strengthens selfishness, strengthens egotism.

The performance of one's duties results in the establishment of love and peace, the attempted extortion of one's rights in the outbreak of hatred and violence. Duties unite, rights divide. Duties are cooperative, rights competitive. The former depend upon our own selves, and are therefore swift and easy of accomplishment; the latter depend on others, and are therefore tardy and difficult, if not impossible, of achievement. Rights are wrested forcibly from other human beings outside, but duties are softly and sweetly laid upon us by the voice of the Divine—of our own potential Buddhahood—reverberating within.

Buddhism, being based upon the realization of emptiness, upon egolessness, upon unselfishness, teaches the doctrine of the mutual interpenetration of all things, inculcates the practice of love and compassion, exhorts men and women to perform their duties in every walk of life, and therefore tends naturally toward the ultimate establishment of peace, both in the hearts and minds of men and in the world of events outside us. Western political systems, on the contrary, however different or even antagonistic they may outwardly seem, are all based upon the concept, ultimately of dogmatic origin, of the existence of separate, mutually exclusive ego-entities which are socially, politically, and even spiritually valuable and significant in themselves. All such systems therefore justify hatred and excuse violence, all insist on the intrinsic reasonableness of clamorous agitation for rights, and all, without exception—despite emphatic protestations to the contrary—result in the eventual outbreak of war, both in the individual psyche and in the life of societies and nations. Emptiness, egolessness, the performance of duties, and internal and external peace and harmony are members of the same Nirvanic series, just as egotism, individualism, the claiming of rights, and external violence and warfare are the indissoluble links of the same Samsaric chain.

The world today truly needs peace, but does not sincerely desire it. For peace is sought not in the dynamic equilibrium of selfless mutual performance of duties, but in the mechanical manipulation of merely superficial and therefore unstable adjustments between a host of conflicting egotistic claims. There can be peace in the world between people and between nations only when the hidden roots of disharmony—the concept of a separate soul, self, or ego—are ruthlessly dug up and cast into the blazing fire of selflessness. There can be peace in the world only when doing one's duty is stressed more emphatically than getting one's rights, when it is considered more intrinsically valuable to confer a benefit upon one's fellow human beings than to receive one from them. It is no more possible to get peace by means of the egotistic assertion of rights than it is possible to gather grapes of thistles or figs of thorns. But peace springs naturally and spontaneously from duties quietly and unobtrusively done, just as from the rose tree comes the rose, or as the lotus rises from the lotus lake.

"But," some will protest, "if we simply perform our duties, without demanding our rights in return, we shall be taken advantage of and exploited by unscrupulous politicians and crooked capitalists; we shall be abused and trampled upon by people on every side." This objection would be valid only if the performance of duty were envisaged as something which applied not to all sections of society, but to some only. But since the two ends of a human relationship are as inseparable as the two ends of a stick, and since our rights become duties when looked at from the other end, and since no one will consider himself to be without rights, the performance of duties is an obligation which rests equally upon the shoulders of all of us and from which none can escape. The remedy for any injustice or inequality in human relationships, whether domestic, social, civic, political, cultural, racial, or religious, is an insistence not upon the rights of one party, but on the duties of the other. The reminder of their duties appeals to all that is best and noblest in people and nations, to their innate selflessness and love; whereas the reminder of our rights appeals to all that is basest and worst in us, to our innate selfishness and greed, hatred, and violence. The appeal to the performance of duties is constructive and positive, and results in cooperation, harmony, and peace. The appeal to the claiming of rights is destructive and negative, and issues eventually in competition, discord, and open war. The former is based upon the Wisdom and Compassion of all the Buddhas, the latter upon the sophistry and mutual antagonism of the founders of the various schools of Western political thought. One is profound, the other superficial; one transcendental, the other mundane.

8. Mindfulness of Purpose

If we are to act skillfully, we need to focus our attention on the objective situation rather than on ourselves and how we feel about what we are doing.

IF WE DO NOT stay continually aware of our purpose and aim in life— which for a Buddhist is ultimately the attainment of Enlightenment—

we will succumb to *asamprajanya,* which could be described as a sort of neurotic introspection with no clear purpose or point. We can be aware in some degree of what is going on in our minds, we can even have a measure of faith in the possibility of attaining to higher states of being, but if we aren't fully mindful—that is, if we aren't watchful with regard to our mental states, our speech, and our actions—we will "fall from our level of being" to a lower level of existence through the process of karma and rebirth.

If we do not bring our activities of body, speech, and mind into line with our discriminating awareness and our faith—that is, if our approach is purely psychological—we will come to grief. If we are careless or cavalier with regard to ethics, no amount of discriminating awareness will save us. The point is that it is possible to examine and analyze our mental states without actually being mindful or watchful with regard to them any more than to our speech and physical actions. If we are preoccupied with our mental states in this unhealthy, even neurotic way to such an extent that we don't heed the ethical implications of those mental states in terms of our actions of body, speech, and mind, there is bound to be an overall deterioration in our level of being.

This is because our level of being is determined by our volitional actions, by whether they are skillful or unskillful, not by whether or not we feel good while performing those actions. Unfortunately, there is a tendency in the West to be far more concerned about the complexities of our inner psychological states than about the much simpler questions of how to live an ethical life. One may perhaps fear, for example, that giving up some unskillful activity may disrupt the free flow of one's energies: it may well do this, but one should then be able to redirect that energy into a more skillful activity.

It is true that Buddhist ethics are ethics of intention, but this does not mean that they are simply about how we feel; rather, they are about our intentions with regard to objective situations. If we are to act skillfully, we need to focus our attention on the objective situation rather than on ourselves and how we feel about what we are doing. It may be reasonable to expect to get something out of what we do, at least occasionally, but the paradox is that we are going to get something out of it only to the extent that our focus is not on getting something out of it.

9. WHY WE CONCEAL THINGS

What prevents many of us from confessing and from being more open generally is the feeling that if other people knew us as we were, then they would no longer accept us.

WE OFTEN CONCEAL things not just from other people, but even from ourselves. We don't like to admit that we have done something wrong, that we have made a mistake. It's a form of humiliation to feel that you have not lived up to your image of yourself. Someone once said that when you sit down to write your autobiography, the first thing you become aware of is what you are going to leave out. Almost inevitably you don't tell the whole story. "Oh no, I'm not going to say that. I'll say everything else, but not that." To be happy for others to see you exactly as you are, warts and all, is very difficult. Usually there is some little nook or cranny of your character or your life or your past that you don't want anybody to know about. You don't even think about it yourself very much; you hide it even from yourself. Nietzsche said, "Memory says I did such and such, pride says I couldn't possibly have done it, and pride wins." Ideally, of course, it should be possible to lead such a life that you can be open with everybody—one's life should ideally be an open book—but most people have at least a few pages, not to say the odd chapter or two, which they would prefer other people not to look at.

It's a strain relating to others with only a part of yourself, keeping back another part that they are never allowed to see. If you never relate to them as a complete, whole person, they don't know who you are, or at least they don't know the whole of you. This doesn't mean that if you have committed a crime you should tell it to everybody—that might be unwise—but certainly there should be a few people with whom you can be completely frank. Assuming you share with them a common spiritual ideal, they will be for you the spiritual community in the full sense. If you don't have friends whom you can trust totally, you are in quite a difficult position.

What prevents many of us from confessing and from being more open generally is the feeling that if other people knew us as we were, then they would no longer accept us. "If people knew what I was really like, they wouldn't want to have any more to do with me." But within the context of the spiritual community you are still accepted, even though people may strongly disapprove of what you have done. You may find it difficult to make that distinction—and it may be difficult for your friends in practice—but in principle they will try to retain the same metta for you even though they may be very grieved at what you have done. To be open, you have got to have this kind of confidence in other people's genuine, basic goodwill toward you, which you are convinced will remain unchanged under all circumstances. Even if they tell you off, it will be with basic good will.

Of course, trust—the confidence that people will deal with you from a basis of love rather than from a basis of power—cannot be forced, even in the spiritual community. True confession cannot be the kind of mechanical procedure which goes under the name of confession in so many parts of the Buddhist world. You need to be in close, trustful communication with the person to whom you confess. And you can only trust people if you feel they are not going to hurt you, not going to take advantage of your openness. In a way you need to feel that their attitude toward you is basically like that of the Buddha. Whatever you have done, they are going to forgive you. Their basic attitude toward you is not going to change; they will have the same metta for you even after you have confessed, when they know the worst about you.

10. BUDDHIST CONFESSION

Ideally we should be open with our friends all the time, and anything obstructing communication should be cleared up at once, so confession should be an everyday practice.

YOU MAY DISCOVER that there is something in your life which is incompatible with your spiritual commitment, but which you are unwilling to give up. It becomes a sore and sensitive area that you are not prepared to discuss with anybody, especially not with your spiritual friends. Yes, you feel guilty; you know that what you are doing is unskillful. But you are determined to hang on to this pet weakness. You don't come clean and confess it because you would then be openly confronting the fact that you were doing something unskillful—and you would also be urged by your friends to give it up, so as to clear the path to more positive states.

In concealing your fault from others you are also in a sense concealing it from yourself, in that you are not really facing up to its implications, which are that it is obstructing the realization of the positive. You are sort of hoping to muddle through somehow. Thus it is not unconnected with *vicikitsa,* doubt and indecision. You may even start to rationalize your unskillful behavior, find all sorts of arguments to justify it. Because you are avoiding clarity, your state of mind becomes duller and duller. Your friends may be aware that there is something wrong, that you are not making progress for some reason, and they may try to get you to bring your difficulty out into the open. But you stubbornly pretend that there's nothing the matter.

As long as there is this sacred area of your life that is off-limits as far as your friends are concerned, you are effectively closing yourself off from them. You become increasingly out of touch—not because of your unskillful activity (otherwise we should all be out of touch with each other most of the time) but because you insist on holding back from communicating, to those who are supposed to be your friends, something that is evidently a very pressing problem. The longer you put off coming clean with your friends, the more difficult it becomes to do it, and the stronger becomes your commitment to your pet weakness. So this upaklesa of slyness-concealment (as it is defined by the Abhidharma), once it becomes entrenched, is one of the most problematic to deal with.

The danger is that you will eventually break off contact with your spiritual friends altogether, in favor of people who are less demanding. At this point, the most important thing is to feel that your spiritual friends are on your side, that they are not against you. If they really are your friends, they will do their best to maintain contact even though you may be getting quite defensive and isolated as a result of your secrecy and feelings of guilt.

The principal antidote to this is confession of faults. Ideally we should be open with our friends all the time, and anything obstructing communication should be cleared up at once, so confession should be an everyday practice. But what is confession? It is not just admission or acknowledgement of what we have done. It is true that in a legal context admission and confession are more or less interchangeable expressions; they are interchangeable, however, only if they are both taken to have only a psychological significance. But confession in a spiritual context is primarily not a psychological but an ethical act. If we confess to a spiritually unskillful action there is obviously a psychological element there, inasmuch as we are referring to a mental attitude, something pertaining to our own psyche. But there is more to it than this. Indeed, the psychology of the Abhidharma as a whole is not just about psychology. Although it does involve becoming a healthy human being, it is also about developing beyond that level.

When we confess to an unskillful action we are confessing to a failure to live up to our own ideals. We are invoking a norm, a set of ethical and spiritual ideals that we have accepted for ourselves, and that we share with other members of the spiritual community. These ideals are not imposed upon us. There is no veiled threat behind them that if we don't try to live by them we'll be in big trouble. It is this, in fact, that makes them truly ethical and spiritual ideals. And it is this also that makes a refusal to confess one's ethical failures so damaging toward one's integrity as an individual.

A general confession—"I'm afraid I sometimes behave rather badly"—is not enough. To be effective, confession should be very specific, and it should be addressed to someone who understands the seriousness of what we are confessing. If we have any doubt about whether or not to confess something, we need to make a particular point of confessing it, because that doubt is quite likely to be the first stirrings of slyness-concealment. As its name suggests, it is a slippery customer that has to be watched out for carefully.

We should ideally confess to the people we have offended, but if they don't share our ideals, all we can really do is make an *admission* to them. To make our confession in the spiritual sense, we will need to talk to someone else who understands the Buddhist distinction between skillful and unskillful. In this case it is more important to make the confession than to make the admission.

Confession has been an aspect of the relationship between teacher and disciple in the Buddhist tradition from the earliest times. It is customary in any well-ordered monastic situation for the pupils to go to the teacher every morning and evening and confess any unskillful actions they are aware of having committed during those twelve hours, and ask for forgiveness for any that they are not aware of. One says, "Whatever faults I have committed of body, speech, and mind, please forgive me." And the teacher says "*Khamami, khamami*," "I forgive, I forgive."

This practice differs from Catholic confession and absolution in that the teacher doesn't forgive on behalf of God; in fact, he doesn't forgive offenses committed against anyone apart from himself. It is a purely personal exchange. One is asking forgiveness for any offenses committed against him personally. If, for example, one had committed an offense against the rules of the order, then that would be dealt with by the order as a whole. However, in respect of offenses that don't concern him personally, the teacher can, if not forgive, certainly listen to one's confession and advise one what to do, or what practice to take up, to help one avoid repeating that particular fault.

If—as is usual among Western Buddhists—you are not in a traditional teacher-disciple situation but part of a spiritual community, confession can still be very much part of your spiritual life. Spiritual friends (*kalyana mitras*) can help one another a great deal through mutual confession and exploration of how to act more skillfully in future.

There is a Tibetan practice of confessing to the thirty-five Buddhas of confession, who each preside over a different set of the monastic rules. That is, one confesses to whichever Buddha presides over the set of rules that includes the rule that one has transgressed. It is important, though, not to misunderstand this idea of confessing to the Buddhas. When Buddhist texts speak of asking forgiveness of the Buddhas and Bodhisattvas, this is not to say that the Buddhas might not forgive one if one didn't placate them.

After all, what is forgiveness? It is to let someone off the consequences of their action in terms of one's own personal reaction to it. It is to say that in effect the matter is now closed, the slate is wiped clean. No vicious circle of action and reaction, offense and retaliation has been initiated. But as far as the Buddhas are concerned, your breaking a precept is no offense to them. It is essentially an offense against yourself, because you will be reaping the *vipaka* (the fruit) of your karma in the future. In that sense you are going to have to forgive yourself. Of course, as already discussed, one should be careful not to be too self-referential; as well as harming yourself through your action you will in most cases have caused harm to someone else. You cannot forgive yourself on their behalf, so to speak. Nor can you effectively confess to yourself—though it may be a start.

11. "THE OPPRESSION OF EXISTENCE"

It's as though there is some force at work in the world almost compelling us
to do unskillful things against our better judgment and our own wishes.

> In the oppression of existence or through foolish thought,
> whatever severe evil I have done, in the presence of the
> Buddha, I confess all this evil. And I confess that evil which
> has been heaped up by me in the oppression of birth, by the
> various oppressions of bodily activity, in the oppression of
> existence, in the oppression of the world, in the oppression
> of the fleeting mind, in the oppression of impurities caused
> by the foolish and stupid thoughts, and in the oppression
> of the arrival of evil friends, in the oppression of fear, in the
> oppression of passion, in the oppression of hatred and by
> the oppressions of folly and darkness, in the oppression of
> the instant, in the oppression of time, by the oppressions of
> gaining merits, standing before and in the presence of the
> Buddha, I confess all this evil.[156]

THE WORD TRANSLATED as "oppression" is the Sanskrit *samkata*,
for which the dictionary gives the following definitions: "brought
together, contracted, closed, narrow, strait, crowded together, dense,
impervious, impassable, crowded with, full of; a strait, difficulty, critical condition, danger to or from." That gives one quite a good idea of
what *samkata* means, and makes it clear that this term "oppression,"
though not bad, is not a fully adequate translation by any means.

The *samkatas* are those factors by which we are surrounded, which
crowd in upon us, which oppress us, which squeeze and limit us. This
suggests that there are all sorts of unskillful acts that we do, as it were,
under duress. Our unskillful acts are not those of a free untrammeled
will, and if only conditions had been a bit more favorable, we might
not have done them at all. There are so many factors in existence
which oppress us, making it more likely that we will do something

unskillful and more difficult for us to act skillfully. Circumstances are so often against us. Our surroundings tend almost to compel us to do what is unskillful. Not that that is really any excuse, ultimately, because it is due to our weakness that we feel the oppression *as* oppression. But people are not deliberately wicked; it's more that they are weak and give in to pressure.

The list of oppressions is a long one: existence, birth, bodily activity, the world, the fleeting mind, impurities caused by the foolish thought, the arrival of evil friends, fear, passion, hatred, folly and darkness, the instant, time, gaining merits. The sutra confesses evil committed under the oppression of all these things. So clearly they are not factors that we occasionally encounter and have to resist; they are things that surround us and almost crush us all the time. It's not as though they are just there but don't bother us; they are all around us, hemming us in, breaking in upon us, weighing upon us, and restricting our movements. They are a constant chronic danger, and if we are not conscious of the fact it is because we go along with them to such an extent that there is nothing in us to be oppressed.

The list begins with "the oppression of existence." This implies that conditioned existence itself—just being a human being—is pressurizing us to perform unskillful actions. All you have to do is go out for a little walk and you see all sorts of things that cannot but give rise to unskillful thoughts, even unskillful activities, on your part. To be more specific, city life, we could say, is an oppression. In the city, we have to put so much energy into keeping the world at bay—keeping the world from encroaching upon what we have gained already in the way of mindfulness and positivity—that we don't have much left over with which to make real progress. Still, we have to admit that this only happens because something within us has an affinity with these oppressions of the world.

The sense in which "foolish thought" might become an oppression is fairly obvious. Thoughts are running through our minds involuntarily all the time. We don't deliberately set out to think an unskillful thought; it just pops into our head. We didn't ask it to come, we didn't want it to be there; it just came. This is our experience. We call it "our" thought, but sometimes it seems as though it is coming from outside, invading us. When we sit to meditate, we try to concentrate our minds, keep them clear and pure, and all these unskillful foolish thoughts keep rushing in and undoing all our best efforts. This is how we feel. And yet we cannot escape the fact that these thoughts are our own; they belong to us.

Then there is "the oppression of birth." According to some psychologists, birth itself is a traumatic experience. There you are in the womb before birth: warm, relatively quiet, quite comfortable. Then suddenly you are violently squeezed through a narrow aperture, and come out at the other end into a terrible bright light to be seized, slapped, and plunged into water. This must surely be a very traumatic experience. You are slapped to make you breathe, rubbed with a rough towel, then dressed, all tied up. And then you start feeling hungry. This might well be described as the oppression of birth.

But next, in what way might bodily activity be an oppression, or even "various oppressions"? Well, think about it. You wake up in the morning, you've got to get up and dress yourself, go to the toilet, brush your teeth, and then you've got to eat. All these are bodily activities which are needed to keep you going. Sometimes there seem to be so many of them that you forget what you are living *for*. As you get older, physical existence becomes more and more of a burden. In the end you can hardly walk, or even get up from a chair without help. You can't get onto a bus without a helping hand. Maybe you can't dress yourself or go to the toilet without help. This is when this oppression really strikes home—although when you are young, you sometimes get a foretaste of it when you are ill. You can't think of very much at all beyond your physical state, your aches and pains, your medicine, and so on.

As for "the oppression of the world," this could be taken in a narrower sense than the oppression of existence, to mean the whole of social life. Indeed, whatever the specific oppression may be, it is all-pervasive. Take, for instance, "the arrival of evil friends." It is not

624 ~ THE ESSENTIAL SANGHARAKSHITA

that we occasionally meet an evil friend, someone who is going to try to induce us to perform unskillful actions; we are surrounded by them. Go for a ride on a bus; there they all are. Go to watch a soccer game; there they all are. We are surrounded by people who are in a sense "evil friends," in that their influence on us is not a positive, skillful one.

Then there is "the oppression of the instant," having to act or make a decision when one may be off guard, and "the oppression of time," or as we would say "pressure of time," which is what so often seems to keep us from skillful action. Certainly under the conditions of modern life we often feel that we don't have enough time to do things properly, or think about what the skillful way to act would be. We act hastily, and the chances are that we act unskillfully.

Even gaining merits, according to the sutra, is an oppression—odd as that may sound. What the sutra is pointing to is the danger of getting too attached to our merit. If we think of the spiritual life in terms of acquiring merits too much then that becomes quite oppressive so far as our real spiritual life is concerned. The text doesn't explicitly say so, but I take it that the merits referred to here are of the lower kind, the kind which guarantee you a place in a higher heavenly world after death. I don't see how merits which are dedicated to Enlightenment could be an oppression. Oppression, after all, only arises when you are trying to do something skillful and external factors are getting in the way. Life itself can get in the way, time can get in the way, but merits that are dedicated to Enlightenment surely can't get in the way.

This list draws attention to the fact that there are all sorts of unskillful factors in existence which are always pressing in on us, and from which it is very difficult for us to escape, because we are experiencing them all the time. They never let up. It's as though there is some force at work in the world almost compelling us to do unskillful things against our better judgment and our own wishes. If we are surrounded by these things, sooner or later they are going to have some definite effect. It is not that they give rise to unskillfulness in some mysterious, indirect way. If we are constantly surrounded by evil friends, sooner or later they will have some influence on us. The list is of course selective; all unskillful or unhelpful factors are of this nature.

This is not to suggest that as an individual you are absolved from responsibility for your behavior. In confessing the evil you have committed, you accept responsibility for it. It may be understandable when you fail to stand up to the oppressions, but it is your responsibility to stand up to them. If something is not your fault, why should you confess it? There would be no point. The fact that you confess means that you accept responsibility, even though you were strongly tempted. To make a technical distinction, one could say that these oppressions are the occasion of unskillful actions, but not their cause. You are their cause, and therefore the responsibility is yours. Perhaps you are very strongly tempted, but you still have the capacity to resist.

3 ← The Nature of Spiritual Effort

1. LIVING WITH PURPOSE

The question is always the same: what effect is this going to have on my development as a human being?

WHATEVER SITUATION confronts us, whatever experience befalls us, whatever opportunity presents itself to us, we always have to ask ourselves: "What bearing does this have—directly or indirectly—on the higher purpose I have set myself?" We have to raise this question in relation to our work, our personal relationships, our social, cultural, and sporting activities, our interests—the books we read, the music we listen to, the films we watch. The question is always the same: what effect is this going to have on my development as a human being?

Making the living of a religious or even spiritual life in a conventional sense our main consideration will not necessarily have any kind of positive impact on our development. But if we make the development of consciousness the primary motivation in everything we do, we will make sure progress. And if we don't—well, we won't.

2. The Spiral Path

No doubt it is good to have the concept of Enlightenment before us, but it needs to be brought down to earth.

ACCORDING TO Buddhist tradition, our mundane experience naturally consists in action and reaction between opposite factors: pleasure and pain, love and hatred, and so on. Upon taking up the spiritual life—which in this context means becoming a novice Bodhisattva—you get the same process of interaction between factors, but one factor augments rather than opposes the other. One traditional description of this process is in terms of the sequence of positive nidanas or links: awareness of the inherently unsatisfactory nature of existence, in dependence upon which arises faith, then joy, rapture, bliss, calm, meditative concentration, and "knowledge and vision of things as they really are."[157] However, although this sequence is progressive or spiral rather than cyclical, it is reversible; you can revert back through the sequence until you are back where you started. It's a bit like playing snakes and ladders.

So the crucial point of the spiritual life is the point at which one passes from this skillful but reversible state to a state that is irreversible. This is the point of insight, the point at which one enters the Stream, the point at which—in terms of the sequence outlined above—one gains knowledge and vision of things as they really are. This is the real object of the spiritual life. There is no need to think in terms of Enlightenment or Buddhahood; that is simply the inevitable culmination of the irreversible sequence of skillful mental states that ensues from insight. Once you have entered the Stream, you are irreversibly bound for Enlightenment, one could say; you have sufficient spiritual momentum to take you all the way. You may still have a long way to go, but you are now safe from any danger of losing what you have gained.

It is therefore said of the Buddha's "victory," his attainment of Enlightenment, that it is irreversible. It cannot be undone. There is no outside power that can make a Buddha no longer a Buddha. This applies not only to the Buddha, but also to the Arahant, the Once-Returner, and the Stream-entrant—and of course the irreversible Bodhisattva.

But until we have passed through that gate of irreversibility we are in a precarious position. This is why we need to make a constant effort in our spiritual life and also make sure that we are living and working in conditions that support our spiritual efforts. Until we have reached that point of no return, we need the most positive situation, the most helpful environment, we can possibly get.

This is what the Buddha was getting at in his last words, *appamadena sampadetha,* which can be translated "With mindfulness, strive."[158] To reach the point of irreversibility one has to go on making an effort—including the effort to be mindful and aware enough to ensure that the conditions you live in are conducive to your making the best effort you possibly can. You can make a great deal of effort, but if it does not include an effort to create more favorable conditions, you are almost wasting your energy. On the other hand, you can be in the most favorable conditions imaginable, but if you are not making an effort, what use are those conditions? Both are necessary.

Many people become aware of the effect of positive conditions when they go on retreat for the first time. The degree to which one can change in the course of just a few days is remarkable. Just leaving the city and staying in the country, being undisturbed by the pull of trivial distractions, and doing a bit more meditation and Dharma study than you usually have time for can transform you into quite a different person—much happier, much more positive. So it isn't enough to try to change one's mental state through meditation; one needs the cooperation of one's environment. Without this it is very difficult, even impossible, to develop spiritually up to the point of irreversibility.

This fundamental concept of irreversibility—the point at which one's commitment to the spiritual path is so strong that no conditions can sway it—has been lost sight of to some extent, both in the Theravada and in the Mahayana. This is a pity. No doubt it is good to have the concept of Enlightenment before us, but it needs to be brought down to earth; and thinking in terms of Stream-entry—in the broad sense, not in the narrow sense which opposes it to the Bodhisattva ideal—helps us to do that, reminds us that we cannot afford to slacken off our spiritual effort until we have reached the point of irreversibility.

3. THE FOUR EXERTIONS

Most of us have our own private dream-picture of ourselves. Closing our eyes we see ourselves as though in a mirror and think, "How beautiful! How noble!"

PERFECT EFFORT, the sixth stage of the Noble Eightfold Path, consists of a set of exercises known as the four exertions. These consist in (1) Preventing, (2) Eradicating, (3) Developing, and (4) Maintaining, and their common object is good and bad thoughts, or as we say in Buddhism, skillful and unskillful mental states. The effort which consists in *preventing* means the effort to prevent the arising in our minds of those unskillful thoughts or mental states which have not yet arisen. Similarly, *eradicating* means eradicating from our minds those unskillful states which are already present therein. *Developing* means developing within our minds skillful states which are not there already, while *maintaining* means maintaining within our minds those skillful states which already exist there. Thus Perfect Effort is primarily psychological. It consists in unremitting work on oneself and upon one's own mind by means of these four exertions.

This classification is given as an incentive and a reminder, because it is so easy to slacken off. People start with lots of enthusiasm: they are all for Buddhism, all for meditation, all for the spiritual life; but very often it quickly wears off. Enthusiasm wanes, and after a while it is almost as though it had never been at all. This is because the forces of inertia within ourselves, the forces holding us back and keeping us down, are very strong indeed—even in simple matters like getting up early in the morning to meditate. You might make a resolution to get up half an hour earlier, and you might succeed once or twice, or even three times; but by the fourth morning temptation will almost certainly have set in, and it will be a matter of quite serious mental struggle and conflict whether you get up or whether you stay a few minutes longer in that warm, cozy bed. You are nearly always the loser, of course, because the forces of inertia are so strong. It is so easy for enthusiasm to wane, dwindle, and vanish.

Before any consideration of these four exertions there is one very important observation to be made. We cannot even begin to prevent, eradicate, develop, or maintain unless to begin with we know ourselves; that is to say unless we know which way our minds are going, or know what the contents of our minds are; and to know ourselves requires great honesty—at least, great honesty with ourselves. It is not perhaps to be expected that we should be able to be completely honest with other people, but at least so far as the four exertions are concerned we should be honest with ourselves.

If we want to practice the four exertions we must at least try to see ourselves as we truly are, so that we know what needs to be prevented, or eradicated, or developed, or maintained. Most of us have our own private dream-picture of ourselves. Closing our eyes we see ourselves as though in a mirror and think, "How beautiful! How noble!" This is the highly idealized picture which most of the time we have of ourselves. Not endowed, perhaps, with *all* the virtues, not *quite* perfect, but a really warm, lovable, sympathetic, intelligent, kind, well-intentioned, honest, industrious human being—*that* is what we usually see. What we have to try to develop, what we have to demand and almost to pray for is, in the words of the poet, the grace "to see ourselves as others see us";[159] and to see ourselves as others see us is not easy. We have to undertake a mental stocktaking of our own skillful and unskillful mental states—our own "vices" and "virtues." Though no moral absolutes are involved here, we at least have to understand our own minds, or our own mental states and mental qualities, very seriously and honestly before we can even think of applying the four exertions. Otherwise we shall not know how to proceed, and no real improvement—no real development—will be possible.

4. What Counts as Laziness?

Being lazy really means being busy doing something that is not conducive to skillful mental states.

We tend to think of laziness as being about lack of exertion, but the Buddhist idea of laziness is quite different—and quite revealing. For Gampopa, for example, the most extreme form of laziness is devoting oneself day and night to defeating enemies and making money.[160]

Being lazy really means being busy doing something that is not conducive to skillful mental states: one's busyness actually prevents one from being aware of what one might otherwise be engaging in. In fact, Tsongkhapa goes further than that: laziness, he is saying, is taking delight in the fact that one is *not* occupying oneself with something of higher value. It involves a sort of complacency and satisfaction in the fact that one is occupying oneself with lower things. To overcome laziness we need to be able to distinguish that which is worthwhile from that which is less so. This means that we need to think deeply about the implications of attaining concentrated mental states (*dhyana*): what it will mean to attain *dhyana* and what it will mean *not* to attain it. Eagerness (*chanda*) is based on this, and it is established to counteract laziness.

Tsongkhapa's remarks on laziness are especially important for those who are tempted to immerse themselves so deeply in various discussions and arguments about the teachings of Buddhism that they miss the whole point of them. However conscientiously you occupy yourself with the teachings, if you don't put them into practice, such occupation is no more than a form of laziness. This is not at all to say that Dharma study and Dharma practice are necessarily two different things. Study can be a method of practice just as meditation is. Study is, after all, an aspect of the first of the three wisdoms (listening, reflecting, and meditating).[161] Laziness sets in when you do not go on to reflect and meditate on the teachings you have studied.

5. DISCIPLINE

Following a system of discipline doesn't necessarily have any spiritual value at all.

IT IS A GOOD THING to have a definite framework of behavior, definite guidelines, especially when one is young, and it is even a good thing to be quite strict in observing those guidelines. An old brahmin lawyer I used to know in India, a very rigid, orthodox old man, was fond of saying, "A disciplined life gives strength," and this is true. In the case of this old man, he derived his strength from following the brahminical rules, with some of which I would violently disagree because they involved the strict observance of the caste system. But they did make him into a very strong character, because he believed that he was following a divinely inspired way of life.

But following a system of discipline doesn't necessarily have any spiritual value at all. You develop a kind of strength in the army, in which you are governed by a certain ethos and have to observe certain rules. And even the "rules" of Buddhism, the guidelines which you find in the traditional Vinaya-Pitaka, are not necessarily helpful to us now. The principle behind all of them is probably still valid, but it may require a different application, a different expression. It might be a useful exercise to go through all the Vinaya rules systematically, examining each rule to see what principle is involved, how it was applied or formulated in the Buddha's day, whether that formulation still applies, and, if not, what fresh formulation of that principle might be helpful.

Some would argue that one should continue to observe the rules out of faith in the Buddha. This sort of attitude cannot be disregarded altogether, but one could argue that it could not be the result of faith, because the Buddha encouraged his followers to think for themselves. The value of observing rules is not to be underestimated, but one has to give careful thought to what rules one does observe and why; one should not be inflexible about it.

It is no good trying to defend the Vinaya rules by saying, "If it was good enough for the Buddha, it's good enough for me." We shouldn't just accept the tradition unthinkingly. It's a question of finding a middle way. You can't go it alone, relying in a one-sided, individualistic way on your own judgment, your own opinion; you need to consult with those who are wiser and more experienced than yourself. On the other hand, you don't want to submit unquestioningly to authority. It is not easy to follow this middle path, but we have to try. There has to be a place for faith and there has to be a place for healthy skepticism. It is very easy to go from one extreme to the other, rather than searching for the middle way. But if we are going to accept some authority unquestioningly, why bother with Buddhism? Why not just go and join the Catholic Church, which is so much closer to us in culture? Why give ourselves the trouble of going to the East and setting up an infallible authority there? And on the other hand, if you're going to be a thoroughgoing skeptic, why bother with Buddhism at all? Go and be a humanist, go and be an agnostic. The way to advance in the Dharma is a middle way between the extreme of authoritarianism and the extreme of individualistic thinking for oneself.

6. A Regular Routine

It is strange that people are often reluctant to adopt regular habits, because these do in fact make life easier.

IN THE *Satipatthana Sutta* the Buddha exhorts the monks to apply clear comprehension in all the activities of daily life. Bending and stretching, wearing robes, carrying the begging-bowl, eating, drinking, chewing, savoring, attending to the calls of nature, speaking and keeping silent are all carried out with awareness of what you are doing and why, so that that aspiration is allowed to permeate everything you do. Any activity, however small or apparently insignificant, can be done with a sense of purpose. You can even fall asleep mindfully, with a sense of when and why your period of rest is necessary. If you have to be up in the morning at six-thirty for meditation, your clear comprehension might take the form of making sure that you get to bed in good time so that you have enough sleep and won't just feel like a lie-in when the time comes to meditate.

If you are serious and passionate about reaching your spiritual goal, it is absolutely necessary to take a regular, disciplined approach to what you do. Success, as in any other enterprise—sport or art or business—depends on establishing a disciplined and committed lifestyle. It is strange that people are often reluctant to adopt regular habits, because these do in fact make life easier. If you live haphazardly, just doing what you feel like when you feel like it, you can end up not finding the time or inclination for things you know will benefit you. But with a regular routine you will still, for example, sit to meditate even when you don't feel like it, because you are aware of the benefits of doing so. You can take the likely outcomes of particular courses of action for granted—you don't have to re-assess them every time you think about doing them.

It is equally important, however, not to get too rigid about this. The "path" is not a set of rules that you can stick to mechanically and be sure of getting the results you want. At dinner time you might be able to get away with shovelling food into your mouth in the knowledge that your stomach will take care of the rest of the process, but it isn't like that with meditation, puja, or Dharma study. These practices are designed to be liberating, but if you lose touch with why you are doing them, they become so many obstacles to your progress. Mindfulness is an intelligent, responsive awareness to ever-changing conditions. If the urgent need to develop insight gets lost in the lackluster business of keeping everything ticking over, it is time to look again at the balance of your life.

7. Certainty of Success

Our tendency is perhaps to think of spiritual life as difficult and worldly life as easy, but there is no objective reason for this view.

IN HIS *Bodhicaryavatara* Santideva says that the effect of giving, of puja—in short, of committing yourself to the spiritual life—is that you become "without fear of being or becoming."[162] The would-be Bodhisattva has no more worries. You just give yourself to the spiritual life. You aren't bothered whether you are going to live or die, be rich or poor, be praised or blamed, or anything like that. You are just on the spiritual path and that's that. So long as you are still wondering what to do with your life—perhaps weighing up how much time to give to spiritual things and how much to worldly things—you remain unsure, unclear, and therefore unconfident. But once you have made up your mind and committed yourself, in a sense everything is looked after and there's nothing to worry about.

Our tendency is perhaps to think of spiritual life as difficult and worldly life as easy, but there is no objective reason for this view. Sometimes it is less trouble just to lead a spiritual life than to try to put things right in the world or even to try to have a successful and happy worldly career. In a way, it takes less effort to gain Enlightenment. It's very difficult to be successful in the world—there are all sorts of factors that might upset one's plans—but if one follows the spiritual path one knows that, if one makes the effort, sooner or later success will come.

8. Encountering the Dakini

Sometimes it is said that the dakini throws herself into the spiritual life just as a passionate woman flings herself into the arms of her lover.

Dakinis are mysterious female figures who appear in the Tantric tradition. The word *dakini* is derived from a Sanskrit root meaning direction, space, sky; and when Tantric texts were translated into Tibetan, dakini was rendered as *khadroma*, which is usually translated "sky-walker" or "traveler in space." Empty space represents absence of obstruction and therefore freedom of movement. This is not, of course, literal movement within space. Space or sky also represents mind in its absolute aspect; so the dakinis represent the free-moving energies of the mind itself—they are the thrills or tremors of emotional energy that pass quivering through the mind, bubbling up from its very depths.

In developed Tantric Buddhism, especially in its Tibetan form, there are said to be three kinds of dakini, representing three levels on which the dakini principle, as we may call it, is experienced. First, there is the dakini as female Buddha form. In early Buddhism, the Enlightenment principle, Buddhahood, was usually represented in the form of a perfect human body sitting cross-legged as though in meditation—and the body was usually male. But there is no reason why it should be male rather than female, and in the case of the dakini as female Buddha, it happens to be female. Secondly, the dakini is the embodiment of one's own upsurging energies. And thirdly, the dakini can be seen as a spiritual companion and as representing the esoteric Tantric form of the Third Refuge—the Refuge in the Sangha. The dakini in this sense, as encountered in, for example, *The Life and*

Liberation of Padmasambhava, is a highly advanced female spiritual practitioner in association with whom a male practitioner practices the Dharma and whose company is spiritually inspiring. She has a highly developed moral awareness, though not in a conventional sense. Dakinis are usually described as being youthful and extremely beautiful, as well as having intense faith and devotion, and being pure-minded and given to meditation. As such, they are not at all common.

To get a real feeling for the dakini, we can do no better than encounter one. I propose, therefore, simply to give a description of a particular dakini figure, one who occupies an important place in the Tantra as practiced in Tibet. She is known as Vajrayogini, and, in Tibetan, Narokhacho, and she is also described as Sarvabuddhadakini. Sarva means "all" and Buddha of course means "Enlightened one," so Sarvabuddhadakini is the dakini of all the Buddhas, the embodiment of all the energies that have carried all the Buddhas, past, present, and future, to Enlightenment. She is thus a very powerful figure indeed, as her appearance dramatically demonstrates. She is also, in a way, a Buddha figure in her own right.

She is not depicted sitting down meditating. She stands with her legs wide apart, her right leg straight and her left knee bent. She is moving toward the right, with her breasts, which are very full, thrust out, and her head tilted back. Her right arm hangs a little away from her side, while her left arm is raised above her head and bent back, the hand almost touching the head. The whole figure is brilliant red in color and completely naked. She wears only a few ornaments—which are of human bone—and an enormous garland of human skulls which hangs down below her knees. She has long dishevelled hair which falls straight down her back to her waist. In her right hand she holds a chopper with a vajra handle, while with her left hand she lifts a skull-cup filled with blood to her mouth and drinks it with evident enjoyment. She has what is called a wrathful smile, and three eyes, the extra one being in the middle of her forehead. She wears a crown of five human skulls and on her left shoulder, lying horizontal and passing behind her upturned head, is a long staff, from the top of which there hangs down a type of small drum, called a *damaru,* and a bell, with streamers. The head of the staff is formed by the vase of initiation, which is surmounted by crossed vajras and, above them, three human heads, one on top of the other: a freshly severed head, a head that has been severed for some time and allowed to go yellow, and—at the top—a skull, on top of which a vajra stands upright. She tramples underfoot two figures, one red, the other black. Each has four arms. Usually the red figure holds a skull-cup filled with blood and a staff like the dakini's, while the black figure holds a small drum and a curved sword. Each has one pair of hands raised in supplication. And surrounding the naked red figure of the dakini is a halo of flames.

I am not going to say what the dakini "means"—the figure makes its own impact. I will just elaborate a little on some aspects of the symbolism and suggest a few associations. First of all, the dakini is red in color. In Tantric Buddhism, red is the color of love, passion, and emotional arousal—which, in the case of any dakini, is total. Blood suffuses not only her face; her whole body blushes crimson. So the dakini represents the state of total emotional involvement in the spiritual life. This is also why her hair is dishevelled. She doesn't care about decorum, about keeping herself tidy, about what people may think or say. She just abandons herself. Sometimes it is said that the dakini throws herself into the spiritual life just as a passionate woman flings herself into the arms of her lover. She represents the spiritual ideal of self-abandonment to the Three Jewels.

Usually people find it very difficult to give themselves in this way, not just to the spiritual life, but to anything. They find it difficult to plunge in, commit themselves, get totally involved, put all their emotions into what they are doing. As a result they don't achieve much in any direction, certainly not in a spiritual one. In many cases people can't give themselves in this way because they are emotionally blocked. They have to learn to loosen up, get their emotions flowing more freely—flowing, ultimately, in the direction of Enlightenment. This is what the red color of the dakini suggests—that in the spiritual life one should not be afraid to feel.

And the dakini is naked. She is concerned only with direct experience, reality, truth. She has nothing to hide. She is completely open, completely honest. Nakedness is a prominent feature of Tantric symbolism, to underline the importance in the Tantra of being direct, unveiled, radical. In Tantric art, yogis, dakas (dakinis' male counterparts), and dakinis, even Buddhas, are often depicted naked, which is entirely scandalous from the point of view of Theravada Buddhism, or even Zen. The nakedness is, of course, spiritual nakedness, nakedness of one's being. However, it is not in the spirit of the Tantra to hide behind the idea of symbolism, and sometimes even literal nakedness is not without its significance and even value.

4 ⊱ Great Buddhists of the Twentieth Century

Buddhism began with lives; it didn't begin with books.

HERO-WORSHIP is not in fashion at this time in history, at the end of the twentieth century—except, perhaps, in a perverted, degenerate, or trivial form. History is nowadays presented—even to children—in terms of the small doings of ordinary people rather than the momentous actions of great individuals. It would appear that children are offered facts and figures—and of course pocket calculators—rather than the inspirational examples of heroes like Nelson and Florence Nightingale. And this does seem to me a very unfortunate development. We need people we can look up to, people on whom we can model ourselves, and from whom we can derive inspiration. We need, in short, heroes in the true, positive sense.

Above all, we need spiritual heroes; and not only heroes—even legendary heroes—from the dim and distant past, but also heroic exemplars from our own time. Nor is there any dearth of contemporary or near-contemporary ones. I have to say that I started turning over in my mind this subject of great Buddhists of the twentieth century with the assumption that there would be no more than a handful of individuals to consider. But it did not take me long to realize that I had a problem. There seemed to have been dozens upon dozens of them.

Unless one is going to attempt an exhaustive guide to the great Buddhists of the twentieth century one has to select. And unless one is going to do this according to mere whim, then one has to look around for some meaningful principles by which to make one's selection. On what basis could I focus on certain individuals and not others?

In the end I allowed two principles to direct my choice. First, I decided not to touch upon any great Buddhists who were still alive. After all, there is always the faint possibility of great Buddhists ceasing to be so, either by changing their religion or by losing their greatness of character—and then where would that leave us? Such things happen from time to time, unfortunately. We should heed Sophocles' warning: "Call no man happy until he is dead," and be wary of calling someone a great Buddhist too definitively before he or she is safely dead.

As for my second principle of selection, this was to consider no one with whom I had not had some kind of personal contact. I did, however, make an exception for Anagarika Dharmapala, the first of my great Buddhists, who died in India in 1933 when I was still a small boy living in Tooting, London. I feel justified in making this exception because I do have the sense that I lived with him for several weeks while composing my biography of him in 1952, having spent this time among the many volumes of his diaries.

Just one preliminary question remains to be cleared up, but it is quite an important one. How do we define a great Buddhist? Well, in the first place, great Buddhists have to be Buddhists. That is, they have to go for Refuge to the Three Jewels, to the Buddha, the Dharma, and the Sangha. It is not enough in itself to be a great scholar of Buddhism, to be learned in Sanskrit and Pali, to make outstanding and original contributions to Buddhist studies.

It's not enough, either, to occupy a prominent position in a Buddhist organization. During my time in the East it was a recurring puzzle to me, when I came into contact with various Buddhist organizations, and met their presidents and secretaries, to discover that these dignitaries weren't actually Buddhists. So it is not enough to have a position of influence in the Buddhist world. Nor of course is it enough to have been born into a position of influence in the Buddhist world—to have been born into a Buddhist royal family, say.

Moreover, a great Buddhist is not just a great individual with Buddhist leanings. To be a great Buddhist, one would have to possess at least some of the characteristically Buddhist qualities to an eminent degree. Great Buddhists possess not just a little bit of *metta,* not just an occasional burst of *virya,* not just the beginnings of *prajna.* They have, we may say, at least some of these qualities "in spades."

Naturally, it goes without saying that they have, too, the basic human virtues—straightforward kindness and awareness of the needs of others, an integrated personality, self-knowledge, and so on—and these also to an eminent degree. One can't be a great—or even a good—Buddhist without being a great or good human being.

Besides having at least some of these virtues, they should deploy them in their life and work in such a way as to influence many other people, especially many other Buddhists. Thus a great Buddhist contributes to the making of Buddhist history. Furthermore, a great Buddhist is a paradigmatic figure, providing a model or an example for other Buddhists, both when alive and after death. That is, he or she functions as a source of permanent inspiration and guidance for other Buddhists.

Not all the people mentioned here could be said to be equally great—though it is difficult to compare them very accurately in that way as they were great in very different ways. And I must also say that I personally don't necessarily agree with everything that each of them said or did or wrote. But they were all undoubtedly great in the sense that I have defined.

Finally, in our definition of terms, we come to "twentieth century." Strictly speaking, from a Buddhist point of view we should perhaps be talking about the "twenty-fifth century" (after the Buddha's Enlightenment)—which concluded in 1956–7 CE—rather than the twentieth century (after the birth of Christ). But never mind. "Twentieth century" can be taken simply as convenient shorthand for "more or less within living memory." The first four of our great Buddhists were, in fact, all born in the nineteenth century, though they did most, if not all, their significant work for Buddhism in the twentieth.

My concern in these biographical sketches is not so much with the everyday biographical details—what they used to have for breakfast, say. It is rather with the significance of their lives for us, living as we do in the fresh wake of their achievements and in something of the same world as they did.

Anagarika Dharmapala

Dharmapala, the future "Lion of Lanka" as he came to be called, was born in 1864 in Colombo, Sri Lanka—except that here we must call this island "Ceylon," because that is the name it had in those days. His father was the proprietor of a furniture manufacturing business, so he had a solid, middle-class background; and his parents were good, pious Buddhists, so one might have thought that he would have had a solid Buddhist background as well.

However, he was christened "David"—his name was David Hewavitarne. And from the time he was five until the time he was eight, and again from ten to eighteen, he attended a series of Christian schools, both Catholic and Protestant. So this calls for some explanation. Why did his pious Buddhist parents send him to Christian schools?

The reason is simply that they had no choice. Ceylon had been a British colony since 1802, and before that, between 1505 and 1796, large parts of the island had been ruled first by the Portuguese and then by the Dutch. The result was that Buddhism and Buddhist culture at the time of Dharmapala's birth were at a very low ebb in Ceylon. In fact, it was not possible to be a Buddhist at all—at least, not officially. Children of Buddhist parents had to be taken for registration of their birth to a church—either Catholic or Protestant—and there given a Christian name. Otherwise, according to a law which was not repealed until 1884, the child would be illegitimate and unable to inherit property. And all education beyond primary level was in the hands of the missionaries.

So by the time he was in his early teens, Dharmapala knew by heart four complete books of the Old Testament, all four Gospels, and the Acts of the Apostles. However, he never lost faith in the Dharma. Dharmapala picked up a basic understanding of Buddhism at home, and being unusually argumentative, even for an adolescent boy, he used to get into trouble with his teachers for the persistence with which he picked away at inconsistencies in Christian doctrine. A much more serious offense, however, was his insistence on celebrating Wesak, the festival in honor of the Buddha's attainment of Enlightenment. At that time, of course, it wasn't a public holiday. Christmas was a public holiday, Easter was a public holiday, but Wesak wasn't.

But when Dharmapala was in his early teens he realized that as a Buddhist he ought to celebrate Wesak, and in order to do this he would have to be given the day off school. So he went to the headmaster and asked to have the day off in order to celebrate the most important festival in the Buddhist calendar. Unsurprisingly, the headmaster said, "No." Equally unsurprisingly, Dharmapala took his umbrella, walked out of the school, and simply didn't turn up for school the next day. He celebrated Wesak, and the following day was soundly thrashed. This little drama was enacted between Dharmapala and his headmaster once a year for three consecutive years. This was how obstinate and determined he was, even as a boy.

We know a lot of details about Dharmapala's life, even before he became well-known, because he kept a diary more or less from the time he left school until his death in 1933. He also wrote some memoirs later on in life, and in these we find described another incident from his schooldays that shows a deeper side to his character.

It so happened that one of his schoolfellows died, and the corpse was laid out in the school. The teachers apparently invited the students to gather round the dead body of the boy and offer up prayers, and Dharmapala joined them. But as he looked around, a question came into his mind. He asked himself, "Why are they praying?" And as he continued to look at the faces of his schoolfellows, at the faces of the teachers, the answer came to him quite clearly that they were afraid; they were afraid of death. This was why they were praying. He saw that prayer—petitionary prayer—was born of fear. And from that day onward he had no temptation to pray in that sort of way.

This uppish, confrontational teenager, however, was also a rather dreamy lover of poetry, reading widely in English literature, especially the Romantics, and particularly Shelley. He read Keats and Shelley constantly. And this poetic streak went in counterpoint with marked mystical and ascetic tendencies.

Fortunately for this idealistic youth, things were changing, even in colonial Ceylon, and the tide was beginning to turn in Buddhism's favor. In 1875 in New York, Madame Blavatsky and Colonel Olcott had founded the Theosophical Society. They were both very sympathetic to what they understood of Buddhism, and in 1880 they arrived in Ceylon, declared themselves to be Buddhists, and publicly took the Refuges and precepts from a prominent Sinhalese bhikkhu. This created a tremendous sensation from one end of the island to the other, because they were the first Europeans publicly to embrace Buddhism.

The Christian missionaries were understandably very upset, and they continued to be upset because Colonel Olcott took rather a liking to Ceylon. He stayed on and devoted himself to the cause of Buddhist education, eventually setting up more than three hundred Buddhist schools, some of which are still in existence. Sri Lankans still celebrate his work on "Olcott Day."

As for the still very young Dharmapala, he helped Colonel Olcott in his work, particularly by acting as his translator. Dharmapala also became quite close to Madame Blavatsky. In his late teens he had wanted to study occultism, as so many Theosophists did, but Madame Blavatsky advised him to follow a very different course. She advised him to study Pali and to work for the good of humanity—which is what he did. And it was at this time that he changed his name from David to Dharmapala (meaning "the Guardian of the Dharma").

In 1891 he paid his first visit to the holy places of northern India and found them in a shockingly neglected condition. Some of them were no more than ruins. This should not really have been any cause for surprise because Buddhism had disappeared from India several centuries before. Whatever was left of Buddhism that had not been absorbed by Hinduism had been destroyed by Muslim invaders.

The ancient Maha Bodhi Temple at Bodh Gaya, the most sacred of all the Buddhist holy places, had been restored by General Sir Alexander Cunningham. However, there was no one to look after the place, and when Dharmapala arrived there he was profoundly saddened by its desolate aspect. He sought out the Vajrasana, or "Diamond Throne," the carved black marble slab that marks the spot where the Buddha, according to tradition, actually sat when he attained supreme Enlightenment, and bowing down before it he touched the edge with his forehead. As he did so he was seized with a sudden inspiration. He would stay and look after the place until Buddhist monks could arrive and take over. At the age of 29 he had found his life's work.

It was not going to be as straightforward as he had thought it would be. Legally, the temple belonged to a Hindu monk, who was not pleased to have Dharmapala there, and at one point even had him thrown out and beaten up. Out of this ensued a long legal battle, which Dharmapala finally lost in 1906. Meanwhile, however, Dharmapala founded the Maha Bodhi Society to help him in his work. Initially, this work comprised the task of restoring Bodh Gaya to something of its former splendor; but the scope of the society's activities soon expanded to involve the promotion of Buddhism in India and eventually the development of Buddhism throughout the world. A natural extension of this work was to set up, in 1892, the *Maha Bodhi Journal*.

In 1893 Dharmapala was invited to attend the Parliament of World Religions in Chicago as representative of "Southern Buddhism"— which was the term applied at that time to the Theravada. He was a great success. In fact some journalists paid him what to them was the ultimate compliment, and compared him to Jesus. By his early thirties he was already a global figure, and he continued to travel and give lectures and establish viharas around the world during the next forty years. At the same time he concentrated on establishing schools and hospitals in Ceylon and building temples and viharas in India. Among the most important of the temples he built was one at Sarnath, where the Buddha first taught the Dharma. Here, in 1933, when he was already a very sick man in a wheelchair, he was ordained a bhikkhu, and he died there in December of the same year, aged sixty-nine.

Dharmapala was a leading figure in initiating two outstanding features of Buddhism in the twentieth century. He was a great pioneer in the revival of Buddhism in India after it had been virtually extinct there for several centuries. And he was the first Buddhist in modern times to preach the Dharma in three continents, in Asia, in America, and in Europe.

Clearly, Dharmapala led a very active life. However, he invariably started his day, often before dawn, with two hours of meditation. In his younger days in Ceylon he had failed to find a meditation teacher; for various reasons, the practice of meditation there had simply died out. But in his twenties he met a Burmese lay yogi who was able to give him some instruction. And the practice that we may say fuelled his life and work was the metta bhavana, the cultivation of universal loving-kindness. This is a vitally important aspect of his life. He wasn't simply a Buddhist activist, flitting from one Buddhist conference to another. His work for Buddhism sprang out of a deep experience of Buddhism—an experience that is enormously difficult to achieve without regular meditation.

One other significant aspect of his life was that he was the first *ana-garika*—that is, a celibate, full-time worker for Buddhism—in modern times. He wasn't, until his last months, a bhikkhu—but he wasn't a layman in the ordinary sense either. It seems that he took a vow of celibacy or brahmacharya at the age of eight and remained faithful to it all his life. And he also wore a yellow robe. However, it wasn't of the traditional bhikkhu pattern, and he didn't shave his head. He felt, it would appear, that the observance of all the vinaya rules would have got in the way of his work, especially as he flew around the world.

Ultimately, the key to Dharmapala's life and work is before one's eyes wherever one opens his voluminous diaries. At the top of every alternate page he wrote: "The only Refuge for him who aspires to true perfection is the Buddha alone." This is what he reminded himself, every day of the year, year after year. Going for Refuge is the fundamental, decisive, definitive act of the Buddhist life. It is what makes us Buddhists, and it is what unites us all as Buddhists.

Alexandra David-Néel

Born in Paris in 1868, at the time of the Emperor Napoleon III, Alexandra David-Néel died in southern France in 1969, when Pompidou was President of France. She would have worn crinolines as a young woman, and she survived to see young women in mini-skirts. So this gives us some idea of the historical parameters of her very long life.

Her father was a wealthy middle-class Protestant, socialist, and an ardent republican, whereas her mother was a Belgian Catholic and an ardent supporter of the Belgian monarchy. Alexandra David—as she was originally called—seems to have been very much closer to her father. Her mother had wanted a son who would become a Catholic bishop, and a daughter was a bitter disappointment to her. So Alexandra grew up in these circumstances something of a tomboy. She was educated in various Catholic convent schools, but she remained a tomboy, and from the age of sixteen she started running away from home. She would come back again, but before long she was bicycling—this was in the 1880s—all the way to Spain. She also visited Holland, England, Italy, again all on her own, and still a teenager.

On her second visit to England she came in contact with Theosophists. In the library of the British Museum she started reading up the more alternative mystical traditions—Gnosticism, Catharism, and so on. And on her return to France she settled in Paris with a group of French Theosophists. She started to study Sanskrit, and in doing so came across the Lalita-vistara, an imaginative and poetic, not to say legendary, life of the Buddha. However, this was not her first contact with Buddhism. At the age of thirteen she had apparently come across one of the most ancient and beautiful Buddhist legends, the Jataka tale of how the Buddha, in one of his previous incarnations, had given his body to a starving tigress and her cubs. She had thought, at thirteen, that this was the most beautiful story she had ever heard.

Living in Paris she was also in contact with Buddhist art, because the Musée Guimet in Paris housed one of the most famous collections of oriental art in the world. There, one day, she stood before a magnificent Japanese Buddha image, joined her hands together and bowed in salutation before it. She continued to study other religions, especially Hinduism, but she already regarded herself as a Buddhist.

At the age of twenty-one she came of age and inherited some money, which she spent on a trip to India, on her own, where she met maharajahs and swamis. She returned to Europe virtually penniless. She made a little money out of the occasional bit of journalism, but it wasn't enough. So she trained as a singer, and supported herself in this way for seven years. She had quite a successful and rather colorful career as a singer, and in the course of it learned a lot about human nature. But her voice was evidently not very well trained because it started to deteriorate. And so she decided, regretfully, that she would have to get married.

In 1904, at the age of thirty-six, Alexandra David married Philippe Néel, an aristocratic French engineer, then aged forty. They lived in French North Africa for a number of years, during which her beloved father died and she published her first book on Buddhism, called *Buddhist Modernism and the Buddhism of the Buddha*.

Alexandra David-Néel left for the East again in 1911, and she did not return for fourteen years. She traveled in Ceylon, India, Sikkim, Nepal, Japan, China, and Tibet, and continued her study of Buddhism. Not only that: she was putting what she studied into practice, which was unusual at that time. Not only was it unusual for a student of Buddhism to practice it; what she was doing was also unusual in another way. She met the thirteenth Dalai Lama—in exile in

Kalimpong after an invasion by the Chinese—and he was astonished, on asking how she had become a Buddhist, to be told that it had been by reading books. He had never heard of such a thing.

In Sikkim she met the Gomchen of Lhachen, who was famous as a meditator and yogi (Gomchen meaning "great meditator"). She became his disciple and spent two years there, practicing meditation and studying Tibetan. She also adopted a Sikkimese boy—Lama Yongden as he afterward became—and he remained with her for the rest of his life.

David-Néel's husband seems to have taken her extended absence very well. She wrote to him every day, so clearly she was fond of him, though equally clearly she could be fond of him only from a distance. In return he sent her money regularly—and she evidently needed plenty of it, to be frank. She usually traveled in some style, with a number of servants and a good deal of equipment.

There was one journey she took in rather less than grand style, and that was her famous journey to Lhasa. At that time foreigners were prohibited from entering Tibet, so she traveled in disguise. Her only companion was Yongden, who took the part of a traveling lama, with herself as his old mother. They were four months traveling on foot. They traveled through China to approach Lhasa from the northeast, crossing vast deserts, scaling lofty mountains, and braving bandits, starvation, and landslides to reach their destination. They spent two months in Lhasa and David-Néel subsequently wrote *The Journey of a Parisienne to Lhasa*.

In 1925 she returned to France with Yongden and settled in the Alps of Provence, at Digne. By now she was a rather famous elderly lady, giving lectures and writing books. She took a journey east just once more, in 1939, but this proved to be ill-timed. The Second World War broke out and she and Yongden were stranded in a small town in southeast Tibet called Darsendo (or Dhartsendo) for six years. Her husband was dead by the time they returned and Yongden died in 1955. She continued to write. It was during this last period of her life that I had some contact with her. We exchanged letters and she contributed to magazines I was editing; and I noticed that her handwriting, despite her years, remained firm and clear.

Her life was noteworthy in three particular respects. First of all, she was one of the first Westerners to take Buddhism seriously—that is, to take it as a way of life, not just as a subject for scholarly study. Secondly, there was her readiness to defy convention, especially when convention stood in the way of the realization of her cherished ideals. Nowadays, when defying convention is often a meaningless convention in itself, it is difficult for us to realize how strong, how rigid, certain conventions were during her lifetime. For her, being unconventional took real courage. Thirdly and lastly, she showed what a really determined woman is capable of. Her life is thus an inspiration to all Buddhists, but perhaps to Buddhist women in particular.

Lama Govinda

Lama Govinda was rather a mysterious figure—particularly when he was Ernst Lothar Hoffmann—which is the name with which he began life. We know very little about his early years. He was born in 1898 in Germany, into a middle-class family of partly Spanish descent, but his mother died when he was three, and he was brought up by her sister. He originally wanted to be a mining engineer, but developed an increasing interest in philosophy, especially the work of Schopenhauer. He went on to study comparative religion, and Buddhism in particular, until, toward the end of the First World War, he was called up to spend two years in the German army.

After the war he took up residence in Capri, where began a very important period in his life. He studied Pali, he took up art and a bit of archaeological research, and he met an elderly German lady who became, for much of the rest of his life, a sort of foster-mother. He started practicing meditation, and he started as well to make pastel drawings of the meditative states he experienced. So he was evidently already making the connection between meditation and art which would later be the subject of much of his thinking.

In 1928, aged thirty, Govinda moved to Ceylon—with his foster-mother as well, of course. For a couple of years he studied Pali and Abhidhamma with the famous German bhikkhu Nyanatiloka, during which period he took the name of Govinda and became an anagarika (anagarika literally means "homeless one"; becoming an anagarika usually implies celibacy). He also visited Burma and researched cases of alleged recollection of previous lives, a subject he was always interested in.

His next move was to India, and at a Buddhist conference in Darjeeling he came into contact for the first time with Tibetan Buddhism, which thereafter exercised a compelling influence on his life and work. There are not many firm dates in what we know of Govinda's life, but about 1930 he settled—again with his foster-mother—in Ghoom near Darjeeling, where he met his Tibetan guru, the famous Tomo Geshe Rinpoche. During the next few years he was based partly in Ghoom and partly in Shantiniketan, the forest university established by Rabindranath Tagore a hundred miles north of Calcutta [Kolkata].

Govinda lectured, he wrote, he traveled—until in 1942 he was interned by the British because of his German descent. Conditions in the camp near Dehradun were very mild: he studied Chinese, he studied the I Ching, and he enjoyed the companionship of Nyanaponika, another German disciple of Nyanatiloka. After the war he returned to Ghoom and to Shantiniketan, and in 1947 he married a former student of his at Shantiniketan, Rati Petit, who became known as Li Gotami.

In 1948 they made their celebrated journey to Tsaparang in western Tibet, and they made it just in time, because within a year or two the Chinese had occupied the whole of Tibet. The two of them spent several months working in conditions of great hardship, sketching, and photographing ruined Buddhist temples and monasteries, and copying ancient frescoes. They were greatly impressed, not so much by the religious life they found there as by the vastness of the open spaces, by the views, by the brilliant colors, by the light, and of course by the ancient art that they discovered.

In 1952 Govinda announced the formation of the Arya Maitreya Mandala, an organization through which he hoped to spread Buddhism, especially Tibetan Buddhism, in the West. Shortly afterward, he and Li Gotami moved to Almora in the foothills of the western Himalayas, where they remained for the next twenty-five years, and where Govinda had the most creative phase of his career, producing at least two Buddhist literary classics: the semi-autobiographical *Way of the White Clouds,* documenting the journey to western Tibet; and *Foundations of Tibetan Mysticism.* In the sixties and seventies they made several trips to Europe and America, where there was a growing interest in Buddhism, and they spent their last years in San Francisco, where Govinda died in 1985, aged 87. Li Gotami died in India about three years later.

I got to know Lama Govinda quite well. We discovered that we had a good deal in common, especially in our approach to Buddhism. In a letter he wrote to me four days before he died he made a couple of points that seem to indicate what the overall direction of his life and work had been. Firstly: "I'm a great admirer of Italian art and, like you, I always uphold the importance of European culture. Without knowing the roots of our own culture how can we absorb the essence of Buddhist culture?" And secondly: "Now it is up to the next generation to take Buddhism out of the merely academic atmosphere and make it a living experience."

Lama Anagarika Govinda always emphasized that intellectual understanding and the observance of rules wasn't enough, but that Buddhism could be made a living experience by means of meditation, together with ritual and particularly color—color in the full, literal sense—in the spiritual life. He also stressed the importance of what he called "creative imagination" and thus the importance of art. As a meditator and an artist himself, he did not see these two activities as completely different. In fact, he saw a sort of parallelism between them. The way he put it was that in meditation we pass from the world of outward expression to the world of inner experience; and in art we pass from the world of inner experience to the world of outward expression.

Edward Conze

Eberhart Julius Dietrich Conze was born in London in 1904 of mixed German, French, and Dutch ancestry. His father belonged to the German landed aristocracy, and his mother to what he himself would have called the "plutocracy." His background was Protestant, though his mother became a Roman Catholic in later life. He seems to have had a rather bad relationship with his mother.

He was born in England simply because his father happened to be posted there as German Vice-Consul, but this meant that he had British nationality, should he ever need it (which he would). He was educated at various German universities and with a flair for languages picked up a command of fourteen of them, including Sanskrit, by the age of twenty-four. Like many other Europeans, he came into contact with Theosophy quite early on. But he also took up astrology. He took it seriously, remaining a keen astrologer all his life. And while still a young man, he wrote a very substantial book called *The Principle of Contradiction*. Apparently his mother said that she was not surprised he'd written such a book since he himself was a bundle of contradictions.

During the rise to power of Hitler, Conze found himself so strongly opposed to the Nazi ideology that he joined the Communist Party and even made a serious study of Marxist thought. It seems that for a while he was the leader of the communist movement in Bonn, and his life was consequently in some danger.

In 1933 he came to England, having earlier taken the precaution of renewing his British nationality, and he arrived at the age of twenty-nine, virtually without money or possessions. He supported himself by teaching German and taking evening classes, and he became a member of the Labor Party. He met a lot of prominent figures and intellectuals in the Labor movement and was not impressed. He had, after all, been to a whole series of German universities. He met Trades Union leaders and he met Pandit Nehru and Krishna Menon of the India League and he was not impressed by any of them either. He was not easily impressed.

He became very active in the socialist movement in Britain, lecturing and writing books and pamphlets, until eventually he became disillusioned with politics. At the age of thirty-five he found himself in a state of intellectual turmoil and collapse. Even his marriage had failed. Indeed, in his memoirs he admits, "I am one of those unfortunate people who can neither live with women nor without them."

At this point he discovered—or rather rediscovered—Buddhism. At the age of thirteen he had read *Gleanings in Buddha Fields* by Lafcadio Hearn (and at the beginning of each chapter he would have read quotations from the *Diamond Sutra,* as if presaging his future life's work). However, Conze's first significant contact with Buddhism was at this mid-point in his life, at the beginning of the Second World War, and it was through the writings of D.T. Suzuki. They were literally his salvation.

After this there was no turning back. Conze devoted the rest of his life to Buddhism and in particular to translating the Prajnaparamita or Perfection of Wisdom sutras, which are the fundamental scriptures of the Mahayana. But he wasn't just a scholar in the academic sense. During the war he lived on his own in a trailer in the New Forest, and he practiced meditation, following very seriously the instructions given by Buddhaghosha in the *Visuddhimagga,* and achieving some degree of meditative experience.

After the war he moved to Oxford and re-married. In 1951 he brought out *Buddhism: Its Essence and Development,* a very successful book which is still in print. However, his real achievement over the following twenty years was to translate altogether more than thirty texts comprising the Prajnaparamita sutras, including of course two of the most well-known of all Buddhist texts, the *Diamond Sutra* and the *Heart Sutra.*

It was in connection with these translations that I myself came into contact with him. I started publishing his *Selected Sayings from the Perfection of Wisdom* in a magazine I was editing called *Stepping Stones* in about 1951. We corresponded, and when I came to England in 1964 we met a number of times and found that we agreed on quite a lot of issues.

In the sixties and seventies he lectured at several universities in the United States, and he went down well with the students. However, he was very outspoken, and gained the disapproval of the university authorities and some of his colleagues. With the combination of his communist past and his candid criticism of the American involvement in Vietnam, he was eventually obliged to take his talents elsewhere. He died in 1979.

Dr. Conze was a complex figure, and it is not easy to assess his overall significance. He was of course a Middle European intellectual refugee, fleeing from Germany before the war like so many others. But he wasn't at all representative of this dominant strain in twentieth century intellectual life, because he was very critical of many trends in modern thought. He was a self-confessed elitist, which is usually something people are ashamed of nowadays, but he wasn't ashamed of it at all. Indeed, he entitled his autobiography *Memoirs of a Modern Gnostic,* believing as he did that Gnosticism was essentially elitist. Nor did he approve of either democracy or feminism, which makes him a veritable ogre of "political incorrectness."

He is certainly representative of a whole pre-war generation in the West which became disillusioned with Marxism, especially with Marxism in its Soviet form. Where he differed from others was in the fact that he did not really lose his sense of faith. He did not simply become disillusioned while carrying on within the milieu he was familiar with. He transferred his uncompromising idealism from politics to Buddhism.

Dr. Conze was one of the great Buddhist translators, comparable with the indefatigable Chinese translators Kumarajiva and Hsuan-tsang of the fifth and seventh centuries respectively. It is especially significant, I think, that as a scholar of Buddhism he also tried to practice it, especially through meditation. This was very unusual at the time he started his work, and he was regarded then—in the forties and fifties—as being something of an eccentric. Scholars were not supposed to have any personal involvement in their subject. They were supposed to be "objective." So he was a forerunner of a whole new breed of Western scholars in Buddhism who are actually practicing Buddhists.

This overview of some great Buddhist lives does not in any way provide a comprehensive view of the achievements of the great Buddhists of the twentieth century. For that, we would have to introduce many others. The thirteenth Dalai Lama, the Zen scholar and translator D.T. Suzuki, Dr. G.P. Malalasekera of Sri Lanka, Bhikkhu Buddhadasa of Thailand, the great Chinese Ch'an meditation master the Venerable Hsu Yun, and the great Chinese abbot Tai Hsu are just some of them.

However, I hope I have been able to suggest what we may gain, as Buddhists, from reading, studying, reflecting, and meditating on the lives, the biographies, and memoirs of Buddhists who have lived, in one way or another, truly inspiring lives. They enable us to see Buddhism being actually lived. Purely doctrinal studies—good and necessary though they may be—sometimes give us the impression that Buddhism is rather remote from our own modern lives. Biographies help to redress this balance. After all, Buddhism began with lives; it didn't begin with books. Buddhism began with the lives of the Buddha and his Enlightened disciples.

While preparing these sketches of great Buddhists I noticed two things. I noticed first of all that these men and women were all very different. They had very different characters and they grew up in very different circumstances. In many ways they did very different things. But they were all great Buddhists. This is very important. It reminds us that though we are all Buddhists, though we all go for Refuge, we don't all have to be the same; we don't have to live in the same way; we don't have to do the same things. This is because what unites us is more important than what divides us.

The second thing I noticed was that there were certain qualities which, despite their differences, all of them seemed to possess. To begin with, they were all very single-minded. Once they had discovered their purpose in life, they never wavered. Then, they were all characterized by fearlessness. They were also all unconventional. And they were self-motivated. They were autonomous individuals, they "did their own thing," they went their own way, sometimes in the face of tremendous opposition. They were all true individuals.

In short, they were all heroes, in the best sense of the term. We need to cherish our heroes. We need to admire them, we need to cherish their memory, we need to rejoice in their merits. We need to appreciate that our great Buddhists, whether of the twentieth or any other century, are among our greatest and most precious possessions.

5 ← Living in the World

1. THE IDEAL SOCIETY

Even in political affairs ethical and spiritual considerations and values should be paramount.

THOUGH MOST daydreaming is what may be described as unproductive fantasy, occasionally daydreams are blueprints for the future. Today's dream may be, in some cases, tomorrow's reality. Looking at the history of the world, at the history of culture, religions, the arts, and philosophy, we find that the greatest men and women of the past have sometimes been the greatest daydreamers. If we go back to the days of ancient Greece, to Plato—surely one of the greatest men who ever lived—we find that Plato too dreamed his dreams. The most famous of his dreams is *The Republic,* the great dialogue in twelve books in which Plato dreams his dream of an ideal society, the society based upon Justice. Moving to other times and cultures—and other dreams—we have in the book of *Revelation,* the last book of the Bible, the marvelous vision of the new Jerusalem with its walls of jasper and gates of pearl—a vision of great archetypal and mythic significance. Coming nearer to our own times there is More's *Utopia,* Bacon's *New Atlantis,* Campanella's *City of the Sun,* and so on, down to H.G. Wells' *Men Like Gods.* These are all daydreams of an ideal society, daydreams of a world transfigured and transformed.

Buddhism too has its daydreams. One Buddhist daydream of the ideal society is found in the conception—or vision—of Sukhavati, the "Pure Land" of Amitabha, the Buddha of Infinite Light, as described in some of the great Mahayana sutras. Especially as taught by the Shin schools of Japanese Buddhism, a Pure Land of the type represented by Sukhavati—the "Happy Land"—is a place, a world, a plane of existence where there is no pain, no suffering, no misery, no separation, no bereavement, no loss of any kind. It is a place where there is no old age, no sickness, and no death. It is a place of perfect peace in which there is no conflict, no war, no battle, nor even any misunderstanding—it is as perfect and happy as that! These great Mahayana sutras also tell us that the Pure Land or Happy Land is a place where there is no distinction of male and female, where the weather is always perfect, and where no one ever has to do any work. Food and clothing appear of their own accord whenever they are needed. In the Pure Land no one has anything to do except sit on their golden or purple or blue lotus at the feet of the Buddha and listen to his exposition of the Dharma. This is a Buddhist daydream, a vision of an ideal society and an ideal world.

This may all seem rather remote, rather archetypal and mythical, and not of much direct concern to us; but Buddhism, although it can dream, and dream very beautifully, is not content to leave it at that. The whole approach of the Buddha's teaching to these questions is very sane, very practical and very realistic. Buddhism is not content to dream about some ideal society of the future, or some ideal world on another plane; it tries to create the ideal society, the ideal community, here and now on this earth. It tries, therefore, to transform, to transfigure, this society and this world into the image of the future, into the image of the Ideal; and it tries to do this in a number of different ways. One of these ways is the teaching of Right Livelihood, the fifth step of the Buddha's Noble Eightfold Path.

The preceding stages of the Noble Eightfold Path are concerned with our initial spiritual experience of insight into the nature of existence, including ourselves, and the transformation by that experience of our emotional life, our communication with one another, and our ordinary everyday behavior. In other words, up to this point the Eightfold Path has been concerned with the transformation of our separate, individual selves. With this step, Perfect Livelihood, we are concerned with the transformation of the collective life, the life of the community, the life of society. This is an aspect of Buddhism which is not very much emphasized, in fact it is sometimes rather played down; but the idea that we should transform not only our individual lives but also society at large is very definitely a part of the total teaching.

Buddhism stands for the creation of an ideal society as well as for the creation of an ideal individual. After all, we are all parts of society, all members one of another, and it is very difficult for us to change ourselves while society remains unchanged. The Indians have a proverb, "You can't work in the kitchen without getting a bit of soot on you." (Cooking in India is apt to be a rather messy affair.) In the same way you cannot live and work in a corrupt, basically unethical society without to some extent being besmirched by it. So even in the interests of one's own individual moral and spiritual life one has to make some effort to transform the society in which one lives. It is all very well to talk about the lotus blooming in the midst of the mire, but it is very difficult to be a lotus when the mire is particularly nasty and all-pervasive.

Our collective existence has three principal aspects—the strictly social aspect, the political aspect, and the economic aspect—and Buddhism has teachings which cover all three.

Buddhism has various social teachings, especially in the context of ancient Indian life. For example we find that the Buddha was not at all in favor of the caste system, which was a dominant feature of social life in India at his time and still exists today. According to this system your position in society was dependent on your birth. If you were the son of a brahmin you were a brahmin, if you were the son of a trader you were a trader, and there was nothing you could do to change your status. Even now this system is very strong and all-pervasive in India, especially in the villages, and it has a stultifying effect upon human initiative generally. For this reason the Buddha said clearly and emphatically that the criterion which determines a person's position in society should not be birth, but worth. This is just one example of his social teaching.

In the same way we find that in the political sphere Buddhism upholds—or rather upheld in ancient times—the ideal of what is called Dharmaraja, a number of sutras being devoted to this topic. Dharma means truth, righteousness, reality. Raja means king, or even government. Thus the ideal of the Dharmaraja represents the ideal of government by righteousness: the ideal that even in political affairs ethical and spiritual considerations and values should be paramount. It represents the idea that politics should not just be a cockpit of rival interests and factions, not just a question of manipulation and string-pulling, but that one should try to see the ethical and spiritual principles involved, and apply these to this aspect of one's collective existence.

In India the greatest example of this political ideal was the Emperor Ashoka. He was a great ruler of the Maurya dynasty, and lived about two hundred years after the Buddha. He inherited from his father the kingdom of Magadha, which he proceeded to expand, promptly swallowing up nearly all the other states of the subcontinent. A series of mopping-up operations increased the dimensions of Magadha even beyond those of present-day India and Pakistan. The last state left for Ashoka to subdue, in the days before he became a Buddhist, was the state of Kalinga on the east coast, roughly corresponding to the modern state of Orissa. As Ashoka himself recorded in one of his Rock Edicts, "One-hundred-and-fifty thousand persons were carried away captive, one hundred thousand were slain, and many times that number died."

Seeing the havoc that had been wrought, Ashoka realized the misery brought about by war and by his own conquests. In his own words he "felt profound sorrow and regret because the conquest of a people previously unconquered involved slaughter, death, and deportation . . . even those who escaped calamity themselves are deeply afflicted by the misfortunes suffered by those friends, acquaintances, companions, and relatives for whom they feel an undiminished affection." So he gave up this career of conquest—possibly the only example in history of a great conqueror who stopped in mid-career because he realized the moral wickedness of his actions. He stopped and he completely reversed. Instead of being known as Chandashoka or Ashoka the Fierce, as he was before his "conversion," he became known as Dharmashoka or Ashoka the Righteous, and from that day onward seems to have considered himself the father of his people.

Ashoka did not give up his political path, but he quite explicitly proclaimed as his ideal the service of those he was supposed to be governing and upheld their welfare as the main object of his administration. He also gave great support to Buddhism, dispatching missionaries not only to different parts of India and Sri Lanka but also to Alexandria, Palestine, and Greece. Unfortunately, so-called Buddhist rulers have not always followed in the footsteps of Ashoka. He is perhaps the only real example in Indian history of someone trying to apply Buddhist teaching directly to political life, and for that he deserves much credit. H.G. Wells gives a moving tribute to Ashoka in his *Outline of History*. "Amidst the tens of thousands of names of monarchs that crowd the pages of history," he writes, "their majesties and graciousnesses and serenities and royal highnesses and the like, the name Ashoka shines, and shines almost alone, a star."

The third aspect of our collective existence is the economic aspect. In this sphere Buddhism teaches Perfect Livelihood, that is to say it teaches the complete transformation, in the light of Perfect Vision, of the whole economic aspect of our collective life.

Now at this point a question arises. We have seen that our collective existence has three principal aspects, the social, the political, and the economic; but Perfect Livelihood represents only one of these, the economic. Why is this? Assuming that the fifth stage of the Noble Eightfold Path deals with our collective existence, why does it deal only with the economic aspect? If the Path is concerned with our whole collective as well as our individual existence, why include only Perfect Livelihood, and not Perfect Citizenship or Perfect Administration?

The answer to this question is partly to be found in the conditions obtaining in India in the Buddha's day. The social system was comparatively simple and unorganized—luckily—and apart from the caste system there was not much in this area which needed revision. In the political sphere, the Buddha taught and propagated the Dharma mainly in areas where monarchy was the only existing form of government, which means that ordinary people had little if any share in political life and activity. So in those days there was not much point in asking people in general to practice Perfect Government or Perfect Administration, or even Perfect Citizenship, when they had very little say in these matters. Everyone, however, had to work. They may not have had a vote or known what the king was up to, but they all had to earn a living, so the question of Perfect Livelihood was one which concerned everybody, even in the Buddha's day; and for this reason, no doubt, Perfect Livelihood was included in the Noble Eightfold Path. We might even hazard a speculation and suggest that the Buddha himself felt that the economic aspect of our collective existence was more basic than either the social or the political aspect, and that for this reason too he included Perfect Livelihood, as representing that aspect, in the Noble Eightfold Path.

2. The Basis of Ethical Work

The economic relationship is one of the commonest fields of exploitation in the whole range of human life.

THE PRINCIPLE of non-exploitation should ideally hold good in all the relationships of life. It should be possible for us to take what we need, whether food, clothing, education, or anything else, and give whatever we can. There is no need for there to be any connection between what we give and what we receive. Unfortunately, however, the way things usually work is that each person involved in any transaction, whether as the giver or as the receiver, thinks only of himself or herself, giving as little as possible in exchange for as much as possible. This is how ordinary life generally works: we negotiate transactions in which what we give is determined by what we can get for it, not by any regard for the consequences of the transaction for other people.

Beyond a certain point, any commercial profit made is necessarily at the expense of someone else; but the plight of the losers in the game does not generally bother the winners. A particularly brazen form of this universal phenomenon is to be found in poor places like India, where hugely wealthy dealers in grain, especially rice, hoard their stocks, refusing to admit that they have anything to sell, so as to force prices up. This may go on for weeks at a time, especially in remote parts of the country, to the point where people are actually starving, yet the merchants will hold on to those stocks as long as they possibly can, before slowly releasing them at extortionate prices on the black market. The poor have then to scrape together every penny in order to buy enough food to live on. Such exploitation happens—albeit usually in more subtle ways—in all walks of life, in all parts of the world.

The idea of non-exploitation is clearly related to the second of the five precepts (the precepts which form the basis for the ethical life of all Buddhists). The second precept asks that one undertake not to take what is not given. This is more than simply a roundabout way of saying "not to steal." Not stealing isn't enough. It leaves too many loopholes. Someone may be a perfectly honest person according to the letter of the law, but they may still build up their business in all sorts of irregular, dubious or downright shady ways. Thus a great deal of wealth is amassed through highly unethical means without the breaking of any conventional ethical codes.

But the Buddhist precept is an undertaking not to take something unless those who are its present owners, whether individuals or the community as a whole, are willing and ready to give it to you. If it has not been given to you, you do not take it. I mentioned that there should be no connection between what we give and what we take. However, what we take must at the same time be given—in this respect giving and taking are two aspects of the same action. In some Buddhist countries monks are supposed to be so strict in the observance of this precept that when food is given to them on formal occasions, they are not allowed to eat it unless the plate containing the food is lifted up and actually placed in their hands.

The same principle finds application in the fifth stage of the Buddha's Noble Eightfold Path: right or perfect livelihood. The very fact that right livelihood is included in the list gives an idea of the importance given within Buddhism to the way one earns one's living. People may talk of getting the perfect job, but we can guess that this is not what is meant by "perfect livelihood." But how does something as apparently mundane as employment find a place in this august collection of ideals?

We all have to earn a living—those who are not monks, anyway—but however we do it, no harm should come either to others or to ourselves through the work we do. The early scriptures even offer a rough and ready guide to right livelihood in the form of a list of occupations which are prohibited for those following the spiritual path.[163] The first of these concerns any commercial activity that involves trading in living beings, whether humans or animals. Slavery is and always has been condemned and prohibited in Buddhist countries—Buddhists did not have to wait until the eighteenth or nineteenth century for a clear line on this issue. Of course, trading in human beings still goes on in the world today, but even more widespread is trading in animals for slaughter, also prohibited in Buddhist societies: you will never find a Buddhist butcher or slaughterman. This form of livelihood is harmful not only—of course—to the animals being slaughtered, but also to those doing the slaughtering. To spend eight hours a day killing pigs, cows, sheep, or chickens will necessarily bring about some degree of mental or emotional damage to the slaughterman, as a result of stifling his natural feelings of compassion for other living beings.

Another early Buddhist prohibition was placed upon trade in poisons—not of course medicinal poisons, but poisons used to take life. Before the days of autopsies, this was an almost foolproof way to dispose of someone; a dealer in poisons would give you a phial of the requisite potion—whether fast or slow working, painful or painless—and you would then dose that inconvenient person's curry with it. Like slavers, dealers in poisons are, in a sense, found less frequently today than they used to be. But, of course, the modern equivalent—the widespread dealing in what are called class A drugs (like heroin and cocaine)—is just as harmful. Also, many people are involved in the manufacture and sale of cigarettes and other indisputably harmful drugs, including advertising them and dealing in shares in them.

The third prohibition was against making or trading in weapons. For the early Buddhists this meant bows and arrows, spears and swords. From these primitive beginnings of the arms trade, however, our more advanced cultures have made considerable progress—so they would say—in the development of wonderfully safe and refined methods of ensuring victory over the enemies of civilized values. But any involvement in making these means of destruction, however "intelligent" they may be, is to be condemned as wrong livelihood. There is no question of justifying any war, any idea that weapons are a deterrent, any bombs, however "smart."

These prohibitions are of course directed at the laity, but there are also certain ways of earning of living which are forbidden specifically to monks. For example, various forms of fortune-telling, of which there were very many in the Buddha's day, are enumerated and roundly condemned in the scriptures. However, all over the Buddhist world monks to this day are relied on by the laity to foretell the future, and unfortunately many monks take advantage of this trust in their powers of prognostication.

Monks are also prohibited from earning a living through the display of psychic powers, or by promising psychic powers to others. The reason for this is obvious, really. People are naturally very interested in psychic phenomena, supernormal powers, and so on. Such things are generally taken more seriously on an everyday level in the East, but in certain circles in the West there is also an intense—and unhealthy—fascination with the idea of acquiring mysterious and occult powers that other people don't possess. If you dangle psychic powers in front of someone's nose, you can, if they are easily led, lead them almost anywhere.

I was once presented with an opportunity of doing this myself. When I lived in Kalimpong in the 1950s, an Englishman arrived on my doorstep one evening in the midst of the rainy season. I was quite accustomed to unexpected visitors, so I invited him in and he introduced himself. He was a medical man who had trained in Dublin. Quite soon I got round to asking him what had brought him to Kalimpong. He said straight out, "I want to develop psychic powers." This was not the first time someone had expressed this kind of interest to me, so I just said, "What sort of psychic powers do you want to develop?" He said, "I want to be able to read other people's thoughts, and to see the future." He was not at all coy about it; he was quite open about what he wanted. I then asked him, "Why do you want to develop these powers?" He simply said, "It will help me in my work." What that work turned out to be is not germane to this specific issue; I will mention only that he was a disciple—or had been a disciple— of Lobsang Rampa, who wrote a lot of books about the more fabulous and fanciful aspects of Tibetan Buddhism. Inspired by one of the most successful of these books, *The Third Eye,* my visitor was searching for a Tibetan lama who could perform an operation to open his third eye. It involved, he believed, drilling a little hole in the middle of his forehead and thereby endowing him with the clairvoyant vision he wanted.

One can see the temptation that this kind of person puts in the way of monks and lamas. He could have been milked by any unscrupulous teacher who was ready to pander to his desire for developing psychic powers. What he said to me made this very clear: "If anyone can teach me these things I'm quite prepared to place at their disposal a very large sum of money." He came to an untimely end, unfortunately, but before he did so, several people got quite a lot of money out of him in one way or another.

So much for general prohibitions as regards earning a living. The Buddha did not leave it at that, for, as we know, the economic relationship is one of the commonest fields of exploitation in the whole range of human life. Employers exploit employees if they can, and employees exploit their employers whenever they get the chance. We tend to think that problems of suspicion and exploitation between management and workforce, capital and labor, boardroom and factory floor are peculiarly modern. But the Buddha gave considerable attention to this issue, in his advice to Sigalaka as recorded in the *Sigalaka Sutta*. In the section of the discourse devoted to the employer-employee relationship the Buddha enumerates five duties of the employer toward the employee, and five duties of the employee toward the employer.[164] Together these amount to a general guide to capital and labor relationships, and a business code of economic ethics for Buddhists.

Taking the duties of the employer first, the Buddha says that the employer must give the employee work according to his bodily and mental strength—that is, work he or she can do without injury. Unfortunately, two thousand five hundred years later, this principle is still not being observed—certainly not in India. In India today, thousands of men and women earn their living as coolies, that is, as unskilled laborers. They are treated as beasts of burden, carrying heavy loads on their backs, or more usually on their heads, and anybody who ever goes to India will see them at work. Coolies are at the very bottom of the economic ladder, and they have virtually no hope of rising above that level, even though they may have to support a growing family as well as themselves.

The problem from the point of view of the merchant hiring a number of coolies to carry, say, sacks of rice is that some coolies cannot carry as much as others, and they do not move as fast, particularly if they are old or unwell. It is shocking to say that the solution for a great many well-to-do merchants is to make sure they get their money's worth out of all their coolies equally. This is a pitiable sight indeed— some old man, old before his time, staggering along, his veins standing out, muscles stretched like whipcord, and the perspiration streaming down, under loads which he has no business to be carrying at all. It's the same with the rickshaw pullers that you used to find all over Asia (though not any more, I am glad to say). Their life-expectancy was no more than a few years. They used to start pulling rickshaws when they were fifteen or sixteen; by the time they were twenty-five they usually had tuberculosis, and that would be the end of them within a few months. Their inadequate diet and the huge physical stress of their work quite literally killed them.

But for a very long time it was not an issue that bothered anyone. I remember vividly the first time I was in Sri Lanka, taking a ride in a rickshaw—rather against my will. As we moved smartly through the streets I kept telling the coolie to go slower, but he didn't understand me—he thought I was telling him, as most of his fares must have done, to go faster. The more I expostulated with him, the faster he went, until I had to tell him to stop altogether. Thereafter I used a rickshaw only in an emergency; and even then I would pick someone who was fairly strong and sturdy, and insist that he went at a reasonably leisurely pace. In retrospect, I should not, probably, have used them at all, but at the time it seemed there was no other work for them to do. However, the Buddha was quite clear that no human being should be hired to work beyond his or her natural capacity.

Secondly, the Buddha said that the employer should give the employee sufficient food and pay. This is still the custom in certain parts of India. If you employ someone you give him or her food and clothes, plus some cash, rather than a salary. But the operative principle is to give food and pay that is sufficient in terms of enabling the employee to live a full and decent human existence, not simply sufficient in relation to the work done. There shouldn't be any correlation between the amount of work done and the amount of pay received. Even if the employee is strong and healthy, and his output is prodigious, he should not get paid more than his weaker or even lazier fellows; he should just get what he needs by way of remuneration. We have become accustomed to thinking in terms of rewarding hard work and penalizing those who underperform: so much work done, so much pay received. But while this is an effective incentive to invention and enterprise, a Buddhist should ideally find that incentive somewhere else. If the incentive is greed, you are feeding that mental poison.

The employee is enjoined by the Buddha to work as faithfully as he can, and the employer is enjoined to provide for the employee's needs. These needs constitute not just a bare subsistence, but the means to live a richly human existence. We no longer have a society that divides quite so rigidly into employer and employee as the society of the Buddha's day, but the Buddha was not of course recommending the particular social structure of his day; he was simply pointing out the essential principle by which the people in his society could make an economic relationship an essentially human one.

We have to try to do the same within our own society. One radical plan that gets an airing from time to time, and does seem to express the principle of non-exploitation very effectively, is the idea that on the attainment of their majority everyone should be given by the government a basic stipend to cover the cost of food, clothing, and shelter, regardless of whether they work or not. If they want more than this—if they want to travel, buy expensive electronic equipment, go out to cinemas and restaurants, have the luxury lifestyle that most people see as a virtual necessity—they will have to work. But in a luxury culture people should work because they want to—because they want to make a creative contribution to their society, or because they want a few extras, or both—not simply in order to live. In this way the state would support the spiritual community, enabling individuals who wanted to devote themselves to creative but financially unremunerative activity—to meditation, study, even the arts—to do so, if they were prepared to live a very simple, even monastic life.

Thirdly, the Buddha says that the employer should provide the employee with medical treatment and support after retirement. This we do have nowadays, with pensions, insurance, and so on, but it has taken two millennia for us to get round to this scheme of the Buddha's. Fourthly, the Buddha says that the employer should share with the employee any extra profit he makes. That is, you don't take the profits for your own purposes while telling your employees that they must make do with a basic level of support. Once again, we have caught up with this idea rather late in the day, in the form of bonus schemes. Fifthly and lastly, it is the duty of the employer, according to the Buddha, to grant the employee holidays and special allowances—and this, too, has something of a modern ring to it. However, we should not lose sight of the essential principle expressed in the Buddha's advice—that of establishing the human dimension of the economic relationship—which is not always what bonus schemes, holiday allowances, and pension schemes are about.

So these are the five points made by the Buddha for the guidance of the employer in relationship to the employee. The employee also has certain duties. The first of these is that he or she should be punctual. Indians are notorious for their lack of punctuality. Trains can be two or three hours late. Someone may say, "I'm coming to see you at three o'clock," and you'll see them the following week. A meeting may be advertised to begin at eight o'clock sharp, but if you are naive enough to turn up at that time, you may find the place deserted. The meeting has not been cancelled: if you wait until nine o'clock the organizers will arrive; by ten o'clock the platform is being erected. At eleven o'clock the audience is beginning to arrive, and at half past eleven you will be invited to begin your talk. In the West we are a lot more punctual than this; but the Buddha's principle is not just about clocking in on time, but of not needing to clock in at all. Indeed, the Buddha suggests that you try to be already working before your employer arrives: you are not coming to work simply to be seen to be working.

Secondly, the employee should finish work after the employer. You should try to become free of the whole clock-watching mentality. You don't fling down your tools as soon as the clock strikes. Thirdly, the employee should be sincere and trustworthy. This is quite obvious, as is the fourth point, which is that the employee should perform his or her duties to the satisfaction of the employer. Fifthly, the employee should speak in praise of his employer. The Buddha must have been aware of how readily workers abuse the boss behind his or her back, then as now. They may be dutiful and respectful during working hours, but what you hear outside the company gates can tell a different story.

The Buddha is reminding us that, as with any relationship, the economic relationship should not be one of antagonism, in which all you feel you can express is impotent frustration. Ideally, it is a happy, harmonious relationship, in which there is no exploitation on either side. Each takes from the other what he or she needs, without causing harm, and gives what he or she can. If you are an employer, you make use of the labor and skills of your workers and also take responsibility for seeing that their needs are met. And if you are an employee, you work to the best of your ability and take what you need from that work situation. There is then no need for a grim, protracted bargaining between employers and unions, as though they were in opposite camps, arranging a truce between opposing armies.

3. RIGHT LIVELIHOOD BUSINESSES

We have to be prepared to live in a capitalist world without partaking in capitalist values, practices, and objectives.

THERE IS WORK which is not in accordance with the principles of Right Livelihood, and there is work which is. Most people are only too familiar with the first kind: work which is concerned with the production of harmful or frivolous things, work which is boring, repetitive, and non-creative, work which is done under conditions that are unfavorable to personal development, and in the company of people who are indifferent or even hostile to spiritual life. But there is an alternative: work done for the sake of the Dharma, not for the sake of a wage or one's own creature comforts. It is done so that the wealth produced or acquired can be given to the Dharma. And it is ideally done with others similarly committed to the spiritual life.

Of course, efforts are being made in the direction of more ethical work practices even within the capitalist system. There is now some ethical stockbroking: companies that advertise themselves as guaranteeing that any money you invest won't go into arms dealing, tobacco, or any other unethical enterprise. This would suggest that some non-capitalist ideology must have got a toehold; usually capitalists want to make money at any price, regardless of ethical considerations. Ethical investment is at least a step in the right direction, even though it is a modification of the system rather than a replacement of it by something more ethical and idealistic.

But I am doubtful as to whether there is an alternative economic system that can supply us with consumer goods in the way and to the extent that the capitalist system does. People tend to assume that we could change from the capitalist system to some other ethically more desirable one and still have the consumer goodies coming in just as before. I personally rather doubt that. I don't even know that one could come up with a viable alternative, but if there *were* an alternative, I think it would be at the expense of at least some of the consumer goodies. It would therefore be an alternative that most people would not be prepared to contemplate—at least, not without a great deal of education, perhaps over a period of centuries.

To give a crude example, suppose everybody did go back to the land and grow their own food. To do that they would probably have to give up their cars and televisions, and most people simply wouldn't be prepared to do that. There is a price to be paid if you want to introduce a more ethical system, and I doubt whether most people would be prepared to pay that price. So we have to be prepared to live in a capitalist world without partaking in capitalist values, practices, and objectives.

I regard the cooperative structure as being opposed to the capitalist one, and that is one reason I favor it. But it is not at all easy to apply. In a team-based Right Livelihood situation, as distinct from a business of the ordinary capitalist type, there is an equal sharing of responsibility—or rather, everybody has responsibility to the measure of their understanding and experience of the business. This principle gives rise to a lot of difficulty, because for various reasons people don't find it easy to cooperate with each other in the way that is essential if the business is to work. Some people want to be bosses, although the co-op structure doesn't really allow for that, and others want to be told what to do rather than taking a share of the responsibility. These opposite tendencies both detract from the application of the cooperative principle. It is important, therefore, to be realistic about what setting up a Right Livelihood business involves. People sometimes get starry-eyed about how easy and lovely it will be just because you are all working together, but it isn't really as simple as that. However, it is well worth making the effort and having faith in the cooperative principle that you take what you need and give what you can.

A Buddhist team-based Right Livelihood project has three aims. First, it aims to provide its workers with a means of support—that is, it aims to provide for their needs: not just their need for food, clothing, and shelter, but also their need to go on retreat, buy Dharma books, and so on. Second, it aims to provide a working situation that is conducive to spiritual progress. This means that it functions, within that particular economic context, as a sort of spiritual community, inasmuch as its workers are friends with one another and share the ideals of the project. In short, it should provide the people working within it with an experience of *kalyana mitrata,* spiritual friendship. And the third aim is to help finance Buddhist activities: Buddhist centers, publications, and so on. To be considered fully successful, the Right Livelihood business needs to fulfill all these three objectives.

4. BEING EASY TO SUPPORT

We do not necessarily have to accept the traditions as they have come down to us, especially when these are influenced by the Indian social and cultural conditions of some two thousand five hundred years ago.

AMONG THE DESIRABLE qualities of a meditator, according to the *Karaniya Metta Sutta* is that he or she should be subharo—"easy to support." In the context of the sutta, this refers to the economic situation of the monk. The suggestion seems to be that we renounce work and commit ourselves to a life of contemplation, relying on the support of others to give us the necessities of life. The fact is that in the Buddha's time, the monks were completely dependent upon lay people, who provided them with food, clothing, and sometimes even shelter. With the basic necessities of life taken care of, the monks and nuns were free to devote their energies to meditation, study, and devotional practice. This being the case, it was the responsibility of the monks to be easy to support, and not to make life difficult for those who were considerate enough to provide them with their material needs.

The tradition of the homeless wanderer being supported by society at large was not instituted by the Buddha. He inherited it; it existed in Indian society already. In the Buddha's day, the renunciation of social identity was a common and accepted practice all over northern India, and the homeless wanderer or *paribbajaka* was thus an accepted outsider. When the Buddha started out on his journey to Enlightenment, he too left the home life to become a *paribbajaka,* and after the Enlightenment many of his disciples came from that same casteless social category or rather non-category, and continued to go on foot from village to village with their alms bowls, accepting whatever food they were given. In the early days of the Buddhist community, the Sangha, the priority was to establish a spiritual community on principles that transcended the worldly concerns of the wider society. As the figure of the itinerant spiritual practitioner was already a feature of Indian society, and the support of such individuals by the wider community an accepted tradition, the Buddhist Sangha adopted this model quite naturally.

The withdrawal of the bhikkhu from the world of work went with an attitude to work, particularly manual labor, which still persists in Indian society today: the view that it is inherently unspiritual. The ancient Indians had a similar view to that of the ancient Greeks, except that whereas the Athenian state relied upon a class of slaves to carry out any manual labor that might be necessary, Indian society depended upon a number of lower castes. The Greeks have of course given up slavery, but to a large extent India continues to run on the basis that physical work is inherently degrading, and that no respectable person would do such work if he or she could possibly avoid it.

Thus, in the India of the Buddha's day the possibility of taking up the spiritual life and continuing to do physical work simply did not arise. You could not be a full-time spiritual practitioner and continue to support yourself. But by virtue of the same attitude, you could rely on the lay people to support you. Indeed, the religious renunciant was almost compelled to depend for alms on the lay community if he was to form any kind of socially acceptable relationship with them. Nor did the Buddha think it worth challenging this convention. It is not after all such a bad thing in principle for the more spiritually committed to be supported by the less committed, and he accepted the customary division between monks or wanderers and lay communities as a reasonable way to make this happen, and a way of propagating the Dharma in the process. But as Buddhism developed and spread, the range of activities that the full-timers were able to take up expanded. In the beginning, they were expected to devote all their energies to meditation, study, and teaching. For the first five hundred years the teaching was passed on entirely through oral transmission, so a good deal of the time would have been spent in learning the suttas by heart and chanting them communally to impress the doctrine on the memory of every monk. Then, when the suttas began to be written down, a great deal of literary activity ensued. Later still, with the building of the great monasteries, monks would have been involved in the sculpting and gilding of images, as well as in the design and decoration of the monasteries and temples themselves.

Later, when Buddhism, especially in its Mahayana form, traveled to China and Tibet, whose cultures had a more practical inclination than that of India, monks began to take up everyday physical tasks. Tibet, for example, has no cultural prejudice against manual labor, and in a Tibetan Buddhist monastery you will find monks energetically engaged in all manner of necessary activities according to their various abilities. In the Ch'an and Zen schools, work is considered to be an integral part of a fully committed spiritual training. As in Tibetan monasteries, monks are expected to throw themselves wholeheartedly into every task that needs to be done, from cooking, cleaning, chopping wood, and drawing water to the printing of Buddhist sutras.

So we have to be careful not to be trapped by our respect for ancient texts such as the *Karaniya Metta Sutta* into thinking of practical, physical, and even economic activity as being necessarily worldly or unspiritual. A human being is not only a mind, but also a body inhabiting a sensory, physical universe. We need productive activity for our physical and psychological well-being. If our mind is the only part of us that gets any real exercise, whether through study or teaching or at an office desk or computer, there will be an imbalance in our being as a whole, and we will be in need of physical work and exercise to bring it back into balance.

I know from my own contact with bhikkhus in Southeast Asia (admittedly as far back as the 1950s) that monks can get into quite an unhealthy state—not just physically or psychologically, but also spiritually—from lack of exercise. Their dependence upon the laity, who in most cases looked after them extremely well, was such that even though the monks would have liked to have done more for themselves, the laypeople would not let them. As I remember it, the laypeople felt embarrassed, or even affronted, if the bhikkhus tried to do things for themselves. It is after all through service to the monks that laypeople traditionally express their devotion to the ideal of Enlightenment.

On the face of it, the dependence of the full-time spiritual practitioners on the laity ought to contribute to the simplicity of their lifestyle,
enabling them to concentrate more of their energy on purely spiritual
matters. But in reality it can hinder them from engaging their energies
at all. Perhaps in the early days of Buddhism this unequal distribution of
labor between monks and laity was necessary. The dawn-to-dusk burden of physical labor was no doubt so heavy that a degree of freedom
from such duties was essential if one was to have the time and energy for
reflection and other higher pursuits. It is understandable that a conflict
emerged between the demands of farm and field on the one hand and
those of spiritual pursuits on the other, and an outright separation of the
two was probably the most straightforward solution. However, the cost
was a certain alienation: from worldly affairs on the part of the monks,
and from any real spiritual life on the part of the laity.

It would seem then that this concept of *subharo,* being "easy to support," owes its appearance in the sutta to the social conventions prevalent in India at the time of the Buddha. In view of this it would be a
mistake to interpret the term as suggesting that someone committed
to leading the spiritual life must be materially supported by others,
and should not get involved in practical or economic activity. In the
market economies of the modern world, we are very fortunate in
being able to be full-time Buddhists while at the same time involving
ourselves unashamedly in straightforward, practical tasks. We should
take that opportunity. In our practice of the Dharma there is invariably a healthy tension between the need to be involved in the sphere
of worldly human activity, and thus practice the other-regarding
aspect of the Dharma, and the need to withdraw from worldly activity
for the purposes of meditation and reflection. As modern Buddhists
we have a unique opportunity to decide for ourselves how this balance may be struck in our lives. In doing so, we need to return to the
basic principles of Buddhism, and specifically to the principle of right
livelihood—that is, ethical work.

To practice right livelihood, we may have to question our overall
attitude to work. Like ancient cultures, industrialized societies have

their own conventional attitudes to work, these attitudes being based in the case of the latter on the strict division between paid work and leisure. For many of us, work is an activity we don't *want* to do but *have* to do in order to support ourselves, and leisure time is "our own time," in which we are free to pursue our personal interests. This unhappy distinction seems to affect much that we do. Jobs, tasks, and physical activities with some practical purpose or end in view, like cleaning or cooking, are considered a burden, a chore, and resented as such; and we imagine that when we are not working we should be continuously diverted. We certainly don't want to have to do "chores."

However, all human beings, even spiritual full-timers, need work, in the sense of some productive, useful activity, whether paid or unpaid, that is beneficial to themselves and to others; and simple, practical physical work may be better than intellectual work from the point of view of fulfilling this human and spiritual need. If you are able to devote all your time and energy to meditation, study, teaching, and writing, all well and good. But not everyone is able to meditate or study the Dharma day in day out. Many people, including many monks, are quite unsuited to teaching or writing; so for them, an injunction to refrain from working and physical activity would be quite unhelpful. Of course, this means that we have to be able to carry out such work without resentment, without considering it demeaning or a burdensome imposition.

Today we have the opportunity to reappraise the whole question of work and financial support. We do not necessarily have to accept the traditions as they have come down to us, especially when these are influenced by the Indian social and cultural conditions of some two thousand five hundred years ago. In modern post-traditional societies, you can renounce family life and worldly occupation without having to rely for your livelihood on those who have chosen to engage with them. You can choose to work with other Buddhists—that is, others who share your aspirations—in such a way as to support one another's spiritual development and at the same time provide for the material needs of each one of you. The necessity of supporting oneself financially can become an opportunity to deepen communication, share skills, and learn new ways of cooperation and mutual support. Working in such a situation you can take full account of individual temperaments and attitudes to allow each person to work in a way that is appropriate to their spiritual needs. Some people might find it suited them best to do mainly manual work, while others would benefit from gradually taking on more managerial responsibility. Of course everyone would need to have time for meditation and Dharma study.

In the modern world, it is up to the individual to choose their own way, to make their own decisions, according to whatever principles they wish to live by. There can no longer be blanket rules for spiritual life and practice. What is appropriate at one time and in one place may not work in another. We need a new kind of Buddhist culture in which economic relations can be constantly recreated to meet a constantly changing world. This is probably as close to the Mahayana ideal of the Pure Land—the perfect environment for spiritual practice—that we can hope for.

Taking the sutta at face value, therefore, we can interpret the term *subharo,* "easy to support," as referring to how a monk should behave in terms of his economically dependent role with respect to the laity. But there is a deeper and less historically specific principle at work in this part of the sutta. Whether we are monk or lay, or neither one nor the other, we are supported by society at large, and dependent upon the labor of innumerable other people for the necessities of life. We do not grow all our own food or draw our own water; we do not build and furnish our own houses or weave and sew all our own clothes.

If we reflect on how it is that we can enjoy so many consumer products for so little outlay—if we think of the hours of cheap labor that go into what we are able to buy for next to nothing—we will find that we are not at all easily supported. There are also environmental and ecological considerations to take into account. The natural and human resources available to our society should not be expended heedlessly or needlessly. The fact that we have the financial resources to help ourselves to what we fancy does not justify our consuming the wealth of the world without consideration for the claims of others—both in the present and in the future—to those same resources. We owe it to the society that supports us to give what we can to support others. There are very few people who would benefit spiritually from being entirely supported by others in the way that the traditional monastic Sangha was.

The principle behind this term *subharo* therefore comes down to taking from the world and from society no more than you need, and freely contributing whatever you can. You are entitled to rely upon others for the help and support that one human being can be reasonably expected to give another, but you also need to be prepared to stand on your own two feet, as far as you can. You cannot expect to be propped up by others as a right.

This principle operates on all levels of exchange, not only on the material and economic level. We need the emotional support of others, for example, but we should not expect from our friends what we are capable of providing for ourselves, with a little effort. Once they have helped us back onto our feet, we shouldn't expect them to prop us up indefinitely. If you are emotionally needy, you are clearly not yet "capable," and as such you are not "easy to support." You are therefore unlikely to make much progress in meditation. Of course, if you are such a person it is quite possible that you will not understand that you are making undue emotional demands upon others, and that their time and energy might be better spent in other ways. In that case it is up to your friends to help you to see the truth of your situation, and perhaps direct you toward getting some therapeutic help, rather than offering "support" that will just perpetuate the problem.

If you are aiming to be easy to support, the way to do it is to keep your wants and needs to a manageable level, however you manage to do so. This is the ideal to which the term *sallahukavutti* refers: a livelihood, *vutti*, that is *lahuka*, literally "trifling" or "lightweight." It suggests a basic simplicity in one's attitude to life, a determination not to be weighed down by a multiplicity of wants and desires or onerous material commitments. Clearly a taste for hard work, and a relish for the challenge of practical tasks and problems to be overcome, is a virtue, but it is possible to like these things too much for one's own good, especially if they become distractions from more spiritually pressing challenges. So the sutta goes on to say that one should be *appakicco*, "with little work" or "with few duties."

The fact is that one can become too busy even with religious or spiritual activities. Again with reference to the monastic context of early Indian Buddhism, the sutta warns against giving oneself too many things to do. The monk shouldn't be too occupied with performing ceremonies for the laity or running errands for his teachers or preceptors, or even with teaching his own pupils. He should allow himself enough time for study, meditation, reflection, and just spending time quietly by himself—all the things that the lay people in fact support him to do.

Work, in the sense of pleasurable, productive, ideally physical activity, is a necessary part of life for most people. But there is a difference between this and a kind of neurotic, compulsive activity that masquerades as work but is really a way of keeping the deeper emotions at bay. Work can be an unhealthy means by which to escape from being alone with oneself and one's feelings. We should beware of feeling that we have to keep busy, that we can never be without something to do. So yes, by all means work, but don't let busyness be an escape from your true self. Be occupied only with those activities that are really necessary.

The division of labor between monk and layperson has other disadvantages. Relying completely on other people for your support puts you in a passive relationship with regard to them. There is a suggestion of this danger in the sutta, in which the Buddha now enjoins the bhikkhu to be *apagabbho kulesu ananugiddho*. Like *subharo*, the term *apagabbho* clearly has to do with the relationship between wandering monks and the lay people upon whom they depend. It is the negative form of *pagabbho*, which means "impudent," "over bold," "tending to push oneself forward," and Saddhatissa translates it quite neatly as "modesty." Together with the term that follows, *kulesu ananugiddho*, "greedy after gifts" it would seem to refer to the danger of monks insinuating themselves into special relationships with particular families. It could happen that a family would end up adopting a particular monk and in a way "domesticating" him. To avoid this, the sutta directs the monk to avoid making strong connections with anyone or soliciting special favors from them when on his alms round, as this is against the whole spirit of renunciation for which he stands.

Reading between the lines of the sutta, we can see that even the homeless wanderer of the Buddha's day was not necessarily free from attachment to the things that came his way, few as these must have been. He might well be tempted to secure creature comforts and a certain sense of belonging by getting to know certain families, out of a yearning for the approval and acceptance of ordinary people. To guard against this, he is counselled to cultivate a sense of identity based upon inner stability and contentment.

But how should we ourselves interpret this exhortation? After all, we don't knock on doors for alms. For us, perhaps, the danger is of depending for our sense of identity upon the acceptance or approbation of others, being afraid of exclusion. The possible result of such dependence is that one is unable to make decisions, hold opinions, dress, eat, or do all manner of other things without reference to the norms of the group whose approval one seeks. To protect ourselves from this, we should avoid making ourselves too much at home in any one human grouping, or identifying with a group too rigidly. We should avoid becoming too comfortable with the feeling that we "belong" in the course of our involvement with groups, systems, and ideologies. If you are skilled in working for your own good and wish to attain nirvana (which is the assumption with which this teaching starts), you cannot afford to be too attached to the approval of any group, whether it is your biological family, your cultural or ethnic group, your caste or nationality. A mature individual has an existence, as it were, in his or her own right, without needing to have recourse to the affirmation of any group, be it a family, a community, or even a religious movement. Such a person is capable of finding a sense of fulfillment within the experience of his or her own being, independent of external circumstances.

5. The Group and the Individual

Where there are no individuals, there will be no spiritual community, call it by whatever name you please.

WANTING TO BELONG to a group is in our bones, in our blood. We have a long history of gathering together in groups. If we include our primate ancestors, we have about twenty million years of group conditioning, as ape-man, man-ape, and human. To begin with we used to live in something like an extended family group or small tribe of perhaps fifty individuals, with just occasional encounters with other small tribes. With the development of language we have been able to accommodate a somewhat larger tribal grouping than this. But almost all our relationships would have been within this home group, and in some ways this is the sort of group that we would all naturally like to get back to.

It is only within the last few thousand years (which is really no time at all by comparison) that we have developed all sorts of much more complicated social groupings. Today we find ourselves struggling to get what we need from ever more distorted, even aberrant social institutions. It is more and more difficult to find groups of the right scale. On the one hand we have the isolated nuclear family, which can be so cramping as to be—as some psychologists say—a breeding ground for neurosis; and on the other, we belong to a group—the nation state—which is so big as to be meaningless on a personal level.

Between these two institutions we establish, in a partial and intermittent fashion, membership of or loyalty to all sorts of other groups. But none of these seem to satisfy our ancient need to belong to a small tribe of between thirty and sixty people, a group in which we can live and work, in genuine and continuous personal relationship with all its members.

We have all been born into groups, and we are all therefore subject to the conditioning arising from those affiliations. Our ideas, our views, our feelings, the way we react to people and situations, our convictions—all these will tend to be determined by group conditioning of one kind or another, except insofar as we become conscious of such conditioning and distance ourselves from its influence. The groups themselves often overlap or even cohere. And all these overlapping groups together make up "the world."

Groups fear individuality and all its manifestations, and always tend to discourage it. The group requires conformity. This is because it is based on power, which whether physical, intellectual, or economic is always the power of the strong over the weak, the power of those who have the resources, the cunning, or the knowledge to be able to impose their will on others, deploying brute force or subtle manipulation in order to exploit others for their own, usually selfish, purposes. The group consists of those who wield that power, as well as those who give it to them. Such power is exercised within any group, whether political, cultural, tribal, familial, or even religious.

The Spiritual Community

The purposes of a community of individuals—or spiritual community—are utterly different from those of the group. They are twofold: firstly, its members help one another to develop spiritually; secondly, in whatever way they can, they help others outside the community to develop their individuality. In essence, a spiritual community is a free association of individuals. To form one, therefore, the first requirement is a number of individuals. You can no more have a spiritual community without individuals than you can have an omelette without eggs. A spiritual community is not created by getting a building, an exotic form of dress, and a long list of rules. You don't need a building, you don't need an "authentic tradition"; you don't even need a religion. What you need are individuals; that is the basic ingredient. In other words, you need a number of people who are relatively emancipated from the group, relatively integrated and aware, and with an inner direction and positive purpose to their lives. Where there are no individuals, there will be no spiritual community, call it by whatever name you please.

6. The Integration of Buddhism into Western Society

We cannot isolate ourselves from society or ignore the conditions in which we and others live.

THE INTEGRATION of Buddhism into Western society involves changing Western society. Inasmuch as our level of consciousness is affected by external conditions, it is not enough for us to work directly on the mind itself through meditation. We cannot isolate ourselves from society or ignore the conditions in which we and others live. We must make it easier for anyone within that society who wants to live a life dedicated to the Dharma to do so. To the extent that Western society has not been changed by Buddhism, to that extent Buddhism has not been integrated into Western society. In order to change Western society it is necessary to create Western Buddhist institutions and Western Buddhist lifestyles.

In general, Buddhist movements try to create conditions that are conducive to human development. They do this in three main ways corresponding to three central aspects of ordinary human life which on balance are not conducive to spiritual development—the conventional nuclear family, work, and leisure activities. The idea is to open up and revolutionize these keystones of modern life, and where appropriate offer a more positive alternative to them.

Firstly, residential communities are meant to offer an alternative to stagnant relationships, particularly those of the tightly-knit family unit—or rather, the claustrophobic and neurotic closed system of a couple who no longer communicate with each other, orbited by one or two children, two cars, three television sets, a dog, a cat, and a parakeet. Secondly, team-based right-livelihood projects are meant to offer an alternative to earning money in ways which are harmful to one's own development and which exploit others. And thirdly, the various activities provided and promoted by the spiritual community, both those which are directly Dharmic and those which are more indirectly helpful to spiritual growth, give us something positive to do with our free time. They give us an alternative to activities which merely enable us to pass the time, to forget about the stresses of work or family life, and all too often to forget about our own selves. These three things between them constitute the nucleus of the new society; they represent the transformation of conditions that tend to be unconducive to spiritual development into conditions that are conducive.

How each project goes about this work is up to the individuals concerned. Every one of these institutions is meant to function autonomously. Those who run it have to make their own decisions and take responsibility for them. At the same time, as an aspect of the development of this Sangha, people with similar responsibilities for similar institutions make sure that they meet regularly to swap notes, and support and advise each other.

It is also important to communicate the fundamental concepts of Buddhism in a way that is both intelligible to a Western audience and faithful to the Buddhist tradition. This is yet another point of interaction with Western society: the introduction of Buddhist ideas into Western intellectual discourse. By Buddhist ideas I do not mean doctrinal refinements or philosophical subtleties. I mean ideas so fundamental that Buddhists themselves often take them for granted, and fail to realize their full significance. Such, for example, is the idea that religion does not necessarily involve belief in the existence of God, of a creator and ruler of the universe. Another, related, idea is that it is possible for us to lead an ethical life, to raise the level of our consciousness, and to realize a transcendent reality, without invoking the aid of any outside supernatural power. If Buddhism is to be integrated into Western society, ideas of this fundamental kind will have to become familiar to all educated Westerners.

However, the most important kind of integration—without which the other kinds cannot exist—is the integration of the individual Buddhist into Western society. It is, after all, the individual Buddhist who meditates—meditation does not exist in the abstract. Likewise, it is the individual Buddhist who goes on retreat, who works in a right-livelihood business, who communicates the fundamental ideas of Buddhism. Without the individual Buddhist there can be no integration of Buddhism into Western society.

The individual Buddhist is someone who goes for Refuge to the Three Jewels. He or she does so not in isolation but in the company of other individuals who are also Going for Refuge. That is, he or she belongs to the Sangha or spiritual community in the widest sense. It is this Sangha rather than the individual Buddhist which will raise the level of consciousness of people living in Western society, which will change that society by creating Buddhist social and economic institutions, and which will introduce fundamental Buddhist ideas into Western intellectual discourse. It is this wider spiritual community that will effect the psychological, social, economic, and intellectual integration of Buddhism into Western society. This is what the Sangha is really for; this is what the Sangha really is.

7. GETTING COMFORTABLE IN THE PURE LAND?

The Bodhisattva cannot keep people in the Buddha-land against their will.

According to the Mahayana, an advanced Bodhisattva is quite capable of purifying or building the Buddha-land single-handed, just as a magician is capable of creating a magical elephant through his own power. But what would be the use? Yes, you can create a Buddha-land and give people a glimpse of it. You may even be able to keep them in it for a little while. But you cannot keep them there indefinitely—not even if you are a Bodhisattva. This is because they are not going to cooperate, they are not going to want to stay there indefinitely, or even for very long, because they will not feel at home there. They are not ready for it.

There's a little Indian story that illustrates this point. The story is about a woman who sold fish. She lived in a small village on the banks of a big Indian river, and every week she took her fish to the market in a big basket. Now, one week, for some reason or other, it took her rather a long time to sell all her fish. She decided that rather than make her way back to the village so late at night, she had better stay in town. Fortunately she found a flower shop still open, and the flower-seller was sympathetic to her plight and said she could spend the night in his shop. Indian flower shops don't sell cut flowers in bunches as Western ones do; they sell sweet-smelling garlands, and little bunches of sweet-scented flowers for the ladies to put in their hair. The fish-seller lay down to sleep among all those sweet-smelling flowers, but she tossed and turned, and couldn't get to sleep. She couldn't bear the scent of the flowers—they were so sweet, so beautiful. In the end, she got her old fish basket, which of course smelled strongly of fish, and put it right next to her, right by her nose. And after that, she slept quite soundly.

We might laugh at the fish-seller's plight, but we ourselves are in much the same position. She felt uncomfortable in the flower shop among all those sweet-smelling flowers; but we would feel no less uncomfortable in the Pure Land. We could manage a short visit, perhaps a weekend, but eventually we would want to introduce some equivalent of her smelly old fish basket into the Pure Land. We would want to bring along some physical or mental distraction—perhaps our television set, our motor bike, our record collection, our lover, or our office files. Then we would feel more comfortable, more at home. But then, of course, the Pure Land would no longer be the Pure Land.

So the Bodhisattva cannot keep people in the Buddha-land against their will. In any case, that would be a contradiction in terms, because the spiritual life is essentially the autonomous life, the free life, the emancipated life. So what is the Bodhisattva to do? He cannot create a Buddha-land by magical power and then hold people in it—at least, not for very long. They will soon start getting uncomfortable and then—no more Buddha-land.

The answer is that the Buddha-land has to be a joint creation. It has to be built by a number of people—Bodhisattvas and would-be Bodhisattvas—working together. One of them may be more advanced than the others, may have more vision, may even be the first to attain Enlightenment and then help the others to take that final step. But all must be inspired by the same ideal, the ideal of supreme perfect Enlightenment for the benefit of all beings. They all therefore follow the Bodhisattva path, follow it for thousands of lives—and all follow it together. This is a truly wonderful conception: the whole spiritual community being reborn together as a spiritual community, living and working together, helping one another, life after life, until the Buddha-land is established.

6 ← Buddhism and the Future of the World

1. BUDDHISM AND WORLD PEACE

The failure of communication which is so striking a feature of our times is based, ultimately, on a breakdown of the notion of objective truth, that is to say, on a breakdown of the notion that truth is truth regardless of our subjective feelings about it and regardless of the way in which it affects our personal interests.

GAUTAMA THE BUDDHA gained Enlightenment at about the same time that Cyrus the Great captured the city of Babylon and founded the Persian Empire. Five years later the Buddha paid a visit to his home town, Kapilavastu, just inside the modern state boundary of Nepal. (This was his second visit. His first seems to have taken place within a year of the Enlightenment.) It was fortunate that he did so. A dispute had arisen between the Shakyans of Kapilavastu and their neighbors the Koliyans of Devadaha, to whom the Buddha was related through his mother, and, as a result of this, war was about to break out between the two peoples. The original cause of the dispute was comparatively trivial. Both the Shakyans and the Koliyans were accustomed to irrigate their fields with water from the River Rohini, which flowed between their respective territories, but that year it was obvious that there would not be enough water for them both. The Koliyans therefore proposed that they should have the

696 ~ THE ESSENTIAL SANGHARAKSHITA

water, on the grounds that their crops would ripen with a single watering. This proposal the Shakyans flatly rejected, saying that they would
have no mind to beg food from the Koliyans later on in the year and
that in any case their crops too would ripen with a single watering.
Since neither side would give way, the dispute became very bitter and
eventually blows were exchanged. To make matters worse, the
Koliyans started casting aspersions on the origins of the leading
Shakya families, saying that they had cohabited with their own sisters
like dogs and jackals, while the Shakyans cast aspersions on the leading Koliya families, saying that they were destitute outcasts who had
lived in the hollows of trees like animals. Reports of these aspersions
soon reached the ears of the leading families themselves, who immediately came forth armed for battle, the Shakya warriors shouting,
"We will show the strength of those who have cohabited with their sisters!" and the Koliya warriors shouting, "We will show the strength of
those who live in the hollows of trees!"

Thus it was that, one fine morning, the Buddha came to know that
war was about to break out between his paternal and maternal relations. Realizing that unless he intervened they would destroy each
other, he at once went to the place where the two armies were gathered. As soon as they saw him his kinsmen on both sides threw away
their weapons and respectfully saluted him. When the Buddha asked
them what the quarrel was all about, however, they were unable to tell
him. Eventually, after cross-examining various people, the Buddha
succeeded in establishing that the cause of the quarrel was water. Having established this, he asked, "How much is water worth?" "Very little, Reverend Sir." "How much are warriors worth?" "Warriors are
beyond price, Reverend Sir." Then said the Buddha, "It is not fitting
that because of a little water you should destroy warriors who are
beyond price," and they were silent.

Some features of this "Rohini incident" are only too sickeningly
familiar to us today. They are, in fact, characteristic of disputes and
wars from the Stone Age down to modern times. There is the same
clash of vital interests between different groups of people, the same

unwillingness to compromise, the same dreadful escalation from harsh words to isolated acts of violence, and from isolated acts of violence to preparations for full-scale war. There is the same fatal spirit of belligerence, the same readiness, on the part of large numbers of people, to fight without really knowing what they are fighting for. There is even, we note, the same irrelevant mutual vilification, suggestive of antipathies that have long lurked beneath the surface and now have an opportunity of breaking out. But there is also—and this is more encouraging—the same solitary voice of sanity and compassion that, if only we listen carefully enough, we can hear even today. There is the same appeal to reason, the same reminder of what is truly most valuable, that has been heard if not from the Stone Age then at least from the Axial Age, and heard, perhaps, with increasing frequency—regardless of whether people paid attention to it or not.

But although there are similarities between the Rohini incident and the situation in which we find ourselves today, there are differences too. The quarrel between the Shakyans and the Koliyans involved only the inhabitants of two small city states living side by side at the foot of the Himalayas. The quarrel between the superpowers of the twentieth century involves hundreds of millions of people occupying continents separated by vast oceans and it affects, directly or indirectly, the whole world. The Shakyans and the Koliyans were armed, like the heroes of Ancient Greece, with swords and spears and bows and arrows, and they fought either on foot or from horse-drawn chariots. The superpowers are armed with a variety of nuclear weapons, that is, they are armed with a variety of weapons capable of destroying life on a scale not only unprecedented in history but not even imaginable before the present century. The Shakyans and Koliyans could actually see each other across the waters of the River Rohini. They spoke the same language, even as they worshipped the same gods, and it was possible for one man to make himself heard by the warriors on both sides. Now it is possible for hundreds of millions of people to quarrel without actually seeing one another, and even to prepare to destroy one another without knowing, humanly speaking, who it is they are preparing to destroy. As for their all speaking the same language, they speak it neither literally nor metaphorically, even as they certainly do not worship the same gods, and despite our marvelously improved facilities of communication it is not really possible for one man to make himself heard by them all. Indeed, those same marvelously improved facilities of communication are used, only too often, either for the exchange of insults or for the reiteration of positions known to be unacceptable to the other side. Thus facilities of communication are used for purposes of non-communication.

Peace has become a seamless garment, and the world has either to wear the whole garment or go naked to destruction. There can no longer be any question of a scrap of peace covering one part of the world's nakedness and not another. This makes it impossible for us to think in merely geo-political terms. We have also to think in geo-ethical, geo-humanitarian, or geo-philanthropic terms. Since peace is indivisible, so that the stark choice before us is either world peace or no peace, one world or no world, we shall be able to achieve peace only if we realize that humanity too is indivisible, and if we consistently act on that realization. In other words, we shall be able to achieve peace only by regarding ourselves as citizens of the world, and learning to think not in terms of what is good for this or that nation-state, this or that political system, this or that ideology, but simply and solely in terms of what is good for the world, or for humanity, as a whole. There can be no peace—no world peace—so long as the governments and peoples of sovereign nation-states insist on regarding their separate, sometimes mutually exclusive, interests as paramount and to be pursued at all costs.

Nationalism is in fact the curse of modern history. It is nationalism that was responsible for the rise of sovereign nation-states, and it is sovereign nation-states that produced nuclear weapons in the first place, that produce and possess them now, and that have the power to unleash their destructive capacity upon mankind. Peace and nationalism are therefore incompatible. Nationalism is not, of course, the same thing as patriotism. Nationalism is an exaggerated, passionate and fanatical devotion to one's national community at the expense of all other national communities and even at the expense of all other interests and loyalties. It is a pseudo-religion, an idolatrous cult that demands bloody sacrifices. Patriotism, on the other hand, is simply love of one's country, in the sense of an attachment to, and a desire to care for and protect, the place where one was born and grew up, and it does not exclude smaller or larger interests and loyalties, or honest pride in such things as one's own history and culture. Thus patriotism, unlike nationalism, is not incompatible with peace, even though peace goes beyond patriotism which, in the famous words of Edith Cavell, is "not enough."(Nurse Edith Cavell was shot by the Germans in 1914 for helping English, French, and Belgian soldiers reach the Dutch frontier. On the eve of her execution she said, "I realize that patriotism is not enough. I must have no hatred or bitterness toward anyone.")

This does not mean that in order to achieve peace we have to stop loving our own village or city, our own province, our own country or our own continent, but rather that we have to love them because they are all parts of the world and because we love the world. It means that we have to identify ourselves with humanity rather than with any particular section of it, and love humanity as ourselves. We have to feel for the different national communities, and the different ethnic and linguistic groups, the same kind of love that we feel for the different limbs of our own bodies.

Of this kind of love the Buddha, as he stands between the opposing Shakya and Koliya forces, is the supreme exemplar. The Buddha identified himself with both the Shakyans and the Koliyans, and because he identified himself with them both he could love them both. After all, even apart from the fact that he had attained Enlightenment and thus identified himself with all living things, not in any abstract, metaphysical sense, but in the sense of experiencing the joys and sorrows of others as his own, he was related by blood to both parties in the dispute. Through his father he was related to the Shakyans and through his mother to the Koliyans. Among the warriors on both sides he had uncles, cousins, and nephews, besides old friends and childhood companions. Thus the Buddha's position was similar to our own. We too stand between opposing forces, though the forces with which we have to deal are as much superior to those of the Shakyans and Koliyans as the Buddha's sanity and compassion are superior to ours. Moreover, in our case we do not stand unambiguously between these forces but only too often identify ourselves with one or the other of them and are perceived so to identify ourselves. If peace is to be achieved, however, we have to identify ourselves with both parties, just as the Buddha identified himself with both the Shakyans and the Koliyans. Though we may not be related to them by blood in the way that the Buddha was related to his embattled paternal and maternal relatives, nevertheless we are related to them, inasmuch as we all belong to the same organic species, *homo sapiens,* and it should not be necessary for us to attain Enlightenment in order to realize this fact. If we identify ourselves with both parties and with humanity in this manner, then we shall be able to stand cleanly and unambiguously between the "fell incensed points" of the mighty opposites of our day. We shall be able to speak as the Buddha spoke, because we shall love as the Buddha loved. We shall be a voice of sanity and compassion in the world. We shall be able to appeal to reason. We shall be able to remind humanity, in its own name, what things are of greater value and what of less. We may even be able to remind it what is the most valuable thing of all.

When the Buddha asked the Shakya and Koliya warriors to tell him what the quarrel was all about they could understand the meaning of his question, and were eventually able to give him a reply. He in his turn could understand their reply, and when he went on to ask them how much water was worth and how much warriors were worth they knew exactly what he was talking about and could reply accordingly. Similarly, they knew exactly what he was talking about when he told them it was not fitting that because of a little water they should destroy warriors who were beyond price. There was no problem of communication, as we call it nowadays. The Shakyans and the

Koliyans, and the Buddha himself, all spoke the same language, both literally and metaphorically. When the Buddha wanted to know what the quarrel was all about, neither the Shakya nor the Koliya warriors denied that they were quarrelling. Neither protested that *they* had simply staged a peaceful demonstration on which the warriors on the other side had proceeded to launch a vicious and entirely unprovoked attack. In the same way, neither the Shakya nor the Koliya warriors attempted to argue that "water" could mean "earth" or that in the case of the warriors on the other side "beyond price" really meant "worthless," or that there was in any case no question of destroying warriors but only of *eliminating* them.

The failure of communication which is so striking a feature of our times is based, ultimately, on a breakdown of the notion of objective truth, that is to say, on a breakdown of the notion that truth is truth regardless of our subjective feelings about it and regardless of the way in which it affects our personal interests. That people do not, in practice, exhibit total loyalty to the notion of objective truth, even though they may uphold it in theory, is of course well known and widely accepted. Indeed, in the ordinary transactions of life due allowance is generally made for this fact. We no more expect the used car dealer or the estate agent to dwell as much on the less favorable features of the car or the house he is trying to sell us than we expect him to tell us a deliberate, downright lie. But even if people do not, in practice, exhibit total loyalty to the notion of objective truth, it is important that such loyalty as they do display to it is not allowed to fall below a certain point, since otherwise the transactions of ordinary life will become impossible. Unfortunately, it often does fall below that point. Loyalty to the notion of objective truth becomes *selective*. Actual lies may not be told, but those facts which are not in accordance with the feelings and interests of this or that individual or group are increasingly ignored, misrepresented, distorted, and suppressed. In extreme cases such facts are not allowed ever to have existed at all.

From the stage where loyalty to the notion of objective truth becomes selective—that is to say, becomes that which is in accordance

702 ~ THE ESSENTIAL SANGHARAKSHITA

with certain personal or sectional interests—it is not a very big step to the stage where that which is in accordance with those interests becomes the truth. At this stage, therefore, there is a breakdown of the notion of objective truth. "Truth" is whatever happens to be in accordance with the interests of a particular class, sovereign nation-state, or ideology. Since there are many classes, sovereign nation-states, and ideologies, and therefore many different, even conflicting, interests, there will be not one truth but many truths. Thus there is not only a breakdown of the notion of objective truth but also a substitution of the notion of objective truth by the notion of subjective truth. Subjective truth in effect becomes, for a particular group, objective truth, and since there can be only one objective truth, the objective truth of all other groups—including what might be termed objectively objective truth—necessarily becomes untruth. Under these circumstances communication is impossible. Words no longer have the same meaning for everybody, and what one group regards as facts another regards as non-facts. There is a "failure" of communication. Indeed, those whose views and attitudes are not in accordance with the interests of a particular group are treated as non-individuals in the same way that facts that are not in accordance with these same interests are regarded as non-facts. Such an individual is not so much wrong as, in theory, non-existent, and since he is non-existent in theory it is only natural that he should very quickly become non-existent in practice too. Thus we arrive at a state of affairs such as is characteristic of the nightmare totalitarian world of George Orwell's *1984*, where the three slogans of the Party are "War is Peace," "Freedom is Slavery," and "Ignorance is Strength," where Newspeak is fast replacing Oldspeak, where history is being continually rewritten, and where a word from Big Brother can turn a person into an unperson overnight.

Fortunately, the 1984 which has actually come to pass is not wholly that of Orwell's grim foreboding. The nightmare has not yet come true to more than a limited extent. Nevertheless, the situation in which we find ourselves today is sufficiently alarming, and one of its most dangerous features is that we are faced by a failure of communication between large and important sections of the human race. As I have tried to show, this failure is based, ultimately, on a breakdown of the notion of objective truth, so that if communication is to be restored, and if we are all are to learn to speak the same "language," the notion of objective truth will have to be reinstated in its former central position in human affairs. Only if the notion of objective truth is reinstated in this way shall we be able to speak to the opposing forces of our day as the Buddha spoke to the Shakyans and Koliyans, because only then will it be possible for us really to communicate with them. Only then will it be possible to ascertain the facts of the situation. Only then will it be possible for the voice of sanity and compassion to make itself heard at last. Only then will it be possible to appeal to reason.

Ever since the dawn of history—perhaps from the very beginning of the present cosmic cycle itself—two great principles have been at work in the world: the principle of violence and the principle of non-violence or, as we may also call it, the principle of love—though love in the sense of *agape* rather than in the sense of *eros*. The principle of violence finds expression in force and fraud, as well as in such things as oppression, exploitation, intimidation, and blackmail. The principle of non-violence finds expression in friendliness and openness, as well as in such things as gentleness and helpfulness, and the giving of encouragement, sympathy, and appreciation. The principle of violence is reactive and ultimately destructive; the principle of non-violence is creative. The principle of violence is a principle of Darkness, the principle of non-violence a principle of Light. Whereas to live in accordance with the principle of violence is to be either an animal or a devil or a combination of the two, to live in accordance with the principle of non-violence is to be a human being in the full sense of the term, or even an angel. So far, of course, people have lived in accordance with the principle of violence rather than in accordance with the principle of non-violence. They could do this because it was possible for them to live in accordance with the principle of violence without destroying themselves completely. But now this is no longer the case. Owing to the emergence of nuclear weapons it is now virtually impossible for us to live in accordance with the principle of violence without, sooner or later, annihilating ourselves. We are therefore faced with the necessity of either learning to live in accordance with the principle of non-violence or not living at all. Thus the possibility of nuclear holocaust has not only enabled us to realize the true nature of violence, by showing us what the consequences of violence on the biggest conceivable scale would be, but it has also given us a much deeper appreciation of the real value of non-violence.

It is because of this deeper appreciation of the real value of non-violence that we are able to realize what peace in the full sense of the term really means, as well as how the problem of its achievement is to be solved. Peace—world peace—is something we can hardly imagine today. We can hardly imagine a state of affairs in which disputes between groups and between individuals are settled entirely by non-violent means because all people alike are committed to the principle of non-violence and live in accordance with its precepts. Such a world, in which the principle of Light had overcome the principle of Darkness to so great an extent, would be a world that surpassed More's *Utopia*, Bacon's *New Atlantis*, Campanella's *City of the Sun*, and Morris's *Nowhere* as much as these dreams of an ideal world surpassed the real worlds of their respective days. Such a world would be a heaven on earth. It would be a world of the gods.

But even the gods have their problems. Even if we achieved world peace in the full sense of the term we still would not have solved all our problems by any means. One problem that the gods have to face is the problem of leisure, or the problem of what to do with their time, and even though we have less leisure than the gods this is the kind of problem that faces us too. Indeed, it faces us in the still more acute form of what we are to do with our lives. It would be a thousand pities if, having achieved world peace in the full sense of the term, we were to make no better use of our time, or of our lives, than many of us do at present. In Tennyson's "The Lotos-Eaters," the gods—the gods of Homeric Greece—are imagined as lying beside their nectar and looking over lands wasted by plague, famine, earthquake, and war, and on a human race subject to the painful necessity of wringing a laborious subsistence from the cultivation of the soil. It would be a thousand pities if, when we had solved the problem of world peace, the gods were to look down on a world that in many respects resembled theirs only to see us playing bingo or watching third-rate television programs. Idealists—or cynics—might even be tempted to wonder whether it was really worthwhile delivering humanity from the horrors of nuclear war only that it might fall victim to trivial interests and worthless pursuits. Thus, even if we succeed in solving the problem of peace in the full sense of the term we shall still be faced— as we are now faced—with the even greater problem of what to do with our lives.

But even if that problem too had been solved, and we were living in a manner that was truly worthy of a human being, there would still be one problem that we had not solved. It would not be strange that we had not solved it, for it is a problem that the gods themselves, despite their nectar, are unable to solve. Indeed, it is a problem that no form of sentient conditioned existence is able to solve—so long as it remains merely conditioned. As we know from Tibetan Buddhist scroll-paintings of the Wheel of Life, there are six main forms of conditioned existence, or six main classes of sentient beings: gods, demigods or titans, men, animals, hungry ghosts, and beings in states of torment. These six classes of sentient beings occupy the six principal "worlds" or "spheres," and these worlds are depicted as occupying the six segments into which the third—and widest—circle of the Wheel of Life is divided. The first (and innermost) circle is depicted as being occupied by a cock, a snake, and a pig, symbolizing greed, aversion, and delusion, the three unskillful mental states that keep the Wheel of Life turning; the second circle is divided into two segments, one representing the Path of Light, the other the Path of Darkness; while the fourth and outermost circle is divided into twelve segments representing the twelve "links" that make up the entire process in accordance with which one passes from one form of sentient conditioned existence to another. All four circles, and thus the Wheel of Life in its entirety, are supported from behind by a dreadful monster, whose four sets of claws are seen curving round the edge of the Wheel, while his scaly reptilian tail protrudes below and his bared fangs project over the top of the Wheel beneath fiercely glaring eyeballs and locks crowned with skulls. This dreadful monster is the demon of Impermanence, the demon of Death, who holds in his inexorable grasp not only the six worlds but the whole of conditioned existence, from the electron spinning about its nucleus to the extragalactic nebula receding from us at an unimaginable rate. He holds in his grasp the highest as well as the lowest heavens, the least evolved as well as the most highly evolved forms of earthly life, from the amoeba to *homo sapiens.* Even if we succeed in abolishing nuclear weapons, even if we achieve world peace in the full sense of the term, even if we live in a way that is meaningful and purposeful, we shall still have to face the problem of death. Whether we live in a hell or in a heaven on earth, we shall still see the demon of Impermanence, the demon of Death, glaring down at us over the edge of the Wheel.

More than that. The demon of Death glares at us not only individually but collectively. He glares not only at you and at me but at the whole world, the whole earth. Whether or not nuclear war is averted, we shall still have to die, each one of us; the human race will still have to go the way of the dinosaurs; civilization will still have to collapse, the earth itself will still have to come to an end, even if after thousands of millions of years. Indeed, the very solar system to which the earth belongs will come to an end, as will the galaxy of which that solar system forms part. All conditioned things are impermanent. Whatever comes into existence must one day cease to exist. Thus the solution of the problem of world peace and nuclear war does not really solve anything at all. We still have to face the problem of death. Even though the Buddha was able to prevent the Shakyans and Koliyans from destroying each other on that morning twenty-five centuries ago, he could not save them from death itself. In the case of the Shakyans, he could not even save them from an untimely death at the hands of their

enemies. So thoroughly had his paternal relations been converted to
the principle of non-violence that when, some years later, they were
attacked by the King of Kosala, they decided to offer no resistance
and were massacred to a man—thus giving us, for the first time in history, an example of personal—as distinct from political—pacifism.
(According to some accounts, a remnant of the Shakyans survived
the massacre.) It was not fitting, they declared, that the relations of
the Enlightened One should commit the sin of taking life.

Not only could the Buddha not save the Shakyans and Koliyans
from death, he could not save himself from death. Truth to tell, he did
not wish to save himself from death or even to prolong his earthly
existence to the extent that, according to tradition, he could have prolonged it had he been requested to do so. Forty years after the Rohini
incident, therefore, when the Shakyans themselves were dead and
when the ashes of his two chief disciples, Sariputra and Maudgalyayana, lay beneath their memorial mounds, the Buddha came to the
little wattle-and-daub township of Kusinagara and lay down between
the two sal trees in the sal grove of the Mallas to die or, in the traditional Buddhist phrase, to enter into *parinirvana,* a state as much
beyond non-existence as it is beyond what we call existence. And having lain down between the twin sal trees, with his head to the north
and his feet to the south, he did, at the age of eighty, die. No miracle
intervened to save him. Having traversed all eight *dhyanas* or "meditations," his consciousness came down to the first *dhyana;* having
come down to the first *dhyana* it traversed the first four *dhyanas* a second time and then, as it passed from the fourth *dhyana* and entered
parinirvana, the Buddha died. His body was cremated, and the ashes
placed beneath a memorial mound. The Buddha had to die, as we all
have to die, and there was no resurrection. He had to die, as we all
have to die, because he had been born, and because even for him there
could be no exception to the rule that, birth having taken place, death
must inevitably follow. Even his Enlightenment could not save him,
any more than our knowledge, or virtue, or riches, or friends and relations, can save us. When the messengers of death come, willing or

unwilling, ready or unready, Enlightened or un-Enlightened, we have to go.

Only too often we try to ignore this fact. We refuse to face the problem of death, as though we hoped that by our not looking at the monster with the fiercely glaring eyeballs we could ensure his not looking at us. We may even try to convince ourselves, and others, that it is morbid to think about death. The truth of the matter is that it is morbid *not* to think about death. Not only do we in fact know that we must die, but it is the one thing about ourselves that we really do know. However unsure we may be about other things, we can at least be quite sure of this. Not to think about death is therefore to deprive ourselves of the most certain knowledge that it is possible for us to have. It is to deprive ourselves of the one thing on which we can rely absolutely. Moreover, not to think about death is to deprive ourselves of the possibility of knowing what we really and truly are. Indeed, it is to deprive ourselves of our very humanity. All conditioned things are impermanent. All sentient beings are subject to death. Humans are the only beings (in the sense of the only form of terrestrial life) who are not only subject to death but also aware that they are subject to death. Humans are the only beings for whom death is a problem. Indeed, human beings may be *defined* as the beings for whom death is a problem. For us to ignore the fact of death, or to refuse actually to face the problem of death, is therefore to be untrue to our own nature. It is not to be a human being in the real sense of the term.

The Buddha certainly did not refuse to face the problem of death. He faced it, in fact, quite early in life. According to what became the standard traditional account, he faced it when, as a young Shakya warrior of the ruling class, he drove out from the luxurious mansion in which he lived with his wife and infant son and saw, for the first time in his life, an old man, a sick man, and a corpse. On seeing them he realized that although young, healthy, and very much alive, he too was subject to old age, disease, and death. He also realized that being himself subject to birth, old age, disease, and death, sorrow and corruption, he sought what was subject to birth, old age, disease, death, sorrow, and corruption, and thus lived an unethical and unspiritual life. In other words the Buddha, or Buddha-to-be, became aware of the fact of death. He faced the problem of death. But there was another sight that he saw for the first time, and that was a yellow-robed wandering "monk" who had gone forth from home into the homeless life. On seeing him, the Buddha-to-be realized something else about himself. He realized that although he was subject to birth, old age, disease, death, and corruption, and sought what was of like nature, he could change; he could seek, instead, what was *not* subject to birth, old age, disease, death, and corruption, and thus lead an ethical and spiritual life. He could seek nirvana. He could seek the Unconditioned. In other words, he became aware of the possibility of there being a solution to the problem of death and that the finding of that solution was somehow connected with the homeless life. Accordingly he left home, sat at the feet of various teachers, none of whom could satisfy him for long, practiced extreme self-mortification, realized the futility of self-mortification, adopted a middle way, refused a half share of a kingdom, and eventually, at the age of thirty-five, sat down under a pipal tree at what afterward became known as Bodh Gaya. While meditating he realized that death arises in dependence on birth, and that birth—that is, rebirth—arises in dependence on craving—the craving for continued existence on this or that plane of conditioned being. He realized that when craving ceases birth ceases, and that when birth ceases death ceases. With the cessation of craving one attains nirvana, or the Unconditioned. One attains a state of irreversible spiritual creativity in which there is no birth and no death because in passing beyond the "cyclical" and entering upon the "spiral" order of existence one has transcended all such pairs of opposites. Paradoxically, though the Buddha had solved the problem of death, he still had to die beneath the twin sal trees forty-five years later. But it did not really matter that he had to die. Because he had eradicated craving and the other unskillful mental states that make for birth—i.e. for rebirth—he had solved the problem of birth, and because he had solved the problem of birth he had solved the problem of death in the sense that he would not have to die again.

Thus the Buddha could face the problem of death when he saw his first corpse, and because he could face it—because he could look at the monster with fiercely glaring eyeballs without shrinking—he could also find the solution to the problem of death. In our case it usually takes much more than the sight of a single corpse to make us realize that we too are subject to death. It takes much more than the sight of a single corpse to convince us that death is a problem. In our case we are able to ignore any number of corpses, especially if we only read about them in the newspapers or see them on television. Even if we do become vaguely aware of the problem of death we usually hope, no less vaguely, that we can somehow solve it without having to solve the problem of birth, just as we usually hope, with the same vagueness, that we can somehow achieve peace without having to give up violence. In other words, we usually become aware of the problem of death only to the extent of hoping—or perhaps praying—for the impossible. So far as the problem of death, at least, is concerned, it is a true saying that "What men usually ask of God when they pray is that two and two should not make four." But now all that has changed. We have begun to realize that we cannot have peace without abolishing war. We have begun to realize that we cannot have birth without also having death. We have, in short, woken up to the problem of death. In fact, we have woken up to it to a greater extent than ever before in history.

The reason for this is not far to seek. The reason is that we, the human race, are now faced by the possibility of full-scale nuclear war. We are faced by the fact that each one of us may at any time meet with a premature, painful, and horrible death, and that the whole human race may be destroyed. It is the realization of this frightful fact that has had, upon some of us at least, the same kind of effect that the sight of his first corpse had upon the Buddha. It has made us aware of the problem of death. It has made us aware that the fundamental problem is not the abolition of nuclear weapons, or even the achievement of world peace in the full sense of the term. The fundamental problem is not living in a way that is worthy of a human being in a purely material sense. For a human being worthy of the name, the fundamental problem is the problem of death, and the real significance of the possibility of nuclear holocaust that now confronts us is that it sharpens our awareness of this problem to a greater extent than has ever before been the case. The possibility of nuclear holocaust thus represents not only the greatest threat that humanity has ever faced but also the greatest opportunity. Formerly it was possible for some people to dwell in peace while others were at war. It was possible for some people to live in accordance with the principle of non-violence while others lived in accordance with the principle of violence. It was possible for some people to face the problem of death while others ignored it. Now this is no longer the case. The possibility of nuclear holocaust means that we must all dwell in peace, all learn to live in accordance with the principle of non-violence, all become more aware of the fundamental problem of death. It means that we must all rise to our full stature as human beings—or perish.

What, then, are we to do? Once again we look at the figure of the Buddha, not only as he stands between the Shakyans and the Koliyans but as he stands beside—and above—the Wheel of Life. In some Tibetan Buddhist scroll-paintings the Buddha is depicted in the top right-hand corner, well outside the Wheel, with one arm raised, and pointing in an upward direction. He is pointing out the Way—the Way to nirvana, the state where there is no death because there is no birth. What we have to do is to realize not only the significance of the Rohini incident, and the meaning of the Buddha's exchange with the Shakyans and Koliyans, but also the significance of that solitary wordless gesture. We have to solve both the problem of world peace and nuclear war *and* the problem of death. The very immensity of the problem of world peace and nuclear war indeed serves to make us— if we have any imagination at all—more aware than ever of the problem of death, and unless we can solve the problem of death even the solving of the problem of world peace and nuclear war would, despite the unexampled magnitude of such an achievement, be only the most magnificent of our failures. We must therefore not only abolish

nuclear weapons, achieve peace in the full sense of the term, and learn
to live in accordance with the principle of non-violence, as well as
deepen our realization of the indivisibility of humanity and restore
communication by the reinstatement of the notion of the objectivity
of truth, but we must also eradicate craving, transcend both birth and
death, and attain nirvana.

The situation in which we find ourselves today is dangerous in the
extreme, perhaps more dangerous for humanity than that at any other
period in history, and time is running out. Whether we shall be able to
achieve world peace and avert nuclear war we do not know. We can
but do our best in a situation which, to a great extent, is not of our own
personal making. But whether we succeed in achieving world peace
and averting nuclear war or not we shall still have to die, still have to
face the problem of death. If we solve the problem of death it will not,
in the most fundamental sense, matter whether we solve the problem
of world peace and nuclear war or not—though, paradoxically, if we
do succeed in solving the problem of death then we shall, in all probability, succeed in solving the problem of world peace and nuclear war
too. In any case, if we solve the problem of death, the problem of birth,
the problem of craving, then we shall be able to live in the world as the
Buddha and his disciples lived. We shall be able to join them in chanting those celebrated verses of the *Dhammapada,* the first three of
which the Buddha, according to tradition, recited to the Shakyans and
Koliyans by way of admonition immediately after he had prevented
them from destroying each other:

> Happy indeed we live, friendly amid the hateful. Among
> people who hate we dwell free from hate. Happy indeed we
> live, healthy among the sick. Among people who are sick
> (with craving) we dwell free from sickness.
>
> Happy indeed we live, content amid the greedy. Among
> people who are greedy we dwell free from greed. Happy
> indeed we live, we for whom there is no attachment. Feed-
> ers on rapture shall we be, like the Gods of Brilliant Light.

Victory begets hatred, (for) the defeated experiences suffering. The tranquil one experiences happiness, giving up (both) victory and defeat.[165]

2. A BUDDHIST APPROACH TO WORLD PROBLEMS

The central problem for all of us is: how do we ourselves, individually, react to whatever we perceive to be the world's problems?

IN 1943 I was posted to India as a signals operator, and after the war I stayed on to spend the next twenty years in the East, seventeen of them as a Buddhist monk. During this time I had the opportunity—I might say I was under the obligation—of attending a large number of public meetings. It is probably fair to say that Indians have a positive weakness for public meetings. Very often these are open air meetings held late at night under the glare of arc lights, and they go on and on. In fact, the bigger they are, and the longer they go on, the better. To be called a success a meeting needs to be distinguished by a long line of speakers, each speaking for at least an hour. I can remember on one of these occasions being enjoined, in an authoritative whisper from behind me as I rose to my feet, to "speak for at least two hours."

People in India can be very generous with their time (and, it must be said, with other people's time as well), so I used to hear a lot of speeches. Some of the topics—and even their treatment—became very familiar to me indeed. For example, I got used to the idea that at some point during an evening of talks on Buddhist subjects you had a reasonable expectation of hearing a talk on Buddhism and world peace. This subject would come round regularly, and it didn't matter who was giving it, it was practically always the same talk.

First of all you would be treated to a graphic description of the terrible plight of mankind in the modern world, and the usual suspects would be rounded up. You would be reminded of the prevalence of flood, fire, pestilence, and war; then you would be led through the various incontrovertible signs of a universal and unprecedented breakdown of moral and spiritual values, focusing in particular on the behavior and attitudes of young people today. Then, when you were judged to be fully reconciled to an altogether bleak prospect culminating in nuclear holocaust and no solution in sight, Buddhism would be brought in to save the day. Buddhism, you would be told, teaches non-violence; it teaches peace, love, and compassion. If everybody in the world followed the teachings of the Buddha you would have world peace, and all our problems would be solved automatically. And that would be it—end of talk. Spontaneous applause would break out, the speaker would sit down, beaming with satisfaction, the audience would clap away, happy in the knowledge that there was hope for the world after all. And, of course, the world would go on just as before.

The problem with this sort of analysis of our situation is not that it isn't true. If everybody in the world meditated every day and tried to develop kindness and love and compassion and joy, and worked at the precepts and followed the Noble Eightfold Path, then—well, we wouldn't just have peace, we'd have heaven on earth. No, the problem with this line of argument is that it's an oversimplification of both problem and solution. In the abstract, it's beautiful, but that is where it remains: in the abstract.

Another big difficulty with talking about Buddhism and world peace is that Buddhists are not the only people with values that support world peace. If everyone in the world followed the teachings of Jainism, or Taoism, or certain forms of Hinduism, you would still get world peace, without any need to mention Buddhism. There's no need, in fact, to bring in any religion at all—religions don't have a monopoly on peaceful values. If everybody followed the teachings of Plato, or even Bertrand Russell, you would have world peace on the spot.

So if one is not simply going to present Buddhism as a universal panacea for the world's ills, what *does* Buddhism offer? One cannot talk about *the* Buddhist view of world problems because there isn't an official Buddhist party-line on these or any other issues. All one is left with is *a* Buddhist view of world problems. One can talk about world problems only from one's individual standpoint. And as a Buddhist standpoint, its validity can only be measured by how deeply one has been influenced by Buddhist teachings.

There is still, however, the question of what an individual Buddhist can have to say that is truly relevant to world problems. All I can say for myself is that the work I have engaged in as a Buddhist has arisen, to some considerable extent, out of the view I take of current world problems. This topic is not of academic or peripheral interest to me. In approaching it I am in some sense trying to make clear the *raison d'être* of my own existence as a practical working Buddhist; that is, as a Buddhist not just inwardly, in faith and conviction, but also as far as outward activities are concerned. My view of current world problems constitutes a sort of philosophical autobiography, even a confession of faith. It will, I hope, show where I stand and perhaps, to some extent, why I stand there.

We can probably all make our own list of world problems, and we hardly need reminding of them: most of them have been with us since the dawn of history, and the news industry keeps us abreast of those that are of more recent provenance. What is new about the problems of today is the very fact that we hear about them. They are global in character, world-scale problems. It really is as though we live in a global village, and although this is a matter of common knowledge, even a truism, it perhaps does not sink as decisively and deeply into our awareness as it should.

The result of "globalization" is that all world problems affect all of us in some way, either directly or indirectly, either potentially or in actuality. Not very long ago, the vast majority of people knew absolutely nothing about the problems of people who lived just a few valleys away, let alone people on the other side of the world. Catastrophic events hardly impinged at all on the lives of those who were not directly and immediately involved. Even in a country ravaged by years of terrible warfare there would be peasants within its borders going about their everyday lives knowing nothing whatso-ever about it.

But not any more. We have the world's problems at our fingertips. The real problem for us is how to respond to them personally. How do we ensure that every individual citizen in the world grows up healthy and sound in body and mind? What can be done about the apparently increasing incidence of mental illness in the West? What is the role of women—and what is the role of men—in modern society? How do people with jobs avoid making themselves ill through over-work? How do people without work make the best use of their enforced leisure? How do we ensure that people are not discrimi-nated against or abused on account of their racial origin? How do we reconcile the claims of law and order with those of individual free-dom? How do we reconcile the conflicting interests of sovereign nation states? How can we all get along with one another?

Fresh outbreaks of hostilities between rival factions in some former European colony, food-shortages and unrest in some ex-communist state, inner-city deprivation and crime, drug-dependency and alco-holism, child-labor, racial violence, industrial pollution, nuclear acci-dents, disease, drought, famine, starvation, "ethnic cleansing"—these are just a few of the problems and crises that confront us, or at least pluck at our sleeves every now and then, and are recorded for us on the television and analyzed for us in the newspapers. No doubt there are many others, equally pressing, which I have failed to mention. We all have our own pet world problems which seem more crucial than oth-ers. But the central problem for all of us is: how do we ourselves, indi-vidually, react to whatever we perceive to be the world's problems?

Sometimes our initial reaction will be very strong. For a while we may get quite carried away by our indignation: we are outraged; this should never be allowed to happen; something must be done; those responsible—if particular perpetrators can be identified—should be brought to justice; and so on. And we may be anxious on our own account, if the problem seems likely to affect us directly at some point. In the end, however, when that initial reaction has exhausted itself, we are overtaken—overpowered—by a different kind of reaction: help-lessness. The problem is too big, too involved, for us to do anything about it. So we try to forget about it and get on with our own lives, and deal with our own problems. We are very sorry that others suffer, but at least we can try to enjoy our own lives.

This is, I suspect, how many people react to world problems. How-ever, my own view is that such an attitude of withdrawal from public concerns into purely personal ones is one that is not worthy of a human being—not worthy, at least, of someone who is trying to be a human being in the full sense of the term. It represents an abdication of responsibility. So, given that one is helpless to effect any kind of solution to these large issues, and given too that one can't turn aside and ignore them either, what is one to do?

World problems, by their very nature, are essentially group prob-lems, as they always have been. What is new today is the size of the groups involved and the destructive power available to them. But whatever their size, the problems arising from these groups cannot be solved on the group level. All that can be achieved on the level of the group is a precarious balance of power between conflicting interests. And that balance, as we know only too well, can be disturbed at any moment.

The only hope for humanity is therefore necessarily a long-term solution, involving more people becoming clearer about how they need to develop as individuals and cooperating in the context of spir-itual communities in order to make, in their various ways, a significant impact on the world, or on "the group." The alternatives before us are, in my opinion, evolution—that is, the higher evolution of the indi-vidual—or extinction. That would be my overall diagnosis of the sit-uation facing us. As for practical ways to effect a remedy, I would prescribe four courses of action for the individual to undertake.

1. Self-development

This means essentially the development of the mind, the raising of consciousness to ever higher levels of awareness. Human development essentially consists in this, and for most people the route to achieving it is through meditation. The practice of meditation essentially involves three things. Firstly, it involves concentration, the integration of all our energies, conscious and unconscious. Secondly, it involves the raising of consciousness to supra-personal states, leaving the ego-realm for higher, wider, even cosmic dimensions. And thirdly, it involves contemplation: the direct insight of the uncluttered mind—the mind in a state of higher consciousness—into the ultimate depths of existence, the seeing of reality face to face. Meditation is concerned with achieving all this. There are many different methods; you just need to find a teacher who will introduce you to one or two of them. After that, you stick with the methods and practice them regularly. That's all there is to it, really.

The more demanding aspect of self-development consists in what you do with the rest of your life in order to support your meditation practice. You will look after your health. You will simplify your life as far as possible, dropping all those activities, interests, and social contacts which you know to be a waste of time. You will try to base your life, and in particular your livelihood, on ethical principles. You will make time—perhaps by working part-time—for study; for study of the Dharma, of course, but also for study of other subjects of general human interest: philosophy, history, science, comparative religion. Finally, you will find opportunities to refine and develop your emotions, especially through the fine arts.

Self-development always comes first. However active you might be in all sorts of external areas—political, social, educational, or whatever—if you are not trying to develop yourself, you are not going to be able to make any truly positive contribution to anything or anyone.

2. Join a Spiritual Community

This does not necessarily mean joining some kind of organized body or living under the same roof as other aspiring individuals. It simply means being in personal, regular, and substantial contact with others who are trying to develop as individuals. It means being able to enjoy, and seeking out, not just the psychological warmth of the herd but the challenge of real communication, genuine spiritual exchange.

3. Withdraw Support from All Groups or Agencies that Actually Discourage, Directly or Indirectly, the Development of the Individual

Groups derive their strength from their members, so it is a basic first step to weaken the power of the group by removing yourself from among its contributing members. Otherwise you are pulling in two directions at once: on the one hand trying to be an individual, and on the other lending your support to the very forces that hinder this process. If you wanted to take this principle to its ultimate conclusion you would withdraw support from the state, as the ultimate group of groups, though this would clearly be extremely difficult, however desirable.

4. Encourage the Development of Individuality within All the Groups to which One Unavoidably Belongs

It may be that you cannot help having a circle of friends or acquaintances, whether at home or at work, who are not interested in any kind of self-development. You may have to remain very nominally a member of a group. Still, you can stand up for what you believe in, and speak up whenever it is appropriate to do so. It is always possible to act in accordance with one's ideals even when others cannot—or do not appear to—understand what one is doing. The way to disrupt a group is simply to encourage people within it to think for themselves, develop minds of their own. So in the context of the group one can still work to undermine it. Even in the enemy camp, so to speak, one need not surrender one's individuality.

These, then, are four strategies to get under way in order to begin to make a meaningful impact on world problems. A network of spiritual communities of all kinds, many of whose members would be in contact with one another, could exert a significant degree of influence, such as might—just possibly—shift the center of gravity in world affairs. Spiritual communities have had a crucial impact in the past, and they may, with sufficient vitality, do so again.

It doesn't matter how humble a level we are operating at, or how undramatic our work may be. The true individual is not so much the king of the jungle as the indefatigable earthworm. If enough earthworms burrow away under the foundations of even the most substantial building, the soil begins to loosen, it starts to crumble away, the foundations subside, and the whole building is liable to crack and collapse. Likewise, however powerful the existing order may seem, it is not invulnerable to the undermining influence of enough individuals working—whether directly or indirectly—in cooperation.

A spiritual community is necessarily small, so the best we can hope for is a multiplicity of spiritual communities, forming a sort of network through personal contact between their members. A silent, unseen influence is exerted in this way, which we must hope will be able, at some point, to shift the center of gravity in world affairs from the conflict of groups to the cooperation of communities. If this were achieved, if the influence of the spiritual community were to outweigh that of the group, then humanity as a whole would have passed into a new, higher stage of development, a kind of higher evolution as I like to call it—into what we might even describe as a new period of human history.

Such a shift in the governing values of the world is probably all that can save us from extinction as a species in the not very distant future. There are certainly signs of hope, but there is also perhaps little time left. In this situation it becomes the duty of every thinking human being to take stock of his or her position, and the responsibilities that it implies. We have to appreciate that it is, without exception, the most important issue we shall ever face, either individually or collectively. It is certainly more important than any merely religious question, anything that concerns Buddhism in the sense of a formal or established religion. It concerns both the purpose and the very survival of human life.

3. The Miracle of Spiritual Development

Dissatisfaction—if it is not just disgruntlement but a genuine and creative mood of inner revolt—is a positive and powerful impulse.

WHAT ONE BRINGS to the Buddhist center, at least initially, is a sense of dissatisfaction. This might seem an unlikely attitude for Buddhists to encourage—we are all surely familiar enough with dissatisfaction. Anyone who has ever picked up a mail order catalogue, pored over its glossy pages, found something depicted therein that is too tempting to resist, and filled in a form and sent it off, waiting for that winter coat or that electric drill with its guarantee of full and complete satisfaction, will know the meaning of dissatisfaction. When it finally arrives and you unwrap it, somehow it seems less glamorous, less luxurious, flimsier, smaller than in the photograph. Sometimes it is even the wrong color, or there's a part missing. Our disappointment may be such that we have no hesitation in sending the offending article, unsatisfactory as it is, back for a refund, perhaps accompanied by a strongly-worded note.

But we have all taken delivery of one article which, when we compare it with the design specifications, is clearly incomplete or botched, and yet we seem more than satisfied with it. That article is, of course, ourselves. We want everything else in our lives to be properly made, polished and shiny, but we cherish ourselves in our imperfect state. So how can we become dissatisfied? Quite simply, we become dissatisfied when we compare ourselves as we are here and now with how we could be in the future. We become dissatisfied when we get a glimpse of a potential which is without any limit and see that by comparison we are at present distinctly unsatisfactory and limited. When we espouse that vision we are in a sense taking the first steps toward sending ourselves back in disgust and demanding a properly functioning human individuality.

Dissatisfaction—if it is not just disgruntlement but a genuine and creative mood of inner revolt—is a positive and powerful impulse.

Indeed, such a mood is the starting point. You are dissatisfied, perhaps, with the quality of your relationships, with your work, with your leisure activities—and perhaps, more often than not, you are pretty fed up with yourself as well. You start looking around for a new direction, and you hear, perhaps, about Buddhism, and then about the Buddhist center, about meditation classes, and you start going along to those classes, and to listen to talks. You may even go on a weekend retreat. And as a result of all this, you start to change.

Such change is quite noticeable. I have seen it taking place many times. One sees people visibly changing almost before one's eyes—and this, one might say, is a miracle: that people can change, not just piecemeal, but from top to bottom. Indeed, the Buddha himself referred to this as the greatest of all miracles.[166] In general he condemned the display of so-called miracles or supernormal powers. The ancient Indians were very interested in these things, and even now people tend to perk up and take notice as soon as the subject comes up. The Buddha was often asked to demonstrate miraculous powers, and sometimes he did, if he saw good reason to do so. But for him they were entirely insignificant, and if he thought that they were being taken too seriously, he refused to have anything to do with them. He even went so far as to say, "I condemn and abhor them, I look down upon them." "These," he went on to say, "are not real miracles. The real miracle is when someone who was following the dark path changes and starts following the bright path, the path of skillful activities, the path of the spiritual life: that is the real miracle."

It is a miracle which continues to occur—often, it seems, against all the odds. People come along quite literally off the street, looking hopeless and dejected, as if they carried all the cares of the world on their shoulders. They start meditating, they become more aware, and in the course of a few weeks, sometimes in the course of a weekend retreat away in the country, you see them beginning to look bright and cheerful. They begin to see something of the Buddha's vision of existence, and they change. One might think that when someone has traveled along the same old rut for decades, it is too late. But that is a great mistake. If you find the right sort of encouragement and the right sort of conditions, you can change at any time of your life.

Notes

PART ONE

1 *Anguttara Nikaya* II, 37–9, quoted in *Buddhist Texts through the Ages,* ed. E. Conze, I.B. Horner etc., Harper & Row, New York 1954, pp.104–5.

2 *Majjhima Nikaya* 26; see Bhikkhu Nanamoli, *The Life of the Buddha,* Buddhist Publication Society, Kandy 1984, p.10.

3 See *Mahagovinda Sutta (Majjhima Nikaya* 19), verse 45.

4 The three laksanas are enumerated in many places in the Pali Canon—see, for example, *Samyutta Nikaya* xxxv.1 and xxii.46; *Udana* iii.10; *Anguttara Nikaya* iii.47; *Dhammapada* 277–9.

5 See Nanamoli, p.43 for a brief reference. Of the many canonical references, perhaps the reflections of the Buddha in section 18 of the *Mahasatipatthana Sutta (Digha Nikaya* 22) are especially worth consulting.

6 Shakespeare, *Measure for Measure,* III.i.128–31.

7 *Majjjima Nikaya,* i.135.

8 See, for example, *Itivuttaka* section 100.

9 See Edward Conze, *Buddhism,* Cassirer, Oxford 1957, pp.46–8.

10 See *Vinaya Pitaka, Culavagga* i.

11 Nanamoli, p.230; *Samyutta Nikaya* xii.61.

12 Of the many texts which bear the name Upanishad, there are thirteen principal ones. They originate from the period eighth to fourth century BCE, and form the basis of the school of Hindu philosophy known as the Vedanta. The *atman* is one of their main themes.

13 *Majjhima Nikaya* I (Middle Length Sayings), *Ariyapariyesana Sutta,* trans. I.B. Horner, Pali Text Society, London, 1967, p.207.

14 Ibid. p.213.

15 *Sutta-Nipata* ii, 103–4, from *Some Sayings of the Buddha,* trans. F.L. Woodward, Oxford University Press, London 1939.

16 A famous quotation from the Smaragdine Tablet, an ancient alchemical document ascribed to Hermes Trismegistus states the "Hermetic correspondence" between higher and lower levels of reality: "That which is above is like that which is below and that which is below is like that which is above, to accomplish the miracle of one thing."

17 *Jatakas* (literally "belonging to, or connected with, what has happened") and *Avadanas* (literally "glorious or heroic deeds") are stories illustrating the workings of the law of karma, showing how the spiritual stature of the Buddha and his disciples is consequent upon their skillful actions in former lives. The *Jatakas* are devoted mainly to the previous lives of the Buddha, in which the Bodhisatta practices the Perfections. They incorporate much material from Indian folklore in the form of fables, fairy tales, and so on. In the canonical *Jatakas*, the Buddha is invariably a wise ruler or famous teacher; in the non-canonical stories, he is also depicted as an animal. The *Avadanas* deal mainly with the careers of the Buddha's disciples or other famous Buddhist figures.

18 Nagarjuna, the author of *The Precious Garland,* lived in the second century CE in India. He is credited with establishing the doctrinal basis of the Mahayana and in particular is regarded as the founder of the Madhyamika School. Legend has it that he descended to the depths of the ocean to receive the Perfection of Wisdom teaching from the king of the *nagas.*

19 Padmasambhava was a great Indian teacher who was mainly responsible, in a short visit, for establishing Buddhism in Tibet in the eighth century CE. His life story is made up almost entirely of miraculous events, not least of which is his birth from a huge lotus flower. The highly symbolic but deeply stirring account of his life can be read in Yeshe Tsogyal's *The Life and Liberation of Padmasambhava,* Dharma Publishing, Emeryville 1978.

20 Milarepa was a Tibetan Buddhist master of the eleventh century CE from whom the various Kagyu lineages are descended. He is famous for his asceticism, living on nettles in a cave in the snow-mountains and wearing only a thin cotton garment. His songs and the stories of the circumstances in which they were sung provide some of the best-loved literature of Buddhist Tibet.

21 *Vajra* (Sanskrit) literally means "diamond" or "thunderbolt." In Indian mythology, it is wielded by Indra, the king of the gods; it is similar to the thunderbolt wielded by Zeus. The vajra is also like a diamond in that it can cut through anything but is itself indestructible. In Tantric Buddhism, known as "Vajrayana," the vajra became a symbol for the nature of Reality. The vajra is extensively used in Tantric ritual and various figures in Tantric iconography—the most famous being Vajrapani and Vajrasattva—are depicted holding or wielding it.

22 The Buddha's victory over Mara is described in several texts—for example in the *Ariyapariyesana Sutta* (*Majjhima Nikaya*); the Book of the Kindred Sayings (*Samyutta Nikaya*) Pt.1, Ch.4; The *Buddhacarita,* Canto xiii; The *Lalita-vistara,* published as *The Voice of the Buddha,* Dharma Publishing, Oakland 1983, Vol.II, Ch.21.

23 See *The Voice of the Buddha,* pp.481–2.

24 In early Buddhism, the Perfections are the moral observances which the Buddha has practiced and brought to perfection in the course of his thousands of lives as a Bodhisatta; they are an essential ingredient in his preparation for Buddhahood. In the Mahayana, the practicing of the Six or Ten Perfections is a crucial aspect of the Bodhisattva's spiritual career.

25 The word *mudra* (Sanskrit) literally means "gesture" or "seal." A *mudra* is a symbolic gesture of the hands either performed in the course of a ritual or depicted iconographically in the statues and pictures of Buddhas, Bodhisattvas, or other eminent Buddhist figures.

26 I.B. Horner (trans.), *The Book of the Discipline (Vinaya-Pitaka)*, Vol. IV (*Maha-vagga*), Pali Text Society, London 1982, I, 5.

27 Ibid., I, 3.

28 For the position, names, and significance of the psychic centers, see Lama Anagarika Govinda, *Foundations of Tibetan Mysticism*, Century, London 1987, pp.138–46.

29 *Mahaparinibbana Sutta* in Maurice Walshe (trans.), *The Long Discourses of the Buddha (Digha Nikaya)*, Wisdom Publications, Boston 1995, Sutta 16, p.272.

30 The Abhidharma (the word simply means "about Dharma," though its adherents came to think of it as "the higher Dharma") began as a project to systematize the Buddha's teachings, including establishing the meaning of technical terms, collating references to the same topics, and so on. In the course of its history—which lasted several hundred years—it developed an exhaustive analysis of mind and mental events, a kind of "Buddhist psychology." See Sangharakshita, *The Eternal Legacy*, Tharpa, London 1985, chapter 7: "The Fundamental Abhidharma"; and Sangharakshita, *Know Your Mind*, Windhorse, Cambridge, UK 2002, chapter 1: "The First Buddhist Analysts."

31 The story is told in *Mahavagga* viii.26 of the *Vinaya Pitaka*. See also Sangharakshita, *The Buddha's Victory*, Windhorse, Glasgow 1991, chapter 4, "A Case of Dysentery."

32 See Mrs. C.A.F. Rhys Davids and K.R. Norman (trans.), *Poems of Early Buddhist Nuns (Therigatha)*, Pali Text Society, Oxford 1997, pp.88–91.

33 See *The Long Discourses of the Buddha (Digha Nikaya)*, Sutta 16, p.265.

34 According to the Vinaya Pitaka, the first two people to encounter the Buddha after his Enlightenment (they were two merchants called Tapussa and Bhalluka) declared: "We go for refuge to the Blessed One, and to the Dhamma." See Nanamoli, p.34.

35 *Majjhima Nikaya* 39, *Maha-Assapura Sutta*.

36 *Dhammapada*, verses 189–92.

37 Lin Yutang (trans.), *Tao-Teh-King* xxv.

38 *Udana* v.5.

39 Herbert V. Guenther and Leslie S. Kawamura (trans.), *Mind in Buddhist Psychology: A Translation of Ye-shes rgyal-mtshan's "The Necklace of Clear Understanding,"* Dharma, Berkeley 1975, p.xvi.

40 The term is *maggam bhaveti*. See Nyanatiloka, *Buddhist Dictionary*, Buddhist Publication Society, Kandy 1988, p.169, "The Progress of the Disciple."

41 This is referred to in Case 46 of the Zen classic *Mumonkan, The Gateless Gate*. See Katsuki Sekida (trans.), *Two Zen Classics*, Weatherhill, New York 1996, pp.128–31.

42 Saint Simeon Stylites (387–459 CE) lived for the last forty or so years of his life at Telanessa, near Antioch, on top of a pillar about twenty meters high from which he preached to visiting crowds. His name comes from the Greek *stulos*, meaning column or pillar.

43 Nanamoli p.224; *Samyutta Nikaya* xxxviii.1; *Anguttara Nikaya* iii.53.

44 *Dhammapada* 204: *nibbanam paramam sukham*, "Nirvana is the highest bliss."

45 *Klesa nirvana* is synonymous with the attainment of Arahantship; *skandha nirvana* is synonymous with *parinirvana* ("full" nirvana), a term which is usually used to refer to the death of the Buddha but in fact is applicable to the death of any Arahant.

46 This is from Blake's poem "London," in *Songs of Innocence and Experience.*
47 *Udana* vi.4.
48 E. Conze, *Buddhism: Its Essence and Development,* Windhorse, Birmingham, UK 2001, p.16.
49 E.g. *Vajracchedika-prajna-paramita* 3.
50 *Vinaya Pitaka* i.182.
51 *Samyutta Nikaya* XLVIII.IV.II.ii.
52 *Siksa-samuccaya* 316.
53 *Hevajra Tantra* II.viii.c.8–9.

Part Two

54 Yeshe Tsogyal, *The Life and Liberation of Padmasambhava,* Dharma, Berkeley 1978, Part ii, Canto 103, p.690.
55 According to Heinrich Dumoulin in *Zen Buddhism: A History—India and China* (Macmillan, New York 1988, p.8), the earliest version of this apocryphal story is told in a Rinzai School text, The *T'ien-sheng Record of the Widely Extending Lamp.*
56 Mentioned at the beginning of the preface to *Dhyana for Beginners,* in *A Buddhist Bible,* ed. Dwight Goddard, Beacon Press, Boston 1966, p.437.
57 *The Table Talk and Omniana of Samuel Taylor Coleridge,* ed. T. Ashe, George Bell & Sons, London 1905.
58 See Goethe's *Criticisms, Reflections, and Maxims,* trans. W.B. Ronnfeldt, The Scott Library, London 1982.
59 This was an aspect of the Buddha's first teachings after his Enlightenment. See *Vinaya,* book 4 (*Mahavagga*), chapter 1; or Nanamoli, p.42.
60 "Cromwell was about to ravage the whole of Christendom; the royal family had been brought down, and his own would have been established forever but for a small grain of sand that formed in his bladder. Rome would have trembled beneath him, but once that little gravel was there, he died, his family fell from power, peace reigned, and the King was restored." Blaise Pascal, *The Pensees,* trans. and introduction by J.M. Cohen, Penguin, Harmondsworth 1961.
61 Rabindranath Tagore, *Gitanjali (Song Offerings),* no.95.
62 The Buddha is widely referred to by this title, which literally translates as "Thus-come" or "Thus-gone," so it means one who has "gone beyond" conditioned existence—one who leaves no trace.
63 A *sramana* is someone who has taken up a homeless religious life. *Sramana* literally means "one who is washed, purified," and it shares this literal meaning with the words "Sufi" and "Cathar." The quotation is from *Vinaya Mahavagga* i.23.
64 Thomas Gray, "Elegy in a Country Churchyard," 1750.
65 According to Buddhist tradition a *kalpa* is the time taken for a world system to evolve and involve; a *kalpa* is divided into four *asamkheyya-kalpas* (Pali *asankheyya-kappas*).
66 See, for example, *Samyutta Nikaya* iv.229.
67 *Dhammapada,* verses 1–2.
68 *Anguttara Nikaya* i.188.
69 *Vinaya* ii.10.
70 *Digha Nikaya* ii.81.

Part Three

71 T.S. Eliot, "The Dry Salvages" part 5, in "Four Quartets".

72 F.L. Woodward (trans.), Anguttara Nikaya i.259, in *Gradual Sayings* vol.1, Pali Text Society, Oxford 1995, p.239.

73 "The smile of the Arahant" is listed in the Theravada Abhidhamma classification of mental events as one of the karmically neutral mental events, and as being among a group of mental events that are "automatic"—that is, not the result of past karma.

74 Sigmund Freud, *Jokes and their Relation to the Unconscious,* Penguin, Harmondsworth 1978, p.199.

75 M. Winternitz, *A History of Indian Literature,* University of Calcutta 1933, vol.2, p.149.

76 "Never did eye see sun unless it had first become sunlike, and never can the Soul have vision of the First Beauty unless itself be beautiful." Plotinus, *The Enneads,* trans. Stephen MacKenna, Penguin, Harmondsworth 1991, I.vi.9, p.55.

77 See Sutta 16 of Walshe (trans.), p.266.

78 Ibid., Sutta 17, 1.2 et seq.

79 See *The Larger Sukhavati-vyuha Sutra,* section 16, pp.33–6, in *Buddhist Mahayana Texts,* ed. E.B. Cowell et al., Dover Publications, New York 1969.

80 This essay appears in Conze's *Thirty Years of Buddhist Studies,* Cassirer, London 1967, pp.185–90.

81 sGam.po.pa (Gampopa), *The Jewel Ornament of Liberation,* trans. H.V. Guenther, Rider, London 1970, p.41.

82 *Dhammapada* verse 182.

83 *Majjhima Nikaya* 129.24 (*Balapandita Sutta*); and elsewhere.

84 *Jataka* 316.

85 For the parable in the sutra, see *The Threefold Lotus Sutra,* trans. Bunno Kato, Yoshiro Tamura, and Kojiro Miyasaka, with revisions by W.E. Soothill, Wilhelm Schiffer, and Pier P. Del Campana, Weatherhill/Kosei, New York and Tokyo 1980, pp.85–109.

86 See *The Book of the Discipline,* vol. 4 (*Vinaya-Pitaka*), trans. I.B. Horner, Pali Text Society, London 1982, pp.35–45; and *The Book of the Kindred Sayings* (*Samyutta Nikaya*), vol. 4, trans. F.L. Woodward, Pali Text Society, London 1956, p.28.

87 The story of Krishna's flute is told in the *Srimad-Bhagavata*—see, for example, Radhakamal Mukerjee, *The Lord of the Autumn Moons,* Asia Publishing House, Mumbai 1957, pp.97–102.

88 For a fuller account of these three *yanas,* see Sangharakshita, *A Survey of Buddhism,* Windhorse, Birmingham 2001, pp.241ff.

89 Here "universalism" refers to the view that all religious teachings are equally true and lead equally to salvation. This sense of the term has nothing to do with the usage of the term Universalism within a specifically Christian context.

90 For the parable in the sutra, see *The Threefold Lotus Sutra,* pp.110–25.

91 For a translation of the "Hymn of the Pearl," see, for example, Hans Jonas, *The Gnostic Religion,* Beacon Press, Boston 1958, pp.113–16.

92 *Majjhima Nikaya* Sutta 63 (*Culamalunkya Sutta*).

PART FOUR

93 Romans 7:19.

94 See J. Blofield (Chu Ch'an) (trans.), *The Sutra of Forty-two Sections and Two Other Scriptures of the Mahayana School,* Buddhist Society, London 1977, section 8, p.13.

95 Shantideva, *Bodhicaryavatara,* chapter 6, verse 43.

96 See Har Dayal, *The Bodhisattva Doctrine in Buddhist Sanskrit Literature,* Motilal Banarsidass, Delhi 1978, pp.209–13.

97 For canonical references, see Nanamoli p.131; Udana iv.1; *Anguttara Nikaya* ix.3.

98 For a canonical account of the mindfulness of breathing, see Nanamoli pp.122–3; *Majjhima Nikaya* 62.

99 This meditation is described by Buddhaghosa in the *Visuddhimagga,* trans. Pe Maung Tin, Pali Text Society, London 1975. pp.342–3.

100 Nanamoli p.242; *Mahasatipatthana Sutta (Digha Nikaya* 22), vv.6–10.

101 This is related in the "Parajika": trans. I.B. Horner, *Book of the Discipline,* part I, Pali Text Society, London 1949, p.117.

102 This meditation practice is a recapitulation of the process the Buddha describes himself as having undergone just before his Enlightenment. "I thought: What is there when aging and death come to be? What is their necessary condition? Then with ordered attention I came to understand: Birth is there when aging and death come to be; birth is a necessary condition for them." In this way he traced back each of the links of conditioned co-production. See Nanamoli pp.25–7; *Samyutta Nikaya* xii.65.

103 A canonical reference to the "six element practice" is to be found in Nanamoli pp.214–5; *Majjhima Nikaya* 62.

104 For an explanation of the *alaya-vijnana,* see Sangharakshita, *The Meaning of Conversion in Buddhism,* Windhorse, Birmingham 1994, chapter 4.

105 *Digha Nikaya* 2 in, for example, *The Long Discourses of the Buddha,* trans. Maurice Walshe, Wisdom Publications, Boston 1995, pp.91ff.

106 See, for example, *Dhammapada* verse 23.

107 In the Tibetan tradition a dakini ("sky-dancer") is a female figure representing the energies of Enlightenment.

108 *Ratana Sutta,* trans. Sangharakshita, in *Complete Poems 1941–94,* Windhorse, Birmingham 1995.

109 "The Tale of Red Rock Jewel Valley" in *The Hundred Thousand Songs of Milarepa,* Shambhala, Boulder and London 1999, p.5.

110 *Mahaparinibbana Sutta* 5.14, Sutta 16 of the *Digha Nikaya,* trans. Maurice Walshe, Wisdom Publications, Boston 1987, p.265.

111 *Vinaya* I, 301ff.

112 *Digha Nikaya* 31.

113 *Digha Nikaya* 16. Quoted in Nanamoli, pp.286–9.

114 *Samyutta Nikaya* iii.18.

115 For an account of pratyekabuddhas, see Reginald Ray, *Buddhist Saints in India,* Oxford University Press, Oxford 1994, chapter 7.

116 "Suppose, monks, an ass follows close behind a herd of cows, thinking: I'm a cow too! I'm a cow too! But he is not like cows in color, voice or hoof. He just follows close behind a herd of cows thinking: I'm a cow too! I'm a cow too! Just in the same

way, monks, we have some monk who follows close behind the Order of Monks thinking: I'm a monk too! I'm a monk too! But he has not the desire to undertake the training in the higher morality which the other monks possess, nor in the higher thought, nor that in the higher insight which other monks possess. He just follows close behind thinking: I'm a monk too! I'm a monk too!" *Samyutta Nikaya* iii.9.81 in *The Book of Gradual Sayings vol.1* trans. F.L. Woodward, Pali Text Society, Oxford 1995, p.209.

117 *Dhammapada* 194.

118 *Digha Nikaya* iii.190.

119 Santideva, *The Bodhicaryavatara,* trans. Kate Crosby and Andrew Skilton, Oxford University Press, Oxford 1995, chapter 8, verses 112ff.

120 See, for example, Sangharakshita, *The Inconceivable Emancipation,* Windhorse, Birmingham 1995, pp.51–4.

121 William Blake, *Jerusalem,* plate 57, lines 10–11.

122 *Udana,* IV.1.

123 *Digha Nikaya* 19.

124 *Brahmajala Sutta,* Sutta 1 in *Digha Nikaya,* Maurice Walshe (trans.), The Long Discourses of the Buddha, pp.67–8.

125 *Majjhima Nikaya* 72.

126 "Subhuti, what do you think? Has the Tathagata attained the consummation of incomparable enlightenment? Has the Tathagata a teaching to enunciate?"

Subhuti answered: "As I understand Buddha's meaning there is no formulation of truth called consummation of incomparable enlightenment. Moreover, the Tathagata has no formulated teaching to enunciate. Wherefore? Because the Tathagata has said that truth is uncontainable and inexpressible. It neither is nor is not."

A.F. Price (trans.), *The Diamond Sutra,* Shambhala, Boston 1990, p.24.

127 See *The Lankavatara Scripture* in *A Buddhist Bible,* Beacon Press, Boston 1970, p.348.

128 An account of Sangharakshita's meeting with Anandamayi, "the blissful mother," is to be found in *The Rainbow Road,* Windhorse, Birmingham 1997, chapter 20.

129 *Porphyry,* in *Plotinus,* trans. A.H. Armstrong, Heinemann, London 1966, vol. 1, p.3 et seq.

130 *Digha Nikaya* 25, section 22.

131 See *Samyutta Nikaya* vi.2; *Anguttara Nikaya* iv.21. For further commentary, see Sangharakshita, *Who Is the Buddha?,* Windhorse, Cambridge, UK 2002 chapter 5, "From Hero-worship to the Worshipping Buddha."

132 These are listed (in Pali) in the *Sangiti Sutta,* Sutta 33 of *The Long Discourses of the Buddha (Digha Nikaya),* section 1.9, point 43.

133 *Loka* means "place," "plane," or "world," and Buddhist cosmology envisages an ascending hierarchy of these: hell realms at the bottom, then the abode of human beings (and various abodes of non-human beings), and then various heavenly realms. The *kamaloka,* the plane of sense-desire, encompasses all non-heavenly realms, and some of the heavens also; the higher heavens belong to the *rupaloka,* the plane of (archetypal) form, and—higher still—the *arupaloka,* the formless plane. The fact that the *rupaloka* and the *arupaloka* are associated with various higher states of consciousness suggests that this "cosmology" can be taken to refer to inner psychological and trans-psychological realities, as well as to the external world.

134 Early Buddhist tradition enumerates a hierarchy of eight *ariya-puggalas,* "noble persons," often listed as "four pairs of persons": the Stream-entrant and the one who has won the fruits of Stream-entry; the Once-Returner (that is, the one who will live only one more human existence before Enlightenment) and the one who has realized the fruition of that stage; the Non-Returner (who will gain Enlightenment from a heavenly realm) and the one who has realized its fruition; and the Arahant, who has attained Enlightenment, and the one who has realized the fruits of Arahantship.

135 *Anguttara Nikaya* i.14.

136 See s.Gam.po.pa (Gampopa), *The Jewel Ornament of Liberation,* trans. H.V. Guenther, Shambhala, Boston 1986, p.32–3.

137 This is from Sutta 7, the *Sela Sutta,* of the *Sutta-Nipata*'s "Great Chapter." E.M. Hare (in *Woven Cadences of Early Buddhists,* Oxford, London 1947, p.87) gives: "I have heard it said by brahmans of old, venerable teachers of teachers, that those who have become men-of-worth, all-awakened, manifest the self when praise is uttered about them. What if I were to chant seemly verses in the presence of the recluse Gotama?"

138 See, for example, the *Lalita-vistara* in *The Voice of the Buddha,* trans. Gwendolyn Bays, Dharma Publishing, Berkeley 1983, vol.ii, p.570; or the *Abhiniskramana Sutra* in *The Romantic Legend of Sakya Buddha,* trans. Samuel Beal, Motilal Banarsidass, Delhi 1985 (first published 1875), p.237.

139 Huien Tsiang, in *Buddhist Records of the Western World,* trans. Samuel Beal, Motilal Banarsidass, Delhi 1981 (first published 1884), part ii, p.123.

140 "Reverence, humility, contentment, gratitude and timely hearing of the Dhamma; this is the most auspicious performance." *Mahamangala Sutta* in *Sutta-Nipata* verse 265. This translation is by H. Saddhatissa, Curzon Press, London 1985, p.29.

141 From *Sigalaka Sutta, Digha Nikaya* iii.188. This translation is from *The Long Discourses of the Buddha,* trans. Maurice Walshe, Wisdom Publications, Boston 1995, p.467.

142 *Dhammapada* 354.

143 *Anguttara Nikaya* IV.xxii.213.

PART FIVE

144 Quoted in Sangharakshita, *The Buddha's Victory,* Windhorse, Glasgow 1991, pp.62–4; also in *Some Sayings of the Buddha,* trans. F.L. Woodward, The Buddhist Society, London 1975, p.103; and *The Book of the Discipline (Vinaya Pitaka)* Part 4, trans. I.B. Horner, Pali Text Society, London 1982, *Mahavagga* VIII, pp.431–2.

145 Walt Whitman, "Song of Myself," part 40.

146 See E.B. Cowell (trans.), *The Jataka Book* xii, *Jataka Stories,* vols.v and vi, Pali Text Society, London 1973, no.547, *Vessantara-jataka.* See also Har Dayal, *The Bodhisattva Doctrine in Sanskrit Literature,* Motilal Banarsidass, Delhi 1978, p.185.

147 This story is told in the *Jataka-mala,* and also in a Mahayana sutra, R.E. Emmerick (trans.), *The Sutra of Golden Light,* Pali Text Society, Oxford 1996, pp.90–6.

148 See *Samyutta Nikaya* ii.178.

149 s.Gampopa, *The Jewel Ornament of Liberation,* p.184.

150 Nagarjuna, *The Precious Garland,* trans. Jeffrey Hopkins and Lati Rinpoche, Harper and Row, New York 1975, verse 219.

151 *The Precious Garland,* verse 398.

152 See D.T. Suzuki, *Outlines of Mahayana Buddhism,* Schocken, New York 1970, pp.297–8.

153 D.T. Suzuki (trans.), *Lankavatara Sutra,* chapter 8, "On Meat Eating," Motilal Banarsidass, Delhi 1999, pp.211–21.

154 *Vinaya Mahavagga* vi.23.9–15.

155 William Wordsworth in "Ode to Duty."

156 *The Sutra of Golden Light,* trans. R.E.Emmerick, Pali Text Society, London 1979, p.12.

157 These are the first eight links of the twelve-fold spiral path. The twelve links relating to the Wheel of Life are much better known than the twelve links of the spiral. It was Mrs. C.A.F. Rhys Davids who first drew attention in modern times to the existence of the latter, and Sangharakshita has brought this teaching into greater prominence. For more on these two types of conditionality, see Sangharakshita, *What Is the Dharma?,* Windhorse, Cambridge, UK 2007, chapter 7, "The Spiral Path."

158 *Mahaparinibbana Sutta, Digha Nikaya* ii.156.

159 Robert Burns in "To a Louse."

160 See *The Jewel Ornament of Liberation,* p.183.

161 The three levels of wisdom are enumerated in, for example, *Digha Nikaya* 16:iii.219.

162 See Santideva, *Bodhicaryavatara,* chapter 2, verse 9.

163 This list is to be found in the *Anguttara Nikaya* (v.177), and is quoted in Nanamoli, p.239.

164 *Digha Nikaya* 31, section 32.

165 *Dhammapada* 197–201.

166 This is what the Buddha (in *Digha Nikaya* 11) calls "the miracle of instruction."

Page References in Source Works for Extracts Quoted

Bibliography

This list does not include early publications that have been republished in later collections of Sangharakshita's writings. In the case of titles that have been printed several times, the date given is not necessarily the date of first publication but that of the copy used to select extracts for this book. Almost all titles are still available from Windhorse Publications (www.windhorsepublications.com) and several can be found online at www.sangharakshita.org.

BUDDHISM: INTRODUCTORY AND GENERAL WORKS

Ambedkar and Buddhism, 2005
The Bodhisattva Ideal: Wisdom and Compassion in Buddhism,
    1999
Buddha Mind, 2001
The Buddha's Victory, 1991
Buddhism for Today—and Tomorrow, 1996
Crossing the Stream, 1996
The Essence of Zen, 1985
The Eternal Legacy: An Introduction to the Canonical Literature
    of Buddhism, Tharpa 1985
Going for Refuge, 1997
A Guide to the Buddhist Path, 1996

*Human Enlightenment: Encounter with the Ideals and Methods
of Buddhism*, 1987

A Survey of Buddhism: Its Doctrines and Methods Through the Ages,
2001

The Taste of Freedom: Approaches to the Buddhist Path, 1997

The Three Jewels: Central Ideals of Buddhism, 1998

The Ten Pillars of Buddhism, 1996

Tibetan Buddhism: An Introduction, 1996

*Vision and Transformation: An Introduction to the Buddha's Noble
Eightfold Path*, 1999

What Is the Dharma?: The Essential Teachings of the Buddha, 2007

What Is the Sangha?: The Nature of Spiritual Community, 2005

Who Is the Buddha?, 2002

COMMENTARIES ON BUDDHIST TEXTS

Auspicious Signs: A Seminar on the Mangala Sutta, 1988

*The Drama of Cosmic Enlightenment: Parables, Myths, and Symbols of
the White Lotus Sutra*, 1993

*The Inconceivable Emancipation: Themes from the Vimalakirti-
Nirdeśa*, 1995

Know Your Mind: The Psychological Dimension of Ethics in Buddhism,
2002

Knowing How to Live: The Ethics of the Mahayana, 2008

Living with Awareness: A Guide to the Satipatthana Sutta, 2003

Living with Kindness: The Buddha's Teaching on Metta, 2004

Transforming Self and World: Themes from the Sutra of Golden Light,
1995

Wisdom Beyond Words: The Buddhist Vision of Ultimate Reality,
2000

The Yogi's Joy: Three Songs of Milarepa, 2006

RITUAL, MYTH, AND SYMBOLISM

Creative Symbols of Tantric Buddhism, 2002
The FWBO Puja Book: A Book of Buddhist Devotional Texts, 1989
Ritual and Devotion in Buddhism: An Introduction, 1995

ART AND CULTURE

Alternative Traditions, 1986
*Buddhism and the West: The Integration of Buddhism into
    Western Society*, 1992
The Priceless Jewel, 1993
*In the Realm of the Lotus: Conversation about Art, Beauty,
    and the Spiritual Life*, 1995
The Religion of Art, 1988

POETRY AND TRANSLATION

The Call of the Forest, 2000
Complete Poems 1941–94, 1995
Conquering New Worlds, 1986
The Dhammapada: The Way of Truth, 2001
Hercules and the Birds and Other Poems, 1990

MEMOIRS AND OTHER PERSONAL WRITINGS

*Facing Mount Kanchenjunga: An English Buddhist in the Eastern
    Himalayas*, 1991
*Forty-three Years Ago: Reflections on My Bhikkhu Ordination, on the
    Occasion of the 25th Anniversary of the Western Buddhist Order*,
    1993
*From Genesis to the Diamond Sutra: A Western Buddhist's
    Encounters with Christianity*, 2007
The History of My Going for Refuge, 1988

In the Sign of the Golden Wheel: Indian Memoirs of an English Buddhist, 1996

Moving Against the Stream: The Birth of a New Buddhist Movement, 2003

My Relation to the Order, 1990

Precious Teachers: Indian Memoirs of an English Buddhist, 2007

The Rainbow Road: From Tooting Broadway to Kalimpong—Memoirs of an English Buddhist, 1997

Through Buddhist Eyes: Travel Letters, 2000

Travel Letters, 1985

Was the Buddha a Bhikkhu?, 1994

THE WESTERN BUDDHIST ORDER

Extending the Hand of Fellowship: The Relation of the Western Buddhist Order to the Rest of the Buddhist World, 1996

The FWBO and Protestant Buddhism: An Affirmation and a Protest, 1992

New Currents in Western Buddhism: The Inner Meaning of the Friends of the Western Buddhist Order, 1990

Index

devotion, 25, 105–106, 125–126, 165–167, 441, 447–448, 451–452, 465–468, 470–472, 473, 540. *See also* ritual

Dhammapada, 43, 45, 47, 88, 130, 180, 225, 250, 351, 444, 504, 551, 712–713

Dhardo Rinpoche, 459, 460

Dharma, 83, 233–234
  definition, 83, 91–96, 179, 231, 481, 611
  emotional impact of, 389–392
  giving, 572
  practical nature of, 94–96, 102
  taste of freedom, 406–407

Dharma study, 249, 510, 633
  in a non-traditional society, 481–483

Dharmapala, Anagarika, 644–649

Dharmaraja, 664

dhyanas. See meditation

Diamond Sutra, 80, 186–187, 188, 236, 264–265, 389–392, 517, 656

Dickens, Charles, 391, 496

Digha Nikaya, 232, 330, 514

discipline, 152–153, 359, 400, 439–440, 633–636

dissatisfaction, 721–722

distractedness, 56, 413, 360–361, 430–432

distractions, 360–361

dogmatism, 151–152, 194–195

Dona, 23–25

dorje. See vajra

doubt and indecision, 153–155, 200–201

dreams, 28, 98, 113, 324, 327–329

drugs, 590, 669

dukkha/duhkha, 32–39, 43–44, 349, 567–568

duties, 610–613

dysentery, a case of, 75, 487–489, 565, 727

early Buddhism, 308, 309, 732. *See also* Pali Canon; Buddhist schools and traditions: Theravada

Earth Goddess, 67–68, 71, 73

earth-touching mudra, 68

Ecclesiastes, 213

Edman, Irwin, 292

effort, 277, 458, 628–633, 636–637
  four exertions, 95, 510, 630–632

ego, 197, 276, 291, 380–381, 422, 511, 553–554, 611

elements, 422–424, 477–478

Eliot, T.S., 271, 380

emotional blackmail, 509

emotions, 387–389
  being moved by the Dharma, 81–82, 389–392, 407–409, 639
  as distinct from feelings, 393–394
  free-flowing, 639
  lack of involvement, 200
  positive, 240, 395–398, 414–417, 470–472, 474–475, 588–589
  synthetic, 151

energy, 70, 145, 153–154, 185–186, 191, 396–397, 436

Enlightenment, 21–22, 104–105, 111–112, 278, 401–402, 487. *See also* nibbana/nirvana
  dependence upon conditions, 452–453

environment, 266–267, 683–684. *See also* nature

escapism, 85–88, 365–367

eternalism, 196

ethics, 170, 278, 510, 583
  basis of Buddhist ethics, 586–587
  conventional and natural morality, 591–593, 599–601
  and eating, 593–596
  ethical formalism, 131
  ethical investment, 676
  an ethical universe, 218
  factors which provoke unskillfulness, 621–625
  Five Precepts, 587–591, 593, 667–668
  intention, 614–615
  Judeo-Christian ethics, 583–586
  and karma, 216–218
  marriage, 598–599
  moral relativism, 131–133
  skillfulness and unskillfulness, definitions, 587
  speech, 300–302, 505–506, 602–610
  Ten Precepts, 146, 593
  Vinaya, 633–634, 648
  and work, 596–598

"evil friends", 623–624

metta (Sanskrit *maitri*) 32, 270, 414–415,
  458, 508, 537, 588–589, 616
  importance of metta for oneself, 566
metta bhavana. *See* meditation
miccha-ditthis. See views: wrong
middle way, 115, 196, 232, 349, 454, 634
Milarepa, 65, 475, 538, 601, 726
mind, 40, 108, 216, 469
  absolute, 181
  definition of, 180–181
  effect of art on the mind, 290–292
  reactive and creative, 179–186, 421
  unconscious, 61–62, 67, 121, 389, 461
mindfulness, 145, 432, 590, 636
  being too mindful, 434
  of the body, 425, 434
  of breathing. *See* meditation
  in everyday life, 205, 430–432, 433–434,
    590–591, 596
  of feelings, 393–395
  four foundations of, 95, 425
  rational, 155
  in ritual, 458–459
  silence of, 178
  and spontaneity, 434–435, 636
mindfulness of purpose, 156, 278, 432,
  613–615, 627, 635
modern life. *See* society
monastic life, 124, 127–128, 132, 146,
  439–440, 488, 591–592, 600, 619,
  669–671, 678–681, 685–686
morality. *See* ethics
motivation, 121–122, 249, 429
Mucalinda, 69–70, 542
mudita, 539
mudra, 68, 332, 459, 726
music, 275–276, 400–401
myth, 61–74, 322–324, 329–335, 461

nakedness, 640
Nagarjuna, 65
nagas, 70
Narokhacho, 638
nationalism, 698–699
nature, 97–98, 265–267, 405, 422–423,
  474–479, 480
Neo-Platonism, 324

nibbana/nirvana, 54, 106, 113–122, 169.
  See also Enlightenment
nidanas, twelve. *See* meditation; Wheel of
  Life
Nietzsche, Friedrich, 615
nihilism, 196–197
niraya, 552
niyamas, five, 215–219
Noble Eightfold Path. *See* path
noble quest, 31–32
non-conceptual approach, 61–62, 167,
  326, 461, 478
non-duality, 106–107, 570
non-exploitation, 666–668, 673
non-violence, 593, 669, 703–704, 707,
  711
no-self. *See anatta/anatman*
Nyanatiloka, 653
Nyingma school, 252

Olcott, Colonel, 646
old age, 14–16, 33, 98, 406, 579, 623
oppressions, 621–625
optimism, 184–185
organization, 303–304
original face, 376
other-power (*tariki*), 227

Padmasambhava, 65, 160, 447, 475, 638,
  726
paganism, 473–479
Pali Canon, 141–142, 321–322, 330, 578
  descriptions of Going for Refuge, 81–82
  inclusion of supernatural beings, 477
  parables and similes, 39, 59–60, 86–87,
    93–94, 140, 503–504
  stories and teachings, 23–25, 58, 75, 76,
    93–95, 145, 209–210, 230, 231, 246–
    247, 274, 330, 356, 377, 427, 473,
    487–489, 492–493, 500, 509–510,
    514–515, 533, 635
pancendriya. See spiritual faculties, five
Paradise Lost, 479
paramitas. See Six Perfections
paribbajaka, 678–679
parinibbana/parinirvana. See Buddha
  Shakyamuni

About the Editor

KAREN STOUT (Vidyadevi) has worked with Sangharakshita as an editor since 1987, as well as editing many other books for Windhorse Publications, UK. She became a member of the Western Buddhist Order in 1993 and was given the ordination name Vidyadevi. The Sanskrit translates as "shining one or goddess of intuitive wisdom and aesthetic appreciation"—an aspiration, not a description, she hastens to add!—but an appropriate one because of her interest in the affinities between Buddhism and Western culture. She has traveled widely and feels special connections with Aryaloka Buddhist Center in New Hampshire and the Buddhist movement in India, both of which continue to be the source of joy and inspiration. She lives with her partner in rural Herefordshire, UK, close to the border between England and Wales.

About the FWBO

THE FWBO (Friends of the Western Buddhist Order) is the Buddhist movement founded by Sangharakshita in London in 1967. It seeks to create all of the conditions needed for the effective practice of Buddhism in modern society, and has grown into a varied and energetic tradition of practice.

Drawing on twenty years' experience in Asia, studying under teachers of the Theravada, Chinese Ch'an, and Tibetan Vajrayana traditions, since his return to the UK, Sangharakshita has spent the last forty years drawing out the essence of these teachings as a guide to the Buddhist path for today's Dharma practitioners, wherever they live. The FWBO draws inspiration from many Buddhist traditions but does not identify itself exclusively with any one of them, preferring to consider its approach as simply "Buddhist."

There are FWBO centers in twenty countries worldwide, including Mexico, Venezuela, and a number of locations in North America, and also India (where the movement is known as TBMSG). Centers teach meditation and Buddhism through classes, courses, and retreats, as well as celebrating Buddhist festival days and acting as a focus for the local Buddhist community. There are a number of FWBO retreat centers, and activities in many fields, including the arts, health, and social activism. At the heart of the FWBO is the Western Buddhist Order (WBO), a community of men and women who have formally committed themselves to pursuing their own spiritual development and supporting that of others. Preparation for ordination is undertaken with the support of the Order's network of spiritual friendship, and ordination is conferred on women and men on the same basis. Order members, Mitras (people who are deepening their contact with Buddhism and the Order), and Friends (those who participate in FWBO activities but have made no formal commitment to practicing the Dharma within the context of the FWBO) often live, work, and practice together—some of them running public Dharma centers, some working in team-based right livelihood businesses, and many living in Buddhist residential communities.

The FWBO is a diverse organization, including people of many nationalities, from all walks of life, and living a wide range of lifestyles, both lay and monastic. Practice within the FWBO does not require a monastic lifestyle, and many Order members, Mitras, and Friends are married or have children. The essence of membership of the Order is simply a commitment to put Buddhist principles into action in one's life.

For more information and contact details, see www.fwbo.org; and for online meditation courses and advice, see www.wildmind.org.

About Wisdom Publications

WISDOM PUBLICATIONS, a nonprofit publisher, is dedicated to making available authentic works relating to Buddhism for the benefit of all. We publish books by ancient and modern masters in all traditions of Buddhism, translations of important texts, and original scholarship. Additionally, we offer books that explore East-West themes unfolding as traditional Buddhism encounters our modern culture in all its aspects. Our titles are published with the appreciation of Buddhism as a living philosophy, and with the special commitment to preserve and transmit important works from Buddhism's many traditions.

To learn more about Wisdom, or to browse books online, visit our website at www.wisdompubs.org.

You may request a copy of our catalog online or by writing to this address:

Wisdom Publications
199 Elm Street
Somerville, Massachusetts 02144 USA
Telephone: 617-776-7416
Fax: 617-776-7841
Email: info@wisdompubs.org
www.wisdompubs.org

THE WISDOM TRUST

As a nonprofit publisher, Wisdom is dedicated to the publication of Dharma books for the benefit of all sentient beings and dependent upon the kindness and generosity of sponsors in order to do so. If you would like to make a donation to Wisdom, you may do so through our website or our Somerville office. If you would like to help sponsor the publication of a book, please write or email us at the address above.

Thank you.

Wisdom is a nonprofit, charitable 501(c)(3) organization affiliated with the Foundation for the Preservation of the Mahayana Tradition (FPMT).